MOMAN PRUIETT

CRIMINAL LAWYER

The life story of the man who defended 343 persons
charged with murder. The record shows 303 acquittals
and the only client to hear the death sentence pronounced
was saved by Presidential clemency.

Printed in the United States
by
HARLOW PUBLISHING CORPORATION
Oklahoma City, Okla.

PRUIETT IN HIS PRIME

Dedicated to
The memory of my mother
ELIZABETH LOUISA
My most cherished possession

ACKNOWLEDGMENT

The publication of this book has been made possible by the cooperation and assistance of many of my friends. They have given freely of their time and advice. Special acknowledgment is made to Mr. Howard Berry for his assistance in preparing the manuscript and to Mr. Howard Parker for his careful work in editing the same. Mr. Ben Preston by his financial assistance, made the publication a reality. To all who have had a part in making the publication of this book possible I extend my heart-felt thanks and appreciation.

MOMAN PRUIETT

FOREWORD

The history of mankind reveals a long, continuous violent struggle for freedom, to establish and protect the dignity and rights of the individual and to resist tyranny and oppression. The history of the United States of America shows that the lawyers of the country have played a leading role in establishing and protecting the freedom and rights of the citizen. When we read the history of the early day lawyers and picture their courage, initiative, ability and ingenuity we sometimes wonder if the present crop is not letting the standard fall. How many people remember that we have a Constitution with a Bill of Rights guaranteeing certain fundamental rights to every citizen? And how many remember that these guaranteed rights include freedom of speech and religion, the right of peaceable assembly and the right to petition the government for redress of grievances; the right to bear arms; the right not to have soldiers quartered in any house; security against unreasonable searches and seizures; the provision that no person shall be held to answer for a capital crime unless on presentment or indictment of a grand jury; protection against double jeopardy, and against being compelled to be a witness against himself; the right to a speedy trial by an impartial jury of the state and district wherein the crime shall have been committed and to be informed of the nature and cause of the accusation and to be confronted with witnesses against him and to have compulsory process to procure witnesses in his favor and to have the assistance of counsel for his defense; the provision against excessive bail and cruel and unusual punishment and the reservation of all other rights not expressly delegated.

Moman Pruiett knew what the rights of the citizens were and he likewise knew the cunning and ingenuity employed by many officials and other persons in position of power or authority to thwart such rights. The universal tendency of those in power is to take away, not to preserve, the rights of the individual. Pruiett has said, "I never enter a court room to try a case without offering up a prayer—not a prayer to win the case, understand, but a prayer directing me to try it right, so that my client will have the best chance of getting what he needed when he showed confidence in me by hiring me."

Clients knew when they hired Moman Pruiett to represent

them he swept all other interests aside and concentrated all his tremendous energy on the presentation in the most effective manner of any and every defense they were entitled to under the law.

Blackstone says, "It is better that ten guilty persons escape than that one innocent suffer." Pruiett knew his Blackstone and it was a safe bet that if one of his clients was convicted the prosecution had made a case which left no possibility of doubt as to the defendant's guilt. Pruiett may have cleared a guilty man occasionally but it is doubtful if he ever had an innocent client convicted.

In these days of tyranny and dictatorship and disregard of the simplest rights of the individual it is refreshing to read a book like this which makes you realize that freedom still exists and the right to it can be enforced by insisting upon the observance by those in authority of the safeguards laid down by our lawmakers for the protection of human rights.

C. W. VAN EATON

PROLOGUE

Attempting to pay tribute to Moman Pruiett, author of the following pages, is as difficult as to etch a discord, "Gild refined gold, throw a perfume upon the violet, add another hue into the rainbow, or with taper light seek the beauteous eye of heaven to garnish." As there are depths of the sea to which the plummit will not descend, there are depths of my thoughts for Mr. Pruiett which language cannot express.

Stigmatized with two prison sentences before he reached eighteen years and thus bearing the whips and scorns of time, "the oppressors wrongs," the viperous tongues of falsehood and slander, with no education or legal training, and without assistance from any source but his own energy, determination and courage, he rose from those miasmic swamps in which he was engulfed, like the phoenix, and now, at the age of seventy-three is conceded to have been one (among the few) of the greatest and most successful defense lawyers found in the annals of criminal jurisprudence.

When Moman weighed anchor and set sail amid the uncharted rocks and reefs dotting the tempestuous sea of his life, his bark was leaky, masts down and canvas rent,—the result of dissappointment after disappointment. Did he resent the spurns, the insults and humiliations heaped upon him in his tireless, uphill fight to succeed, and give up in disgust? He did not; the handicaps that beset him on every hand served to make him another Anteas, gaining new strength with each contact with earth. While his ship was tossed from the crest of the wave to the sinus of the trough, back and forth, he never left the bridge until she was safely moored in a haven of peace—realizing that he had defeated the most powerful enemy known—rumor, scandal, and half truth.

In criminal trials he was a master at cross-examination; and bowed to no one in his argument to a jury. His brain was an intellectual ocean whose waves touched every shore of legal technique and finesse, though unschooled and untrained in legal procedure.

Now, at the age of seventy-three, he can play with his grandchildren and relate to them with pardonable pride how, single handed and alone, he licked the most formidable enemy known to man.

It is with pardonable pride, that after an unbroken friend-

ix

ship lasting more than forty years, I have the privilege and honor to write, in my humble way, the prologue to the following recital of your life, and to offer you my sincere thanks, and allow me to place upon your hoary head the wealth of spring—the flowers and blossoms of love and respect.

Sincerely,
F. A. ROBERTSON

October 8, 1944.

No section of our country has had a history more spectacular or more fascinating than the history of old Indian Territory. It was our last frontier. It was the greatest opportunity for souls rugged enough to meet its tests and conquer the obstacles it presented. It was the last harbor for the violent who came to this virgin land because of its near freedom from repressive laws. Hence the entire territory became a battleground between the law abiding and the lawless—a land of incessant combat in which only the strong of heart could survive.

It was in this boiling caldron of conflicting passions that Moman Pruiett won his laurels as a veritable Napoleon of the bar. And there could be no greater error than to conclude that Pruiett became eminent among mediocres—that he became famous because frontier competitors were poorly endowed. The old bar of the Indian Territory was equal to any that ever appeared in a courtroom anywhere west of the Mississippi. Truly there were giants in those days. And it was among lawyers who would have adorned any bar in America that Moman Pruiett won a place at the very head of the line.

To think of Indian Territory is to think of Moman Pruiett. Of course he achieved many of his greatest triumphs at the bar in the courtrooms of Oklahoma during the years that followed statehood, but he was a giant in reputation and professional stature long before the two territories were fused into a single state. Certainly the story of his life should be written. And who is better equipped to write that story than the dynamic man who made the story so fascinating?

Very truly,

L. H. HARRISON

"The newspapers made Moman Pruiett." Such was the statement of Omer K. Benedict, who was editor of the Oklahoma City Times when Pruiett was at the peak of his career, and who subsequently was a Republican nominee for Governor. "That is," explained Benedict, "the press helped very materially to make Moman the big figure he became. Moman was always good for a story; he was good copy. And of course the publicity he got never hurt his business."

Pruiett generously concedes the part played by the press in establishing him as an outstanding criminal lawyer. "When the reporters came around I always tried to hand 'em out enough data for 'em to build a more or less colorful story," commented Pruiett. "I realized theirs was a business from which a living had to come, just as was mine. In giving out stuff acceptable to each reporter I didn't go to the extreme said to have been reached by Dizzy Dean, of baseball fame. When Dizzy was in his prime as a colorful pitcher for the St. Louis Cardinals, naturally he was much sought after by sports writers. Dizzy's manager, seeking to be helpful, tipped him off to the fact that reporters liked to be fed with different dope so that their published stories would not read too much alike. Well, as the story goes, one day Diz was approached at different hours by two sports writers, each seeking biographical data concerning the ace pitcher. The next day one newspaper featured a story relating that Diz was born in a log cabin on a little barren farm in Arkansas, and as a barefoot boy he chewed tobacco and plowed corn and hoed cotton and fished in the creek for mudcat and 'went in washin.' And the same day another leading paper printed a story which pictured Diz as born in Louisiana, in a small town, where he played marbles 'for keeps,' smoked cigarettes on the sly, killed neighbors' chickens with well aimed rocks, and engaged in other village pranks such as pushing over privies late at night. When Diz was called down about the contradictory sketches of himself, he blandly replied: 'Well, they told me these writers wanted different stuff, and that's what I gave 'em.'

"No, I never was as raw as Diz in my relations with the press," continued Moman, "though I always tried to give the boys somethin' to work on. I'm mindful that there are good lawyers who, when approached by reporters about a case, close up like a clam, set back on their professional dignity and announce they try their cases in court, not in the newspapers. As for me, I could co-operate with the press for the most part without revealing my important 'military secrets' and jeopardizing the interests of my clients. And besides, to be perfectly frank, that publicity tickled Ole Moman's vanity and helped him to get more business."

TABLE OF CONTENTS

Wherein a hasty jaunt into retrospect is taken, and after the Pruiett progenitors are given a casual glance, the story of a trip aboard a river packet, is told. And how the scenes shift from the Ohio River to Arkansas, and from river boats to railroad trains, but the transient characteristics of the Pruiett family remain unchanged. And how a mother's dream of a pre-natal gift is confided in her off-spring, as she charges him with the responsibility of winning acclaim for himself in the court rooms, but how she sorrowfully sees him there, not the acclaimed, as she had dreamed, but as the lowly culprit, pausing in the parade to prison.

Wherein current events, as indicated by the notices of the National Press, are contrasted with those of a day when Pruiett, an adolescent youth, returns from prison to a mother still determined to push him into the law. And how he has his first view of the Tall Sycamore of the Wabash, in action in a celebrated Indian murder case. And how his connection with the railroad laboring crew takes him, with the wandering Pruietts, to North Texas, and wherein, he expresses his doubts and fears concerning the effect of the felon's brand he carries. How it forthwith confronts him, to carry him down for a second time under a felony conviction, and how the boy who went to prison is a man when he returns, and how hard work, a thick skin and the generosity of a federal judge combine to make a new lawyer in Texas.

Wherein rumblings from the dungeons of Rusk and Little Rock begin to reverberate, as Pruiett's plan for courtroom procedure is discussed and put into operation. How he tries his first case and wins—and tries a murder case and wins—and tries for the hand of a maiden and is likewise successful. And how his aptitude attracts the attention of a pair of powers from the dark and wild Territory, and how he goes, on their invitation, recommendation, and capital, to try it as a proving ground for his long-nourished desire for a place to cast his lot.

Wherein Lawyer Pruiett makes definite location in the Indian Territory, and begins, forthwith, to keep apace with the so-called rougher element of the section. And how he goes back to Texas to try a murder case and, after having jailed himself for his lack of respect for the local court, frees himself and wrests a verdict of acquittal from the jury. And, wherein he lets the Territory's light of promise blind him against an attractive offer of partnership from a distinguished Dallas attorney, and he goes back to the Valley to

hood dawn again for the despairing territorials. He hurried home to
try the Matlock and Danna murder cases, and got them acquitted.
And how his versatility takes him to a Constitutional Convention, and
he sees the subdivision of government, named "Moman" in his honor,
changed to suit the caprice of a political boss . . . and, wherein, he
restates his views on the ills of the prevailing penal system, and
announces his discontent with the confines of the Valley.

Wherein Pruiett abandons the Valley and attempts to abandon
a portion of his criminal law practice, but is catapulted back into its
maelstrom by his brilliance in the reluctant defense of a certain
Rudolph Tegeler. And how he tips the scales in a difficult non-murder
case by well calculated psychological maneuver, and delivers, along
with the deliverance of his client from the clutches of the law, District Judge W. N. Maben, a fatal blow to the gubernatorial aspirations
of a favorably considered little Attorney General, and, wherein he
lends his efforts to a policeman, Crow, who is charged with murder,
and acquires his acquittal with little, if any, evidence of justification,
pleading confusional insanity.

How Pruiett encounters an enemy in need, and saves him, for a
valuable consideration, from the penalty which is usually provided
for the crime of murder. And how he displays his prowess in the
scenes of his childhood, to postpone, and render more sweet and
profound, his vengeance for an old, but never-to-be-forgotten injury.
The Red Fox case in Fayetteville, Arkansas, and told the blue
barrow story in a speech to the law class in the University of
Arkansas.

How Pruiett is deprived of a fat fee and two clients at the
same time, by the intervention of old Judge Lynch, and a group of
murder cases, with possibilities, are never tried. And wherein the
murderer's friend sits at the wrong side of the counsel table, and a
theatrical killer is sentenced to the henceforward in confinement for
his misdeeds. And how Pruiett atones for his assistance to the system
as the jury says "not guilty." And how it begins to appear that good
murder cases are not produced without Pruiett, and that, although
a pretty murderess goes up for life despite his defensive effort.

Wherein Pruiett loses a hard fought contest before the Canadian
King's bench, and sees his accused Murderess extradited to the United
States for trial. And how he couples virtue and vice together to raise
funds in old Seattle, and treats the Pacific slope press to a liberal
portion of his pre-trial propaganda before he astounds the western
citizenry, and his friend the Governor, by wringing a verdict of
acquittal for his client, from a hostile jury.

LIST OF ILLUSTRATIONS

CHAPTER ONE

MOMAN PRUIETT'S MOTHER'S DIARY:

Wherein a hasty jaunt into retrospect is taken, and after the Pruiett progenitors are given a casual glance, the story of a trip aboard a river packet, is told. And how the scenes shift from the Ohio River to Arkansas, and from river boats to railroad trains, but the transient characteristics of the Pruiett family remain unchanged. And how a mother's dream of a pre-natal gift is confided in her off-spring, as she charges him with the responsibility of winning acclaim for himself in the court rooms, but how she sorrowfully sees him there, not the acclaimed, as she had dreamed, but as the lowly culprit, pausing in the parade to the prison.

Warren Legrande Pruiett had been a Confederate, but it was the Union Prison Army that mustered him out. When the war was over, and Camp Chase's luckless inmates were released, he was starting his fifteenth month as a captive of the North. It was a long way to Leitchfield, Ky., and Captain Pruiett was sick of body and heart. He skulked and begged his way out of the hated Yankee territory and back into Kentucky, with little spirit or hope. It was well for him he despaired, for it served to prepare him. Martha Harris Pruiett, his wife, had been dead for almost a year. Oscar, Albert, and Anna, the happy kids he had left behind, were gaunt, backward starvelings.

The Moormans, near Elizabethtown, in Hardin County, had suffered the complete reduction which accompanied Confederate defeat. The elegance of the plantation, flourishing when old Colonel Moorman exhibited Elizabeth Louisa, the new grandchild, in 1850, and still maintained by slave cultured tobacco wealth in '62, had become a sad memory. In cheerless December, of the year '68, the grandchild stood above a fresh mound on the plantation grounds, beside a group of older stones. Grandpa Moorman was dead. Little Betty Moorman's heart would break, if her violent sobbing was an indicator, before the crumbling columns of the old balcony fell.

Betty Moorman had been born Elizabeth Louisa Laws. When Mary, the Colonel's only child, married Thomas Laws, no objections were made. The Laws were aristocrats, and southern Ohio wasn't so far north as to amount to a complete disqualification. Black-haired and black-eyed Betty, when she came, made up for

[1]

her father's various minor shortcomings. After her pudgy hand had given the Colonel's black beard a single jerk, Tommy Laws had a permanent home. But when he went north, with the coming of the war, and thence to a Yankee regiment, he committed the unpardonable sin. The seldom invoked Hardin County divorcement act was brought forth, and with the stern Colonel Moorman guiding her, Mary Laws insisted, that despite her matronly status and pigtailed Betty, she be divorced, and restored to the name of Moorman.

A Tennessee slug put an end to Tommy Laws and the speculation on what his attitude toward Mary's maneuvers would be, on returning. Elizabeth Louisa Laws moved into adolescence as Betty Moorman.

No one knew, and no one was concerned, in fact, how elderly Captain Pruiett and the dejected orphan of the Moormans came together. Pasts weren't important, with presents so difficult to maintain and futures so hard to predict. Men were scarce after the war. Niggers and white trash terrified unescorted women. A man with three sick and hungry kids had to have a mother for them, whether a dowery went with the deal or not. There was no magnolia scented romance on the columned veranda of the manor house, at least not the Moorman manor house, for the official county records of 1869 revealed that the long delinquent mortgage on it had been cancelled in foreclosure during the summer of the preceding year. The records said that Warren Legrande Pruiett and Elizabeth Louisa Moorman were united in Elizabethtown, on March 23, 1869. She was 19; he was 42.

The Gray Eagle, serving points on the Ohio between Louisville, and Cincinnati, was showering cinders and soot through the Kentucky side of the soft spring atmosphere.

"That's Looeyville, ain't it?" A young woman, with a pretty face, was asking the question of the man beside her, a man much taller, and older than she. It was Betty Pruiett, and the former Captain of the Confederacy. As they looked down the river they each cast quick and constant glances toward two ponderously bundled infants sitting back to back on the rough-planked deck beside them.

"That's her," the man said. He was leaning against the rail of the upper deck and staring at a black smudge visible above the bending green of the river bank. "That's old Looeyville, an' we'll be dockin' in less than an hour. Ain't seen her since I was through on my way home—after the war." There was a touch of sadness, and bitterness, with the addition of the phrase.

They stood together, watching the smudge in the sky, the verdant shore and the foaming muddy water. "You better set down," he cautioned. The attempted style in the cut of her home made coat didn't conceal her abnormal contour. She was advanced with child. "It ain't good to ride on these rough boats, nohow, the way you are. Let's set."

As he led her toward a wooden bench on the deck, near the babies, she clung to a small imitation-leather accessory bag. "I just had to come with you, even if we did have to bring the babies," she said. "It's kinda like a vacation, gettin' back in this part of Kentucky—just for a day. I'm glad the lawyers an' creditors for Bruner Brothers decided to have a meetin'. I couldn't 'ave stood that Indiana winter much longer, without a little rest."

"It ain't been no worse at Alton than it's been at Looeyville, or Leitchfield, this winter," he said. "You've been homesick, an' run down with takin' care of these twins, an' gettin' ready to have another one, maybe more, so soon."

"We've done perty good at Alton," she agreed. "Makin' our own expenses an' gettin' all this cash out of an' old bankrupt store stock. You done real good, to do that, Warren."

"There's three thousand in greenbacks in that old didy satchel," he grinned. "Three thousand dollars, an' that's about all anybody could milk out of the old junk. It won't surprise me a damn bit if they don't close her up and turn me loose, when they take this money an' examine my accounts. Then we're out a work again. What the hell we goin' t' do?"

"You'll find somethin'," she said. "Maybe the tobacco price'll be better, or—."

"Maybe I can get me another butcher shop an' go back to cuttin' meat—'til I go broke. It's funny I can make money out of a worn-out stock someone else has gone busted in, but if it's for me, I can't get over."

Betty looked sad. "Bad luck," she said. "Bad luck. That's all I've seen since the war came. There's Grandpa Moorman, with his big house an' his money, an' mother an' me havin' ever'thing we need. Then he loses his money an' the niggers, then his property, an' finally dyin'. I remember that, an' me an' mother bein' left in that big house, until they took it away from us an' moved us out. It's just one misfortune after another, 'til you came to Elizabethtown, Ky., an' we met—."

"Misfortune was what brought us together," the Captain said. "Hard luck—misfortune—was what done it, an' it looks like the two of us together have been gettin' a double dose ever since. You was just a kid when the war came, just a girl when it was over. Why, I was grown, had a good business an' was making good money, classin' tobacco there in Leitchfield, raisin' three kids. I thought I was gettin' some place. Two years in the army—one year in that damn Union Army Prison, sick to death all the time in the filthy prison camp, an' what do I find when the war's over an' I get home? Wife dead. Kids sick an' half starved. Business blowed. The wife's folks helpin' to push the damned niggers in so the poor devils like me'll be sure to finish our starvin' to death. I ain't never coming out of it—an' I'm getting to be a' old man."

"I ain't goin' to let you get discouraged," Betty said. "We was on starvation when we married. You remember, we agreed to join forces an' fight it out, because it seemed ever' one an' ever'thing was against us? It was my fault you quit the tobacco business in Brandenburg an' went into the meat market. If times hadn't been so unnatural tough you'd a'made money, instead of losin' it. An' just remember, Oscar an' Albert are gettin' big enough, almost, to get a little job here an' there, an' Anna's a heap of help to me about the house. The—."

"Them poor kids," he lamented. "They're perty near like you, only you had a little better care when you was little. They've had sadness to live on since they was born. They ain't had no chance an' it looks—."

They each held a pudgy year-old twin on their laps. "No," Betty objected, "it don't, neither. We're goin' to do better, an' these kids of ours is goin' to know a little happiness, an' have a little education. I'm goin' to see to that."

"Let's quit croakin' an' watch her dock," he interrupted. The green fringe of the west bank had disappeared. In its place was an expanse of churned water with dingy house-boats and coal barges. Beyond and above them were smoking stacks, dirty windows and the streaked sides of flat industrial buildings.

"Listen to her blow." The Gray Eagle was letting it out. Her hoarse, grunting whistle was blowing almost constantly. Holding a child apiece in their arms—Betty holding tight the diaper bag— they moved to the rail to watch the noon-day bustle of the river traffic. "Ain't I glad to see old Looeyville." Betty said.

"Say," said the Captain. "Lois's wet. She's got to have a dry napkin afore we get off'en this boat. She feels like she fell over-board."

"Ain't she a dandy, now," Betty said. "Jessie's a lady; she's dry, an' clean, too. Here—let's trade, an' I'll change her. We'll be gettin' off in a minute. I'll take a didy an' go inside with her, an' you hang onto this bag."

She placed the flat bottom of the bag on the flat rail of the boat, and holding the handle with her left hand, the hand and arm supporting the baby, she flipped the spring and opened the bag.

"I'm goin' to put two of 'em on this young lady, for the city," she laughed, as she jerked the white clothes out of the bag. A worn leather wallet, the one containing Bruner Brothers' green-backs, leaped out with a white fold, and balanced for an instant on the lip of the satchel.

"Good God," gasped the Captain, with a wild lunge forward. He caught it after it started its fall toward the muddy water. "I got it. Say, what the hell?"

Betty and Lois were flat on the deck. Lois was making pro-test with frantic screams, but the mother lay quite still.

"Drive us up to the Gault."

"We shouldn't go to such an expensive place, Warren," Betty protested from the interior of the hack. "Let's go some place that ain't so high."

"This is a kind of vacation for us, an' I'll try to get it allowed on my expense account," he said. "An' besides, if them pains keep up you'll need a doctor. The Cap'in of the boat says they got a house man at the Gault."

"I feel awful silly, faintin' like a plumb ninny, but I never was so scared in all my life. I saw that money start to fall, an' it seemed like an eternity I was froze there. I couldn't move, an' I couldn't scream. All I could see was both of us goin' to prison for stealin' it. Nobody would of ever believed we lost it, if we did. Are you sure you caught it?"

"I showed it to you a dozen times now," he laughed. "I'll take it out an' count it if it'll make you feel better. Ain't them pains goin' away any?"

"They are—some," she said. "But if they got a doctor, an' it don't cost extra, why let's have him look at me. They go away—an' then they come back, an' I feel awful weak."

"It's just what I told you," the Captain said, as he came into their rooms at the Gault House that evening. "The court says to close her out. We'll auction off what's left when we get back. I get half o' what she brings for my commission, an' old Bruner Brothers is buttoned up. How you feelin'? Has the doctor been back?"

"The doctor's been here, an' he says I'm havin' early labor pains. He says the scare I got, an' the fall, almost brought the baby. It ain't hardly seven months yet, either."

"I knew it wasn't right, ridin' that rough boat an' all," he said. "I'm supposed to get right back, an' the Gray Eagle goes at noon tomorrow. How you goin' to make the trip?"

"I'll be all right," she said. "The doctor said to stay still tonight; that's a fine vacation, ain't it? I can get up all right in the mornin.' You go out somewhere tonight, an' see how old Looeyville looks, an' then tell me about it in the mornin'."

"Nope, I'll stay in an' rest, an' try to make some plans with you. What we goin' to do after I wind up this liquidatin' job I got now?"

"What you goin' to have when you get through?"

"The stockholders was tickled to death with the report I made 'em, an' with that three thousand. They hadn't thought anybody could do it, an' they admitted it. I got ten per cent, three hundred dollars, out of it. They said I could have half of what the sale of the balance brought, an' I know it'll do for fifteen hundred. That'll make us better than a thousand dollars an' our expenses, out'a this job."

"Why, that's a good year, after all." Betty's face was glowing. "With a thousand, you can go in business. You can get a good start with that."

"There's somethin' I been thinkin' about for quite awhile," the Captain said slowly. "I been thinkin', with business so bad around here—me failin' in ever' thing I try, well—maybe we ought to move plumb out an' start over fresh somewhere. Out—."

"Go ahead, Warren," she urged. "Don't be afraid to talk to me. What you been thinkin'?"

"Well," he repeated, "I was in the west once, it was with Van Dorn. They transferred me to a Tennessee outfit, an' moved us into Missouri, an' south from there into Arkansas. We fought at a place called Elk Horn Tavern, an' got whipped, of course, an' scattered all over that Ozark hill country. I hid out in the woods and caves for a couple of months. It's a lot like east Kentucky, lots of fast-runnin' streams, rough, hilly as hell, an' the soil's shallow and rocky. There's lots of it, an' it's awful cheap. I got the idea right then that it would raise tobacco, same as Kentucky soil, an' that the bird to start it would get richer'n hell."

"If it was good for tobacco, they'd be raisin' it out there," Betty observed. "They wouldn't be crowdin' up an' wearin' .these pore old hills out, if there was all that good land to work on."

"Maybe nobody ain't thought of it," he said doggedly.

One of the twins fretted in the adjoining room. "We got little babies, an' goin' to have more, Warren," she said. "It'd be awful hard on me, goin' to a strange country, an' a wild one, with the babies. I think we better think about investin' in a little business, an' startin' over again around here. We get awful homesick, both of us, when we get out of Kentucky."

The soot sifted over the river docks. The black laborers cursed the white ones, and the white laborers cursed the black ones. Cursing truckers beat big-footed horses as the huge wagons were backed into unloading positions at the Gray Eagle's side. Passengers with luggage were climbing from horse-drawn hacks and scrambling up the plank runway.

"Be careful," Betty said, as the Captain helped her from the step of the hack. "I'm awful sore. I'm still havin' a touch of them pains."

"I don't think you'd better try it, makin' this trip," he told her. "I can arrange for you to stay with some one here. I'll go up and hold this sale, an' get the other kids, an' come back here. We was plannin' to come anyway."

"Just let me lay down in the cabin, an' ever' thing's all right," she said. "You ain't leavin' me here by myself. You got your hands so full of kids now you can't hardly help me up the boards. What'd we do? You take Lois an' Jessie, or leave 'em with me? Let's get in where I can lay down, an' get home."

The Eagle cleared the docks at two o'clock, an hour later. At six, with her wheels churning the flood-stage muddy current she was well above Louisville, vibrating in every joint and timber as she struggled to make way against the current's pull. Betty Pruiett, trying to smile through the anguish-seamed lines of her face, shivered as a helpful passenger held a wet cloth to her forehead. Captain Pruiett, with bloody wrists and cuffs, stood awkardly beside her. She lay in the bunk of their cabin. He held a squirming infant in his hands. It was swaddled in a boat towel on the 12th day of July, 1872.

"Ain't he got the awfulest head of hair you ever seen?" he said, "an' just a seven monthser, too."

"Just like Grandpa Moorman," Betty was able to whisper.

"What we goin' to call him?" he inquired.

"I'd like to name him for Grandpa Moorman," she said.

"That's good for me," the Captain agreed. "His name's Moorman. Moorman Pruiett. That's name enough for anybody, I guess."

"God bless his little soul," the mother whispered, as she looked at the ugly infant. The wide mouth, which was partly covered by the long ropes of birth-wet black hair, stringing down from its head and about its face, flew open, and a lusty wail arose. "God bless his soul," she whispered again.

Hovering genius swung low and clipped the ear of the infant with a mark reserving him to her as her own. While the big mouth was open and the tiny pointed tongue protruded between the toothless gums, the muse of eloquence dropped down to touch it with his magic wand. The deity of all the paradoxes stopped long enough, as gliding by on the cool river mists, she endowed the scrawny being with the strangest mixture of impulse and motive ever assembled under a single section of human flesh and skin.

The soft light of heavenly presence illuminated the dusky ripples of the muddy water in its beam, and over the dark waves, emissaries from above and below met to touch the squalling, squirming body at the same instant. When he was laid in the improvised crib, furnished by gaping passengers, there rested the best, the most kind, the most considerate, of all the curiosities ever assembled in human form.

Five years of assorted failures—Pruiett luck was gaining momentum as it rolled from bad to worse—was enough to convince Betty. She followed the Captain on his long considered experiment into the southwestern hills of Missouri and northwestern hills of Arkansas. Her brood, with increases and losses, remained the same in number. Lois and Jessie had died; they had been buried side by side at Evansville, Indiana. The step-children, the war-stunted get of the Captain's first marriage, were plodding through adolescence, still awkward and stunned by the tragedies of their infancy. The boy Moorman was thriving. Two boys,

named White and Boyd, were born before the Kentucky exodus
began in 1879.

The Captain tried his tobacco in '80, and followed it in
'81 and '82. "She just won't work," he complained disconsolately.
"The climate's about the same, the rainfall's about the same, an'
the ground's just like Hardin County ground, all but the smell, but
she sure as hell won't sprout tobacco. I've worked my damn head
off, an' here I am. Rented farm with no rent paid, no crop out,
a house full of kids an' no money. I'm at the end of my row."

"Oh, no, you ain't," Betty argued. "This here's a great country. It's good for the children, an' our health's better since we
came out here. We'll sell this furniture an' these tools, an' move
down to Fort Smith. We'll just quit the farm, an' you an' Oscar
an' Albert can get jobs."

"Whose team's that?" the Captain interrupted, peering through
the window. A wagon had stopped in the road in front of the
house.

"It's old man Sykes," she answered.

"Wants his rent, I guess," the Captain growled. "Well, I'll
just have to owe him, or he can—."

Betty showed Sykes into the kitchen, where they had been
talking. It was Silas Sykes, the owner of the farm they had
worked for three years.

"I guess you won't be wantin' the farm any more, Pruiett,"
he said. "I ain't goin' to have the whole thing to let, now."

"That won't be botherin' us, I reckon," Pruiett replied. "We
was—"

"We're broke," Betty cut in, bluntly. "We was goin' to give
you notice. We're goin' to move to Fort Smith."

"It ain't my affair, but you're goin' at the wrong time,"
Sykes said. "I'm givin' up a lot of my farms to get things
opened around here; you're here workin' your heads off an' goin'
broke, an' then when she's ready to hum, you get up an' get.
But it ain't my business."

"Ain't you said you was sellin' part of the farm?" Betty
inquired.

"Nope, I ain't sellin' her; I'm givin' her away. Just deedin'
forty acres away, an' a strip two rods wide through another
forty. Just deedin' her away, free."

"You mean you got that railroad survey turned this way,
after all?" guessed the Captain.

"The Frisco's cuttin' right through the north eighty, an' I'm deedin' forty to the townsite company to go to make a town. You're goin' to see a city right in the Sykes farm, what I'm tellin' you."

"I'm glad for you, Mr. Sykes," Betty said. "You worked hard to get these farms, an' to keep 'em. I know that. You worked hard, an' you're entitled to get your values up with the railroad I'm mighty glad for you."

"I'm glad, too, Sykes," the Captain said. "Some fellows get all the luck—all the good luck. I get all the tough. I hope it makes you double rich, Sykes."

"Are you bound to make this move to Fort Smith?"

"Well," answered the Captain, looking doubtfully toward Betty, "we ain't got much choice. It's like Betty just said, we're busted. We're down to the bottom of the pan, an' we got to try a new trick."

"You got a little choice," Sykes said. "I knew you was broke. I watched you work this farm, an' seen how hard you tried to make tobacco grow on it, an' I hated to see you fail time after time. But I seen you was a good worker, an' good to your family, an' it ain't ever' body that's got that much to his credit. I came over to make you a little proposition."

"It'll have to be a little one for me to consider it," the Captain said. Betty smiled.

"You told me you was in the meat business, a time or two?"

"I cut meat all over Kentucky, an' never made a cent out of it," agreed the Captain.

"Was it grocery-store meat business—retail business?"

"Yep. Just little business, but I never could make it go. Went broke ever' time."

"These railroad contractors have to have a lot of fresh meat," Sykes explained. "Bridge gangs, steel gangs, flocks of laborers. Live beef's cheap and easy to get, but killed meat ain't, an' won't be. The man that gets the beef contracts with the construction is goin' to make a lot of money."

"We got a milk cow an' a calf, an' we can butcher in the bed-room," the Captain said, dolefully. "I'm afraid I ain' got nothin' to start on."

"We're goin' to have a town," Sykes said, "an' these new towns are cracker-jacks. An' this one, right here in this good country, this farmin' country, an' with the minerals an' timber we got, is goin' to be a big one. You'll have to have a shop, an' do it right."

"What they goin' to call the town?" Betty inquired. "Sykesville?"

"I wanted 'em to, but the townsite company wouldn't hear of it. They're callin' it 'Rogers.' "

"What for?" asked the Captain.

"Some muckety-muck in the Frisco," said Sykes. "A big stockholder, or somethin'."

"You really think it'll make a big settlement?"

"Hell, yes, Pruiett. The promoters come in an' promote each other, an' some of the natives'll fall for it, but the smart guy'll get some holdin's an' let 'em go up in value. Property values'll sky rocket."

"I wisht we could stay for it an' make some money, but I guess it ain't for me," said the Captain. "We ain't got nothin' to start on."

"You ain't never let me make my proposition," Sykes said. "I gave 'em the forty for part of the townsite. They gave me back my pick of some of the choice town lots. I got some good cnes facin' the depot an' the right-of-way. I'm goin' to build a two-story frame on the best ones, with store room downstairs an' rentin' rooms upstairs. You an' the missus is good workers, an' you ought to have first shot, seein' as the town starts on your farm—anyway, the one you been farmin' for three years. Put in a butcher shop, with a roomin' an' boardin' house. I'll help you get started, an' we'll go after them railroad meat contracts. Missus Pruiett can feed the promoters an' the new ones that come to town. We'll clean up."

The transit-born Pruiett child, the Gray Eagle's unbooked passenger, was eleven. He was average in size, but odd of act and appearance. He had a glittering, dark eye, and a crowning mop of crow-black hair. The Captain cut it and Betty cut it, the neighbors cut it, and he hacked at it himself, until the shears were dulled, but the black flag continued to wave defiantly. It was of prodigious thickness.

Moorman was Mawman in Betty's Kentucky accent. He moved with the Captain and Betty to a large new house with rooms upstairs. He had watched it grow from the stacks of yellow lumber dumped about from the six-and eight-horse wagon-freighters. He saw men with soft hats and laced leather boots come and go on their horses, and in wagons and buggies, and he heard them talk to his father, and to Mr. Sykes, about depots, and streets and sidewalks. He played in the shavings, when he could get away from minding the ever-troublesome Boyd, and walked the rafters of the line of new one-story buldings, which the men, who were becoming more numerous about the farm, were building.

And then one day he saw the square yellow ties being swung and dropped along the fresh ridge of earth in front of the new buildings, and he saw sweating, straining men, with queer clam-like tools, carrying heavy steel rails and laying them, with cursing and swearing, across the picket lines of the square ties.

The new house was full of the strange men who shoveled the dirt and carried the rails, or who carried great rolls of blue paper with white and red lines on it, and who sat around the house at night, smoking pipes and uttering unnecessary oaths as they talked about the railroad. Anna was helping Betty with the work, and it was good that she could. He knew that. Betty didn't stop to pet him, and run her hands through his hair and tell him how nice it was. He was glad. He hated to be coddled. She didn't have the time—he knew that, too—for the big sign hanging out over the muddy street in front, unpainted, like the house, brought constant crowds to eat the food which Betty and Anna took from their great iron stove.

The Line of the St. Louis and San Francisco Railway Company was pressing out of southern Missouri toward Fort Smith, with north Texas its ultimate objective. The peaceful beauty of the hills, cut by the foaming lines of spring-fed streams, was being revealed to the increasing tide of settlers and speculators who followed the extension of the rails. Settlements strove to get the survey to head their way. They tempted the road with land grants. Where the trains went, increased values and prosperity followed. Towns were established by an executive's pen dot upon a blue diagram. What had been a wooded tract or a cultivated field became a bustling camp.

Captain Pruiett had the best thing in Rogers. (The name of the new town was painted with black letters on the boxed-ends of the dung-colored depot.) A downstair's stall of Pruiett's board-ing house was his butcher shop. The men who toiled on the fills and in the cuts had to have red meat, and he worked at night, trimming bones and stuffing guts for the morning wagon load to the camp. He whistled and counted his money. Sure, he went broke cuttin' meat at Hawesville, Kentucky—but what the hell? Sure he flunked trying to make tobacco grow in Benton County.

What about now? Them railroad contractors have got plenty
of money, an' you can buy fat calves for whatever you want to
pay.

Rogers became a town overnight. Within a year it had a
staid and established appearance, with the unpainted houses and
buildings near the depot adopting a duller shade of dung than that
of the railroad station. The yellow pine walls and roofs faded
and blended. They appeared to be as indigenous to the landscape
as the small oaks and granite boulders. Professor Arnold came
to take charge of classes in the new school, and Betty Pruiett
smiled one of her rare smiles. Mawman would get some book
learnin'.

"Don't coddle me, Ma. Keep your hands to yourself."

A plain woman, with a slightly pained expression, sat beside
a scowling boy. They were in a plain room, on the side of a
red-quilted iron bed.

"Don't resent your mother, son, she loves you," she said.
"You're not too big for mother to touch you, even if you are
thirteen."

She attempted to run her hands through his hair. It was
coal black, bulky and uncut, but shiningly smooth and sleek. He
recoiled from her again. "I wisht you wouldn't do that all the
time, Ma."

"Paw says you fought with the teacher today, hit him with
the water bucket and cut his head. That's what I called you in
here to talk about."

"Old Arnold ain't fit to be a teacher. He ought to be a mule-
skinner—the bully. I wish I'd a-killed him."

"Don't say things like that, Mawman," the mother said. "It's
sinful to say it—even think it. The Bible says 'thou shalt not kill.'
It's been hard, draggin' about from place to place, not hardly
settled long enough to get you into school, but I've tried."

"It ain't your fault, Ma, but I just can't get along in school.
It's no use."

"Why?" she asked, wearily. "The other boys ain't always in
trouble, comin' home with their clothes torn and bloody, with their
faces all scratched up. Fightin'! Always fightin'! An' now it's
the teacher, so you can't ever go back to this school."

"Mutton-chops," he answered laconically. "Mutton-chops.
They call me that 'cause paw's a meat-cutter, an' I don't like it.

"Betty"

"THE CAPTAIN"

I said I'd whip ever' one that called me that, an' I done it—all but a few girls. I hate that school."

"But why the teacher? Why did you have to hit the professor with the water bucket, an—."

"He called me white-trash," the boy said, still defiant, "called me white-trash, an' all the time he's floggin' me, cuttin' the blood out of me. I can lick him—even if he is growed. He squalled like an old girl when I swung that bucket."

"You've got to get yourself educated, son," the mother persisted. "Let me tell you a story. I've wanted to tell you for a long time, but I just never could get up to it. We was livin' up at Alton, in Indiana, just before you was born, an' I had a dream. It was just about the time for you to come to us—your paw an' me— an' I hadn't been feelin' so well. There was a big case bein' tried at the courthouse. Dan'l Voorhees was on one side, and Judge Vallandingham was on the other. Missus Shellenbarger got me to go down to the courthouse with her, just to sit an' listen to the case, to listen to the big lawyers that was tryin' it."

A beautiful light shone in her eyes, and a work-worn hand moved to the child's shoulder. He nestled to her, unconsciously. "I won't never forget it," she went on. "It was Senator Voorhees, they called him the Tall Sycamore of the Wabash, that interested me. He was seven foot tall, it seemed, with a long frock coat on, and long cut hair. An' how he could talk. Low, an' real confidential like, at times, an' then he'd stand up to his full height, an' roar like the thunder. He'd been to college, an' been to Congress, an' he was smart. He had educated his self. An' there he was, a leader, a leader of men, with his hands full of wonderful power. I closed my eyes, right there while he was cryin' out with his great voice, an' prayed that my baby would be a boy, an' that I'd be able to get him educated, for a great lawyer like Senator Voorhees.

"An' that night I dreamed," she said, her face glowing and the dirty urchin held close to her bosom, "that I was in the same courtroom, an' that my son, my own flesh an' blood, was standin' before the jury makin' the rafters sing with his great voice—an' makin' the people think with his great learnin'. It was just a few days later, son, that you was born to me. I thought it had been a sign, a vision I was havin', an' that it would be a part of you, an' you'd help to make it come true. I've dreamed an' prayed that it would, but son, you've got to have schoolin'. You got to have schoolin' to be a great lawyer."

He jerked away defiantly. "I ain't goin' to no more school, an' I ain't in for bein' a lawyer. I can work on the railroad when I'm a little bigger. I'll—."

"But you got to learn," she interrupted. "You can't lay naked in White River all summer, with the gang of no 'count town boys, an' loaf with the old men on the sidewalk all winter, or ride with your paw on that meat wagon. You're growin', an' you got to improve yourself."

Moorman stood up and stretched. "I'm leavin' home," he said. "I'm goin' to the city an' get me a job."

"I'll thrash you myself, if I ever think you're serious about leavin' me, an' goin' to Fort Smith—."

" 'Tain't Fort Smith, it's Fayetteville," he said. "Big mills an' fine buildings, an' swell people with lots of money. I guess I could get along all right—other boys have done it. I ain't a baby no more. I'll show 'em who's the Mutton-chops."

After a despondent shake of her head, the mother laughed. "Don't think, Mister Smarty, that 'cause you can whip the professor, you can run me. I'll cut me a hickory, an' whip you ever' step of the way home, just you try it."

Fayetteville, the Arkansas Athens, hung like a weird, smoky painting on the maple covered drops of the Boston Mountains. On two slopes, and in a portion of one gully, the old buildings of the State University covered easily-accessible learning. The living-places, built before the war, scaled their paint in sullen defiance behind huge lawn trees. Bright colors, and bright lights and sounds, proceeded from the smaller and more moderate homes which rested amongst smaller trees, fresh set along neat, narrow streets. Carriages and carts and freight-wagons rolled regularly around the well kept central square. The business buildings facing the square enjoyed brisk patronage.

Business was good. The pine and hard-timber from Fayetteville's adjoining hillsides was being hurried to market. New steel of the various railroads was literally strapping the countryside. Money was easy to get; every one seemed to have it. Crops were good; provender was plentiful; fish from the flashing mountain streams and game from the brush along their banks made high living commonplace.

Colonel Henry Van Winkle owned the War Eagle Mills on old War Eagle. River boat owner, mine promoter and capitalist, general man of ease, he had graded the lumber at his

FRISCO EQUIPMENT OF THE EARLY PRUIETT PERIOD

"Settlements strove to get the survey to head their way. Where the trains
went, increased values, and prosperity followed."

big mill on the mountain creek with a purpose. The best of the piles, planks and siding, he held unto himself. The Van Winkle House, something special in Boston Mountain's extravagance, was being built just west of the public square in Fayetteville. "She ain't got a knot in her," the colonel boasted. He was dreaming dreams of hospitality a la Memphis, and Nashville.

Wire nails and metal bolts took the place of wooden pegs. Mill-turned columns of ornate complexity supported the roof of the two-sided veranda. Gingerbread, as the natives called it, spiraled and curley-cued about the veranda rails, the shutters and the cornices. The Colonel christened it "The Van Winkle House— the Pride of the South." Its massive outline encompassed three full stories, with ceilings eighteen feet tall in every room on every floor. Southern food served southern style contributed to the fame of the Van Winkle. It became the mingling place of the society which flourished with Fayetteville's new prosperity, and the base for the operation of the drummers and speculators who had business with the industrial developers of the wild territory to the south and west.

"How much y' make today?" Ed Graves, owner of the Fayetteville Livery Barn, was addressing a serious-faced boy.

"Forty cents," came a prompt, proud answer. "Thirty for shines and a dime for holdin' the horses. Them folks at the Van Winkle are some sports."

"I could take a shinin' box and a rag an' make it better than I can with this damn barn," Graves grumbled. "Guess I'll have to take to chargin' you for sleepin' in that hay loft. I didn't spose you'd get wealthy so fast."

The boy grinned. "It *is* pretty good, now, ain't it?" he inquired.

"It's damn good," Graves admitted. "Say, there's a half a san'wich in that bucket of mine. The old lady put in too much. You can have it, if you want."

"Thank you, Mr. Graves, you're awful nice, but you don't need to leave me nothin' out of your dinner bucket. You know what? I'm goin' back tonight an' wash dishes in the kitchen, and get a dinin' room dinner when I get through."

"At the Van Winkle?" the amazed Graves gasped.

"Yep, an' I don't want to ruin my belly with no san'wich. I get a whiff out of that dinin' room once in awhile when I'm shinin' on the veranda, an' I see them swells—through the window—in there eatin'. They carried a little pig, cooked whole, with a' apple in his mouth, right out where I could see it. An' you should've smelled that pork." He rubbed his lank mid-section in anticipation. "I'm goin' go eat so much pork tonight—."

"Look out for them teams," Graves shouted, yanking him aside. A rumbling freighter, pulled by four lathering black mules, rolled through the wide doorway.

"Hi, Mawman, how you makin' out?" the dirty driver sung out from the high seat.

"I'm all right, Lane," the boy chirped. "How you makin' out?"

"I saw your maw an' paw," the driver replied, ignoring the inquiry. "They was out to see me when I pulled in Rogers this trip."

"Were they mad?"

"Nope," the driver said.

"Worried?"

"Nope. Jest asked a few questions and walked off. Not mad an' not worried. I guess they know old Mawman's a man. A grown man."

Young Pruiett swelled with importance. "Well— what did they say?" Man or not, he had to have a word from home.

"Well," came the reply, "your maw comes up—I've got the bits out, waterin' the mules—an' she says, 'Lane Robberson,' 'my boy Mawman's been gone for six days, an' he left the same day as you was through here last. I want to know if you know where he's at?' I says—you know me, Mawman, I don't tell nobody no lies, an' I says, 'Missus Pruiett, Mawman is down to Fayetteville, livin' at Ed Graves' place, an' makin' his livin' a-shinin' shoes.' That's what I says. She says, 'What do you mean, haulin' my boy off on your ole rickety freight wagon. You, helpin' a little boy run away from home?' "

Lane Robberson spat on the wagon spokes before he resumed the narrative. "The Captain comes up about that time, an' your maw tells him I said you was down here. 'Why, hell, yes,' the Captain says, 'I told you where he was. The boy at the wagon yard told me he rode off with Lane. He ain't no baby no more. He's able to take keer of hisself.' That's what the old man says. He ain't worried a bit."

"Are they a'comin' after me?" the boy inquired.

"Nope," said Lane. "They says to tell you if you get to makin' more money than you need, offen these pine-lumber swells around here, not to forget 'em. The Captain says his business ain't none too good. An' your maw says," he lowered his voice, as if to keep a privileged communication from Graves, who had the mules in stalls and was hanging up the last of the harness, "she says if you need a little cash, for me to give it to you, an' she'll pay me back when I come in next trip."

The boy beamed. "You tell 'em I got a good place to stay, an' that I'm makin' money. I made three an' a half in five days, an' I got a job at the hotel now, washin' dishes for my supper. I guess I won't need no help from nobody."

"I'll tell 'em I seen you, kid," Robberson waved as he swung off toward a saloon on the square. "An' you can ride back with me any time you want."

"I ain't goin' home," the boy shouted. "I ain't goin' home— not for a long time."

"That's pretty strong language for a kid," Graves observed from a mule stall.

"I'm goin' on fourteen," Pruiett said.

"Excuse me," said Graves.

"When I get rich," he said, "I'm goin' to have me a room at the Van Winkle, an' eat three meals a day in the dinin' room. I'll keep my buggy an' team here with you, Mr. Graves, an' I'll have a derby an' patent leathers. Say, Mr. Graves, who's the old coot at the hotel that keeps the fancy team up the street— an' wears such flashy clothes?"

"The one with the mustaches an' the loud band on his sailor?"

"Yeah, the city dude."

"His name's Van Zant," Graves answered. "He's from Pennsylvania. Ain't he a dandy?"

"I shined him three times today, an' a different pair of kicks ever' time. He changed his suit before dinner an' had on a fresh one this evenin' when I started down here. He must be awful rich."

"He is," said Graves. "Some one died an' left it to him. He's investin' it in timber land an' coal mines. He's goin' to live in Fayetteville an' take care of his property from here. He's got a few farms an' some railroad stock besides."

"He's got the handsomest vests an' the biggest watch chain I ever seen," the boy said. "An' I'll bet ya that I get the regular job of holdin' his horses, 'fore very long."

The summer sun was half out of sight behind the wood-covered slopes of town when Pruiett trudged up to the side veranda of the Van Winkle House. His strap was over his shoulder and his box hung at his side. Ed Graves had reminded him that he might pick up some shine money after supper. The elegant Van Zant, with a straight cheroot slanting down from his mustaches, was leaving the hotel by the side steps.

"Hi, sonny," Van Zant said. "Hit'em a few licks for me."

Pruiett looked at his boots. "Ain't I just shined 'em for you?" he asked.

"They get dusty awful quick in this dry weather," Van Zant answered. "Shine 'em up." The boy was already on his knees, lifting a shoe to the foot-rest on the box. "When you're comin' by the hotel, an' have your buggy out, I'd like to hold your horses," he said. "I like horses awful well, an' always get along easy with 'em. I sleep in a livery stable."

"I'll see about it," said the easterner. He was smiling at the boy's frankness. "Hurry up with that shine."

"Yes, sir. Pull up your pant-leg a little—up off'n your shoes an' I can go faster." Van Zant complied, exposing a dazzling expanse of pure white sock. The flying paste-brush was covering the leather with happy strokes.

"I'll keep your shoes shined, an' your buggy wheels, too, Mister." The boy smiled, looking up enraptured. "I'll take—."

"Look what you're doin'," Van Zant cried. The unwatched brush had traced an ugly trail across the white of the sock. "You little fool. What's the matter with you?"

The boy continued to kneel before him, a perfect pose for the penitence and pain which showed in the expression of his face. "I'm awful sorry, Mister. I'm just terribly sorry."

Van Zant scowled blackly. He would damn himself for a spot of soup dribbled on a cravat. He might overlook a foul name, but he would fight for the continued beauty of his fine raiment. He lashed out with his open hand, not to strike, but in a gesture of his extreme annoyance. He slapped at the flopping brim of the shoe-shiner's nickel straw hat.

"You've hurt me," came a loud wail, as the kneeling shiner doubled up in a Hindu bend. "You put my eye out. Call the doctor."

"Shut up, you little whelp, or I'll stomp your head off," Van Zant grated, looking about to see if he was being made into a spectacle. There was no one on the veranda. "Shut up—an' get out of here."

"Oh! Oh, my eye. I'm goin' blind! You've hurt me bad."

A flake of pressed straw from the brittle brim of the hat had been driven into his eye. The sudden pain, with the humiliation that went with blacking a customer's sock, was bringing out some hitherto undisclosed dramatic talent in the boy Pruiett. "Call the doctor," he moaned. "Call the doctor."

Van Zant dropped a dime in the gravel of the path. "I'll get you a doctor, you dirty little bastard," he said. "You'd better shut that God damn clack—." Looking about, and still being unable to see any one about, he aimed a kick at the upturned rump, "There's your doctor." The kick turned him over. Van Zant ran up the steps and into the side door of the hotel.

It was ten o'clock at night. Ed Graves rapped cautiously at the door of the Van Zant's room in the Van Winkle. "I thought I'd better tell you, sir, about the kid," he mumbled, apologetically. "He's perty bad off. He's sick. Maybe he ought to have a doctor."

"What kid?" Van Zant demanded.

"The boot-black," Graves persisted. "I saw it—well—I saw you out there this evenin'—well, when you kicked him. I seen it. I had to carry him back to the stable, an' he ain't gettin' over it too quick. I think he's hurt bad."

"Jesus Christ," Van Zant gritted. "I might 'ave killed him. What's the matter with me? Them drinks I had with supper must 've made me crazy. Where is he?"

Graves led the way to the canvas covered straw bed in the loft of the livery barn. "I'm awful sorry about them white socks," the boy whimpered as they came in. "An' I'm sorry about this—too. I know you didn't mean to, an'—."

"That boy's hurt," Van Zant said, 'with one look at his streaked, suffering countenance. "Get a doctor, an' have him come to my room at the hotel. I'll carry the kid over there an' put him to bed."

"Am I really goin' to sleep in the Van Winkle?" Pruiett inquired, as Van Zant was carrying him up the hotel stairs. "In your room at the Van Sickle?" The affirmative answer he received relieved the bruised and sprained rump more than did the arnica and tape which the doctor applied.

Betty and the Captain arrived from Rogers two days later.

"This here twelve dollars, I'm givin' you," Van Zant said, "is for damages, damages for the injury I done to your fine boy.

Of course, it was an accident, but I want to do what's right, an'—."

"It seems like an awful lot, Mr. Van Zant," Betty demurred.

"Not a'tall," Van Zant flourished. "An' I want you to sign this little paper, sayin' that it's all right, an' that you don't expect me to pay no more. My lawyer fixed it up. You sign the paper and take the money. Then I got it all fixed for the Graves stage to haul you home."

"You mean—you mean we're goin' plumb to Rogers in the Van Winkle bus?" Young Pruiett had risen on two elbows in the big bed, and was staring incredulously.

"'Tain't no sense in such extravagance, with such good train connections," the Captain opined. "You're spoilin' us."

"One seat's just right for a bed for the kid," Van Zant explained. "You have plenty of room for yourselves, an' for takin' care of him."

"Good God," the boy sighed, falling backward. "Plumb to Rogers—on the stage."

The conveyance consisted of four fancy horses, a surplus of brass-trapped harness, a veneer covered and varnished box, and an enclosure upholstered with real leather drawn by four horses. "She's stuffed with horse-hair," Moorman observed as they bounced over the gravel toward Rogers.

"Mr. Van Zant's a fine gentleman," Betty said.

"The folks'll set up an' take notice when they see us rollin' up in this trap," the Captain said. "We ought to have a carriage ourselves. They don' cost so much, an' horses ain't expensive to keep, but it just seems ever' time I get about ready, why somethin' has to happen. Right now, we ain't makin' expenses. The construction has run too far from us, an' that's all there is to my meat business. If it wasn't for your boardin' house we'd be in a hell—."

"I know," Betty nodded. "I been seein' it in your eyes for a long spell. Them pastures across the valley are lookin' greener. I guess it's about time to get movin' again."

"Well," he said, defensively, "the Frisco's done fifty miles southwest, an' them paddies is eatin' beef down there just the same as they was when they was buildin' through these hills. Ever' one says that the goin' is slowin' down while they make them mountains through the Indian Territory. The rougher it gets, the better prices the supply men will get for their stuff. So—."

"I seen that look on your face at Elizabethtown, an' at

Brandenburg, an' Alton. I can tell when you get to thinkin' about how much better you could do if you was just some place else. I know."

"I ain't no quitter," he replied. "But there ain't no sense in lettin' a mistake starve you to death. I thought tobacco would do good in this country, but I was wrong. I thought sellin' meat to the damn railroad would make us rich, an' it did make us a good livin', but it didn't last. I can't get a contract, an' ship the stuff down on the supply trains. They want it fresh; killed an' delivered right on the job. We got to move with the road, or get into somethin' else."

"Yes," Betty agreed, listlessly. "There's more people than ever on them trains, but they ain't none of 'em stoppin.' They just go right on through, an' my rooms stay empty. We ain't doin' no good where we are. Where we headed?"

The Captain grinned. "Hackett City's a comer," he said, jerking his head for emphasis. "Four miles from the territory boundary, good timber all around, coal mines openin' up all around it, an' the Frisco headed for her big middle. I'll get the meat contract back. We'll put the kids in school, an' we'll save up some money. We're gettin' old."

Betty looked at the sleeping boy on the seat of the hack. The bouncing had shaken a black lock from his bulky crown, and it lay carelessly across his handsome features. Her expression softened.

"Then Mawman can go back to school. He can't go back to that old Arnold. He's too tough. Always fightin'. Always got to have his own way. In trouble all the time. He's most big enough to put on the section. We'll get him to work, an' help him save his pay. Educatin' ain't goin' to do a kid like him no good."

Betty's eyes flashed. "He'll have educatin' if I have to take a pick on the section myself," she said. "He's smart. Just eleven months, that's all the schoolin' he's had in his whole life, an' it's done him more good than all the years the other children has got. He's got a good brain; he don't never forget nothin'. He can repeat ever' word the professor says, just as fancy as he says it himself, if he wants to. He remembers, an' he imitates. He could draw a better paper right now than Mr. Van Zant's lawyer had us sign—only he wanted to. He just thinks it's sissy to be smart, so he hides his smartness. I'm goin' to make a lawyer out of Mawman."

"You'll play hell makin' a lawyer out of that one," the Captain laughed. "He's just another wild colt. He comes in slick in the springtime, an' runs perty fast around the barn lot, but put him up side a real race horse an' he'll fall down. If you don't get such high an' mighty ideas, you won't get such hefty disappointments. Mawman'll always be just like he is right now. He'll fight like hell just for the right to be sulky an' stupid."

The law firm of Brewer and Hale, with offices above Press Cole's Hardware Store, contained the cream of the Hackett City bar. A pot-bellied stove, surrounded by tin spit-buckets, ash boxes and straight backed chairs, stood in the center of the principal room. Phil Brewer's big desk set in a corner near the windows.

"Would you tell me, please, what the requirements for bein' a successful lawyer are?" An awkward boy, with fuzz and pimples, was speaking an obviously rehearsed speech to Brewer. Brewer stared in amazement.

"Hey, Jap," he bawled, "Come 'ere. Come 'ere quick."

Jap Hale appeared in the frame of the open doorway into his adjoining room. "What's the trouble?" he inquired.

"I been practicin' law for near to twenty years," Brewer said. "I've had some tough questions put to me, an' if I do say so myself, I ain't never had one I couldn't answer, 'till right now. Mawman's asked me one that beats me."

Hale feigned interest. "I can't imagine," he said.

"Mawman walks in an' asks me, right out of a clear sky, 'what's the requisites of a successful lawyer?' I hadn't never thought of it."

"I'll be god-damned," Hale acknowledged. "Now there's one that ain't in the book. It never occurred to me, neither. Set down, Mawman, an' we'll worry over it together." He pulled up a straight chair and sat down beside Brewer.

"Abe Lincoln got ahead by bein' honest, an' chargin' his clients starvation fees," Brewer ruminated.

"An' he'd a starved to death as a lawyer, if he'd a stayed with it long enough," Hale objected. "That's part of the background for a successful politician, not a lawyer. That's out."

"My maw says I'd make a good lawyer," Pruiett said, complacently. "But she says that lawyers has got to have a lot of education—if they're successful."

"Well," said Hale, "mothers are most usually right."

"I can't remember ever seein' a successful lawyer," Brewer interrupted. "About the time you get it all learned, why some damn fool up an' changes the law, or somethin' happens to ruin you. There was one that was almost successful, one time. He came down to Fort Smith, from back east, an' he hadn't never lost a case. But when he got through tryin' his case before old Ike Parker he was so turned around he had to hire a nigger to lead him from the courthouse back to his hotel. They hung his client the next day, an' by God, they'd a hung him, too, if he hadn't a' got out of town on the night train. This success business is just awful hard to figger."

"There was an old Texas lawyer through this country one time," Jap Hale recalled, "who had some damn good ideas on the subject. He said if the evidence was agin' you to raise hell with the law, and if the law was agin' you to raise hell with the evidence. 'An',' he says, 'if the law and the evidence is both agin' you, raise hell with the lawyer on the other side of the case.' Well—he won his case all right, but he raised so much hell he made the other lawyer sore, an' he shot him dead on the steps as he was walkin' out of the courthouse."

Pruiett joined with Brewer in a laugh. "Have you read all them books?" he inquired, pointing toward the crowded wall-shelves.

Brewer and Hale laughed again. "Hell, no," said Hale. "You don't need to read 'em. You get in an' get started—you wait till you get a problem, an' then you look it up in the books. You got to start tryin' cases before you learn anything about law."

"Then I don't see why you need to spend so much time studyin'," the boy said. "All you need is a few books, an' to know where to look. Is that it?"

"That's almost it," Brewer agreed. "You see, I ain't had a lot of education, an' neither has Jap. We just got enough to get by with. But we can see now, with the opportunity gone, how much it'd help if we just had it. Good grammar; knowledge of how to make correct sentences, an' paragraphs. That helps when you go to drawin' your pleadings, an' gettin' ready to try your case. An' history, an' literature, an' the classics. You can spot a' educated lawyer in court by the material like that he has to draw on when he's makin' his speeches. But the little feller, that just knows how to look it up, an' make a dry, ignorant argument on a measly state of facts, like me an' Jap, they ain't successful.

We ain't jokin', right now, Mawman. We ain't qualified to answer your question."

"I see what you mean," the boy answered. "My maw told me the same thing, but I didn't think she knew what she was talkin' about. I see it, the way you put it. But I don't get along good in school. I could learn all right, but I hate the kids. Always foolin'—always teasin'. The boys is worse than the girls, an' they don't teach no law at the Hackett City school. Where am I goin' to learn?"

"What's your main trouble?" Hale inquired.

"They call me Mutton-Chops, 'cause paw's a butcher, an' they holler, 'get yore hair cut or pay yore dog-tax!' It ain't my fault about this hair, or paw bein' a butcher, neither."

"Knock it down their throats," Hale grinned, "that's easy—."

"I've licked ever' kid in school," he interrupted, "an' I thought I had things where I could go ahead about my learnin'. I told the teacher I'd speak a piece at the exercises last night—I like to do that kind of stuff—an' so I got up before the school, an' started. 'No more shall smoke curl from the teepee of the lowly American Indian,' I says, an' that's as far as I got. Ever' kid in the room yells, 'Shut up, Mutton-Chops! Go pay your dog-tax' an' they keep it up, throwin' chalk an' paper wads, 'til the teacher makes me set down. I ain't never goin' back to that school."

"The boys are just jealous, about the hair cuts," Brewer observed, "but I believe I would cut more of it off if I was you. You got more damn hair on your head than any boy I ever saw."

"I took Gay Forbes home from the exercises," Pruiett went on. "When we got up to the front gate she told me that Doc Forbes says for her to stop walkin' home from school with me, that he didn't want his girl runnin' around with a butcher's boy. She said—."

Brewer laughed. "You been a hell of a time gettin' around to the point," he said. "There's a woman in the case. I might'a known that any one with his hair brushed that oily would have a gal. I never seen a crow with blacker an' shinier feathers. You want to show ole Doc Forbes that you can get rich, an' successful, in a hurry, an' make him sorry for what he said about you."

"Well," he hesitated, a little embarrassed, "my maw has

told me of how bad she wanted me to be a lawyer. I just wisht I knew how to get started."

"Blackstone was supposed to know somethin' about law, an' he wrote that big book right there in the corner of the shelf," Hale said. "Start out by readin' it—come up any time you want —an' when I get time I'll go over some of these indexes with you, an' show you how to look up cases. An' hang around court— watchin'. That's the way to get started."

"I'll come up an' read ever' day," the boy agreed, "but I got to do somethin' for the trouble I'll be. I'm a good worker. What can I do?"

Brewer looked at Hale before he answered. "You can take charge of the heatin' department," he said, pointing toward the pot-bellied item in the room's center. "Empty the cat-boxes an' spittoons, an' sweep the floor down once in a while. We'll try you out as a new member, for that much work."

"I'll do 'er," he said. "An' them buckets is damn near full, right now."

John Sebastian Little, with full speed on toward the Arkansas governorship, was District Judge for Sebastian County. The courthouse was at Greenwood. "In the case of State versus Pruiett, the parties will please come forward," he said.

Four persons moved into position before his rough bench. One was C. B. Neal, lawyer, who had previously held the position then occupied by Little. One was a bushy-headed boy in his 'teens. The real sufferers, whose sad-eyed misery was unconcealed, were the parents of the youth, Betty and the stooped Captain.

"How old are you, young man?" the court inquired.

"I'm sixteen, sir." There was no quaver in the stout voice.

"You've been convicted by a jury composed of citizens of this county—they've found you guilty of the crime of forgery— an' recommended that you be sentenced to two years in the penitentiary. It is my unpleasant duty to pass sentence on you, and if you've got anything to say—got any reasons for me not doin' my duty—I want to hear about it. You got anything to say?"

The convicted boy looked toward his counsel; contempt was unconcealed in his face as the painful silence continued. A woman's voice was heard.

"Mawman ain't guilty, judge, your honor," Betty said. "Even if the jury says so, he ain't. He's a good boy, he's always worked hard an' always obedient. An' he's so young. Why, he's only sixteen. Penitentiaries ain't built for little boys—they're meant for criminals—an' Mawman ain't no criminal."

The court leaned back and reflected. "The proof in this case showed that your boy was workin' for a Mr. Patterson, that he was the station agent for the railroad spur line, an' it showed that he was drivin' the express wagon, makin' freight and express deliveries from the depot, an' collectin' the freight an' express bills on the stuff delivered."

"He wasn't workin' for Patterson," Betty interrupted. The defendant shot another contempt-laden look at his lawyer, who stood in stupid silence while the miserable woman begged. "He owned the wagon an' the mule too, hisself. Just a boy, an' doin' a man's work. Why—in a year he's bought the outfit an' paid for it, helped me and his paw, an' managed to save money for hisself. An' all the time he's readin' law, an' workin' in the lawyer's office, tryin' to learn law just to please me."

"Why ain't he been in school?" the judge asked.

"Just because we—." Betty was interrupted by the boy, who pushed her aside.

"Don't beg 'em no more," he directed. Then he turned to the court. "I can do all the time you got for me," he said. "I ain't no baby. I told you I wasn't guilty in the first place, an' this thing you called a trial wasn't nothing but a farce. If I got to go to Little Rock, let's get it over with, only don't mistreat my maw. She ain't done nothin'."

"The evidence showed that you were kitin' freight bills; that you made threes look like eights, an' ones look like nines, an' was holdin' out the exorbitant amounts you collected in these raised bills. That is a serious offense, an' it continued over a considerable time. You were takin' advantage of the confidence that your friends an' neighbors put in you, when they hired you to do their haulin'."

"Nobody saw Mawman do it," Betty pleaded. "Maybe Mr. Patterson done it. Maybe some of the other railroad men done it. An' Mawman's just a child. Ain't the law big enough to give a little child another chance?"

"The special agents for the Frisco had convincin' evidence. I can see how the jury was able to agree on your boy's bein' guilty. I was satisfied he was guilty, by their evidence." The court was leaning across the bench with an unfriendly light in his eye.

"The other boys Mawman's age is walkin' across the platform at the Hackett school today—gettin' their diplomas—just startin' out in life, the right way. It ain't fair to send my boy away, for such a little thing; mark him for life. Please don't make a criminal out of my boy." Betty was pleading; great tears were streaming down her careworn face.

"Let's have it over with, judge," the defendant said, gruffly, as he pushed her aside again. He looked toward his still silent, obviously confused attorney. He thought of what Phil Brewer and Jap Hale had told him: "The little feller, that just knows how to look it up, an' make a dry, ignorant argument on a measly state of facts, he ain't successful." "I ain't guilty, yer honor, but you can't hurt me. Let's have it over."

"I sentence you to confinement in the State Penitentiary at Little Rock, for a period of two years. The sheriff is directed to deliver you to the warden, an' the sentence begins to run with your delivery." Little set his sharp chin. Betty sobbed, miserable uncontrollable sobs.

The kids at Hackett, with unintelligible giggles, took their graduation certificates and shuffled from the platform. Mutton-Chops, manfully defiant, walked erect from the presence of the stern court and his distressed parents, with the sheriff. He had protested his guilt, and his plea had been spurned. The State had its judgment to execute.

CHAPTER TWO

Wherein current events, as indicated by the notices of the
National Press, are contrasted with those of a day when Pruiett,
an adolescent youth, returns from prison to a mother still deter-
mined to push him into the law. And how he has his first view
of the Tall Sycamore of the Wabash, in action in a celebrated
Indian murder case. And how his connection with the railroad
laboring crew takes him, with the wandering Pruietts, to North
Texas, and, wherein, he expresses his doubts and fears concerning
the effect of the felon's brand he carries. How it forthwith con-
fronts him, to carry him down for a second time under a felony
conviction, and how the boy who went to prison is a man when
he returns, and how hard work, a thick skin and the generosity
of a federal judge combine to make a new lawyer in Texas.

"The men of the southwest were living wide-open lives in
the days when Pruiett, by the sheer force of his appeals to the
emotions of his juries, was setting out to unlock the doors for prisoners who faced the hangman's noose." The New York Sun, three
and a half decades after the professional beginning of the strange
career, was reproducing a part of the legend which had sprung up
about the man Pruiett.

Thirty-six hundred miles away the Long Beach Sun, impressed by the news value of the same subject observed ". . . then
began the career which has stamped Pruiett a genius at defending
criminals before the bar. In 36 years he defended 342 men accused
of murder. Of this number, 304 went free. Thirty-eight were
found guilty and were given sentences ranging from four years
to life. Not a single sentence of death in 342 cases!" (A correction,
please, Mr. Reporter. One death sentence, but no execution of it.
President McKinley saved him his record.) "He often boasted that
he would quit whenever the death sentence was passed on one
of his clients."

Where is the lawyer in America—in the universe—who has
defied the dark angel's retribution and walked arm in arm through
the valley of the shadow with so many accused murderers? Let
him who knows stand and proclaim the fame of the advocate
who has gained half the number of acquittals, for faith, he is
entitled to it. The Suns, on Long Island's smelly sound and the
Pacific's sunny slope, could have truthfully charged that Pruiett's
deliverances were gained over the undeniable, and often obvious,

guilt of his clients. Brutal murder—single, triple, five at a time, with poison, axe and firearm, he could clothe it with the white robe of justification and procure, in some manner, the acquittal of his clients.

". . . It needed no unusual reportorial perspicacity to spot him as the best story on the courthouse beat," the western cub who rose to the editorship of the Saturday Evening Post once observed in a letter in retrospect on Pruiett. "I worked in Oklahoma City only a little more than three months, but in that brief time Moman defended and acquitted four or five men whose guilt was as obvious as the clock in the tower. Once I thought he was stuck. He feared so, too, and tried a move of desperation. It worked. The assistant prosecuting attorney was a Jew, named Gus Paul. I had not even been conscious that he was a Jew. I never had encountered anti-Jewish feeling. When he took the jury, Moman launched into a savage Jew-baiting harangue and soon had the twelve good men and true eager to lynch Paul for the betrayal of Jesus Christ."

Lemuel F. Parton, publishing the Tammany Hall corruption trial which banished boss Hines to Sing Sing and moved the ambitious and trust-busting Tom Dewey a notch nearer to the White House, couldn't keep the old Washita campaigner out of his mind—or copy. Commenting upon the able but unsuccessful efforts of Lloyd Paul Stryker, Hines's counsel, Parton said, ". . . Old-timers around here tell me that only Morton Rutherford and Moman Pruiett, of Oklahoma, have ever topped him in courtroom decibels, metaphors, similies and all-around tear-jerking."

But back to Gotham's reverie on Pruiett. "In the foreword of her novel 'Cimarron' Edna Ferber wrote: 'There was no Yancy Cravat—he is a blending of a number of dashing Oklahoma figures of a past and present day.' In that foreword she had explained, too, that only the more fantastic and improbable events contained in her book were true. But in the pen picture of the various characters who figure in the book Oklahomans who have lived through any of the fantastic or improbable incidents which form its structure have no difficulty in identifying many of its personalities."

". . . Oklahoma Territorial juries first came under Pruiett's spell thirty-six years ago. He was graduated from the school of the streets of Rogers, Fayetteville and Fort Smith as a bootblack and took to books. He admits that the culture of the frontier was deeply ingrained in him. Men were being put to death daily at the Federal hanging pen for crimes they might not have committed. 'I studied backwoods psychology,' he once said, 'by watching juries and noting the reaction of the lawyers' arguments. The Government had all the best of them. The defendants for the most part were so poor or so ignorant they didn't hire lawyers, and those who were hired made their appeals on dry facts, alone. The jury would go to sleep and the bailiff would have to wake them up. Sometimes they'd bring in a verdict without leaving their seats. I made up my mind that I'd be a lawyer and that no jury would ever go to sleep on me.' "

"Possibly that process of applied jury psychology has something to do with the record of this remarkable lawyer, who during his career at the bar has defended 342 persons accused of murder, 304 of whom have been acquitted . . ."

"Moman Pruiett is the last of his type. The swashbuckler, with his turgid appeal to the frail sentiments of the prairie folks, is vanishing along the lines that once marked t'e frontier. In his best days he (Yancy Cravat, of course) was only a feeble imitator of Moman Pruiett, or Temple Houston, 'scion of a nobler forebear who made his word into law,' or Morton Rutherford, the Virginia Aristocrat, who carried respect for law into the Indian Territory at the end of his sixshooter. From the Arkansas to the Panhandle, from the Strip to Red River, no man, qualified to venture an opinion, will deny that these three stood at the head of the Southwest's list of criminal lawyers."

Pruiett methods, with the story of his prowess, and success, were woven into the fabric of legend which lived and grew after age and adversity had pulled him from active conflict. A Pruiett conducted trial was a continuing chord of climaxes. What the promoter did to keep the jury, and an invariably packed courtroom, laughing, wondering and crying, was of some benefit to the accused culprit, of course, but Pruiett's client was always the victor.

"During the last decade of his career, Pruiett and his ability to win acquittals have made him the subject of many legends accounting his ability and his readiness to act on the spur of the moment. . . ."

And not all of the tons of newsprint and barrels of printers' ink used on the Pruiett process were turned into favorable or flattering comment. His capacity for making bitter enemies was as great as was his acumen for winning lasting friendships. Criminal

law was his bower; politics was his hobby. Such a strange com-
pound was emblematic of the extremes of his nature.

"Last week was a strenuous one in the big political circus;
big guns, little guns, and some we would be inclined to call sons-
of-guns, appeared on the horizon, shed their little lights and disappeared, probably never to be seen again. As we might be
prejudiced in our views, however, we will content ourselves with
giving a brief description of some of the animals and leave their
classification to a candid world."

"In the latter class may be mentioned Moman Pruiett of
Oklahoma City, who denounced socialism as the 'red-handed enemy
of the government,' and in the next breath damned the federal
officials for the way they administered the law. If a socialist had
used the language he did in his condemnation of the officials he
would probably have been run in by the police."

. . . "To the visiting spectators, the opposing counsel, the
court and jury Moman's brilliant and spectacular mannerism was
always a curiosity to them in his arguments before a jury.
He has admirable qualities, energy and courage, of medium height,
a shock of coal black hair extending far down toward a prominent nose over a broad forehead, glittering, deep set eyes, and a
stooping, crouching gesture. He makes you feel that he is the
embodiment of a loving father pleading for a wayward son. He
prides himself on his reputation as a criminal lawyer, and he is
probably deserving of that reputation to a greater extent than
even he realizes."

"Mawman's comin' home tomorrow." Betty tried to keep
elation out of her tone. Her hands were in a steaming washtub
full of dirty dishes. She spoke to the Captain, who smoked
and rocked in an old chair beside the kitchen stove.

"I'll be glad to see the boy," he said. "Been a long time
since he went away."

"It has not been much over six months, but it seems much
longer. It seems like a year, almost, just between visits I have
been makin'."

"How many times have you been up there?"

"I have been up there every month, six times, and you
haven't been a single time. You oughta have gone with me."

He said, "I'm gettin' old. Too old to be goin' that far to
see anybody. An' anyway, some one's got to run that meat wagon
out ever' day. It's pore enough with it runnin' regular. Between

it and the boardin' house we are not hardly makin' it. I managed to lay enough away every month to get you up there on it, and it's a good thing that Anna's so much help, and knows how to run things around here."

"I just had to see Mawman, and I had to see that Governor."

"Governor Hughes is a gentleman," Betty retorted. "He's awful stern, an' awful stubborn, all right, but he's honest and fair. I knew that I would be able to make him see the right if I went after him long enough."

"It took him a long time to make up his mind," the Captain said.

"He started out by sayin' he'd have to serve his term. After three or four months, an' me comin' in ever' month, an' just settin' 'til I got to talk to him, he got to askin' questions—about where I was tryin' to get with Mawman, an' who was payin' all the cost it took for me to make the trips up there. Then he visited the prison an' had them bring Mawman in to see him. That was what got the pardon. He saw that Mawman wasn't really nothin' but a child, an' that he was awful sick."

"It just don't sound like Mawman—bein' sick."

"He can't stand bein' shut up," she said. "He's like a wild animal, a wild colt, like you said. He started wastin' and fadin' from the day they locked him up, just turnin' yeller an' gettin' thin. An' then his knees an' ankles started swellin', an' they had to put him in the hospital. It ain't natural for a kid to be havin' inflammatory rheumatism, so I tell's the Governor that the cold and damp of them cells is what is causin' it, an' he just can't get better unless he can get back with me for nursin'."

"Have you thought any about what we was goin' to do with him, after we get him home?" There was a doleful look on the Captain's face. "You know how it is, an' if he'd fight the whole county 'cause they called him mutton-chops, what's he goin' to do when someone calls him a' ex-convict?"

"I'll cure him up an' get him well before I go to worryin' about such stuff as that," she answered. "I guess we can manage. For one thing, that big Boudinot case is comin' up at Fort Smith, an' Senator Voorhees is goin' to be there. I'm goin' to see that Mawman gets to see him—an' hear him."

"Who's Voorhees?" inquired the Captain.

"He's the finest lawyer that ever banged a table," she said. "He's the Tall Sycamore of the Wabash. I heard him at Alton, an' it seems I been hearin' him ever' since. Them rich Boudinots is payin' five thousand dollars for him to come from the United States Senate, just to defend that wild Cornelius. I read all about it in a Fort Smith Sunday paper. Voorhees says that Ike Parker ain't goin' to get to sentence this Indian to hang."

"You still got them law notions in your head?"

"You bet I have, an' I ain't gettin' 'em out, neither. That Mawman has got a brain for a lawyer, an' don't you forget it."

"Gettin' jailin' for schoolin' ain't going to help his lawin' none," observed the Captain. "If I can get him on one of them crews in the territory, he'd better take it an' get to makin' some money. That cut an' trestle work they're doin' in the Windin' Stair Mountain is goin' to last a long time. It's a hell of a job, with flood an' cave-ins an' slides. They need men, an' if Mawman's in any kind of shape at all, I can get him on."

"Sure, he can help us by workin' when he's able, but first he goes to Fort Smith. Phil Brewer told me he could get right back to his law readin', as soon as he got back an' got able, an' workin' on the road won't last forever. They've almost run away from our boardin' house an' meat market again, an' it won't be long now before we got to move, or think about doin' somethin' else."

The Captain removed his pipe from his mouth and pointed it at her. "Now," he said, "you're talkin'. You took the words right outa my mouth. When they get through them hills in the Injun country an' hit the Texas flats they's goin' to be some fast track layin'. Old Hackett's blowed up. We gotta go to Texas."

"I guess we gotta keep movin'," Betty sighed. "I wisht we could get a nice little business somewhere where we could get the kids in school, so's they could learn to be somethin', but the line keeps movin', an' all we got is a workin' interest in it. When they get through the hills I guess we'll be movin' on south."

The gang camps on the banks of Kiamichi River and Black Fork were embracing the virgin fastnesses of the Choctaw Nation, preparatory to making the first violation of its maidenliness. The fox-squirrels that darted and chattered in the treetops and invaded the grounds of the camps for scraps of food were no less commonplace than the spotted deer that would not give up their watering place to the noisy white men. They came back in large droves, to sniff statuesquely of the aroma of the shacks and tents, and to drink long and freely before scampering back into the wooded oblivion of the hillsides.

A wood fire reflected red and yellow upon a variety of faces in the ring about it. The bushy-headed Pruiett kid, with sun-color back in his skin and with his great brown eyes out-flashing the gleam of the fire, had the floor.

"You should have heard it, and seen it," he said. "He had iron gray hair, an' a long, square chin. He paced up an' down in front of that jury like a tiger in a cage, talkin' to 'em all the time, low, an' soothin' like—an' then all of a sudden he would throw back his arms, wide, like Jesus on the cross, an' beller like a bull in a wrecked box-car. He was a great big feller, tall an' slim, an' with the clearest voice you ever heard. Had a high collar an' a Prince Albert coat, an' wore a white carnation in his button-hole. When he says that it'll be a prostitution of justice if they hang that Cherokee, an' how purity would be dragged through the muck an' mire, he walks over to the ash box beside the stove, an' he takes the white carnation out of his coat button. Then he winds up like he was goin' to throw a fast curve, an' he throws the flower down in the ash box with all his might. The dust flew up an' drifted around in the room, an' he just walks over to the table an' sits down, with his arms folded an' a superior look on his mug. He looks just like he don't give a damn."

"You got a good way of rememberin' it, an' tellin' it," a bearded listener observed, with a spew of tobacco. "How do you remember all that fancy language?"

"I been to school a few days, I guess," came the answer.

"An' a damn few," came from the half-lighted circle. There were more youngsters than Pruiett working with the railroad crew.

"Mawman's got a right to be excited over Dan'l Voorhees," one of the old men opined. "They ain't kept him in the Senate all these years for bein' a damn fool. Mawman's right—if it ain't for him they'd a hung that Injun."

"What was all the ruckus about in the first place?" came an inquiry from the fringe. "I ain't never heard of it before."

"It was murder," said Pruiett carelessly. "Old Elias Boudi-not, who's the uncle of Cornelius, is way up there in the Cherokee Council, an' been to Washington a lot of times on Indian business. That's how he knows who to pick, an' he picks Voorhees. This Cornelius is a wild Indian that's about half smart, an' double-tough. He was runnin' a little newspaper up to Tahlequah an' he gets in a fuss with another Indian, named Stone. He shoots hell out of him an' the marshals move him up to Fort Smith an' toss him in the cooler. Ever'body says old Ike Parker'll hang hell out of him, so the rich Indians jar aloose. They hire Voorhees."

"How much?" some one inquired.

"Five thousand bucks is what they said around the courthouse, an' if one Indian's worth five thousand, they got their money's worth. Oscar Miles an' old man Sandels, that was prosecutin' for the government, ain't no green hands, an' they wasn't pullin' no punches. The Boudinots have got lawyers in the family, an' they was there worryin' an' workin', and they had old Judge Rutherford in the case, an' old Blair from Kansas City. But they're all scrub timber up to the side of Voorhees. He pulled their biscuits out of the fire. They call him the Tall Sycamore of the Wabash, up in the east."

"Where you gettin' all this crap?" a listener inquired.

"Anyone that knows how to wipe his face knows about Voorhees," he scoffed. "Why, damn it, I was there. I rode up on a lumber wagon, an' I'll tell you that courtroom was packed to the rafters ever'day. Half the people didn't get in that tried to, but I had a good seat. Old Voorhees, when he was windin' her up, stood up real straight, an' it looked like he was as tall as a windmill. He stuck his hands up in the air an' just stood there, an' it got still in the room just like it does in that cut before the fuse gets up to the dynamite."

Pruiett, carried away by his own unconscious eloquence, jumped up and stood in the center of the circle, with a clenched fist above his head, and a wild flame dancing in his eyes.

"'I spurn the charge on assault! I spurn the charge on manslaughter! Better, it would be, to end the life of this noble red man on the scaffold, than to grind his spirit out with his life— to wring his liberty-loving life out by degrees in a felon's dungeon. I defy you to sentence him to the rope. If you lack the courage required to do your duty, to acquit him, then hang him and be done with it.' He says it so loud it's like a hundred an' fifty pound charge goin' off in the granite. Then he says, 'Let the great God of the universe, the keeper of men's souls and consciences, be your guide, an' I shall have no fear.' It came in like an echo, kinda like the pines an' little rocks slidin' down the mountainside after the blast. God, but he had the power!"

"It musta been ketchin', to get you to goin' like that over it, Mawman," the old man said. "Air you goin' in for law now?"

The boy slid back into his place, abashed. "I can if I want, or I can do somethin' else. It's just what I please. Jap Hale says I got a good head for lawin' an' I done quite a bit of readin' in his office, but maw says it takes a lot of schoolin', an' I ain't got too much of that."

"If you can carry all that fancy language back, just after hearin' it once, you don't need no educatin'. Just loaf in the court-house awhile, an' listen to the big windy ones, an' then go to chargin' for the spoutin' yourself. I ain't heered much better speeches anywhere, afore, than that one you just put on."

"I guess bein' a powder monkey's better pay, between it an' the kind of lawyer I'd make. But at that, I could beat some I've heard, right now, an' not half try." A hard look tightened about his dark eyes, and they bored into the smoky fire. "I'm goin' to keep on readin', when I get the chance, 'cause it may come in handy in some other kind of business. Maw says she always dreamed I'd get to lawin', an' it'd suit her, but I ain't sure about it. I'm goin' to do some lookin' before I say whether I will or not."

South of the swamps of the southeastern Indian Territory, below the ever-changing sweep of Red River, Paris, Texas, was the terminus of the Frisco's extension. Pruiett's boarding house, in the western part of the sprawling prairie town, was one of the new enterprises to come in with the new railroad. Paris had grown from a depot on the Texas and Pacific into a robust town. It wouldn't let another line inflate it. Like a new chew, the Frisco and its followers were maneuvered into a handy place in the cheek, and Paris browsed casually along.

"Did you get a job, Mawman?"

"Not just exactly, Ma, I didn't. I got all the work I want to do cleanin' a law office, but there's no pay in it. Just the right to hang around and read."

The Captain said, "Don't lawyers ever pay anything? What's wrong with a lawyer payin' for service he gets, like any one else?"

"I have never seen one that was very prosperous," Moorman said. "I was with Brewer an' Hale for most a year an' all I ever saw pass over the counter for fees was butter an' vegetables an' cured meats. Ma hollers about gettin' to be a lawyer, an' then you'll be somethin', but the lawyers is the brokest bunch I ever saw."

"You have never been in with the right kind, that's all,"

Pruiett Boarding House at Paris

Moman, with the watch chain, leans against the post. Betty and the Captain are at the right.

Betty retorted. "You just work an' learn for me, an' the pay'll take care of itself."

"Who you goin' to work for?" the Captain inquired.

"Colonel Jake Hodges," he answered.

"There's a lawyer that is not broke," the elder Pruiett replied. "What he can't make tryin' murder an' cow thief cases, he can make playin' poker. I've heard of him ever since the railroad got across Red River. He's the best lawyer in this part of Texas."

"That's what I heard, an' if droves of clients callin' is any evidence of office business, he's got all he can handle. It's the busiest place I ever seen."

"How'd you happen to get in with him, Mawman?" Betty inquired.

"He's got a brother, an' I ran into him down at the Peterson Hotel, where I've been tryin' to get a job. He got to braggin' about his brother bein' the best lawyer in Paris. I told him I cleaned offices for lawyers back in Hackett, an' that as soon as I got lined up I was goin' to get back into it, an' do some more law readin'. He took me up to the office, an' there was a big poker game goin' on. The spittoons an' buckets are so full they're runnin' over, an' the whole bunch is spittin' out the windows an' on the floor. Bob, that's the Colonel's brother, says, 'Jake, here's a friend of mine from Arkansas that read some law with Jap Hale, up at Hackett City,' an' Colonel Jake looks up from his hand for just a minute, an' he says, 'Tell him to take off his wig an' make hisself at home.' The bunch started to laugh, an' I says, 'Ever' country son of a gun in Arkansas has pulled that one on me. If you want to get up to date, ask me if I got my dog-tax paid.' They all gave Jake the horse laugh, an' I started to walk out. 'I was joshin',' Jake called. 'Hang around here with Bob 'til I get this hand down. I want to talk to you.' "

"It don't sound just like the right kind of a place, to me," Betty observed.

"Jake Hodges is a good man, Maw. He's rough, an' don't take nobody's backwater, but he's all right. He talked to me awhile, an' asked about my plans, real polite like, an' then he tells me to clean 'er up, so's he can see what I can do. When I got through, in about two hours, he says it's the best the offices have looked for thirteen years. He gives me some money, an' sends me to the DeShong's bar for some whiskey for the bunch. When I get back he gives me a key an' a quarter, an' he tells me I'm a member. I got the run of the office an' it's got plenty of books. All I got to do is keep her clean."

"I wisht he had a good payin' job, an' had these law ideas out of his head," the Captain said. "Hard work is what pays in the long run. An' look at me, gettin' too old to cut meat or chop ties, an' nothin' but a broke lawyer as prospects for support."

"You keep outa this, Paw," Betty said. "Mawman don't need to work as long as I can cook an' scrub floors. My slavin' an' prayin' is not goin' to waste. You read in Colonel Hodges' office, an' apply yourself, 'til you get to know the law. Then you can take care of your maw an' pay her back."

She ran her hand through his black brush and caressed him. He didn't pull away from her. "Ever' time I ask for a job, an' get turned down, it just feels like some one is lookin' down my windpipe," he said. "I get to wonderin' if they know about my trouble in Arkansas."

"One reason I was so glad to come out here, when your paw got to talkin' about it, was to get away from that," Betty answered. "Just you forget about it. You're young, an' you have not got the hard look that goes with that awful experience you had. Keep your head up, an' keep lookin' ahead; think about what there is to be done, an' how easy it's goin' to be for a boy with a clear head like yourn to do it. That's been a bad dream, somethin' that is not true, an' look at it that way. Nobody knows about it out here."

"There was an old man in Little Rock prison that was older'n paw, an' he'd spent the biggest part of his life there, or some other prison. He said he was doin' his ninth term. He said he got homesick if he was out very long."

"I said for you to forget about that, son," Betty persisted.

"The old man didn't care much about bein' inside, like I did, most of the time. He just set around, an' didn't care what day of the week it was, an' he was always glad when the Salvation Army church was over on Sunday. But once in awhile they slipped a little dope in to him—morphine—an' after he'd had his shot, he seemed to come to life, an' really worry an' hurt. One time, when he was high on the needle, an' cryin' soft to hisself, we was together in the cell block, an' I ask him how in Christ's name he stood it, bein' locked up an' pushed around all his life. He said—."

"Please, Mawman, let's don't keep talkin' about such things. We—."

"I been thinkin' about this, lately, an' I want to tell you

an' paw," he persisted. "This old codger, he grew up an' got old in solitary, he told me. One time, he says, 'Son, I used to be chock full of hope like you are, an' while I was that a'way, it hurt me somethin' awful. I made a mistake, an' I paid for it. I done my full stretch, an' they turned me out, but I was just a damned ex-con. Ever' place I went, it got out that I'd done a rap, that I was a one-time loser. I'd get a job, maybe, but I couldn't keep it. I left the serpent's trail behind me, an' no matter where I went, the damned bluenoses would dig it up on me. When that snake's trail's behind you, you don't need to do nothin' to get in trouble. If somethin's missin', you stole it, 'cause you're a ex-con. Somebody's house burns down, an' you're the son of a gun whether you got matches in your pocket or not. They held me in jail investigatin' me for murder one time, 'cause a drunk stumbled in front of a freight train, an' I had done two stretches in the penitentiary before, an' I happened to be in their damn town. Ain't that a fine system?' he says. The pore old man cried like a baby, an' when I tells him to cheer up, that maybe it won't be so tough on him next time he says, 'Jesus Christ, I ain't worrin' about that. I'm upset about you. You got the trail of the serpent behind you, an' just as sure as hell, you'll keep comin' back to the joints as long as you live. I got mine most done, but hell, you're just sixteen, an' you got a lot of misery ahead of you.'"

"I told you to hush, Mawman," Betty said, crying softly. "The prison hurt your knees, an' made them swell up, an' almost crippled you, but it didn't do nothin' to you inside. It's different in your case, 'cause you wasn't bad in the first place. You went for somethin' you didn't do."

"Is that goin' to make any difference if some one finds out about it, an' there's somethin' goin' on that looks bad for somebody?"

"I ain't goin' to argue. I don't want to hear no more about it, an' that's final with me. Now you hush."

"Mawman, will you run down to DeShong's an' get me a quart of whiskey before you go home?" Jake Hodges was calling from his private office. Pruiett was reading under the gas light in the waiting room.

"I hope you'll excuse me, Colonel, but I couldn't help over-hearing your discussion," Pruiett answered, coming to the door. "I believe I can find you some cases that will help you."

"Meet Judge Russell from Dallas," Hodges said carelessly.

"How are you, son?" Russell inquired with gravity, rising and shaking hands.

"I just happened to read some cases on the same subject a week or so ago," Pruiett repeated, half in apology.

"Well," Hodges grinned, "me an' the judge is right about it, ain't we?"

"No, sir, you're not," came the frank answer. "You're wrong. That's why I thought I'd better butt in an' tell you about these cases I read."

"This is Stilwell H. Russell, you're talkin' to," Hodges suggested, with mock politeness. "He's supposed to know a little law hisself."

"It's a pretty fine point, an' an easy one to go wrong on. You don't want no error in your record if you can keep it out, I'm sure," Pruiett persisted.

"You're absolutely right, young man," Russell agreed. "Now, look here—maybe we don't understand each other. Do you know what our question is?"

"I think I do," Pruiett replied. "You're here as special prosecutor in the Williams murder case. Buck Williams is pleadin' self defense; that he killed Mitchell after Mitchell tried to slug him in the head with a bar off of a binder. You say, now that Williams has said Mitchell jumped him, that Mitchell's reputation has been put in issue, an' that the state's entitled to prove Michell's reputation for bein' quiet an' peaceable, an' so forth. Is that it?"

"That's it, just exactly," Russell acknowledged. "An' Colonel Jake says, and I quite agree, that when Williams testified that Mitchell attacked him, that he opened up the gate. He assaulted Mitchell's character—his reputation—and now we can prove that Mitchell was a man with a reputation for being peaceable and law abiding, and not usually expected to act like Williams said he did on this occasion."

"It's reversible error if you do it," Pruiett said, with finality. "You just got to suggest an assault in a self-defense plea, an' that alone don't put reputations in issue. I can remember the book numbers, an' I think I can remember the page. Want to see 'em?"

"I want a drink of whiskey," Hodges interrupted. "That's what I called you about. What do you say?"

"I'll be back in a jiffy," Pruiett answered from the doorway.

"Who's the boy?" Stilwell Russell asked.

"Just a pore folks kid. Good worker, though, an' tryin' hard. He's a little too fresh, an' talks back a little too quick. That's the worst thing I see in him."

"It's not a fault, if it's handled right," Russell said. "How old is he?"

"He's only seventeen or eighteen, but he looks older. I'm watchin' him pretty close here lately. I heard he was convicted in Arkansas on a forgery. Maybe that's what makes him look older than he actually is.

"It's that heavy black hair, for one thing, and that agate eye. I'm a fair judge of men an' horses, an' I'd say a kid with a cold eye like that—when a kid eye can bore you like a gimlet— is either plumb good or plumb bad. And it takes a lot of guts to tell your elders they're wrong, right to their faces, even if you don't know what you're talkin' about."

"It's just like I was tellin' you," Hodges answered. "He keeps these offices shined, an' reads law in spurts. I think the eye's bad. He's been makin' the joints a lot with that wild brother of mine, an' he's had a helluva fight or two. He most beat a guy from Arkansas to death in the Peterson bar—bigger'n older'n him—an' it's talked about that the guy was mouthin' about this Arkansas conviction. I am not passin' judgment; I'm just watchin'. If he'll keep the place clean, an' his nose clean, too, we'll be able to get along all right together."

Pruiett banged a big bottle on the desk, smiled and went out. "He's got a nice appearance, an' a likeable manner," Russell observed.

"Yeah, he's got personality. Makes friends quick, an' gets along with ever'body. If he'd just gone to school, an' prepared himself, I mighta been able to make a lawyer outa him."

"Here's a Texas case that illustrates my position," Pruiett said, walking between them and laying a volume on the desk. "An' here are two more, from other states, that follow the same rule. They reversed this case and sent it back for a new trial, just because the court let the prosecution prove exactly what you want to prove about Mitchell, against Williams."

"I'll be god damned," Hodges grunted, without looking up from the pages.

"With Pruiett and the Supreme Court against us, we are in ineffective minority, Colonel," Russell said. "As little as I like to do it, I am going to confess to error, and apologize to your assistant."

"I think I'll run along, Colonel," Pruiett said. "It's gettin' pretty late, an' I ought—."

"You ought to go home, not to that Peterson saloon an' gamblin' room," Hodges interrupted. "An' quit running around with Bob so damn late at night. He can drink beer an' shoot craps all night, an' wake up daisy fresh in the morning, but you can't. You are too young."

With a wave and an infectious grin the black-haired boy was away. "That boy keeps facts in his head better than you or I," Russell said. "It didn't take him a minute to apply the rule in this case, just overhearin' our conversation, an' he knew exactly where to go for the case. Was it an accident, or is he that good?"

"I really don't know," Hodges confessed. "This makes me think—. He's slipped up on me a time or two, with material suggestions, on things I was overlookin'. An' it's always memory stuff. He don't seem to forget nothin'. Maybe he's got somethin'."

Killings, and murder trials, were like cotton-picking and beef-shipping time, in Paris. Liquor and easy money made the stock raisers and speculators hot headed and quick to shoot. The Indian Territory north of Red River was dry, and visitors from across that line were usually saloon bound. The United States District Court, with jurisdiction over the territory, met and tried cases at Paris, to add variety to the local brand of felony displays. In the northern extermity of the territory, in the "no man's land" sector of the Texas-Oklahoma panhandle, the hay meadow massacre had occurred. The victorious element of the Woodsdale and Hugoton County seat feud, of Stevens County, Kansas, had erred in extinguishing Sheriff Cross and his posse on land under Federal jurisdiction. And they had made one slight additional error. One of the dead victims, perforated with Winchester slugs and buckshot, got well. Their victory, in the light of his testimony from the witness stand, was sour and hollow.

With the venue of the crimes in the Federal Court's jurisdiction in the territory, the cases were heard at Paris. Colonel Jake Hodges, acknowledged best of the criminal lawyers of the section, was counsel for the defendants. The Colonel was a typical frontier type. His voice was deep and booming; his identifying gesture was a big-fisted slap on the back, accompanied by a roaring laugh.

He had memorized all of the Henry W. Grady orations on the Old South, the Constitution of the United States and the Declaration of Independence. His jury arguments in criminal cases were hybrid composites of these three sources, embellished with the homely delivery he had acquired with his years of experience. With a huge gold chain draped across his portly paunch, and with his wrinkled, freckled neck flushed with effort, he waved the bloody shirt in front of the cowman jury.

The six defendants, Charles Edward Cook and his brother, Oran Cook, and John J. Chamberlain, Cyrus Fields, John Jackson and Jack Lawrence, were convicted of murder in spite of the Colonel's lusty bawling, and were sentenced to hang. Young Pruiett heard every syllable of the evidence, the court's charge and the arguments of counsel. He had correctly predicted the outcome before the jury returned its verdict.

"The Colonel didn't have much chance to win those cases." He and Bob Hodges were having beer at the far end of the Peterson Hotel's bar.

"They was guilty, wasn't they?" Hodges inquired. "Why the hell shouldn't they have been stuck?"

"Well, now," Pruiett mused. "If you're convicted when you're guilty, an' acquitted when you are not—why have lawyers, a'tall? Why have courts? Just call a guy in an' ask him 'Are you guilty or are you not?' and then lock him up or turn him a'loose. Is that your idea of how to work it?"

"It's all the same to me, lawyers or no lawyers," Bob answered. "They're all grafters, anyway. That cheap brother of mine is a crook, an' he don't split none of the dough he makes with me. He's tryin' to starve me to death, so I don't give a damn whether he goes good or not."

"I wisht I could get it straight in my head, just once," Pruiett said. "There's times when I get in heat over the prospects, an' then times when just thinkin' about tryin' a lawsuit makes me sick. Have you got any idea how hard a job it is, to get up an' vouch for a bunch of dirty bastards like Colonel Jake did today, knowin' all the time they're guilty? Do you think it's easy to stand up an' beg an' argue for acquittal, when you can see conviction in ever' expression in ever' juror's face? You got to be an actor, an' you got to be a hypocrite, an' you got to be a faker, to be a good lawyer. An' if you are not goin' to be a good one, then you have no business bein' one at all, 'cause then you double your clients and take pay for somethin' you can't deliver—an' in the long run you're a party to spreadin' misery, an' sufferin' an' distress. Did you know that?"

"I don't know nothin' about it, an' I don't care. I do know that old Jake'll raise a lot of hell with me for bein' out so late. It's past midnight. We better go."

"I'm ready," Pruiett said, and they started toward the exit. As they walked by the tender motioned for them to stop.

"I got a drunk over there that ought to be put to bed, an' I ain't got no one to look after the place while I do it," he said, indicating a limp figure bending over a small table. "It's old Pat Riley from Bonham, an' I been tryin' to send him to his room all evenin'. Couldn't you boys help him up the stairs an' into bed?"

"I've poured plenty of drunks into bed," Bob Hodges answered. "Grab an arm, Mawman, an' we'll hist him up. Let's go!"

Riley was an old tailor who had sold his business in Bonham, preparatory to opening a shop in Paris. "You boys is awful nice to old Pat," he mumbled, as they half-carried him up the stairway.

"Maybe you can do as much for us sometime, when we get in the same fix," Moorman suggested.

"You boys is too nice to drink old nasty licker," Pat said. "You are good fellows. I'm goin' to pay you a nice reward for helpin' me to bed. I got plenty of dough."

"You'd better keep your mouth shut about it 'til you sober up a little," one of the boys suggested. They unlocked the door to his room, lighted the lamp on the dresser, and started unbuttoning his shoes. He began to kick.

"Let's all go back an' have just one more drink," he suggested.

"You ain't goin' nowhere but to bed," Hodges said.

"One of you good boys go down an' get old Pat a bottle of whiskey, then," he said. "I'll need a drink for sure in the mornin'."

"We ain't gettin' you nothin'." Pruiett was holding his shoulders off the bed while Hodges peeled off his coat.

Riley managed to drag a bulging wallet from the inside pocket of the coat. Spreading its frayed jaws apart he exhibited its contents, with pride. "I got plenty of money, an' I want to pay you nice boys a reward. An' I want you to buy me a bottle of whiskey. Just help yourself." Hodges and Pruiett looked at each other in amazement. The case was crowded with hundred dollar bills.

"Where do you suppose the old son of a bitch got all that jack?" Hodges whispered.

"It's a wonder he ain't been rolled, drunk as he is. I guess nobody thought he had the price of another drink," Pruiett answered, in the same tone.

"I don't want you nice boys to run out an' leave me," Riley whimpered. "I got the shakes comin' on, an' I have 'em awful bad once they start. They's snakes an' wildcats an' ever'thing gets after me."

"Maybe we ought to stay an' kinda watch out for him," Hodges suggested. "But I'd never make Jake believe me, tellin' him what I was doin'."

"We'd do pretty good, three in one bed, an' one limber drunk, now, wouldn't we?" Pruiett inquired.

"You could stay an' look out for him, Mawman," said Hodges. "Your folks don't know when you get in, anyway; they don't know whether it's you or some of the roomers, an' the two of you could make out all right in that big bed. Do you think so?"

"I guess I could, if it's necessary," Pruiett agreed. "What do you say?"

"I say take good care of Uncle Pat an' get him sober, an' then if he wants to pay off a little, in appreciation, it'll be all right to take it. I'll see you tomorrow." Hodges waved and disappeared into the darkness of the hallway.

It was visitors' day at the jail. Betty Pruiett was there to see her Mawman.

"Colonel Jake says he won't defend you, honey," she said, through the bars. "I begged him, an' offered to pay him good, too, but he just said no. He said the deal kind of involved Bob, an' that Bob would have to be a witness. He said he just couldn't afford to take it at all."

"There ain't much use to fight it," the boy said. "You remember what I told you,—the trail of the serpent? The old codger was just exactly right. When somethin' happens, the first one they jump on is the fellow with snake's tracks behind him."

"I got H. B. Birmingham hired," she said. "An' there's plenty use to fight it, if you're innocent. Tell me the truth, Mawman, what happened? What was you doin' in the old man's room?"

"I told you once, Maw, an' you got to believe me whether

any one else does or not. Bob an' me helped him upstairs an' we put him to bed. He had about three thousand dollars in hundred dollar bills, an' he was dog-drunk an' talkin' about goin' after some more whiskey. We decided I'd better stay all night in the room an' watch him an' take care of him. I went to bed with him. He was asleep when I dozed off, an' the next thing I knew they was throwin' water in my face in the Hotel Hallway, an' the place was full of smoke. I ran back into the room an' it was burnt up inside. The mattress, an' the bed clothes an' the curtains all burned up, an' the smoke must have knocked me out. I was unconscious when they pulled me out of the room, an' I don't know nothin' about his money."

"No, but that room clerk at the Hotel Peterson says he got kinda worried about the old man, an' looked across the court in the room about two o'clock. He says the light was burnin', an' he saw you sittin' on the side of the bed countin' bills, an' that in about fifteen minutes he saw the smoke, an' ran up an' found you an' the old man in bed together. He says he doesn't think you were really unconscious when he hauled you out."

"There's a man I'll kill if I ever get out of jail," Pruiett gritted. "Why, he or Bob Hodges is the one's that stole Riley's money. He's the one that done it, an' he's cooked up that tale to cover up his own stealin'. Nobody would believe it was me, though, if it wasn't for the deal I got in Arkansas."

"The money might have burned up in his coat pocket," Betty suggested.

"If that thievin' clerk hadn't a-lied on me, I'd a-thought the same thing," he said. "There was no way on God Almighty's earth to tell, the shape the room was in. The bedding, and the curtains, was solid char; just black an' gray flakes all over the room. The old wallet an' the bills might have been there, burned to flakes, but so long as they got a' ex-convict around, why not send him back to hell? Why not make the serpent's trail a little heavier behind him, so's that he won't never have no chance to do nothin' but bust back into prison."

"Don't get bitter, Mawman," she said, wiping her eyes. "Your paw and I'll be behind you, an' Mr. Birmingham will be over to see you right away, about the trial. Just you tell the truth, an' I'll pray. There's got to be some justice in the world somewhere, for us."

"It's damn scarce, the kind you're lookin' for," he told her, as she turned to leave.

The prosecuting attorney toyed with a one-page document in his hand and smiled, tolerantly. A sad faced boy with piercing eyes and shining black hair was telling his story of the fire in Riley's room at the Peterson Hotel. The paper was proof of a conviction in Arkansas; it was a certified copy of the Sebastian Court record. It would soon be time to cross-examine. He glanced at the record and smiled like a miser counting his money.

Birmingham, the defense attorney, had a listless sincerity and perseverance which barely kept him in practice. "You may cross-examine," he mumbled when Pruiett had concluded his account.

"May I inquire," the prosecutor drawled, rising to his feet, "Have you ever been convicted of a felony?"

The witness' eyes flashed. "Well, it was like this—."

"That calls for a 'yes' or 'no' answer, your honor," the prosecutor interrupted.

"Yes," came the crisp answer. There was a dangerous glint of defiance in the dark eyes, and his lips were set in a hard, straight line.

Betty cried and the bailiff had to take the Captain out of the court room. His caustic comment, when state's witnesses were on the stand interrupted the process of justice. The jurors slept or pondered over their own personal problems after the defendant acknowledged the prior conviction. If he's been convicted once, what more was to be said? Write him a ticket to Rusk and save the state the expense of trying him.

"We find the defendant Moorman Pruiett guilty of robbery, as charged, and fix his punishment at imprisonment in the State Penitentiary at Rusk, for a period of five years," droned the court clerk, reading the verdict while the jurors looked indifferently at the opposite wall of the court room. Betty continued to cry. The defendant leaped to his feet.

"You'll all regret this," he cried, shaking a clenched fist in the jury's face. "Ever' damn one of you'll regret it. You never would have arrested me in this case if I hadn't a-had that term in Arkansas, an' you never would have convicted me, neither, if it hadn't a-been for that. It's the trail of the serpent, following me from Little Rock, an' takin' me back to prison. You think you can break me with it, but by God, you can't. As sure as I live I'll make you sorry. I'll empty your damned jails, an' I'll turn the murderers an' thieves a'loose in your midst. But I'll do it in a legal way."

A deputy grabbed him and pulled him from the court room. There was a look of fiendish hatred on his face as he passed from his sobbing mother's sight.

The following is a story told to young Pruiett, by his mother, which he always remembered after his release from the prison in Arkansas:

Back in Hardin County, Kentucky, there lived a family by the name of Lowery, a very old and aristocratic family of Hardin County. Young Tobe Lowery was arrested, charged with stealing a hog, a blue-barrow. His nearest relative was old Colonel Tobe Lowery, an old patriarch who was young Tobe's grandfather. Colonel Tobe Lowery secured the services of Colonel P. Watt Hardin, one of Kentucky's great criminal lawyers. After Hardin's employment the grandfather said: "Tell me, tell me, Colonel Hardin, tell me in God's name can you clear young Tobe?" Colonel Hardin replied: "I don't know, I will talk to the witnesses. The trial starts under yonder chestnut tree, meet me here in my office at two o'clock." At two o'clock Colonel Lowery met Colonel Hardin, and said in a very nervous excited manner: "Tell, tell me, Colonel Hardin, will you be able to save young Tobe?" "Yes," replied Colonel Hardin. "Thank God, thank God," replied Colonel Lowery, "the family's name is saved." "Hold on Colonel Tobe," said Colonel Hardin, "I will save young Tobe, but by-God so long as the name of Kentucky exists, and the name of Lowery lasts, the blue-barrow will always squeal." The story of the blue barrow has followed young Moman Pruiett throughout his lifetime.

Moman did two years of the five-year term. Charles A. Culberson, who was governor of Texas, had been receiving visits from Betty Pruiett, periodically, during the time he stayed in confinement.

Betty had changed. The bloom of her blue grass beauty had been washed away by the stream of sweat in her years of transient toil. Her once proud shoulders, graceful and square, emulated old Sugar Loaf, the mountain which had separated the burst of the summer sunrise at Hackett City.

She had grown old and unlovely, but there was an intangible beauty about her year-seamed face and labor-bent body. Her eyes were like those of a crusader. The dream of the future for the confined son had lost none of its reality; her prayers for his development were as fervent each night as they had been while he writhed within her womb.

"I'm sorry that I wasn't able to see you yesterday," Culberson was saying. "I noticed you in the waiting room, and I thought—."

"You thought I might get tired and go away?" she interrupted.

"Frankly—yes, Mrs. Pruiett. I'm thoroughly familiar with the nature of your business, and it's impossible for me to help you."

Betty gave him a wan smile. "When you're thoroughly familiar with the case, Governor, you'll pardon him," she said.

"How many times have we gone over this application, Mrs. Pruiett?" the Governor inquired.

She smiled again. "I don't remember," she said, "but we'll have to do it again. I was going to come back tomorrow if you didn't let me in today. It's too far down here, from where we live, for me to come an' then get chicken-hearted."

"Yes, I know that, and I felt bad about it at home last night. I thought of you waiting there, as I slipped out the side door and went away. You come from Paris to Austin—from the Red to the Colorado. It's almost like travel between foreign countries. Who pays for it?

"I do," she said simply. "I start savin' as soon as I get back, for the next trip to visit him. I go to Rusk first; then I come on down to Austin to see you. We're poor, an' the boardin' house doesn't make a lot, but we've cut down on our livin' since Mawman got in this trouble."

"You spoil him," the governor said. "Look here—if you hadn't prevailed on Simon Hughes, and I know you worked on him just like you're workin' on me right now, and had just let him serve that two years he got, then maybe he'd a-learned his lesson. Maybe he wouldn't be back in now. If he thinks the law can be trifled with, an' that he won't have to pay for his violations of it, he'll be more apt to take chances, and do things that he knows shouldn't be done."

"You've told me that before, Governor," she said, "but I say if he hadn't been mistreated the first time, an' sent up for somethin' he didn't do, that he never would have been suspected in this case. Why, they never did prove that a crime had been committed, much less that Mawman done it. That room was full of waste, an' char, an' the burned money might have been there all the time, an' the officers never would have known it."

Culberson shook his head. "We always come right back to the place where we started," he said. "I had my own attorney make an investigation of this case, and ask for recommendations, but he couldn't get them. The judge that tried the case says his conduct was brazen and hardened, both when the jury convicted him and later when sentence was passed. The warden says that he's not made a good prisoner, that he's an agitator, an' makes speeches in the prison yard that disturbs the other prisoners. My man, that went down and talked to him, said he was a little off. All he would say, in answer to questions, was something about the serpent's trail, and the squeal of the blue barrow, and to ask another question. 'If an innocent man can be convicted, then why can't a guilty man be acquitted?' To ever' question they ask him he answers the same, 'If an innocent man can be convicted, then why can't a guilty man be acquitted?' You see, Mrs. Pruiett, that there's really not much that I can do."

"He's not makin' speeches in the prison yard any more," Betty answered, daubing a soiled handkerchief to her eyes. "He's in the hospital, an' his knees are swole up as big as his head, an' his ankles are so swole it looks like he hasn't got any feet— just big chunks of flesh at the end of his legs. He didn't hardly know me, his fever was so high, an' he's talkin' about the trail of the serpent, all right, but there is not many around to hear. It was the same way after they kept him caged up at Little Rock. You got to turn him loose, or you got to bury him, an' I know your great big state did not mean to sentence a little boy to death for somethin' he didn't do."

Culberson drummed on his desk and looked out of the big windows. "I heard he was sick, too, but I can't turn 'em out as fast as they get sick. That's an old gag to get out of the work routine."

"It's a long way to Rusk, Governor, but it is not too far to go to find out the truth," she said. "I'll leave it up to you. You're fair and honest, an' tryin' to do the right thing. I know that. You go down an' talk to him. See how sick he is, an' what them old damp cells is doin' to that inflammatory rheumatism, and then you look him in the eye an' ask him to tell you what happened up at the Peterson Hotel that night. If you think he's lyin' about it, an' if you think he is not goin' to die if he stays in your prison, then you just tell me. If you say no after seein' him an' talkin' to him, I promise I won't bother you any more. I'll just make my visits to Rusk, as long as he lasts—an' I got some one there to visit."

She was laboring to speak without breaking. Culberson walked to her side and patted her shoulder. "All right," he said. "I'll go to Rusk, and I'll see your boy. If he's the flesh and blood of a suffering soul like you, there must be something in him worth saving. I'll go down and take a look."

Summer of 1894 was burning its Texas best. The mistress of the Pruiett Boarding House rocked listlessly on the porch as she read a pencil-written letter she had just taken from the postman. Her wayward son, more mature of face but less robust of physique, sat on the rough planks of the porch floor. Shaggier brows matched the still abundant raven growth which adorned his bare head, and shone in the dust-laden heat of the early afternoon. His feet, which he permitted to rest below the floor level on the crust of the grassless yard, were covered with shoes not conforming to the style of the place and period. He was consciously holding them there, so they would be out of the mother's vision. They were prison cut.

"What's the trouble, Ma?" He thought he had seen her brush a tear away.

"Nothing," she said. "Nothing at all." She folded the letter, and after placing it in her apron pocket, walked over to where he was sitting. With her characteristic gesture of indulgence she ran her rough hands through his thick hair before she stooped and kissed him. He had not been mistaken. Tears were in her eyes and on her cheeks.

When he heard her busy in the kitchen he went to the place where he knew she would place the letter. He took it and after locking himself in the outhouse on the rear of the lot, sat down to read. The quivering hand suggested the great age of the writer. It was from Aunt Millie Huff of Kentucky, the sister of the long departed Colonel Moorman.

"My dear Betty:" it said. "We have all heard about Moorman being in trouble *again*. I know how you must feel with your flesh and blood turning out bad, an' causing you so much expense and trouble. It is the first time that the good name of Moorman has ever been connected with shame and disgrace, and Lucy and I were saying that we wish you had named your boy something else. It makes me sick to think of what your good mother, and her father would say, if they heard . . ."

The letter went quietly back to its place, and the subject quietly about his business. Then the regular mail brought Betty another letter, addressed in a familiar hand. "My dear Mother," she read. "Please try to excuse the liberty I took in reading Aunt Millie's letter to you. She expressed some of the same sentiments that I have felt, along those lines, for a long time. I would gladly abandon the name of Moorman, and even that of Pruiett, if I could get away from the hardships that seem to go with the disgrace I have brought it."

The formal discourse was a well formed scroll. He was drawing upon his remarkable memory and capacity for imitation in presenting words and phrases. ". . . I feel that I have no right to carry the name of the Moormans further, and you may so advise Aunt Millie and the meddling Lucy. Every tub must stand on its own bottom, and I am convinced that the time has come for me to get along without your constant support, and *to make a name for myself.* I am, and will continue to be, your devoted son, MOMAN Pruiett."

The United States District Court for the Eastern District of Texas held an occasional term at Paris. David E. Bryant, of Sherman, was the judge. During the court session at Paris, he stopped at the Hotel Lamar, and on the warm evenings of spring and fall he would pull his chair from the lobby to the sidewalk in front, drummer fashion. In the way that a good man of position knows of the little man of misfortune, Judge Bryant knew of the reborn Moman.

"Moman," he called. "Come here. Got time to stop a minute an' talk?"

The boy, hurrying in the September twilight, hesitated before he stopped or turned. Had something happened? Were the snake's tracks behind ready to involve him again? He walked back, slowly.

"I'm Judge Bryant, of Sherman," the judge said. "I been in town holdin' a term of court."

Pruiett accepted his cordial handshake with suspicion. "I know you well enough, Judge Bryant. My name's Pruiett— Moman Pruiett."

"Sure it is," agreed the judge. "I know you, an' I know about you. First time I heard of you was through Stilwell Russell. I

FEDERAL JUDGE DAVID E. BRYANT,
who admitted Pruiett to practice on his own motion.

been talkin' to Jake Hodges about you since I been in town this trip. Have you got time to set down here, an' talk to me for a little while?"

"I got plenty of time," he said, dropping into a wooden rocker. "An' I'm right proud to talk to a judge."

"Stilwell Russell was tellin' me about you showin' him an' Colonel Jake some law when he was down here tryin' a murder case three years ago—an' then a little later he told me about your tough luck, an' about you gettin' sent away. Russell said the whole thing sounded like a big mistake, an' Stilwell Russell is one of the best lawyers, and one of the best all round men, we got in Texas. Do you know that?"

"He was very kind to me, and I heard him try the Williams case; that was all I heard him try. I'd say he was a fine lawyer."

Bryant laughed. "You got a nice way of expressin' yourself, Moman, an' of lettin' the praise kind of glance off. It isn't every kid reading law in a country law office that Stilwell Russell remembers to talk about, after he gets away from 'em."

Pruiett smiled and said nothing.

"Jake Hodges brought it up in a little session we was havin' in chambers this afternoon. He says that it looks kind of funny, nobody never findin' that money the old Irishman lost, an' then the room clerk quittin' his job an' leavin' town all of a sudden, when the word gets out that Culberson's givin' you a pardon an' sendin' you home. He thought."

"I was goin' to make him and Bob explain," Pruiett interrupted.

Bryant laughed again. "An' Jake says if you surprised Stilwell Russell with how you could remember citations an' opinions two years ago, he ought to come back an' try you now. He says you have not visited a joint since you came home, an' that you've read about ever' book in his whole library."

"I made up my mind I was goin' to make up for lost time," Pruiett answered.

"How you gettin' along? I mean, what you doin' to make your livin'? Does this conviction make it hard on you that way?"

"Well," he answered slowly. "I had a pretty hard time. an' I'd a'either had to leave town or really go to hard labor if it wasn't for old man Ambrose Long. He runs the Lamar County Warehouse, you know, an' I finally told him right out that nobody in town would hire me 'cause I was a ex-convict. He says, 'Well, I don't really need help at the warehouse, but if that's the way

these Christians are around here, I'll just put you to work.'
I'm wrasslin' cotton bales an' goods boxes for Long, an' makin'
thirty dollars a month. I read law ever' night, an' keep busy
all the time. I don't think they'll be able to hang anything on
me, no matter what happens around here. But I am not sure."

"Did you ever try a lawsuit?" Bryant inquired.

"Not to really try one," he answered. "I fronted for a farmer
one time in a horse-deal squabble up at Hackett City, Arkansas.
Just a scrap before a country squire, but I read 'em some law an'
made a little speech. I was just a kid."

"Do you actually want to be a lawyer?" the judge asked.
"I mean, if you got to be one, would you work at it, an' try to
make something out of yourself?"

"It's serious business with me, Judge," he said. There was a
dangerous glint in his eye which Bryant could not see there in
the half-darkness. "I'm goin' to learn how to try cases an' I'm
going to learn to try 'em right. You watch me an' see."

"How you fixed for clothes?" was the next question.

"These overalls is the best I got right now, but I got a pay
day comin' so's I can get me a suit. But while I am not goin' no
place, I don't need no clothes, much."

There was a silence between them for several minutes. Then
Judge Bryant pressed something into the boy's hand and arose
from his chair.

"Fix yourself up, an' spend a day in my court before the
session's over," he said. "Tell old man Long I said to give you a
day off."

"This here's a twenty, Judge," Pruiett said, peering at it in the
light of the hotel window.

"I know it, son," he answered. "Some one ought to try to
make up for the way these crooks around here been usin' you.
I want to help that much. Get you a suit, an' spend a day in
court with me. That's all I want you to do for the twenty."

So Pruiett went to court. Before adjournment at noon Judge
Bryant looked uncertainly at him, and then, after pointing his
finger, crooked it in a beckoning gesture.

"Come up here, Moman, he said, loudly.

When the boy reached the space in front of his desk, the
judge extended his hand for a handshake, and then turned to
the surprised clerk.

"Swear Moman in, an' place his name on the rolls, as a

lawyer, an' as an officer of my court. See that it shows that it's done on the court's own motion."

Thus did Moorman Pruiett become Moman Pruiett, and thus did Moman Pruiett become a lawyer. Twenty-three years had fled since his unscheduled arrival on the old Gray Eagle. Ten months he had spent in institutions of learning. Thrice as many months had he spent in institutions of correction. The hopes and prayers of a sacrificing mother and the invisible touch of pure genius made up his stock in trade. A smoldering hatred for the system which had wrongfully taken away his liberty, a tongue of unsurpassed, although untried, eloquence, a psychological flair for the dramatic and unexpected, were some of the intangible attributes of his unorthodox personality. Without fear; if the straits of his client were difficult enough, he was to become the most formidable obstacle in the path of the prosecution which would attempt to obtain and maintain a conviction.

There is no question but what if it had not been for the conviction of stealing old man Riley's three thousand dollars, when he was innocent of the offense, that Moman would not have become one of the most successful criminal lawyers that ever defended a client in the south or in any other part of the United States. In every trial he lived and breathed an atmosphere of innocence, defense or mitigation for every client.

CHAPTER THREE

Wherein rumblings from the dungeons of Rusk and Little Rock begin to reverberate, as Pruiett's plan for courtroom procedure is discussed and put into operation. How he tries his first case and wins—and tries a murder case and wins—and tries for the hand of a maiden and is likewise successful. And how his aptitude attracts the attention of a pair of powers from the dark and wild Territory, and how he goes, on their invitation, recommendation, and capital, to try it as a proving ground for his long-nourished desire for a place to cast his lot.

"The case against S. C. Brashier, who was arrested some weeks ago charged with the robbery of an intoxicated stranger in a restaurant on the east side of the square, and which since then has attracted a great deal of interest, was tried yesterday, and resulted in a speedy acquittal of the accused. The defense was by Moman Pruiett, and it was most brilliantly conducted under most unpromising circumstances . . . He displayed superb skill at every juncture, and made one of the most forcible and eloquent speeches heard in the courthouse here in a long time . . ."

Pruiett stood on the walk in front of the Lynch Building, reading his notice in the Paris Daily News.

"That was a nice job of work you did in the Brashier case," a man said, walking up and stopping beside him. It was Enoch Fagan, of the local law firm of Brants and Fagan. "That guy was generally considered as guilty. I didn't have any idea he'd come clear."

"Thanks," Pruiett responded, indifferently. "What you're generally considered an' what you are, is two different things. If you'd a asked me, I'd a told you he was comin' out all right."

"I guess you knew it all the time," Fagan suggested, with a touch of sarcasm.

"I ain't braggin', I'm just makin' conversation. I tried him to acquit him, not to stick him."

"That was pretty neat, all right, takin' that little baby off his wife's lap, there when you was arguin' to the jury, an' holdin' it in your arms all the time you was makin' your speech. Did Jake Hodges put you wise to that?"

"Jake Hodges told me to plead him guilty."

"Who wrote that speech for you?" Fagan persisted.

"Nobody," Pruiett answered. "I wrote a speech for that jury, all right, but I didn't use it. I changed my mind at the last minute, and let 'em have just what came to me. I heard a good lawyer try a case at Fort Smith when I was a kid, an' I was just apin' him, mostly."

Fagan took on a confused look. He didn't know whether the brown-eyed boy was making fun, or in earnest.

"Brants and I got plenty of room in our offices, an' if you want to use the library any time, or meet a client up there, you're welcome. We want to see you get along."

"Thanks, much obliged," Pruiett said.

He was trying to be indifferent when he walked into the boarding house that evening. He knew Betty would be elated, and that she would probably make an embarrassing scene in her elation. "I'm awful glad you won your case, Mawman," was all she said. "I knew you could do it."

"Thanks, Ma," he replied. "I really don't see nothin' to it. Ever' trick I had figured worked just right. I was givin' the jury somethin' to keep 'em awake, an' to keep 'em from thinkin' about that guy Brashier. I took that month-old kid, an' I kept it in my arms, wrapped in its blanket, an' I says, 'Could you hold a precious bundle like this to your heart an' utter an untruth?' I says, 'Could you lie to the Savior with an angel sittin' on your knee? When that little woman, with this little baby in her arms, testified that its daddy was home all evenin' that evenin', she was tellin' the truth like God loves it. Straight and untarnished. The men that says they saw Brashier hangin' around the front of the restaurant that night are mistaken, or,' I says, 'or they got a guilty motive for bein' so positive it was him.' I poured it on the deputies that arrested him, an' I poured it on old Taliaferro an' Frank Lee, the prosecutors. Old Frank twisted an' the jurors grinned. They liked it, so I keep goin'. They smiled when I ate the sheriff up, an' they cried when I pulled the flap back an' showed 'em that baby's face. The jury wasn't out fifteen minutes, an' they said Brashier's not guilty."

"You're pretty proud, are you not, son?" she asked.

"It's a start for me," he said. "A little start on a big job I got to do. Tissie Hotubby might as well of got off, as gettin' life, is what I still say."

"A good lawyer's got a wonderful power," she said. "All I've been through with has not shaken my faith in my vision. I knew it was goin' to be, ever since I heard Dan'l Voorhees make that wonderful speech at Alton, July 1, before you was born.

You was born to be a lawyer, an' nothin' could keep you from it, not even your 'serpent's trail,' as you call it."

"Keep me from it?" he whispered, with a black look. "Keep me from it? Why, Ma, that's what pulled me into it. You know that. I am not goin' to fool you."

She kissed him and ran her fingers through his black hair. "That's good enough for an excuse, if you need one, but when you soften up you'll find you was the one that was fooled, yourself. It's your gift, not this foolish hate you got, that's pullin' you on."

Let's not talk about it," he smiled. "I wouldn't even have said that much to any one else."

"How'd you like to have a murder case? Maybe two of 'em?"

"I'll land one, an' when I do I'll show that swelled-up Jake Hodges how to try it," he said. "I'll—."

"I think I got you one."

"What?"

"I think I got you one. There's two women from the Territory rented the back room this mornin', an' they're here for court. There's two men in the Federal jail charged with murder, one's a wife, an' the other's the sister of these two. I told 'em there was a lawyer in the house, an' they seemed interested. I'll call an' tell 'em that you're home."

"Just a minute, Ma," he said. "There's something else I want to talk to you about first. You know it's important with me if I'd let a chance at a real murder case wait, don't you?"

"There's not any trouble comin' from tryin' this Brashier case, is there? You ain't in trouble again?"

He smiled and hesitated, awkwardly. "Not the kind of trouble that worries you," he answered.

"That's right," she agreed. "There's nothin' wrong with them."

"You know Lilly Belle, don't you?

"She's a sweet girl," Betty said.

"Did you ever notice that her hair was really red, instead of black, like it usually looks?"

"Why, no, I hadn't," Betty laughed. "But I never looked very close to see. Do you mean to tell me that it's actually dark red?"

"It really is," he said, earnestly, "an' her skin's so thin that you can see right through it. You can see the bottom side of those little freckles on the side of her nose, if you look real close, an' the pink flesh of her face, underneath." His dark eyes and hair sparkled with his complete animation.

"I noticed her clear skin, all right," Betty agreed. "She's a lovely girl, but she's awful young. She is not more than fifteen, now, is she?"

"She's almost eighteen," he answered. "I've been goin' over to their place in the evenin's, an' she an' her mother have been like real folks with me. They have not got the old poker in their back like a lot of these hypocrites around here have ever' time they see me a-comin'. I think I'll ask Lilly Belle to marry me, if you think it'd be all right."

"If it'd make you happy, son, it's goin' to be all right with me," she said. "It's nice of you to tell me about it, an' I'm glad you trust me an' tell me things like that, but I really have not got any right to say. You're a grown man now, an' you do what you know's the best for you."

"You are not exactly old, Ma, but you are not young, neither, an' Pa—he's gettin' old. He's countin' a lot on me, even if he does think I'm makin' a big mistake in tryin' to be a lawyer. You have not done nothin' since I was born but worry with me an' about me, an' try to keep me out of scrapes. I won't have nothin' in my life that is not yours, an' havin' a wife an' home is not goin' to interfere with that. If she'll have me, it'll be subject to my takin' care of you an' tryin' to make things comfortable for you in the future. I'll have that out, the first thing."

"Don't you worry about me," Betty smiled at him. "If she's what you want, just take her, don't ask nobody about it. The girl that gets married to you is never goin' to regret it, bein' married to the best lawyer in the country."

"Run your murder case in here," he cried, "while I got the big head from your braggin'. I'll make 'em think they're talkin' to Stilwell Russell."

"I'm John Evans's sister, an' this is Missus Richards. She's Doc Richards's wife."

"I've heard about them cases," Pruiett answered, with professional gravity. "They're charged with killin' Armon V. Beatty up in the Indian Territory, are they not?"

"That's right," the prospects agreed. Pruiett was interviewing them in the parlor of the boarding house.

"I thought they had lawyers defendin' 'em," he said. "They're set for trial ahead of the John Stevenson case, an' that's on the docket for week after next."

"They ain't been able to raise no money," the Evans woman

said. "We had some lawyers at Fort Worth that was goin' to try 'em, but when we didn't raise the money, they got awful busy an' wrote us that they couldn't make it over here for the trial."

"Don't you have no money at all?" he inquired.

The women shook their heads despondently.

"Bein' in jail charged with murder in that kind of a case is bad, an' bein' broke makes it worse," Pruiett observed. No one disagreed, so he continued. "I am not takin' no murder case under false pretenses; there's too much involved. I've just been practicin' less than a year, an' I have not had a lot of experience in court. I'd like to help you, but I want you to know that before we say any more."

"Your Ma showed us what they said about you in the papers down here, an' besides, I can see you're a lawyer, a good lawyer, just to look at you an' listen to you. If I had plenty of money I'd still hire you." Richard's simple wife was frank in her praise.

"I'll do the best I can for 'em, if you say take it," he said.

"I want you to represent Doc," she said.

"An' if John says it's all right, I say take 'em both together," her companion agreed.

"There ought to be a little expense money advanced for me to work on," he said.

"We can give you ten dollars, an' that's all we got over our two weeks room an' board," Mrs. Richards told him. "We'll put that up if it'll do you any good, but that's the best we can do."

"I want a note, signed by all four of you, for a hundred dollars," he said, trying to look unconcerned with the mention of notes and amounts. "I'll take the ten an' the note, an' see what I can do with the cases. Now, I want to know all about the facts, so just tell me all you can about it."

"Well," John Evans' sister began. "Armon Beatty was killed at John's house up near Emmett, in the Chickasaw country. John an' Clara, his wife, had been havin' trouble almost ever since John brought Beatty home an' gave him a job on the ranch as a hired man. Clara an' Armon was cheatin' on John for a long time, an' ever'body knew it, it seemed like, but John. But finally him an' Clara has a fallin' out, an' John goes to drinkin', an' stayin' away from home while he runs around with Doc Richards. About daylight, one mornin' last summer, two men walked up in the yard with a shotgun, an' Armon's sleepin' out, it's so hot, you know, he's got his mattress on a wagon box in the yard. Well, some one blows Armon's head plumb off with a shotgun. That's about all there is to tell."

"Is there any witnesses, or is it a circumstantial case?" Pruiett almost fumbled the high sounding final phrase of the question.

"There's two witnesses, Clara an' Clarence. Clara's his wife, an' Clarence is a nine year old orphan nephew of Clara's they was a' raisin'. They both claim they seen it, an' that it was John an' Doc that walked up in the yard. They say John did the shootin.'"

"Clara can't testify. She's his wife, an' a wife can't testify against a husband in a criminal prosecution," Pruiett said. "That's cuttin' it down to Clarence. Is he smart?"

"He's a pretty smart kid."

"Is he friendly or unfriendly."

"He'd be friendly, if it wasn't for Clara, but she's seein' that he stays plenty mad at his uncle John. They're goin' to prove that he was awake when the two of 'em walked up, an' that when John pulled the trigger Clarence jumped up an' says, 'Why Uncle John, what did you want to do that for?' Clara wants to see 'em hang, an' she won't let Clarence cool off."

"A jury won't never hang two men on the testimony of a kid like that," Pruiett observed. "A kid's too changeable; he's too likely to be excited, an' mistaken. He'd admit in a minute, on cross-examination, that the light was bad an' he was sleepy, an' that he could have been mistaken about who it was.' I wouldn't be afraid of him so much. What else they got?"

"They're goin' to prove that John an' Doc were in that neighborhood the night Armon was killed, by John's horse. He had a big stallion, a big roan, an' it's a easy horse to remember. Well, Clara's neighbors are goin' to testify that their mares were cuttin' up an' restless, between midnight and dawn, like there was a stud around the lot somewheres. The marshals found a tree on the creek a quarter from where Beatty was shot, where some horses had been tied with short lines that night. One was rubbed up an' the bark was full of roan hair. The shoe prints all around it was big, like stud prints. The marshals saved a lot of that hair, an' they took some samples from John's horse after they arrested him, an' they say they match up perfect."

"That's pretty smart prosecutin'," Pruiett admitted. "It's damn clever an' that'll hurt the case worse than little Clarence. That's somethin' a cowman jury will understand. Is that all they got now?"

"Well," she pondered, "Doc's place, up on Pennington, is about forty miles north of John's place at Emmett. There was a couple of ranch hands camped about half way between, an' along after sun up, according to their story, John an' Doc rode through the brush an' helped them drink their can of coffee. They say the roan an' the black was showin' signs of awful hard ridin', an' the marshals say that the trail, from the creek back of the house where Armon was shot, up to this camp, was clear, an' especially of the big horse. Them cowboys are government witnesses."

"Is that all?" he persisted.

"Yes," they agreed, "that's all, unless John an' Doc can think of somethin'."

"I'm goin' down to the jail to see 'em an' tell 'em I'm hired in the case, an' I may not be back 'til kind of late," Pruiett said. "Would you please tell Maw at supper that I won't be home to eat?"

The Paris Tribune made official note of the only interruption permitted in the preparation of the John Evans and Doc Richards murder case. "Merrily the wedding bells pealed at the Congregational Church last night, when at 8 o'clock Mr. Moman Pruiett led to the altar Miss Lillie Belle Thrasher, where, in the impressive silence which followed the strains of the wedding march, Rev. Luther Reese read the service which made the happy young couple man and wife. Both are well known in the city, and their friends join the TRIBUNE in wishing them a long, happy and prosperous journey down the rugged pathway of life."

"How many recesses has Pruiett had to have in this case, Judge?" Jake Hodges was showing unmistakable signs of peevishness.

"I've lost track, a long time ago," Judge Bryant answered. "But I feel like I got to give him all the time he wants. This is a capital case, an' that Pruiett kid is making a hell of a record on me. They'll sentence Evans an' Richards to hang as sure as the world, an' he'll be just as sure to take an appeal on it. I don't want any error in the record."

"We got fifty witnesses here for that Stevenson case; had 'em here for two days, an' it's costin' like the devil," Hodges complained. "It's—."

"I don't mind the waitin', so long as it's so edifyin'," Stilwell Russell interrupted. "I'd rather watch that bushy-headed devil work than listen to Bob Ingersoll. If we'd a had him in the Stevenson case the last time we tried it, we might have got better than a hangin' sentence out of it for our client."

"Yes, and if I had been as careful with the record then as I'm being in this one, the Circuit Court wouldn't have reversed it, and John Stevenson would have been dead, like he ought to be, instead of back here running up the government's cost bill," the judge said.

"That janitor of Jake's is nobody's damn fool," Russell continued. "I don't agree when you say his men will get death."

"They haven't a chance in a million," Bryant scoffed.

"What about that old man Washington, the old white-haired stockman?" Russell reminded. "How's the jury goin' to discount his testimony."

"Hell," Hodges said. "He was fixed. There ain't nobody goin' to believe that kind of stuff."

"He sounded good to me," Russell persisted. "He said he was over to Richards at sunup the mornin' of the killin', an' that Evans an' Richards was there, an' helped him have his mare served by John's stud. Them old stock owners keep records of their breeding dates, ever' one of 'em does, an' there's eight or ten stockmen on that jury. When the old man pulled that record book, with the date in it in John Evan's handwritin', an' the receipt for the stud fee, I thought old Taliaferro was goin' to drop his uppers."

"I notice you are not lettin' none of your ideas on that subject get in the record, like you did on Stevenson," Russell laughed. "An' if it's perjury, it's a long ways ahead of the type you'd normally expect of this section of the country to produce. I think it's the truth, an' the government hasn't got a sign of a case."

"I guess you believed that damned old blacksmith?" Jake Hodges put in.

"Why not?" countered Russell. "He's got no more motive for lyin' than them deputy marshals that are testifyin' to ever' thing the government wants 'em to. The marshals claim they followed the killer's trail up toward the Pennington country, an' that he was ridin' a big horse, with heavy calks on his shoes. The old blacksmith swears that he put the shoes on Evans' stud four days after Beatty got his head blowed off, an' that he could tell from the hooves that there never had been a nail in 'em before he put his in. If that is not competent an' credible proof, I have never learned nothin' about lawsuits in these years I been tryin' 'em.''

"It'd be good if it wasn't so obviously hand tooled," Bryant said.

"Who tooled it?" Russell demanded. "These boys have been in jail for almost a year. They got a green country kid that's tryin' his first murder case defendin' 'em, an' ever'body knows it. Just on the surface, I'd say the government was in for a trimmin'."

"I know who tooled it," Jake Hodges interrupted.

"You have not been on the stand yet, an' what's more, you're not goin'." Russell retorted.

"It doesn't make a damn bit of difference to me how she goes," Bryant began. "I'm just the trial judge—."

Russell interrupted again. "When Pruiett asked that old white haired codger if John's stud was shod the morning he stood his mare to him, an' he swelled up an' said, 'hell no, there ain't no shod stallion goin' to claw up my mare's flanks,' the jury caught it. I saw Pruiett had made a point, an' I think Taliaferro an' Lee did too. It's things like that, that wins or loses cases."

"Like I said, it don't make a damn to me," Bryant said. "You know how I feel about Moman. He's my baby, whether he makes a go or not. He's practicin' law on my own motion, an' old Judge McClelland, in the state court, hated like hell to give him a license down there. Why, McClelland tried him for robbery, an' sentenced him to five years at Rusk. When I admitted him here, Mac said he felt like he almost had to send him down there, but he gave him a temporary license. I think he'll make good, and I'm not apologizing to anybody for what I did."

"He ain't human, in some respects," Jake Hodges said. "He's got a filin' cabinet for a head an' ice water in his veins instead of blood. When he's in the courtroom you'd swear he was graduated out of Harvard or Princeton, an' down at the office or at the DeShong's saloon, you'd think he was a gutter-monkey. An' another thing, he carries a grudge, on account of the way he was convicted and sent to Rusk."

"I been wonderin' about that fine courtroom manner of his," Bryant said. "I know he is not educated. I've heard he hadn't had a full year's schoolin' in his life. Where does that come in?"

"It's imitation; nothin' but imitation," Hodges states. "Ask Russell about how he can remember things. He reads a case, an' he notices a citation, an' he sticks it in that filin' case with all the wild hair on it, and he keeps it there 'till he needs it. Then he yanks it out. I've had him around me for better'n three years, off an' on, an' I tell you he's a bear on memory. He stood up in the office one time, an' he made my speech back to me, the one I made in the Tissy Hotubby case, an' I swear to Christ it was word for word, an' with ever' gesture. I asked him how he kept it in his mind so long, an' he took a drink out of my bottle an' started recitin' another speech, an' I recognized it right off as the one I made in them Haymeadow Massacre cases. He told me once that if he just had a chance to follow Dan Voorhees, an' watch him try a few cases, that he'd show the boys around Lamar County how lawsuits ought to be tried."

"That's right," Russell agreed. "He's a kind of genius that way. He don't forget nothin,' an' even when you think he's asleep, he's watchin' out of them slit eyes an' storin' stuff up for use in the future. He's a goin' to make an' awful good trial man, if I'm any judge of lawyers at all."

"I wish to Christ he'd hurry this case up," Hodges sighed. "This witness expense is eatin' me up."

Pruiett technique, as it was subsequently perfected and nationally recognized, was marked by a slow gathering attack in the opening period, a well calculated stall through the intervening rounds, and an annihilating final attack. He would take more time to qualify a jury than the average lawyer took to try an entire case. He studied prospective jurors with a cold and deliberate eye; he boasted that he could tell a bad eye from a good one, by the way it reflected his own cold stare. He took enough time with the individual juror to place him, at least partially, under the spell of the personality which seemed to make people feel that they would like to do something for him.

Court baiting, although occasionally indulged in, was not practiced to the same extent as counsel baiting. He quickly acquired a capacity for exciting and haranguing a prosecutor which was unsurpassed. He liked to have the stage exactly right for the particular brand of final eloquence he intended to deliver up to the jury. The final appeal was the master's touch. He stood to win or lose, in most of his cases, on the blistering heat of his closing plea.

The Evans-Richards alibi didn't afford a footing for his subsequently developed flights into eloquence. He had to have some unwritten law, or self-defense, for that. His stock and stencil from the scriptures and the classics was not employed; he gave the jury a cold, logical analysis of the conflicting—or coinciding—facts in evidence.

Frank Lee, the assistant to the district attorney, was closing the case. He assembled the breeding books, the stud receipts and the blacksmith's receipt before him on the counsel table and began to soliloquize.

"We can discern here," he said, "the alibi for two murderers, penned in fine Italian hand. No novice drew this device. No amateur laid this trap to ensnare the feet of stumbling justice. The cunning brain of a man who would see murder go un-punished, the smooth tongue of a man who would prostitute truth has brought this perjury before you. Justice cannot be deceived by this cunning Italian hand."

Frank Lee was in error, in at least one respect. Justice aborted. Evans and Richards were found guiltless by the jury.

"Moman, I want'a introduce you to a couple friends of mine," Colonel Jake condescended. "This here's Sam Garvin, an' Cal Grant. They're from Pauls Valley, in the Chickasaw Nation."

"I'm feelin' good about it," he said. "It was my first murder case, an' I was worried sick 'til the jury came in. When they says 'not guilty,' I bet I felt more relieved than Evans and Rich-ards did."

"You mean that's the first murder case you tried?" Calvin Grant's question was accompanied by a look of surprise.

"He's been in plenty of 'em with me," Hodges interrupted, "but that's the first one he took over by hisself."

"That's right," Pruiett agreed. If Hodges wanted to take a little credit for what he had accomplished, it was all right with him. He wasn't going to tell that Hodges had done his best to keep him out of the cases, because "there wasn't a chance in a million to get anything but a pulled neck."

"You ought to get in a few with him," Grant suggested, flatly. Garvin laughed and Hodges grinned weakly. Pruiett said nothing. "We wouldn't a'had to be back here for another trial if you'd a put a little life in that last one we had."

"You got a lawsuit?" Pruiett inquired.

"We're witnesses in the John Stevenson case," Garvin said. "That's where he killed Joe Gaines, up at the Valley."

"What you doin' down at the office tonight?" Colonel Jake asked

"I been so excited this evenin' over the verdict I couldn't set still," Pruiett answered. "An' I thought about a question or two that come up during the trial that I wanted to look up. I didn't expect to run into a crowd up here, though."

"I'm goin' to be workin' with witnesses," Hodges replied. "I got some people in the private office. Garvin an' Grant is just killin' time, waitin' for this case to get over with so's they can go home. Tell 'em about what's been goin' on till I get through, will you?"

Pruiett dropped into a chair and threw his feet to a table top. "What kind of business you gen'lemen in?" he inquired, carelessly. All the time he was making a slit-eyed survey.

"Mr. Grant here, he's the banker at the Valley," Garvin said. "I'm in the cattle business, I guess you'd call it. Land and cattle. How old are you, son?"

"I'm twenty-three," Pruiett answered.

"God almighty," Garvin said. "By the time you get grown you ought to be somethin' of a lawyer. I ain't foolin'. You got the world by the tail an' she's scramblin' on a slick hillside. If I could make a speech like you I'd stay up all night, just talkin' an' listenin' to myself."

"There's a bill through Congress an' about ready to go into effect, givin' us courts of our own up in the territory," Grant said. "They's goin' to be one hell of a lot of litigatin' up there, an' a hell of a lot of money for good lawyers to make. Now if I was young like you, an' with your ability, I'd—."

"What kind of a country you got up there?" Pruiett interrupted. "I made a trip or two across the river, workin' on this murder case, but I didn't see much."

Garvin was a huge man, with a bulging belly and fat face. He started a process of pride-expansion before he started to speak in reply.

"You ain't seen no country till you get in the Washita bottoms," he beamed, rubbing his fat hands over the tight-stretched trousers on his thighs. "That little old river is as crooked as a pan of hog guts; she bends an' doubles back on herself like she's afraid somebody is goin' to slip a little upland in on her. Six cuttin's of Alfalfa for feed a season an' the last one makes a whale of a seed harvest. A bale an' a half of cotton to the acre; corn that beats Iowa all holler, that's what she does. The main line of the Santa Fe from Wichita to Fort Worth splits her right down the middle, an' when the cattle is ready to ship, the buyers come in from both ends an' fight on the depot platform to see who gets to pay the most for beef. There's—."

"Lay off, Sam, for Christ's sake," Grant chuckled. "Don't—."

"What about this Valley you talk about?" asked Pruiett. "What's that?"

"It's our town," Grant explained. "It's on the Santa Fe, in one of them bends of the Washita. Some call it Smith Pauls, and some call it Pauls Valley, but us old timers are cuttin' it down to just the Valley."

"Smith Paul was a' old Englishman that settled there in the early days; married a Chickasaw an' grabbed off a choice batch of land," Garvin interrupted. "Ain't nothin' wrong with that. I married a Choctaw myself, an' I wouldn't trade her for a European duchess. Paul puts in a tradin' post an' store, an' starts gettin' wealthy. The Chickasaws let their intermarried citizens have all the ground they can fence an' keep away from the nesters. The post growed an' settlers started to buildin' around, especially after they got the railroad through. It's the finest little old town right now, you ever saw."

"You got a town with a bank?" Pruiett inquired, looking at Grant.

"You're damn right, an' I just wisht my customers didn't pay their notes so prompt," Grant said. "I'd like to take over a little land on the mortgages, but they won't let me. That land's sure hard to grab."

"You live in town?"

"I do, but Sam don't," Grant said. "He's up west in the Washita valley; calls his place "White Bear Hill." Just to tell the truth about it, he had a store an' tradin' post an' was about to run Smith Paul out of business, 'til the Santa Fe lit where she did. When Smith Paul got the depot, Sam gave up. All he's got is a nice start toward a little town that he calls his ranch. White Bear is perty complete."

"My folks has always been movers," said Pruiett. "They came to this town in easy hitches. Just followed the Frisco as she came out of southern Missouri, across Arkansas, an' right into Texas. I don't like it none too well here, an' I'm lookin' for a place where I can settle an' work, an' make some money."

"You married? Got a family?" Garvin inquired.

"Yeah," he answered. "I got a wife. I have no children— yet."

"You'd be just as at home in the Valley as a cottonwood

sprout," Grant said. "An' I'm tellin' the truth when I say that the folks up there has put off their suin' a long time, just 'cause court is so inconvenient an' far away. Hell, comin' to Texas, or Arkansas or Kansas, just to law with some fellow, ain't worth it. But if they get that territorial court started, an' go to tryin' cases up an' down that Washita bottom, just look out. It'll be the place for a smart lawyer to get wealthy."

The United States District Court for the Oklahoma and Indian Territories was established by the Congressional Act of 1895. Known familiarly as "The Sandy Land Court," it invoked and attempted to enforce, as the law, the statutes of the state of Arkansas. (Mansfield's Arkansas Digest was the Sandy Land Bible). For a limited period it held concurrent jurisdiction with the Federal Courts of the Eastern District of Texas—Judge Bryant's court—and with the Western District of Arkansas, the domain of hanging Ike Parker. President Cleveland appointed Constantine B. (Buck) Kilgore, of northeast Texas, as judge over the southern division of the new court. This division included the Chickasaw country, or the territory west of Fort Smith and north of Paris.

Pruiett took the Texas and Pacific from Paris to Gainesville, and the Santa Fe north to Smith Pauls. Calvin Grant and Sam Garvin were together in Grant's bank when he sauntered in.

"It's Jake Hodges's spittoon cleaner that tries lawsuits in his spare time," Grant greeted, rising and grinning.

"I'll be damned if it ain't," the ponderous Garvin agreed. "Hi, son! Is there anybody with you? You got some law business up here?"

"Nope," Pruiett answered. "I come up at your invitation. Ever since you been down there, talkin' about your Valley garden I been restless. I got to strike out for myself in a place that's growin'. Paris is about as big as it's goin' to get, an' just as long as the old timers like Colonel Jake, an' Enoch Fagan, an' old man Brants keep livin' they'll get the choice business. Competition's too strong for me. I'm prospectin' an' if this place is half what you say it is, I'm goin' to hang out my shingle."

Garvin shook his hand the second time. "Son," he said, "the last time I'm talkin' to you I says you are a real lawyer, one with real ability an' a future. Well, I had just seen you try a tough case an' win it, an' that's the test that decides, more'n any other, whether a lawyer's got the stuff or not. Right after that I seen Jake Hodges try one, not any tougher, neither, an' Jake's

THE MARSHALS-ENFORCEMENT ARM OF THE SANDY LAND COURT
"The hills up off the bottom are chock full of horse thieves and cattle thieves."

got a reputation for bein' a smooth trial lawyer. He got a hung jury an' thought he was doin' perty good. You got Jake skinned a mile in a comparison, an' I'll promise you right now that if you stay in the Valley you got one client, an' that's old Sam Garvin."

"That's mighty nice of you, to say that, Colonel Garvin," he said.

"An' if there's a lawyer in town that I know's got the guts to fight an' head enough to do it right, then I'm through runnin' plumb to Ardmore to hire my work done," Grant smiled. "An' ever once in a while Garvin gets to recommend his lawyer to folks that ain't just sure which one's the best in town."

"I like that kind of talk whether you mean it or not," Pruiett said. "But there's things I got to think about, an' decide on, before I take up anybody's proposition. Is this place goin' to last, an' is she goin' to keep good business, or is she goin' to stall an' stagger an' wind up with a bunch of hungry bums playin' against each other, an' none of them got enough to get out an' move to the next place? How much is it goin' to take to start, an' to hold on 'til the money season comes around?"

"You mean 'til they hold a term of court here?" Grant inquired.

"Yeah, an' 'til some stealin' an' shootin' starts? Fightin' fence rows an' suin' on notes is goin' to be all right, on the side, but I'm goin' in for criminal law. How's the field for that?"

"This has been the longest quiet spell we had in years, just since we been talkin' here," Garvin said. "Shootin's and killin's is everyday stuff on Paul Avenue. The hills up off the bottom are chock full of horse thieves an' cattle thieves, mostly crossed between Indians an' their old nigger slaves. If you're lookin' for that kind of stuff, you shore don't need to go no farther. Didn't John Stevenson take a Winchester to Joe Gaines right in front of this buildin', an' Joe a deputy United States marshal, too?"

"I haven't got enough cash to start on," Pruiett said, frankly. "How'm I goin' to get credit around here for a little while, a stranger to ever'body but you?"

"I'll hire you for my lawyer, an' I'll stake you in the business," Garvin agreed. "If I ain't got enough, I'll sign your note an' let my bankin' friend here spend a little of his money. I'd take the risk just to get to hear you defend some wild Chickasaw halfbreed when the travelin' court comes to town."

AULS VALLEY, CHICKASAW NATION. I T

Photo by J J.I. Wood
PAULS VALLEY COURT HOUSE

The Valley Court House where Pruiett practiced law.

"I am not jokin', Colonel Garvin," Pruiett insisted. "I mean—."

"An' I ain't either," Garvin interrupted. "You see that little box shack with the big window in front, across there an' down the street a little?"

"The shoe shop?"

"Yeah. Where the shoe-shop sign is. It ain't no shoe shop no more, on account of the cobbler that was runnin' it got lickered up one night an' got in a scrape in one of these damn Uno joints. He didn't have enough change on his body to start to pay back rent."

"What's a Uno joint?"

"Uno stands for one; one per cent alcohol, that's all the kick the government lets 'em put in beer in the territory. It's mostly

Longhorn brand, shipped in here from Fort Worth, an' some of the Chicks say Longhorn, an' others just plain Uno. A Uno joint is a beer joint where they sell beer that won't make nobody drunk, but where you find ever' son of a gun on the inside dog drunk."

"Well," Pruiett encouraged, "what about the shoe shop?"

"They killed this damn cobbler in the fight, is what I'm tellin' you an' he didn't have enough on him to pay the rent. I own the damn buildin' an' I'll put a table an' some chairs in it; you can paint your lawyer sign over that shoe shop sign, an' you'll have one of the best damned locations for startin' in this town."

"If you're on the level, I'm takin' you up. The rent is to be charged."

"I'm right square on the level, an' the rent's to be charged. She's ten dollars a month, an' the chairs an' table'll be in there in the mornin'. What you goin' to do about your wife?"

"She's carryin' a baby," Pruiett explained, a little embarrassed. "I'll have to go back to her in a month or six weeks. In the meantime, I'll batch up here an' see how things are goin' to go. After she's up again, if I think I'll be able to make it, I'll have her up here with me."

"MOMAN PRUIETT—LAWYER." Smear paint made from lampblack mixed with kerosene and painted roughly on a tan pine board announced the willingness of the box-building's inmate to be of service. Rusting bailing wire nailed to the plank siding kept the sign from swinging too far about in a gusty morning wind.

"How you makin' out, son?" Two pairs of muddy boots covered the table top and Sam Garvin was speaking. An iron cot, with a rough quilt neatly arranged, stretched across the back wall. The shoe shop had become a combination law-office and dwelling.

"It's perty good," Pruiett replied. "I have not made any money, but I got it on the book, an' just as soon as a term of court hits town, I'm goin' to settle up a little of it an' collect some fees."

"When you goin' back to Paris?"

"Won't be but a day or two. Lilly Belle's bound to be comin' around perty soon, an' I want to be sure an' be there with her."

"Are you comin' back?"

"You mean to the Valley?"

"Yeah."

"Why, hell, yes, Colonel. What you think I am? Think I'm goin' to get down there owin' you an' Grant, an' a bunch of others, an' not come back to settle?"

"I ain't even thinkin' about that," Grant growled. "What I'm tryin' to ask you, do you think this Valley's got a future for your kind of business? You been awful quiet the last couple of weeks, an' you ain't looked exactly contented. I just wanted to know."

"I can do more learnin' when I keep my mouth shut," Pruiett said. "I wanted to learn as much as I could as quick as I could, in decidin' whether to bring my wife and kid up here to live. That's—."

"Well, if you been learnin', let me in on it. What you picked up since you been here?"

A great drove of spotted steers pushed and slid past the front of the office, hoof deep in the mire of Paul Avenue. Men on horseback whooped and swore and banged their big hats on their horses' flanks, hurrying them on. A drunk ambled past the front window.

" I learned that they got this country named wrong," Pruiett observed. "It is not the Indian Territory; it's the white man's territory."

"Ain't that the damn truth," Garvin agreed.

"I've found out why all the old lawyers that used to come to the boardin' house at Paris, when they was here for court, carried a big pistol in their carpet bag. These birds around here can't see the lawyer in a disinterested position. They get as mad at their adversary's lawyer as they do at their adversary."

"She's tough as a boot," Garvin acknowledged.

"I found out that this government whiskey regulation is a lot of bull. It's as easy to get liquor here as it is at Fort Smith, an' this white lightnin' they still off in the hills, an' the alky they run in from Texas, makes a man crazy instead of plain drunk."

"You ain't missed yet," said Garvin.

"They're fallin' off these Santa Fe trains an' drivin' in—in wagon gangs so fast, an' nestin' around on this black land, that the damned old Indians are goin' to have to fight or move on again. I say this government's goin' to have to make a better arrangement for 'em than they got now."

"I'd a said the same thing, if you'd a ask me."

"An' another thing that occurs to me," Pruiett continued, "is that this territorial court is a temporary move, just to fill in a gap until somethin' permanent is worked out. I'm talkin' about statehood."

Garvin smiled and nodded.

"I found out that my luck is not all bad," Pruiett mused. "I fell into the hottest little spot left in the west, an' got adopted by two of the biggest men in the place. I learned that you an' Grant are not hot air, like a lot of the bunch I been thrown in with, an' that when men like you say somethin', that I can depend on it bein' so."

"Have you discovered the why for that?" Garvin inquired. "That you got an exceptional way about you, your face, an' your eyes, an' a voice an' manner that excites attention, an' makes friends. Have you found that out?"

"You an' Grant have woke me up, in a way," he admitted. "I got more self-confidence now than I ever did have."

"Have you discovered that the main thing it's goin' to take in the next few years, with the territorial government runnin', an' with things gradually workin' around to statehood, is guts? Do you understand that the man with brains an' guts together is goin' to be the one to get on top in this mess?"

"I was gettin' ready to tell you that, Colonel," he laughed. "The fellow that can get the toughest, an' is luckiest, is the one that's goin' to get along. I say lucky, 'cause it's goin' to take more than brains. It's goin' to take plain luck, to dodge all the stray lead that's goin' to be flyin' around this valley in the next few years."

CHAPTER FOUR

Wherein Lawyer Pruiett makes definite location in the Indian Territory, and begins, forthwith, to keep apace with the so-called tougher element of the section. And how he goes back to Texas to try a murder case and, after having jailed himself for his lack of respect for the local court, frees himself and wrests a verdict of acquittal from the jury. And, wherein he lets the Territory's light of promise blind him against an attractive offer of partnership from a distinguished Dallas attorney, and he goes back to the Valley to find a surplus of assorted criminal business awaiting. And how begins an offensive against the serpent's trail, and he receives commendation from a friendly jury for having cracked a skull in the fray.

Late April had the Washita valley in its spring finest when he brought Lilly and the baby there for trial inspection. The inhabitants, even the Indians, were abustle with the promise of plenty in the atmosphere. The sprouting corn in the fertile bottoms was racing to overtake the dark bulk of the alfalfa and clover in adjoining fields. Sleek well-fed beef moved restlessly in the unpainted pens along the railroad tracks, as if impatient to be off and away to market. The crated poultry, stacked high on four-wheeled trucks, cackled a dual hello and goodbye as it rattled over the rough brick of the platform toward the forward portion of the freight train on the passing track.

The Garvins, Colonel Sam and his Choctaw princess, Susan, as he called her, were waiting at the depot with a buggy.

"Let me see the shaver," Garvin said, as Lilly pulled the blanket back. "Perty good. Is it a boy or girl?"

"It's a boy," Pruiett said.

"What you name him?" Garvin inquired.

"Hayden Warren. The Hayden's for my mother's uncle; my father's name is Warren," Pruiett explained.

"I got a house vacant for you to take over," Garvin said.

"We have got no furniture—yet," Lilly Belle reminded.

"Well, this place ain't furnished, but you got to have furniture sooner or later. I'll help you make arrangements to buy some." Sam Garvin was willing to help in any way at any time.

"Thanks, Colonel," Pruiett said, "but I made a deal with Mrs. Scrivener before I left, to take some of her light-housekeepin' rooms. They'll do us for a while, 'til I can get straightened up a little."

"Court opens here in ten days, an' things are goin' to hum," Garvin said. "An' I got you some more business while you was gone. The marshal has arrested Sam Willingham an' Ocie Collins for breakin' enclosures, an' I signed their bonds. I wouldn't go for 'em 'til they agreed to hire you to defend 'em. An' old Uncle Henry Gordon's been askin' when you'd be back. One of his boys is in jail at Ardmore, charged with stealin' cattle."

"That's the kind of friends I got here in the Valley!" Pruiett beamed, aside to Lilly Belle. "How am I goin' to keep from gettin' along with that kind of backin'?"

Fortune, long indifferent, began to bear a faint semblance of a smile. As the judge, court clerk, and lawyers began to gather for the first local session of the territorial court, he was able to collect on the J. C. Harmon note, the subject of his first Valley cases. He got the full fifty dollars reserved on its face for legal services. Vancie Wyatt, who had employed him to sue E. J., her husband, decided to abandon her suit for divorce and incidental relief, and to take him back regardless of his shortcomings. She paid Pruiett twenty dollars to dismiss the case she had on file. Rose and Jack Goodwin, who lived above the Valley on the South Canadian, agreed to disagree, and divided thirty-five dollars from the proceeds of the sale of a load of beef with Pruiett, for taking care of the technical points of unhitching them. Willingham and Collins, up for trial for violating government rules, paid twenty-five dollars apiece, in advance, for his services.

He bought a stock of furniture and moved into Garvin's box house on a side street, three blocks from the office. He took a shaggy saddle pony for services in adjusting a difference over shares of crops for farm rent, and kept it in a three-sided shed behind the house. Uncle Henry brought a bushel of pecans and a burlap bag of apples as part payment of the fee for defending his cow-stealing son. Bill Ticker owed him twenty dollars for the replevin of a span of mules; Pruiett rode the pony eight miles east to Bill's place and took a red milk cow in full payment. He took half the night riding back. The cow had such a bulging udder that she lagged and held the pony back. Lilly Belle wasn't able to supply enough milk and the baby wouldn't make modification of his constant demands upon her, and the milk from the cow made up for the deficiency.

"When Pruiett located at Pauls Valley that village was just a little wilder, a little woolier, and a little rougher than any stomping ground in the Chickasaw Nation or any other nation. It was in the period of municipal career in the frontier west when a six-shooter acted as the town clock and the sexton of the cemetery was the most important officer. The saloons, or rather, the 'uno joints', never closed, and the merry din of the festive liquor glass and the rattle of the festive poker chip blended together into a weird music that only those who have known the early days in Oklahoma appreciated as music."

Sam Paul, surviving eldest son of old Smith Paul, the settlement's founder and heaviest landholder, kept the John Stevenson standard aloft by shooting and wounding his own son, Joe, in a muddy Paul Avenue uno joint. Joe was able to recover, and as soon as he was about, he shot Sam (his father), in the same den where his own assassination had been attempted. Sam died. Jennison McClure, a Chickasaw cousin of the Pauls, shot Joe Paul to death with a six-shooter. Bill Paul, Sam's boy, who was attending boarding school at Sherman, Texas, was sent word of Joe's demise with advice not to come home to the funeral.

Pruiett was playing poker upstairs at Swift Hotel. Claude Weaver, who went to Congress from the Fifth Oklahoma District, and Dave Langdon and Scott Jones, were holding hands. The half-breed Jennison was in the game and it was late—or early.

"It's damn near mornin'," Pruiett reminded them.

"Ain't no use to quit now, before breakfast time," Weaver said.

"Keep dealin'," Jones said. "Who's comin' up? Somebody's wife thinks he's stayin' out too late, an' comin' after him?"

The door to the outside-stair approach opened and a squatty half-breed sidled in. He stood beside the table for several minutes, watching the play indifferently, before he spoke.

"Bill Paul in town; I just seen him," the half-breed Indian said.

The players exchanged significant glances and continued their play. When the hand was finished Jennison McClure pushed his stack of chips toward Weaver, who was banking, and arched his eyebrows.

"You quittin'?"

"I go home now," he said.

"It's almost daylight, Mac," Pruiett suggested. "Hadn't you better play a couple more before you leave?"

"I go home now," he repeated.

"Look here, now, Jennison," Weaver said. "It ain't hardly safe to be runnin' around here in the dark, without knowin' where he is. Why don't you stick around a little longer. You know damn well he ain't comin' up here."

"I go home now," McClure said, without changing tone or expression.

"Pay him off," said Pruiett. "He says he go home."

The squatty informer was already dozing in a chair. New hands were dealt and McClure walked carelessly out the side door.

"It's gettin' light, now, as sure as hell," Pruiett observed. "Let's go an' get some breakfast after this hand. How long's Jennison been gone?"

"Listen!"

"That was a shot!" Pruiett whispered.

There was a short silence, then two more shots. The players glanced toward the little half-breed Indian, who slouched low in his chair with his dirty hands folded peacefully across his pot belly. His eyes opened wide and understandingly. With a significant shrug of his shoulders he closed them again and began to nod.

"Damn it," Pruiett gritted. "I'm out. If you fellows want to play any more it's all right, but I'm quittin'. What the hell's that?" He jumped and started.

"You're all upset," Weaver laughed. "It's just a train whistle. It's the mornin' Santa Fe. I'm out, too."

"Come on, Shorty; coffee." Pruiett called to the little Indian. He was close at the heels of the quartet as it reached the bottom of the staircase which ran up the side of the stone building. A woman hurried up Paul Avenue from the east, from the direction of the Santa Fe Depot. "Is Doc Young up here?" she inquired, breathlessly.

"No, he ain't," one of the men said. "What's wrong?"

"The mornin' train just ran over a man," she said. "You want Doc for professional service, or official service?" Pruiett asked. Young was the mayor and chief magistrate, as well as the principal M. D.

"It ain't for treatment," she answered. "He's mince meat. We just want him there for the identification, an' to watch the pickin' up."

The four looked understandingly at each other, and then at the Indian. He shrugged his shoulders again.

"I'll give you three guesses, an' the first two don't count," Pruiett said. They were walking toward the railroad property. "Perty bloody mess," Weaver observed.

"Somebody ought to have a basket ready for Doc to use when he gets here," Pruiett suggested.

"Anybody know who it was?" some one asked. The curious were arriving from every direction. "Was it a bum? Did he fall under gettin' off?"

Pruiett picked up a blood colored fragment of coarse cloth. He held it in front of the short Indian. "Jennison?" he asked.

"Jennison home now," was the answer. The little Indian was gazing placidly up the tracks toward the north. The rails were beginning to glimmer with the rising light in the east.

"If we was to look, we might find some little round holes in them biggest pieces, holes that a Santa Fe engine couldn't make," Pruiett said.

"An' if we keep our damn noses out of other people's business we ain't liable to catch a stink that turns our stomach," Weaver replied. Langdon laughed and said, "You'll learn somethin' worthwhile ever' day, if you keep your eyes open. Claude's taught you a damn good lesson, already this mornin', Moman. I'm gettin' some eggs an' ham. What you fellows say?"

When Weaver and Moman arrived at the scene where pieces of Jennison McClure's body was scattered around over the ground, and while waiting for Dr. Young, the mayor, and other officers to arrive, Ex-Governor Tecumseh McClure of the Chickasaw Nation, who was the father of Jennison McClure who had just been killed, appeared upon the scene, looked all around and said, "Jennison he's cut up bad. Well, he's all right. He, Fred Wade, Sam and Joe Paul, all now in Injun's Happy Hunting Ground."

The government met the recklessness of its territorial populace by meting out, measure for measure, the same heedless and heartless conduct. The gallows in the yard of the Federal jail at Ardmore worked overtime. The color of the neck being pulled until it popped was of no consequence to the hangman. White ones, red ones and black ones, and occasionally one of foreign stripe, were stretched with indifference. The swinging tactics of Arkansas Ike Parker were adopted. William B. Johnson, a vigorous and vicious prosecutor, was assigned to try the outlaws and murderers

THE GALLOWS IN THE FEDERAL JAIL AT ARDMORE
"The color of the neck being pulled until it popped
was of no consequence to the hangman."

as such enforcement officers as Bill Tilghman, Chris Madsen, and
Heck Thomas were able to apprehend. The fact that murder and
robbery was rife didn't mean that it went unwhipped or un-

censored. If you killed a man but missed the getaway, you were a better than even bet to drop through a Federal gallows' trap.

Success in the Valley put the slow-blossoming Pruiett into full bloom. He was naturally fearless, non-conforming, and tough. The opportunity, the desire, and the necessity to be tougher suited him. The contempt which he had previously expressed for the courts and the administration of justice had grown within him. His hatred for the system which had wronged him had climbed and spread like the poison ivy on the river cottonwoods.

He developed into a definite type. His appearance was something to distinguish him, to make him stand out, in the gatherings of the wild community. He permitted his black hair to grow to a bushy, unwieldly bulk; he brushed and groomed it until it outshone the dress of the crows that circled and roosted on the river through the Valley. He was quick to fight or shoot; to curse and swear and was consumed by fits of useless rage. For the frontier, his dress was the finest. He shaved daily. He wore bat-wing high collars and bulging hard cuffs, and he changed so often that they were usually spotlessly white. He went in debt for store clothes, fancy alpacas and broadcloths, and his shoe-string tie wasn't real shoe string. It was tight-stitched genuine silk.

He came into court with his custom-tailored suit and shining high-collar in faultless fashion. In an hour he was roaring and ranting from a surrounding circle of ashes and stubs and brown expectoration.

Pruiett and his eatin' tobacco were legendary before his prowess for holding hard liquor was proved. "Quid pro Quo!" was the title of a hastily concocted courtroom sonnet, typifying Pruiett engrossed in the practice of his life work.

> "Oh, Mister Moman Pruiett,
>   We've watched you as you do it;
>   Watched you closely as you stack
>   Away tobacco by the sack;
>   Seems so easy for you, too—
>   Double handful for a chew;
>   Gives you so much pleasure,
>   Commensurate with measure,
>   That we very often rue
>   That we cannot do it too.
>   Oh, Mister Moman Pruiett,
>   Please tell us how you chew it."

"This here's a perty good party, you're havin', Moman." John Stevenson, the marshal killer, pulled his face from a mug of Choctaw beer to compliment his host.

"Christmas don't come but once a year," Pruiett replied.

"It's all right to play poker an' drink Choc, but don't make so much noise," Lilly Belle complained. "You'll have the baby awake again if you keep on."

Sam Garvin gathered her to his bulging belly in a fatherly embrace. "It ain't just a Christmas party, don't forget. It's a fare-well party, too. Ain't your old man leavin' for Texas tomorrow to try a big murder case?"

"I guess I'll be goin' back for trial again before long," John Stevenson said. "An' I'm gettin' awful tired of that case. Sentenced to hang once, an' gettin' a hung jury after the conviction was reversed—. I got ever' thing I own mortgaged to pay costs, an' bills an' lawyers, an' it looks like I'm just ruined for nothin'."

"Ever' since I went to Paris with you the second time, I been tellin' you you ought to reorganize your defense. Stilwell Russell an' Jake Hodges ain't effective like my lawyer. If you'd a had Pruiett to that last jury you'd a come clear."

"Don't be slanderin' Stilwell Russell," Lilly Belle said. "He's my favorite lawyer, that is, all but one." She caressed her young husband.

"You're just like my poor old mother," Pruiett laughed. "Can't keep her paws out of my wool. Always runnin' your fingers through it an' mussin' it up."

"Russell's all right; he's a damn good lawyer, an' Jake Hodges is too," Garvin said. "I didn't have nobody representin' me for a long time but them, but ain't I been doin' better since Moman came to the Valley?"

"It seems like just one murder after another, to me," Lilly Belle observed. "I see 'em, an' I hear about 'em 'till I dream about 'em. I'm scared all the time."

"How many you had since you been here, Moman, an' how long you been here?" Stevenson asked two questions at once.

"I come in February, an' then I went back for Lilly an' the baby. Let's see, it was April, '96, an' this Christmas, '99, makes it most three years," he mused and sipped his drink. "It don't seem that long to me, but I tried Bud Nolan and Jake Henson at Ardmore, an' old Pink Bruner here, an' Charley Bias—."

"Time gets away when you're busy," Garvin explained. "I had a little trouble weanin' these fellows that was mixed up serious with the law away from old Henry Furman, an' them Cruce brothers, at Ardmore—an' from old Stilwell Russell, but they done took care of that for me now. Since yon won that Douglas case for 'em, you'll get their criminal business—all of it."

"Maybe not," Pruiett grinned, complacently.

"They had old man Ledbetter an' C. L. Potter in there too, didn't they?" Stevenson asked.

"Yeah, they damn near had too many lawyers," Garvin answered. "I heard an old cuss up there at Purcell sayin' 'it looks to me like Douglas is guilty, or he wouldn't have so many lawyers to try to prove he ain't.' They hired you last, didn't they, Moman?

"I didn't hardly have time to get ready," Pruiett said.

"How come they try it at Purcell, when he killed Williams at Ardmore?"

"Cruces took care of that; a change of venue," Pruiett answered. "There was some prejudice down there, an' here in the Valley, too. We took it up on the South Canadian, right to the boundary of the Chickasaw nation, so's that we'd be as far away as we could get."

"Self-defense'll work for anybody but me," lamented Stevenson. "That was as thin as hell, what you put over for Douglas. A pencil lookin' like a knife—? Hell's fire!"

"What did he really want to kill him for, Moman?" Garvin inquired.

"That defense was on the level," Pruiett answered. "I saw a case tried before Ike Parker, at Fort Smith, that was damn near a ringer for this one. Boudinot killed Stone up at Tahlequah, an' they were editors of rival papers. Jimmy Williams was runnin' the Ardmore Chronicle, an' Douglas was writin' for some other sheet when this happened. Williams says in a' editorial that Douglas considered himself eligible for service cleanin' spittoons in the court house or a uno joint or as a member of the Dawes Commission. That started feelin' between 'em, an' they was both on edge, watchin' for the other to make a move. If Douglas made a mistake in killin' him—in bein' too hasty—it was a' honest mistake. He really thought Jimmy was pullin' a knife."

"Apologizin' for them kind of mistakes don't help much," Garvin grunted.

"You ought to see what the 'Register' says about Moman," Lilly Belle said. "I cut it out an' I'm goin' to save it."

"I saw the real thing," Garvin laughed, "an' it was good

enough to write up. Old Ledbetter an' Potter had been mumblin' around for the defense, an' old Humphrey had been stumblin' around for the government, 'til they had that farmer jury dozin' off about right. Moman had told me what he was goin' to do, an' I was watchin' for it. He had a pencil, exactly like the defense had introduced in evidence, in his pocket. It was one of them bullet-lookin' affairs that you pull in two in the middle an' reverse ends, for carryin' around in your pocket. It was made out of metal all right, an' it was perty big. Well—that jury was restin' an' wishin' they was at home lookin' after the cattle, an' Moman just kept a talkin', low an' smooth, about that pencil he had in his hand. That was the real pencil. Then he tossed it right into the middle of the table, an' left it there where ever'body could see it, an' he went on talkin' real careless like about somethin' else. Then, he lets out a squeal like a steer-hooked nigger, an' he jumps right straight up in the air. When he hits the floor his hair's down in his eyes an' he looks like a maniac, an' he grabs a juror, right in the middle of the front row, by the throat. All the time he's doin' his yellin' an' jumpin' he's haulin' out this other pencil he's got, the one that the jury don't know about, an' he raises that over his head like he's goin' to stab the juror with it. You should've seen them scramble."

Garvin paused to laugh and slap his fat thighs. Pruiett cut in. "Them wild antics is what gets the results. The men that come to the courthouse for jury service, they're just farmers an' clerks out of grocery stores, an' things like that; they want to see somethin.' When a stockman goes to Kansas City with a load of beef he don't go out to the packin' plant to see what the best way of killin' an' dressin' is. He gets him a jug an' goes to a leg show. Jury service is just somethin' the boys have to endure, an' if you'll liven things up for 'em they'll show their appreciation for it. Have a fit, or shoot off a blank cartridge, or carry the baby. A jury is a musical instrument with twelve keys; if you can play it, and secure a responsive chord, you win."

"Moman either entertained 'em out of the verdict, or he scared them out of it," Garvin laughed. "He says, 'Why, gentlemen, don't be scared. I haven't got no dangerous weepun; I just got a little pencil. It's just a little pencil exactly like the one that James Williams was carryin', and you knew it was a layin' there on the table. But you thought it was a knife, an' that I was a'goin to slash your throats. Don't deny me that 'under some circumstances the slightest movement justifies instant ac-

tion, viewing it from the defendant's standpoint alone,'' referring to the court's charge to the jury, 'because it's evident in
your faces,' he says, an' it was. They were scared out of their
chairs,'' Garvin said. "Pruiett replied, 'It wasn't so much what
I had in my hand, as the way I handled it an' the expression I
had on my face while I was doing it. Unless you are able to
conclude beyond all reasonable doubt that Douglas was not justi-
fiably scared, and that he was not frightened for his life, and
safety, then it's your duty to acquit him—to turn him loose.' That
was all Moman said. His whole speech didn't last ten minutes.''

"I'm goin' to read a part of his clippin' on it," Lilly Belle
insisted. "About four o'clock on Thursday afternoon the jury
in the case against Clarence B. Douglas, charged with the murder
of James Williams, was brought into court, and when asked
by the judge if they had arrived at a verdict stated that they
had, and the foreman, W. C. Henry, handed in same, which was
read as follows: 'We find the defendant C. B. Douglas not
guilty as charged in the indictment' . . . The case was stated to
the jury last Friday night, after which the jurors were put in
charge of the bailiffs. On Saturday morning witnesses were
examined . . . Court was resumed at 3 o'clock Monday afternoon,
the train from the south being late. . . . The arguments by the
attorneys began Tuesday afternoon, Assistant Prosecuting Attorney Jas. E. Humphrey, of this place, opening for the government, presenting the case in a forceful manner. He was followed
by C. L. Potter, of Ardmore, who spoke for an hour, very ably
presenting his side of the defense. At the evening session W. A.
Ledbetter took up the entire time with an eloquent address for the
defense. At the morning session Wednesday Mr. J. F. Sharp
gave a succinct and lucid exposition of the government's position.
He was followed by Messrs. W. I. Cruce of Ardmore and Moman
Pruiett of Pauls Valley, who spoke very briefly for the defense.
. . . Mr. Pruiett's speech was especially complimented, members
of the jury stating at the close of the case that it had a very
strong effect in determining the verdict."

"It had ever'thing to do with it," Garvin said.

"I didn't know a hell of a lot about the evidence in the case,"
Pruiett said. "I was hired to do two things, empanel the jury an'
make one of the arguments. I wasn't to examine no witnesses.
When I got the jury in the box I had to come home. Lilly Belle
was havin' the baby, an' I was here a few hours. I just got back
in time to hear the second witness."

DOUGLAS, HIS ATTORNEYS, AND THE JURY THAT ACQUITTED HIM

Douglas with the beard, is in the center Pruiett is at his right; A. C. Cruce at his left.

"Is Cruce still talkin' to you about namin' the baby," Stevenson inquired.

"Yes, his daughter is named Gail Hamilton Cruce. I love A. C. Cruce, as dearly as one man can love another not to be related, so he virtually has named my baby Gail Hamilton Pruiett, and it meets Lilly's approbation."

"This is a perty tough case you got at Wichita Falls, ain't it Moman?" Stevenson inquired.

"Why hell, no," John Webb put in. Webb was a quiet fellow who liked to listen. He was head ranch hand for the Garvin properties. His judgment in livestock matters, especially in horses, was considered infallible. "Old Doll Wilson just shot a deputy sheriff in two with a shotgun. It ain't very tough, killin' deputy sheriffs in Texas."

"Did he have any good reason for doin' it?" Stevenson asked. "I had a little experience in that kind of case. Maybe there was some excuse—or maybe he thought he had some excuse for doin' it."

"The only reason I see for it is that the deputy was cuttin' in on his girl," Webb replied. "I guess Moman, now, ain't goin' to let it go to the jury just that a'way, but that's the way I heard it."

"Doll Wilson's sister an' brother-in-law rents one of my places on the river," Garvin explained to Stevenson. "I heard about it so many times from them that I know it by heart. The gal's name was Maude Crumpacker. Doll got stuck on her an' wanted to marry her, but she didn't want to be limited so much. She'd tried marryin' a time or two before. She an' Doll was kind of livin' together—Doll says he considered her the same as his wife, that it was a common law marriage—an' one night he come home an' sees Sam Abbott Mosely, the deputy, sneakin out the side door. Doll just happened to have a twelve gauge in his hands, wasn't figgerin' on doin' no killin', and asks Sam real polite like where he's been an' what he's been a'doin'. Sam give him a cussin' an' starts to pull a hog leg outa its holster, an' Doll shoots the shotgun from his hip."

"Now, that sounds like Moman Pruiett," Webb grinned. "Has he got the explanation for carryin' the shotgun around with him all the time worked out?"

"That' part's a little more difficult," Pruiett supplied. "The shotgun belonged to Billy Dees, a guy that runs a saloon where Doll hung out, an' he says he don't know what Doll was doin' with it. Billy says he kept it leanin' in the corner just inside the back room, an' that he didn't give it to Doll. Doll ain't explained it, not even to me, yet."

"What you goin' down so early for?" Stevenson asked.

"Just on a writ," Pruiett answered. "Garvin an' Grant an' a lot of people around Wichita'll sign his bond if the court'll allow it. We got to get him out of jail an' out of town for awhile. The way feelin' is around there right now, they'd vote to hang him in a minute."

"You ought to try him somewhere away from Wichita Falls," Garvin said.

"How the hell you goin' to arrange for that?" Pruiett inquired.

"You're the lawyer, not me," Garvin said. "But if you think it oughta be done, then you'll think of a way of doin' it. You win that case an' these local outlaws'll make up. It's too bad you got to go clear to Texas to try murder cases, when we got some of the best ones in the country right here at home."

"I got to go to St. Joe as soon as I get back," Pruiett said. "I got to go up there an' try Wade Hampton—."

"Wade Hampton, hell," Garvin exploded. "What the hell you want to get mixed up with that cow thief, for?"

" 'Cause he's got the money to pay a damn good fee, principally," Pruiett answered.

"He's as guilty as hell," Garvin insisted.

"It's my business to prove that he is not," Pruiett laughed.

"Wade Hampton was a southern gen'leman an' a great soldier," John Webb interrupted. "What right's this cow thief got to be usin' his name?"

Pruiett laughed again. "That is not any of my business," he said. "It may be yours, but it isn't mine. I did mention it to him, an' he says they made it so hot for him he had to run off an' leave his real name, an' that Wade Hampton was dead an' the name was a good one, so he just adopted it for himself. He said people that was born with big names had life a lot easier, an' so long as he had to have a new one, he was just goin' to snatch a good one while he was at it. It sounded perty smart to me."

"He stole them cattle in the first place, an' he stole the feed he half-fattened 'em for more than they was worth, an' then he sold 'em to them Saint Joe packers for twict as much as they was worth. Well, when that Kansas City Livestock Association gets after somebody, they're blowed up."

"He's got a right to a trial by jury, whether a big outfit like the K. C. is tryin' to railroad him, or not. That's all he's askin' for, an' if they can convict him, I guess Wade can do the time they give him."

"Wade, hell," Garvin fumed.

There was a distinct odor of hostility in the Texas atmosphere when Pruiett, accompanied by John R. Flood, an attorney he had engaged to assist him, presented his writ of habeas corpus in an attempt to compel the court to permit bail for Wilson. George Miller, judge of the district court, made no effort to conceal the disapprobation he contained for anyone who appeared in behalf of the killer of his friend, Sam Moseley. Pruiett arose as an officer led the prisoner into the room.

"We have invoked this right on a strict proceedings to have bond fixed," he said quietly.

"Our laws don't permit bond in capital cases, an' I understand this is one." Miller looked calmly and defiantly over his thick lensed glasses.

"Your honor is familiar with the way that section has been construed by the Supreme Court," Pruiett replied, still low and respectful. "We are in a position to show that this case comes within that rule."

"No man is in a position to show this court something he knows is not true," Miller cried, rising from his chair with the color that mounted from his collar. "Before you take any more of our time, make a statement as to what you expect to offer."

Pruiett's color was rising, too. He looked to Flood for some kind of assistance, but Flood was engaged in tracing a pattern on the linoleum of the courtroom floor with the toe of his boot.

"We expect to show that the proof of the defendant's guilt is not evident, nor the presumption of his guilt great," he said. "Our courts have stated that in such cases—."

An angry court interrupted him. "That might be your law up in the Injun Territory where murderers and horse thieves go unwhipped of justice," he roared "But it ain't the law in Texas. If that's all you got, the writ is denied."

Miller expected his listener to fold up his scant collection of papers and retire, as Flood or the local advocate, more familiar with his style, would have done. Instead, Pruiett advanced and stood defiant in the vacant space between the plain counsel tables and the bench.

"I am a member of the Texas bar and I know that the laws of Texas are as fair and just as those of the Injun Land, as you call it, or any other state or territory in the Union. The trouble is that Texas has to have an occasional judge who lacks the mental and judicial capacity to understand and interpret the law. I'll file this writ in the Court of Criminal Appeals, an' an'—."

Miller had resumed the pose which his act had required that he temporarily abandon. He eyed the attorney coolly.

"Your remarks are deliberately contemptuous, Mr. Pruiett," he said. "You may withdraw them, or it will be the court's duty to levy punishment against you."

"My remarks are for the record of this hearing," Pruiett replied. "The record will reflect that they were invited and provoked by the unwarranted statements of the court; I have nothin' to withdraw, or say further."

"Very well, young man." The court was now painfully deliberate. "You are sentenced to confinement in the jail of this county, until you have purged yourself of contempt by paying a twenty-five dollar fine, and withdrawing your contemptuous remarks."

Flood watched with dismay as Pruiett followed the sheriff from the courthouse and into the square red-brick jail behind the building. When he went to talk to him, through the rusty bars. he found him jubilant and radiant, instead of crestfallen and dis- couraged. As soon as the jailer was out of hearing, Pruiett grasped his lapels and pulled him close.

"File a motion for a change of venue and set up prejudice on the court's part, in connection with this contempt," he whispered. "As soon as you have it filed, I'll apologize to the old judge, an' pay the fine. He'll either have to change it or disqualify, an' in either case we'll be ahead. I believe he'll change the venue rather than see some one else assigned here to try the case in his court."

Flood whistled in frank admiration and amazement. "Did you do that on purpose? Did you have it figured this way before you went in there?"

"Hell, no," Pruiett replied. "When I saw how tough he wanted to get about it, I knew somethin' had to be done. When

I saw the opening I just pushed my little stack of chips in. Go on, now, get started."

The kid lawyer defending the Doll Wilson murder case was attracting considerable notice and attention at Decatur, Texas, in Wise county.

"Ain't that Pruiett awful young to be tryin' this kind of case."

"Watch him an' see. He don't act like no school boy, does he?"

"He's the one that old Miller put in jail at Wichita Falls for contempt. That's why they're tryin' it out here, because Miller lost his temper an' was goin' to have to disqualify."

"I've heered how Pruiett done that on purpose. He knew that Moseley's friends was so strong at Wichita that Wilson didn't have a show, so he just made old Miller disqualify."

"Well, Pruiett's tried murder cases before. He beat a couple tough ones in Lamar County, they tell me."

"He might be good an' he might be smart, but he's a long way from winnin' this case. Killin' a deputy sheriff ain't no safer in Wise County that it is up at Wichita Falls. 'Honest Pat' an' these old nesters they got on this jury panel ain't no cinch for any killer."

J. W. Patterson, "Honest Pat," was the trial judge. Pruiett was working on the voir dire examination of prospective jurors. He was tying up progress with his customary detailed questioning of each juror.

"Some one ought to tell the kid about old Baldy, that fellow he's examinin' now," one courtroom lounger whispered to another. "He's a sticker."

"Let him handle his own troubles," came the answer. "Let Baldy stick 'em."

The bald-headed prospect was from nearby Paradise, Texas. His name was Conner. He was tall and gaunt and bald, with a sharp and eagle-like countenance.

"What is your native state, Mr. Conner?" Pruiett inquired, never looking for so much as an instant from the prospect's glassy gray optics.

"Kentucky," was the passive, cold reply, as the level stare was returned.

"Have you had previous jury service?"

"Yes, sir."

"Have you served on the jury in a capital case?"

"Yes, sir."

"And what was the jury's judgment in it?" Pruiett continued.

"The state objects," the prosecutor said. "It's improper examination of the juror."

"Sustained." 'Honest Pat' made the ruling with finality.

"But Pruiett had more than one way of getting at the subject. He thanked the court and put another quesion. "Do you know wheher or not the defendant in that case is living at this time?" he inquired. The state's attorney objected again.

"Overruled," Pat stated. "You may answer the question."

The venireman had never taken his cold gaze from his examiner's face. "He is dead," he said evenly. "I saw him die." The heavy silence which followed was broken only by the sound cf an uncomfortable spectator in the crowded courtroom, shifting his boots over the rough pine floor.

"Is that the only capital case you've been in?" Pruiett was being painfully deliberate, A local lawyer near the door whispered to another standing against him. He said that Pruiett was unwise in pursuing such an examination, for it prejudiced his client with the other jurors. He was assuming that Conner would unquestionably be challenged by the defense.

"No," was the barely communicative reply he received.

"Do you know whether the second defendant you tried is alive or dead?" Pruiett was being careful to draw his inquiries so as to comply with the previously expressed idea of the trial court.

"He is living, so far as I know. We only gave him life."

He was forced to smile with this declaration, and the tension of the room was broken. A wave of relieved laughter swept over it. Pruiett proceeded to questioning the prospect seated next to Conner.

It was growing late in the day and the early darkness of western January was enveloping the corridors of the old court building, but the spectators and interested parties in case of the State of Texas against Doll Wilson remained each in their places in the courtroom. The day had been consumed in selecting a jury, and each side, state and defendant, still had a lone peremptory challenge to assert. Baldy Conner of Paradise was still sitting defiantly in the box.

Pruiett was conferring with his client, preparatory to excusing his last man.

"Baldy has got a damn good eye," he whispered. "I never saw a better one in a man's head. I hate to excuse him, but you know what he is by what he said here in court. Ever'body in the courthouse has warned me against him and told me to take him off, but I like him. What do you say?"

"I'd as soon hang as stay in this lousy jail any longer," Wilson replied. "It makes no difference to me. If you like him let him stay; if not, kick him off."

The answer left Pruiett in a difficult position; he tried Conner with one more question. "Mr. Conner," he inquired, "do you believe in the old sayin' 'it's a long lane that has no turnin'?"

The prosecutor's objection was overruled. Judge Patterson was too tired to interfere. "Answer the question if you can, Mr. Juror," he said wearily.

Conner gazed long and unwaveringly at Pruiett, as if pondering over a weighty problem. "Why, sure," he said, slowly, as he gazed for a moment out the window and over the tops of the trees of the square. "It'd have to be a' awful long one that never did turn."

"The defendant will waive his last peremptory challenge," Pruiett announced, rising to address the court.

"Swear the jury."

It was on the fourth day after the trial began that Pruiett began to pace the floor in the delivery of his final argument. His defense of Doll had been home-spun and simple. A mutual friend of Billy Dees, and of the accused, swore that he had removed the gun, on the license of his friendship with Billy, for use in a bird hunt, and that he had asked Wilson to carry it home for him. There was no suggestion of premeditation of murder in the handy possession of the shotgun. Moseley had made the fatal hip-pocket pass. He had commenced the assault by grabbing for the iron. What red-blooded American citizen would have done less than long-suffering Doll Wilson?

Pruiett called down the wrath of the Texas Gods, to plague and destroy all those who had lost their fundamental sense of justice and fair play. The peace and tranquility of the placid Ohio, and of his early days in the Kentucky hills, he recalled and called back, and shed a tear for them. He talked of love, and of peace, and of hate and fear. He reminded his hearers of Texas's resplendent past and its encouraging future. He talked about everything but his case; of everything but the guilt or innocence of Doll Wilson.

Four hours, hours, that slipped away like minutes, were engaged and filled with a brand of eloquence and oratory that had theretofore been unheard by the western court fans. Now as in the Brashier case, with a crying child, he enlisted the attention and sympathy of his listeners, and drew their interest from the only issue in the case.

He was a free spirit, safe from the narrowing confines of boyhood weaknesses and adolescent indiscretions. He was trying a man for his life, charged with murder, and he had a jury to work on. Like the true genius, first realizing the power of his gift, he gained poise and power with each prompt response which he received from the untried brain and voice box. He shamed the court and jury and made them cry; then he sat down. He even knew the time and place to quit.

A Mamie Taylor cocktail was the proper and stylish thing to order in west Texas saloons in 1899. Pruiett was proper in style until the bar on the corner closed at midnight. Then the poker players moved down the street to an available hotel room. As they walked past the square, Pruiett saw the light burning in the upstairs room of the courthouse. The jury was still deliberating.

There was no sleep for him that night. At ten the next morning the report went about announcing that the jury was coming in. The trial of another case was interrupted as the twelve bedraggled jurors, one with a bruised face and black eye, stood in line in front of the bench.

Pruiett heard a whisper. "Old Baldy beat hell out of that Dutchman," some one said.

The bailiff had passed the verdict to the clerk and the clerk had transmitted it to the judge.

The state's attorney arose, cautiously. "If the court please," he said, "the defendant isn't in the room. He hasn't been brought from the jail yet."

"Honest Pat was staring at the verdict, the jury, and the state's attorney, all at the same time. "It ain't necessary for him to be here," he said in loud tones. "The jury has done turned him a'loose."

Stilwell H. Russell, the Dallas lawyer, had business on the Wise County docket. He had been in the courtroom throughout the trial of the Dorsey (Doll) Wilson case, and had followed Pruiett's process of handling it with more than casual concern. He and Pruiett were riding the train together, as far as Fort Worth, where Pruiett changed to take the cars north to the Territory.

Doll Wilson was going back with Pruiett, "to pay his respects to his sister and thank her for giving him a hand," as he called it. Pruiett's private, although unexpressed, opinion was that he was going back to make a touch. They were sitting side by side in the chaircar, neither speaking, when Russell came through and spoke to them. Pruiett nudged Wilson and whispered something; Wilson got up and walked away. Pruiett shook hands with Russell and invited him to take the newly vacated chair beside him. Russell accepted.

"You handled the Wilson case very capably," Russell said. "I could see a touch or two of Colonel Jake's handiwork in it. However, I don't believe he would have ever had the nerve to leave Conner on."

Pruiett smiled as he thanked him. "Colonel Hodges was very kind to me. I'll always owe him a debt of gratitude for his kindness." That was all of his reply. He chose to ignore the reference to his success.

Russell persisted. "You won Conner completely," he said. "He stood for acquittal from the beginning, and he had a fight with one of the jurors over you. I talked to the bailiff."

"Is that so?" he asked, registering mild surprise. "I hadn't heard of it. I was so glad to win that I scarcely thought to thank them for the verdict. I didn't have much time to make the train, either."

"He said that a Dutchman that was for conviction said something unbecoming of you, something about that trouble you had in Paris, and that Conner swung on him. He did such a good job that the Dutchman and another fellow that had been stayin' came over and signed the verdict. We all thought that Conner was a sticker; he's hung a few in his time."

Pruiett was meditating. Even that far from Paris, and so long afterward, the serpent's track was still discernible in the dry soil. He continued to look out the window as he answered.

"He had a' awful' good eye," he said. "I never saw such a keen eye in a man's head before. He had a' awful' good eye."

"That long lane stuff was pretty good. At first I thought it was too deep for him, but it was all right. It showed him what a narrow viewpoint he was goin' to have if he kept lookin' in the same knot-hole all the time. It was a good way to wake him up."

Pruiett was looking far out into the moving prairie, and saying nothing. Russell was not sure now that he was listening.

"Would you be interested in movin' to Dallas, and making an association with me?"

"I beg your pardon, sir, but I was studyin' for a moment. What did you say?"

"I asked if you would be interested in comin' to Dallas, into my office. I could offer you an association where you could make four thousand a year, possibly more."

Pruiett shook his head. "No, sir, but thank you," he said. "I'm honored, and hardly know what to say, except—. I have other plans, and I just can't. I just simply can't."

Russell, with his carefully developed poise and control, was unable to conceal all of the surprise he felt at receiving so prompt a rejection. While he was not inclined to be self-admiring, he knew of Pruiett's background and previous circumstances. He knew that the same offer would have been relished by many a more successful and accomplished lawyer. It was his turn to gaze away, and to ponder.

"I've got my plans worked out quite a ways ahead," Pruiett said doggedly. "I've got a little start up in the Valley where my family is, and some friends that are helpin' me along. I don't think I'd like it back in Texas. My father and mother are growing old very fast, and if fortune should smile upon me one of my real purposes is to see that they are made comfortable in their declining years."

"But you'll have friends wherever you go," Russell said assuringly. "Dallas is a good town, and it's growing. You can make more money there in the next year than you can in five in the Sandy Land courts. There's money for you in Dallas."

"I'm thinkin' about statehood," Pruiett replied. "At the rate the whites are takin' up land and crowdin' the Indians out, it won't be long before the government'll see the futility of tryin' to protect 'em and their property. I look for the government to settle with the tribes, an' open all the unassigned land to settlers. If they do, it means there'll be another state in the Union."

"We've pushed the Indians as far as we're goin' to be able to," Russell replied. "What you get in the territory will be temporary, like the nesters that marry the squaws for a good place to lay down, or the traders that run those dinky little stores. The marshals'll get tired of the squaw-robbers an' bootleggers some of these days, and run every damned white person out of there. Then they'll disband that funny little court, and you and all the other lawyers will have to come back to Texas, or take a chance on Arkansas."

Pruiett smiled at him, conscious of a feeling of superiority, and shook his head. Was it possible that the great Russell, with his experience and wisdom, could have such a narrow and warped idea of what was going to come? If he did, he would have to continue to labor under it, for he was too big a man to be informed or corrected by a Sandy Land practitioner. He smiled again, but made no spoken reply.

Pruiett climbed into Garvin's waiting buggy beside the depot. "It was grapes," he laughed. "I took after the toughest hand they had on the jury, an' started sellin' him stock. He brought the verdict in just like I thought he would."

"I got the wire," Garvin said, "an' I sure was proud of you. You got to get down to Ardmore. There's—."

"I got to go to Saint Joe," he interrupted. "Hell, I told you that. How's Lilly Belle an' the kid?"

"They're fine, but ain't you interested in this Ardmore business I got you? It's murder."

"What?"

"You're damn right. Murder, right here on the home diamond. You know Frank Henderson and his boy, the boy's name's Mike? The tall ganglin' boy? They're bein' held by the Federals; goin' to be indicted for murder. They killed Charley Anderson an' Fred Stevens from up around Paoli, an' it's a hell of a case."

"You mean they killed 'em both?"

"Yes, sir, I sure as hell do," Garvin said. His excitement was obvious. "Soon as anybody gets in trouble around here they come hightailin' to me for a bond. I told their folks right to their faces that if Furman or Cruce or any of that bunch got the cases ahead of you, that I don't schedule a hoss, steer or cow. They promised to give it to you."

"What's the dope?" Pruiett asked. "What brought it up?"

"Frank's got a girl named Virginia; it's his baby girl," Garvin explained. "Maybe you don't know her. She's a' overgrowed gal about sixteen that looks like she's twenty, an' she's been runnin' around. Frank an' Mike caught her out with both of these boys, an' in a hell of a fix. She did about all she could do, under the circumstances, an' bein' caught by her paw an' her brother. She started to bawl an' said that Charley and Fred used force on her. They shot 'em both dead."

"The unwritten law," Pruiett whispered. "The unwritten law—."

"Don't it sound good to you?" Garvin inquired.

"Hell, yes, it does," he answered. "I'll make this trip with you an' get 'em released on bond, if the commissioner'll allow it. I suppose we won't have no trouble on that? Then I'll have to hustle up to Missouri."

"He's indicated to their folks that under the circumstances, he's willin' to set bail, but it'll have to be kinda high."

"Has these folks got any money?" Pruiett asked. "Do they expect to lay out a perty fair fee?"

"They're able to pay," Garvin grinned. "When you learn to fix fees as well as you can try cases, then you are goin' to be a genuine lawyer."

"You know more about law an' business, for bein' a cattle breeder than anybody else I ever saw," Pruiett laughed. "You should be a lawyer yourself."

"Did you want to see me, Moman?" Claude Weaver, Pruiett's poker playing colleague, walked into the converted shoe-shop. "I thought you was out of town 'til John Webb saw me in the street an' said you was lookin' for me."

"I got in on the night train," Pruiett explained.

"How'd you get along with your case?"

"I won it," he answered, shortly.

"What?" Weaver demanded. "You don't mean you got an acquittal for Wade Hampton?" He smiled with his use of the alias.

"Hell, yes, I did. The jury turned him loose. He rode back as far as Guthrie with us on the train."

"How in the hell did you do it?" Weaver asked.

"I don't know exactly how I did do it," Moman answered. "You probably wouldn't believe me if I was to tell you. I found a long lost uncle's son-in-law on the jury panel for one thing, an' Buchanan County's the home of Fightin' Joe Shelby. Wade Hampton stood ace high with the Shelby gang," Moman stated. "I proceeded by sayin' that: 'Here is another funny thing that happened in 1879, my Father and I had walked all over St. Louis, Missouri, looking for an uncle of mine, father's brother, who was supposed to own and operate the Buckhorn Livery Stable.' After the Hampton jury had retired to consider his case, the sheriff said to me, Mr. Pruiett, I went to school with a Martha Pruiett. Come with me. We went into his office, where he picked up the telephone, and called either his father or grandfather, and inquired what was the name of the livery stable that Uncle Bobby Pruiett owned at one time here in St. Joe? The Buckhorn, came the reply. The sheriff turned to me. Come get in the sleigh with me, and we will go down on Darby Street, and I believe that I can introduce you to your uncle. When we arrived at the Pruiett residence on Darby Street, there I met my long-lost uncle, and the cousin Martha, that the sheriff had gone to school with, who's husband's name was Mr. Isenberger, a cigar manufacturer. It so happened that he was a member of the jury that was trying Wade Hampton. I learned this at about ten o'clock that night before I left my Uncle's home. The jury returned a verdict the following morning of 'not guilty.' Just such damned coincidences as this has often played a part in my past life."

"Claude, I am so damned mad I don't believe I can trust myself when I meet old L. C. Andrews," Moman remarked.

"If you cleared that cow thief you ain't justified being mad at anybody," Weaver observed. "And if it's murder, count me out. I am not encouraging none of that, not even for my friends."

"Would you consider assault an' battery?" Moman inquired.

"I might stay with you if you was goin' to beat hell out of somebody, but this killin' is out with me. I don't believe in it."

"Here is the layout," Moman said. "I get up to St. Joe an' they got Louis C. Boyle, ex-Attorney General of Kansas, there to prosecute the case against Hampton. The Livestock Association hired him special, and he is an able prosecutor.

"Boyle gets a letter. It say that Pruiett is a two-time convict from Arkansas an' Texas, an' to bring it out an' the defense will be blowed up. Can you believe it? He writes 'em I'm a ex-convict."

"Well," Weaver waited. "What happened? Did you get in any trouble?"

"Billy Morrison, a local lawyer, informed me of its contents. He didn't wait, and he didn't take it to anybody else. He brought it right to me. He says, "Look what some scoundrel down in the Territory says about you. It's an outrage."

"I looked at him for a minute, and I says, 'It's true, Judge, as far as it goes.'"

"I disagree with you, sir. It's a insufferable lie. You are a gentleman, and a worthy member of the bar—and my friend," Morrison stated.

"Well—that's the way it was. The judge was friendlier than ever, and I really think he was sincere," Pruiett declared.

"You are not hurt much then," Weaver said.

"But I didn't think old L. C. Andrews was built that way," Pruiett replied. "That misfortune is not going to follow me around, and keep draggin' me down," Pruiett declared. "My friends know how it's hurt me. They won't talk it, and don't like to hear me mention it. The others, my enemies or the ones that think they can repeat it, have got to learn that it is not healthy. I'm going to resent it," Pruiett persisted.

"You can do a sight more good by cripplin' 'em," Weaver observed.

"Who's that comin' down the walk?" Pruiett asked. Henry Carr, my partner, just appeared. "It's old L. C. Andrews," Carr answered.

"Here's where we settle," Pruiett grated. He opened the drawer of his table and pulled out a blue barreled pistol.

"Don't do no murder," Weaver cautioned. Pruiett slid the gun into a coat pocket and started up the board walk.

"I read that letter you sent to Saint Joe about me," Pruiett began, fishing out the weapon. L. C. Andrews was a big man, powerful of mind and body, but he turned to flee. Pruiett clubbed him on the side of the head with the barrel and cylinder. The first blow dropped him like a beef. He fell to his knees and elbows, but he scrambled up; blood was spurting from a great gash above his neck. Pruiett was in front of him as he regained his feet, with the big gun high above his head. He brought it crashing down between Andrew's eyes, and Andrews went down again.

The second blow—the combination of blows—should have disabled the victim. But Andrews was big and strong, and he was conscious enough to know that he was in a precarious predicament. If he lay still he stood to be stomped or beaten to death. With an unnatural effort, he lurched to his feet, charged into Murray's grocery on his right and raced for the back door. Pruiett was in close pursuit, sliding in the blood that gushed from Andrews' battered head. Proprietor Murray grabbed the pursuer and struggled with him; the pursued found painful safety behind the locked door of Doctor J. A. Young's office—the office of the combination doctor and mayor. Pruiett was rounded up by the city marshal and charged with assault and battery.

The trial of the case of the Town of Pauls Valley versus Moman Pruiett was representative of the Pruiett theory. Four of the six men on the jury were merchants and two preachers,

Rev. E. D. Cameron and Rev. Duncan McCruer. During the trial Pruiett introduced as evidence the letter that L. C. Andrews, wrote to L. C. Boyle, relative to Pruiett being a two-time convict, and testified that he heard that Andrews was carrying a pistol for him. THE JURY FOUND PRUIETT NOT GUILTY OF ASSAULT AND BATTERY.

"I ain't satisfied with that verdict," Mayor Young stormed. "It's agin' the clear weight of the evidence, an' it's a reflection on the peaceful natur' of this here community."

"I object," Weaver howled.

"This town ain't goin' to be made a joke of, this a'way," Young insisted. "Call another jury an' let's try'er again."

Pruiett grinned as he pulled Weaver close and whispered into his ear.

"I object," Weaver repeated. "It's agin' the Constitution of the United States. No man can be put in jeopardy twict for the same offense. I can show it to you, in Mansfield's Arkansas Digest."

"I reckon that's right," Young ruminated, scratching his chin. "But there ain't nothin' wrong with tryin' him again on somethin' else. Where's the city marshal?"

"I'm here," the officer called from his seat in the window.

"Put Moman under arrest an' charge him with carryin' concealed weapons. Charge him as on the date of this assault on L. C., an' his bond will be fixed at two hundred an' fifty dollars." Young slammed his table with a book, for emphasis.

Sam Garvin signed the bond and the same witnesses were called back when the case was reset. Pruiett kept up the insolent grin. Weaver reappeared as the attorney for the defense, and the routine of the trial was put on. The prosecution introduced the pistol and Pruiett acknowledged that it was his, that he heard that Andrews was armed for him, and that he was carrying the pistol for his own protection. The jury found Pruiett not guilty. Mayor Young despaired and gave up.

But life in the Valley wasn't all glitter. "Friday morning, after an illness of two weeks, little Hayden Pruiett, son of Mr. and Mrs. Moman Pruiett, departed this life . . . Mrs. Pruiett was nearly crazed by the death of her babe, and were it not for the ministration of Dr. Young and Dr. Davenport it might have been our sad duty to chronicle two deaths instead of one. Saturday morning all that was earthly of the little one was taken to Paris, Texas, accompanied by the father and mother and Dr. Davenport."

The reunion with Betty and the Captain, the first in almost two years, was a sorrowful one.

"Things ain't lookin' good around here," Pruiett observed, bluntly.

"The money you been sendin' us, Moman, from time to time, has come in handy, all right," Betty answered, with a wan, wrinkled smile.

"Pa is just too old to be any help to you at all, isn't he, Mother?"

"He's almost like a child," Betty confessed. "He gets around all right, but he's forgetful, an' I have to watch out for him. He starts the garden in the spring, but he usually forgets about it, or gets tired of it, before long, an' I have to either mind it or let the weeds have it. My eatin' customers has just about all quit me, by now."

"You an' Pa will have to go back with us, up to the Valley."

"I ain't aimin' to get in your way, son," she said. "We can—."

"You can do what I say," he interrupted. "I own a good house with six or eight lots about a block an' a half away from our new house. I took it for a fee in a murder case, an' it ain't rentin' for hardly nothin'. You see the fix Lilly's in. If losin' this one don't kill 'er, she's goin' to have another one in days or weeks, an' you can help her durin' the bedfast period. Don't argue with me, now. Just get ready to go back with us. When Pa turns over a spadeful of that Valley ground for his garden, he won't walk off an' leave it. You won't be able to run him off."

There was a letter for the Pruietts when they returned. It was from Luther Reese, the preacher who had married them at Paris.

"My dear Brother and Sister in Christ," he began. "I was shocked when Mrs. Reese handed me, on my return from South Louisiana, the telegram containing the sad news that your dear little babe had fallen asleep . . . Was so sorry that I did not get to see you and especially was I sorry that I was away when the message came. I could not have done any good, but I did long for fellowship with you in your deep sorrow. In it all, it is blessed to know that the sweet babe is with the Lord, 'Safe in the arms of Jesus,' which Paul, by the Holy Spirit says, 'is far better,' . . . . I am on my way to Cleveland, Ohio, where I am to speak at the annual meeting of the Congregational Home Missionary Society in behalf of our work in Texas and Louisiana. Pray for me—both of you. Praying that you may receive this affliction from your Father as one of the 'All things that work together for the good of His children,' I am, Yours in Christ Jesus—-Luther Reese."

CHAPTER FIVE

Wherein a country lawyer goes to Washington, and meets, under circumstances vastly dissimilar, a man who had known and befriended him in a day not so prodigal. And how he offends the Attorney General of the United States, but captures the fancy and good will of the Senators—and the President—by his quick wit, his sharp tongue and gruff manner, to make himself the savior of a convict condemned to die and the subject of some flattering comment in the Capital Press.

Culberson of Texas and Beveridge of Indiana lounged in the Senate offices of the latter. Their short conversation had dealt with such ponderous topics as the prospect for prosperity in Nineteen Hundred, the century whose recent beginning was revealed across the face of a brass-plated calendar pad on the senator's desk, and how long the steady fall of snow, as discernible through the slightly sooty windows, might continue. Senator Culberson's original intention of a brief visit, evidenced by his failure to have removed his long black coat, was further indicated by a slow ascension from the deep chair he had been occupying, and a cautious sidewise movement toward the corridor exit.

"I promised Hare I'd meet him in the Court for opening," he said. "I want to be there when he moves the admission of one of my former—er—constituents, a young lawyer from the Indian Territory. He used to live in Texas. But if you've got time I'd like for you to meet this youngster. He even claims a branch connection with Indiana—besides Kentucky and Texas. Unless I'm badly mistaken, you'll agree that the business won't be overcrowded with his kind."

"All right," he replied. "I was going out anyway. I'll drop in with you and see what you and Hare can produce from this place you call Texas and bring it to Washington without even offering an apology."

Court was opening and the justices were filing to their places as the two senators entered the Supreme Court chambers. Taking seats they waited, hats in hand, until that item of business was called which excited the idle curiosity of one, but a strange, half-mournful and half-pleasant glance into retrospection, for the other.

Silas Hare, former member of Congress from the Lone

Star State—and who had relinquished his seat there only after a close contest to the inimitable Joseph Bailey—was addressing the court. Hare, a lawyer, maintained offices in the National Capital.

"With your Honor's pleasure," he said, "I move the admission of Mr. Moman Pruiett, licensed attorney of Texas and the Indian Territory—now residing in the Indian Territory—to practice before the Supreme Court."

After the routine observation and inquiry, Chief Justice White directed the clerk to administer the oath. When the young man who had been sitting quietly behind Hare arose and took the oath, the senator from Texas nudged his Indiana colleague.

"That's the one," he said in a hoarse whisper. A stronger emotion than the one of apparent pride was evident in his tone and manner.

The object of his attention and concern was a young man of not more than 27 or 28 years, and obviously from that rapidly vanishing sector called the frontier. His suit was neat and well pressed, but of a cut which suggested an origin different from that of the Washington tailored array of Hare. He was of but average height. Heavy square shoulders and a robust brown neck lent him the appearance of physical strength and endurance, while the color of his hands and face, as brown and leathery as his neck, marked him at once as a man more than casually acquainted with the outdoors.

An amazing crop of coal-black hair extended backward and about his close-set ears to a point immediately above his coat collar. There, by the ingenuity of a territorial tonsorial artist, it ended abruptly and proceeded neckward in a solid wall of the severed ends of black wire strands. The bulk, the glow and the faultless array of the remarkable growth was matched by black brows, unnaturally shaggy and prominent. The coarse bronze texture of the skin over the countenance underneath caused the head to appear to be much too large for the body, and to give it an aura of animal-like power and strength.

Beveridge and Culberson waited in the hall for Hare and his companion. Pruiett was aware of Culberson's presence, and he was looking about for him as he came out. He proceeded directly to the senator and connected with a powerful handclasp. Then they stood apart—without speaking—gazing intently into each other's faces. The gentleman from Indiana was not certain, on subsequent reflection, whether it was a tear he saw on Culberson's cheek as he brushed it with the back of his hand, or but a trick of his own imagination, as produced by the uncanny tenseness of the atmosphere.

"Beveridge," the taller of the two said, "this is Moorman Pruiett, whom I first knew in Texas. I have quite an interest in his future—and his success. I guess I don't need to tell you again that I'm very proud of him."

"I have long anticipated the pleasure of your acquaintance, Senator Beveridge," Pruiett responded, in a deep, well-modulated voice. The oratorical flourish, of both the language and delivery, was not forced or out of place. "To have made it through Senator Culberson is doubly agreeable."

Culberson interrupted, but the interruption was not to place the younger man at his ease. That indefinable quality of charm and personality radiated from the young lawyer as spontaneously as the gleam of the corridor lights reflected from the shiny blackness of his hair. As an office associate was to say of him later, "There was that something about him—he could get a total stranger to do more for *him,* than I could get my best friend to do for *me.*"

"If you remember, Bailey was talking about the fellow who raised so much hell with Griggs?" Culberson was saying, "Well, this is the one—."

Beveridge whistled a surprised interruption. Then he laughed. "Young man," he said, "it's bad business to offend Griggs, even when you have no business with him. I'm surprised, after what Joe Bailey told me about that deal, that your motion for admission here wasn't refused. That Attorney General's as tough as hell—an' he'll even fix the Supreme Court on you if you don't watch him."

Pruiett exhibited his good taste and judgment by saying nothing—and smiling agreeably. The other members of the group laughed. He didn't have to be told that his advisor was not inclined to censor him for the scraps he had with John W. Griggs, the cabinet member, a whispered report of which had been traveling about the Capitol. With Hare's approach to the group and a renewed exchange of greetings, Pruiett shook hands with the senators again, and departed. As he and Hare walked out of hearing down the hallway, Beveridge turned to Culberson.

"That's a fine boy," he said, warmly. "Nice appearance. Nice manners—and smart as hell. Got regular senatorial polish and culture. What school is he from—and what's the story behind all the feeling between you and him? Has he some orphan kinfolks, who's struggled through college, or something like that?"

Culberson was silent for a moment. He held searching eyes full into those of the friend he knew he could trust.

"On your Indiana honor, Beveridge, don't repeat this," he said. "I shouldn't say it, and don't misunderstand me when I do, but this thing here this morning has torn me up, and by George, I got to tell somebody what I know. Six years ago, while I was governor of Texas, I pardoned that kid from the state penitentiary at Rusk. He's had no schooling, an' I'll be damned if he hadn't served a term in Arkansas, before gettin' in trouble in Texas. He had three years left, out of a five-year sentence, when I turned him over to his mother—an' she was one of the most persistent and devoted women I ever saw. That Pruiett is a genius—just a natural-born genius. He's got a head full of the damndest brain I ever came in contact with, an' a belly plumb full of guts. No education, a'tall, but you just watch him. He's learned his lesson the hard way, an' he'll stay out of trouble from now on. You'll see him at the top—an' in damn short order."

The Washington Post made note of the more formal part of the proceeding in a casual item. "Hon. Bryan Houston, of New York, formerly of San Antonio and Wichita Falls, was in Washington. . . Mr. Houston was admitted to practice before the Supreme Court yesterday, as was Moman Pruiett of Pauls Valley, I. T., formerly of Paris, Texas."

Pruiett's admission to practice before the Supreme Court was but incidental to his real business in Washington—as in the case of Hon. Bryan Houston. Charley Bias, a stoic Negro, was in the Federal Prison at Ardmore, Indian Territory, sentenced to be hanged. The scaffold was built and the inhabitants of the countryside, white, black, and Indian alike, were straining the accommodations of the settlement's hotels and rooms as they came to town for the execution.

"People of the Indian Territory," announced the Ardmorite, "should not fail to be at Ardmore on the 19th (January, 1900), for there the great government of the United States, represented by Marshal Hammer, will provide a festival which will bring to the mind tender suggestions of ancient Israel and Rome. . . . Take your children with you and wait with them, exposed to the elements, as the people of Jerusalem were wont to wait outside the gates for the coming of their victim . . . Of course, the sport will be less exciting than in the days of Moses, when everybody who could throw a stone was allowed to take part in the execution, or in Nero's time when the victims were torn by wild beasts 'to make a Roman Holiday,' or in the later days of our own Anglo-Saxon race, when ignorant Negroes were artistically tortured to death by refined and civilized men."

Bias and a young African named Gus Wright differed over the respective rights of each to a community Negro girl. They were freedmen descendants, a strain which began as half Indian-half Negro, as the male Indian owner impregnated his female Negro slave, but which rapidly graduated toward a black pre-dominance as the half-caste get was taken up by the black slave associates. According to custom, the young bucks rode their poor ponies to the weedy flats of Wild Horse Creek to fight it out—fist and skull. Bias, a battered and bruised victor, had started to remount and ride away when Wright, with enough of the vengeful red man's blood under his black hide to make his lacing doubly distasteful, violated the rules by grabbing a knife and reopening the fracas. Bias killed him.

"I've always been an optimist, Bill, but I have got no idea I can clear Charley Bias," Pruiett said. "An' I didn't ask that damned old carpet-bagger court to appoint me to defend him. I'll plead him guilty an' take twenty-five years."

"I might consider life for him if you want'a make a trade, but that's all," the prosecutor replied. It was W. B. Johnson, the government's hob-nailed vice-destroyer on the last frontier. Offi-cially, he was District Attorney for the Southern District of the Indian Territory. "The evidence in this case is goin' to shock even the roughest element of this little old community. I've never heard of a murder so brutal, an' I heard about this one from the guy that done it. I got a full confession out of him, an' it's wit-nessed."

"That's my best talkin' point," Pruiett answered. "He's so utterly ignorant an' brutal that we shouldn't measure him by cur law, that makes hangin' or life in the pen the punishment for murder. Charley wouldn't kill a rabbit unless it hurt him first—but after he got started he'd just as soon kill a dozen men as one rabbit. He's not mean—he's just ignorant. He won't never learn no better."

"I'll recommend life, but I don't think Judge Townsend'll

let Charley have it," Johnson persisted. "This is an awful bad case."

Pruiett reflected. "I hate to do it—but I think I'd better," he said. "Tell Townsend that all the case I got's based on the nigger's savage ignorance. He's never been near a school—never seen a railroad train, an' the Santa Fe to Fort Worth runs sixteen miles from their shack. His folks are awful poor an' awful ignorant. Tell him we'll take life an' save the government the cost of tryin' him. That's all a jury will give him, anyway."

But the Bias case came on for trial before a jury. Hosea Townsend refused to accept the guilty plea. Self-defense refused to fit the vicious conduct exhibited by the evidence, but Pruiett put the dull Negro on the stand, and turned him over to Johnson for cross-examination.

"So you say he rushed up behind your back with this weepun in his hand?" Johnson bellowed, as he began. "Uh-huh," Charley replied. His languid gaze enveloped a vista of green-budding cottonwoods through the open window.

"An' you took this chunk and knocked him down with it?"

"Uh-huh."

"He was layin' there at your feet, unconscious, was he?"

"Uh-huh."

"So you took his knife from his hand and stuck it into his heart, like this?" Johnson roared, as he flourished the death-knife through the air and brought it up sharply as though he had a body before him on the floor.

"Uh-huh."

"An' you took him by the hair, an' pulled his head this a-way, and cut his throat on this side?" "Uh-huh." "An' then you pulled his head over this a-way and cut his throat on the other side?" "Uh-huh." "Then you stabbed him in the right eye, did you?" he inquired. "Uh-huh." "An' then you stuck the knife in to the handle in his left eye?" "Uh-huh."

"You can stand aside." Johnson mopped the perspiration produced through the horror of his own device from his brow and head, as he walked slowly to his chair.

The government won the case. The jury convicted Bias and sentenced him to hang, but Pruiett hadn't been a push-over. No agency or individual, opposing Pruiett in a jury trial, had an instant's peace from the time the case was called until the last word was said and the court room was cleared. He charged Johnson with using the walls of the temple of justice for a canvas, and the blood of the underprivileged chattel for oils, while he painted a gory picture of hate and vengeance to obstruct the jurors' view of the right. He roared and tore, he emulated black Charley, on Wild Horse, but it was wasted effort.

The condemned Negro, a pauper, had the same kind of representation at South McAlester, where the Territorial Court of Criminal Appeals was in session. Pruiett duplicated, even embellished, the fierce forensics of the trial court, but the result was the same. He was drooped and dejected when he returned to the Valley. Charley's death sentence was affirmed; the date of the hanging was fixed.

Pruiett was telling his troubles to the Cruce brothers, attorneys at Ardmore, "I am not goin' to let that nigger hang," he said doggedly. "It's just like torturin' a cat, or dog. He's just a plain animal. He don't know anything about civilized conduct, or the law we got to regulate conduct."

"What you aim to do about it?" A. C. Cruce inquired.

"I don't know," Pruiett answered. "What have I got left to do?"

"Make yourself a little trip to Washington, an' talk Bill McKinley out of a reprieve, or a commutation of sentence." Will Cruce suggested, a trifle sarcastically. "It won't cost you much, an' he can't do no more than sick the White House dog on you."

Pruiett reflected. "I'd like to go to Washington," he said. "How much would it cost?"

"It ain't what it costs to go that counts," Will Cruce said. "It's what it takes to get along while you're there, an' what it costs to check out. What them pauper niggers of yours could raise wouldn't get you to Wichita." Pruiett continued to reflect. "Suppose you was goin' to Washington—to get a sentence commuted. What would you do the first thing?"

"Get me a lot of pull," A. C. answered. "A few senators—an' a few representatives, to put the pressure on. Big time politics ain't much different from backwoods politics. It's the pull and the fix that gets the results."

"Know any big guns up there?" Pruiett inquired, innocently.

The Cruces laughed in unison. "There's an old man up there from Kentucky—we're from Kentucky, you know—that's a senator and Bill McKinley's right hand man. Senator DeBoe, they call him." A. C. was still laughing. "He was the doctor with my mother when I was born, an' when all the Cruce kids were born. We know him pretty well."

"Would he help a friend of yours, if you asked him to?"

"I ain't sure," Cruce replied, "but I think Old Doc would do anything on earth he could for us. If he won't help, I ain't got a friend in the world."

"I know a senator, too," Pruiett said.

"Which one do you know?" Will Cruce inquired.

"Culberson, from Texas," Pruiett answered.

The Cruce brows arched, with a suggestion of a little more respect. "I forgot you was from Texas," A. C. said. "Do you know him very well? Ever have any business with him?"

"Yeah—I had a little business with him," Pruiett said, slowly. "An' I believe he'd help me. I may call on him—but I don't guess it's any use to figure that far ahead. Bill Johnson told me he was conscientiously opposed to capital punishment—an' that if the Department of Justice asked for it, he'd tell them so, and agree that my application for commutation be allowed. I think he'll take care of ever' thing for me."

"Did Bill Johnson tell you that?" Will Cruce asked, showing his surprise. "Did he—really?" "Hell, yes, he did." Pruiett showed his complacence with his answer.

"Let me tell you something," Will said earnestly. "He's offered to do that before—lots of times—but they keep wearin' out the ropes over at the hangin' pen. He wants you to rest on that written application to the department. When they write him, he turns it down, an' then it's too late to do anything else. They hang your nigger before you can catch a train out of town."

"You mean that?"

"Hell, yes, I mean it. Everybody around here knows it. You ought to, by this time."

"Write me a letter of introduction to DeBoe, will you?" Pruiett asked. "An' ask him to do his best for me with the president. I'm goin' to the Valley, an' catch me a train to the capital. I always wanted to go up there, anyway."

"Who's goin' to pay your expenses?"

"Old man Grant at the Pauls Valley bank," Pruiett laughed.

"You ain't goin' to borrow money an' make such an expensive trip—for a pauper nigger, are you, Pruiett?" A. C. Cruce inquired.

"I'm goin' to save that nigger's life, or I'll never try another lawsuit as long as I live," Pruiett said. "I didn't ask for this

case—but I got it—an' I'm stayin' with it. That nigger is not
goin' to swing."

Pruiett left the Valley on the day after Christmas, 1899. He
made the Oxford Hotel, at 14th Street and New York Avenue,
his stopping place in Washington, and set out to get his work
done.

"I got a letter from the Cruce brothers, in the Indian Territory, Senator," he grinned at the tall Kentuckian. "They said
to tell you 'hello', an' to try to get you interested. Do you remember 'em?"

"I caught 'em," DeBoe said. "Ever' damn one of the Cruce
kids, an' ever' damn one is a good one. Good stock—good timber.
Waited on 'em while they was children, sick, an' watched 'em
grow up. The Cruces were genuine Kentucky."

"My people was from Kentucky," Pruiett suggested, hopefully.

DeBoe was a man of some 65 years, with a tall brow which
extended, uninterrupted, into an expanse of oily baldness. He
stopped the conversation to read the letter from the Cruce boys.
"It says here," DeBoe observed, "that you're up here on your
own expense; got a pauper client. How can you do that?"

"I can't," Pruiett answered with a doleful look. DeBoe
laughed. "Have you got your application filed with the Department
of Justice?" he asked.

"I sent that in by mail," Pruiett said.

"John Griggs is a good friend of mine," DeBoe said. "He's
the Attorney General. Do you want a personal hearin'?"

"I want ever'thing that it takes to get a nigger a reprieve,"
Pruiett answered. "The Attorney General, the Supreme Court,
the President of the United States. Can you help me?"

DeBoe laughed again. "I am nothin' but a senator," he said.
"But if you got the guts to make it up here at your own cost,
son, I sure can't afford to turn you down. When do we go to see
Griggs?"

"How about right now?"

"Maybe I ought to make an appointment," DeBoe said. "Let's
make it tomorrow. Where are you stayin'?"

"At the Oxford. It's not so fancy, but—."

"It's a good place," DeBoe interrupted. "Gilbert, from Kentucky, stays there. Get acquainted with him as soon as you can.
An' old ex-Senator Kenna from West Virginia lives there, too.

Work on 'em. Make friends, 'cause I can see it's easy for you, an' you may need all the help on this thing you can get, before you're through."

DeBoe went for the Pruiett personality. "He got stuck on me," Pruiett explained it, later. The Kentucky Senator made him acquainted with the best people in Washington. He gave him a big send-off with the Attorney General, who promised to send for the records of the case and to give them a hearing. Pruiett told him that Bill Johnson would agree, if solicited, that the death penalty be commuted to life imprisonment. He thought of what the Cruces had told him, and wished that he hadn't said it, before the words were out of his mouth. The delay connected with the production of the letters and records from the Washita was neither noted nor despaired of by Pruiett. DeBoe took him around; the Charley Bias cause gained a few converts. There was Congressman John L. Sheppard, of Texas, and his colleague, Reese C. DeGraffenreid. Pruiett tried to enlist Joe Bailey.

"The trouble is," Bailey declared, "you won't be able to get anyone to believe you're up here at your own expense—that you are not tryin' to make a fee out of it." It was obvious from his tone and manner that he doubted it himself.

When Pruiett reappeared before Griggs, accompanied by DeBoe, the hope and cheerfulness he had carried with him since DeBoe's welcome was chilled by a hostile face and manner. Without a greeting or an introductory declaration, Griggs lifted a paper from his desk and threw it across at Pruiett.

"I was sorry to find that you are not worthy of confidence," he said. "I admit I was favorably impressed by you—and the nature of your business—but I see now that you have deliberately misstated the facts, in an effort to deceive me."

Pruiett was pale, but without retort as he read the letter. It was from Bill Johnson. "Replying to your inquiry of Jan. 3rd," it said, "regarding Chas. S. Bias, awaiting execution here after murder conviction, I must advise that I have no recommendation to make . . . The trial disclosed the most atrocious murder recorded in territorial criminal history. The record is without justification or extenuating circumstances of any kind. This is the one case, in my experience, which requires the infliction of the death penalty."

Johnson's treachery, and Grigg's abuse, were ringing in his head as he turned. "If you or Johnson or any other man mean to say I deliberately misrepresented the facts in this case you're a damn liar," he roared, as he hurled the letter into the face of the astonished Attorney General. Griggs had presumed that his official rank would insure him against such an outburst.

"You're just a damned liar, an' Bill Johnson's a damned liar, an' the records of this case will prove it," Pruiett howled. "Show me the record—let me show you the record. Show me some facts, not a letter from a damned lyin' hypocrite—."

"Get out of here," Griggs shouted, keeping the desk between himself and Pruiett. "Get out—an' don't let me see you in my office again."

"You played hell, now," DeBoe exploded, as they stalked through the slushy snow. "Jesus Christ!" That's the Attorney General you're talkin' to. You've got us both in a fix."

"I guess so," Pruiett growled, "but you can't afford to let 'em get started with that kind of language, where I have to make my livin'. I should have broke his dirty neck."

"You just the same as broke your nigger's neck," DeBoe corrected him.

"Yeah, I guess I did," he agreed. "I made a mistake in mentionin' Bill Johnson. Cruce told me he wasn't to be trusted. I sure hate to see 'em murder that ignorant nigger, but I've done about all I can do."

"Griggs isn't really such a bad sort," DeBoe said. "He lost his temper, like you did, an' said some things he didn't mean, or expect to say. But he told me, before I came out, to tell you that you had an appeal direct to the President—this being a capital case—and that he was forwarding his unfavorable report to him this afternoon."

Pruiett's manner brightened. "Will you help me arrange—?"

"I can't be responsible for you before the President," DeBoe said, dubiously. "It's a miracle you got by with what you did before Griggs. He may decide to give you some trouble over it yet, after he thinks about it a bit. Talk to some of the other boys, an' see if they can't work something out for you."

Pruiett had dinner that evening at the Metropolitan with Congressman Sheppard and Mrs. Sheppard. It was both pleasant and profitable.

"And," he wound up the narrative of the day's events, "he threw me out of his office an' told me not to come back. They'll hang that nigger, and they hadn't ought to do it—an' I've sworn to quit practicing law if he swings. How's that?"

The Sheppards were concerned. "It's a pity," Mrs. Sheppard opined.

"It's a damned outrage," the congressman said. "What's your next move? What have you got in your mind for me to do?"

"Well," said Pruiett, "DeBoe is scared off—a little. I know how he feels. I'd be embarrassed myself if some one I was sponsorin' blew up in my face, like I did this morning. What I want—I want to get this before the President."

"I can do that for you. I can get you in," Sheppard said, "but you ought to have DeBoe, too. He's strong with McKinley. The President thinks a lot of the old boy. Can you get DeBoe to come back?"

"I think I can—if you'll go with me," Pruiett said.

"I'll meet you in the lobby of the Riggs in the morning, an' we'll go up to his room. We'll make him go along with us."

Pruiett, without question or interruption, retold the Charley Bias case to the President, DeBoe and Sheppard sat quietly—apprehensively—as if in dread of what might occur. Perhaps it was the congenital kindliness of the executive, and not the charm of the young lawyer who was telling the long story. It may have been that the peculiar nature of the facts involved held his interest.

"Your Excellency," Pruiett concluded dramatically, "this has become a question now of veracity. I want mine tested. I said there are extenuating circumstances in that record, circumstances which justify, and require a commutation of sentence. Johnson has told the Attorney General that there is none. The official record will show which of us has told the truth."

President McKinley was impressed. "Cortelyou," he said to the secretary who answered his ring, "get me the file in this case of the government against Charley Bias. It's in the Department of Justice."

"I have them here," Cortelyou said. "They came from the Attorney General today. There is a recommendation that no action be taken, attached."

"Griggs is mad," Pruiett interrupted. "He's sore. The only way you can find out about this is to study the official record, yourself."

"Have the Department forward the official record," the President said, "and leave it with the file, on my desk."

Pruiett interrupted again. "By the record, I mean the transcript of the testimony in the case," he said, "and it's never been sent to Washington. Griggs wants to dispose of this case on the correspondence of interested parties in the Indian Territory. That's no way to get information."

"Where is this record?" McKinley inquired, showing signs of impatience.

"Where we tried the appeal," Pruiett said, "at South Mc-Alester, in the territory."

The President studied. "Direct the Department of Justice to send for it, Cortelyou," he said, "and write Mr. Griggs to the effect that Mr. Pruiett is to have another hearing on this matter, ON THE OFFICIAL RECORD, as soon as it reaches Washington."

The Indian Territory was bone dry, but on the Arkansas, and in Texas, liquor was abundant. As a boy, and as a young man, the saloons and joints in the fringe of the states had never interested Pruiett. He had, innately, an insatiable yen to see another card, or to watch the wheel spin. The bulk of his contact with alcoholic liquors, prior to his first eastern trip, had been in the occasional drink which went along with his visits to the gambling hall bars.

But it was different in Washington. There was a brilliance about the gaudy interiors of the cafes and lounges, with their gay and smart talking patrons, which captivated him. On the wings of the stimulated eloquence of Culberson and Beveridge, of DeBoe, Sheppard and DeGraffenreid, Pruiett suffered a fascination for the refined convivialities which went with the stimulation of the cafe liquor. The slightest suggestion of a cause or excuse, in his later and more profitable years, was all that was necessary to cause him to pack and start for what he invariably called "business in Washington."

"The Attorney General desires to give you a hearing at 2:30 today." The terse communication, reaching Pruiett on January 12, was signed by J. S. Easby Smith, Pardon Attorney. Pruiett attempted to apologize to Griggs—DeBoe had insisetd—but the cabinet member was cold.

"We must be brief, gentlemen," he said. Turning on Pruiett he thrust the voluminous transcript of the Territorial Court proceedings at him, in the same manner as he had previously tendered Johnson's letter. "This is the official record. I have read most of it, and fail to find anything to substantiate your position. Where, if you please, is there a suggestion of evidence to support your contention that there are circumstances either mitigating or extenuating?"

Pruiett was game. Thumbing the pages, he stopped long enough to extract an old envelope from his coat pocket and insert it between the pages for a book mark, as he turned on to find substance for argument. He had repeated those movements some four or five times, when an orderly entered the room. It was a welcome interruption, for the silence, unbroken save for the slight rustling of the pages in Pruiett's hands—was more than painful. The messenger handed a yellow slip—a telegram or cable—to the Attorney General, who casually directed his cold gaze into it.

"My God," he exclaimed with feeling which Pruiett would have sworn he lacked, "she's dead."

Griggs gazed beyond his audience and into the intricate design of the handsome door of his chamber. Rising, he walked around his desk, took the record from Pruiett, and handed it to the still silent pardon attorney.

"I'll be unable to continue the hearing of this matter," he said. "Please transmit the entire proceedings to Solicitor General Richards, with the suggestion that he hear it and make a recommendation to the President, for the department."

"This is indeed fortunate for you," Easby Smith said to Pruiett as they moved down the corridor toward the Solicitor-General's offices. "Mr. Richards is a very considerate gentleman, and directly opposed to capital punishment."

"But who's dead? To whom am I indebted for this good fortune?" Pruiett's inquiry was in a tone of ripe sarcasm.

"Mrs. Griggs' mother has been very low for several days," Smith explained. "I rather believe that the telegram was the advice of her death."

"God bless her," Pruiett said. "I hope she's in heaven, although I'd be burdened to say as much for her son-in-law. The Lord giveth and He taketh away. The old lady's death may mean that my nigger can live a little longer. That's the compensation of nature, for you."

The strange caprices of fate which dogged the career of Pruiett, to attach an almost uncanny glamor to his successes or defeats were already beginning to appear. Scarcely had the act of good fortune which removed the hostile Griggs from the problem been assimilated, then another appeared. Easby Smith told him that Judge William M. Springer of the Northern District of the Territory, one of the members of the appellate body that heard the territorial appeal of Bias, was in town. Pruiett determined to see him, in an attempt to get a favorable recommenda-

tion for his application, at least more favorable than the one
he had acquired from the District Attorney at home.

He called on Judge Springer on the following morning. "Have
you been able to make any one believe you are here on your
own expense?" he inquired.

"Joe Bailey wouldn't believe it, an' he said that nobody else
would," Pruiett replied. "But men like Senator DeBoe and Senator
Culberson have been very kind to me. President McKinley was
very considerate."

"What did Johnson do about it?" Springer inquired.

"He turned me down, and after he had—." Pruiett launched
into the details of the Johnson letter and the episode in the Attorney General's office. It was highly amusing to his listener.

"Johnson doesn't want to disappoint the crowd," the Judge
laughed, as he scratched his chin through a sparse gray beard.
"They're all set to have a big time at the Charley Bias party.
But did you know that Johnson told me the same thing at Mc-
Alester, after that sentence was affirmed? I mean all that about
having conscientious scruples and stuff?"

Pruiett admitted that he hadn't known of it.

"And did you know that I thought the penalty too stiff at
the review, and told old Townsend and Clayton so? I felt that
you were right about him bein' too ignorant and savage to
have a real murderous intent. I couldn't convince the others,
an' I was in the minority, so I had to keep quiet."

The gleam in Pruiett's eye was indicative of the new impetus
being added to his rapidly ascending hopes. "Could you say now
that there were circumstances in that record which might be
considered as extenuating?" he asked.

"Well—yes," the judge said, slowly. "I consider the proof
of the crime, in connection with the evidence of his utter lack of
intelligence and contact with the outside world, sufficient to establish that he should not be measured by the same standards as
that employed in the measuring of a civilized man's conduct."

"Will you give me a letter to the Department of Justice to
that effect?" Pruiett almost whispered?"

"I'll be glad to, my boy," Springer said. "It's refreshing to
find an occasional person with a noble motive and the courage
to stand up and fight for it. Don't build your hopes too high,
because the men here who have the say don't pay much attention
to an old judge from the territory, and I may not do you and
Charley much good."

Execution time was drawing unpleasantly close. The greater part of the 17th (January, 1900) Pruiett spent in the waiting room of Solicitor General Richards' office, or in pacing the corridor, outside. No information was being put out. On the same date and under the forbidding black head of "DEATH WATCH SET" the Daily Ardmoreite, back in the territory, carried related Pruiett news.

"This forenoon the Negro Chas. Bias was taken from among his fellow-prisoners in the United States jail and furnished more comfortable quarters wherein to spend the few remaining days of his existence. . . . During his removal today Marshal Hammer notified the prisoner of the nearness of death, and advised him to employ his time in making peace with his Maker. . . . He partakes heartily of food, and when informed that he could get anything he desired to order in the way of food, replied that he was getting all he wanted and had no desire for anything else. In his cell Bias seems perfectly content, has nothing to say, and seems wholly indifferent to the fate which awaits him, on next Friday, when he will hang by the neck until he is dead, unless perchance the President's clemency intervenes.

At four the next day the Solicitor General, acting as Attorney General in charge of the Bias case, completed and forwarded his report to the President. Pruiett, with his senatorial connections, couldn't get the grapevine on its content. The Times-Herald, in a special article of the late edition, made public the text of the report.

"A remarkable fight to save a human life ended successfully this evening when Attorney General Griggs, through Solicitor General Richards, to whom the matter had been referred, decided to recommend commutation of sentence for a colored boy named Chas. S. Bias. Bias is incarcerated at Ardmore, I. T., and was to have been hanged for murder next Friday. Only the efforts of his attorney, Moman Pruiett of Ardmore, will give the prisoner commutation of sentence from hanging to life imprisonment. . . . Pruiett sought many senators and they became interested, chiefly because his mission was purely charitable and because they were told the boy had really killed Wright in a fair fight and in self-defense. Great pressure was brought to bear, and the Attorney General undoubtedly gave exceptional attention to the case."

The full column front gave the gory details of the affray, the conviction and sentence, and the names of all the participants. The Washington press was taking out a charter membership certificate in the national organization which was to engage in plastering Pruiett on the front page for more than a quarter century.

"Pruiett is 27 years old and has defended men in twenty murder cases in the country, and has acquitted all but Bias, and now has saved that boy's neck by almost a miracle . . . Pruiett himself is a typical southerner—slouch hat, but his heart is full of charity as his head is full of brains. Many of the notables of Washington who have become interested in his case were congratulating the young lawyer tonight."

The bottle was off the shelf. The notables were before the bar at the Metropolitan, and the congratulations were prolix and verbose. Sheppard and DeGraffenreid were vieing with each other, and all with Pruiett, for the coinage of an oratorical expression sublime enough to fit the occasion. Pruiett was learning to like his liquor, and to hear the boys talk about Pruiett.

The Ardmoreite, the sheet which had previously decried the contemplated hanging and Roman holiday, was more descriptive than exultant. "Seated in the death cell, with his two guards, never speaking one word and evidently suffering no mental anguish, when informed last evening that the President had commuted his sentence to life imprisonment and that he would not be hanged, with muscles unmoved and without apparent expression from gladness or joy, his only answer was 'all right.' "

The Chickasaw Enterprise (weekly), Pauls Valley paper, tried to emulate its more established and influential kin-organs. "Word was received in Ardmore Monday from Washington that the sentence of Chas. Bias had been commuted to life imprisonment. Bias would have been hanged tomorrow. Attorney Moman Pruiett of this city has been in Washington the last two weeks working on this case."

CHAPTER SIX

Wherein Pruiett clears a man charged with double murder in a single trial, and although he offends his best friend and benefactor, he earns a cash fee which relieves his slightly damaged conscience. And that the bent sapling not only grows with the crook in it, but that it grows, and grows and grows.

Sam Ashton, in the Federal jail at Ardmore, was charged with shooting Charley Dismukes and his aged father to death. The double killing occurred in the Dismukes' country store and post-office at Hickory, Indian Territory. The one redeeming feature, if any, of the bloody fracas, rested in the existence of two wealthy uncles and a willingness on their part to spend some money to keep Sam from being hung.

Pruiett, back from Washington and enjoying a profitable run of practice from the attention attracted by his successful efforts in the Bias case, swore profusely as he saw old Uncle Hugh Forhand, from Lexington, on the South Canadian, and Uncle Matt Wolfe, of the Valley, pass him up and go on to Ardmore. They employed Henry Furman and A. C. Cruce to defend their nephew charged with murder.

The case was about ready for trial, when Sam's attorneys came to town ahead of schedule to argue a motion for a change of venue. "There's a lot of feelin' against old Sam, for one thing," A. C. Cruce told Pruiett as the two of them stood near the entrance of the court building. "And for another—."

"That's hell, now, isn't it?" mocked Pruiett. "Old Sam just goes out to Dismukes' country post-office, shoots Charley down in cold blood, and plugs his daddy in the back because he's runnin' away, and they get some feelin' up about it. Isn't it funny how people are?"

"Old Man Garvin's too bitter," Cruce continued, ignoring the interruption. "He's agitated opinion around here, knockin' Sam and boostin' the Dismukes, 'till we haven't got a chance for a fair trial, at all."

"The Colonel was awful fond of Charley Dismukes," Pruiett agreed, "an' he hates Sam's guts. Just between me and you, he says he'll pull up and leave the Valley if Sam don't hang, an' I believe he means it. You know me. I don't like the prosecution side of the table a bit, but they're makin' it mighty interestin'. The Colonel's puttin' up some of his own money."

"You mean—Garvin is tryin' to hire you?"

"That's just what I mean."

"Listen, Moman," Cruce hastened. "Henry Furman and I been talkin' about local counsel—about you. If we don't get this motion for a change of scenery over, we want you to help us and we'll make old Uncle Matt, dad-burn him, pay you a fee. He's awful tight, but we can work him. Leave that to me."

"Old man Garvin would run me out of town," Pruiett said.

"Forhand and Wolfe will pay you more than Garvin, an' you don't want to get in with the prosecution. You'd be all out of place, tryin' to send a man to the gallows."

Pruiett studied. The look of hybrid anguish and hatred, which had faded somewhat with the years since Rusk, passed across his face. "How come I have not been consulted about this before? What's the reason that nothin's been said?"

"You know how old Matt Wolfe and Sam Garvin hate each other," Cruce said. "That's why Garvin is persecutin' Ashton, and why Wolfe is willin' to spend money. Garvin says he'll hang him, mainly because he hates old Matt so much. Wolfe says he'll save him, just to spite old man Garvin. I told Matt, an' old Forhand, too, that we ought to get you in this case, but Matt says you're Garvin's man; that you'd work to get him stuck, even if he paid you. You know how it is, but if we got to try it here, I'll get you in or get out myself."

"Suppose I get in, what you got to work with?" Pruiett was being practical and matter-of-fact. "Here's the way I get it. Sam Ashton goes on Charley Dismukes' bond, when Charley gets charged with assault an' attempt to kill. Then Charley gets drunk again an' tries to kill somebody else, an' they get another warrant out for him, so Sam thinks his bond's in trouble—that Charley's liable to jump. He gets a certified copy of the bond and goes out to arrest Charley; he's got the right to do that, just take him in an' surrender him, but he don't get any authority like a regular officer, to use force, an' kill if he meets resistance. He didn't have no right to kill Charley."

"No, he didn't have no right to kill him, just to get off his bond," Cruce agreed, "but it shows you Sam was properly motivated when he went out there. That's our best point. When Sam told him what he wanted, Charley got tough. They got in an argument and Charley reached for his gun. Sam shot him in self-defense."

"What did he shoot the old man in the back for, as he ran

out the front door?" Pruiett inquired casually. "He wasn't on his bond, too, was he?"

"Well—," Cruce began, "well—. Let's cross that bridge when we come to it. Sam don't have to stand trial in but one case at a time, and the one for killin' Charley is set first. Maybe killin' the old man makes it bad, in the long run, but right now, just remember he was the only witness, an' he can't testify through them clods piled up in his face."

"You don't know much about your case," Pruiett observed. "Charley's wife saw the whole thing, and so did her sister. They're goin' to say that the guns were in the back, where they lived, an' that there wasn't any guns up in the front part 'of the store."

"Do you know what you're talkin' about?" Cruce demanded.

"You're damn right, I do," Pruiett answered.

"You stick close to your office this afternoon, and tomorrow mornin'." Cruce said. "You are goin' to get a visit from Mr. Wolfe and Mr. Forhand, and if you don't take care of yourself on the fee, it's your own fault. Don't make any deals with Garvin 'til you talk to them."

Pruiett smiled softly, midway of the following morning, as he saw two men in a buckboard stop in the shade outside the window of his office. It was Wolfe and Forhand. He planted his shoes amongst the papers on his desk with professional indifference as he saw them alight and move toward his door.

Forhand introduced himself. "An' this is Mr. Wolfe, Mr. Matt Wolfe," he said, stepping to one side so that Pruiett could reach him for the handshake. Forhand acted as spokesman, and was to the point, according to his nature, in an instant.

"Would you be able to take employment in the Sam Ashton case, next week?" he blurted.

Pruiett was deliberate and studious. "I'm afraid it would be embarrassin' for me to go into that case," he said, watching his callers closely. "While I have not been employed, I've been talked to. Colonel Garvin said the Dismukes wanted to hire me as a special prosecutor." Matt Wolfe uttered a grunt that was near to a groan.

"We been sent here by A. C. Cruce. He said he had worked with you before in cases." Forhand was trying to speak lightly and persuasively at the same time. "He said that you would give us a consideration on his account, that is, if you could."

"I would've been glad to, with a little more notice," Pruiett

said, carelessly, "but I wouldn't have time to prepare for trial—
that is—on the defense. No, gentlemen, I'm afraid I can't be
of any service to you." Neither of the callers was inclined to
abandon his purpose so early. Wolfe finally spoke.

"Now, if it's money, Mr. Pruiett, I think Mr. Forhand and I
can interest you. Maybe you can get a continuance, so as to be
able to get ready. We'll pay a fee, just for continuance of the
trial."

Pruiett was well acquainted with the unsuccessful efforts
made to continue the case, and knew why they had failed. He
knew that a continuance of the case for the term was out of
the question.

"No," he said. "My friend Garvin would be sore if I went
into it. I heard him say that Ashton was guilty as hell, an'
what he thought the punishment ought to be. I couldn't afford to
get myself in such a position."

"We'll pay you five hundred to sit in the case with Cruce
and Furman," Wolfe said, desperately.

"Yes," said Forhand.

"No," said Pruiett, "I wouldn't be interested. I'm sorry but
I'm just not interested."

"We'll pay you a thousand to try the case," said Wolfe,
with real pain and desperation in his coarse face. "A thousand
dollars." That was money. That was money for the territorial
days, or any other days, and Pruiett had to look again. Turning
squarely upon his callers, he studied them for a moment before
he spoke. "I'll try him for twenty-five hundred. I'll go in for
twenty-five hundred. I'll go in for twenty-five hundred dollars—
cash."

The gleam in Pruiett's eye indicated a quiet enjoyment of
the discomfort he beheld. Forhand looked at Wolfe and Wolfe
looked at Forhand. "It's plum' out of reason," Wolfe exploded.
"Why, we only paid Furman and Cruce fifteen hundred. Why,
why—."

Forhand, giving Wolfe a dark look for disclosing the terms
of their previous contract for legal services, interrupted him. "Mr.
Cruce told us you would be reasonable, at least," he said. "That
kind of fee is ridiculous. It's impossible." He and Wolfe arose
to go. In a last and final effort, Wolfe turned. "I'll still pay
the thousand. That's cash. A thousand bucks."

Pruiett wanted that thousand. He was beginning to believe
he was carrying the fee fixing bluff a little too far, so he changed

his tactics. "Do you want Sam Ashton acquitted," he inquired patronizingly, "or do you just want to save him from swingin'?"

"Acquitted," the two uncles answered in chorus. "We want him turned a' loose."

"Well, sit down. Maybe I can make you a different proposition," Pruiett suggested. "Maybe I can make a deal with you where you don't pay unless you get what you want."

Wolfe and Forhand resumed their seats, a little more cheerful and hopeful. "Mr. Cruce told us you would be reasonable." That was all Forhand could think of, so he said it again.

"I'll tell you, now," Pruiett began, "I can take this case for the thousand, and try to get it continued. If I do, or if I don't, I sit in with A. C. an' Furman, and help try it when it comes up. If Sam's acquitted, you pay me four thousand more. If he isn't, you don't pay me any more."

The plan didn't appeal to Forhand, but it did to Wolfe. He turned to his companion. "We should've made a deal something like that with the other lawyers," he said. "It would've been cheaper, and then they would have worked harder."

"It's too much. Five thousand is too much money. A thousand ought to be enough." Forhand was yanking his short whiskers as he jerked out the short sentence.

"I couldn't afford to have old man Garvin on me for the thousand," Pruiett explained. "I'd take my chances with him if you made it that interestin.' Pay me the thousand an' I start to work, an' if your man doesn't come clear, you don't owe me another cent. I can get the thousand out of the Dismukes."

Wolfe winced with the mention of the Dismukes. Having to try the case in the Valley, with Garvin hostile, was all that he could stand. His hatred for the proprietor of White Bear, as much as interest in his kin by marriage, had prompted his activity in the case thus far. He spoke hastily. "Could we have a word in private, Mr. Forhand and I?" Just a word or two, to talk it over?"

"Of course, of course," Pruiett assured him. "Use this room right here. I'd be glad for you to discuss it."

Pruiett ushered them into a small room adjoining the office. A few old books and papers, a rack and a chair, were discernible in the scant light admitted by a small, high window. When they had closed the door behind them, he resumed his chair behind the table, which served as a desk, the principal piece of furniture of the room, and placed his feet back amid the litter of papers on its top. Gazing through the open door and up the unobstructed street, he could see the olive coaches of the Santa Fe's regular train from the north, passing as it pulled into the Valley station.

Forhand and Wolfe came out slowly. Forhand was still attempting to serve as spokesman. "We can agree to twenty-five hundred," he said. "The thousand in cash, and if you clear him you get fifteen hundred more; just as soon as Sam comes clear."

"Hell, no!" Pruiett exploded. "Hell, no! I won't represent you at all." He was finally and genuinely mad. "Just tell Cruce and Furman that if I'm in the Ashton case I'll be with Johnson, on the other side of the table."

As the two stockmen went out, Pruiett looked over their heads and up the street again. He was vaguely conscious of the dark green railroad cars, which had been blocking the street, slowly moving again, as the train's brief stop ended and it resumed its journey southward into the Territory and Texas. He had let a good fee get away, and at a time when he could have used it, but by God, he wasn't goin' to be prostituted by a pair of misers. He had made them a fair proposition, and they had made light of it. After all, he could tell Sam Garvin he had turned down a twenty-five hundred dollar fee in the case, and it would put him in there more solidly than ever. He might cause Garvin to get the Dismukes up a little, after this, and—.

His musings were cut short. Forhand and his friend were standing in the open door. They had gone as far as the hitching rail under the tree, conferred further on the matter, and retraced their steps to his office.

"We decided it was a deal," Forhand said. "We pay you a thousand dollars, an' you get in the case with Furman and Cruce. If Sam comes out free, we pay four thousand more. If he doesn't—."

"If he don't, you don't pay me another dime," Pruiett supplied for the somewhat deliberate speaker. "Not another damned dime."

A brief memorandum of the agreement was drawn up in Pruiett's long-hand, and signed by the visitors. Forhand gave a check on the Lexington bank for a thousand dollars. Pruiett, with his feet back on the table, had hardly time to contemplate what, if anything, could be done to make good for the four thousand, when the door was opened. He glanced up, half provoked, expecting to see Wolfe and Forhand back again. He looked, instead, into the inquiring face of an unusually attractive woman.

She was a stranger in town. He knew by her dress and manner. She had just arrived on the train he had seen pass through, he surmised, as his gaze traveled slowly down past a shapely mid-structure to the hand at her side, which held a small leather traveling bag. Pruiett arose, stuffing the check into his pocket, and rendered his most charming of bows and smiles.

"This is Mr. Pruiett," she said, not inquiringly, but with finality. "Mr. Moman Pruiett, the criminal lawyer."

Pruiett's chest swelled, and the black foliage atop his handsome head sparkled as though charged with an electric current. "Yes. Yes, this is Mr. Pruiett. I am at your service." He dusted off one of the straight-back chairs before offering it to her and after she had daintily deposited the rhythmically shifting hips upon it, he stood in the middle of the floor and stared at her.

"I'm a stranger in this part of the country," she said. "I'm from Colorado."

"I've never seen that part of the country," Pruiett replied. "I've just got back from a trip east. I—."

"Yes, I know of that," she interrupted. "I read of it in the papers at Denver. That's what brought me to your office, reading of the things you did for that poor, unfortunate Negro. I think it was wonderful of you to do that, Mr. Pruiett. Just simply wonderful." She was throwing a lot of feeling in with her flattery and Pruiett was catching it all. He could scarcely stammer a word or two about it "being nothing at all." His ability to do the right thing under pressure, as in court and pressed for a maneuver before the judge or jury, didn't include a situation such as this. Here was a creature in his own little office, with a face as faultless and with hair as fluffy as Lillian Russell's whom he had seen on the stage in the east. The eyes which beamed her undisguised admiration upon him were inviting and compelling.

"I'm here to see if I could interest you in the defense of Sam Ashton," she said. "Sam Ashton, the man who's to be tried for killing two men. I came down here to help him, if I could."

"You mean," he inquired, "that you want to hire me to defend Sam?"

"Why, yes," she said. "That is, I—."

"I know quite a bit about that case," he said. "He looks as guilty as hell to me, an' ever' one's bettin' he gets the rope, on one trial."

Pruiett's temporary confusion was gone. He was in full

HOTEL HAMPTON; PAULS VALLEY

THE HAMPTON HOUSE IN THE VALLEY
"Where the success of Sam Ashton's defense was guaranteed."

control. She didn't expect to pay him—in money, at least, and he didn't want her to. He relished the look of anguish that passed across her handsome face as he baited her.

"Please don't say that," she whimpered.

"What you got in mind for me to do?" he demanded, gruffly.

"I'm looking for some money by mail, in a few days," she said lamely, "and I could pay you something on the fee then. I read in the papers about you bein' such a wonderful lawyer, and—."

"What's Sam Ashton to you?" Pruiett asked.

She hesitated. "He's my half brother," she answered.

Pruiett whistled. "Is that a stall, or is—."

"He's my half-brother," she insisted.

"Does anybody in town know you?" he inquired.

"They don't know me, and they don't know about me, either," she said. "I don't think—."

"I'll take the case for you," Pruiett announced. "How far'll you go to get Sam acquitted?" His agile brain was wheeling.

"As far as it's necessary to go," she replied, coolly.

"Any limits?"

"No limits."

"You just came in on that Santa Fe, didn't you?" Pruiett inquired. She nodded.

"When that rattler left here yesterday, it hauled a whole car load of prisoners south, for hangin' an' for jail at Ardmore, an' for keeps at Atlanta. They been havin' a term of court here that's rough as hell. Springin' Sam isn't goin' to be no cinch."

"What can I do to help?" she asked.

"They got a bird on this panel named Tom Adkins. They call him Squire Adkins. He's a body-boss an' he's the foreman of ever' jury he gets on. He'd vote for life for chicken-stealin', an' he's high on himself. He's an old bachelor." She nodded again. "That's the Hampton House across there," Pruiett said, pointing toward the town's principal hotel. "The squire stays there, an' that's where you're to stay. I want you to get acquainted with him, study his characteristics, never breathing to him who you are, or why you are here. Can you do that?"

She smiled, "I think so."

Pruiett grinned, as he appraised her with a frank stare. "Now, listen, I want to be able to keep him on the jury. You understand what I mean?"

"I'll take care of him," she said, simply.

Stilwell H. Russell sauntered into Pruiett's office. "Hello, Judge," Pruiett grinned. "I been expectin' you to come to town."

"I didn't send any word in advance, that I was coming," Russell answered, shaking hands with him.

"When I told old man Garvin I had gone into the Sam Ashton case he damn near came unwell. When he couldn't talk me out of it he took out for the telegraph office. I figured he was wirin' for you to come an' help him."

"You wasn't wrong," Russell agreed. "I'm hired as special prosecutor, to help Bill Johnson."

"You can thank me for a nice fee," Pruiett said. "If I hadn't a crossed the old man he wouldn't have come across."

"Much obliged," Russell acknowledged.

"How's things in Texas?" Pruiett inquired.

"Not so good," Russell answered. "I was over to Paris a couple of weeks ago and saw Colonel Jake. We was talkin' about the Doll Wilson case, and about you. Jake told me to watch you, if I ever go in a case against you. He said you'd fix a jury, with the other side lookin' right at you."

"I didn't fix no jury in the Doll Wilson case, did I?" Pruiett laughed. "How's Jake's poker?"

"He's gradually givin' up his law for it," Russell replied. "I had to go over to the Peterson Hotel to see him, when I was in town. He was layin' out of the office and when I went over to the hotel, there he was, in a game."

"You know I lost one of my babies, didn't you?"

"Yeah, and I'm sorry," Russell answered. "How's Lilly?"

"She's not well at all, an' she's carryin' another. We're all worried about her. She can't pick up a bit."

"I got to be sure an' see her before I leave town," Russell said.

"Let's go out for supper," Pruiett suggested.

"I got to see Sam Garvin," Russell said. "I was supposed to see my principal first, I guess, instead of my adversary, but you was the handiest. What about this Ashton case the old man's so worked up about?"

"The colonel's gettin' childish," Pruiett laughed.

"Is it tough for you, or me?" Russell demanded.

"For you, I'm sorry to say," Pruiett said, indulgently. "Sam's innocent."

"Do I rely on you, or Garvin?" Russell inquired. "There seems to be quite a conflict in the reports that come to me."

"Take my word for it," Pruiett said. "The old man's biased. If he wasn't payin' good, I'd advise you to let this case alone. I'm goin' to win it."

"Come on over to the Hampton with me, an' let's visit with Garvin," Russell suggested. "I don't guess it'll make him mad for me to bring you along."

"He gets sore easy, but he gets over it easy," Pruiett said. "If you think it's safe, I'll go along with you."

"Come on. We'll all eat supper together," Russell agreed. "If the colonel won't pay for it, I will. We can outline the prosecution, and the defense, at the same time."

So the three of them grabbed their viands, served up the family style way, at the Hampton. Pruiett could see that Garvin's attention, and Russell's too, was being attracted by a handsome woman seated at a long table opposite them.

"Who's the flashy lookin' dame?" Pruiett inquired.

"Don't know," grunted Garvin.

"The squire's wife?" he persisted.

"You know damn well the squire ain't never been married."

"He's got ideas in his mind then," answered Pruiett. "The old boy keeps pilin' them potatoes on her plate like he thought she was starvin'."

"A damn fool, if I know anything about it," growled Garvin, "Just a damned old fool."

"If I know anything about it," Russell interrupted, "he's a pretty smart man. That girl's got some class."

"No good looker like that would make eyes at an old fool like Adkins, except for one thing. It's his money. She'll take some of it away from him, if he don't watch out."

"Do you reckon that's what it is?" Pruiett inquired, innocently.

"Hell, yes," Garvin said, as he watched the squire and his shapely companion leave the table. They walked onto the veranda, arm in arm.

"It was Kipling, wasn't it," Pruiett inquired, "who said 'When the devil can't get a man any other way, he sends a woman?' Wasn't that it?"

"What the devil's that got to do with it?" Garvin demanded.

"Maybe it ain't," Pruiett grinned. "You ain't feelin' so well these days, Colonel. You better watch your indigestion."

Pruiett asked the court for a continuance because asking for a continuance was part of his contract with Wolfe and Forhand. He knew he wouldn't get it, and he didn't want it, for word from his ally at the Hampton House was in. If they call Squire Adkins, keep him.

"What we goin' to do about John Webb?" Cruce whispered.

"He's one of the best friends I got on earth," Pruiett answered.

"He's Garvin's ranch overseer, an' he's been workin' for him for ten years. What about that?"

"John comes as near to bein' a honest man as I ever want to see," Pruiett persisted.

"Can you trust him to be right?"

"I think I can trust him to be fair," Pruiett answered.

"I said right," Cruce hissed. "Who gives a dad burn about a man's fairness when he's on the jury. If he's fair he'll vote for hangin'."

"I couldn't fix him, I know that, so I don't think Garvin could, not even with him drawin' his pay from him. I may be wrong, but I say, leave him on." Pruiett reflected. "If they don't kick him off we can afford to keep him on."

"I heard old Stilwell whisper to Johnson to take Adkins off," Cruce said. "What do you think of that?"

"He's suspicious 'cause we ain't knocked him off already," Pruiett answered. "What did Johnson say?"

"He told him he was a damn fool."

Pruiett smiled, understandingly. "Russell's settin' on more brains than Bill could pick up above his shoulders, countin' ears an' dandruff," he said. "Don't worry. Johnson won't let 'em take Adkins off, an' if he stays, we're satisfied."

The clerk swore John Webb and Squire Adkins, and ten others, to try the issues to be submitted to them in Territory versus Samuel Ashton. Cruce moved the court for a short recess. Pruiett crammed a huge cut of tobacco into his jaw and moved a rusty cuspidor into convenient range.

"If at first you don't succeed, try, try, again," he observed, as he tested his aim on the nearest one. "If you can't make it the first time, maybe your luck'll be better next time."

"What do you mean by that?" Johnson inquired from across the board. "What you drivin' at?"

"Oh, just that other charge you got against Sam, for pluggin' the old man," Pruiett grinned, insolently. "If you don't fool this jury, maybe you will the next one. Too bad you haven't got three or four."

"You're as crazy as hell," Johnson cried. "That second one's a case the government'll waste. You can't hang a man but once, or we'd just try Mr. Sam twict. We'd like to drop him through the trap, stiff and dead."

"You haven't got a chance to convict him this time, an' you know it," Pruiett persisted. "If Sam ever gets as much as five years it'll be because the law of average lets you win a case once in a while. Why don't you admit it? What you got a special assistant for?"

Johnson's face was livid. "It ain't 'cause I want a special prosecutor, or need one, either, that I got one. I ain't got nothin' to say about what these damned relatives, an' others, do about hirin' some one. I just—."

"I know," Pruiett interrupted. "You got a' alibi for this case, and then you'll show 'em how good you are by winnin' the next one single-handed. Why, ever'body knows the case for shootin' the old man is the worst case." Johnson shook his head in rage, unable to trust himself to reply. "I got a good notion to waive my rights and stand trial on both indictments, just to take your grandstand play away from you," Pruiett continued, grinning insolently. "I know how to turn up your bottom ace."

"You mean," stammered Johnson, "that you'll agree in the record to dispose of both cases at once? Let the government make proof on both killin's?"

"You mean you got the guts to try 'em that way, if I would agree?"

"Hell, yes," Johnson howled.

Pruiett feigned confusion. "I guess I better talk to my client, an' his folks," he said. "Let me talk to them, an' I'll let you know."

While Pruiett was whispering with Sam, his uncles and the other members of the counsel, Stilwell Russell called Johnson aside. "You better go easy," he said. "There's something fishy in this business, as sure as hell. I know that boy better'n you, an' he's too smart to leave Squire Adkins on a jury when he's got challenges, if he didn't know somethin'. An' what he's offerin' to do now is foolhardy, or awful smart, an' Pruiett ain't no fool. Don't be afraid to back up. If he offers to stipulate that the verdict in this case goes in both—if he accepts to go in jeopardy on both of 'em at once—don't do it. It ain't natural, and something's wrong."

"He's swell-head crazy, that's all," Johnson growled. "He won a case or two, an' it went to his head. This case is a cinch as it is; throw in the evidence on shootin' the old man in the back, an' it'll be very bad for his client. I just hope he falls for it."

Pruiett fell. "The defendant will stipulate," he announced to the astonished judge, when court had reconvened, "that the government may present both of its indictments at this trial, and that the verdict in this case may be considered as the verdict in each of them."

Pruiett, in the Sam Ashton case was Pruiett, the frontier lawyer, at his best. Progress, which was to lift the frontier into the field of more decorous manner and appearance of refinement, was to carry him with it and see him keep apace. But here, tanned and animal-like, with the bristling bulk of his bushy black hair creating a veritable shaft of light for him to shine in—with the fresh notices of the Washington press to require his utmost—with a hitherto unheard of fee in his grasp, he was the romantic representative of a vanished era.

His heavy lapeled coat and waistcoat, buttoned so high in the front as to almost conceal the black shoe string bow tie which encircled the white collar, gave him a disproportionate massiveness and breadth of upper trunk. This effect was accentuated by the narrowness of the pant legs which extended but slightly past his shoe tops. As he grasped classic utterances from the rank aroma of the crowded room and decorated them with polished gestures, he was as impressive as Dan Voorhees had been, there at the Boudinot trial in Fort Smith, when he had torn the white rose from the lapel of his satin trimmed Prince Albert and had hurled it, for emphasis, into the waste of the ash box.

And old P. Watt Hardin had never been more subtle, crouched in the faces of the jurors, and whispering, instead of shouting, to make a point. But when Pruiett shouted, his voice and its eloquence was amplified by an immobile trance or a mechanical frenzy, as he stood or paraded. He shook the rafters with the reverberations of his great voice.

And he had the witnesses. The four days that had seen the trial drag out, before the final arguments began, had seen a great number of witnesses, for both sides. Sam was relying

on self-defense, and he had to have a corroborating witness to
that theory of justification.   Pruiett had the evidence of unimpeached testimony to refer to and analyze as he delivered his
blazing final argument.

The jury acquitted Sam Ashton. Squire Adkins was its foreman, and led a two day fight for the verdict which it finally
reached. John Webb was the last to sign. It had been Webb's
lone vote from the beginning that had kept them out. Colonel
Garvin was a member of the crowd which gathered—it was
Sunday evening—when word of the jury's report was circulated
about. He was purple and shaking with rage as he stalked out,
and there was a perplexed, confused expression on the face of
John Webb as he filed slowly out into the dusk with the other
jurors. Thomas, the trial judge, had berated them for the effrontery of their verdict, as he directed his clerk to see that
none of them was summoned for jury duty in his court again.

Garvin and Webb met in the wagon yard around the corner
from the court building.   Murder was written in every seam
of Garvin's tanned countenance.

"You double-crossin' coward," he choked. "After all I've
done for you, and you turn me down. Get your pay and get
your stuff out of my house, and don't let me see you on one
of my places again as long as I live."

"But Sam," the perplexed Webb managed to say, "I got
your note an' I only did what you said. I wouldn't go against
you for anything in the —."

"Don't lie," Garvin cried. "Don't lie to me. You sold me
out to that young pup, and by God—." He caught himself and
lowered his voice. He realized that he was in no position to make
public the details of his plan and plot, even if they did miscarry.

"You told me not to hold out any longer; it was your writin,'
or I'd have been there yet, Sam." Webb's manner and tone was
impressive.

"What the hell are you talkin' about?" Garvin demanded.

"The note the bailiff slipped me this evenin'. It was from
you, an' I did just what you said in it."

"Who gave it to you?"

"The bailiff, Jim Mays."

"And who signed it?

"You did. It was your writin', an' signed S. J. G."

"And what did it say?" Garvin was near to the exploding point again.

"It said, 'don't hold out any longer—turn the poor devil loose.'"

"Let me see it," Garvin demanded.

"But I couldn't keep a thing like that, Sam. I couldn't do that. I was protectin' you, an' I tore it up and chewed it up. I wasn't goin' to have anything like that around."

Webb was speaking both wisely and truthfully, and Garvin could doubt it no longer.

"I'll have that son of a sea cock in jail by mornin'," he groaned, "just as soon as I can get this to Johnson. An' you're fired, Webb, don't forget that. You're dumb as a nigger Indian, an' you're fired."

Garvin and Bill Johnson were waiting in front of Pruiett's office when he drove up in his new phaeton. He was stopping by to pick up the Forhand-Wolfe agreement before the drive up to Lexington, twenty miles north, for collection.

His smile of complacency was not affected by the blackness of the cloud over the faces of his two visitors. The storm broke as soon as the three were inside the office and the door was securely closed. "Did you write that note?" Johnson thundered.

"What note?" Pruiett was unruffled.

"I'll tell you what note," Johnson continued in the same loud tone.

Pruiett was perfectly serene as he asked, "Who? What note?"

"Me, that's who," Garvin chimed in. He could stand the suffocating pain of the situation no longer. "Me, the man who befriended you, and got you started. An' I won't stop 'til I see somebody suffer for writin' that note. We got John Webb," Garvin screamed. "Webb, an' what he told me already."

"It'd be awful damn smart to get John Webb," Pruiett replied, "to tell the folks he was your sinker on the jury, Colonel. It'd do you a lot of good to let the court know that when John qualified he was a directed delegate from your camp, on to convict or hang the jury. It would sure look good when it came out that he changed his vote just because he thought you wanted him to, and that he wouldn't have done it if he thought you hadn't. You hired Russell, an' I know it. Russell knew you had Webb fixed against me, an' he told Johnson so, or Johnson never would have let him stay. If you put Russell on the stand, you know he'll tell the truth. Now, to both of you. Let me alone and I say to both of you that silence is golden."

It was evolution—It was development—It was progress. The boy of the neglected and misspent youth was a man with power, and he was using it as he had told his elders he would use it, when they inflicted upon him the punishment of their doctrines. It was the fine Italian hand, writing with a stroke more bold The message could not be misunderstood.

CHAPTER SEVEN

Wherein Pruiett's prominence and prosperity has to be noted, and Pruiett's excellence cannot be ignored as indicated by an invitation to make the principal address at the Old Settlers Reunion September 4th, 1900, as men charged with murder and thievery are brought into court, tried, and liberated through power.

How tragedy returns to detract from the contentment of the new home in the pecan orchard, and sending him on a business holiday in quest of forgetfulness back to Washington, D. C., and how the same unwelcome visitor calls him back to the Valley, and he pigeon-holes his grief to plunge into bloody murder cases which are clamoring for attention on his docket. And wherein a Pruiett client is convicted, and he congratulates himself and feels full well, as the jury sentences him to confinement for the balance of his life.

"The fellows who only stole chickens were soon turned away from the office of Pruiett, counselor of criminal law, and none but those charged with murder, and horse stealing were accepted."

Victory in the Douglas and Wilson cases, and the delivery of Sam Ashton, made Pruiett. The little incident of a conviction and death sentence in between them, for black Charley Bias, didn't detract from his popularity. Charges for services went up. L. J. Robberson, charged with the killing of Jeff Rose, had to deed him a quarter section of valley land before he'd front for him. Stilwell Russell, employed by George Hancock, who was charged with taking the Winchester to Charles Lidell, the marshal at Thackerville, split his fat fee with Pruiett to get him to come into the case. Frank Hunt, delinquent son of a wealthy family west of the Valley, was charged with armed robbery, and Pruiett was retained to defend him. Dave Putty, territorial whiskey runner and horse thief, shot Deputy United States Marshal Ed Thurlow to death. Pruiett took a thousand dollars cash, and agreed to defend him in the federal court back at Paris, where he had been charged.

"Moman Pruiett received a fine office safe of the Bauhm make, which weighs about 5000 pounds. This, with other new furniture which Mr. Pruiett has been getting, makes his office more than ordinary, and is far above the average in point of elegance and convenience." The big publisher of the weekly Chicka-

THE HOUSE IN THE PECAN ORCHARD—LILLY THOUGHT IT WAS A PALACE
Pruiett and wife are in the background; Gail Hamilton is the baby.

saw Enterprise was noting Pruiett's prosperity, the inevitable accompanist of accomplishment.

Pruiett's expansion extended in another direction. In an angle made by the intersection of Paul Avenue with Rush Creek, in the western extremity of the town, the Pruietts built their new home. Native young pecans shaded the Bermuda grass lawn behind a white picket fence. A mortgage at Grant's bank shadowed the entire premises.

"Frank an' Mike Henderson owe me a thousand. Frank Hunt'll have to raise more than that for me before trial. Why, hell, I got plenty o' money; I just can't collect it right now, an' that trip to Washington for the nigger cost me a lot." Pruiett was closing a loan with his banker.

"I ain't objectin' to loanin' you the money," Grant insisted. "You can have twict as much if you want to sign up for it. I'm just tellin' you, in a friendly sort of way, that there ain't no sense in a man that's made the money you have in the last year havin' to borrow. You ought to be loanin' it out, on interest."

"I never was much for chargin' interest," Pruiett grinned. "I haven't hardly got the heart to ask 'em to pay me when they're overdue, much less charge 'em for the use of it."

"I got them six hundred dollars worth of checks you wrote at Madill charged against you. You was a damn fool for makin' me pay."

"I'm twenty-one years old an' I'm supposed to know what I'm doin'," Pruiett answered, "but I ought to have a guardian. I went over there an' collected seventeen hundred an' fifty bucks that I made fair an' square, clearin' Jeff Aiken of murder an' what do I do with it? Lose it ever' damn cent in a crooked poker game; write checks for a hundred apiece, an' drop them in the game, an' then come home an' borrow two thousand to finish payin' for my new house."

"All you had to do was to follow my advice an' stop payment on the checks, an' you could've saved six hundred. They never could collect 'em against you."

"I am not a welsher," Pruiett answered. "I wrote 'em an' I meant to pay 'em. I'll straighten the account up in a few weeks."

"That's a classy house you built," Grant said. "Where'd you get the idea of that cupelo and the curvin' porch all the way around the side that way?"

"The lumber company furnished the plans," Pruiett said.

Lilly picked 'em out. It isn't near as big as that place of yours, an' it hasn't got all the outbuildings an' grounds that Sam Garvin's got with his place, but it's goin' to be damn nice for us an' the children.''

"Speakin' of Sam Garvin, it's about time for you an' him to make up. He's cooled off on that Sam Ashton deal.'' Grant was hurt by the hostility between his friends.

"He sure got his fire hot all of a sudden,'' Pruiett grinned.

"Look him up an' talk to him,'' Grant suggested. "He'll shake hands and start over—that is, if you want to.''

"I love the old boy like he was my pa,'' Pruiett said, earnestly. "He looks at things from my perch, usually, an' I couldn't understand how he could get so set on gettin' a conviction against Sam. But hell, I'll crawl on my hands an' knees if he'll pay me a little attention.''

"He'll do it, said Grant. "He was just sayin', the last time I talked to him, that that was the fastest beating he ever got, an' that nobody but a mental freak like you could've ever done it to him.''

Pruiett laughed. "Me an' the old man feels the same way about those kind of things. He wants to help the dog under the heap; that's why he took me under his wing. I wouldn't have gone against him in any case but that one, but it was a lot for me an' a little for him. I had fee, an' principle, an' a good chance to make some more reputation for myself. All he had up was a grudge he's been carryin' against Sam Ashton. You see the difference, don't you Mr. Grant?''

"I been seein' it all the time, an' don't think I'm carin' about you gettin' Sam off. I was damn proud to see it. An' I think that now, seein' that the sting's goin' out of the beatin', old man Garvin sees it too. You apologize to him, an' I'll bet he says he was the one that was in the wrong, an' apologizes to you. I'd like to have a three handed wind-jammin' session in here again, like we used to have.''

"I'll look him up today,'' Pruiett promised. "You an' the missus drive by an' see the new shanty.''

"We'll do it Sunday,'' Grant said. "Say, how many lightnin' rods you got on that place, anyway?''

Pruiett ignored Grant's flattery. "You remember,'' he mused, "when I pulled in, an' opened up the office in the shoe shop? You an' the missus loaned me an iron cot, an' I batched in the same room.''

"You've done damn good," Grant agreed. "Them new offices upstairs are perty up-to-date."

"We just got this house done in time," Pruiett said. "Lilly's goin' to have another baby in about a month, an' she ain't none too strong for it. You been noticin' how she looks?"

"She ain't lookin' good, by no means," Grant said. "Better be careful of her. Give her a rest on havin' them kids."

"I took her to Hot Springs with me last fall, when that damned swellin' rheumatism hit me, an' just made her take a rest. But it didn't help her like it did me. I think there's something wrong that Doc Young can't locate. I'm awful worried."

On September 4th, 1900, Pruiett's prominence as a lawyer and citizen was evidenced by the invitation he received to make the principal address at the Old Settlers Reunion. The reunion, rodeo and basket lunch was the foremost function of the cattle country's social season, and was being held, that year, at Hull's Crossing (across the Washita) west of the Valley. Garvin and Grant nodded with approval when he told them that he had selected, for a subject, "The Bounty of Nature in the Valley."

Pruiett mounted the platform. After a flowery introductory he got down to the "meat of the cocoanut," as he chose to call it, as follows:

PRUIETT'S ADDRESS

Delivered at the Old Settlers Reunion at Hull's Crossing
September 4, 1900

"Ladies and Gentlemen: It fills my heart with emotion when I look out over this sea of humanity gathered here from every state of our glorious Union, gathered here to celebrate with feast and good cheer, with song, story and reminiscence, our coming together into this unknown land a few years since for the purpose of founding a new commonwealth. The sons of Japheth have been moving westward ever since their first migration from the highlands of central Asia, when the fierce herds of Huns, Goths, Visigoths and Vandals poured themselves into the valleys of the Danube and the Rhine. Then as now they were impelled by an irresistible impulse to rule, to govern, to conquer; to communicate the principles and practice of self-government, to organize society, to regenerate mankind. Their genius for empire, for government, for all that goes to refine, ennoble and make man better has never been approached, much less equalled by the offspring of either of the other sons of Noah.

To them it is given to claim and possess the earth, to build shrines and monasteries, to establish governments; and above all things they have been chosen as the sacred medium through which the revelations of God's will to man should be made known; that such is true. Behold our four hundred years of settlement! When Columbus landed at San Salvador, his were the first white man's eyes that ever gazed upon this splendid waste; today we have a republic, the only republic that has ever existed, with 80,000,000 souls, with the most perfect form of government ever established by man, with education without money and without price at the hand of every child; a nation whose wealth surpasses that of any other country, whose production of gold and silver, iron and coal is more in one decade that has ever been produced by all the world four thousand years in the past; a nation whose armies eclipse those of any other nation in the world, and whose navy, from John Paul Jones with the Bon Homme Richard to Dewey at Manila, has been our pride and the envy of every other power on earth. In the past three years our exports have exceeded our imports by more than one billion dollars. We are the store house and granary of the world, and in my opinion we have but commenced that splendid work which God has set before us, and which will ultimately bring all nations together under the cross of a Christian civilization.

My friends, this is truly a marvelous age. I sometimes think the gifted author of the Arabian Nights was endowed with a supernatural power and ken, and in some way Aladdin's Lamp was intended as a prototype of what man was ultimately intended to accomplish in this age; for have we not seen transformations in the material world about us greater, more wonderful and more lasting than any thing pictured by the fiery imagination of the author of those enchanting stories.

"When the battle of Marengo was fought the soil upon which we now stand was a part of the great conqueror Napoleon's empire, but then it was a wild, dreary waste beyond the sea, in the heart of an unknown continent, filled and peopled with everything horrid the imagination could conjure. As for value, it was considered practically worthless. Jefferson paid about $15,000,000 for the entire purchase, and the Indian Territory is an inconsiderable portion of it. Let me see; that was in 1804, ninety-six years ago. From the purchase twelve states have been carved, twelve bright and shining stars, set in the diadem of our united greatness, a very empire within themselves; leaving Oklahoma and the Indian Territory yet to be added. What have we in the Indian Territory to offer to the world, what advantages, if any, has the land which you and I have selected and in which we expect to live and die, to commend itself to the settler and homeseeker?

Its climate, to begin with, is the finest in the world, equal to that of lovely Greece and the renowned Italy. Its winters are never too cold nor its summers too hot. The fragrant ozone of its atmosphere and the steady, bracing breezes that ever blow from the south and east add a zest and pleasure to life that can be found nowhere else; truly, I would not be surprised to learn some day that Mount Olympus, the abode of the Gods, was somewhere in the Arbuckle mountains that skirt us on the south. The faces of the fair and lovely women here present show that Venus, the goddess of love and beauty, must have some time in the distant past have made her home here in the classic vale of the winding Washita, and bequeathed as a heritage to her daughters that beauty of face and form and that loveliness of character which made her the universal favorite of the Gods.

I have read of the delta of the Nile, the fame of whose fertility has come down to us from biblical days; I have read of the Congo and the fertile valleys of the Ganges, upon whose broad acres the teeming millions of India have subsisted since Buddha and Vashti lived and taught their moral precepts. I have taken the wings of the morning and crossed the undulating prairies of Kansas, Missouri and Illinois. I have viewed the rich, dark loam that borders the banks of the great Mississippi for two thousand miles. I have read the learned in song and story of lands far away where rivers bright wander o'er sands of gold, where ruby lights up the secret of mine, where frail man had but to stretch forth his hand, to garner the richest bounty nature could bestow, but the lovely sunlit vale extending from the Llano Estacado on the west to Red River on the south, through which the sinuous Washita winds itself like a silver thread, is far and away the crown jewel of all the lands of which I have ever read and been blessed with a vision of, may we not believe that the poet had this valley in his mind's eye when he sang:

"Know ye the land of the cedar and vine,
Where the flowers ever blossom, the stars ever shine,
Where the light wings of zephyr oppressed by perfume,
Wax taint o'er the gardens of Gull in her bloom;
Where the citron and olive are fairest of fruit,
And the song of the nightingale never is mute,
Where the tints of the ocean and hues of the sky
In color though varied in beauty may vie."

My friends, we have here a foundation upon which to rear a great empire, a commonwealth that will be the peer of any in our proud galaxy of states. Civilization is pressing us from all sides and asks admittance to come in and transform these great grass-grown prairies, these rich wooded alluvial lands into an agricultural paradise; to make the wild waste blossom like the roses in the valley of Sharon. Let the question of land titles be once settled and there will be an influx of people here from every point of the compass, the east and west will be brought into competition and side by side they will vie with each other to outstrip in the race of material progress. The whirr and hum of industry will be heard on every side and smiling mother earth will beneath our sunny skies and vernal showers pour into our laps wealth beyond the dream of avarice. This is the last great undeveloped section on our continent and we whose lots have been cast in such fair lines should feel proud indeed, for to generations yet unborn we will tell the thrilling story at a larger and grander Old Settlers picnic of how we, the old settlers, laid deep and strong foundations of a mighty state.

After Pruiett located in the Valley in 1896, he incorporated the town of Pauls Valley, Oklahoma, and became its first city attorney; its second mayor and chairman of the city school board immediately afterwards. From the very start of his residence in the city he became very active in all civic and fraternal affairs and the economic development of the community, as well as one of its leading citizens.

Pruiett hammered at a local jury until it turned Frank and Mike Henderson out of the prisoner's pen, to freedom. He went back to Paris to defend Dave Putty.

"Old Judge Bryant was the one that admitted me on his

own motion," he explained to Claude Weaver, on his return. "I went up to shake hands with him an' tell him good-bye, after the jury came in, an' he was stiff-necked as hell. 'I didn't believe that proof you put on,' he says. 'The jury believed it—they turned Dave a'loose,' I says, laughin' an' tryin' to thaw him out a little. But he wouldn't thaw. He acted like he was sore at me 'cause I won it."

"Some of them old Federal Judges gets funny ideas," Weaver winked. "Are you lettin' Henry Furman get you in the Bud Watkins case?"

"I agreed to help him try it," Pruiett answered. "He wanted to try it up here in the Valley, instead of down at Ardmore."

"You know why, don't you?" Weaver asked. "That's where they convicted him the last trial, an' they sentenced him to hang. It's a damn nasty case."

"I know all about it," Pruiett said. "I knew Wyatt Williams, the man he killed, an' I'm entitled to say that Bud done a noble public service when he killed him. I know why Henry Furman asked me to get in the case with him, too."

"How's that?"

"Old Sobe Love down at Marietta made him do it," Pruiett answered. "Sobe's the old Chickasaw envoy, an' he's Bud Watkins' granddaddy. He owns most of the land south of the Arbuckle Mountains an' north of Red River, an' he couldn't tell you within a hundred thousand of how many head of beef he's got. He helped Furman to reverse that hanging conviction, an' he's heard about y' 'r uncle Fuller. He's hirin' him to empanel the jury this time."

"Bud was the first duck to get a capital sentence in the Sandy Land Court," Weaver observed.

"An' he's still out runnin' around alive an' loose, but that buryin' ground at Ardmore is runnin' over with dead convicts right now," Pruiett said. "My ideas on that subject isn't all wrong. Have a little jack—get a little extra consideration. Have the bad judgment to be busted, an' you get your neck pulled in two. Dave Putty paid me a thousand cash to pull him out of that fire."

"Tuesday and Wednesday were consumed in the trial of the notorious Roberson murder case, and this morning the jury brought in a verdict of not guilty. . . W. B. Johnson, prosecuting attorney, was assisted by Max Hill of Texas and T. M. Robnett. For the defense was Moman Pruiett. . . Mr. Hill opened the argument for the government, Moman Pruiett, for the defense, followed with an impassioned oration which is said by all who heard it to be Mr. Pruiett at his best. If the case lacked evidence on behalf of the defense, and it seemed that the issues were closely joined, Pruiett's masterful speech tipped the beam in Roberson's favor. For forty minutes he seemed to have blended his own identity with that of his client, and certainly he could not have been moved to greater eloquence or deeper earnestness had he himself stood like Roberson in the very shadow of the gallows."

"'Gentlemen of the jury,' said Judge Townsend, 'it is a matter of regret to me—to see this verdict. It will be utterly useless to attempt to enforce the criminal law in this country so long as murderers can be turned loose when they are without a shadow of a legal defense. You can be discharged, and I never want any of you on a jury in this court again."

He shifted into the trial of the Hancock case at Ardmore. Stilwell Russell, chief counsel, came up from Dallas.

"I been hearin' things," Russell told him. "There's rumblin's of another government commission to settle with the Indians, an' statehood for the Indian an' Oklahoma Territories. I get it straight from Washington."

"What was I tellin' you on the train from Decatur?" Pruiett reminded. "Didn't I say statehood? She's comin' as sure as hell, an' there I am, got me a hell of a practice, a new house paid for; own a half a dozen bottom farms I took in for fees, an' all I got to do is to let statehood skyrocket my values. I'm settin' pretty."

"I been thinkin' about gettin' out of Texas an' comin' up here—somewhere. Where's a good place?"

"The hot spot's Oklahoma City, a hundred miles north, in Oklahoma Territory," Pruiett replied. "They say she's a laudy. Liquor an' gamblin' and prostitution wide open. Killin' an' robbin' on ever' corner. She isn't twelve years old an' goin' to twict the territory of Ardmore, here. Two railroads an' goin' to get more. If I didn't have such an investment in the Valley, I'd pull out an' get up there. I mean it."

"This here Ardmore looks awful good to me," Russell said.

"She may make it, but she's stalled here for five years. With all the government business they've had, it looks like she should have grown more than she has."

"I'm thinkin' serious about leavin' Dallas," Russell said.

"How are we fixed for this Hancock case? Know any of the jury panel?"

"I never seen a one of 'em."

"The Hancock murder trial at Ardmore last week resulted in the acquittal of the defendant, who was represented by Moman Pruiett and Stilwell H. Russell of Dallas. Hancock was charged with killing City Marshal Chas. Lidell of Thackerville." The Enterprise was matter-of-fact about it. In its following weekly issue it said: "Moman Pruiett is stepping high these days. In addition to the glory he won in the Hancock case, Mrs. Pruiett has presented him with a son and heir. We understand the young Mr. Pruiett will be named after that brilliant lawyer, Stilwell H. Russell, of Dallas."

Pruiett was stepping high, and he had to be. The inflamation of his knees and ankles was beginning to recur, and he couldn't find time to give them the rest and mineral baths that they needed. He had a new son and a sick wife, and murder on the docket. His mother was able to help Mrs. Fisher with Lilly and the children and the housework, but Lilly wasn't coming out of it. Something was wrong.

He and Furman tried Bud Watkins; the jury disagreed. Pruiett traveled to the Pontotoc country, to Ada, and defended Lawrence Walker, charged with murder. "Moman Pruiett of Pauls Valley, made a masterful defense in the Lawrence Walker murder case last week, in which the defendant was acquitted," the Ada News observed.

Molly and Jack Lanier were jailed by the government at Ardmore. Molly's seven year old daughter, Jack's step-child, died in fits, and a strychnine bottle was dug up near the back door of their farm home.

He made bond for the accused pair and accompanied them— he had brought Colonel Garvin along—to the farm, where he collected his fee. Molly, and Jack were later acquitted of a charge of poisoning their daughter. He sat carelessly in the saddle while he watched Lanier's and Garvin's riders cut two hundred head of young beef from the big herd. A south breeze rumpled the shining contour of his bulky hair.

"That's four-footed gold; solid gold on the hoof," Garvin grunted, leaning forward so that his ponderous belly rested on the saddle horn. "What you goin' to do with it?"

"Have the boys drive it up to the old Walter Bennett place, above here on Rush Creek," he answered carelessly.

"What the hell for? You got it sold already?"

"Nope—that's my place now. I took a deed to it."

"How's that? I could've sold you better property than that."

"I didn't buy it. I took it for services."

"You mean," Garvin asked incredulously, "that Indian gave you sixteen hundred acres for gettin' him out of that cattle stealin' jam?"

"Yep."

"An' now Jack an' Molly are stockin' it for you, with two hundred head of beef—for services rendered?"

"That's right, Colonel," Pruiett laughed.

"I sure did get in the wrong business," Garvin lamented. "They must ever' damn one be guilty, to be willin' to put up so much for legal services."

"You told me one time that all I needed to do, to make a lawyer out of myself, was to learn to fix fees, didn't you? How am I gettin' along?"

"You ain't no amateur no more," Garvin replied. "You ain't no amateur."

The South Canadian River was the boundary between legal and illegal drinking liquor. The Oklahoma Territory on the north side was wet. The Indian Territory, on the south, was dry—at least it was dry within the intentions of the United States Government. The Box Saloon, on stilts in the sandy bed of the stream, brought the spirits as near to the sheltered Chickasaw Nation as it could. The line was the center of the usually dry sandy bed. The Box was perched in the middle of the river, barely north of the survey.

A cattle man named Choate, with a fresh roll, was there; Bert Casey, outlaw, with Jack Swofford, of the same vocation, and Joe Mobley and Tom Powell, two weak, shiftless kids, were there, also. Everybody was drunk. Powell, youngest and weakest of the Casey group, was afflicted with a ponderous pair of flat feet which flapped inward. He was so shiftless that he didn't object to being called "Pigeon Foot."

Choate and the roll went whooping out the door. Powell and his flapping feet skulked quietly out after him. Silence, two shots and more silence followed; when the gang from the Box got out with their lanterns Choate was dead and his pockets were empty. Great, pigeon-toed tracks of one man led across the moist sand of the river bed toward the north bank and solid ground.

"I realize he's your brother, Nora, an' you're a nice girl.

I'd like to help you, but I can't perform miracles," Pruiett was saying between coughs and squirts of tobacco juice. "I ain't feelin' good, here of late, an'—."

"You've just got to defend him, Mr. Pruiett," Nora Powell insisted. "You cleared Clarence Douglas and you cleared George Hancock, didn't you? Why—?"

"This is different, that's why," he answered. "Those were bad murder cases, but there was some foundation in 'em for buildin' a defense. Hancock killed a marshal, but he was able to prove the marshal had been pushin' him around an' mistreatin' him. Douglas had that bad blood between him an' James Williams for stackin' a self-defense plea on. But here, you got a robbery for a motive. That's bad. It's as bad, if not worse, as the killin'. They got them tracks in the quick sand, and they got lots of witnesses to swear they was big an' toein' in. Tom was there, he left just before Choate was shot, an' when they caught him up in the Creek Nation he was drunk an' had a part of Choate's big roll still on him. If I could make roses bloom on a black-jack sprout, I might get him off with life, but that's the best anybody could do."

We've always been honorable people, Judge," Nora said. "I can't stand to have Tommy hung. I'll pay you three hundred dollars—cash. Won't you take it?"

"Where you goin' to get that kind of money, Nora?"

"I've already got it. I've saved it from my school teachin' job. I've been savin' an' a' hoardin' it for years."

"You ought to keep on savin' it, honey," Pruiett said. "Plead him guilty an' take a chance on the court givin' him leniency. He'll get life, an' that's all you can expect for him. I got to go to Paris this week. That Bud Watkins case, the one I got a hung jury in here last term, is set down there. We got a change of venue. I got to go to South McAlester an' argue my appeal in the Frank Hunt case. I got stuck there for fifteen years. Doc Tyree's killed another man an' I got to work out a defense for him, an' I got a sick wife. Aren't you goin' to let me out of tryin' Tommy?"

"You got to take the case, Mr. Pruiett," Nora cried. "You just got to. I'm goin' right from here to Mr. Garvin's about it if you turn me down."

"Give the money to the girl out there an' have her give you a receipt for it," he said, wearily. "I hate to walk into one like this, but I'm the guy that can swallow the sour right along with the sweet. Pay your money in an' watch close to see what comes out. There won't be no refunds. I can't guarantee to win one like this."

Doc Young hailed him and stopped him on the street.

"Moman," he said, "Davenport an' I are agreed on what's the matter with Lilly, an' it's perty serious. We ain't goin' to be able to help her."

"What you mean—you can't help?" Pruiett asked, with alarm.

"Not that. Don't get excited. I mean it's goin' to take a surgeon; some one that's equipped to perform a serious operation. She's strained down there from havin' her first baby, an' she's got a little worse, gradually, ever' time. There's Doctor Bacon Sanders and Doctor Thompson at Fort Worth, they're specialists on that kind of work, an' if they was to get a hold of her right away they could straighten her up."

"I got to try a case down at Paris next week," Pruiett said. "Could we figure on takin' her to Fort Worth the next week after that?"

Young shook his head. "She's awful weak an' run down, an' here the last few days she's been losin' fast. Davenport an' I both say if we don't get her worked on in a day or two, it's goin' to be too late."

"Let's catch the train in the mornin,' then, an' get it over with. If she's in shape, after the operation, I can leave there an' go to Paris. If not, I can pass the case or get out of it. I'll phone down for a reservation. Bacon Sanders? Is that what you said?"

"Yeah, an' Thompson. They both ought to take part in it," Young replied.

Pruiett looked hopefully across the white bed in the half-dark room. A carved crucifix, above the head of the bed, stood out in the dim light. "What about it, Doctor?" he inquired.

"It was quite satisfactory," the doctor answered. "Quite a delicate operation, and not a moment too soon, but we agree that it was quite satisfactory. She should recover quickly."

"Let me see you in the hall a minute, will you, Doc?" he suggested.

When they were outside the room Pruiett got to the point.

"I got a murder case set in Paris tomorrow," he said. "If she's bad, or if I can help here, I'll wire 'em to get along without me. But if it's all right, I could run down there for three or four days, an' then get right back—."

"If you'd pardon my being frank, Pruiett, I don't think you ought to go down—."

"Then you wasn't tellin' me the truth in there?" he interrupted. "She's bad? She's—."

"She's all right like I said she was," Doctor Thompson said. "It's you I'm talking about. You haven't had any rest or sleep for three days, two, anyway, and you've been drinking a lot. I really don't think you'd be in very good condition to try a man for his life."

"Hell," Pruiett grunted. "I'm as fresh as a wild onion sproutin' through a fresh chip. Don't bother yourself about me. When I have a murder case to try I don't want to sleep."

Doctor Thompson looked at Pruiett seriously, and said: "If you want to consider this strictly on Mrs. Pruiett's condition, you may as well go. She has her special nurses and the hospital will provide everything she needs. She must have complete rest; no visitors, and it would probably be best for her for you to go away for a few days."

"Thanks, Doc," he answered. "I can make enough out of Old Sobe Love on this trip to take care of most of your bill."

Pruiett's charm on the Paris juries was still working. Bud Watkins came clear, but Pruiett wasn't there to hear the verdict, or to collect the bonus he had coming from Bud's Chickasaw grandpa. His blistering final argument had been bawled with an empty, aching dread in his heart. A wire in his pocket, from Fort Worth, had said that Lilly was worse and for him to come as soon as he could. He had the time before the train, so he made his speech, and counsel, prosecutors, jurors and spectators winced at its ragged viciousness. He didn't look back as he rushed out of the courtroom.

"What is it, Doc?" he begged in the hospital corridor. "She looks like wax, like she was dead, an' she hardly knows me. What's wrong?"

"She started hemorrhaging right after you left, Pruiett," Thompson said. "Sanders and I couldn't stop it. At first we didn't think it was serious, but she kept on, an' she almost bled to death. There wasn't anything spared. Everything we had, and everything we knew, we tried, but nothing worked. We wired you when she got—."

"She's all right now, ain't she?"

"I'm afraid not," Thompson answered, shaking his head. "I'm afraid that there's no hope. There's nothing can be done."

Stilwell Russell had abandoned Dallas and opened offices in Ardmore. After the funeral he pronounced an eulogy over Lilly's grave.

"Our sister and friend whose body now rests within the open grave will have all that is mortal of her soon mixing with the elements of the earth; the clods will soon cover her, and that which is natural of her will be hidden from sight. But to those to whom she was near and dear—her spirit will escape from its tenement of clay, and will shine as a beacon light beckoning them to follow the paths of right. The manly youth, whom she as a girl selected as her heart's mate, is still amongst you. These two came years ago as a matter of choice, and cast their lots in this beautiful valley, amongst these good people. I knew them in their earlier days, and I knew them well. They struggled hard to establish themselves in the good opinion and esteem of this people . . . The picture is now somewhat changed. The right hand of the husband is gone, and obligations a thousand fold are added to his already heavy responsibilities. It will be your privilege, my friends, as it is your duty, to aid and encourage him to do right. Let him know that it is your will and desire that he live in your good opinion, and, by conduct warmly manifested, make him feel that in every purpose and endeavor to do right, he will receive your hearty commendation . . . Let us revere the dead; let us love the living."

Russell's thoughts were winging, as he spoke from the open grave, to the events of the years before at Paris, and of what he knew, and what he had heard. It was a frail thread, that line between genius and lunacy—between good and evil. He dreaded to see what the result of this loss would be.

"I'm checkin' out for a few weeks." Pruiett, with muddy boots on a banker's table, was talking to Garvin and Grant.

"You been needin' a rest," Garvin agreed. "Where you goin'? Hot Springs?"

"I'm goin' to Washington," he replied. "I want to see Charley Culberson, an' I can get well if I can get a parole from the President for Frank Hunt. I—."

"Won't that be a hell of a rest, now?" Grant observed.

"Right now, when it looks like you're blowin', you got business to take care of."

"Business in Washington is the best rest I can get," Pruiett answered, with a wan smile.

"It's the kind you don't need," said Garvin. "You're drinkin' too much."

"That's what ever'body says, but I'm doin' all right. I just need to relax."

"What you doin' about the kids?" Grant asked.

"I moved my mother and father into my house," he answered. "With the hired help I got an' them two the children will be in good hands. I got to get away from here for awhile."

"It was too bad about Lilly," Garvin suggested, cautiously.

"She didn't hate to die; she wasn't afraid of dyin'," Pruiett said, easily. "She just enjoyed life so much. That's why it was hard to see her go. She thought I was the greatest lawyer in the world. She thought our kids were smarter, an' pertier than anybody else's an' that that house down there was a palace. Just happy an' contented with livin'—an' she had to die." He looked casually into the distance.

"It looks like them high-priced doctors could've done something. Why did you bring her back so soon?"

"They told me when I got back from Paris that it was a matter of a few days, a few weeks at the most. I wanted to argue about it, an' to call more doctors in, but after I talked to Lilly I knew it was no use. She told me just what the doctors had said, an' they hadn't been talkin' to her about it, neither. She said she wanted to be near the babies, an' to see the green of the valley, an' hear the thrush an' the larks in the alfalfa across the creek. I could see it in her eyes, so we fixed it up for movin' her on the trains. I wanted her to have what she wanted."

"Old Stilwell Russell spoke a perty piece for her," Grant said.

"He's my friend," said Pruiett.

"What about business while you're gone?" Garvin inquired. "There's liable to be a little shootin' an' cuttin', an' maybe a little cow an' horse stealin'. Shall I tell 'em to hold their guts in 'til you get back, or just let 'em go ahead and puke 'em up?"

"I'm not licked by a hell of a lot," Pruiett assured him. "I'll take all I can get when I get back, an' nobody'll have to hire new counsel in these cases pendin'. I am not sure when I'll be back, but I am not goin' to be gone long."

"Ain't he the damndest feller you ever saw?" Grant mused as Pruiett swung slowly down Paul Avenue.

"He told me after he come here that he was goin' to keep a vow he made to turn criminals aloose on society which wasn't fair in dealin' with people that was charged with violatin' its rules. I thought he was foolin'. I thought he wanted to work all the time 'cause he wanted the jack, but hell's fire! He keeps pluggin' in his damn criminal cases, an' workin' all the time, when his legs swell up as big as watermelons, an' when his heart's busted like it is right now."

"He's takin' this loss of his wife perty easy, it looks like to me," Grant said.

"Pruiett's like a damn Chickasaw," Garvin replied. "They look the same all the time, when they feel good or when they back into a brandin' iron. You couldn't tell by the way he looks what he's thinkin'. I knew how close he was to that girl, an' what plans he had for his children through her. He's makin' this little business trip to Washington to keep from goin' plumb loco. That business is part of the act."

Pruiett's Washington visit was terminated by tragedy. He had been there all summer, it was September, 1902, when he got the bad news from his mother. The baby boy named for Stilwell Russell was dead.

"I was out at Cabin John's with Charley Culberson," Pruiett said, "and I heard that rumblin', ringin', noise in my ears that had bothered me off an' on since before little Hayden died. I had 'em a few years ago, an' right afterward my baby died. They started ringin' again on me this spring, an' Lilly Belle up an' died. They kind of got me bothered; I've called 'em the bells of death. Do you believe in that kind of stuff?" The Senator laughs in my face, an' he says, 'Son, I call 'em the whiskey bucks, when my head goes to blastin' like a light house bell. That's all that's the matter with you.' So I kind of pass off, but my head keeps ringin'. I think when I get back to the hotel I'll wire home, an' find out if everything's running smooth, an' what do I find when I ask for my key? A telegram that my baby is dead."

"It's a coincidence, that's all," Claude Weaver assured him. They were visiting in Pruiett's Valley office. "I don't believe in this mental telepathy."

"I feel like I can trust them bells," Pruiett answered. "The next time I get to hummin' in my head like that I'm goin' to start lookin' an' dodgin'. Us Pruietts is down to me an' a' orphan girl, an' we got to look out."

"An' I've had plenty of good, too. I learned a long time ago that the sun don't shine under the same dog's tail all the time. If you got a dollar, spend it. If you got a drink, drink it. If you don't you'll be sorry when hard luck overtakes you, an' she's bound to catch up sooner or later."

"You're in a nice peaceable frame of mind," Weaver observed.

"Haven't I got a right to be?"

"I ain't sayin' you ain't," the agreeable Weaver acknowledged. "There's a term of court comin' up an' you got an awful batch of cases set. What you doin' with 'em?"

"I'm continuin' all I can an' tryin' all I can't," Pruiett answered. "Bill Johnson ought to do some good this session. He's holdin' Tom Powell over my head, an' I ain't got a chance to get away."

Bail had been arranged for Tom Powell. Pruiett and Nora and Tom were having daily rehearsals in the lawyer's office.

"Good God, Nora, can you stand there an' say you love him, even if he is your brother?" Pruiett stormed, pulling his black wool. "Good God, Tommy, use your head. Can't you remember nothin'?"

"Pay attention to Mr. Pruiett," Nora begged. "Why don't you listen. We're tryin' our best to help you. This case is comin' up next week, an' he wants to be sure you know what to do an' say in front of the jury."

"Well, what is it now?" Tom sulked.

"You are not pigeon-toed," Pruiett bellowed. "That's all a mistake. When you walk you stick your toes out at right angles like a goose full of clabber. These reports around here that you're pigeon-toed are all a mistake—see? Nora's got witnesses to prove that you was born with good feet an' never did walk pigeon-toed. Do you understand? I got to have somethin' to argue to this jury."

"It ain't my fault I was born with feet like that," Tom said, rolling a cigarette.

"Let 'im hang. Let me kill 'im myself," Pruiett raged "What's the use of us goin' to all this trouble for this no good lout?"

"Please, Tommy," said Nora. "Can't you understand? They got those government witnesses that testified at the preliminary, before the commissioner. They say that the tracks of the man that killed Choate were pigeon-toed. They expect to connect you up with it that way."

"My head ain't no sack," Tom answered. "I know what you're gettin' at, an' I'm doin' just what you want me to."

"There isn't a thing the matter with his feet, Nora, except they're so damn big," Pruiett insisted. "I took his shoes off and showed you. He's just so damn triflin' an' lazy and sloven that he don't pick em' up or care how they flop. He'd ought to be hung."

"Help Mr. Pruiett, Tommy," Nora placated.

"Help Pruiett, hell," Pruiett gritted. "All right, Tom, pull off them boots. Now walk over to the door. Point 'em out. Out, damn it; out, not in. Duck walk! Point 'em out. There—that's it."

Pruiett met Johnson's brigade of witnesses man for man. For every one to swear that they knew Tom Powell, had known him for a long time, and that he was unusually and noticeably pigeon-toed, the defense produced two witnesses who testified to the contrary. They proved a good alibi for him besides, and when it came time, at the practical close of the evidence, to put the accused on the stand, the case was in good shape. Pruiett whispered a final admonition on "turning those damned toes out when you show 'em to the jury," and put him on the witness stand.

Concluding a satisfactory examination of his own witness, Pruiett inquired: "Now, Tommy, certain people in this community, who don't know you very well, have intimated that you are pigeon-toed. Are you?

"Naw, sir," answered Tom.

"Have you ever walked with a pigeon-toed gait, that is, with your toes turned in, like this?" Pruiett made a gesture with his hands and fingers, laying them across the table pointing inward.

"Naw, sir," Tom answered.

"Tommy, I want you to take your shoes and stockings off, and walk down here to where I am." Pruiett asked the question and waited. The awkward youth twisted about in the witness chair, removing his heavy shoes and coarse socks. When Tom had completed, Pruiett put the final touch of polish to him.

"Now, son," he said. "I want you to walk down here to where I am, an' remember walk in your most natural way. I mean, the way you walked when you took your first steps, hanging to the hem of your mother's apron, an' as you've walked about naturally, to this good day."

The question was too strong for Tom; it had been formulated for the jury. But Tom, studying a moment, followed the directions literally. He stepped down with his big feet toed in in a natural step, the toe nails raking the ankles of the opposite foot with each languid stride. Even the resourceful Pruiett couldn't think of a quick question to ask, in an attempt to recover and cover up.

"No cross-examination," was all the grinning Johnson had to say.

The jury gave Tommy life, and Nora, with tears in her eyes, thanked Pruiett for saving him from the gallows.

"That's the first case I ever lost an' was damn glad of it," Pruiett confided, patting her consolingly.

"I'm glad you lost it, too, Mr. Pruiett," she sniffled. "You were right. They should have hung him."

Casey, and Joe Mobley, his youthful apprentices in the field of frontier crime, were murdering and pillaging in the ranch houses and on the roads of the Oklahoma Territory north of the river, while their friend Powell was being tried. Near the town of Anadarko, in Caddo County, they were engaged in a gun battle with Sheriff Beck and Deputy Smith, and a posse of farmers and ranchers. Both Beck and Smith were killed in the battle, and although the tough Casey managed to escape again, young Mobley was captured. Pruiett took employment in the case, merely to flaunt the gallows. The tears of Joe's mother, rather than any considerable fee, moved him to attempt the difficult defense.

He changed the venue and tried the case in Kiowa County, at Hobart, the principal town of the Kiowa country, southwest of the Valley. Frank Gillette was the Federal Judge. The government was represented by Horace Speed, an able running mate for Bill Johnson. He had an enviable string of convictions behind him. The court, prosecutor and the bulk of the populace, shook their heads in disgust and despair when the jury forsook their gallows, and meted out a measly five years on a manslaughter conviction for little Joe.

But Casey didn't fare so well. With Fred Hudson, an apparent escape from the Federal Jail at Guthrie, and Ben Hughes, sufficiently calloused to pal with Casey, they started an expedition up the Canadian to rob the bank at Cleo Springs. Gathered around a guarded fire in a rocky canyon, and with Hughes asleep in his saddle blanket, Hudson and Casey methodically cleaned and shined their six-shooters. Hudson, noting that all of Casey's cartridges were lying on the blanket beside him, and that he was squinting through the cylinder of his pistol as he slowly turned it between his eye and the flickering fire, slipped a single lead slug into his own gun and let Casey have it, low. Hughes, jumping up, saw what had transpired, but couldn't see where it was any of his business. He adjusted his saddle pillow and went back to sleep. It developed that Hudson was not an escape. He had been liberated by government authorities tired of being eluded by Casey, to perform the particular job. Some one else got Hudson, but that was the way it went. It was the story of the territory.

CHAPTER EIGHT

How Pruiett shoots a man for pulling a pistol upon him. And how his destiny, and his faultless luck is proven, as the cartridge which failed to explode over his heart is ready to go when given a second and subsequent test. And wherein he clears a cross-breed Indian woman with jury box appeal, and saves a murderous doctor from penalty for his latest killing, and is caused to appeal an unsuccessful murder case to the upper court. And how his infant daughter acquires a new mother, and the Pruietts and the Garvins tour the Pacific Northwest, to forget the Valley and give it a rest.

When the English walking coat came, he put it on and strutted before the hall-tree mirror. His mother bit her lip and patted her foot.

"Put it in the box an' ship it back," she said, threateningly.

"Ship it back, nothin'," said Pruiett. "Them big houses in Saint Looey don't make exchanges an' give money back like Kendall does. What's wrong with this walkin' coat? I like it."

"You ain't wearin' it out of this house," she retorted. "Look at the yellow an' green in them big plaid checks, an' them buttons is as big as saucers. You look plumb ridiculous."

Pruiett grinned. "This here's the style," he said. "See that split up the back, an' how she stands open when I button her up tight."

"That waist-line is under your armpits, an' the split starts right between your shoulder blades," Betty sniffed. "A man that would wear a double-breasted barber pole like that ought to be examined by a head doctor. You look like you had a bustle on."

"She cost me seventy-five bucks, an' I done paid for her at the C.O.D. window. I say I ought to wear it."

"An' I say if you ever go on the street in that outfit I move out of the Valley," Betty challenged.

"I can set that outfit off right," the Captain called from his rocker. "Give 'er to me. I need a' overcoat anyway."

"You two are framin' me," Pruiett laughed. "That's the reason why you won't let me wear it, Maw, you want it for Paw."

"He can get his old army bonnet out an' wear it with that coat, an' look like somethin'—a Chickasaw chief or a Mexican general; but you ain't wearin' it. I wouldn't be surprised to see it on one of these wild Indians that wear red an' green blankets

[167]

around here, or a town dandy, but not you, Mawman. You're a big lawyer now."

"She's a fine lookin' garment," the Captain said.

"Maybe White could wear the coat," Pruiett said. "I'm joshin' with you about it, Maw, but it's a damn shame to let it go plumb to waste. It's expensive wool, an' it'll keep somebody warm when the cold weather hits."

"The Captain's got to have a' overcoat an' nobody but a man like him could get by with wearin' such a garment," Betty concluded. The argument was over. The Captain got the coat.

"Is that louse friend of White's still eatin' an' sleepin' on us?" Pruiett inquired.

"Yes, an' I don't like it," she answered. "He keeps White out all night, an' they come in drunk ever' mornin'. Then they pile up in his bed an' sleep 'til afternoon, an' then get up an' holler for food."

"I'll stomp his head off," Pruiett grated. "What's his name?"

"It's Charley Wiseman," Betty answered. "Let me try to straighten it out before you start anything. You lose your temper too quick. I'll see if I can't freeze him out without no trouble."

"How's Gail been doin'?" Pruiett asked. "How's her appetite?"

"She's the liveliest kid I ever seen," the Captain said.

"She's fine, but she's awful spoiled," Betty said. "She—."

"She needs a mother," Pruiett said. "She's goin' to have all the advantages you an' I didn't get, Maw, an' she's got to have a mother for that."

"Ain't I takin' proper care to suit you?" she began.

"The best in the world," he interrupted, grabbing her and hugging her. "A kid like Gail is entitled to a mother, an' a grandmother, too—not just a combination. She lost a good mother, but I'm goin' to get her another one. I wisht you'd let me wear that English walkin' coat."

The winter term of court, and cold weather, came to the Valley together. Pruiett was immersed in the preparation of two murder defenses; one for Izora Alexander, the statuesque cross-breed who had slain her black lover, and the other for Jim Moorehead, who killed the husband of the woman he was handling in a sordid rural love affair.

Moorehead had become enamored by the corpulent charm of Elsie, the middle-aged wife of Frank McMenimen, who farmed in the bottoms south of town. Elsie was no bargain on the adultery board, but Frank loved her, and he wanted to keep those paths he had trod alone those fourteen years since the marriage unsullied by the track of a libertine. He designed a premature return after an announced absence of considerable length, and upon executing it, found Jim and Elsie in the kitchen—instead of the iron bedstead boudoir as anticipated—and Jim, unorthodox always, had off his shirt instead of the item usually missing when disarray of raiment becomes justification for attempted homicide. As the evidence indicated, Jim and Elsie were seated opposite each other with a tub between them, paring apples and letting the shavings drop into its intervening abyss.

When Frank came in and caught them together, Jim attacked him with the apple knife. He didn't stab him with a well directed thrust, or even a pair of them. He cut him down like a wormy apple, until even the hardened officers, who came in to try to identify the bloody hulk, shuddered and backed away. Moorehead had literally hacked him to pieces while Elsie ran gibbering to the neighbors, a mile away, to tell them of what was going on at home.

The jury disagreed in the J. W. Moorehead case. Izora received twelve stares of ill-concealed admiration, and a vote of acquittal, from the good men who heard the evidence in her case. Pruiett packed his necessaries in the old carpet bag and followed the court east to the Pontotoc Country. There were killings there, as in the Valley, and the Pruiett fame had traveled up and down the rivers and across the hills and gullies. Gold Brady, a wealthy rancher, had been shot-gunned to death. Lon Goff and Frank Driggers, rival cattle raisers, were being held, without bond, for Brady's murder.

Ada, in the eastern edge of the Chickasaw Nation, was the principal town and the seat of government. Pruiett had a room at the Byrd Hotel, the fanciest hostelry in town.

"What you doin' down here?" he hailed across the narrow lobby. He had seen A. C. Cruce, his varying colleague and adversary, from Ardmore. "You come over for court?"

"I got a little case set that I'm tryin' to continue," Cruce explained. "You here for Lon Goff and Frank Driggers?"

"Yeah, an' I'm ready for trial," Pruiett answered. "If the government's ready, we ought to start in the mornin'. I figger on bein' in town all week."

They talked together of business and Ardmore, of Stilwell

Russell, and prospects for statehood. "What's the matter with you?" Cruce demanded. Pruiett was slapping violently at his ear and neck.

"It's these bells," he answered, deliberately. "My head goes to buzzin' an' ringin'."

"What do you mean, these bells?" Cruce inquired.

"The bells of death," Pruiett said. "They don't fail me. They mean trouble; serious trouble. Tragedy."

"You ain't drunk, are you?" asked Cruce.

Pruiett laughed. "No, I am not, but that's an idea for me. I got some licker in my suit case, an' it's most time to eat. Let's step up an' have a shot, an' then go eat supper together."

"You're talkin' sense now," Cruce agreed, as they walked into Pruiett's room from the lobby. "Say, what is it about these bells? You got my curiosity excited."

"If you don't believe in predestation, an' the supernatural transfer of thoughts an' wishes, you are not goin' to take any stock in what I mean by it," Pruiett laughed, trying to lead him away from the subject.

"Stilwell Russell told me not long ago that you hypnotized the jury in the George Hancock case. He said you threw yourself into a trance, an' gave 'em that cold, glitterin' eye, an' that they was in your power. You are not pleadin' guilty of bein' a hocus-pocus feller, are you?"

"People with lunky heads are just like country telephone exchanges with weak batteries," Pruiett confided, lighting the lamp in the room and pulling the blind down. "They can carry a little distance, but not very far. People with strong minds shoot out a lot of current, an' they got a faculty for pickin' current up out of the atmosphere. With a little reasoning, an' a little understanding of the circumstances you see a man, an' you ought to know perty well what he's a' thinkin'."

"You mean you got one of them telegraph heads on you?"

"Don't be funny, A. C.," Pruiett insisted. "I'm serious. I hear them bells ringin' right now, while I'm tellin' you this. I am not braggin'. I'm just tellin' you that I can understand people's thoughts up to a certain point, an' I get flashes that put me on my guard. I've learned to trust 'em."

"You said somethin' about the bells of death. What did you mean by that?"

"I feel tragedy a'comin'," he answered. "I've had three deaths on my hands in just a few years, an' ever' one was told to me before it came. I didn't understand what the message was the first time—or the second. That's why my experience is such a good teacher. If you got any sense at all you learn after you've been knocked down a few times. I heard the bells ever' time, just before the trouble came."

"That's bunk, if you'll pardon my sayin' what comes to my mind first," Cruce grinned.

Pruiett had fished his bag from under the bed and thrown it across the quilts. The blue six-shooter nestled amongst his rumpled clothing; a bottle of whiskey lay snugly in a protected spot away from it. Pruiett handed the bottle to Cruce while he put the pistol in his hip pocket.

"What you goin' to carry the iron for?" Cruce inquired.

"Just in case," Pruiett replied. "The bells may be for me, this time. It won't hurt to carry it around for awhile."

One drink called for another, and each demanded and required a story. The two lawyers had entertained each other for an hour, when Pruiett jumped up from his seat on the bed.

"I can't keep these flashes out of my head," he muttered. "You wait here an' I'll go out an' make a 'phone call to home. I got to ask my Maw if Gail's all right, and' if the rest of 'em is all right. There's something wrong, or there's somethin' goin' to be wrong. I got to find out."

The assurance he received from his mother didn't relieve him. Gail was fine. Everything was quiet and satisfactory. There was no need to worry at all. Just work hard and win the case, and hurry back to them. His mother was still dreaming and praying him up the path he was climbing.

A man was pounding the clerk's desk as Pruiett passed. "I got to have a room," he demanded. "I drove in here from Allen in my buggy, an' I'm tired. I want a room so I can go to bed."

Pruiett recognized the speaker as Doctor Walter C. Threldkeld, a casual acquaintance. "How are you, Doctor?" he said, offering his hand.

"Hello," the Doctor answered, uncertainly. As he shook hands he swayed, and the lids of his glassy eyes sagged. "What's your name?"

"It's Pruiett—Moman Pruiett," he said, smiling. He could see that Doctor Threldkeld was carrying a heavy load. "I was goin' to say that I had a nice room with a big bed, an' if the hotel is crowded, it'd be all right for you to use the room with me."

"You're the man that defended Sam Ashton, ain't you?" Threld-keld asked, still swaying unsteadily.

"Why, yes, I tried the Ashton case," he answered.

"Charley Dismukes was a personal friend of mine, an' that Sam was a dirty son of a gun," Threldkeld cried. "He ought to have been hung."

"I am not discussin' my business here in the hotel lobby," Pruiett said, shortly. "I just wanted to offer you an accommodation—."

"Who the hell asked you for it?" Threldkeld demanded.

"I beg your pardon," Pruiett said, starting to walk on past him. Threldkeld suddenly pulled a pistol from his coat pocket, pushed the muzzle of it against Pruiett's chest, and pulled the trigger at the same time. Instead of an explosion there was a metallic click, hollow, and faint. Pruiett jumped behind the counter, and pulled his pistol. As he did so Threldkeld jumped behind a square column which supported the upper floor. And Threldkeld's second shot produced better results. There was a deafening report, and from Pruiett's pistol shot, a handful of splinters flew from the beam by Dr. Threldkeld's head.

The battle was on. The clerk was down behind the counter, and guests huddled behind chairs and couches, or ran for the two street openings. Pruiett, sighting around the protecting column, was hitting Threldkeld every time he pulled the trigger, but the Doctor wouldn't go down. Through the smoke of the lobby he could be plainly seen, holding his gun in both hands and firing deliberately; with feet wide spread he trembled from head to feet each time Pruiett's lead entered his body. When his six shots were gone he walked across the room and out the door to Dr. Ligon's office. Those who followed him, cautiously, by his bloody trail, found him half way up a stairway leading from the street. He was unconscious, but alive. There were two gaping wounds in his body. By the efforts of close friends there was no prosecution, and the two became fast friends, with the Doctor getting well from his wounds.

"Pruiett was sore as hell at the jury's givin' Lon Goff eight years for manslaughter for killin' Brady." Grant was talking to Garvin. They had their customary box in the front window of Grant's bank, where they could watch life on Paul Avenue.

"The jury's got to say 'not guilty' unless they want to hear Moman belly-ache," Garvin replied. "He ain't satisfied with workin' his head off tryin' to beat the law. He wants to win 'em all. His wife dies an' his kids dies, an' he won't quit. He ain't satisfied to beat the ropes; he want's 'em all to be turned out, Scot free. I was surprised he went up to the Cherokee Strip to help prosecute that Riggin, in the cattle war cases."

"He done a fair job of turnin' murderers loose in that last thirty day term here. He made a plumb fool out of Bill Johnson. Hung the jury for Moorehead, an' there wasn't a defense in the world to that case. There was Russell and Henry Furman, an' them high sailin' Cruce brothers, a'gettin' fifty years, an' life sentence, an' hangin', an' then old bush-headed Moman comes in an' spits all over the courtroom, bellers 'til the jury thinks the roof is comin' down, an' they say 'Not Guilty.' He's a dandy."

"When he tried that cross-breed that killed her sweetie at the festivule," Garvin began. "Her name was Izora Alexander," he continued:

"Zack Follis walked into Pruiett's office, and said, 'Mr. Moman, Cousin Zora wants you to come up to Purcell.' 'What does she want me to come to Purcell for?' Pruiett said. 'She killed a Negro out there at a festivule.' 'Where was the festivule?' Pruiett asked. 'Out in the settlement on the Canadian River.'" Pruiett went to Purcell, and conferred with Izora. He was employed, and secured bond for her through some Creek freedmen who lived in the Creek and Seminole Nations. Leta, a half-sister, assisted her in securing her bondsmen. Pruiett says at this writing that Izora Alexander Lee, and her two nephews—sons of Leta, have just inherited $7,000,000 accumulated over a period of years from oil royalties, from Leta's land, who is now deceased. Pruiett says the most amusing and interesting incident connected with Izora's trial was the testimony of an old Negro woman by the name of Dora Willis, who testified that when Izora entered the dug-out with her, 'Izora had her forty-five six-shooter in her hand and that it was full-roostered.' The court asked her what she meant. She replied, 'Well Judge, you see the thing that makes it shoot was pulled clear back, and when she pulled that trigger it was all over, he falls.' The government brought a white school teacher from Pine Knot, Kentucky, who testified that he 'happened to be present on the festival grounds and saw Izora go into the dug-out with the forty-five six-shooter in her hand.' Izora's attorney, Pruiett, had her to plead self-defense, the results was the usual verdict, *NOT GUILTY*."

PRUIETT AND UNCLE HENRY GORDON
"He defended four of his sons, charged with murder,
and preached the old man's funeral."

"Yeah," said Garvin, "Izora, she killed that buck in one of them voodoo fits, an' there wasn't no particular reason for it, that I could see."

"What's the idea of them festivules?" Grant said. "Somebody gets killed or hurt ever'time. The government ought to stop 'em."

"As long as I been in the Chickasaw country they have been having festivules," Garvin laughed. "The niggers never did have 'em an' the Indians never did have 'em. The cross breeds just cross bred 'em a name, an' startin' 'em regular as a good excuse for gettin' drunk. They get a barrel an' fill it full of candy and apples —mostly candy. They get rock candy an' old-fashion stick candy an' then they melt candy in their corn licker an' they eat candy all the time they drink. When they get a certain heat, along about morning, they start to ring aroun' the candy barrel—a whoopin' an' a skippin'. I been to 'em an' seen how they go. They dance an' kick 'em an' skid off a waist or a jacket as they go. When the inside of the shack gets to foggin' about like a boar's nest they start droppin' out, a buck an' a wench here an' a buck an' wench there, headin' for the bushes. Izora caught her buck slippin' out with one of them."

"I wasn't so surprised to see 'em turn her aloose," Grant said.

"Pruiett can think of more ways of getting a person charged with murder out of jail, an' keepin' 'em out, than a hungry freed-man can of milkin' a fresh jenny," Grant grinned. "How come he tells you so much about his business?"

"He's my friend," Garvin answered. "He never crossed me but once—in that damn Sam Ashton case—an' I just couldn't stay mad at him about that. He comes out ever' Sunday and we fry up chickens, an' loaf around all day. He says he likes to get my slant on the cases he's goin' to try."

"That's his secret," said Grant. "He don't ask the other law-yers about what to do in a case. He goes to the home-folks, like you an' me, an' the boys in the barber shop. When he gets that slant on a question, he's damn near got a jury's slant, an' he knows just what to offer in his case."

Jake Hodges had succeeded in getting John Stevenson a ten year sentence in the third trial of his case at Paris. With Gaines's ghost partially avenged, Jake withdrew, and Stilwell Russell, sur-viving counsel, took Pruiett into the case. Pruiett and Russell took another appeal, and following it to a hearing before the

Circuit Court at New Orleans, obtained another reversal. Stevenson's mistake had ruined him, financially, but he wouldn't give up. He wasn't going to jail.

"A letter received here yesterday morning from St. Luke's Hospital, St. Louis, where Mr. C. J. Grant was taken recently, states that he is not improving, and it is thought he might as well be cared for at home. Dr. Young, Moman Pruiett and Cody Witten left at once for St. Louis."

The Santa Fe rocked northward. "It's too bad about old Cal," the Doctor observed. "Maybe he ought to stay in the hospital awhile."

"I know how he feels," Pruiett responded. "Lilly Belle insisted on bein' brought back to the Valley, when she knew that she had to die. I guess we'll all feel the same way."

"We could've made these arrangements for bringin' him back, without it interferin' with your trial docket." Witten suggested. "You didn't hardly have time to catch the train."

"I got time to serve my friends, an' men like Grant an' old man Garvin and Judge David E. Bryant don't come along ever' day," he said. "When I got through with that Mobley case at Hobart, I came right home. I got off lucky to that jury up there, too."

"Joe was just as guilty as Bert Casey, an' if they ever catch him he won't get a trial. A mob'll tear him to pieces." That was Witten's appraisal of the situation.

"I never did have the details of that murder straight, exactly," Doctor Young said.

"You remember Tom Powell, the pigeon footed little devil I defended, an' they gave a life sentence to?" Pruiett said. "Well, Casey put him up to killin' Choate that night, an' he took part of the money Tom stole. Tom an' Joe Mobley was just kids. Casey took Joe an' drifted out into the Arapahoe country, an' they got to robbin' an' mistreatin' farmers, an' burnin' down their houses an' so on. The sheriff, his name was Frank Smith, an' deputy George Beck organized a posse an' cornered 'em in a farm house, over near Anadarko. There was a hell of a gunfight, an' Smith an' Beck was both killed. Bert Casey got away, as usual, but they caught Joe. They tried him before Frank Gillette for murder."

"An' the jury gave him five years?" Young said.

"That's all they gave him—just five," Pruiett laughed.

"How come?" Witten inquired.

"We just made a good show out of it," Pruiett answered. "I made 'em think about Joe's poor old mother instead of the dead sheriff an' his deputy. They was feelin' right sorry for Joe's maw before we got through."

"You didn't do so good in the Riggins case, up at Enid, did you?" Young wanted to puncture his ego.

"I can't get my dander up in a prosecution," he answered. "The jury turned Riggins loose, an' I knew they was goin' to. We wasn't tryin' Riggins for murder, we was tryin' Temple Houston for bein' a good fellow, an' his daddy for being a great national figure. Old Temple is a great lawyer all right, an' with his ability, an' havin' a favorable jury, the blind goddess gets the prong put to her."

"The Ardmore paper said that that was one of the most important cases in the country; that it was a test, to determine whether the big cattle companies were goin' to be able to hold the ranges, or whether the farmers that were comin' in an' fencin' homesteads were goin' to be able to break 'em up. What about that?"

"It might look that way, Doc, but I don't agree with it," Pruiett replied. "Sears was a nester all right, an' Riggins killed him because he homesteaded a hunk of his range. Temple Houston cleared him of murder, an' gave me a nice little court trimmin' along with it, but that don't take care of the livin' an' eatin' question. The families are comin' in fast, an' they all got to have a roof over their head an' food for their hungry kids. Them government ranges are fit for farmin' an' the majority wants to break 'em up an' let the farmers have 'em. That's what's goin' to happen, no matter how many of the farmers get shot before it's finally done."

"You ain't been at home in the Valley but a few days in months," Young said. "Does your folks take care of the kid to suit you, an' keep her all right?"

"It was good while she was a baby, but she's gettin' a little older, an' she's got to have a mother. I'm gettin' married as soon as I get back to the Valley."

"Who's the lady?" Witten inquired.

"Leda Sniggs," he answered.

"She's workin' in your office, ain't she?" Young asked.

"I had her quit her teachin' job and go to work in the office, so's I could find out whether she's got the qualities I need for Gail. She's educated an' refined, an' out of good stock. She's loyal, an' she's terribly fond of me. She understands the situation I'm in, an' about what will be required after she marries me. We got it all worked out, on a' intelligent basis, an' I know character when I see it an' study it awhile. She's a good girl."

"I hope you'll be happy," Young replied. "Say—by the way. How much did you get for defendin' Joe Mobley?"

"Not a damn cent," Pruiett grinned. "In fact, I paid the expenses of goin' up there, an' transportin' some witnesses—an' the old lady. It really cost me about two hundred of my own money to try it."

The ceremony was over. Leda Pruiett was in charge of the house with the curving veranda and the pecan orchard. The first frost of fall brought a creak and clatter to the side yard. "What's that?" Leda inquired.

Pruiett looked out the window. "It's old Spencer Bias," he laughed. "He's makin' his annual payment on my fee for defendin' Charley."

"How's that?" she asked.

"It's his first bale of cotton," he explained. "For three or four years, he's been skiddin' that first bale off in my yard. He ain't the only one that does it. Old Uncle Henry Gordon delivers me a bale, an' so does Caesar Franklin. You'll know Caesar when he comes by in his coon-skin cap. Bill Yoder usually dumps a bale, an' old Uncle Henry always brings a sack of apples an' a sack of pecans or hickory nuts with his payment. All that stuff goes to you."

"The cotton, too?"

"I'll watch the market for you, an' when it's right, sell it," he answered. "It goes for things for the house, or for Gail. Lilly used to send to Dallas an' get things like them Dresden china pieces, on the sideboard, there, an' one year she bought that cherry secretary. You just do whatever you want with it. It runs into perty good money."

"Why do they leave it here for you like that?"

"It's for services," he said. "I defended Yoder's brother up in Oklahoma Territory, an' I went to Washington to keep Spencer's boy from bein' hung. Old Caesar Franklin killed a nigger an' I defended him for murder. They didn't none of 'em have money, but I went ahead an' defended 'em anyway. They're under eternal obligation, so they'll pay as long as they live, I guess. Ever' year they dump me one bale of cotton."

"How long do you think the jury'll be out, Moman?"

"There isn't any way of tellin'," he answered. "We must've waited two hours at the court house before we came to the office. They might be hung up, and the court might keep 'em together for a couple of days."

The customary entourage had trailed him from the court. There was Weaver, Doc Young and John Webb, and Tyree, the defendant. Doctor F. B. Tyree, from Magee, an inland settlement east of the Valley, was the principal in the production. The jury was deliberating over what should be his punishment, if any, for killing Joe Mode, a recent citizen of Magee.

"What you think they'll do?" Webb inquired.

"You can't tell," Pruiett answered, carelessly. "A damn jury can't be figgered. For instance,—."

"What do you think about it, Doc?" Webb asked Tyree. "How do you feel?"

Tyree looked up from the floor with an evil gleam in his weasel eye. He opened his thin lips, as if to speak, and then clamped them back together again.

"You see this cartridge?" Pruiett hastened, as if to avert an inquiry into Tyree's black frame of mind. "This here cartridge is what old Doctor Threldkeld gave me for a souvenir. When they were sure the old man wasn't goin' to die, they let me in to see him, an' he gave it to me. You see the little hole drilled in the middle of that cap? That's where the firin' pin hit 'er. It damn near run through the cap, but she didn't explode, an' the muzzle of that pistol was pushed half way through my tit, right over the heart. Ever' other bullet in the cylinder was fired, five of 'em, but this first one missed."

"What was the matter with that old fool?" Young asked.

"On a mean drunk," Pruiett said. "He bawled an' carried on like he was broken-hearted, an' said he loved me like a brother. He made a statement assumin' full blame for the fracas an' said that he wisht I'd a killed him. He says, 'Son, take this here ca'tridge an' save it for a lucky piece—not for yourself but for me. If that cap had a' popped it would'a got you all right, but it would a'got me too. If they hadn't hung me for murder I'd a' committed suicide over it.' The old man was as sick on remorse as he was from loss of blood."

Will Jones, city marshal, examined the metal cylinder. "That cap had hell rapped out of her, all right," he said. "Do you suppose that it's a dud, or do you think she just didn't tickle the right spot?"

"Let's try 'er out," Webb suggested. "Ever'thing quiet out here in the back. Put it in the chamber an' point it out the winder. See what she does."

Pruiett unlocked his table drawer and brought out the forty-five. Dumping the contents of the full cylinder into the palm of his hand and transferring them into his side pocket, he placed the single shell into the cylinder and slid it back into place. When he squeezed the trigger, with the barrel pointing toward the ground outside the open window, a cannon-like roar shook the interior of the room. The gun leaped upward with the recoil. "Jesus Christ!" Pruiett muttered through the blue smoke. "I knew I heard them bells a'ringin' that day."

"You must keep your pledge paid at the church," Weaver observed.

"A guy with that kind of luck can't lose," Young said, aside to Tyree, "an' here you are a'ridin' on his shirt-tail. You're as bound to come clear as a nickel is for a barlow."

"I got a belly full of you stupid bastards," Tyree cried. "Ain't you got sense enough to keep still an' let a man alone?" He looked about the room with quick jerks of his head, like a cornered animal, and then turned and ran out the door.

"That varmint ain't got no right to be out on bond," Webb said. "He's plumb wild. What's got the matter with him, do you suppose?"

"Doc's jumpy. He's been actin' queer for two or three days," Pruiett explained.

"Shootin' that gun off didn't do his nerves any good," Weaver said. "I guess I'd be jumpy too, if I had as much killin' on my conscience as Tyree's got."

"He hasn't got no conscience, or nerves, neither." Pruiett laughed. "He's hot at somebody about somethin', an' I think it's me, over the way I defended him. He don't seem to think I did it right."

"He didn't seem to object to your gettin' him an acquittal two years ago, when he killed that poor kid he claimed was prowlin' his young wife's drawers," Webb said.

"He just had got his fee paid in that case when he killed Joe Mode," Pruiett said. "I think he put it off several months, just 'til he got able to afford another killin'. Old Doc is a murderin' maniac—as long as he's out he's a menace to the peace and safety of society."

"Then he ought to be hung an' put out of the way," Weaver interrupted. "If that's——."

"This here's a democracy we're livin' in," Pruiett reminded, with mock gravity, "an every citizen accused of a crime is entitled to a trial by jury. If the jury says you're not guilty, when you are, then you're not guilty. An' vice versa, if you're innocent, but the jury says you are not, then you're a damn felon. Let's make the rule work both ways, boys. Don't let's try to substitute our own little opinions for the majesty of the law."

"You better watch your client," Webb advised. "He's got a murder in him that may not wait 'til he's saved up another defense fee. He might kill his lawyer."

"He's not so tough, I can't handle him," Pruiett grinned. "I'll take my chances with him. Old Doc got in a killin' up in Missouri, around Springfield, an' things got so hot he had to leave out, real sudden an' unannounced, like. He got over to El Dorado, Arkansas, an' when that old Tucker-Parnell feud got hot, Doc couldn't hold his fidgits, so's he kills himself another man or two. The law wasn't worryin' him, in that case; it was some of the tough birds in the other camp. Doc shoved off an' settled over at Magee."

"Nice background he's got, but I don't need his history to know he's a killer. It's wrote all over his mean, evil face," said Young. "The jury ought to convict, just on his face."

"They've convicted on a hell of a lot less, lots of times," Pruiett agreed. "Say, it's startin' to get dark. The sun's plumb down. What do you say we move down to Kimberlin's drugstore, an' see if we can't shake up a drink or two? If that jury don't report perty soon, I'm goin' home for supper."

Pruiett furnished the money; Kimberlin furnished the ingredients. The proprietor didn't try to compete with the saddlery, the Hampton dining room and Alexander's Hardware Store. His line was drugs, prescriptions and pills. Chewing and smoking tobacco constituted his only digression from type.

"Ain't you got too much distilled water for that much alky?" Webb half asked, half suggested.

"Don't try to tell Uncle Fuller how to make his licker," Pruiett grunted, shaking the quart bottle vigorously under the counter.

"I know damn well you got it too sweet," Webb complained. "You put too much pepsin syrup in it."

Pruiett pulled the cork out and gulped from the neck of the bottle. "If it isn't as good as Manhattan Club I'll drink it all myself," he said, passing the bottle.

"I don't care if the damn jury stays out all night," Doctor Young volunteered, as the bottle was going around the second time.

"I'm going home to supper when this bottle's gone," Pruiett said. "Wait a minute. There's my client comin' in. Hey, Doc. Wanta little drink?"

Tyree leaned on the front counter, staring at the men in the back. There was evil written on his furtive face. He said nothing.

"He might as well be civil; I was not goin' to charge him extra for that," Pruiett muttered. "I think I'll just call his hand. I might as well hear his yelp now as later."

Pruiett marched up to where Tyree was slouching. "What the hell's the matter with you, Doc?" he demanded. "What you so nasty about?"

"You know what's the matter," Tyree retorted, sullenly.

"Get it out of your guts," Pruiett challenged. "If you got a kick to make, let's hear it. I want to keep my record straight."

"You double-crossin' son of a bitch," Tyree cried, "don't try to get wise about it, after you sold me out—."

Tyree grabbed a heavy glass bottle from the nearby case and hurled it at Pruiett's head. Pruiett ducked, and taking the quart liquor bottle, which he had been holding beneath his coat, he smote the doctor squarely between the flaming little eyes. The men who had been standing in the rear of the store rushed between them, but Tyree needed little restraint. The blow had stunned him, and had opened a free-bleeding gash down his forehead.

"What's got the matter with that damn fool?" Pruiett demanded. "Hasn't he got brains enough to understand that nobody besides me's crazy enough to represent him? If he was to kill me he'd have to cut out his permiscious murderin'."

Kimberlin was holding his needle in the flame of the gas light. He didn't want any microbes to interfere with the operation he was preparing to perform.

"What you want to jump Moman for, Doc?" the druggist asked, while he bored suture holes through the tough hide on the injured man's forehead. "Look's to me like he'd be the last one for you to fall out with."

"He made a deal with the government for me to be convicted, this time," Tyree stormed. "He never tried to get me off. He was layin' down all the time he was actin' like he was pleadin' to that jury. But I'll get him before I swing, the dirty sell-out bastard. I'll kill him as—."

"Isn't that gratitude for you?" Pruiett demanded, as he led his crew out into the darkness of Paul Avenue. "A clean outlook like his is almost indispensable in our friendly sociable little world."

The jury reported at ten that night; the Enterprise made brief comment upon its findings in a current issue. "Jury in the F. B. Tyree case returned a verdict of not guilty." There was nothing said about the defendant, with his head swathed in a white bandage, rushing to thank—and apologize to—his counsel. Tyree stalked out of the court room with his ugly lip raised at one corner in an insolent sneer, and a defiant look of hatred in his eye.

"It ain't been six months since old Doc Tyree was acquitted over here, has it?" Sam Garvin inquired.

"I was in the court room when the jury came in," Doctor Young replied. "An' now he's dead. He got tough once too often."

"That Leonard Hyden won't back up for nobody, whether they got a reputation for bein' a killer or not. They say old Doc was shot up somethin' terrible."

"Hyden's a client of Pruiett's," Young said. "I tried to patch Tyree up, but it weren't any use. He was too leaky."

"I guess old Moman's got him another murder case to try," Garvin grinned.

"I'll bet he don't charge Leonard a damn cent for defendin' him in this case."

"You don't suppose,"—?"

"No, I don't suppose," Young supplied, "but I'll bet you a calf he clears him."

"I'll give you a calf if you need it," Garvin laughed, "but I ain't makin' no fool bets. Come over an' see me."

"Things are gettin' in a hell of a shape with me," Pruiett growled. "I'm gettin' stale. Two cases to take to that lousy appeals court, an' I ought to have won 'em both."

"You did win 'em," Garvin's Choctaw princess assured him. "The men can thank you for saving their lives."

Pruiett rocked in the shade and gnawed a chicken bone. "I try 'em to win 'em," he said. "When I get through representin' a man I want to see him go walkin' down Paul Avenue a free man."

"He rolls an' pitches an' tosses all night while these murder cases are goin' on," Leda, Gail's new mother, said. "He makes the child so nervous she can't eat. I want him to get a room at the Hampton, or stay over with Betty an' his paw. It's terrible."

"Your damn joints'll start risin' with a little of that," Garvin predicted. "Take a little time off an' get down to Mineral Wells. Don't try to run the wagon without grease."

"I felt so bad about old Cal Grant dyin' that I got behind with a case or two, an' before I knew it they had slammed hell out of me. They like to have whipped my ears off."

"Cal's counted his last stack of buggy washers," Garvin mused. "He's somewhere where they extend the note ever' time it comes due, an' that's what'll tickle the old banker. He sure hated to crowd a customer."

"Yep," Pruiett agreed. "Instead of collectin', he's payin'; throwin' the gold out to them that needs it. No more mortgages to foreclose. The stockholders won't get to hurt him no more by tellin' him to move a farmer off."

"Sam misses him more'n anybody, even if he tries to be hard an' indifferent," Mrs. Garvin smiled. "I see it, an' I understand it. Calvin was such a nice man."

"We all need a rest—a change," Pruiett declared. "I been handlin' murder an' distress for ever'body, an' my friends an' people have been dyin' on me, 'til I'm gettin' a morbid twist to all my thinkin'."

"That ain't out of the ordinary for you," Garvin interrupted.

"There's a big fair goin' on up Northwest, the Lewis and Clark Exposition, up in Portland, Oregon. I'll pay the expenses, an' the four of us, an' Gail, will take 'er in. What do you think about that?"

"Would you actually take a little time off from your murder cases, if the rest of us would agree to it?" Garvin said.

"I can get away in a week," he replied.

"Say, there's a bright spot for you, clearin' old Buck Garrett."

"Buck's a privileged character," Pruiett said. "He's got a

technique to his killin' that makes it artistic. People don't mind gettin' killed by Buck Garrett."

"They say that there's quite a city up there," Mrs. Garvin said. "A cattle buyer that was out here said it was spreadin' out an' shootin' up. He said it was looking big city-like, like Dallas."

"I gave it a close inspection, for reasons," Pruiett answered. "They got five-an' six-story buildings up already, an' more on the way. I been thinkin' about movin' my practice up there. She's got ever'thing it takes to make a city; railroads, markets, an' rich land. The Kickapoo flats out east of the main settlement are damn near as rich as these river bottoms. They got upland, out west in what they call Mustang section, that's as rich as the bottom. You remember my speech at Hull's Crossing?"

Pruiett said, "Remember what I said about the roses bloomin' in the Valley of the Sharon, an' wealth beyond the wildest dream of avarice, ready to pour into your lap?"

"That's what you said," Garvin agreed.

"I thought about it when I got in that rush up in that town," Pruiett confided. "Maybe I had my lines crossed, an' was goin the wrong way. After I had an eye full of the way business is rushin', an' got pushed around on them nice dry brick sidewalks, with the Indians an' niggers. Jews an' chinks, I says to myself that maybe the Valley isn't the best spot on earth. There's some awful good pickin's, for a good lawyer up there."

"Do we take the vacation trip together?" Garvin interrupted, softly. "Fifty-fifty on the expenses, an' we go up the California coast seein' the scenery an' enjoyin' ourselves. It would help us all."

"Yes," Pruiett said, running greasy fingers through his glossy hair. "Let's go away for awhile an' rest, or maybe give the Old Valley a little rest."

CHAPTER NINE

*Wherein Pruiett finds more business in Washington, and
how he takes the long-flourishing Hamilton Bill from its hock,
through the indirect medium of his censored past, and sees the
promise of statehood dawn again for the despairing territorials.
He hurried home to try the Matlock and Danna murder cases, and
got them acquitted. And how his versatility takes him to a Constitutional Convention, and he sees the subdivision of government,
named "Moman" in his honor, changed to suit the caprice of a
political boss . . . and, wherein, he restates his views on the ills
of the prevailing penal system, and announces his discontent with
the confines of the Valley.*

Early January, 1905, found Pruiett back in Washington. It
was one of his few trips there which did not involve, directly or
indirectly, executive clemency for a convicted criminal, or special
privilege for a political ally. He was lobbying—"creating interest in and good will for"—the Hamilton Bill, which was before
the Congress, and as the territorial residents complained, was staying before it too long. Stopping at the elegant Raleigh, he was
making up the constant deficit in his expense account with con-
tributions from his own purse.

An organization known as the Democratic Executive Committee of the Indian Territory had been gasping an inactive and
useless existence since its sun-dried birth by mishap. Pruiett
grasped it by the ears, and blowing a gust of his own breath into
its failing lungs, gave it a figurative boot with a substantial cash
contribution and the presence of his own vigorous person. The
Committee sent him as a delegate to promote action at the Capitol.
George Barefoot, lawyer and land man of Chickasha, west of the
Valley, accompanied him as a delegate.

'I see the Oklahoma outlaw is back in town," Senator Beveridge observed over his evening paper.

"How's that?" his companion across the table inquired. It
was Senator Culberson. The senators were dining at the Willard.

"Pruiett," said Beveridge, "and he's still getting that front
page. How does he keep doing it?"

"He's just as smart as hell," Culberson smiled. "What's he
doing now?"

Beveridge began to read: "The people of the Indian Territory are as a unit in favoring the Hamilton Statehood Bill, said Judge Moman Pruiett of Pauls Valley, who is in the city . . ."

"The press boys didn't call him judge the first time he was here; the time he jumped on the Attorney General, and tried to whip him in his own office. So it's judge now?"

". . . The action of some senators on this question passes all understanding," the senator continued reading. "Just why they will get up and talk and talk and talk for months at a time, day in and day out, about the Philippines, and Filippinos, and about Panama and other foreign matters and things, when there are 700,000 patriotic American citizens in the Indian Territory, who are clamoring for admission as a state in the Union is beyond my ken."

"Sounds like he's talking about me," said Culberson. "I hope the judge's in a better humor when I run into him. He's got his fire hot over something."

Beveridge kept reading: "Just what the Republicans will eventually do I cannot guess. But I am shocked and surprised that a large number of Democratic Senators, comparatively speaking, are opposing a law to admit Oklahoma and Indian Territory into the galaxy of the states. Of course, we will not guarantee that the new state will be either Democratic or Republican, but the congressman who will let this fact stand in the way of 700,000 citizens enjoying those privileges which are theirs by divine right, is a demagogue, and nothing more."

They both laughed as Beveridge concluded. "He's got your number, as sure as hell," he agreed. "If he really knew how you and Bailey were blocking him, with your stupid plan to have two states out of the territories instead of one, so that you could have four senators out of it instead of two, he'd have you impeached. But how does he get so loud, all of a sudden?"

"Pruiett's quite a big man in the territory, now. I've watched him pretty close since, well, it's been five years that he was here in the Bias case. Five years; maybe a little more. He's had a lot of success as a criminal lawyer, and he's made a lot of money." Culberson was talking earnestly. "That's all it takes to upset an otherwise sensible young man, and turn him into politics, and that's all that's the matter with Mister Pruiett. The Bias case made copy out of him, so all he has to do is call in a reporter and go to popping off. Judge! Judge Pruiett! Jesus Christ!"

"Does he want to come to congress, or the senate?" Beveridge inquired.

"No," Culberson answered, "he doesn't want an office for himself; he wants it for someone else. He's smart enough to see that statehood for the territories can't be stalled much longer. He's picked himself a man to be the first governor, and he's giving him a lòt of backing. Guess he's got ideas like some of your friends, and mine. Wants a few quiet contracts, and a pardon or two."

Beveridge took a quick drink. "He can make more damn noise up here than any other rube I ever saw," he said. "He's got a knack for that. He ought to get the governorship for himself. Who's the man he thinks can win?"

"Cruce," the Texas senator said. "Lee Cruce. I got a letter from Pruiett about him not so long ago. Pruiett says he's a natural, a regular Abraham Lincoln. You know how the boy is, gets worked up and excited in a hurry. He said Cruce was just as honest as old Abe, and even looked like him. He's a banker—but Pruiett insisted he's honest in spite of that. He's a friend of a lot of lawyer friends of Pruiett's."

"He jumps on the United States Senate like he was making a speech to a cow-hand jury," Beveridge grinned.

"Who's got more right to cuss the Senate than Pruiett?" Culberson demanded. "If the track's open at Havre, Ollie James has to have him go down there, an' get drunk. You and I will get him drunk out at Cabin John's if we can get him there, just to hear him tell those wild stories. Remember how he could tell about the holler of the screech owl? And down at Marlborough, with John Sharp Williams, and Mark Goodwin. He told me he put old Ollie under the table by swallowing a square of butter between drinks; that the grease pad kept the fumes from coming up to his head and making him drunk. He ought to have a hell of a lot of respect for the senate, all right."

"I'd like to see the little devil," Beveridge said. "If you run into him, and get a chance, bring him around."

Culberson had laid his napkin on the table and was standing. "Here he is now, speaking of the devil. He must have spotted us from the outside."

"Howdy, Governor," Pruiett hailed. "Still careless, I notice, in who you eat with." He was shaking hands, in turn, with the Indiana senator.

"Carrying your own copy around?" Beveridge inquired, nodding toward the bundle of newspapers Pruiett was holding under his arm.

"Hell, yes," he replied promptly. "They sent me up here to make some noise, and I want 'em to know they're gettin' their money's worth. I'm puttin' a big circle around the stuff I got printed today, an' mailin' these copies back to the Valley. Can I eat with you?"

"Pull up a chair," said Beveridge.

"Now look here," Pruiett began, as he was seated and had his elbows planted on the linen, "you two are doin' more to block statehood for us than any other two in Washington. I'm glad I found you together. It won't take me long to show you how wrong you are, and get you straightened—."

"Take yourself a drink," Beveridge invited, waving the bottle. Pruiett paused long enough to accept.

"You got to get right," he continued. "Republicanism is not goin' to benefit from this stallin'. It's goin' to be injured. Look at the national revenue goin' to waste, the difference between what these little old territorial agencies produce and what it costs to operate 'em. Another state, greater national strength, another star in the flag. Hell! Just think about it."

"Play the Star Spangled Banner and I'll stand up for you," Beveridge agreed. "You sound like a Fourth of July speaker. Take another drink."

Pruiett complied. "An' what the hell's the matter with you, Governor?" he said, turning to Culberson. "Here I been writin' you all these letters, an' tellin' you what we want down there, an' why we want it, an' what do I get? A lot of talk that don't say yes or no; just somethin' to put in a free-postage envelope. If you're against us, say so. I been tellin' them nesters you're the right kind of folks; that you'll get us a vote on this damn draggin' bill, and put it over for us. An' what's the fact? You're lined up with a bunch of damned Republicans; playin' right into their hands. They're against any kind of expansion unless it's guaranteed blue-belly. You help 'em out by tryin' to be a hog. Two poor states, beggin' an' scrapin', instead of one rich an' powerful one, just for two more Democrat senators. Ain't that a hell of a note?"

"What did I tell you?" Culberson winked at Beveridge. "Didn't I say the judge would give me hell as soon as he caught me? Say, where do they get that Judge stuff? Gettin' pretty classy, aren't you? Let's all take another drink."

Culberson's pride in Pruiett, and Pruiett's love for Culberson couldn't be concealed under sarcastic banter or affected discontent. "It's like this, son," Culberson continued, "I been in this business a long time. You're all right, you're smart as a tack, and I'll go to the floor with any man that says you're not, but look at it my way. Us good Democrats are in a miserable minority. We got to take what the blue-bellies, as you call 'em, leave over. Northerners. Aristocrats. Federalists, like that evil lookin' one across the table. We need numbers to combat 'em, and by God, let's have more southwestern states. Let's even up—."

"If your plan's so damn practical, let's partition Texas," Pruiett interrupted. Beveridge began to laugh; Culberson squirmed. "Wouldn't take any more than a constitutional amendment, maybe just a bill through congress, an' if it's started, I'd bet my last dollar it'll pass. Ever' one in the country says you're too rich and powerful—just plain too big. Divide it up into six or eight, maybe ten, states, and give each state two votes in the Senate. That way you'd—."

"I got a good notion to give that to the press," Beveridge said as he laughed. "Mark me a bunch of copies an' mail 'em to Texas. I think I'll introduce a bill on—."

"Now, look here, boys," Culberson insisted, "that's different. Why, Texas—."

"A third of the folks in the territory is from Texas," Pruiett said, "an' you won't find a single one of 'em, Oklahoma Territory or any of the Indian Nations, that won't fight over this two state idea of yours an' Joe Bailey's. They all say you're traitors, linin' up with the blue-bellies like you have. Try to divide Texas, an' look at the fight you've got. Try to divide the Oklahomas, an' you'll have just as tough a time."

"He's got you, Charley," Beveridge cut in. "Might as well shut up. Take a drink and admit you're licked in debate."

Pruiett's eyes were shining. "Take it all together," he said, "an' it's a great country. The Washita bottoms are as rich as your Trinity black land, or the Brazos bottoms, either. An' the songs you sing about your Wabash don't make it any richer, or any sweeter, Senator Beveridge than that crooked, muddy stream through the Chickasaw Nation. Minerals, livestock, agriculture, and men. We got some real men down there. Wait till you see Lee Cruce, an' hear him. He's goin' to be the first governor, and by God—."

Culberson reached out and patted the clenched fist which was pounding the white table. "All right, son," he said, "I won't be the one to stand in your way. You can count on me. Do you hear

that, Beveridge? We call this damn thing off. The Hamilton Bill
goes on through."

"I hear you," laughed Beveridge. "I hate to see it go over, but
I see the fix you're in. I'll call off the blue-bellies."

Pruiett swayed to his feet. His bristling black mane looked
purple in the bright dining-room light. "To Oklahoma! To the
State of Oklahoma," he said. "One great commonwealth, with the
fairest portion of nature's vast domain intact; with the blood
of the red and white mingling in the honorable institution of marriage; with the wealthiest and healthiest race of people of all the
states of the Union."

Pruiett left the rest to the Texas senator and hurried back
to Pauls Valley. He had the Matlock and Danna cases to try
there, and word from the office had convinced him that the
effort of his associates, to acquire another continuance because
of his absence in the Capital, was not going to be successful.
The defendants, Alex Matlock and Dan Danna, had been arrested
and charged with the murder of Robert L. Price, almost six
years before. They had been tried once, but the jury hadn't been
able to agree, and every conceivable device for delay had been
successfully employed since that one trial. The Federal Judge was
determined to stop at least a part of the procrastination, and he expressed his determination in such terms that Pruiett received an
urgent wire in Washington. He hurried home.

"The well known and even noted case of the United States
against Alex Matlock and Dan Danna was tried this week and
resulted in an acquittal of the defendants. In 1900 Bob Price was
shot down at his own house at Table Mountain, and said to have
been robbed. There was nobody present but his wife, Belle Price,
who has since married. The conjectures and suspicions as to
who did the deed were many and various. . . . But one thing is
settled, Alex Matlock and Dan Danna were not the men, as the
jury said. . . . As a fact, on the Saturday night of the killing
they were 30 miles away, at Lexington, Oklahoma, as was proved
by several witnesses. . . . A confusing thing in the investigation
was the different description of the murderers by Mrs. Price,
made at different times . . ."

Pruiett read the account with a smile. He could see and
appreciate the uncultivated irony of the hack of that country
paper, who was telling the populace in a nice way that the defendants were secure in their alibi because Pruiett's defense witnesses

said so, and for no other reason. He smiled again at the reference
to Mrs. Price's miserable attempt at identification in the second
trial. He wondered if the writer of the article knew, as he did,
how the lonely and destitute Mrs. Price, after the expiration of
her unfortunate first mate, had married a man under undying
obligation to Pruiett, and how things had brightened about their
humble cabin, in the material way, by her tendency to be utterly
at loss as to faces, on the witness stand.

"The case had in it many peculiar circumstances. It was
presented by U. S. Attorney G. W. Walker, recently appointed, in
a dignified speech . . ." (Bill Johnson, who had lost out with a
shift in the political lineup, had never received such a favorable
notice on his vicious and venomous courtroom attacks, although
his more undignified manner had obtained an occasional conviction.) ". . . and by J. E. Humphreys, First Assistant U. S.
Attorney, who represented and pressed with all his zeal and ability.
The defendants were represented by J. B. Thompson and Moman
Pruiett. Mr. Thompson was not well . . . Moman Pruiett was
at his best and fully grasping the situation, pressed every argument home with his fiery, rugged oratory. It was a great victory
for the defense . . ."

The Chickasaw Nation's proudest contribution to the Oklahoma Constitutional Convention, when it convened at Guthrie,
Oklahoma Territory, on November 20, 1906, was William H.
"Alfalfa William," "Bolivia Bill," "Cockle-burr Bill," Murray.
His occasional contact with the complete library which he kept
'neath the shelter of his log hovel and the frequent expostulations
of what he had gleaned thereby, from the curb in front of
the Indian Courthouse at Tishomingo, had earned him the additional title of "The Sage of Tishomingo." Murray was never
reluctant to exercise the stentorian, fog-horn vocal equipment he
had been endowed with, and it was as much his manner, as much
as what he said, that appealed to the Indians and poor whites.

Pruiett and Murray were bitter enemies, with Pruiett, in
his frequent moments of indiscretion, swearing to "kill Bill
Murray on sight." Murray had referred to him as an "ex-convict"
while delivering a speech from the shallow curb at Maysville,
in a panic-stricken attempt to stop Pruiett's rapidly rising political popularity, which began with his issue of the "Call to
Arms" letter.

Murray's frank observation put Pruiett back to his pen, for
the creation and publication of an epistle which attracted more

comment than the "Call to Arms" letter. The original was registered to Alfalfa Bill. Two hundred thousand copies printed fac-
similies were distributed over the territories and the Indian Na
tions.

"Wm. H. Murray, Esq., Tishomingo," he began. "Sir—In
a speech delivered by you at Maysville some time ago, you took
occasion to speak of me as an ex-convict. For the purpose of
this campaign, my personality, of the past or of the present, is
of no interest to any one. I am not a candidate for public office.
I am supporting for Governor, however, a man who is, in every
respect, mentally, morally, humanely and otherwise, your superior.

"You are a candidate for the office of Governor of this
state, an office which requires much honor, and which should be
filled by a man whose home life and whose treatment of his
family is an example to all the good people of this state. It is
not to be recalled by any one who knows you that your family
life is exemplary, or ever was. Although you are the father
of several children, the bringing into the world of each one has
brought you, coincidentally, some three hundred acres, making
you today master of some seventeen hundred acres of land. (Murray had an Indian wife.) It is not to be recalled that you ever
displayed any great characteristic of affection toward your family
except when you could use your wife or children for political
purposes, as, for instance, when you had your family photographed
barefooted, for the political effect."

The theme then lapsed into a retrospect of Murray's ulterior
motives in sponsoring the "grandfather clause" in the Oklahoma
Constitutional Convention, in helping a Washington firm of lawyers to bilk the Chickasaws during the operation of the Dawes
Commission, and in fixing the election of the Chickasaw governor
in 1902.

". . . . Notwithstanding you, as the first and original ballot
mutilator of this section of the country, had perpetrated a crime
so obnoxious," he continued in the letter, "to every one and
everything decent, still you have the effrontery to charge me, because of a misfortune in my youth, with being an ex-convict. You
certainly must be in a bad way for campaign material, and you
must be forgetful of every sparkle of manhood that is supposed
to exist, even in a man of your character, when you attempt,
in your desire to attain public office, to bring misery to innocent
people.

". . . . You have lied about and villified every man who had

the temerity to disagree with you politically or otherwise. You
have so taken on, politically speaking, the 'Holier than Thou'
character, that at times in your madness, you have shown actual signs of incipient imbecility. With the honors that the people
of this state have heretofore given you, why don't you stand up
like a man and fight your battles fairly, treat all men honestly,
speak of all men properly, and at least be honest with yourself."

". . . I have my weaknesses. So have you—and many of
them. I have erred often. I have been abused and maligned,
but 'In the fell clutch of circumstance, I have not winced nor
cried aloud. Under the bludgeoning of chance my head is bloody,
but unbowed. Beyond this vale of wrath and tears lie but the
horror of the shade; and yet the menace of the years finds, and
shall find me, unafraid.'

"I have tried to help many a man politically. I have done
what I could for my friends, but I have never sought to advance
their interests by bringing down upon the heads of innocent
women and children the burden of brutal sorrow or by picking
out one of my fellow citizens and attempting to besmirch his
good name by resurrecting from the smouldering ashes of the
past, what was, at the worst, a simple youth's misfortune.

". . . . In your rush for political preferment, have you entirely forgotten your manhood? Are you to prove yourself a man
utterly unworthy, utterly insensitive, without character—without
one single sympathetic trait? Have you lost all decency—all pride?
Is your self-respect dead? Has it died in an agony of indecision
and self-reproach? Has it died, struggling in tortured resurrection
—beaten to its knees—lying prone—heedless, insensible to the
alarms of honor, duty and self-respect? I hate to think of a man
seeking the greatest office the people of this state can give, as
profligate in his brutality of speech as you are—passing from
dread of defeat to anger—enduring the ceaseless need of a fair
mind and clean conscience, but never to suffer even the shadow
of their contact; a man who has forgotten the words of the
Master when He said, 'Let him who is without sin cast the first
stone.'

"What manner of ambition is yours, with its birth not in
noble things—not in things of mind—but its beginning, its origin
in everything profane and debasing—founded on nothing—nur-
tured on nothing except your self-conceit and arrogant abuse of
others? . . . If you are an honest man, not entirely devoid of
manhood in its better sense, you will not let this letter pass un-

noticed. If what I have said is true, you will acquiesce by your silence. If it is not true, you will resent it in some way at the very first opportunity. In either event, your silence or your resentment will be synonymous—the last expiring hiss of a bruised and dying political serpent."

Murray was elected President of the Constitutional Convention, which success was all that was needed to render the well salved and greased ego hard to stop. He appointed his committees with an obvious intent of insuring his nomination to the governorship, more than for the efficient accomplishment of the business which the populace was so anxious to have done and accomplished. Word went out with the elevation that Murray should be President of the United States.

Pruiett writhed in agony and distress when he read of Murray's success at the convention, and that with the governorship in his grasp, he was talking himself for the national ticket. The law office was closed; Moman went to the convention. Murder trials had to wait. What he had up in the way of cash on a winner for governor, was secondary to the utter contempt he had for Bill Murray. He went as "a special delegate" representing the Democratic Executive Committee. He declared that the committee had authorized him to lobby at the convention, to see that the fundamental principles of the party were not disregarded in the formulation of the new constitution. As he was the committee, he went self-appointed, and as there was no provision in the enabling act for a special delegate, he was without official authority.

But Pruiett didn't need official authority. His presence, his personality and his force, was authority personified, and the vital issues of the meeting were met, fouled and delayed, as the fiery and oratorical lawyer required, or alternately demanded, that they should be. The local press noted and failed to understand his unofficial influence.

"Moman Pruiett seems to be cutting quite a high dash in the convention, but as he has no connection with it whatever, it is hard to understand why this is. He was allowed to name a new county, and it is the only one that has a Republican name. He was also mixed up in a bribery charge. Isn't he the same Pruiett that used to live at Hackett City, Arkansas? Then whence comes this high flying?"

He read the article and gnashed his teeth. It was the same Pruiett. It was the kid who had blacked the boots at Fayetteville,

and who rode atop the splintery lumber of the wagon truck as he
followed a struggling mother's direction that he go to Fort
Smith and hear the imported Voorhees. It was the same one,
but that wasn't what they were getting at. It was the trail of the
serpent. He thrust out his blunt jaw and glared with venomous
hate. The damned cowards would never let it die.

The delegates were permitted to select a name for a county in
the new state. Pruiett has been accorded the honor, despite his
rather unofficial status, because of what he had accomplished in
Washington. They named it Moman County.

The man whom Pruiett feared and respected, politically, was
Charley Haskell. He had transferred his expansive personality
and extensive financial backing from his native and over-developed
Ohio Valley, to the town of Muskogee, in the Creek Nation. He
was a railroad builder, from which he earned the enduring sobri-
quet of "Railroad" Haskell. While he kept the eastern speculators satisfied with his profitable promotion and development of
the Frisco lines, he formed and developed, for his own use and
benefit, the Midland Valley Railway Company. His intellect and
foresight was much like Pruiett's. He could carry two tunes
at the same time.

But Pruiett liked to stand up and exercise his eloquence; to
proclaim to all his natural brilliance. Haskell kept his mouth
shut. While the other fellow was talking, he was working, and
scheming. A masterful organizer and a wizard at anticipating
the processes of his opponents. Murray and Cruce divided the
majority. Haskell quietly took up the balance, and gathered enough
from the two deadlocked factions to have a passing majority
on hand for every issue.

"Charges of graft were carried into the county boundaries
committee today," stated the Kansas City Journal in a current
issue. "Moman Pruiett, a prominent member of the Democratic
Executive Committee, was accused before the county committee
with favoring Sapulpa for the county seat of Moman County
for an alleged consideration of $1,000. Pruiett heard of this
and appeared before the committee. He denied the charge as absolutely false, and presented a counter charge that a prominent
citizen of Bristow had offered him $5,000 to use his influence to
make Bristow the county seat."

The sponsorship of Moman County was adroitly dissevered
from its namesake, as was its good name, and by official act of

the convention the name was changed to Creek, in memory of the extra-dark aborigines who peopled the shallow soil of its hillsides.

Haskell called for a showdown, and when one called for that with Pruiett, he got it. Haskell was unquestionably stronger in the convention than President Murray, but the margin was not sufficiently wide to permit him to go about without apprehension. The calm of the Cruce group was baffling him. Pruiett acknowledged that he was for Cruce until the last, bar one contingency, and that was the probability of a Murray nomination. Then he was for Haskell.

The railroader advanced a plan of coalition, with the Cruce group behind him for governor and the united strength of the two behind Cruce for United States Senator. Pruiett considered it and submitted it to the Cruce brothers by telegram. He would have liked to see his candidate in the senate, and he knew such a maneuver would insure the defeat of Murray. But the Cruces couldn't be compromised; Pruiett stuck with his guns. Haskell gave his advance notice that he would be sorry. It was open warfare thenceforward, and regardless of the advantage, it was the kind of a fight that Pruiett most enjoyed.

The Wichita Eagle's special representative was quick to perceive and relish the first of what promised to be real activity. ". . . . The manner in which the Cruce contingent of the Democratic party took 'Railroad' Haskell by the seat of the trousers and threw him out of the executive committee meeting at Tulsa, last Tuesday, is still the principal topic of discussion among politicians gathered at the hotel of this city. . . . It develops here today that prior to the meeting at Tulsa, 'Santa Fe' Thompson, of the executive committee, was rather inclined to give Haskell a chance to speak before the committee, but Moman Pruiett went to him on Tuesday last and told him emphatically that if he permitted Haskell to appear before the committee his own political head would be laid on the chopping block. . . . The threat had the desired result, and . . . . the committee went into executive session for the express purpose of keeping Haskell out."

Current sequel installments of the story appeared rapidly. "'Now just for that, Mr. Moman Pruiett, you shan't have any counties in the new state of Oklahoma named after you,' is what 'Railroad' Haskell is stated to have said this morning, when he got revenge on Pruiett for the latter's work against him at the Tulsa meeting of the Democratic Committee . . . Moman County was changed to Creek County as a rebuke to the Pauls Valley Statesman for having opposed the candidacy of 'Railroad' Haskell for Governor.   Silently, but most impressively, Haskell's henchmen in the constitutional convention assented to the decree of their boss, and the change from Moman to Creek went through in easy fashion. . . . At a meeting in Tulsa several weeks ago Pruiett made Haskell look like the proverbial thirty cents. . . . and naturally, he made a solemn vow to get 'even.' The opportunity came today, and when Pruiett wasn't looking he got a heavy swat in an unspeakable portion of his anatomy. Reports reached here this afternoon that Pruiett is on a rampage."

Thus Pruiett saw the monument to the name he had founded and given himself, set up and tumbled down. The right to allocate the seat of government went winging with it. For once, the local press took up the Pruiett cause, and the petty-fogging tactics of Haskell and his efficient majority were broadcast and censored.

The St. Louis Globe Democrat was matter-of-fact about it. ". . . The convention also voted to change the name of Moman county to Creek, in honor of the Creek tribe of Indians. The county was named originally for Moman Pruiett, a democratic politician, who recently bolted Delegate Haskell, democratic floor leader, in his candidacy for governor, and this changing of names was intended as a rebuke to Pruiett."

The Muskogee Phoenix, principal publication of Haskell's home town, was less prosaic, and editorially it berated the favorite son's tactics. "Moman county has been changed to Creek county. Moman Pruiett after whom it was first named became an active Cruce supporter, and this evidently did not suit the machine that made and named the counties, and in order to impress on the country at large the fact that they are statesmen duly impressed with the solemnity of their duty in writing a constitution for a great state, the delegates to the convention, under the lead of the machine, takes this method of administering a personal rebuke to one having the hardihood to oppose its boss for governor."

"Henceforth it will be Creek County. Moman has been completely wiped off the map because he has been an impudent little boy." Thus another territorial organ referred to the farce.

"He didn't fall into line at the crack of the master's whip, so the master proceeded to crack his southern extremities with the aforesaid whip."

All good things must have their endings. "At the adjourning

of the convention Haskell and Murray shed tears, and delegates Pruiett and Henshaw had a fist fight in the Royal hotel bar, thus furnishing the blood to complete the sentiment and spirit of the fiasco. Tears and blood! Blood and tears! O tempore! O molasses! O heck!"

Oklahoma was admitted as a state. Cruce was defeated in his race for the governorship, but Pruiett wasn't crestfallen. Bill Murray didn't beat him; it was "Railroad" Haskell, and he and Pruiett talked the same language. Hadn't Pruiett labored in the ditches of the railroad Haskell had promoted through Arkansas? The bonds of understanding between Pruiett and the governor were like those between Pruiett and Senator Culberson. They could sit down and talk—and reason.

"Among the democrats to call on Mr. Haskell during the evening was Moman Pruiett, of Pauls Valley, a delegate to the constitutional convention and whom Haskell's paper, the New State Tribune, recently characterized as 'an ex-convict and moral and mental pervert.'" Pruiett had raised hell with Bill Murray for less, but Haskell had slipped into the governor's job while no one was looking. Pardons and contracts were going to come from that source. Pruiett paid him a sociable call.

Pruiett was back in the Valley with his murder business, but something was amiss. The musty mists which arose from the Washita sloughs in the morning, to pick up the aroma of the alfalfa bloom and clover and carry it up past the house amongst the pecan trees, were not as sweet as they had been in those years before. The whistle of the quail from the field just beyond his fence annoyed him. He sat in his office alone, brooding and pondering in a morbid reverie.

"What's the matter with you, son?" Sam Garvin inquired, as he sat beside his desk and placed a boot amongst the litter of papers across its top. "You been acting kind of peevish here lately. Ain't you well?"

"Yeah, I'm all right—just a little tired, maybe," he answered, "but I'll be all right. Got a hell of a lot of work to do."

"You've had as much ever since you come to the Valley an' it ain't never made you act this way; not even when your joints swelled up. Why don't you try it over at Hot Springs, or down to Mineral Wells?"

"I been foolin' around too much. I'm way behind with my work. I can't be runnin' off ever' time I get a belly-ache."

"The belly-ache don't make a man look like you been lookin' here lately. You been goin' down for a year. Take my advice an' see a good doctor. Ask old Doc Young what's ailin' you."

"Colonel," Pruiett inquired, earnestly, "don't you ever get tired of this damn place? Two trains a day, bum food, mosquitoes as big as grasshoppers, and mud? Sticky mud on your feet all the time? Don't you get disgusted, an' just not give a damn?"

Garvin studied. "You're gettin' too big for the Valley; is that it?"

"Well, it's not that—exactly," Pruiett hesitated. "Hell, no, I am not too big, but I don't seem to be doin' anything but stand still—."

"You're a liar," Garvin interrupted. "You think you've outgrown this place, an' I do too. With me, it's different. When I fall out with the Valley, it's gonna be because there's too many trains; too many people; not enough open acres for runnin' the cattle. You're a lawyer. I'm a stock raiser. When a country is ideal for me, it's wrong for you. The boom's over here an' we're settled down to holdin' on to what we grabbed during the free settlement period. If you don't get out your're a dam fool."

"I don't want you to think I'm gettin' too good—."

"I won't," Garvin replied simply, "and neither will anyone else with any sense. Don't apologize—just git up and git."

"I think I'd feel better if I did," Pruiett said. "I got Oklahoma City in mind. That's a hell of a town; they got some fast promoters up there. If she don't spread out—if there is not a lot of money goin' around up there I'm badly mistaken."

"What you goin' to do with your stuff down here, the farms an' stuff, an' all the stock? Have a sale?"

"When I pull out, I pull out. I shake the dust off, and scrape the mud off, too," Pruiett said. "I'll sell as fast as I can, 'til it's all gone; that is, all but one piece. The little square lot I own south of town, I'll keep. It'll keep bringin' me back, and prevent my stayin' long, after I come back. The memories are mostly what's makin' me want to leave here."

"How long's Lilly Belle been dead?" Garvin asked. "Been nearly four years, ain't it?"

"Four years," Pruiett replied. "Been a lot happen to me in four years. My baby boy dead; layin' out there with his mother. Say. Did you see the shaft I put up over their graves?"

"Yes, son, I saw it," Garvin said. "I thought it was kinda

flashy for the Valley. We ain't used to that sort of thing down here, even by the ones that can afford it."

"I paid three thousand for it—cash," Pruiett said. "An' I felt a little ashamed, for bein' so cheap. She was a wonderful woman, Colonel."

"I guess it's all right, if you can afford it. The only trouble is it makes neighbors envious; makes 'em distrust you. You ain't supposed to have all the money in the country, you know, even if you are a good lawyer."

"I got it off your friend, Matt Wolfe," Pruiett laughed. "An' you did your best to keep me from makin' it. Like I told you, I had to win that Ashton case to make a profit."

"We're talkin' serious, now, son, and let me tell you somethin'. We was both wrong in the Sam Ashton case. Fixin' juries is like burnin' your own barn; you usually don't cause nobody harm but yourself. I brought you here, an' I don't blame you much for bein' kinda radical in your views. But when you leave here, don't take crooked money. Don't let the crooks capitalize on the wonderful talent you've got. Stay with Lee Cruce, and the things he stands for, like you been doin' this last year, an' you'll do a heap better than you will workin' for murderers like Sam Ashton, and crooks like Matt Wolfe."

"You've been my friend, Colonel, the best one I ever had, I guess, except Judge Bryant, or I wouldn't tell you what I'm thinkin'," Pruiett said. His face was flushed, and there was a hard look in his eye. "The way I feel right now, I don't care whether I ever try another damned lawsuit in my life, or not, but if I stay in it, it'll be for the poor devil that the law is pushin' around. We elect a punk lawyer to a public prosecutor's job an' he thinks he's a damned king. He'll cut ever' corner an' fudge ever' shot, just to convict. He does it to satisfy his own vanity, and dangerous ambition, not to see that justice is done. An' the damned courts help 'em do it. They drink an' play, an' louse together. An' they send innocent men into hell on earth, just to be able to say they won their case."

"I've heard you say that before, son," the old man replied, "but you're wrong. No system is perfect, much less one that ain't been tried no longer than this one we've got; but you got to have law an' order. You got to protect your home, your property an' your kids, from murderers like Sam Ashton. How'd you feel, actually, after they turned that one aloose?"

"I slept like a possum," Pruiett said. "Never had no conscientious scruples about the conduct of the case whatever. How would you have felt if they'd a convicted him and sentenced him to hang?"

"Hell," said Garvin. "that man was guilty. He needed to be convicted. Ever' one knew he was guilty."

"Then what did you want to put a sinker on the jury for? If he was so damn guilty as that, an' our system's so good, was it right for you to butt in, and make sure of his hangin'?"

"No, it wasn't right," Garvin answered. "It wasn't right, but that's what I'm tellin' you. I ain't makin' no excuses. You caught me, but the reason I fixed John Webb was because I knew you was up to somethin'. I never did find out what it was."

"Well," said Pruiett, "I'll just tell you."

"No man on God A'mighty's earth could fix Squire Adkins," Garvin protested.

"Maybe no man could, but a damned woman could," Pruiett chuckled. He was amused at Garvin's complete discomfort. "That little widow was Sam's half-sister, an' she was workin' for Sam in that case."

"I couldn't compliment you on your tactics, even if I believed you," Garvin sniffed. "The old man didn't know it, even if he was fixed."

"Now you've got my point," Pruiett said, rising and walking around beside Garvin. He put his arm about him and patted his shoulder affectionately. "Juries are moved by personal feelings, likes and dislikes, little things that don't have a damn thing to do with guilt or innocence of the one accused. The pens are full of men that were stuck because the jury didn't like the way his lawyer parted his hair, or didn't like the color of his necktie. They fall out with a witness; maybe it's his religion, maybe he made eyes at his wife sometime years ago. So to satisfy his small feelin' he uses his power; he convicts the man in the bull pen. I take a chance on the humane side. If I can get 'em acquitted, society isn't hurt much, even if there is a mistake made. But if it's on your side, an' the one convicted happens to be innocent, then society couldn't straighten it up at all, not if it could mortgage eternity."

CHAPTER TEN

Wherein Pruiett abandons the Valley and attempts to abandon a portion of his criminal law practice, but is catapulted back into its maelstrom by his brilliance in the reluctant defense of a certain Rudolph Tegeler. And how he tips the scales in a difficult non-murder case by well calculated phychological maneuver, and delivers, along with the deliverance of his client from the clutches of the law, District Judge W. N. Maben, a fatal blow to the gubernatorial aspirations of a favorably considered little Attorney General, and, wherein he lends his efforts to a policeman, Crow, who is charged with murder, and acquires his acquittal with little, if any, evidence of justification, pleading confusional insanity.

Introducing Pruiett to speak at a statehood banquet, Chief Justice Monroe Osborn of the Oklahoma Supreme Court observed that "the history of the Sooner State would be incomplete without the life story of Moman Pruiett." The story of his life progressed with the story of the commonwealth, and changed with the changes which came with the dissolution of the Indian Nations and the gradual removal of the customs of the last frontier.

In a remarkably short comparative period the rough pioneer manners had disappeared. The frontier lawyers were gone. P. Watt Hardin had been dead so long that the substance from his mouldering carcass no longer aided the unproductive soil which strove to push a wild flower in the shade of the stone on his grave. Dan Voorhees, the Tall Sycamore of the Wabash, was but a vague, pleasant recollection. The barrister of the boots and pistols was gone. The ones of the frocktailed coats and spoonderbies, who chewed their straight cheroots as they poignantly watched the turning century take all the color that had been theirs from them, had wheeled into the limbo of change and progress. A new type was rapidly assuming their place in the unsettled plan of sectional affairs.

The more sedate practitioners, who winced at the mention of pistol-toting Morton Rutherford or a reference to the peremptory justime of hanging Isaac Parker, were hurrying to their fifth- and sixth-story offices on the jolting and racing trolleys. The free lands were taken up. The runs and land lotteries were over, and their turbulent aftermaths of gunplay and bloodshed had diminished with the gradual regulation of a more pacific populace.

The railroad lawyers, the corporation lawyers, were illustrating to the old school's rough and ready membership that the day of specialization was fast aproaching. Instead of a perfunctory execution or two at the beginning of a boundary dispute, followed as in the old days by a homicide prosecution, the claimants went to court in the beginning in a civil lawsuit, and two groups of lawyers, instead of one, had employment, activity—and emolument.

Pruiett, an old-timer at thirty-five, was definitely not ready for the discard. With the same effortless ease which attended his graduation from the ranks of the lowly to the roster of the Texas bar, he stepped from the shell of his old identity and assumed the most prominent place in the new order of things. As the pioneer's dugout on a windswept prairie grew into a neat and comfortable bungalow, or the commercial institution which opened tent-flaps to trade in its beginning blossomed into a towering building in a metropolitan city, Pruiett grew and developed with the growing commonwealth.

When the more decorous practice required him to discard the shoe-string tie of the cow-country court for the more ornate four-in-hand, he did it without the loss of his innate ease. When the boots had to be replaced by the more conservative buttoned shoes, and the brim of the hat had to be curtailed to conform to the more sedate headgear of the new period, he made the change with a natural grace. When the gradual metamorphosis was complete, the result was the same. He was a masterful and commanding individual, holding, in the new system, the same superior position he had held in the old.

While his manners changed with the requirements of the customs, and were in a sense modulated and toned down, the fierce, smoldering viciousness which had its inception in dungeon cell suffering and physical privation and hardship could not be eradicated. The billowing black brush of hair crowning his shaggy brow was the same—flashing, bristling, and forbidding. Until the fingers of the frost of years began to touch it, and streak it with fern-leaf, glaring white in contrast to its original blackness, no style, craze, custom or regulation could convert or disguise it.

Upstairs over the Florida Bar, on Main Street in Oklahoma City, Pruiett, Lawyer, held forth. A block to the east the Santa Fe, between regular runs, backed and shifted its strings of cars. A block to the north the Choctaw, Oklahoma & Gulf pulled and backed its rumbling trains. To the south, one block, the Bucket of Blood was gasping and clotting. The new constitution had dried the territory. String bands and piano players and dancing girls and free lunch counters couldn't be supported on the revenue brought in by soft drinks and near-beer. The Florida Bar was on the down trail, too.

Progress, and refinement, were discernible in the Pruiett office. Brass cuspidors, girdled in the middle, with wide bottoms and mouths, had supplanted the rusty coffee cans. There was carpet on the floor and a picture, in variations of brown, on the pink calcimined wall. His old table had been replaced by an oak desk with a roll top standing back above pigeon-holes stuffed with a disarray of stained papers. There were traces of brown expectoration in the corners and along the base-boards.

"I'm tryin' to thin out my murder practice," he said. His feet, as usual, were atop his desk. "I'm gettin' to the place where I got to think of my family, an' try to lay up more cash."

His caller was Dan B. Welty, one of his principal competitors for local law business. "You haven't any more chance of gettin' away from defendin' criminal cases than the wagon yard has of gettin' away from the manure pile out behind," Welty said. "You belong in a murder case."

"I been gettin' a good run of civil practice since the constitutional convention," Pruiett argued. "I just had to take that Jim Stephenson case. I'm attorney for the family. That was as tough a murder case as I ever got into, an' I've had some bad ones in my time."

"It was the worst one I ever heard of," Welty agreed, " 'an that's why my clients insist that I take you in to help me try this one."

"Jim Stephenson was the brother of John Stephenson, my client in the Valley," Pruiett explained. "Jake Hodges an' Stilwell Russell defended John for killin' a United States marshal, an' he got a hangin' sentence. They reversed it, an' when they tried it again they got a hung jury. When they tried it a third time an' got him ten years, why, Jake got out an' I went into it with Stilwell Russell, that's the same Stilwell Russell that's the District Judge down at Ardmore now, an' we went down to the Circuit Court at New Orleans for an' appeal. After we reversed it again, I was gettin' ready to go to Paris, to defend old John in another trial, when he got drunk an' went trouble huntin' down on Paul Avenue, carryin' one of his big six-shooters. Old man Kendall, that ran the main grocery, was plumb full of John's foolishness, an' he could see John was paid for, carryin' the gun an' all. Kendall pushed his pistol up over the cake counter an' let John have it. The government didn't have no more case to prosecute."

"You must've had some hellish times down in that Indian Territory in those days," Welty agreed.

"I like to broke my back defendin' Dave Putty, to keep the government from hangin' him for killin' a marshal, an' what was the benefit from it? In about three years from the time Dave come clear he went to a country picnic an' tried to drink up all the licker. The marshals was layin' for him, anyway, so the first time he gets out of line, they give him just enough trouble to get him to start out with his hog-leg. They shot him dead as hell."

"What did Jim Stephenson want to kill a marshal for?" Welty asked

"Those fellers were all fighters," Pruiett said. "On the outside, when they was sober, they was fairly peaceable, but just give 'em a few drinks, an' their true natures began to show up. Jim hated officers 'cause of the way John was pushed around for killin' Joe Gaines. All he needed was a chance to kill Cathey, an' he took it. It just ran in his family to kill officers."

"How in Christ's name could a jury acquit him? There wasn't a man in this town that thought you could win that case."

"I talked 'em out of it—cold turkey," Pruiett said. "I liked to have killed myself doin' it. She was thin on proof, but I had some self-defense to talk on, an' I had to act out that fall that Stephenson took. I wanted to show by the line between bullet holes in the wall that Jim was flat on his back when he shot. Cathey had knocked him down—see? I crumpled up in front of that jury an' sprawled out. My damn head hit the floor so hard I thought I had killed myself, an' I had to lay there. Ever'body thought it was part of my act, my just layin' there so still for so long, but it wasn't. I couldn't get up for a while."

"A man that can try murder cases like you can has no right to deny people in tight places the benefit of your services," Welty said. "And another thing; after all of 'em you've tried, and won, don't it get in your blood? Don't you crave to get into the fight?"

"I'd rather try a good murder case than play stud poker, an' that's sayin' something," Pruiett answered. "But they burn up your energy. I can't sleep; I can't think nothin' but defense schemin' when I get in 'em. Thinking of mercy and liberty takes the place of sleep. Outside of my old clients, like the Stephensons, I been savin' myself, an' turnin' down a lot of murder cases."

"I'm not goin' to let you turn down this Tegeler case," Welty insisted. "These people have got money, and property. You can get a hundred an' sixty acre farm, right close in, an' you know how this town's growin'. That's a good fee."

"It's a good fee if the case isn't too tough," Pruiett agreed. "I don't want to get in one that'll make me look ridiculous."

"I'll tell you all about it," Welty said, lighting a stogie. "Rudolph Tegeler was charged back in 1907. You was probably so busy with your state politics an' elections that you didn't notice it much."

"I noticed it, but I didn't take no stock," Pruiett interrupted. "The facts have slipped my mind. I must've been in Washington."

"Well," Welty continued, "he's charged with killin' James R. Meadows. We tried him to a jury an' they convicted him; gave him life. They slipped him up to Lansing, Kansas, to keep him 'till we get our pen finished, an' I start to take an appeal to the Supreme Court. The district judge that tried the case died before the transcript was certified, an' the upper court said they couldn't affirm an incomplete record, so they ordered a new trial."

"That was almost as lucky for you as statehood was for me in the Frank Driggers case," Pruiett laughed. "They gave Frank life for killin' Gold Brady over by Ada. The old three-man appeals court at South McAlester affirmed the conviction just about the time the state government was ready to take up the territorial slack. Bob Williams was over there, an' I couldn't be there, so I had asked him to watch the case for me an' if it was affirmed, to file a petition for a rehearin'. Bob scratched the petition out in long-hand, on a rough piece of scratch paper, an' filed it right there. The Supreme Court took the business over right after that, an' Jesse Dunn wrote an opinion, allowin' me a rehearin', an' reversin' the conviction. I went back to the Valley to try it, an' won it. Old Frank's aloose today."

"It won't be that easy in Tegeler's case, but his folks swear that you can bring him out with better than a life sentence," Welty said. "I don't want you to go into it under any misapprehensions. It's tough. This fellow Meadows was an employee of the Pioneer 'Phone Company here, an' they thought a lot of him. Sam Harris, their chief counsel, was special prosecutor, an' he's as hard to hold down in the court room as Tegeler's guts.

Tegeler made a confession once, you know, an' he wants to talk, all the time."

"I didn't know nothin' about it," Pruiett answered. "That may make a hell of a lot of difference. How did you get around it?"

"We didn't get around it," Welty answered. "We just kind of evaded it. We had a combination plea of harmless ignorance an' temporary insanity on the signin' of the confession. Here's the way it was. Rudolph was charged along with Lila Meadows —Jim's widow. They proved that Lila an' Rudolph had been hangin' their meat together for two or three years, an' that Jim had a fat insurance policy they wanted to split, in addition to gettin' him out of their way. Meadows disappeared; Rudolph rushes up an' offers a reward for any information on his where-abouts, but he doesn't throw the officers off the track. The tele-phone company tapped the wires at Lila's, an' listened in on some conversations between the two of 'em, to further confirm the suspicion that they already had."

"That's pretty fast work, an' hard stuff to combat in court," Pruiett observed.

"Here's the real sinker," Welty went on, "there's a damned old Sioux fraud out at Elk City that does business as Mother Rosa Myers. She is a medicine-woman—see, a mind reader and future predicter? It was kind of a fad out in Lila's neighbor-hood to write Mother Myers for information; for instance, they had an' argument as to what kind of dress Lila's mother was buried in, an' it seems like the old lady gave them the right answer when somebody wrote an' asked her. They paid a little for the information, you understand? Well, Lila an' Jim were goin' to put the old lady in good; they wrote her a' unsigned letter, tellin' her that Jim Meadows had been murdered an' robbed by a bunch of thieves that had gone to Mexico. They sent along a little map, of a cornfield south of town, where Meadow's body was supposed to be buried."

"I don't get it." Pruiett confessed.

"Nobody got it. It didn't get far enough," Welty replied. "The play was for Lila to suggest that some of the neighbors write Mother Myers an' ask her what had become of Jim Mead-ows. They figured the old lady would pretend to have a vision; wouldn't say anything about this unsigned letter they had sent, an' would send them to the grave. That map was what really disclosed the buried body. It might have worked, but for one thing. Rudolph wrote so bad that the Elk City looked like Oklahoma City, an' they delivered the letter to a Mrs. Rose Meyers, right here in town. She turned it over to the police."

"It sounds plenty bad, so far," Pruiett said, "but not impossible. What's the rest of it?"

"Anybody could see the letter was in Rudolph's handwriting. They picked 'em both up an' put 'em in separate parts of the jail. Then they pulled the old squeeze play—an' it worked. When they told Rudolph that Lila had confessed, an' put all the blame on him, he confessed an' put it all on her. Rudolph signed his statement before he found out that he had been fooled. That's about all there is to it, except the family's been here a long time, an' grabbed off some choice ground. They're pretty well fixed."

"God Almighty usually looks out for a lunk-head, an' I can see that this Tegeler is no mental giant," Pruiett grinned. "I'm kind of itchin' to get in a good rough case. It might advertise the joint. Get me a deed to a good farm, an' leave the complete file up here at the office. I want a chance to do a little work before trial."

The Pruiett home of the period surpassed the Rush Creek manor of the Pecan grove in both external proportion and architectural elegance. Pruiett had it built in the addition being used by the new town's elite. The house was of smooth brick, two stories and a half in height, with sharp sloping gables and carved, ornamented cornices. It stood on a corner. Methodically spaced elm and fir shrubs supplied the neat lawn with the color and shade, which, in the Valley, the volunteer pecans had furnished.

The carriage house and quarters for the Negro servants faced the east on the side street. "The quarters was a damn sight better than the house our whole family lived in at Rogers—or Paris," Pruiett observed. There was an inviting air of subdued richness about the corner which was not exactly like Pruiett. It did not conform to his growing flair for gaudy manifestations of wealth, which he was then entitled to make.

And three blocks down the shady street lived other migrants from the Valley. A white cottage, with hedge fence, and a garden, and trees, was the home of Moman's Maw and Paw. No roomers and boarders to feed and clean up after. Moman was paying all the bills, and they were taking it easy. His mother's dream had finally come true.

THE PRUIETT HOME OF THE PERIOD
"The quarters was a damn sight better than the house our whole family lived in at Rogers."

Rudolph Tegeler ran afoul of the law in 1907. When he was finally discharged, a free man, in 1913, after being twice convicted and sentenced to life imprisonment at hard labor, the trail of the trial had led through the baffling maze of two trips to the appellate court and back, and into the blind bog of two hung juries. When the state's dogs had taken the scent for the fourth time, and had bayed into the court room rafters and the box-car headlines of the southwestern press with all the yowling promise of a catch and kill, only to wind up on the blind trail of another hung jury, they despaired and gave up the chase. Pruiett's client walked out with slightly deferred, but inevitable, Pruiett justice.

A shapely shank had jury box appeal in the shaping period of the southwest, as Pruiett well knew. Hadn't Izora Alexander proved that? Lila Meadows had been tried for murdering her husband, after Rudolph had first been convicted and railroaded, and she had been acquitted. Pruiett capitalized on her acquittal in Rudolph's second trial. His first bomb was loaded with powder scrapings from Lila's hearings.

"The defense will prove," he stated, evenly, making his opening statement to the jury, "that the state is unable to make a semblance of a case; that it is not only unable to prove that Rudolph Tegeler is guilty of the murder of James Meadows, but that it can't even prove that James Meadows is dead."

"I will prove by witnesses who were here for the trial of the Lila Meadows case that as the jury went out Lila said, 'Whether they find me innocent or find me guilty, I'll walk out of this court room a free woman.' She knew that all she had to do was to make known the identity of a disguised man, sitting amongst the spectators in the court room, to insure her release. That man was James R. Meadows."

Pruiett carried the baby. Pruiett popped the blanks in the accused's pistol. Pruiett kept the jury entertained—and awake. The court room was packed. Spectators brought their lunches so they wouldn't lose their places during the noon recess. It was apparent, from the moment Pruiett shook his fist in the face of the giant Sam Harris and shouted that "Tegeler is being persecuted by the soulless telephone trust, on evidence manufactured in the ambition-drunk minds of a bunch of corporation detectives," that the fight was going to be rough, and worth watching.

Sam Harris was a court room wildcat. "He was as mean as Bill Johnson," Pruiett said, "an' twict as smart." Harris had come to Oklahoma from the 'phone company's general offices

THE NOTABLES IN THE TEGELER TRIAL.
"They settled one issue; Pruiett's witness was a terrific liar," so says Harris, the prosecutor.

at St. Louis. He was big and burly, physically and mentally. As special prosecutor, acting at the direction of his company, he took charge of the prosecution and handled it as if the murdered or missing Meadows had been his favorite brother.

Harris's capacity for invective rivaled Pruiett's. He referred to one of the defendant's female witnesses as "a battle-axe harlot." He called Pruiett's star witness "a cigarette pimp." In one of his bawling addresses to the jury he referred to Pruiett as *"the black stud of the Washita."* The name stuck, and Pruiett was known by it thenceforward; thenceforward and long after the blackness of the mane had faded away.

"Should Meadows be found living, beyond the natural consternation which the discovery would create, a condition never before duplicated in criminal annals would come to pass," observed The Daily Oklahoman. "It would establish Meadows as one of the smoothest and cleverest insurance swindlers in the country; it would disclose a nature and disposition never paralleled in that it would reveal that Meadows, becoming annoyed with his wife's immoral relations with Tegeler, had disappeared after securing a dead body and burying it as his own, in order that his unfaithful wife might collect an insurance policy of $5,-000."

"It would reveal a character not only ready to give up friends, position, wife and home, in order that his wife might admit without disturbance a paramour into affections. Not only has such a character never been heard of, but was never conceived until the versatile attorney for Tegeler became interested in the case."

The hack was not only minimizing Pruiett gall; he was letting the theme of the wild defense escape him. "Hell," Pruiett scoffed, "I'm provin' double-barrelled duplicity. I don't know where Meadows got the stiff, an' I don't give a damn. He got one, an' dressed it in his own clothes, put his own shoes on it, an' buried it in the cornfield. Him an' Lila get the insurance that a'way, an' he gets to lay low an' see the guy that was poachin' on his preserves hung for killin' him."

"What about the note to Mother Myers, in Rudolph's handwriting?" a skeptic inquired. "What about that?"

"It's easy," he answered. "Old Rudolph was plain an' simple; fruit for a bunch of fast crooks like Jim Meadows an' Lila. Lila wrote the letters out, took 'em by Rudolph's an' asked him to copy 'em for her. She told him he wrote a better hand than she did, an' she wanted it to look good."

"Is he goin' to testify to that? It sounds pretty thin."

"You're damn right he is."

"What about the signed confession Sam Harris has got layin' on the table, just waitin' for Rudolph to take the stand?"

"The bulls whipped it out of him," Pruiett answered, promptly. He let his thoughts wander, for the instant, to Jake Hodges and drear days at Paris. "Hell, yes, that's what they did. They forced him to sign his name to it while they was third degreein' him. There isn't a word of truth in that statement."

Tegeler's defense produced Mike O'Brien, a self-styled private detective, who swore that he had known Meadows for years prior to his death, and that less than six months before the beginning of the second trial, he had seen him catch a fruit boat at New Orleans, heading for the Canal Zone.

"You mean," Harris inquired, on cross-examination, "that you knew Meadows, intimately, before his disappearance?"

"I certainly did," O'Brien replied, low and out of the corner of his mouth.

"And you want to tell this court and jury that you saw him in New Orleans, alive, as recently as six months ago?"

"That's what I said, ain't it?" O'Brien leered.

"Do you understand any of the obligations of an oath?" Harris demanded.

"I got as much honor as you have," O'Brien shot back.

Harris called him a liar and perjurer. Pruiett charged at Harris, and the bailiffs and other members of counsel rushed between them.

"I want to apologize to the court for that," Harris said to the trial judge, "but I want to limit my expression of regrets. They don't extend to anybody connected with the defense."

"I object to his heroics before the jury," Pruiett bawled.

"I will personally offer a thousand dollars reward for the disclosure of the whereabouts of James Meadows, alive," Harris went on, talking to the court.

"I object, an' move that the court declare a mistrial," Pruiett cried. "Counsel hasn't got that much money, in the first place, an' his bragging before this jury is detrimental to the defendant's right to a fair trial."

Judge Carney rapped in desperation. "I'll have to sustain

Mr. Pruiett's contention," he said. "These matters have no proper place in this trial. Any suggestion of a repetition of mistreatment of witnesses will be censored by this court. The jury is the one to pass on their credibility. Let's proceed."

Harris stood doggedly before the bench. "The state moves the court to grant a continuance, in order for it to send investigators to New Orleans to obtain evidence to impeach this last witness."

"The defendant will agree that his motion be allowed," Pruiett said, jumping from his chair. There was a pause, as the court looked at him in surprise. He went on. "Of course, the defendant will be entitled to a continuance, in order to send to New Orleans for witnesses to impeach the witnesses that the state produces to impeach our witness. Then the state can have another continuance, to get witnesses to impeach—."

Pruiett's point was clear. "There'll be no continuances," Carney cried, slamming his desk. "Court's recessed until tomorrow morning, and unless the state's ready to proceed with this trial then, the court will declare the case dismissed."

With a brown blast at a cuspidor, Pruiett turned and grinned at Harris. A fine mist sprayed the papers on the table. There was murder in Harris's face as he reached for his handkerchief, and walked away.

The advantage shifted back to Harris's side when the first rebuttal witness took the stand the following morning. It was Mrs. J. T. McGraw, who said she lived in Little Rock, Arkansas.

"Do you know the man who testified here yesterday?" Harris inquired, "and who said his name was Mike O'Brien?"

"I do," she answered.

"How long have you known him?"

"For a great number of years."

"Did you know him as Mike O'Brien, or by some other name?"

"I knew him as Milton McGraw—that is his real name."

"And what, if any, relationship is there between you and this witness?"

"I am his mother," she answered, quietly. Pruiett twisted perceptibly.

"Was your son in New Orleans some six or seven months ago?" Harris asked.

"No, he was with me, at Little Rock," she answered.

Harris was thorough in rebuttal. He put her husband, the

purported father of the witness, on the stand, to corroborate her. He did it, and more. He said that Milton, alias Mike, had tried to poison him at Fort Worth.

Did Pruiett care? O'Brien, or McGraw, went back to the stand.

"Without wincing Mike O'Brien sat in the witness chair in the district court room Friday afternoon during the Tegeler trial and met the gaze of the man and woman who claim to be his father and mother, Mr. and Mrs. J. T. McGraw. . . . He denies that he knows the two people who are claiming him as their wayward son, or that he tried to assassinate his father in Fort Worth, Texas, some years before, in order to get hold of a landed estate. . . . . O'Brien referred to the would-be mother as 'that old canary' and to the purported father as 'the old garbage man.' "

"He offered us bribes, at first, and then threats, to keep us from exposing his false identity," the parents responded.

The black stud, Pruiett, the murder specialist, had never hoped to prove that James R. Meadows was still alive. He was artfully engaged in attracting the attention of the jurors from the magnitude of the crime committed and the magnitude of his client's guilt, and in centering it upon a less portentious issue. He succeeded. For a full month the mighty efforts of the able Harris were concentrated, not upon proving that Rudolph Tegeler was a vicious, calculating murderer, but that a broken down old floater named O'Brien, or possibly McGraw, was a prodigious liar.

And over the vicious, pathetic, objection of Big Sam, Pruiett squared off and read a telegram to the gleeful jury. "Mike O'Brien is a man whose reputation for truth and veracity cannot be assailed," he roared. Waving the yellow slip he continued, "This telegram is from Governor J. Y. Sanders, of the State of Louisiana."

While Harris and Pruiett were sparring, reinforcements, marching on the Telephone Company's fat expense account, were coming to the front. As Mike was rubbing his chin in the corridor, Claude Nowlin, lawyer assistant to Harris, and Webb Jones and O. W. Lawler, detectives, were hurrying to the depot. Their ad in the Picayune brought volunteers to the grog-shop in their hotel. A fair per diem and all traveling expenses helped them to know something about the case.

"Under the direction of Sam Harris, the citizens of New

Orleans were brought to Oklahoma City Sunday, and they were on the stand Monday and Tuesday. The testimony they gave supported by public documents, some of which have not as yet been admitted in evidence, went to show that McGraw was never in the employ of the United States as Assistant Labor Inspector of the Port of New Orleans (as he had claimed)." The court, jury, spectators and reading public, had forgotten about Rudolph Tegeler. Just how big a liar was this fellow McGraw—or was the name O'Brien?

The ruinous effect of Pruiett's bombardment was showing—after five weeks—on the mountainous physique of prosecutor Harris. His massive shoulders were drooping dejectedly, and the Indian summer sweat had yellowed the white cuffs of his wilted shirt. But there was an air of malignant, ghoulish revenge about his tired torso as he arose and began to address the court. The state was surely ready to close.

"Your honor," he said painfully, "inasmuch as you permitted Governor Sanders' telegram to be read to the jury, without what I would call proper identification, I feel that I am entitled to announce, in the presence of the jury, that the state rests, except for the proof of one more witness. He will be here tomorrow; it will be Governor Sanders of Louisiana, whom I have just talked with on the 'phone. He will testify that the Mike O'Brien he had reference to in his telegram is a member of the railroad construction firm of O'Brien Brothers, who have been operating in Louisiana for a number of years. Governor Sanders will say that he knows absolutely nothing of the Mike O'Brien who is testifying in this case."

There was no change of expression in Pruiett. He took a fresh chew, stuffed a litter of papers into his brief case, and saluted the jury as he went by. He was unable, however, to control his feeling when the first edition of the evening paper came out.

"While making an alleged attempt to get out of the jurisdiction of the district court Tuesday afternoon, Milton C. McGraw, alias detective Mike O'Brien, was arrested in the alley back of the county jail. He was arrested by Deputy Sheriff Leslie Skaggs. He is being held on a warrant sworn out by Claude Nowlin, charging that he gave false testimony in the Rudolph Tegeler case. . . ."

The stud's tail flew up. He tossed off a huge drink and wheeled on his circle of loungers.

"Why the hell did he have to get caught in the alley?" he

demanded, scowling viciously. "That makes it look bad for the case. That makes it look like we got an alley rat for a witness; a damned alley rat."

When the evidence was all in the court read his instructions of law to the jury, and there was a lull, like the quietude between the stages of a spring storm. But with the night the wind came up again, and the lightning began to flash and roar. "At one time Thursday afternoon Moman Pruiett's rhetorical assault upon Sam Harris was so severe that the court was appealed to, but the speaker was so intensely in his theme that the words of Judge Carney did not reach his ears."

On its first poll the jury was in unanimous accord. Mike O'Brien was the biggest liar in the United States of America. With the second ballot they agreed upon the next issue; Pruiett was just as good as the press had him cracked up to be, and he had put on a whale of a performance. But as to Rudolph? That was different. They played poker, told stories and ate meals being charged to the taxpayers who fumed in the corridors downstairs, waiting for the verdict. When they had been out three days they announced that they were in hopeless disagreement. Six wanted to turn him out, because Lila was free and she was as guilty as he. Six wanted to hang him because he was such a stupid, blundering dolt. The evidence in support of the murder charge was never mentioned. Whether Meadows was living or dead was never considered.

Pruiett always considered his successful defense of W. N. Maben, district judge, indicted and tried for corruption and abuse of authority, one of his most noteworthy accomplishments. The quality of a Pruiett triumph was gauged by the volume and nature of the evidence against the defendant, and by the capacity and ability of the prosecutor handling the people's case. In the Maben case Charles West, Oklahoma's first Attorney General, was conducting the prosecution *in personam*. He was a diminutive, belligerent, little lawyer who had left Georgia for the Territory; he was running over with energy and political ambition. The entire county government, involved in the scandal with Maben, had turned state's evidence, and was lined up as witnesses for the prosecution. The pimps, prostitutes, gamblers and bootleggers were doing the best they could for themselves while the heat was on. They were co-operating with the majesty of the law.

The current press furnished a fairly accurate word-picture of Maben. "Judge Maben has been one of the most prominent Democratic leaders in the state. He was a delegate to the national convention at Denver and has had a great deal to do with shaping the political destiny of the state since the advent of statehood. He was elected judge of the district in 1907 by a large majority. He is a native of Texas and began the practice in Fort Worth several years ago."

Maben was Pruiett's friend; he was capable of doing no wrong. Like Pruiett, he was indefatigable, physically, mentally and morally, and an all night session at whiskey, and poker left no tell-tale mark of wear on his faultless court room bearing next morning. His precise manners, and dress, suggested that he wanted to acquire and keep all of the feminine good will that he could.

As practicing lawyers, they had met as the Sandy Land Court, with its transitory judge, clerk and marshal, shifted about over the Indian Territory. Pruiett would drift east and north to Maben's stronghold in Pottawatomie County, the town of Shawnee. Maben, an authority on relative civil rights, had occasional call to visit the Valley. When they were together there was a bottle, and a good time.

After statehood and Maben's elevation to the bench Pruiett had had occasion to appear before him. He was arguing a motion for a severance for one of his murder clients. They had been together nearly all night at Maben's, and Pruiett had taken a stiff stimulant before he could push himself out of bed that morning. He had taken several more for breakfast. He was hesitant and backward as he tried to express himself in court.

"The court can't hardly hear you, Mr. Pruiett," Maben called from the bench.

"That's perfectly all right, your honor," Pruiett assured him, "I can't hardly *see* you."

"You should have known that a majority like you got would start the wolves to howlin'," Pruiett said to Maben. "Haven't you learned that when you start goin' up that all the bums in the gutter start grabbin' at your coat tails?"

"They've got me in a corner," Maben agreed. "I wasn't lookin' for such a gesture of appreciation for all the hard work I been doin' for these fellows."

"Charley West's got ever'body that was indicted to turn against you," Pruiett said. "He's got leniency to offer, an' all

he wants is you. You got a political future, an' so has he. If he
can ruin you he's made."

"What we goin' to do?"

"We're goin' to raise hell, an' lots of it," Pruiett answered,
vengefully. "This is Oklahoma's first dirty didy. I'll show 'em
that the guy that is changin' this state's first soiled linen is doin'
it for a grandstand act, an' I'll jab his nose in the mess that's in
it. I coined this one on the train down, for a statement to the
press. 'Charley West is tryin' to cover up his own official in-
competency by smoke from the sacrificial fire he has built for
his fellow officer. It is a gigantic conspiracy with two purposes,
one to advance West to the governorship, and the other, to let
Ben Blakeney get the revenge he wants of Maben, because Maben
is an honest and impartial judge. Men of Maben's type are constantly beset by petty conspirators like West and Blakeney.' How's
that?"

"It sounds good, an' it sounds true," Maben replied. "There
I was, partners for years with Ben Blakeney, splittin' fees with
him an' workin' my head off for him, an' just because I got to
be a judge he had to get envious. I can't understand it."

"You don't need to understand but one thing, Bill. Blakeney's
a good lawyer an' he's well thought of down here. With him in
this prosecution it's bad—I mean it's worse. That little Charley
West makes it bad."

"If I ever get out of this mess I'll resign," Maben sighed.
"It ain't worth the trouble it takes, walkin' sideways an' lookin'
back all the time, to see which one of your friends is close enough
to bite a hunk out of your butt. Those politics is dog eat dog,
an' I don't mean like the Seminoles an' Shawnees do it. They
have broiled young bitch an' fricassee of hound pup on their regular menu right out in the open."

"Charley West is runnin' his governor's race right here in
this trial," Pruiett said. "He's usin' your skeleton for a ladder to
climb a notch higher—he thinks. Don't lose your nerve an' start
talkin' about resignin' 'til the scrap's over. You got to stand
behind me an' fight."

"You're the boss hoss," Maben grinned. "What did Sam
Harris say? The black stallion?"

"The black stud horse of the Washita," Pruiett laughed.
"We'll have to do some stampedin' to get over Charley West an'
the organization he's got down here, but watch me trot. A good
farmer's got more'n one way of gettin' to town."

Tecumseh, the council camp of the remnant of Shawnees and Pottawatomies who survived the transfer out of Georgia, had become the seat of government for the county named after the Pottawatomies. The whipping and shooting tree, where stern tribal justice had once been dispensed, was a great elm, shading the spotted and unkempt lawn of the court house. Like the town, and the surrounding countryside and the inhabitants, the brown-stone court building was somber and plain. The sleepy placidity of the place refused to be disturbed by the crowd of curious jamming the rooms and wagon yards, in town for the Maben sacrifice. Mid-May was resting season for the blanket men, and dozing and smoking, they accepted the comfort of the shade or stoically gave it up, as the marching sun dispensed it and retracted it. They ignored the bustling whites who breezed in and out with their important looking brief cases, and their more important gesticulations and loud talk.

The path ahead of Maben was rocky. "The grand jury returned indictments against W. N. Maben, Judge of the Tenth Judicial District, and Virgil R. Biggers, County Attorney of Pottawatomie County, and other county officials, charging them with misconduct in office in conspiring with others to permit unlawful sales of intoxicating liquors, gaming, and other violations of the law within their jurisdiction. They were charged with the acceptance of bribes, and in agreeing and actually taking $2,500 per month, payable on the 15th of each month and beginning September 15, 1908 (ending through discovery of the situation February 15, 1909), thereby indemnifying the bootleggers, gamblers, and other criminals from prosecution from official interference . . . ."

"A Woman Started It All," the Shawnee News had said, explaining the break of the unusual case. "The information which resulted in the trial of Judge Maben on a charge of receiving money to protect bootleggers, dates from the writing of a letter by Mrs. Brown Howell, the wife of a converted jointist. . . . Brown Howell has testified that he is one of the men who gave the $800 which Judge Maben is accused of having accepted to protect bootleggers against indictment. He was converted at the Bulgin revival, and is now a member of the Presbyterian Church. Howell had been a saloon keeper twenty-seven years and after his conversion he drove to his joint and gave all his interest in the establishment to his partner. Mrs. Howell wrote a letter to

the Rev. Mr. Bulgin telling of the alleged corruption in Pottawatomie County. She then put her statement into the form of an
affidavit, the reading of which at the Bulgin revival brought the
earthquake that is still shaking things in this county."

Pruiett and Maben sat on the bridge, watching the rats scurry
down the hawsers. "They're runnin' to Charley West awful fast,"
Pruiett said. "Ever' one that pleads guilty an' agrees to take a
suspended sentence is a witness for Charley, against you."

"There's a few that isn't gone yet," Maben said. "Biggers,
the County Attorney, is still with us, an' he's the main witness."

"I'm afraid of him," Pruiett mused. "He don't look like the
right kind of folks, to me. I predict he'll take the stand against
you before the state rests."

"I might as well try to trade out myself, if he does," Maben
replied jokingly.

"You couldn't benefit if you was to plead guilty to murder
an' agree that they hang you tomorrow," Pruiett scoffed. "Haven't
I told you? This is Charley West's campaign for governor that
is goin' on here, an' our great judicial system is payin' the expenses—what you aren't furnishin'. This trial is front page for
the crusadin' little Attorney General. They don't want the policemen, or the commissioners, or the county attorney. They want
the district judge that has a big political followin', an' that's
you. Charley's got a hand-made basket to catch your head."

"He'll catch a hell of a headache when he does," Maben
grinned. "The stuff you shook up last night like to have killed
me."

The bells had told Pruiett the truth. "Virgil R. Biggers, the
suspended county attorney, and against whom an indictment is
pending, will be called as one of the state's witnesses, according
to a statement from the county attorney's office, and he will likely
be one of the next witnesses to be put on the stand."

"SAYS HE GOT THE BOODLE" proclaimed the News,
of Biggers. "In a sensational statement made to Attorney General West today, County Attorney Virgil Biggers confessed having accepted bribes from gamblers and bootleggers of this city.
He implicated District Judge W. N. Maben and County Commissioner Robert Hager. A rumor is afloat that on Monday Police
Chief Sims will also turn state's evidence, and in case it proves to
be true, it is thought that other prominent officers will be accused."

"What do you say now, my black stallion?" Maben laughed,
shoving the paper toward Pruiett.

"I say pass me a drink," he answered. "Wasn't I right about Mister Biggers. I say Sims'll go the same route. It's all cooked up, an' Charley'll pay 'em back with interest when he gets to be governor."

"Shall we stop the show?" Maben inquired, quietly. "We can throw the towel in any time you say," Freeling suggested. "There isn't any use in lettin' 'em whip our heads plumb off."

"Whip, hell!" Pruiett grated. "I got a hunch, an' I'm the guy that plays his hunches. We're goin' to get a break in this case, an' I think the groggier we are, when it comes, the better off we'll be. Let Sims go, an' all the rest of 'em. We'll try to make the jury understand that the state's case is too perfect—too damn complete to be anything but a well laid an' developed conspiracy. Get my point?"

"I get it," Maben answered, "but I don't think much of it. We haven't got anything to bluff with."

"We'll just let little Charley shoot his wad," Pruiett said. "Sit tight in the buggy an' watch me egg him on. When he gets to steppin' his highest, watch old Moman. Somebody's head, besides yours, may roll into that sawdust."

The trial and progress of the case found the lawyer with the bushy black hair in a most unusual, and unnatural position. He was on the defensive, actually and figuratively. The diminutive Attorney General had beat him to the punch with a scathing statement of what he expected the state's testimony to develop, and he had kept the advantage by constant barrage of leading and suggestive questions put to the already damaging witnesses, and a stream of suggestive, discourteous and insulting comment across the counsel table. He had Pruiett so punch-drunk and bewildered, apparently, during the first week of the trial, that the jury was pitying him. Hadn't the papers said something about this Pruiett --about him being smart, and hard to handle?

West was an effective prosecutor. His lack of physical height—he was scarce more than five feet tall—was never noticed after his energy and activity was once set in motion. His small body was muscular and wiry; he moved about with a nervous, springy stride which made one think that he was bounding to his toes with each step in an effort to increase his deficient perpendicular measurement. His head, large and out of proportion to his body, was indicative in both size and shape of mental prowess. A slight baldness accentuated the height of his brow, while beady black eyes and a large, slightly hooked nose gave the immediate impression of a big bird—a hawk.

The inconsistent booming voice which emanated from his broad mouth caused consternation in the first observer and listener, and invited more careful attention. It was incredible that one of such slight stature should be equipped with such a medium. The store of invective which he had brought to the new state from his native state of Georgia was both revelationary and revolutionary, even to the forked-tongue Pruiett, whose superiority in uttering vicious figures and phrases was generally recognized, and respected.

"He's just like a damned little fightin' chicken," Maben whispered behind the back of his hand. "Watch him bounce. Watch him strut. How are we goin' to stop it?"

"He's the worst I ever saw," Pruiett answered. "That chicken's a good name for him. He's so mean that bein' tough with him won't help a bit. Let's keep on bein' real meek, an' let him go. Maybe he'll wear himself out."

But West's bouncing energy wouldn't be exhausted. He put preacher Bulgin on the stand and kept him there until he had succeeded in parading before the jury the hearsay and gossip of the revival tent. Oats Johnson and L. B. Howell, gambling joint operators who handled whiskey, swore to having delivered various sums of money, at various times, to the defendant district judge. They testified that he agreed to deliver them protection for the payoff. Pruiett's cross-examination failed to cross them up.

Biggers, the deposed and confessed prosecuting attorney, was most liberal with the consideration he was to deliver for the immunity he had been promised. There was no doubt, at the conclusion of his testimony, that if the incrimination of Maben was a part of what he was to deliver, that the state was in his everlasting debt. Hager, the county commissioner, corroborated Biggers, and when he was done a three-day procession of pimps, prostitutes and petty gamblers went by, halting long enough at the witness chair to say a few words against the judge.

"You were good," Pruiett said to Maben, during recess. "You acted so meek an' apologetic, while you are testifyin,' that I like to have cried myself. I'm turning' you over to West for cross-examination as soon as we reconvene, an' remember—our strength is in our utter weakness. Ain't the meek supposed to inherit the earth?"

"I've got a lot of respect for your judgment, Moman."

Maben said. "I turned the defense over to you, an' you're the director, but I sure hate like hell to be pushed around this way."

"Let him go," Pruiett insisted. "Our day's a comin'. He'll make ever' dirty inference that can be made, an' he'll violate ever' rule of evidence in cross-examinin' you, but I am not goin' to object. He's done enough of that while we was tryin' to tell our sides of this story. You are a lawyer, an' ought to be able to take care of yourself. Whatever you do, don't let the jury think you're mad, or that your temper's got away from you. I want your word on that."

"If you say let him rape me, I'll do it," Maben grinned, "an' I'll promise to put on the act. I just can't agree to like it, actually."

"I like it less than you," Pruiett said. "I'm lettin' him build himself up; swell his ego. It'll make him overbalanced, an' easier to handle when I start takin' him apart."

"He'll probably take a poke at you," Maben reminded. "You know what I mean."

Pruiett studied. He had never succeeded in flailing the serpent's trail from the sand behind him. "If he's got that little judgment, let him go," he grated. "You've stood him, an' I can too, for a little longer, anyway."

Charley West proved Pruiett's prediction. When he had concluded his vicious cross-examination he asked, with mock politeness: "Did your consciousness of guilt in this case have anything to do with your selection of a criminal lawyer, for your defense?"

Maben pondered. "No," he answered, meekly and quietly.

"It'll be two convicts instead of one, when the jury gets through with him," West hissed over his shoulder to Blakeney, as Maben stepped down. The whisper could be heard over the entire court room. "Pruiett looks like he needs company."

Both sides had rested when the noon recess was taken, and the court's instructions to the jury had been read. The court room had cleared, and Pruiett was sitting alone at the counsel table. Judge Rosser passed on his way out of his chambers; he paused to speak to the meditating lawyer.

"Aren't you going out to eat, Moman?" he questioned. "With arguments ahead you'll need a lot of vitality. You ought to go out."

"I haven't got any appetite," Pruiett replied. "I feel all right, but I'm just not hungry. I think I'll rest a little during the noon hour."

"Are you too mad to eat?" Rosser inquired, bluntly. Pruiett showed his surprise; the judge had overheard the whisper.

"I never felt so much like killin' a man before in my life," he answered, truthfully. "He's gone out of his way to offer me every insult known to depraved ingenuity, an' then—."

"I heard it," the court interrupted, "and I'm sorry. I can't subscribe to those tactics, but I can't say anything about it in front of the jury. I advise you to keep your head."

Pruiett didn't answer, but continued to look down and scowl. The judge went on: "I want to congratulate you on your defense of Maben. You've done a good job, but there is too much evidence against him. Frankly, I think the jury is going to convict him. But don't lose your own head and make matters any worse If you try to get mean, or get even with West when you talk to this jury, you are apt to do your client an injury."

"I've been savin' up a week, thinkin' up and savin' things to say about that little Georgia cracker an' you know it." Pruiett was laughing and the strain was over. "If Mrs. Rosser needs a new sifter, tell her to come by the court house this evenin' and pick it up. I'm goin' to take Charley West's hide off right in front of that jury, an' punch it so full of holes that it won't hold sand. She'll be able to shake flour or nutmeg through it, and—." Pruiett stopped himself, for the laughing judge had already passed through the court room door.

The court room representative of the Shawnee News noticed that the hide had slipped. "Moman Pruiett of Oklahoma City, attorney for the defense in the Maben case, concluded the afternoon arguments with a scathing arraignment of the Attorney General and Attorney Blakeney. He charged the former with prosecuting the case in the interest of his political ambition, and the latter with having personal animosity toward Judge Maben. Toward the end of his speech he grew extremely vitriolic . . . ."

Pruiett's argument to the jury was sandwiched between the opening and closing arguments of the prosecution. Blakeney opened, and in an able, although unnecessarily brutal manner, interpreted every point in evidence as conclusive proof that Maben was an arch-rascal who should be given a long term in prison. He exhibited bad taste and poor judgment when he offered an insinuating reference to Pruiett and his past, and suggested a similarity in the makeup of the defendant and his counsel. His argument as a whole was an analysis of the evidence, for he was leaving, with abiding trust and confidence, the complete stultification of Maben and Pruiett to the gentleman from Georgia the Attorney General who had the last say to the jury.

Pruiett talked for an hour before he mentioned a phase of the case other than those developed by his own client's testimony. With quiet control he reconstructed the life story of the defendant· an humble birth with a struggle against poverty through childhood, but, gradually gaining, slowly rising, with accomplished position within his grasp, the rafters crashed around him and threatened to crush him. There was an old mother, of course. Pruiett paid a tribute to his mother as he placed roses on the altar of Maben's mother's memory. There was a faithful and steadfast wife, and innocent children. These, all of these were suffering, and why? He pondered, as if uncertain. Then in an instant he became transfixed, rigid, wild-eyed. He wheeled upon the complacent little Attorney General and thrust a trembling finger under his nose.

"You, Judas! You, Brutus! You, Benedict Arnold! he roared. "You, the sum total of cowardice and treachery through the ages! Why have you persecuted this innocent man? Why have you abandoned the courtesies and decencies of court room practice, and vomited up your putrefaction and avarice—by every cheap and despicable violation of the rules of evidence if you don't feel that your case is inadequate to support a conviction on its merits?"

West was obviously searching for an answer as he scrambled from his chair.

"You object, do you, you cowardly little braggart?" Pruiett continued. "You cry for the protection of the court? Why have you stood on your hind legs and objected a thousand times to what a man would introduce in his own defense into a court of justice; when he is fighting a conviction that would ruin him and rob him of his birthright?"

The rising Attorney General was being hauled back into his seat by Blakeney, who was tugging at his short coat, "Let him alone," Blakeney whispered to West. "He's only trying to get error into the record. Don't make an objection. We've already got the case won."

"How many times have you heard it, gentlemen of the jury?" Pruiett inquired, turning to them. "How many times has he said it? 'The State of Oklahoma objects! The State of Oklahoma objects!' I'll tell you—as many times as this defendant has opened his mouth to say a word in his own defense. And West always says. 'The State of Oklahoma,'—have you noticed, gentlemen? 'The

State of Oklahoma objects!' His desire to impress his authority is but a manifestation of his attitude of coercion and intimidation. It is as if to say to the honest judge trying this case, 'this court will take notice that a district judge is now on trial, and if this prosecuting power is crossed, another one, maybe you, will be next—.'"

West was rising again. Pruiett turned on him.

"Stand up and crow, you cowardly little capon. Flap your wings and cry for mercy. I knew you would do it; it's as old as the story of man. When the going gets rough the weakling is the one that begins to cry. You've harassed me throughout this trial by your cowardly interruptions and side remarks. Stand up and object again; stand up and object."

West couldn't afford to take the dare and Pruiett knew it. He sank slowly, wearily, back into his chair. Pruiett went back to the jury.

"This little capon from Georgia, with his yellow comb and loud crow, is being milk fed in a private pen so he can be shown to society company. He wants to be governor. So the gang that thinks he can make it goes out and hatches up their dirty conspiracies, and sets the stage for him to rush in and make a big noise. He's to capitalize on the publicity. That's the deal, and it would be all right, if it wasn't for the fact that innocent men, innocent men and their families, have to be sacrificed for the cheap show that he wants to put on.

"In his sequestered ease the little capon doesn't have to scratch. They crack his corn and warm his milk, and when the time comes for him to get out and rough it—he objects! He objects to an American citizen exercising the right that God Almighty and the Constitution of the United States guarantees to him. The great state objects. It sounds better that way, and he thinks he can intimidate the defendant, and intimidate me. He wouldn't object if Judge Maben were to sit quietly by and let him ram the roast of his crooked conspiracy down the throats of the people; let him ravage and discredit this defendant and his innocent family, for his own selfish political benefit. Stand up and object, little capon, stand up and object!"

But the little lawyer couldn't stir. Uninterrupted for the first time during the two weeks' trial, Pruiett proceeded to take the few favorable circumstances of the case and set them up in such a way that they seemed to surpass, in importance, all of the injurious testimony which the state had produced. He skinned

West without mercy, and punched the sifter holes in his hide with his own small bones. He pilloried Blakeney with his burning vituperation and matchless ridicule, and charged that Biggers and the pimps and prostitutes were a part of the scheme to sacrifice Maben to Charley West's political aspirations.

When Pruiett had worn himself completely out, he thanked the jury and walked out of the court room. He wanted them to understand that he didn't intend to make any objection to West's answer. He wasn't interested in what West thought of his chances to convict to sit in the court room and listen.

Pruiett had struck the Attorney General's most vulnerable spot when he likened him to a Georgia capon. West was not entirely without self-consciousness where his resemblence to the fowl family was generally concerned. Somewhere, and at some time, before, some wag had drawn a similar comparison. Try as he might, the little bantam could not recall the vim he had before Pruiett's denouncement. He floundered through his carefully prepared closing speech.

Maben had his resignation prepared. Three hours later, when the jury returned and announced that they had agreed that the defendant was guiltless of the crime charged, he shook hands with Judge Rosser and handed the document to him.

"I would thank you to submit this to the Supreme Court for me," he said simply.

Maben left town with Pruiett. While he was figuratively shaking the dust of the Pottawatomies from his boots, they were liberally washing it from their dry gullets with whiskey from Maben's grip. As the little train lurched and bumped along they were talking of Charley West and the next election. Their comments were interrupted by frequent flights of laughter, laughter that was unreserved and a little vindictive. Who was going to be governor now?

Action in the Tegeler case re-united Pruiett with his destiny. What was political preferment and fat civil-case fees, when memories of Little Rock and Rusk had to be avenged? Could he be untrue to power which had sustained him, and made him, in the Valley? He thought of his vow as he journeyed back to "White Bead Garvin's Ranch." Sam Garvin had died, and Pruiett went to the burial. He abandoned affectation. He became the murder specialist. "It was along about this time that Pruiett began to get higher types of murders for clients."

Patrolman S. G. Crow blushed as he asked for his ten-day summer vacation. "My wife's about ready to have her baby," he mumbled.

"Don't let 'em clip the end off it, if it's a boy," the Chief roared, slapping him on the back. "He won't be a hundred per cent American that a'way. Good luck to you, son."

The baby came that night. On the next, Patrolman Crow, in plain clothes, was dragged out the back door of Nick Kaufman's Southtown bootleg joint, and deposited amongst the empty tin cans and beer bottles.

"That stuff don't work with me," Nick said, dusting off his fat hands. "They don't shoot craps 'til their money's all gone, an' then pull a star an' demand it back, an' get anywhere with it. We didn't kill him, did we, boys?"

"Naw," one of them growled, "but we done a good job of markin' him up. He'll have you pinched, as soon as someone takes him to town. You know how cops are."

"I can pay a fine in the city court better'n I can give him back all he lost," Nick grinned. When the man with the warrant came, Nick went quietly. "These boys here, one of 'em is my brother; can they go along for makin' my bond?"

"Sure," the officer replied, "there's plenty of room in the wagon. If they don't mind ridin' in the cage, it's fine with me."

"It's fine with us," the bondsmen agreed. "She's nice an' black, like a hearse, an' them fine black horses would look good for a funeral. We'll just play like it's a ceremony, an' we're leavin' the church in the stiff-wagon. You're the head man, Nick. You get in and pick out the best seat."

It was Nick's last ride. "Brawl Ends in Killing," the morning paper announced. "T. Nick Kaufman shot by Patrolman Crow. . . . Suspecting no violence, the customary proceedings of searching the prisoner was started. Kaufman had been brought to the window of the cage, a place about 25 by 20, cut off from the rest of the large basement room by a wire netting. His two friends, Evans and Miller, with others gathered around. They were bunched up at the window, eager for news of the charges to be preferred. . . .

"Crow walked into the room. . . . Very deliberately, he drew his revolver and slipping near the cage window, . . . fired. 'You dirty dog, I've got you, and I want your brother next.'

". . . . A brother rushed to the man's side. In the blood that was streaming to the floor he knelt beside him. He felt his heart, and moaning, mumbled a prayer for life. Kaufman, with blood in mouth and nostrils, clothes soaked with blood, with ghastly, distorted face, was dead. . . ."

Crow had sent three forty-five slugs through Kaufman's midsection before the pistol could be wrested from him. Evans and Miller, innocent bystanders, had been wounded by lead that had already passed through Nick. "After Crow was taken to the county jail and charged with murder, he refused to talk, in accordance with the instructions of his lawyer, Moman Pruiett."

Samuel R. Cunningham was recognized as the new city's ablest medical doctor. He lived in a big house next door to Pruiett.

"I want an expert to testify to Crow's mental condition," Pruiett said, bluntly. "I'm pleadin' insanity, an' I want a doctor to prove it."

Cunningham put his sock-covered feet against the rail of his veranda. He and Pruiett were discussing the case nonpro-fessionally, at home. "I'd have to say that he had a very slight paranoia," Cunningham replied. "I understand that he had been mistreated, and that these men had inflicted a rather serious head injury when they beat him up the day before, but that doesn't make insanity."

"I ain't got no use for that paranoia stuff, an' inferiority in-hibitions an' so forth," Pruiett said. "Like I told 'em at the pre-liminary, Crow was sufferin' from confusional insanity. He didn't know—."

"Confusional insanity?" the doctor inquired. "I never heard of it."

"I never did either, before, but what difference does that make? There had to be a first time for some one to hear of this paranoia stuff you just mentioned."

"What do you mean by 'confusional insanity'?"

"He was confused when he killed Kaufman," Pruiett an-swered. "He was kind of nutty, even after Crow had his ear stomped off, even before that gang out there whipped him. I got witnesses to prove that within an hour after his ears were stomped off, in the police station he was picking up pop bottles, putting straws in them and pouring them little drippin's from the bottle into his ear. He claimed it was a sure cure for earache he always had."

"That sounds silly to me," Cunningham said.

"What's silly about it?" Pruiett demanded. "Here's a man that's off to start with. A sane man don't pour soda water in his ear. He goes out an' a bunch of thugs whip him 'til he comes unwell; 'til they have to take him to a hospital an' patch his head up. If he's a killer, premeditatin' a crime, is he goin' to have his victim arrested, an' hauled up before the police, so's that he can get a pot shot at him? Why hell, no, not if he's normal."

"That's what he did do, isn't it?" Cunningham asked.

"Sure, but don't miss the logic. He signed a complaint an' had Kaufman arrested, just like you, or any other citizen would have done. He was goin' to let the law take its course. When they brought Kaufman in, an' he saw him, a cog slipped somewhere. He got confused. He forgot that the law was in charge of him. He forgot ever'thing but one, an' that was that he had been injured by this fellow Kaufman. He started shootin' an' hit two innocent men while he was doin' it."

"You might be a good lawyer," Cunningham laughed, "but you'd better stick to your own field. You've no business trying to invent a new kind of psychological state. It'll make you ridiculous, this confusional insanity stuff."

"What the hell do I care if it does, so long as I win my case?" Pruiett answered. "Pourin' pop in his ear, an' bein' confused about what was goin' on, is all the defense I'm goin' to have in the Crow case."

Pruiett was ordinarily ready for trial; he trafficked in delays and continuances in only occasional cases. The Crow case came up early for hearing. "The case promises to be one of the hardest fought ever tried at the court house." Pruiett had found the right doctor and was promoting his insanity plea. "At this juncture Attorney Pruiett read a hypothetical question embracing two typewritten pages, for the purpose of eliciting from Dr. Riley and Dr. Duke an answer to prove that Crow was afflicted with confusional insanity after having been terribly beaten and under the influence of whiskey, was irresponsible for shooting Kaufman."

The hard fought ones were the ones that Pruiett liked the best. He had the jury so well in hand that the evidence didn't make much difference. A charming, brilliant fellow like Pruiett was entitled to win his case. They couldn't turn him down. "Not Guilty is Verdict in Crow Murder case. . . . Five minutes after the foreman announced the verdict Crow walked from the court room, a free man."

CHAPTER ELEVEN

How Pruiett encounters an enemy in need, and saves him, for a valuable consideration, from the penalty which is usually provided for the crime of murder. And how he displays his prowess in the scenes of his childhood, to postpone, and render more sweet and profound, his vengeance for an old, but never-to-be-forgotten injury. The Red Fox case in Fayetteville, Arkansas, and told the blue barrow story in a speech to the law class in the University of Arkansas.

"The most shocking and dastardly crime that has occurred in this section of the state in a quarter of a century took place between 3:30 and 5:30 o'clock yesterday afternoon, when Mrs. John Winkleman was brutally murdered at the family residence on Spring Street, three blocks from the public square." The shocking announcement was being made by the Fayetteville Daily, under the bold head, MOST SHOCKING MURDER. "The boldness and audacity of the crime stunned the citizens of Fayetteville with its fiendish enormity."

"In the old two-room house in the back of the yard . . . Mr. White opened the buttoned closet door and a most gruesome sight was presented. There lay the dead body of Mrs. Winkleman, her clothes bespattered with her own blood and her head fearfully crushed. . . . In searching the room this morning a large iron bolt with a nut on the end was found wrapped in a bloody bonnet between the mattresses of the bed. This is undoubtedly the bludgeon the villain used. It has been understood for years that Mrs. Winkleman carried a large amount of money on her person. She lost some money once in a Nebraska bank failure, and she was afraid of banks. She had about $10,000 when she left the restaurant yesterday. Her daughter testified before the coroner's jury to this fact, and that she carried the money in a ducking wallet attached to a belt worn under her clothes."

The reward for the apprehension of Aunt Carrie's murderers, offered by the governor, the family and public-spirited private agencies, totaled $3,500. Two drifters, who had been renting a shack on the back of the Winkleman lot and who were indelibly connected with the crime, were captured. Gus Sartain, with efforts to resist extradition defeated, committed suicide by hanging himself in his Sacramento, California, jail cell. N. H. Fox, an Oklahoma gambler, was arrested at Sulphur and brought back to Fayetteville, charged with murder.

Pruiett, the lawyer, had built a more stately mansion for his soul, or in terms more probably correct, the Baum estate had built a more stately one for his murder clientele, and he was contributing by the month for the use of a portion of its elegant interior. The Baum building was the class of Oklahoma's principal city, six stories of fluted stone blocks, with gray marble slabs about its lower extremities, and marble pillars supporting its ornamented ground floor entrance and arcade. Although the dusty atmosphere was full of talk of taller ones, and finer ones, the natives scoffed. The Baum was real big town. It couldn't be surpassed.

The floor of the fifth story offices was covered with Brussels. The surplus of fine mahogany which furnished the place spoke of extravagance—slightly vulgar extravagance—and explained, after one became familiar with the proprietor's background, how he was attempting to compensate a youth-starved soul with long coveted luxuries.

What the dealers in the young city lacked he had required them to get, because a combination plan of the Washington offices of Silas Hare and J. F. McMurray were what he had in mind when he started out to furnish his new suite, and as the cost was not being considered, he got just what he wanted. Blood-colored drapes, of such voluminous folds as to almost obstruct the passage of sunlight from the outside, curved and drooped from above the tall window casements to the green carpeted floor. Strong electric lamps, close to the ceiling, reflected themselves from the shining polish of the desks, tables and chairs, and caused them to shine like a multitude of mirrors. A great iron cabinet safe, plain of exterior and as high as a man's head, and so broad that it seemed to cover the entire wall space of one end of the office, shouted out to attract the attention of the visitors, so inconsistent was it with the ornamented splendor of the other furnishings within the room. The master was prosperous. He was resplendent, personally, as the equipment of his office. The hair was as shimmering in the light of the lamps as the polished top of his desk, while it carried a congenital quality of luxury about it that could not be reproduced in the inanimate things—even in the superior craftsmanship of the woodwork. His features, a little less bronzed and rugged, yet more mature and handsome, retained their two salient features, the undershot jaw and the shaggy eyebrows. His high white collar was bat-winged, as the prevailing style for men of his position and of the period dictated, while the black four-in-hand, tied loosely beneath his chin, was surmounted by a diamond stud as large as a sling-shot pebble from the shallows of White River. His black Broadcloth coat was outlined at the lapel with black braid; his dark striped trousers were immaculately pressed, while a pair of black shoes were shined in the same efficient manner as he would have shined them himself in the distant day of his boyhood. A hand, which nervously twisted a black cigar, or passed it back and forth from a scowling mouth to the ash-desecrated elegance of the table top, bore a diamond larger than the one in the scarf at his throat.

Pruiett had developed an eloquent scowl. He scowled and glared at his office girls; he practiced it in the mirror or on the neighbors' kids who romped across his immaculate lawn, and on the clients who paid so dearly to see him. He could scoop the chin forward, contract the bushy brows into a single furry line, and bite the big cigar until he had a picture of brutal and abandoned ferocity. He had found that the scowl simplified the handling of business about the office—in weeding out the undesirable element which he couldn't find time to represent.

"Pruiett!" he brawled into the transmitter of the upright telephone which set on the corner of his desk. It was his own way of answering a 'phone. He didn't say "hello" or announce the number; he merely bellowed his name. "Yes—this is Pruiett. If you got any one there that wants to talk to Pruiett, put 'em on the lines. I'm waitin'."

"This is Red Fox, Judge," he heard a coarse voice over the wire. "Remember me? Fox, in the Chickasaw Nation?"

"Hell, yes, I remember you," Pruiett yelled. "How old would I have to get to forget about you? What do you want?"

"I'm in jail, up here at Fayetteville," Fox said. "They got me for—."

"Why certainly," Pruiett interrupted. "They got you for murder an' I know all about it."

"Look here, Judge," Fox pleaded, "I'm in a bad scrape. I got to have some help. What I called you about, I want you to defend me. I want to square up that old trouble; let's forget about it, an' you represent me. I just got to get you to help."

"I am not interested in that old trouble," Pruiett announced, bluntly.

"I got some money—."

The receiver was passing between Pruiett's ear and the 'phone hook, with a vicious gesture of disgust, as Fox said it, but Pruiett heard it. Pruiett paused to reflect. So he had some money, did he? The old woman was supposed to carry ten or twenty thousand around in a pouch under her bustle. Maybe Red had some real money. And wasn't he the kind of a rat that would make the public miserable so long as he was at large? Wouldn't society be better off if Red got his neck stretched? Wouldn't the system gloat, if it put a plug in for justice in Arkansas, the same as in Texas, the Territory, or Oklahoma? Pruiett picked up his 'phone. "Is that you, Red?" he inquired, when the connection was complete again. "This is Pruiett. Maybe I was a little hasty in the way I talked to you; sometimes I pop off a little too quick. Would you like to talk to me?"

"You're damn right, I would," Fox answered.

"I got some other business in Fort Smith in just a few days. I got to come to Arkansas anyway. I'll just get me a ticket on up to Fayetteville, and come in an' see you. We might be able to make a deal."

Pruiett drummed his desk and smoked. He could see through the fog-like haze of the office the rough interior of the old courtroom at Pauls Valley, with a jury in the box and Jeff Aiken in the prisoner's pen. He was fighting for Jeff and the contingent fee that went with Jeff's liberty. The defendant had given him a note for seventeen hundred and fifty American dollars, payable at the Madill Bank, if and when Pruiett set him on the ground a free man. He smiled as he recalled some of the crude, but none the less effective, maneuvers he had resorted to in proving Jeff's innocence. And he remembered the victory. It had been sweeter then, he ruminated. Pay was better now, courts were more refined, more cultured and more discreet, although the juries were just as gullible and he cleared his clients just the same, but there was something lacking from the savor of the winning. Yes; he readily recalled the exhilaration he had experienced when Jeff and Marie, his wife, broke their own long embrace to inflict it, jointly, around his neck, while the woman kissed him and thanked him again and again.

"Jeff," he had said, "that note you made was put up at the Madill bank, by your dad. I wasn't to get any more fee if you didn't come clear, but if you did, the note was to be paid. Is that your understandin'?"

"Yep—an' I'm glad to pay it, Mr. Pruiett. You just don't know how happy I am to pay it."

"Is it good—now?" Pruiett inquired. "Have you got the cash?"

"The bank's got it, an' they'll pay it and hold the note. Any time you want to go over there you can get your money. An' I sure am much obliged to you—."

Pruiett smiled as he remembered the payment; the banker counting out the stack of money and pushing it over to him. But the smile froze, as he chewed his stub cigar savagely, as he recalled the sequel; his visit to a frame shack of a drug store; his customary quest for a drink of whiskey.

The clerk had worn a striped vest. "I'm Moman Pruiett, from Pauls Valley," Pruiett told him.

"How are you today, Mr. Pruiett?" the clerk said. "Seems like I've heard tell of you before."

"I'm no Federal," Pruiett continued.

"No, you're no Federal," the clerk repeated. .

"An' I'm dry as a chip. I got to have a drink."

"Sorry," answered the clerk, shaking his head, "but I ain't got a bit of licker. An' I don't believe you'll find any in town."

"I want it for myself," Pruiett assured him. "I've got no Indians I want to feed it to. I'm dry, an' I've the money to pay for a drink, so why can't I get a drink?"

"I'd be glad to give you one, if I had it, but I just haven't," said the clerk. "I just haven't got it."

"You got a pretty good drug store here," Pruiett observed.

"She's perty good for Madill," the clerk agreed.

"An' you got some alcohol, for filling prescriptions, now haven't you?"

"Yep, I got the alky."

"An' you got some distilled water, for mixin' up stuff to sell to the customers, haven't you?"

"Yep, I got the water; got plenty of water."

"An' you got syrup of pepsin, right there on the shelf, haven't you?"

"I shore have; more than I need by a hell of a lot."

"Then let me have a little of each, an' I'll show you how to mix up the best drink you ever saw," Pruiett urged.

The druggist was unimpressed. "Let me see that prescription," he said. "You know how these Feds are. They get real incon-

siderate of guys sellin' alky in this Injun territory. That's all I
need to see—the prescription."

Pruiett pulled a bulging wallet off his hip and selected a
flapping twenty dollar bill. The druggist's eyes glittered as he
quickly inspected the contents of the purse. "There you are,"
Pruiett grinned. "There's the doctor's orders. Give me the stuff."

"Just step this way, back in the back," the man smiled. I
can see you're the right kind of a feller. We'll mix it up back
here."

"Have one?" Pruiett inquired, as he went through the final
motions of shaking the ingredients together.

"Don't care if I do," was the agreeable answer. Sitting on
a keg, Pruiett had several. The druggist did likewise. "Ever play
any poker?" the druggist inquired casually.

"I play for keeps," Pruiett boasted. "I haven't been beat in a
long time, an' if you got real genuine affection for your money,
stay out of a game when you see me in. I wins."

"They have a game upstairs, ever' once in a while, but I
don't get in much," the confidential friend continued. "I don't
savvy it so much, an' I'm just as unlucky as hell. Some guys
that don't play near as much as I do will win my money ever'
time. The guy that relieves me, owns half the joint, is so lucky
he could fall in the toilet and come out smellin like a tulip. But
not me—."

"What time you get off," Pruiett asked.

"I ought to be off any time now," he said. "I got a relief man
on the way. Supposed to be here at noon. Let's have another
drink out of your bottle."

"You want to see a real poker player in action?"

The druggist laughed. "Maybe I could pick up a little learnin',
watchin' you. What's on your mind?"

"I got plenty of time, an' plenty of money," Pruiett announced. "Maybe you'd take me by an' make me acquainted with
the boys in the game. I'd like to play awhile."

"Well," mused the druggist, "I'll try it for you. I don't know
whether the boys'll like it, but I'm in pretty solid with 'em. Soon
as my man gets here we'll go upstairs an' see about it."

It had been Pruiett's first meeting with N. L. (Red) Fox.
He grimaced at the recollection. The steps of the rickety wooden
stairway up the outside of the frame building were as vivid in his
retrospect as were the notches on the marble staircase there in the
Baum, which he frequently traveled, when the iron-grilled car

that lurched up and down the shaft in the building's entrails was out of order.

Three men were sitting beside a round table in the center of the barren room. "This is Mr. Fox—Mr. Pruiett," the drug man explained. Pruiett, flushed with the rapid drinking he had been doing, was conscious of an involuntary shiver between his shoulder blades as he shook hands with the gambler. "What's the deal?" the druggist inquired.

"No game," Fox said. "Just waitin' for some of the boys to drop in. I'm ready any time."

"I got a little to invest with you in some stud," the man from the drugstore stated, "and Mr. Pruiett wants to make expenses on his trip over here before he starts back. Shall we start somethin'?"

"Whatever you boys say," Fox agreed.

"Let's get started," said Pruiett.

Fox took a box of heavy bone chips from a wooden cabinet on the wall. Pruiett noticed, while the door was open, that a heavy calibre pistol, with white handles, lay on the upper shelf of the cabinet. He cut himself a chew of tobacco and sat down at the table.

"I'm out'a chips again—an' out'a dough, too." The man from the drugstore pushed his chair back. "Deal me out this time. I'll go downstairs and get a lamp, an' bring it up."

"Jesus Christ," Pruiett growled, "been here all afternoon. Say, shake up another quart of that pepsin licker, will you?"

The druggist clattered down the stairway with a coarse laugh. Pruiett and Fox butted it out, head to head. By eleven Pruiett was down his eighteen hundred and had six checks, for a hundred each, in the game. The dim light, and Pruiett's increasing drunkenness, made Fox both bold and careless. Pruiett saw why he was losing—and why he couldn't win. He pushed his chair back. "I'm gettin' cheated," he said, looking Fox intently in the eye.

Fox flushed and assumed a half threatening, half defiant look. "What do you mean by that?" he growled.

"There isn't enough chips in that pot," Pruiett said. "Oh," Fox said, with obvious relief. "Maybe I'm short; maybe you're short. Let's check it up."

Pruiett stood beside the table and pretended to count the heap in the middle. When he had a handful of the heavy chips he drew back and hurled them with all his strength into the face of the gambler. Blinded and dazed, Fox staggered toward the wall cabinet, with blood spurting between the fingers spread over his face. Pruiett, mindful of the gun there, slipped out the door and down the old stairway.

Why not represent the red headed outlaw? He questioned himself, interrupting his reverie. If he was in serious trouble, and had the money, what mode of revenge would be sweeter than making him pay? Would representing him in court make any difference later—if favorable opportunity presented itself—in his killing him, as he had always wanted to do? What would be nicer —a front row seat at Red Fox's hanging, or seeing him walk out a free man, to bilk, and cheat and murder some more?

Fox was in an inside cell on the second floor when the officers ushered Pruiett in to see him. The prisoner, confined and in trouble, had to grin and try to be conciliatory. The visitor was as cold and tough as his superior position entitled him to be. "I'm glad you came, Pruiett," he said, trying to sound cheerful.

"I had some other business over here an' was comin' any-way. I only came a day or two earlier than I had planned," Pruiett had his reason for lying.

"Sure," said Red, "but I'm glad you came. "They're trying to give me a bum rap, an' I need some help."

"All right," said Pruiett. "All right. Where do I come in?"

"Let's forget that other stuff, you know what I mean. Let me square myself an' tell you I'm sorry. Maybe it wasn't all my fault, but I'll say it was, and say I'm sorry besides. What do you say?"

Red was straining to talk through the bars, and talking fast. His manner suggested that he considered a willingness on his own part to admit a fault and apologize, was all that anyone could ask for or expect. "All right," Pruiett repeated the phrase. "Say you do. Where do I come in?"

"Go to bat for me," Fox said. "I want you to take my case. I'll get you five hundred bucks."

Pruiett sneered. "You steal two thousand four hundred dollars from me, and tell every one on the Washita I moved out of the Valley because I was afraid you were goin' to kill me, and you'll pay me five hundred?"

"But I'm broke, Pruiett," the gambler lied and begged. "I've had a lot of tough luck. I lost a lot of money—"

"The old girl had twenty or thirty thousand on her hip and

ever' one in town knows it. You got two or three good farms an' plenty of money stashed away. If you called me up here for a joke, I can't laugh. I got a cracked lip." Pruiett was gathering in the revenge like Red had scooped in the blue chips on that previous occasion well remembered by both of them.

"I didn't do this job, judge," Fox replied, with an offended look on his red countenance. "I told you this was a bum rap. They got me all wrong, an' I can prove it."

"Well, if you've got such a good defense you can put it on by yourself," Pruiett said, as he started to back away from the bars. "You won't need me, an' I haven't got time right now for a charity job."

"How much will it take? Maybe I can get some help," Red said.

"Five thousand, cash, and I hope you can't make it. I don't want to take the job." Pruiett was carelessly rolling a fat cigar between his hands and watching the prisoner.

"You won't double me, will you, Pruiett?" Fox inquired, pleadingly and searchingly. "You won't hold that old grudge agin' me? I know you can get me off if you start into—"

"You come clear," said Pruiett with the finality of a judge passing judgment. "You come clear and you don't even have to thank me, but who puts up that five? I have it in cash before I make a move."

Fox motioned for him to come close to the iron. He whispered the name of a man to see and a message to give him, then dropped heavily to a sitting posture on the metal bunk. What a spot to be in. The way Pruiett hated him he could take his cash and give him the twist. He could lay down and let the jury braid the rope. Red turned his head slowly from side to side and rubbed the bulging swells of his muscular neck with apprehension. He was remembering the stories about old Ike Parker and Arkansas justice. What a hell of a spot to be in.

The day of the trial of the case entitled the State of Arkansas vs. N. L. alias Red Fox, was at hand. The state was demanding its forfeit, for Red, according to the language of the indictment, "did kill and murder one Carrie Winkleman by striking, beating and wounding her, the said Carrie Winkleman, on the head and body with a hard substance, a deadly weapon, the name and character of which is unknown to this Grand Jury."

A group of men stood about the judge's bench in the courtroom. It was time for court to open. Voll and Wythe Walker, distinguished members of the Arkansas bar, had been hired as special prosecutors. Hugh Densmore, and Sam Peel, congressmen, were there to lend the weight of their good position to the prosecution while the jury was being selected. Enoch Fagan, of the old Paris, Texas, firm of Brents and Fagan, was with them.

"Who's the man with the sinister countenance?" Wythe Walker inquired sarcastically, jerking his head in the direction of the main entrance into the room.

They all turned. "I don't know," Voll Walker drawled, toying with the sharp tip of his van dyke, "but from his general cut, I'd say he was a son of a gun that would fight on state occasions. He looks like he's got some guts."

A stylishly dressed man, with shining black hair, was looking about, inquiringly, as he stood near the door. He wore a high bat-wing collar and a black tie. Diamonds sparkled from various points on his make-up. "That's Moman Pruiett," Fagan muttered. "He's our competitor. I heard he'd been hired in this case, but I wasn't sure."

Pruiett was striding toward them. "Do you suppose he heard what I said?" Voll Walker whispered.

Fagan and Pruiett shook hands. "This is Pruiett, from Oklahoma City," Fagan began, introducing him around. "He used to crowd into my little office, down in Paris, whenever he could pick up a stray case. Maybe he'll let me use his, now that he's going so good, after I lose out, and don't have any."

"I remember you, Mr. Walker," Pruiett was saying, as he shook hands with Voll. "I used to shine your shoes, every day, on the porch of the old Van Winkle Hotel. And I remember you, too, Mr. Densmore. I've shined your shoes many a time."

"What you doin' down here, Moman?" Fagan inquired.

"I'm hired in the Red Fox case," Pruiett answered. "What you doin' down here?"

"I'm in the Fox case, too."

"You mean, they got a special prosecutor hired?"

"They got some prosecutors hired, all right," Fagan grinned, "Voll and Wythe, but they ain't hired me. "I'm donatin' my services."

"What the hell for? You're no kin to the Winklemans, are you?" Pruiett asked.

"Nope, but I'm the prosecutin' attorney for Murray County, where Red was arrested, and where he's been livin' for the past five years. I couldn't convict him of nothin' down there, but he's

worn me out tryin.' I figured I'd come over and help the boys.
I know his record—and maybe I can help to get him hung. That
way, I won't have half so much work to do at home next year."

"What if Red comes clear?" Pruiett laughed. "You'll have
a' extra load of ill will to carry. He'll really cause you some
trouble."

"I ain't worryin' about that," Fagan laughed, winking broad-
ly at the Walker brothers.

"Attorney Wythe Walker, assisting with the prosecution,
made the opening statement yesterday afternoon. He said that
the state would prove that Fox was in Fayetteville on Saturday,
before the murder on Wednesday, and that he ate a chicken dinner
at the restaurant which the murdered woman operated; that he
was accompanied by Gus Sartain; that he exhibited $2,000 in
a roll of bills to witnesses at Sulphur, Oklahoma; that he was
overheard telling Sartain in a pool room that 'she carries the
money on her person.'"

Gus Sartain was the hapless hop-head who had saved the
state the trouble and expense of a trial by hanging himself in
his jail cell. He evidently hadn't heard of Pruiett. And try as
he would, Pruiett couldn't keep references to Sartain's self-destruction out of the evidence in the Fox trial. One witness was informed that Sartain died in California, in the city of Sacramento.
Every syllable on Sartain's consciousness of guilt was an extra
load for overloaded old Red Fox to carry.

Pruiett destiny—Pruiett luck—was seated on the defense
side of the table. Seated in the jury box, fully qualified to serve,
were two ancient reminders of the Arkansas wanderings of the
Pruiett family. Pruiett felt that when the time came he would
know how to handle them. One was F. L. Van Zant, the quick
tempered Beau Brummell of his run-away experience, now con-
cealing the stern conceit of his countenance with a network of
furrows and wrinkles and a square-cut white beard. The other
was old Noah Stockburger, of Winslow. Pruiett, as a lad of
twelve or thirteen had gone to the Stockburger farm for a heifer
calf, bought by the itinerant butcher for sale to the railroad
crews.

Van Zant was still the fashion-plate, as preened and immaculate, with his dress and his snow white hair and beard, as he was
in the days of the old Van Winkle's glory. Stockburger was bald,
wrinkled and debilitated; he squinted to see the witnesses and
cupped his hand behind his ear in an attempt to hear the evidence,

but Pruiett knew him. Neither of the jurors had a suspicion of having seen the overbearing defense counsel before, but the counsel recognized them on the instant. The inexorable artist of age and decay could not paint a disguise to deceive the keen eye and the photographic memory of Pruiett.

"The examination of witnesses on the part of the state is being carried on by Wythe Walker, and by Attorney Pruiett for the defense. Judge Maples found it necessary to reprimand the crowd for 'laughing out loud.' It was when Attorney Pruiett asked Mr. King, who was on the stand, if he knew the present whereabouts of Mr. Isgreig, a defense witness. The witness replied that Isgreig was dead, and that he didn't know where he was."

In the face of the disheartening proof, Pruiett set out to make an alibi stand up. While the plan of operation was practically the same as in the old John Evans and Doc Richards case, the technique was immensely improved. Washita witnesses from the Valley swore that Red had been with them, miles removed from the place of the tragedy, at the time when it must have occurred. With self-defense and the unwritten law eliminated, the alibi was about all that he had left to offer. It was enough to raise a fact question, something to talk to the jury about, and that was about all he wanted. He had some things to say to that jury.

Charles Hillman Brough, Arkansas's governor from 1917 to 1921, was holding down the chair of Economics, Law and Sociology at the State University. On the day the Fox case was to go to the jury the courtroom balcony was reserved for Brough and his law class, in order for them to hear the arguments. The Walker brothers were the big guns of the Arkansas Bar. (The Voll Walker Memorial Library on the University campus is an exhibit to support his claim to fame.) The Winklemans were prominent citizens. Red Fox was a no-good Oklahoma ex-convict with an Oklahoma lawyer who didn't show the proper amount of deference toward the Walkers, Judge Maples or the Arkansas courts. With it well settled that censor, in the form of a death sentence for Red, was about to be made, Fayetteville, with its budding lawyers, turned out *en masse*.

Wythe Walker opened the arguments for the state. . . . Then with clear and sweeping words reviewed the testimony of the witnesses, analyzing the testimony and showing the strength and weakness of each. Now and then, in a burst of mighty eloquence, he would tear the testimony of a witness to shreds. Then again, with sarcasm which burnt like red hot caustic, he would show the falsity of the testimony of a witness. Mr. Walker's review of the testimony was masterful and his conclusions were almost irresistible. He has been in nearly every big criminal case that has been tried in this country for the past twenty years, but he has rarely equalled, and never surpassed, his efforts in this case."

By agreement, Wythe Walker was to open, Fagan was to follow him for the state and then the defense was to have time for its plea. D. B. Horseley, the regular prosecutor, who was to begin the rebuttal speeches, was to be followed by Voll Walker. The state wanted the jury to have the strongest medicine just before it went out. Old Voll stroked his pointed mustache and shot his personality across the jury box rail. He was goin' to show old Red, and his insolent, shoe-shinin' graduate, a few tricks in Boston Mountain prosecutin.'

Enoch Fagan had his coat off in a quarter of an hour. In a half he was lathering around the collar and at the armpits like a trotting mare in the breechin'. Enoch's tough Texas manner, cradled with Colonel Jake Hodge's, as was Pruiett's was hardened with the callous of his Indian Territory and early statehood practice. He disheveled his hair, tore off his collar, and ranted and stalked. Prejudices instead of laws; personalities instead of facts. Give the jurors a good time, and raise hell. He tried cases *a la* Pruiett, to the best of his inferior ability. He made a hell of a lot of noise.

"Gentlemen," he cried, rushing up to Pruiett and grabbing him by the arm, "I know this man better than any one of you! He comes from my own state, and there, in the trial of a murder case, a bad case, where the defendant is utterly guilty, his services are indispensable."

Fagan was holding Pruiett's left hand above his head, and turning it so that the reflected brilliance of his diamond shone squarely in the jurors' eyes.

"This man, when he leaves his state to defend a murderer, commands a fabulous fee. Look at that rock! See it sparkle? See it shine? Look at it, and tell me if you see in it any of the money that poor old Aunt Carrie saved to protect her against want in her declining days of helplessness? That's where he got it! That's it! He took the wealth to buy the diamond from the murderous paws of Red Fox, who killed and robbed Aunt Carrie. The red that shines there, with the blue, is the life-blood of the poor old soul, trickling down from the wound which Red Fox made with his iron club."

Pruiett sat quietly, making no effort to draw his decorated digit from Fagan's unnecessarily rough grasp. He assumed an expression of tolerant lack of interest, and patiently waited for such a time as the demonstrator would select for replacing his hand back in his lap.

"He commands fabulous fees," Fagan roared, "because he gets the results the murderer wants. I know him. I have seen him before a jury, and I realize his power. As I have seen it, you will feel it, and permit me to warn you against him. Don't be swayed by his matchless eloquence; do not abandon your understanding of truth, your conviction of right, for a siren song. This man, with his forensic perfection, has been trained and schooled by the great masters of the land, and he comes now on the blood money of our departed sister to gain a pardon for her murderer."

When Fagan released his hand and went into another phase of his argument, Pruiett was happy and his soul was at peace. It was not that he was glad to see Fagan let up on him, but that he had seen Fagan, by his own unsuspecting hand, open the gate of the avenue direct to Van Zant and Stockburger. While he had known how he wanted to approach them, the proper lane had not until then been opened to him.

But the hour, which was, and was to become, the anathema of law and order and the men who had to try to assert it, had come. The master of all fanatical forensics, the advocate who hypnotized his listeners, who fascinated them by his utter abandon in oratory, and who dazed them by the heights he could reach in ragged, uncouth vituperation, had to have his say.

Pruiett realized that regardless of the evidence, his client's unsavory record, known to the jury, and the brutality of the treatment meted out against a worthy citizen, made the balances sag away from him. Some one ought to be punished and Red Fox was the only prisoner in the bull pen. He wasn't worth a damn, anyway, so don't let all the money the state's spent tryin' to hang him go to waste. Pruiett could usually figure pretty close to how a juror viewed a murder case.

He looked the jury in the teeth, told them that his client was guiltless, and demanded that they acquit him. Then he proceeded to tell them why. And when he had thoroughly disposed of the material issues he moved into the realm of his most accomplished endeavor, the manipulation of emotion. The partisan "Daily" wasn't impressed, as it had been by Wythe Walker, but the speech mustn't have been so bad. "Attorney Pruiett made a strong plea for the defendant, reviewing the evidence at considerable length" was all the "Daily" had to say, ten hours before the verdict.

"My friends," he said, warming up to his real task, "Counsel has presented me as a product of the far off lands of the masters, where I have been schooled in law, logic and oratory."

He paused, to press a slightly disturbed black wisp back into the bulk of his exuberant crown. He was speaking low and slow, from a confidential crouch. He was close to his dubious listeners. Gazing sadly at his diamond he continued:

". . . and the luxuries I have obtained at such a dear price, he says I have purchased with the blood of your townswoman. I see blood in it, and that white you see—" he held its shining brilliance in their very faces, "the white you see is sweat from my own brow as I labored and suffered with you to lay the rails that carried the first train through this section of this state. The blood is from my own torn palms, carrin' burdens heavier than my youthful strength would permit me to carry, but toilin' on, an' complainin' not."

The jury was impressed, but not understanding. There was a puzzled interest in their faces which he had purposely put there, preparatory to a climax which they would hear, feel and understand.

"I? I trained by the masters? The sum and total of my life's schooling was ten months; ten months spent in the country schools of Arkansas."

He lifted his face to the listening law class on the balcony above.

"Doctor Brough," he cried, "as a purported product of the masters, I commend you for the development of a wonderful institution. You have made this the Athens of a proud state, a state that is proud of you and your accomplishments here. I have crossed your campus, admired your fine buildin's, and envied your handsome and carefree students, but I must confess, as a former citizen of your state, I have never crossed the threshold of a single one of 'em, nor was I ever, in all my years, within the interior of a school of higher learnin'."

He was masterfully building to his climax. He had purposely avoided the direct gaze of Van Zant, whom he intended to make the brunt of his slow gathering attack. His attention went back to the diamond again.

"The utter privation of my boyhood is responsible for this weakness in me, this vulgarity, which I confess I am unable to control. As I washed dishes in the kitchen of the old Van Winkle Hotel for my supper, breathed the odor of the fine food as it went by me on its way to the dinin' room, and saw the guests on the veranda in their fine clothes, and jewelry, I promised myself that I would overcome my poverty, and that when I did, I would permit my hungry soul to partake of those things which then excited my interest and envy."

He stole a quick glance at Van Zant. He was stroking his white beard with quick nervous jerks. He was ready for the thrust.

"And counsel, who would prostitute the truth to discredit me in my countrymen's eye, for the sole purpose of prejudicing and convicting my innocent client, will say that I lie, and that I borrow these references to the past from my fancy, for an ulterior and unseemly purpose. I should then have corroboration for my story from one of repute; from one who can vouch for the truth and correctness of my statements."

He strode to a position before the nervous Van Zant; he was still stroking the beard and pondering, but unable to penetrate the veil between those things the strange lawyer had suggested, and the indistinct, distant past.

"A fine gentleman strolled the veranda of the old Van Winkle," he barely whispered. "An undernourished boy with a blackin' box was slavin' for nickles, sleepin' in a livery stable loft and washin' dishes in the kitchen for his supper. The kid held the gentleman's horses for pennies and nickels, and shined his fine boots, on the veranda, ever' day. And one day the careless boy let the brush slip, while he was blackin' the gentleman's shoes, and the blackin' smeared his clean white socks. He lost his temper and delivered a kick, and the boy was cryin' in the cinders of the pathway—."

Van Zant saw it with the reference to the white socks. He turned helplessly from side to side in his chair, as if looking for a means of escape. He stroked the white beard frantically as he fought to restrain the tears which threatened to come. He saw the whimpering boy he had mistreated; remembered how he had bathed and aided him; saw Betty, his poorly dressed mother, coming for him and taking him home. "Can you vouch for me, Mr.

Van Zant?" he whispered. "Can you do that much for me now?"

Pruiett whirled and strode to the corner occupied by the aged Stockburger. He pointed his finger at him dramatically, and cried: "And you, Mr. Stockburger, can you vouch for me? The butcher's boy, who came that mornin' in the spring, to lead away your Mary's pet calf?"

The juror was confused. The events of that day were now as clear and complete in the Pruiett brain as they had been the day after. He had worried, childlike, about the grief of the coarse farm woman.

"You fastened my rope around her horns before you took your chain from around her neck," Pruiett reminded. "And I paid you the money my father had given me for you; the seven miserable dollars. You took it, reluctantly, like you felt that you were betrayin' a friend, sellin' your Bess to the butcher. But you were so poor then, my friend. You can understand my vulgar desire to wear this stone now, now that I can afford it, after those years of want and privation? You patted the calf, and when I started away, your wife Mary, called me back, and had me to lead her to the chimney corner, by the rough joint in the logs, while she gave her a farewell pinch of salt—."

A sob broke in the old man's throat as the word picture came suddenly upon his understanding. He cried convulsively.

"I can see her there now, with that salt in her poor work-worn hands, while the heifer licked it out. And she was cryin'. When I saw the tears in her eyes, running down her cheek, I wondered. I was but a child. I wondered how she could be concerned over parting with a yellow calf. And then she told me to go ahead and her voice broke in a sob. I can understand it all now, Mr. Stockburger; we were all so very poor, and she knew that you needed that money so desperately—."

Juror Stockburger had spread both hands across his face and was crying like a child. Fagan jumped up.

"Your honor," he said, "I must object to this line of argument. It is outside of the issues, and is too plainly—."

"You're overruled, Mr. Fagan," the court ordered savagely, "You injected this issue in the case, and he has a right to answer, and I caution you not to interrupt counsel, or the court again—."

"—when I got to the road she was still standin' there, in the same place. She hadn't moved, and as I glanced back, I saw that faded old apron she was wearin' and with those red hands, wipe the tears from her eyes. She waved timidly, an' I know now that she wasn't wavin' at me—."

"I am one of you, gentlemen, and I say counsel is trying to deliberately deceive you when he paints me as a mystic, a spell binder, a product of the masters—."

Voll Walker had risen and walked to the side of Horsely, the state's attorney.

"Pruiett's got his jury, and it's all over," he said. "I won't face them in a final argument. Tell the Winklemans they can keep the part of the fee that was to go to me. And tell that wild bootblack to come by the hotel before he leaves town. I want to get down and give him the best shine he ever got in his life."

He strode to the crowded hooks along the wall, and taking down his broad brimmed black hat, marched from the courtroom.

"For if it is not true, why should he have told you?" Pruiett was concluding his appeal. "His purpose is to degrade me, to the detriment of my client. Unless the prayers of a devoted and sacrificing mother and the unswerving application of an under-privileged boy constitutes a course under the great masters, counsel is wrong and his declarations to you are false. By the same measure his charges against the defendant are unfounded, and crushed truth should rise to its innate glory by your verdict of acquittal!"

The jury returned a verdict of "not guilty."

CHAPTER TWELVE

How Pruiett is deprived of a fat fee and two clients at the same time, by the intervention of old Judge Lynch, and a group of murder cases, with possibilities, are never tried. And wherein the murderer's friend sits at the wrong side of the counsel table, and a theatrical killer is sentenced to the henceforward in confinement for his misdeed. And how Pruiett atones for his assistance to the system as the jury says "not guilty." And how it begins to appear that good murder cases are not produced without Pruiett, and that, although a pretty murderess goes up for life despite his defensive effort.

"Take any of that money? Me? Hell no! Why I ought to kill you." The expression of a man in rough ranch clothes showed that he was seriously considering murder as he spoke.

"Look here, Jesse," the one he addressed answered, "I had to do it. I'm a deputy marshal now, and Jim shouldn't a'come around here, when he was so hot. Hell, anybody could have found out if I'd a' passed him up. That's what you call duty, Jesse. I didn't care a damn about the reward, but I'm goin' to cut it with you; I'll give you—."

"Not none of that blood money, you don't; not a God damn cent. Jim Harbolt was my friend, he thought you was his friend. Maybe he did rob a few banks, an' a few trains, but the Texas laws ought to be able to catch him. That's where he done it. Duty, hell. If you'd doublecross Jim you'd double me, and—."

"You ain't got no call to say that to me, Jesse. We been together too long. Let's cut this reward, and get on about our business. We can't fall out over no damned road agent.

"Jesse West and Gus have fell out—they've split," the word was whispered along the curbs and hitching rails. "Jesse West has gone in partners with his brother-in-law, Joe Allen, out in west Texas, at Canadian, an' he's talkin' pretty dirty about Gus." The town talkers continued to dwell on the old partners' affairs. "Gus Bobbitt got to him in the ranch deal; an' what he says about Jesse an' why they quit doin' business together ain't very complimentary."

Bobbitt couldn't be stopped. His brood mares brought mare colts and his cows dropped heifer calves. "He's so damn lucky they drop twins, lots of times, an' just as sure as he ships a train load out, the market goes up. He must be livin' right," less

PROTEST AGAINST PRUIETT DELIVERANCES
"Jesse's feet were swingin' off the ground like a pendulum."

fortunate stock raisers complained. Adjoining tracts were acquired and added to his already extensive ranch. He hired all his work done and proceeded to lay back and rule the ranch hands. As the years sped by and he lived high, his jowls began to sag and he pushed his prodigious belly out in front of him.

"Jesse West's back in town," the electric word went through the crowded stores and streets. "He's back in town, and Gus Bobbitt's in, too. There's a lot of trouble comin' up; you can watch out for a killin'."

"Who's that Jesse's got with him?" was the quiet inquiry. "That guy that looks like a preacher? Wonder where Jesse an' Joe picked up such a queer looking duck?" "Is that a wig he's got on, or is it real hair?" "Hell, it's real. I've seen it lots of times, down to Fort Worth. You know what it looks like? A damn possum's back, don't it?"

"That's the funniest lookin' guy I ever saw." "That's Jim Miller." "That's who?" "That's Jim Miller. That's why I said to look out for a killin'."

"Jesus Christ! Is that Miller? Looks like a damn preacher like I said, doesn't he?" "Well, Jesse West ain't runnin' with him for nothin'. He brought him here for reasons. I'm gonna lay low, an' I'd lay low as hell, if I was Gus Bobbitt."

Jim Harbolt was still behind steel in Texas. Statehood had come to the territory where he had been betrayed and captured, and where the partners West and Bobbitt had divided their lot. Talk, years of talk, that the talkers wouldn't forego, had augmented the smoldering feeling between the men, so that with the prospect of an ultimate meeting, what had begun as a passive hatred was nearing the verge of an active, murderous feud.

West, in a plaid jumper, leaned against a muddy wagon wheel on the sunny side of the street. It was warm there, in out of reach of the sharp February gusts which made the opposite side uncomfortable. "Been seven or eight years since I seen old Pontotoc," he reflected. "These scrubby hills look pretty good, after all that flat sand out the Panhandle way. Seems pretty good to get back."

Joe Allen, his tractable young brother-in-law, was beside him, as usual. "Ain't changed a bit," he chirped, "Looks just the same to me as it did last time I was here."

A tall, sallow-faced man with splotched black and white hair, stood between Allen and West. He held both hands in the side pockets of a black overcoat. "Just as many of these God damned Indians as ever, an' just as lazy an' dirty," West continued. "Ought to be some way the white folks could get rid of 'em; not have to have 'em around in the way, all the time."

"Ought to kill 'em," the man dressed in the black overcoat observed. "That's the best way. Kill 'em ever' damn one."

West laughed. "That's all you think about, Jim, killin' somebody. But let me tell you, you don't need to waste no lead on these bastards. Just give 'em enough money to buy a little corn, an' they'll kill themselves. Likker, an' T. B. That'll get 'em all an' damn quick, too."

"It'll take too long, that way," Miller disagreed. "Christ, I get tired of seein' 'em ever' place I look. I say, line 'em up an' plug 'em."

"You give me the creeps, Jim," said West, bracing himself as if to suppress a shiver. "Think about somethin' else once in a while. Get them ideas—."

"There's Gus Bobbitt." Joe Allen interrupted them.

West set his jaw, and his eyes narrowed, as he watched the fat form of his old partner saunter out of a store across the street. "I don't know about that; maybe you got the right idea, at that," he said to Miller. "Remind me to talk to you about it—later."

Jim Miller's extensive reputation for being a professional assassin—he would kill anyone anywhere for five hundred dollars—didn't seem to impress Bobbitt. He strolled up and down the opposite side of the Main Street, grinning insolently across at West and his two companions. Like kids, afraid to fight, Bobbitt spent the afternoon on the one side of the Main Street, West on the other, silently daring each other to stick his toe across the line. When Miller, West and Allen drifted off to a liquor joint, Bobbitt moved on down to the wagon yard.

"Jesse West's just as yellow as he always was," he told the man who was working there. "Him an' that god damned murderer he's got with him don't scare old Gus. Hitch them mules up an' get me out of here. I got a long drive out to the ranch ahead of me, an' I want to get started on it before night. An' if anyone asks you, just tell 'em the cow thieves don't scare Gus Bobbitt; not a damned bit."

When the sweating mules pulled the heavy load of cottonseed meal into the ranch yard that night and stopped with their chins over the wooden gate of their pen, no driver ambled down from the wooden seat. A ranch hand, swinging a lantern as he hopped up, recoiled from the headless hulk which sprawled back in the load of yellow feed. Bobbitt's head had been torn off by a shotgun's blast.

Jim Miller was caught in Texas, weeks later, and brought back to Ada. Jesse, with Allen trailing, kept out of sight for over a month, but the search that had been made for Jim Harbolt, those years before, was mild compared to that which was carried on for them. West knew that he'd be implicated in the killing and that he'd have to stand trial for it, eventually, but he wanted to make an arrangement or two before he did. There was a certain lawyer he wanted to have interested in his case.

"My name's Jesse West, an' this here's Joe Allen; I married his sister." He was introducing himself to Pruiett. "I got an idea we're gonna need a lawyer."

"I wouldn't be surprised," Pruiett agreed, dryly, "but you ought to get a premium, instead of a rap, if you really killed Gus Bobbitt. That guy was no good."

"Did you know Bobbitt?" West took the hook and began to run with it, but quickly recovered. "I'm innocent. I didn't have nothing to do with it an' I can prove it."

"Sure, if they'll give you a chance," Pruiett said, "but that's what you'd better make sure of. I knew Bobbitt, an' I knew his gang up there. They tried to shift a cattle stealin' job off onto Caddo Gordon, one of my nigger clients down in the valley, but I cleared him. An' that guy Alexander, that was hired to lie against the nigger, stole the cattle himself, an' I proved it on him. They filed on him, then—."

"I heard somethin' about that, Pruiett, but what about us?" West was under a strain. "I got money, an' I'm innocent. Will you represent me?"

"Such a hell of a question," Pruiett laughed. "From now on I'm your lawyer. An' for your first piece of information an' advice, I'm tellin' you that they've caught Jim Miller, an' got him in Ada. They're tryin' to keep it quiet, but I had a fellow 'phone me. Will he talk?"

"Hell no," answered West.

"I don't know how they've missed you," said Pruiett, "hot as you are. But I got to have a little time to study; to decide on what's the best thing to do. Duck in a roomin' house for tonight an' get me some word about where you are tomorrow. I'll try to see if it's safe to surrender, see if I can get a deal; a good stiff bond for immediate surrender."

West and Allen were captured a short time after stepping from Pruiett's office building onto the sidewalk. West didn't mind the end of the flight, but he did object to being taken back into Bobbitt territory. "When the men were in the police station here (Oklahoma City) they talked quite a little, and both of them said they would be killed if they were taken back to Ada," one of the officers who arrested them said. West, in particular, was sure that his trip to Ada would be his last. West told the officers the only reason he never killed Bobbitt was because he didn't get the chance.

"These deputies say they'll take care of you, an' they're the law," Pruiett consoled him as the train was preparing to pull out. "Miller's preliminary's already set, an' I'll get an early hearin' for you. I'll be through with the case I got here in two days, an' I'll be right on down to Ada. We'll make a deal on the fee, an' leave it to me."

"I see," said Jesse, "an' I got the stuff to make it damn interesting. Just go to work, an' leave the pay to me."

Pruiett whistled gaily as he tipped the depot porter and sauntered up to the confection stand. He was catching the early morning train southeast, to see West and Allen in jail at Ada. It was real business, and real money. "Got the mornin' paper, honey?" he inquired of the girl behind the counter. "Got to have somethin' to read on this rattler. Give me the Oklahoman."

"I just hardly can," said the girl, "they just got in. I haven't had time to look at it myself."

"I like 'em fresh," agreed Pruiett. "Say! What the hell! Jesus Christ! Well, can you imagine that?"

The front page was smeared with the photo of four dead bodies, swinging by distorted necks. Pruiett recognized Jesse West's plaid cowboy shirt; he didn't need to read the accompanying story. He pulled his hat down and hurried out to the line of waiting hacks. He was going back to his office. He hadn't paid for the paper he clutched so viciously; his leather bag sat unnoticed beside the news counter in the station.

"Four men, charged with the murder of A. A. Bobbitt, a wealthy cattle dealer of Ada, were quietly taken from the Pontotoc County jail at 2 o'clock this morning by a mob of sixty men and hanged to the cross-beam of an abandoned barn, a few feet from the jail. The mob dispersed as quietly as it was formed and the town knew nothing of the affair until the bodies were found early this morning. In the undertaking establishment of L. T. Walters lie the bodies of James Miller, B. B. Burrell, Joe Allen and Jesse West."

Pruiett was shaking his head sadly as he read the account under the photograph. Five thousand anyway; maybe he would have been able to hike it to seventy-five hundred, maybe ten thousand. Such a hell of a break. Such a case to try; to rant, and roar and raise hell in. It was gone. Why did he have to have all the hard luck?

"When the mob entered the jail they encountered James McCarthey and Joe Carter, night guards, who upon attempting to prepare for resistance were securely bound and left under guard of a party of masked men. The mob then entered the sleeping apartment of Deputy Sheriffs Walter Goyne and Robert Nester, and compelled Goyne to deliver his keys to the cells. * * * The leaders then entered the cells corridor, opened the cells in which the alleged murderers were kept and took them out without trouble save for West, who fought like a demon. He was struck over the head with a revolver and his skull fractured. The mob then repaired to an old barn forty feet from the jail, strung the men to the cross-beams, and quietly dispersed."

Pruiett grinned as he reflected over the story. Old Jesse West went down battling. He was a real man; tough as buckskin, and always ready to fight. Old Jesse wasn't afraid of their ropes; he wasn't afraid to die. Pruiett knew that. He wanted to see how many of Bobbitt's friends he could mark before they got his feet swingin' off the ground like a big pendulum. Like a demon—was that what it said? Yeah? He could see him crumple —not all at once,—but slow, and defiant, when they broke his head with the gun barrel. Pruiett could have experienced genuine sympathy for his friend of the new and short friendship, if it wasn't for his recollection of the lost fee.

"The crime for which these men were lynched was the murder of A. A. Bobbitt, a very prominent cattleman and former deputy U. S. Marshal. Suspicion pointed to Miller, and after considerable search he was located near Fort Worth. The others were arrested at different places, West and Allen being the last captured, at Oklahoma City."

"The prominence of the parties in the case gives it additional interest. Miller was under indictment for murder committed in Johnston County, and it is talked freely on the streets that he is suspected of numerous other killings. West and Allen, who were brothers-in-law and lived at Canadian, Texas, were well-to-do stockmen. While living in the Seminole Nation a very bitter feeling arose between them and Bobbitt. Burrell lived in Fort Worth, but formerly lived in the Indian Territory, holding at one time a position of cashier of a bank at Duncan."

Pruiett leaned up toward the hack driver. "That's what old dog Tray gets for runnin' with the sheep-stealin' pack," he hollered. "Buck-shot in his butt. That Burrell kid didn't have no connection with the killin' at all, no more than you did."

"I don't know nothin' about it," the driver replied. "Keeps me busy tendin' to my own business. Wouldn't hurt other people to do the same thing."

Pruiett leaned back. "The dumb cluck. Wonder how much interest I ought to have in it,—how much I ought to lose,—before I'd be entitled to just mention it?"

Editorially, the local press approved the mob's conduct and took its customary poke at Pruiett. The satisfaction of getting to hear society's organ howl was all he got out of his experience with the case. "As a sequel to a violent assassination that occurred in Ada, in February, last, four men suspected of the crime were lynched. . . . Lynchings are to be deplored, but Oklahoma juries are permitting too many murderers to escape the penalty of their crime. . . ."

"She killed me!" he gasped, as he propped himself on his hands and looked into the indistinct blur of curious faces around him. "I guess I shouldn't have come back here."

Andrew Gilbert was like the farmer boy grazing the mule. When he got tired of holding the rope he tied it to his leg and laid down for a nap. He realized and admitted, as soon as the mule became frightened and started to run away, that he had made a most serious mistake.

His good wife Agnes, who was rapidly becoming a widow, was standing quietly beside him and over her, a defiant expression on her hard Irish countenance. Wispy smoke was still trickling from the nozzle of the bull-dog revolver she held in her dangling right hand, and was drifting into invisibility with the steam which rose from the wash tub setting across two chairs, on the porch nearby. The hand holding the pistol was big and red. Splotches of wet on the front of her coarse apron suggested that her activities in dispatching a lead slug through her prone mate

ANDREW GILBERT AND AGNES
"You ain't goin' to take him in thar an' bloody up my clean bed."

were but briefly removed from her labors over the tub and wash-board.

There was enough drama in the situation to arouse the literary in the news hound on the police run. "The man fell backward and after a few convulsive movements all was over. A large crowd had collected in the yard, attracted by the sound of the shooting and the sight of the speeding police buggy, and pressed morbidly forward to watch the death throes of the dying man."

Selecting an arm and a foot apiece, a quartet of kindly kibitzers lifted the inert remains and started toward the house. Agnes vaulted the steps ahead of them. With her arms folded across her extensive chest and with the pistol still uncomfortably prominent, she placed her ragged figure across the opening into the kitchen.

"You better lay it on the porch," she said coolly. "He'll be all right there. You ain't goin' to take him in thar, an' bloody up my nice clean bed."

When they locked her up, and later when they filed the murder charge against her, she was as unperturbed as she had been there on the back porch. Her's was a sodden life made listless by long suffering and utter lack of hope. If she saw light in the fruit of her desperation, delivery from the discouraging repetition of seeing Gilbert stagger in at night, stuporous from drink, it did not reflect from her tired eyes. If there was remorse with the realization of his death, a stolid and unwavering chin concealed it.

Pruiett claimed that he offered his services to the washerwoman without figuring a fee, and that the development of a choice piece of cash after the conclusion of the case was but the inevitable reward which follows the righteous.

"Agnes," he said, squinting through the bars at her, "This is Mr. Pruiett . . . Moman Pruiett. I want to talk to you."

"I don't want to talk to you," answered Agnes. "I didn't send for you, so don't bother me. I ain't got no use for lawyers."

"You just think you aint," Pruiett corrected her. "I been at it quite a while, an' I can't remember ever seein' anyone who could use a lawyer to better advantage than you could, right now. You've got a pretty rough road to travel."

"Not so rough that I can't stand it, an' it's my own business," said Agnes. "An' it won't be no rougher than it has been behind me, an' I stood that for a long time. I'm guilty. I ain't got no excuse, an' I ain't got no money. I guess you won't bother me anymore, now."

A soft laugh came in between the rusty bars. "Who said anything about money?" he said. "I'm not lookin' for money. I've got enough to get by on for awhile, an' I've got enough business to keep me busy. I came down to try to help you."

"Then I'll say I'm much obliged to you, Mr. Pruiett, but I don't need none of your help. I know what I want to do, an' it ain't fightin' the case. I want you to let me alone."

There was a minute or two of silence. "I got a little girl out home; just twelve years old, same age as your kid. She reads the papers, an' she saw that little girl of yours with her picture in it. She's made me explain all about the trouble to her."

There was no reply from the interior of the cell in the brief pause which followed, Pruiett continued. "She made me promise I'd come to see you, an' offer to help you, before I left home yesterday morning. When I got home last night an' told her I hadn't done anything about it, why, it hurt her—an' that hurt me. It was that young lady that decided you needed a lawyer."

He paused again, and listened, but he heard nothing. "She's got some dolls an' things together, an' we're takin' 'em by to her in the morning—out at your sister's. It was her idea, understand, not mine. I believe," he almost whispered, "that I couldn't hardly stand to have them take me away from that kid of mine. These bloodthirsty prosecutors around here'll cause you plenty of trouble, even if you fight. But if you just lay down, they'll give you more than you'll be able to stand. Ten or fifteen years ain't so bad, unless it drags you away from someone that means a lot to you, an' then it's worse than life. Say—would you mind if me and my kid picked that girl of yours up tomorrow evening, an' took her out to my house for supper?"

The jailer had to call time on the Pruiett-Gilbert visit that night. Their plans for her defense, started there through the cell bars, promised to last till morning unless interrupted.

An organization known as "The Law and Order League" had sprung into being and was flourishing in the southwest. Its object was to procure a more adequate and proportionate punishment for crime than the regular system was meting out during the period. The liberation of the fiendish Red Fox, the apologetic clean slate given Judge Maben, Jim Stevenson's acquittal, and in short, Pruiett's depredations in gutting the pens and letting the gallows go hungry, was the stimulus for its inception and rapid growth.

"There is always two sides to every story, and God forbid that we should cry aloud for vengeance or demand an eye for an eye, a tooth for a tooth, but if the courts of Oklahoma declare every man innocent who shoots down another then indeed anarchy will reign. . . . No one blames a man for using every effort in his power to be freed, for life and liberty is sweet, but the law abiding people deplore the fact that seemingly it is impossible to convict a man in Oklahoma of homicide, that is, a man who can employ astute lawyers or bring influence to bear on the courts. . . ."

While the editorial writer didn't utter the name, the subject was understood, for Pruiett had just cleared Jim Stevenson, for killing Cathey, the marshal, and the populace as well as the press, was screaming. Pruiett read it and grinned as he thought of Rusk, and Little Rock. He was making money so fast that he couldn't deposit it in the bank; he didn't want them to know how fast he was taking it in. He stowed sheafs of bills and sacks of coin, the origin of which was oftentimes subject to censor, in the massive iron safe in the corner of his office.

The dream that had been his solace in the hours of darkest despair had come true, and the anti-social vow he had uttered as he was being dragged away to his prolonged discontentment he had kept. He ground his teeth and rumpled his raven hair with a trembling hand, as he told himself and the horde of hangers-on who trailed him about, that it was only the beginning; that his best was yet to come.

Ironquill's "Washerwoman" was the nucleus for a premeditated tear jerker which Pruiett delivered, intended for the deliverance, of red-handed Agnes. The defense of the case had exerted an uncanny influence over him, and his conduct through its trial had been unusually brilliant. A banker jury sat in the box. He knew that the propaganda of the Law and Order League, with its constant editorial fortification, would find fertile beds for sprouting and growing in their complacent bellies. Pruiett had realized it and tried to avoid it by a heated attack against the entire panel, charging that individual members were prejudiced by the placards, posters and editorial which the semi-secret organization had succeeded in circulating.

Unsuccessful in his attempt to disqualify the panel, he took up the challenge. By his own main strength, and his exposure of the stupidity of the prosecution, he would make the League, itself, turn one of his clients loose.

Pruiett wouldn't let them forget his connection with the case based on nothing save his client's utter friendliness and innocence.
"Just a trifle lonesome she,
Just as poor as poor could be;
But her spirits always rose,
Like the bubbles in the clothes,
For the woman has a friend,
Who will help her to the end."
The personality was being turned on. Standing close to the front row of the jurors, so they could feel the charm exuding from his well groomed frame, he was engaged in deliberately shoveling spades-full of maudlin sentiment into the eyes of their sound judgment.
"I have seen her rub and scrub,
On the washboard in the tub,
While the baby, sopped in suds,
Rolled and tumbled in the duds,
Or was paddling in the pools,
With old scissors, stuck in spools."
He was bringing back the aching damp of Ozark poverty; Betty, stooped and sweating as she labored for the cursing laborers from tie-cutting camps or the fills of the frontier railroad. The methodical rise and fall of the washboard stroke was in his dogged gestures; anguish of mind, agony of body, suffering of despair, came up with his voice and hung like limp, wet garments about him there in the crowd, even after he had ceased to speak and stood gazing appealingly into the floor or ceiling of the courtroom.
"Human hopes and human creeds
Have their roots in human needs,
And I should not wish to strip
From that washerwoman's lip
Any song that she can sing,
Any hope that songs can bring,—
For the woman has a friend
Who will keep her to the end."
The old Pruiett vanity, after it had recovered from the shock which Agnes's conviction gave it, had to call on a friend to keep her from an unanticipated, and rather ignominious end.

The jury found her guilty of manslaughter and gave her four years. With the verdict coming in late at night, he had sent an office associate to receive it, while he stayed with the celebration he had prematurely opened in a downtown hotel room. He was so sure of another acquittal that he had partially completed the speech of congratulation on himself. When the 'phone message apprised him of the unexpected outcome, he swayed unsteadily, and glass in hand, extemporaneously supplied a brief conclusion.

"The jury cried too easy," he said as he swayed. "When you got a bunch of smooth bellies that sweat easy from the eyes, watch out. A cryin' jury will go out and pray for you, an' cry like old women while they vote to send your soul to hel!. I don't never want another cryin' jury."

Washita farm land on the washerwoman's bond kept her out of jail until the appeal, which reversed the conviction and gave her another trial, was complete. Everyone but Pruiett considered the outcome a victory; that four years for such cold-blooded murder was a triumph and that he was taking an unnecessary risk with the old woman's welfare by exposing her again to a trial that carried a possibility of death, or life imprisonment, with a murder conviction. Pruiett scoffed.

"It is true that appellant is only a poor washerwoman and is without friends, without influence and without money, and is dependent upon the charity of her attorney for her defense; but she is a human being, and her rights are as sacred in the eyes of the law as though she was the wealthiest and most influential society favorite in Oklahoma. It is the duty of this court to see that the poor and friendless are fully protected in the enjoyment of the rights given them by law."

Thus the Criminal Court of Appeals echoed Pruiett's repeated assertion that "the woman has a friend, who will keep her to the end." The next jury to hear Agnes's story had dry eyes and horny hands instead of dripping orbs and agate hearts, and as they opened the figurative gates of prison to the washerwoman they commended her for her steady hand and clear aim. Pruiett took half the night to deliver the congratulatory speech he had prepared to deliver on himself the year and a half before.

Another month rolled by. Rough old Agnes was sitting in Pruiett's office, as conspicuously out of place there as the fashionable lawyer would have been in her steamy kitchen. He was talking on the telephone, and employing his most professional dignity.

"Smith," he was saying, "Mrs. Gilbert is in my office, and she has a paper with her, a paper she says she found in with some of her husband's clothes. It looks like a life insurance policy for one thousand dollars, and so far as I can tell, it was in force two years ago when Gilbert was—er-a-when he died. Would you check up on it, and—.''

"Check up on it, hell," Smith replied. "We did that a long time ago. I've been wondering how long you'd wait after gettin' her off, to spring that policy on us. I've got a letter back from the home office about it, already."

Pruiett abandoned his affectation.

"Well, what do they say about it?" he snapped. "The premiums are all paid and you'll pay on the policy or—."

"The company says pay it," Smith laughed. "If you've got the policy there I'll bring the check over. We've got it made out to you and Mrs. Gilbert jointly. Just a lonesome washerwoman. Just as poor as could be—hello—hello? Hell, he hung up on me."

The history of the Miller murder case, tried in the fall of 1911 in Temple Houston's old bailiwick at Woodward, Oklahoma, presents an example of the versatility of the lawyer Pruiett. Acting as a special prosecutor in one, he obtained a conviction and sentence of life imprisonment. As attorney for the defendant in the other, where the appearance of guilt was so great that he "had to gouge himself in the rump with a peggin' awl," as he himself termed it, before he could get started, he gained the complete acquittal of his client.

Woodward was a plains relay for the endless train shipments of cattle out of Texas into Dodge City and on to Kansas City. The Raven's son selected it as a locale for testing his own deflected genius, because it resembled most the limitless ruggedness of his native Texas. The verdant sod of the buffalo grass had not been violated by the implements which were to pulverize its surface and make it sport for the eddying gusts, and were to ultimately make it barren, dust-blown waste. It was a cattle kingdom in its own right, and the grass pastures which stretched away between and beyond the purple mesas where the headwaters of the North Canadian arose, and on to the sandy stretches of the Cimarron's wide bed, were spotted with great herds of market beef.

Statehood and prohibition had removed the back panel of Woodward's color when its double row of Main Street saloons and sporting houses had been closed, but even after the end of the first decade of the century there was a suggestion of the un- tamed west in the jingling recklessness of the bronzed men who rode clatteringly down the brick pavement on horseback, and left their mounts at the livery barns while they rode away on the cabooses of the cattle trains.

The Indian fights, the overland cattle drives, the building of the Orient and the Santa Fe, were typical reminiscences in gather- ings during court sessions, but the topic which surpassed them all in the fancy of the old-timers was Temple Houston. The memory of the brilliant son of Texas' liberator, who came to Woodward to avoid the confining influence of his sire's greatness in Texas, was fast in the hearts of Woodward.

He was dead, buried in the hard packed earth of the town's Elmwood Cemetery, but the echoing eloquence of his "plea for the prostitute" drifted back like a reverent musical accompani- ment as his admirers retold their stories of his many courtroom achievements.

And as they told the whole story, the muffled roar of his big pistols, blazing death in feud and folly, reverberated like dis- tant thunder along the horizon of the plain. He was reproduced in their provincial phraseology. The collar of his buckskin coat was foul from the grease of his long black hair, which he saturated and twisted into tight rolls, Indian fashion. He stalked into a Main street saloon to settle a difference with the Jennings brothers. Ed Jennings was dead, and Frank, his brother, lay under the same gambling table critically wounded, as Houston holstered a smoking pistol and strolled out into the evening atmosphere. And on the street the children gathered about his boots to play, and to taunt and tease him about his peculiar hairdress. He laughed, and joked, and played with them.

Al Jennings, a brother of Frank and Ed, was a mediocre prairie lawyer. He claimed that he turned outlaw and train robber because a jury refused to convict the killer of his brother, when he was tried for the murder. Speculation on what would occur if and when Temple Houston and Al Jennings came face to face was rife, more abundant than the gossip over the Jesse West-Gus Bobbitt relations, but Al saw to it that a true solution was never available.

"Al wasn't no gun-fighter. He wasn't no lawyer, and so far as that goes, he wasn't no outlaw. He was just a little petty larceny fellow that was willin' to take a plea in a felony case, and do a stretch in the federal penitentiary, just to acquire a bad man's reputation." That was Pruiett's private opinion. He went on record, in his defense of Senator Gore, to charge that Jennings "tendered his reputation as a cow thief as a claim to right of belief." Pruiett even refused to take employment in a good murder case, at Guthrie, because his misguided prospective client wanted him to go in as co-counsel with Al Jennings.

Pruiett was more than casually familiar with the legend of the Al Jennings-Temple Houston feud when he went to Woodward to try the Miller cases. His own relationship to the Panhandle's pride was in the feud fringe, or had been until the time of Houston's death six years before. It had been so since a night in October, 1902, when the two had met in the barroom of the Old Frantz Hotel at Enid, the principal town of the Cherokee Strip country.

Pruiett had traveled the long trail from the Valley to the plains at the insistence of Bill Whittinghill, his friend, who was trying to prosecute cases for the government in the northern territorial district. Houston was getting away with murder in the Cherokee Strip like Pruiett had been on the Washita, and his reputation for being good, and effective, was extending from the south of Kansas across No Man's land and into the stretches of West Texas. Pruiett had hoped that the long-haired Texan would move south into the territory and cross swords with him on his home, or at least a neutral battle-ground, but Houston was too wary for that. Against his better judgment, Pruiett gave in to Whittinghill and agreed to help him prosecute John Riggins, charged with the murder of Harry F. Sears. The Sears family had put up an attractive cash inducement, however, before his great friendship for Bill overpowered him, and the cattle-war case, as it was called, was getting a lot of territorial publicity.

The October 2nd issue of the Enid Events, 1902, chronicled an account of a Pruiett defeat. "Mr. Pruiett made the closing argument in the Riggins case. . . . His remarks were characterized by the fiery zeal for justice and law and order. . . . He made a remarkably analytical argument and wove a web of circumstantial deductions from the evidence which was convincing and conclusive. . . . His 'fiery zeal' caused him to tread on the blunt toes of the figurative Houston boot. He told the jury that 'the defendant's lawyer, who wore buckskins and twisted his hair up like a multitude of rats' tails, had but one virtue and claim to fame,

and that was the undying reputation of an illustrious father.' He
shook his fist under Houston's nose, and cried, 'Spawn of the
tee-pee!'"

Pruiett contended that Houston's attitude of utter contempt
for him throughout the trial of the case had provoked the accusation, one which he well knew would arouse the unconventional
Texan. Judge Beauchamp made a noble gesture. He warned
Pruiett to stay off the streets and to get out of town as soon as
he could, lest Houston kill him, and then under the guise of court
business, took Houston by the arm and insisted that he leave
the court building with him.

Pruiett pondered his problem in his hotel room. He didn't
want to stay, and he hated to leave. The kind of trouble that
appeared to be hovering in the offing wasn't new to him. Outraged ego and offended conceit had been the spark for the violent
physical encounters he had been associated with since early childhood. A paddy who backed off the fill just because his adversary
was approaching with a pick and a wild look wasn't worth keeping. He was yellow. The cowhand who ignored a threat or
backed up at a dare soon had to ride on to another settlement.
The better element of the community shunned a coward. Tossing
his old carpet bag to the bed he unbuckled it and took out the
blue-steel pistol. Pushing the front end of it down into the
waistband of his trousers, he sauntered downstairs for a drink.

Pruiett looked over his bottle and glass and into the back
mirror of the bar, and saw Temple Houston, with three or four
companions, when they came in. They ordered, laughed and
talked in a little group at the opposite end of the bar. Pruiett
knew that Houston was conscious of his presence; had seen him
there as he entered the room and walked up to the rail. He
watched them, by looking into the mirror, and saw that Houston,
with a glass in his hand, was edging down the polished counter
toward him.

"The young gentleman from the Chickasaw country is a
pretty talker," Houston said sarcastically, holding his glass awkwardly in front of him, as if in readiness to toss it into his
listener's face. "He makes a very pretty speech." Having no answer
to make, Pruiett remained silent. He stood looking unwaveringly
into Houston's deep eyes.

"But the jury was not misled by it," Houston continued. "I
guess you have heard that Riggins is at liberty? That he was
found not guilty?"

"I hadn't heard of it, until now," Pruiett replied, using the same terse tones as did Houston, and never letting his stare waver from its level path into Houston's eyes. "I hadn't heard of it, but if that's the jury's verdict, I must necessarily concur in it. The jury is always right."

Houston continued to hold his glass and to stare. "Would the young gentleman from the Chickasaw country condescend to drink with the son of the immortal emancipator of Texas—the cne who wears his hair on his coat collar, like a multitude of rats' tails?" Houston was menacingly sarcastic.

"The young gentleman from the Chickasaw country confines his professional feelings to the courtroom," Pruiett replied. "He tries to give satisfaction to those who trust him enough to employ him. When he has done that he is able to look any man in the face, even his adversary, without an apology. He would be glad to drink with Temple Houston, an able lawyer."

Houston weighed the remarks briefly, and gave a quick nod of approval. "He is indeed a pretty speaker," he murmured. He raised his glass and the drinks were tossed off. Each nodding, they moved away from each other; neither changed the focus of the intense eye-to-eye gaze. Pruiett moved toward the exit; Houston back toward his companions. Each appeared to be uncertain, and cautious and apprehensive, as to what kind of a move to expect from the other.

Pruiett left Erid on the midnight train. Houston dropped into a barber shop on the square, next morning, and left his greasy curls. During the balance of his stormy career he wore his hair close-cropped, in cowboy fashion.

But of the Miller cases—. Pruiett's successful defense of Jim Stevenson, and Judge Maben, and Agnes Gilbert, had broken the morale of his chief heckler, the Law and Order League. The League, persuaded that it couldn't beat him, decided to enlist him, and through the agency of two thousand dollars in cash, engaged him to go to Woodward to act as a special prosecutor.

N. L. Miller, the accused, had purportedly slain a Mable Oakes, long the object of his illicit affection. Always theatrical, Miller had committed his crime on the stage of the "Opera House," an unused theatre in the town of Alva, and set the props so that suicidal end might be deduced. The scene was so crudely laid that it failed to fool anyone but the prosecuting authorities who were politically allied with the prominent Miller, and who wanted to be deceived.

The dead girl's relatives, the populace, and the League, cried for a trial, but Miller leered and grinned, and the county attorney stalled. When Pruiett moved in, the gang around the court house, although they agreed he couldn't compare with Temple Houston, did acknowledge that a lawsuit was going to be tried.

Miller was a strange quantity in himself. He was a typical western villain, with a handle-bar mustaches curling back around large white teeth. He had been educated in medicine, but for unknown reasons had not practiced the profession. He was a studious, scholarly sort of man, well past middle age, who was prominent in the local church, apparently devoted to his plump wife and interested in the welfare of two handsome, nearly grown daughters. He had shifted with the territorial land lotteries and contests as a trader and speculator, and settled, shortly after the last opening, at Alva. In 1911, when the trouble came, he was the justice of the peace, with his office in the building which was principally occupied by the "Opera House."

"Mable Oakes was an innocent country girl who left the farm and entered Miller's office as a stenographer; during the time she was in Miller's employ she was seduced by him. . . . During this time Miller and his wife were separated and he had promised Miss Oakes that he would get a divorce from his wife and marry her . . . ." So did Renfrew's Record, the Woods County paper, view the appalling situation. Miller's villainy was summed up by the ladies of the Missionary Society in a whispered and simple, yet eloquent, charge of shame. "He keeps a COUCH in his office, the wretch," they horrifiedly whispered.

Mable had not been the first to suffer wrong at the hands of the 52-year-old Romeo, although she was the first to lose her life. He was an addict to booze and his own ego. The periodical separation from his wife and family usually lasted during the period of an affair with a new stenographer, who either saw things his way or looked elsewhere for a place of employment. He kept his liquor, which was alternately bootleg or the confiscated evidence of his own constable, secreted in various out-of-the-way places about the old theatre building. When an affair was getting cold and the whiskey bucks were overtaking him, he would repent and go home for forgiveness. His was the life of the typical upland libertine.

Both sides claimed that they were unable to receive a fair

trial at Alva, so by agreement the venue was shifted to Woodward, the adjoining county seat on the west.

"The theory of the state is that Miller wished to put Miss Oakes out of the way as she was about to become a mother, and that he wanted the recent reconciliation with his wife to continue. . . . Miller had approached Dr. Saffold, at that time owner of the Alva Hotel, and tried to persuade him to perform a criminal operation on the girl, which the doctor positively refused to do; that failing in this he informed the doctor that if he had the necessary instruments he could perform the operation himself. . . ." The Record was reproducing a part of the opening statement of Sandor J. Vigg, the son of a Swede farmer, who had worked his way through the law school and had been appointed prosecuting attorney when Claude McCrory had resigned. McCrory quit rather than prosecute Miller, when public sentiment had arisen to such a peak that he had to do one or the other.

Miller had had a medical education. "If he had equipment," as Doctor Saffold quoted him, "he could do the job himself." He had acquired the instrument, a physician's speculum, through a mail order supply house in Chicago, but it had been discreetly ordered, and received, by McCrory, who was then county attorney. Pruiett could prove that the order had been filled and shipped, through the testimony of the employees of the supply firm, but he couldn't prove that Miller ever received it, unless Miller took the stand and gave Pruiett a chance to cross-examine him. The state could prove by McCrory, were he available, how Miller had had him order the appliance, and how he had given it to him on its reception; but McCrory had quit when it appeared the case was actually coming to trial, and the Law and Order League was depleting its stable treasury in a wild but futile effort to run him down.

"Dr. Bilby described the condition of the body and stated the girl would have become a mother in a few months if she had lived. He believed that the girl died from strangulation at the hands of another person, by means of her scarf which was wrapped tightly around her neck. The indications were that it was a case of murder, and not suicide." Renfrow's Record was speaking again—this time commenting on the evidence. "Dr. DeBarr, of the State University at Norman, testified that he had held the chair of chemistry there for 19 years; that he had received the stomach of Mable Oakes from Dr. Bilby by express, and that he

had analyzed it and its contents.   He stated that he found strychnine and morphine there, but not enough to cause death."

The Black Stud was as fully cognizant of the prosecution's
one vulnerable spot as he was aware of the potentialities of the
rest of his case. The fact that the girl was dead, or that Miller
had discovered the dead body, was no circumstance indicating
guilt. Miller and the deceased, as occupants of the rented front
portion of the theatre building, were logically the ones who might
have access to it, and if the girl had wished to kill herself, her
morbidity could not have invited her to a more appropriate spot
than the musty shadows behind the rotting drop. The defense
was not going to deny that the girl was about to reproduce, nor
was it going to admit that the defendant was the one responsible
for her condition. That was part of what had to be proved.

The case hinged on the speculum. If Miller had sent for it,
and if he got it, then the chain of circumstances was complete.
The patient had refused to submit to the operation, so he had
given her a drug in a drink of whiskey. Then he had guided
her, sans the customary white gown and wheeled cot, down the
decaying staircase and through the cob-webb matted passageway to
the improvised surgery table back-stage. When he had removed
a part of her clothing and had proceeded so that his purpose
became apparent in her drug befogged brain, she had rebelled,
and Doctor Miller, instead of administering a little more anaes-
thetic, tightened the struts of the Alpine scarf she was wearing
about her neck, until her remonstrances ceased. Then a conclusion
of the operation had become unnecessary.

The men associated with the prosecution, who scoffed at
Pruiett when he said that Miller would never take the stand
unless McCrory was produced to establish that the surgical instrument which he ordered from Chicago was for the defendant,
looked a trifle less skeptical when the trial judge refused to permit
testimony on the speculum "unless counsel would assure him that
it would be connected, by competent evidence," to the accused.
The League's runners and detectives hadn't located the hiding
ex-county attorney, and hope of finding him had been practically
abandoned.

Thus the state's case was clearly incomplete. The defense
had devoted its time to discrediting the dead girl and proving
that any number of men about town might have been responsible
for her unfortunate condition. The almost savage Pruiett could
feel the reasonable doubt which existed, and which would prob-

ably continue to exist, until he could demonstrate that the accused was the one who first wronged her. When the prosecution was down to routine testimony in support of Miller's general good reputation, he despaired. He knew that the accused was going to claim his constitutional privilege. He wasn't going to testify.

Pruiett touseled his bushy hair as he meditated. Then with apparent languor he arose and walked into the corridor, crowded with curious people craning to see the activity through the open door. After he had been out but a moment he bolted back through the crowd and up to the counsel table.

"Vigg," he said in a hoarse whisper. "Vigg! They've got McCrory. They just brought him in—the sheriff—and took him into your office. Go out and talk to him; I'll watch this record. Have him ready for our first rebuttal witness."

Pruiett was lying, but Vigg didn't know it. He hurried out of the courtroom. Neither did the defendant nor his attorneys know he was lying, and they heard every word of the excited communication. When Pruiett declined to cross-examine the witness, the defense held a brief, whispered conference, and then— Miller, with his black moustaches drooping dejectedly, marched wearily to the stand. He had been well coached for the emergency—the appearance of McCrory—but his dread of Pruiett and the ordeal he was approaching was evident in his every movement and expression. Miller's hope was to beat the prosecution to the punch. What he knew they would prove by McCrory, now that he was there, he would admit himself. He had to acknowledge that he ordered the speculum in McCrory's name and that he was the one who got it. He positively had to deny that he used it, or intended to use it, on dead Mable. But any route he took, away from that denial, led him into a field beset with danger. Miller was no fool; he realized the precariousness of his position.

"And when this speculum came, which you admit you ordered, you attempted an illegal operation on this poor dead girl, didn't you?" The ever accusing, trembling finger was in his face as Pruiett roared at him in cross-examination.

"I did not," he replied with spirit. Miller's wife sat in the courtroom between their two pretty daughters. Pruiett glanced in their direction as he formulated his next question.

"Did you order it for use on your wife?" he inquired.

"No," he answered, "I didn't intend for her to use it."

Pruiett glanced at the innocent looking girls. He saw his

opportunity to further discredit the defendant and at the same time impress the jury with a benevolent gesture on his own part. He took a significant last look at the daughters.

"I won't proceed further in that direction, Mr. Miller. You may stand down."

With one well calculated sentence he had made a beast of Miller and a martyr of himself.

"The State rests." Pruiett made that brief announcement when the trial court invited its rebuttal at the close of Miller's testimony. Then he turned to the defense side of the table and laughed audibly. They understood, without going out to look, that McCrory was not there—had not been there. They knew that they had not only been tricked, but that their position in the case had been speedily reversed. The News at Oklahoma City, in a brief bulletin, concluded the story. "The jury in the N. L. Miller murder case returned a verdict of guilty and fixed the penalty at life imprisonment, after having been out one hour and fifteen minutes."

Pruiett was occupying a room with Dr. Edwin DeBarr, head of the chemistry department of the State University. He had helped to establish that Mable Oakes had been drugged before she was killed. "When can we get a train out of here?" Pruiett asked, as he stirred a drink on the dresser.

"I don't know," answered DeBarr, "but it doesn't make much difference to me. I don't get away for a few days; I'm a witness in another murder case. It's a woman, this time, and her name's Miller, too."

"The Millers up in this country must be a tough outfit," Pruiett observed. "But I'm not in any hurry, an' I've got plenty of liquor. I think I'll wait and see what the jury does to this justice of the peace we just tried. What they got the Miller woman for?"

"You ought to watch that liquor, Moman," DeBarr advised. "It's habit forming, and it's tissue destroying. At the rate you go, and after that speech you just made to the jury, your system shouldn't have any stimulants at all. That stuff will get a hold on you before you know it."

Pruiett laughed. "It can have all the hold on me it wants," he said. "That's what I take it to do. It gives me lots of good ideas. I don't just take 'em after; I take 'em before an' after. When I get so I can see the juror's faces, real clear, I know it's time to ask for a recess, so as to get a drink, or to quit. Forget about me; what about this old Miller girl?"

"Her name's Maggie Miller. She's charged with giving a kid a batch of strychnine. They sent the stomach to me for an analysis, so I've got to be a witness."

"Did you find anything in the stomach?"

"I found enough poison in that kid's belly to kill ever'body in Woodward. Old Dr. Workman, who lives here in town, is goin' to testify that they soaked up three dozen towels, with froth, before the kid died. He had an awful dose."

"Who's kid was it?" Pruiett inquired. "What was her idea? What was her motive?"

"It was her husband's kid; she was the kid's step-mother. It was one of those family fights where the ex-wife and the next wife had trouble ever' time the old man visited with his kid. There's plenty of motive, and it's a cold-blooded one, too."

"Being a step-mother is enough to get her convicted," Pruiett said. "There's a lot of prejudice against step-mothers anywhere you go. Who's defendin' her?"

"I don't know whether she's got a lawyer or not," answered DeBarr. "I believe that Vigg said she couldn't get anyone to defend her. There's a lot of feeling up here in the case."

"Anybody prosecutin' besides Vigg?" Pruiett asked.

"No, not in this case," DeBarr laughed as he answered. "He won't need any help in this case. It's just a case of whether they'll let her off with life, because she's a woman, or whether they'll make the court appoint a lawyer to defend, and then send her to the chair. Between Dr. Workman and me that woman is already convicted."

"Roy Miller died August 5," Oklahoma City's Daily Oklahoman explained in a special article on the case, "and, acting on the advice of his mother, Ellen Miller, the divorced wife of the father of the boy, an examination of the viscera was made by the State Chemist, Dr. DeBarr, and a State Bacteriologist, Ellison. . . . It was claimed that Maggie Miller broke up the home of Miller and his first wife in Chandler five or six years ago. Miller afterward divorced Ellen Miller and married Maggie Miller. . . . The theory of the state is that Maggie Miller poisoned the boy in order to remove the last tie between her husband and his divorced wife. . . ."

Pruiett received his next intelligence on the strychnine murderess, the "tiger lady," as Renfrew's Record had tagged her, while getting a cold water shave in Bill Miller's two chair barber shop. Pruiett had once thrived on worse shaves than the Miller parlor dispensed, but the recent lush years had softened him. When the barber dashed un-cut bay rum on his smarting countenance he squirmed and cursed, and observed that the barber "ought to be down in jail with that tiger bitch that killed her kid." A pained expression, with an uncomfortable silence, told him that he had said the wrong thing.

"I guess I talk too much, old man," he said. "I'm sorry."

"That's my wife," said Bill, frankly and quietly, "and it was my kid, too."

"I'm really sorry," Pruiett repeated. "I had no business sayin' such a thing. Just tryin' to be funny, I guess. I hope—."

"It's all right," said Bill, "but there was a pain in his voice. "It's not the first time I've had to take it."

Pruiett was embarrassed by the effect of his inconsiderate slip. At loss for anything to say, he paid for his service and went out. But he was back in the shop the next day, where he waited until dark, and closing time. Then he and Miller took a walk together, talking in low, confidential tones. When Pruiett got back to the hotel that night he had agreed to defend Maggie Miller, without compensation. It was his way of straightening himself up with Bill.

Pruiett was puzzled. He had agreed to defend Maggie but he couldn't think of a defense. At that stage of his career, agreeing to defend a person charged with murder was synonymous to agreeing that he would gain an acquittal. The dead boy had been but eleven years old. Self-defense or the unwritten law wouldn't work. He couldn't set up an alibi, because dutiful Maggie had stood by and passed up fresh towels to the country doctor who was absorbing the frothy secretion from the convulsed countenance of the child. The boy had been robust and healthy the one day; beset with frothing fits the next. His step-mother had given him the last breakfast he had eaten, and had been alone in the house with him until the doctor was called at mid-morning. DeBarr said—DeBarr said too much. It was no assistance to him, in his quandary for an intelligent explanation, what DeBarr said.

"How long was the boy sick before he began to have the convulsions?"

"I suppose about 24 hours or maybe 36."

This question was propounded by Pruiett, and answered by

the boy's father. "He had been playing with the cat down here at the shop."

At this juncture the Negro boy spoke up and said, "Yes, sir, here is the box," taking the box down from a shelf. The box had a string tied to it.

Pruiett inquired, "Where is the cat?"

The father replied that he had killed the cat.

Pruiett inquired, "Why did you kill the cat?"

The Negro boy spoke up again saying, "Lord God, that cat was havin' fits."

Pruiett inquired, "When did you observe the cat's condition?"

The father replied, "It was when the boy came into the shop crying, complaining that the cat had bit him."

"Did you tell Maggie to call Dr. Workman, when Roy got sick?" Pruiett, addressing Miller. "Did you tell Dr. Workman, or did Maggie tell Dr. Workman?" Pruiett inquired.

"No, I did not, but I tried to, but Maggie did," Miller replied.

"What became of the cat after you killed it?" Pruiett inquired.

The Negro boy chipped in, "I throwed the cat out in the weeds."

Pruiett and the father of the boy walked out to where the dead cat was. Pruiett said, "I wished that I could of got hold of this dead cat earlier, we could of had something material and substantial for the experts to testify to in behalf of the defendant."

Pruiett might have saved his introduction of himself to Doctor Workman.

"We all know you up here now, Mr. Pruiett," the doctor said. "And we are all grateful to you. Your service in that Miller trial was needed, and appreciated."

"Thanks," Pruiett answered, a little dryly. "I'm stayin' over next week, tryin' the other Miller case. I'm appearin' in her defense."

"I'm sorry to hear that; sorry and disappointed," Workman replied. "And I'm sure there are many others here who feel the same as I about it. I know about that case myself, and——."

Pruiett interrupted him. "Don't make a lot of talk before you know what you're talkin' about." He had no restraint to employ in this visit. "I'm interviewin' you professionally. I know you're a witness in this case; you know that I'm the lawyer for the defense. I don't want to hear any of your pet theories. Let's talk facts."

"I'll tell you what I know of the case," Workman said, coldly, "but I don't think it will help you, in your position."

"Doctor," Pruiett said, looking at him keenly, "haven't you reported to Dr. DeBarr that when you first got to the Miller boy he was beginnin' to slobber, an' that you gave him two bella donna tablets from your kit to dry the saliva up?"

"Why, yes, I have," Workman replied. "That's just what I did. I gave him one tablet when I got there, and another in about an hour, where—."

"You didn't get the desired, usual, results from them, did you, Doctor?"

The doctor shook his head.

"No," he answered. "The boy grew steadily—even rapidly, worse. The froth came so fast that we used up all the towels and cloths in Miller's house. I carried the boy to my office, but he got worse. Do you know, Mr. Pruiett, we saturated three dozen towels, thirty-six of them, with froth from that child's lips before he died. He had terrible convulsions. He had a monstrous dose of strychnine."

"I know he did, doctor, an' you gave it to him," Pruiett charged. "That wasn't bella donna you took from your kit—it was strychnine! You gave the boy the strychnine tablets, an' you're the one that killed him. You've killed one person by your stupid blunderin', and now you're tryin' to kill another." Pruiett's voice had risen with the gravity of his subject, and he was shaking the finger accusingly at the doctor.

Workman was pale and trembling. His agitation was being produced by anger, not by fear.

"If that is going to be your attitude, Mr. Pruiett," he cried, "I don't care to discuss this case with you any further. I will have to ask you to leave my office."

"Sure. You'll ask me, but I don't go," stormed Pruiett. "I've been hired to defend this woman, and my position as her lawyer requires that I develop all the facts. I'd hate to ruin you, but I'm goin' to do it. This is a case of one man's reputation against an innocent woman's life, and I'll be damned if she's goin' to die. I'm in a position to prove that that kid was bitten by a rabid cat, two days before he got sick, an' that all you did was to put him out of his misery with an overdose of poison. They found strychnine in his belly, all right. Hell, yes, they did, after you got through blunderin' around with him. But did you test him for rabies? Did you do anything beside cut out his mid-section an' ship it to DeBarr? Hell, no! You were too anxious to cover up your own stupidity."

"I tell you, it won't work," Workman insisted. "You can't bluff me! Get out of here."

"Cant' bluff you, huh?" the lawyer was menacing. "I'm wirin' Carter an' Hollingsworth at Wichita to be here Monday at my expense. I'll let some good doctors testify to what that much bella donna would've done to a kid. It would'a dried him up so that he couldn't have spit for a month. They'll get to answer some questions on the symptoms of hydrophobia, an' when they do, and when Maggie Miller comes clear, you can look out for an indictment, Doctor Workman, for the murder of little Roy Miller!"

"What is it—what about this cat?" The doctor had become interested. "That's the first I ever heard about that. Is there anything to it?"

"Anything to it?" Pruiett was scornful. "Bill Miller says he tried to tell you, but that you wouldn't listen to him."

"No," Workman said, weakly. "I don't know anything about it. I didn't want to talk to him after I learned he was staying with that woman, and she—after his own little boy was—."

"That's just it," Pruiett cut in. "You won't listen to but one side of an issue. That's what's wrong with our system. If you get in jail, you're guilty until you prove yourself innocent, instead of the way the boys put it—that wrote up the Constitution. I venture—."

"What was he going to tell me about the cat?" Workman persisted.

"Well," said Pruiett patronizingly, taking an easy chair, "well, the kid had a shoe box, with a string in it, an' the cat hung around the barber shop. He took—."

Pruiett was concluding the narration an hour later; ". . . an' Miller's still got the box, an' all the boys around the shop remember how the cat had those fits just before the boy took sick. Now, doctor, on that hypothesis and based on your experience with this particular case, what, in your opinion, caused the boy's death?"

Doctor Workman mopped his forehead and looked much further away than his pale eye would carry out through the little window. He wasn't seeing the future alone; he was only considering it, as he looked into the past. All he had worked and striven for, his hopes, for himself and others, was about to end in shame and disgrace.

"Hydrophobia," he whispered, "he died from hydrophobia, a cat bite. And I was about to do that woman a terrible injustice. That's what makes it so bad. A terrible injustice."

"What about DeBarr?" Pruiett pressed on. "He's goin' to swear that he found poison in the stomach. What are we goin' to do with him?"

The doctor shook his head, still gazing limply out the window. Pruiett had his answer ready for him.

"These chemists can make mistakes, can't they? Are their tests infallible? Everybody makes mistakes. DeBarr just gave the stomach the wrong test, and he's mistaken in his conclusions. That's the way it looks to me."

"Yes, that's it," Workman agreed. "I gave the boy bella donna, and he had a cat bite. DeBarr is wrong about it. I'll testify that it's possible, that it's easy for chemical tests to go wrong."

"We'll need help; lots of it," Pruiett said. "Get out in the sagebrush in the morning and round up the country doctors. I want at least ten to testify, and be sure that I have a chance to show them by the medical authorities on hydrophobia before I ask them the hypothetical question. They'll be helping you more than Maggie Miller."

Pruiett won his case. As the staff man for the Oklahoman saw it: "The defense alleged that the boy died of hydrophobia and experts testified that all the symptoms shown by the boy previous to his death denoted that he was suffering from hydro-phobia . . . . It was shown that he was seen playing with a sick kitten a few days before his death and the kitten afterwards died in convulsions."

The Law and Order League rued the day it hired Pruiett to go to Woodward. Their cheers turned to jeers as they followed the progress of Maggie's trial, and to groans as they read its final chapter.

"After deliberating from 10:30 Saturday morning to 4 o'clock in the afternoon, the jury in the case of Maggie Miller, charged with the poisoning of her stepson, Roy Miller, brought in a verdict of not guilty. . . ." At the end of the long column, rehashing the week's events at the trial, it was casually stated that "Moman Pruiett of Oklahoma City was counsel for the defense."

Pruiett traveled three thousand miles to the Pacific coast to try the celebrated Carr-Atkinson murder case at Montesano, Washington. His client was acquitted. He had experienced a gnawing curiosity to try the sector since his trip there in '06 when he and Colonel Garvin had visited the Lewis and Clark Exposition at Portland. After he had cleared the wealthy stockman the matter of the attorney's fee was considered. Pruiett told him that he wouldn't charge a fee; he would just charge mileage. They agreed that a dollar a mile would be both fair and adequate. After the railroad receipts had been figured, Carr gave Pruiett his check for $2,950. He got as far as Denver with it, where he threw a party at the Albany and let his guests carry off what was left as prizes of the poker game.

He got back to Oklahoma in time to stump the state for Lee Cruce, who was out again for governor. When Cruce won, Pruiett assorted seventy-five thousand dollars worth of cancelled checks, representing sums he had spent since the constitutional convention in the furtherance of Cruce and his campaign for governor.

"Moman Pruiett, the renowned criminal lawyer, has been secured by Allison Ooley, the deputy sheriff who is charged with the murder of 'Bronc' Heath, for his attorney. Ooley's release was obtained Wednesday by Pruiett through a habeas corpus proceedings. The release was made on $5,000 bond which was given by local citizens. . . ." The Courier, in the county originally named for Pruiett, was printing what was to be the foreword to another acquittal story for Pruiett and his clients.

Katherine Snodgrass killed husband Frank in their Harvey Street residence in Oklahoma City, and Pruiett got her off with the payment of $17.50 court costs. The house went to Pruiett, along with an assignment of a fair bank account, but she was free, and rid of Frank besides. She acknowledged that it was a bargain.

CHAPTER THIRTEEN

Wherein Pruiett loses a hard fought contest before the Canadian King's bench, and sees his accused client extradited to the United States for trial. And how he couples virtue and vice together to raise funds in old Seattle, and treats the Pacific slope press to a liberal portion of his pre-trial propaganda before he astounds the western citizenry, and his friend the Governor, by wringing a verdict of acquittal for his client, from a hostile jury.

It was June again, and there in the vale of the Swinomish as on the Washita, the air was full of its dank sweetness. Pruiett was in Seattle. The business was murder; the respite, for the instant, was poker. June, with its bracing night application from the Pacific and Puget Sound, bore no comfort to Pruiett. The lights in the bar room of the old Seattle Hotel were bright, and the man with the coal-black hair roached over his ears was puffing and chewing a long cigar at the main table in the adjoining gambling room. A huge diamond glittered in the square black knot at his high-collared throat, while a gaudier one shone from the knuckle of his immobile left hand.

A long-necked quart bottle at his right, with a single glass beside it, was taking his attention away from the game before him. The last portion of its content went out of sight with the last of the chips that had stood before him. He stood disconsolately, and placing a large black hat carelessly atop the bulging contour of hair, he adjusted his tie and stone as he walked toward the bar.

"One more glass of whiskey," he said evenly. "One more an' I'll go on up to bed."

"Yes, the same kind," Pruiett growled.

The boy put the bottle on the polished bar, feigning interest. "Was your luck bad tonight, Mr. Pruiett?" he inquired.

"I lost two hundred dollars," Pruiett said, "an' I never won a pot."

"Yes," he agreed, "your luck must be down a little."

"Either that, or your game's awful damned crooked," Pruiett observed. The bar-keep appeared not to hear. The speaker tossed a coin down on the bar and strolled out.

Pruiett's picture, with a full account of the nature of his business in Seattle, had been in both the Star and the Intelligencer earlier that day. He was acknowledged about the hotel, by guests and employees alike, as a visiting celebrity. Nodding to the girl at the telegraph desk, he sent a telegram to his office associates in Oklahoma City, advising that he was out of funds, and requesting that five hundred be sent immediately. He had already ascertained that the hotel wouldn't like to accommodate him for that amount on a check, even with the big send-off in the press, unless he had a substantial endorser.

His reply was waiting at nine the next morning when he stepped briskly into the lobby from the elevator. It was a frank, even vulgar refusal. Concluding, the missive read, "and why not come home by way of Cape Horn?" Pruiett was evidently off his course, as it was now easy for him to go, and he grinned, biting the end off a cigar. He envisioned the black frame of mind his less imaginative but more profoundly practical associates must have been in on receiving his night message. Instead of going to breakfast, he stepped over the Negro, on hands and knees scrubbing the marble step into the bar, and ordered Green River.

Pruiett was traveling with a client, a middle-aged woman and her fifteen-year-old son, and his lack of cash was embarrassing. His associates at home had turned down his plea for aid. His wife knew how much money he had received with his last wire from home, and how recently he had received it. The bills were running up at the hotel.

It was luck, in place of resourcefulness, that came to aid him first. A lobby bell-hop was paging him. He hurried to the 'phone booth.

"Pruiett?" he heard a male voice over the wire. "Pruiett? Is this Moman Pruiett of Oklahoma City?"

"Yes, this is Pruiett," he replied readily. "Who is this?"

"Doctor ————," the voice supplied.

There was genuine cordiality in Pruiett's tone as he told the caller he was glad to hear his voice. The Doctor or the Reverend was a minister.

He was a man of position and prominence in Seattle, and that was what the Oklahoma lawyer needed more than anything else at the particular time.

"We saw your picture in the paper last evening," the preacher was saying.

"How are you, and how is Mrs. Pruiett, and your mother?"

"I'm a little tired," Pruiett confessed. "I had a bad evening; however, my health is good."

"Can you come out to dinner?"

"No," Pruiett replied. "My train leaves at 1 o'clock and I have a number of things to take care of before. And, by the way, I'm a little embarrassed, out of funds, and was just preparing to wire the bank at home for an order. I was just wondering—."

"Not at all, Mr. Pruiett, not at all," came the prompt and welcome interruption. "My bank is right across from your hotel. If you can't come out here, we'll come down there to see you."

Pruiett and the Reverend met in the hotel lobby a few minutes later. Pruiett wrote a check for five hundred, the preacher endorsed it, and the three of them walked to the hotel desk to present it for cash. The clerk came back with an apologetic expression.

"I'm so sorry," he said. "So very sorry. We don't have enough cash to handle it this morning. If you'll bring it back a little later—."

The Reverend interrupted. "It's the bank right across the street, where I do business," he said, pointing through the plate window. "We can walk over there and cash it."

The obliging clerk had a suggestion to make. "I can call over and identify Mr. Pruiett, and tell them he is coming over with it. It'll save you a trip."

Pruiett agreed. The three chatted a little longer before the minister and his wife departed.

"The Seattle Bank across the street is where I do most of my business," the Reverend advised as he departed, "but if anything goes wrong, you can go to the City National a block up. Our church has a big deposit there, and I know they will be glad to handle it for you."

Complimenting himself on his unfailing good luck, Pruiett hurried to the closest bank. The officer he had been referred to greeted him considerately, but he remained in the back office so long that the waiting applicant's suspicions arose. When he did appear, he wore the same kind of apologetic look as Pruiett had seen on the face of the hotel clerk.

"I'm very sorry, Mr. Pruiett," he said, "but this kind of an item is very unsatisfactory to our officers. The exchange fee is very slight, and while we know of you, and acknowledge the sufficiency of the endorsement, there is always an element of difficulty connected. We would just rather not handle your paper."

Pruiett gave him the poker face as he thanked him, and

Negro Trails Woman 4,000 Miles

Held as Slayer of Her Husband

PRINCIPALS in the chase and capture of Mrs. Laurena Matthews, who is being taken to Oklahoma to stand trial for the murder of her husband four years ago. Above: Mrs. Lurancy Harris, the Canadian police officer, who has Mrs. Matthews in charge. Below: Mrs. Matthews.

Black Gets Revenge After Four Years Dogging Footsteps of White Employer.

LAURENA MATTHEWS AND HER ESCORT
"***guarded by a Canadian policewoman who wore a fur hat."

turned away. Knowledge of another bank where he could take his righteously endorsed check was not enough to keep him from being apprehensive when he reflected over his actual plight, and what he would have to do if this plan didn't work.

The vice-president of the other bank took time for conference and consideration after the check was presented to him, but his decision was the same. As he stroked his white Vandyke, or patted his slick and utterly bald head, he gave Pruiett to understand that while he hated to do it, he was required to turn down the endorsement. Pruiett went back to the bar at the Seattle for a glass of Green River. He was trying to elect between sending a wire to the wife, or one to his banker. Under the circumstances, having to approach either for cash was the same as an admission of extravagance, and what went with it, on the road.

But he retained his Pruiett luck. They were paging him again, and as he began to realize that it was his own name that was drifting in between the velvet portiers, he was not so quick to respond as he had been to the last exploratory bellow. He sipped his drink and mused. It would not be the Doctor. He wouldn't be calling back so soon, and so near to train time. He didn't know any one else in Seattle, unless—. Yes, that was it. The banker had reconsidered; probably had decided that he couldn't face his preacher and admit that he had rejected his friend's check. Surely, that was it. He was going to get the money; be spared that embarrassing appeal to home for relief. He left the bar and hurried from the bar room.

"Pruiett!" He hurled his most business-like bellow into the tilted transmitter. "Pruiett."

"Hello, Moman," a soft sweet voice cooed in his ear. "Is that you, Moman, dear?"

"Who the hell is this?" he cried. He was surprised and disappointed. "This is Pruiett."

"I saw your picture in the paper, and I was scared to death you would get out of town before I got to see you," the sweet voice continued, sweeter than ever, "How are you, dear?"

"I'm all right," he managed to answer, "but who is this?" The caller was playful.

"Don't you know?" she blandly catechized. "You're not at all as flattering as you used to be. How is R. J.? Is he still trying to get hold of all the money in Oklahoma?" That was a cue, and Pruiett almost caught it, but his troubles were resting so heavily that it got away from him. He had to ask her again who she was.

"This is Josephine," she said. "I've married again, since you got my divorce for me, so you wouldn't know my last name. Josephine? Remember?"

Pruiett remembered, with a flood of recollections. "How are you, Moman, dear?" she inquired again. "Well, I'll tell you," he said. "I'm not so good. I'm a long ways from home and I'm flat broke. I was just ready to wire home for cash and I hate like hell to do it, but I can't get a soul out here to cash my check." The frank confession and its dolorous tone brought a peal of merry laughter.

"Bless your heart," she laughed. "Bless your heart. Come on out here and I'll cash your check. I've just got to see you before you go. I'm dying for someone who can answer some questions about some of my old friends. Come on out here."

"Out where?" Pruiett questioned bluntly. "Where are you?" She was still laughing merrily as she answered him. "My place is 2912 Pine," she said, "put it down so you won't forget it. 2912 Pine, and hurry, dear. And bring the check."

Pruiett was taking stock as he went through the wide door of the hotel toward a line of waiting taxicabs. He had less than two dollars. "How much to 2912 Pine?" he inquired of the first driver. "A buck," was the prompt response.

"Let's go," said Pruiett, stepping through the low door into the uncovered, hard seated driver's compartment.

"You'll find it a lot better in the back," the driver volunteered. "These cobblestones is kind of rough, and that seat ain't none too soft."

"Let's go," said Pruiett again, impatiently. "I want to ride up here with you." As soon as they were off Pruiett turned to the driver. He lost no time in getting to the point. "What kind of a place is 2912 Pine, where we're goin?"

"It's the fanciest whore-house in Seattle," was the prompt, proud response.

"Well, hurry it up," said Pruiett. "What are we waiting for?"

The place on Pine set far back from the curb and sidewalk. It was brownstone, a two-tone creation in light and dark brown, with curving glass in the bay windows behind the colonaded porch, and shining green and blue prisms in the diamond-shaped openings and between them.

Pruiett marched to the carved door and pulled the old

fashioned door bell. A yellow wench with pierced ears and straight, oily hair admitted him. The nap of the Brussels carpet covering the floor of the mirrored hallway tickled his ankles, and as he tried to view the magnificence of the tapestry on the walls between the mirrors, and the leaf-work of the elegantly plated chandeliers, he had to shake off a pack of dogs that leaped up about him. There were little ones, with bald bodies tied in bright ribbons; great flat-footed ones that wore steel spiked collars, and dogs of all other colors and sizes ranging in between. The grinning wench helped him to push them down as she guided him into a high ceilinged sitting room, elegantly fitted, and slid the tall panels together behind him.

"Miss Josephine will be down in just a minute," she said. "She told me you was comin', an' to make you comfortable."

"All right," he said. "I need a drink. Can you get me a drink?"

She departed with her grin but without an answer. He had scarcely time to look around at a part of the elegance of the old place when she returned with a pail of ice, with two bottles of champagne, and glasses. Then Josephine came in.

"Moman, dear! I'm so glad to see you," she said, as the twist of her rapid approach across the soft floor caused the feather-trimmed hem of her long skirt to wave and billow. "So glad to see you, again."

He gave her the kind of embrace which the approach suggested, or required. Turning her loose and holding her back for a second look, he could note that the seven years elapsing since he had seen her last had been more than gentle, regardless of what he had just heard and understood about the nature of her business.

"It's been a long time since I saw you, Josie," he said. "But you're as young an' charmin' as ever. I've often wondered what had become of you."

"Don't lie," she smilingly rebuked. "You were as cross as you used to be, when I called you. I really believe it made you mad."

"I'm so damned worried, I can't think," he explained. "What I was tellin' you, about the expenses, is the truth. I lost my roll in a game at the hotel last night, and it's goin' to be embarrassin' as hell if I can't cash a check. I'm worried about it."

Josephine, fondling a bubbling glass, had twisted into the far corner of the silken seat. She was beautiful, with flashing eyes, teeth and diamonds. Her bare arms were plump and white.

Her busts and hips were over, but not disproportionately, developed.

"Whatever became of Joe?" Pruiett inquired.

"I don't know," she said. "I heard he went to California. I guess he's still the proud, struggling baggage clerk."

"How did you happen to marry such a bird?"

"I was stuck on him, an' I thought he was smarter than he turned out to be. I didn't think he was so damned straight."

They laughed together. "Did he ever know who promoted the divorce?" Pruiett asked.

"He knew you were my lawyer, if that's what you mean. He knew that, and cussed you for it."

"That isn't what I mean. I said, who promoted it? I'm talkin' about R. J., the money-bag."

"I don't know whether he did or not," she answered. "But I don't think so. He didn't seem to pay any attention, much, after the divorce."

"When you took up so quick with R. J., afterwards, I thought he might have got suspicious. A lot of people knew that R. J. paid me a good fee for representin' you."

"If Joe knew it, or suspected it, he never let on. He never tried to cause us any trouble," she said.

She cast her glance toward the bubbling glass, while a perceptible flush mounted her fair forehead.

Pruiett looked at his watch and started. "I meet my people at the station, in an hour, an' I've got to get my things out of the hotel. What about this check?"

"How much is it, dear?" she asked.

"Five hundred," he answered. "I'm stoppin' at Denver to take depositions in this case, an' I've got a lot of expenses. I need all of that, an' maybe more."

"Well, all right, you can get it," she said soothingly. "I don't have it here this morning, but it's in the bank. I'll put my name on it and you can stop by on your way to the station. No, I'll have my boy drive you there, and then take you to the hotel." Pruiett handed her the check, dubiously.

She took a gold pen from the tall mahogany secretary. "Now," she said, "you take this to the Bank and present it to Mr. ———, and tell him I sent you. You'll get the money."

"Is he a bald-headed fellow with a Vandyke?" Pruiett inquired.

Josephine smiled and nodded as she answered. "Yes, that's him. He'll take care of you."

"No, he won't, either," Pruiett disagreed. "He's the one who just turned me an' the preacher down. Can't you let me take it to some other place—"

Josephine picked up a small 'phone and called a number from memory.

"Mr. —————?" she said, when she had a response. "Mr. —————, this is Josephine. I have a friend, a very dear friend, from out of town, who wishes to cash a large check, and I've endorsed it for him. I'd like for him to have the money immediately . . . . Do you understand? . . . Thank you, Mr. ————— . . . . thank you, dear."

"I don't like that guy," Pruiett insisted, as she was holding him and helping him toward a big car waiting in the shaded drive. "An' I hate like hell to see him again, but I've got to have that money."

The contents of the champagne bottle were dancing and sparkling in his dark eyes as he reclined in the car seat and mused over the strange, unorthodox happenings. It seemed that there was always an answer, an aid, in his every dilemma; and there was usually a lovely female connected with it. He could recall similar situations, such as—. His thoughts were interrupted by the uniformed Negro who had already opened the car's door in front of the bank.

The banker was no happier to meet him again, under the circumstances, than he was to meet the banker. They smiled and bowed while the banker took the check. He returned almost immediately with the money.

"You forgot to deduct the exchange fee," Pruiett reminded him, very politely.

"No," said the banker, even more politely. "The charge is slight and we are remitting it. We are glad to accommodate you, Mr. Pruiett."

"But I don't like for you to do that," Pruiett insisted. "This is business, and I'd like for it to be handled that way."

The banker was beaming with indulgence. He was stroking his white stub of a beard and smirking. "We have our own way of handling things out here in Seattle," he beamed. "It may seem a little different, or odd, to a stranger, but it's our own way.

We like it, doing it different. Our ways are big. It's the influence of the Rockies, and the Pacific, you know."

Pruiett shook his head as he started to leave. "You will pardon the observation," he drawled, "but I've noticed that you do handle things differently here to any other place where I've been, an' I've been to quite a few places. It's the first damned town I ever saw where a man with money in the bank had to have his check endorsed by the pastor of its biggest church and the madam of its most flourishing whore-house, before he could get it cashed."

"The common law isn't nothin' but common sense," Pruiett maintained. "A successful lawyer's no freak. He's just a level-headed guy with brains enough in his head to reason things out."

Pruiett was a profound, and practical, thinker. He was loud and boisterous, and his sensationalism oftentimes attracted attention away from his learning and understanding, but it was always present to aid him.

"Come right in, Judge," Pruiett exclaimed, rising with unusual deference and shaking hands. His caller was an associate justice on the Oklahoma Criminal Court of Appeals.

"I'm here on serious business, Moman," The Judge said, abruptly. "I want to hire you in a white-slave case."

"You mean—?"

"No, it's not me," the Judge smiled. "I'm not old enough to be gettin' my tail in that kind of a crack. It's my father-in-law; the wife's old man."

"Has he been indicted?" Pruiett inquired

"No, but he's in for it. There's a Federal grand jury in session an' a subpoena out for the gal. I don't see any way of blockin' it, at all, once they get her story in the grand jury room."

"Give me the dope," Pruiett invited, holding a box of cigars toward the judge.

"The old man owns a lot of land down around Cero Gordo, Arkansas," the Judge began. "He's got some poor-folks for tenants, farmin' it on shares, an' they got a buxom daughter. She's a good lookin' girl about seventeen or eighteen. He took 'er up to Kansas City an' bought a bunch of fancy clothes an' stuff, an'—."

"An' when she got home the folks wanted to know who the Santa Claus was? Wasn't that it?" Pruiett inquired.

"That's right," the Judge said. "An—."

"An' then they wanted Santa Claus to come again, or they'd have to protect Sal's virtue with a criminal prosecution?"

"There ain't no use of me tellin' you when you're able to tell me," the Judge laughed. "You must be reading my mind."

"They're all alike," Pruiett said. "The difference between rape an' mutual lust is in the check book. I'll bet I can settle with the outraged parents for less than the old man can defend for in K. C."

"We're willing to pay off," the Judge answered. "Can you handle it for us?"

"I'm on my way to Cero Gordo right now," Pruiett said. "When I wire, shoot me the money order. Maybe that little girl'll have to answer that subpoena the Federal grand jury's tryin' to serve on her, but if I get down there in time I don't think she'll have much to say to 'em."

Pruiett sauntered into the chambers of United States District Judge Van Valkenburg at Kansas City. The insolent grin of perfect confidence was spread across his handsome face.

"The clerk over at the Baltimore Hotel said you called a' hour ago," he smiled. "Sorry to keep a Federal Court waitin' but I was tied up in the barber shop an'—."

"The grand jury's the one being detained," Van Valkenburg said, sternly. "Mr. Wilson has asked me to commit this child for contempt, and it appears that you are the one that is really in contempt of court—and the grand jury. She says she refuses to answer, on your counsel."

Pruiett looked at the frightened Arkansas girl and gave her a reassuring smile. "Our Constitution provides," Pruiett said, speaking to the judge as if he were a law student, "that one does not have to incriminate or degrade one's self. I advised the child of that much."

"The district attorney, and this court, has guaranteed full immunity to the witness," Van Valkenburg gritted. "Did you tell her that when she had her immunity, that she had to testify, or be subject to punishment for contempt?"

"I did, your honor," Pruiett answered. "If this court could grant her *full* immunity, my client would not hesitate to answer, but until that is done, she shall refuse to testify."

"Young lady," the Judge said. "This court assures you again, here in the presence of your attorney, that you need have no fear of criminal prosecution from anything which you disclose in your testimony. Now go back to the jury room and answer the questions the district attorney asks you."

The girl looked at Pruiett. Pruiett shook his head and smiled.

"That isn't full immunity," he said. "That isn't even half—assurance that she won't be prosecuted. She will continue to refuse to answer any questions that you put to her in this investigation."

Van Valkenburg turned purple and red. "You are in contempt yourself, Mr. Pruiett," he choked. "Why shouldn't you be punished for deliberately opposing this court?"

"But I'm not, your honor," Pruiett assured him. "When my client has all the immunity which she is entitled to as a citizen, then I'll tell her to answer."

"What's your point?" the prosecuting attorney demanded.

"You are tryin' to make a white-slave case on this child's testimony," Pruiett replied. "You can guarantee her immunity from criminal prosecution, and liability, but can you immunize her from the badge of disgrace she'll carry to her grave if she gives you the information you want?" Pruiett struck an heroic attitude in the middle of the office floor. His remarks were in a thunderous roar. "You pin the scarlet letter of shame upon her young breast, an' send her out into the world degraded by her own admission, an' you have no semblance of power to guard or protect her. You can refrain from prosecution, but how many wagging tongues can you stop? How many heartaches can you abate? How many dragging strides, as she walks the street peddling the lack of virtue which you exposed to public knowledge, can you retrace?"

"You have your law to enforce, but she has her reputation as a chaste woman to protect. Unless you can enforce your writ without transgressing her holiest right, then you must retire and let your statutes suffer. You are powerless to deliver the immunity which you must guarantee before you can compel her to answer. She will not utter the words which drop the cloak of virtue from about her shoulders, and you may send the child to the dungeon, and her oft-erring counsel along with her, if the laws of the land are so unjust as to require the one or the other."

The court drummed on his desk. "What about that?" he inquired of the district attorney.

"I haven't had the question raised before," Wilson answered, frankly. "It doesn't appeal to me, however, as being sound logic, or law. I—."

"It appeals to me," the court said. "Have you any authority for your position, Mr. Pruiett?"

"The authority of common sense," Pruiett answered. "I haven't read any cases on it, but the law's just. If you want to give me a little time in the library, I'll see about it."

"We'll continue this matter until after lunch," Van Valkenburg said. "I'd like to have some cases on that question."

Woman's virtue was safe in the robed embrace of justice. Pruiett found his cases, although he went back to the courts of Old England. The girl didn't have to talk and the government couldn't make out a case without her. The Washita stallion had dropped another stumbling block in the pathway of law enforcement.

Persistence had its reasonable limits in Pruiett practice. When a jury convicted W. T. Maness of murder, and fixed his punishment at life imprisonment, Pruiett, his lawyer, knew that the time for resistance was past. The state had another charge of the same character, for Maness had murdered two before his blazing pistol had ceased to fire. Pruiett announced, when formal sentence on the first conviction had been made, that his client would plead guilty to the content of the second charge.

"Very well," Judge Clark observed. "It will be the judgment and sentence of the court that you be sentenced to life imprisonment on the second charge."

"Might I inquire," Pruiett asked, rising carelessly, "whether those sentences are to run concurrently, or consecutively?"

There was a titter from the gallery. "Are you trying to make fun of this court, Mr. Pruiett?" Judge Clark demanded, belligerently.

"Not at all, your honor," Pruiett answered. "This is a matter of the utmost gravity both to me and my client. I insist that the record show whether the sentences in the two cases run concurrently or consecutively."

Clark pondered. He didn't want to be ridiculed, and he didn't want to commit judicial error. Pruiett's manner of complete sincerity confused him.

"What difference could it make?" he demanded. "This man's been sentenced to life imprisonment. He hasn't got but one life, so any sentence rendered after that is actually surplusage. I sentenced him to life just to be consistent with the sentence in the case where a jury convicted him. What's the difference?"

"I recall the sweet words of the poet," Pruiett said, advancing into the opening before the bench. "Our lives are old and our loves are old, and death shall come again. Should it come today, what man may say, We shall not live again?

"God wrought our souls from the Tremedoc beds and He furnished them wings to fly; He has sown our spawn in the world's dim dawn, and I know that it shall not die. Though cities have sprung above the grave where the crooked-bone men made war, and the ox-wain creaks o'er the buried caves where the mummied mammoth are. Our lives are old; our loves are old, and death shall come again; Should it come today, what man may say, 'We shall not live again'?"

His tones were like the whispers of time. His gestures, and expressions, gave him the air of utmost sincerity.

"I believe in the Christian religion," Pruiett said, devoutly, "but my client believes in the reincarnation of the soul. He believes that after this misspent life he'll come back to earth again, in some other form, or in some other body. He doesn't want another lifetime of imprisonment hanging over him."

Clark scratched his head. There was something in the argument. Pruiett wasn't poking fun at the court. He was too devout, and too serious for that.

"That may not be much consolation to you, but it is to me," Pruiett said to Maness. "I had to win at least one round of this case, an' they'd beat me at ever' turn up to that one. If you come back as a bird-dog or a jackass, you can look the cops in the eye without a flicker. When you serve that one life sentence you have evened up with the majesty of the law."

Governor Lee Cruce was distressed. His Chickasaw Nation colleague, his former campaign manager and financial backer, —had invaded the Dominion of Canada and was creating such a disturbance with the King's Bench that international complications were threatened. It was Pruiett, resisting the efforts of the State of Oklahoma to extradite a buxom widow wanted for the murder of her wealthy, farmer husband. The Legislature was in session and the sensitive ear of the chief executive could hear the whispers of political opposition—"He's overlooking Pruiett's outrageous conduct because Pruiett backed him in his campaign." Cruce demanded that the legislative body appropriate five thousand dollars to pay the expense of concluding the proceedings, and insuring the return of the accused woman.

The act and its performance was a trifle hard on Pruiett, who, until that time, was having the fun of his life with the white-wigged Canadian justices. He had made four trips to Edmonton, in Alberta province, in one year, and had each time successfully resisted the efforts of the United States authorities to move the woman across the line. They had arrested her again, in Vancouver, British Columbia, and had been holding her there, when the governor gave the push that was to cause her to be extradited.

Back in Oklahoma Pruiett badgered the courts until they set her bond, but they set it so high that they thought she wouldn't be able to make it. Pruiett scheduled a portion of his own unencumbered real estate on the $25,000 bond to make it without assistance. Then he took her on a trip back through the Canadian Northwest, developing evidence by deposition which he intended to use in the actual trial of her case.

When her husband had been put away he was considered to have been the victim of a perfectly legitimate mishap. "On the night of December 5, 1908, between eight and nine o'clock Mrs. Matthews went to a neighbor and told him the mules were kicking him to death in the barn. The neighbors then went back with her and assisted in carrying the body from the barn to the house. . . ." It was the Advance-Democrat of Stillwater, Payne County, recounting and recollecting, as best it could, the strange circumstances around his death.

According to the account ". . . . the farm owned by him at the time of his death lies principally in the Stillwater bottom and is one of the finest in Payne County . . . . His family consisted of himself and his wife, and a boy and a girl about eight and ten years, respectively . . . ." He had actually owned, along with a great variety of livestock, a span of young mules that were unusually mean and vicious, what they called "fighters." The accused woman's version was that on the night of the tragedy the young mules started to fight, causing such a commotion in the barn that he went out to try to stop them. When he was found there were mule-shoe prints on his face and cranium, and the cause of death was perfunctorily attributed to the rough treatment, which it appeared, the mules had given him.

Jim Chapman was a common laborer employed on the farm. He was a stalwart specimen of physical development, with skin as smooth as a billiard ball and with muscle as solid. Chapman was later to tell an amazing story of a love affair between himself and the middle-aged farm woman which culminated in a plot, and its execution, with the murder of her husband. The Negro said that he choked the man as he sat in a chair, while his wife beat him in the head with an iron poker. Then they carried the fresh corpse to the mule's stalls and flung it at the animals' heels, so that the hoof tracks, apparent with his removal, became evident.

It was almost a year after his burial that the first rumble came. The widow and her Negro hired-man had become careless with their relations, in fact, were flaunting them in the community's collective face. A move was started to take the children away from her—"to remove them from the injurious effect of such lascivious conduct." "She and the Negro had unbridled all caution and were constantly together, at her home or at Chapman's house, or at work on her farm. She was seen to take refreshments to him in the field where he was at work, and while Chapman's wife was in Texas she was at Chapman's place almost every night and would leave somewhere from ten to two o'clock in the morning. They were seen to take their fishing rods and go fishing together—she went with him to Perry—she went with him to Negro picnics—she had him constantly with her at her table, and with her family, when he was at work for her. They had been seen together on the creeks west of Stillwater, and were seen to enter a stairway, in Stillwater, which led to some upstairs rooms which were, at the time vacant . . . . They were seen walking through Donart's field one morning with their arms around each other . . . ." The little Advance-Democrat either knew what it was talking about, or had a wholesome contempt for libel suits. It was going pretty strong for her.

Acting under the authority of the state juvenile law a neighbor filed a formal complaint against her. "The trial to take her children away from her lasted twenty-one days. . . . The feeling on both sides was bitter—the colored population armed itself. . . . The jury rendered a verdict taking the children away from her. On the evening that Judge Burns came up from Cushing to pass on her motion for a new trial Chapman and she went to the home of a Negro tenant of hers and wanted to stay overnight together. The public had not lost interest in the case and the Negro would not allow them to stay, but they were furnished some bed quilts and they went into the cotton patch, where they spent the night together. . . . Within a few days Chapman left and went to

Canada—finally landing at Edmonton.   She also left and went to Canada. . . ."

The black and white romance was on the rocks in less than a year. When she tried to shake the Negro, he wouldn't shake. The liberties which he insisted on taking about the Clover Bar Ranch, a wheat farm which she had bought and had been operating with his help, were beginning to embarrass her. "He became such a nuisance to her that she complained to Police Chief Lancey. When spoken to by the chief the Negro stated that he had murdered her husband, and implicated her. His statements were very contradictory when he was placed under a grueling examination by the police, who soon abandoned the case. They did not place any credence in his remarks. Then Chapman went to the mounted police, who arrested him, and the woman also, on his statement. . . ."

The Edmonton Daily Capital had that much, and more, to say. This organ contended that she was being persecuted by the Negro and the officers who persisted in extraditing her. In a later edition it stated: "The life that she led while she was in Edmonton and Calgary and the fact that she had the intimate friendship and good-will of a large circle of eminently respectable and well-to-do people of both cities, should absolutely prove the falseness of the scurrilous attack made on her character by a confessed murderer, who says she conducted a house of ill-repute in this city. . . ."

Chapman waived extradition, went home and started doing the twenty-five years which they gave him on a guilty plea. A public-spirited lawyer named J. L. Springer started a campaign, from Chapman's cell in the State Penitentiary, which was to result in the recovery of the suspected woman, whom they had tried so hard, and for so long, to grab. In an open letter, published over his own signature, Springer told of the progress of his maneuvers.

". . . . A committee of five citizens called on Governor Cruce and the Attorney General for the purpose of interesting them in appointing me special counsel for the prosecution of this case and making a trip to Canada to bring about the extradition of her. . . . They both promised to aid in every way they could and . . . on the 3rd day of October (1912) he appointed me to represent the State of Oklahoma in extradition proceedings. I immediately took the matter up with the State Department at Washington,

D. C., and had the Governor of Oklahoma to request her arrest in Canada. She was arrested on the 16th day of October at Vancouver, B. C., Canada. . . ."

And so they took her back to Oklahoma. The Denver Daily News carried her picture, being guarded by a Canadian policewoman who wore a fur hat. The Canadian good will had extended south from Puget Sound, for the News' attitude was decidedly sympathetic. "Trailed by a Negro, who, twice baffled in efforts to cause her indictment by an Oklahoma grand jury, shadowed her for more than four years and finally brought about her arrest through the Canadian Mounted Police. She is 37, is being taken back to Stillwater to stand trial for the murder of her husband, a crime alleged to have been committed December 8, 1908. In the custody of Mrs. Laurancy Harris, the first woman police constable of Canada, and James Springer of Stillwater, she arrived in Denver yesterday and was confined for several hours in the quarters of the police matron at the city jail. . . ."

Jim Springer lamented the laxity of the American procedure which, in his estimation, was less disciplinary than that of the Dominion. "As soon as she had been committed for extradition she was sent to the penitentiary at New Westminster and put in what they call the death chamber. No one was allowed to see her, not even her counsel, without an order from the King's Bench, and the order would state who it was to see her and just the number of minutes she might talk to any one. When she was brought here it had been arranged that she might be kept guarded in one of the best hotels in the city, and allowed the privilege of receiving whoever wanted to see her. In fact, she kept open house. . . ." Pruiett had made the advance arrangements. He considered those little expressions of thoughtfulness a part of the requirements of his employment. He always tried to keep his client in a peaceful and serene state of mind.

And Pruiett couldn't understand why Springer was so impatient to have the case tried. As he looked at it, her husband had been dead for five years already, and another year or two, to prepare for the trial, shouldn't make much difference. As a final gesture he took his client and made another tour of the northwest, taking statements and depositions of witnesses to be used, one way or another, in the eventual trial.

Back in Edmonton, Pruiett took a final verbal poke at the prosecution. ". . . . That she has been practically ruined financially through the heavy expenditures necessary in her defense of the charge of murdering her husband leveled at her by James Chapman, a Negro farmer, who is now serving a 25 year sentence in the McAlester, Oklahoma penitentiary on the strength of his own confession of the crime, is the statement made to the Capital by Moman Pruiett, Oklahoma City, her attorney. . . ."

They were lionized at every stop on the way back. At Seattle Hotel. "She is the central figure in the sensational murder case which has been before the courts of Oklahoma and Canada for the past number of years. Accompanied by her son and her attorney, Moman Pruiett, of Oklahoma City, she is on her way from Vancouver, B. C., to stand trial. . . . A dishwasher in a restaurant, an old man named Baker, complained to the juvenile court that she was not a fit mother for her children. . . . The prejudice against Negroes is strong in Oklahoma, . . . she, defying prejudice, often ordered Jim to hitch up and take her to town on shopping and business errands. . . . The Negro followed her to Canada. . . . You perhaps know the nature of the southern Negro farmhand. His name has been coupled with that of a white woman, and he was mighty proud. . . ."

The Seattle Post-Intelligencer concluded a similar story with a flattering recollection of the attorney in the affair. "Pruiett, the attorney in the case, is known to the northwest. Two years ago he came to Montaseno for the defense of the Carr-Atkinson murder case, in which case Carr was cleared. . . . She is said to be still wealthy, although a large part of the fortune left by her husband has been spent in the courts of Oklahoma and Canada."

When they laid over in Denver the accused woman had a suite at the Albany Hotel, instead of an iron bunk in the women's ward at the municipal prison, as she had had on her latest visit. The Daily News remembered her. It was still friendly, and solicitous. ". . . . she has spent the bulk of her fortune left to her in defending herself of the charge. The only part of the vast sum left her is a few thousand dollars. . . . With her was Moman Pruiett, an Oklahoma Attorney. Following her release on bond, Pruiett accompanied her to Canada to get certain documentary evidence, which, the defense hopes, will offset the evidence given by Chapman. . . ."

When Pruiett had baited the exponents of justice and order to the point where they were near madness, and had aroused them to such a pitch that they were editorializing him and his client, he knew he had gone far enough. It was as far as he cared, and

had planned to go, at any rate. ". . . It was a great disappointment to those interested in the prosecution of the case to see her
admitted to bail. . . . In England 80 per cent of the murderers
are hanged while in the United States 80 per cent of the murderers
are acquitted. . . . It is because the efforts of those who under-
take to prosecute crime in this country are hampered by the courts
in allowing bail, then continuing the case from time to time, and
efforts of attorneys through newspapers to throw sympathy and a
feeling of persecution about the defendants. . . ."

Pruiett attached a copy of that editorial to a motion for a
change of venue, and got what he asked for. The cause was sent
to Guthrie, first capital of Oklahoma, in Logan County. Once
off of Judge Springer's docket Pruiett was ready for battle. The
trial, which opened on September 1, 1913, continued over two
weeks. "Nearly two hundred witnesses testified in the case and
the defense had fourteen depositions from Canada, where it was
claimed the accused and the Negro went after the death of her
husband. . . ."

Jim Chapman was brought from the penitentiary to testify
for the prosecution. He was a willing witness. "That man died
with my hand over his mouth and my fingers on his neck, and he
knew me, too." Thus the current stories carried it. ". . . . She,"
he said, "is one of the pleasantest women I ever knew, and I
believe she is the smartest woman in this courtroom; but she is the
deceiven'st woman I ever saw, too, ..."

"But from your story," suggested counsel, "you indicate that
she was the principal in the murder, and that she persuaded you
to help."

Said Chapman, "I wouldn't say that. She persuaded me
into it. We arranged the details right by the corner of the court
house, the day before the murder. I got the stuff for her and she
was going to do the job; but she wanted me around. After she
hit him with the poker and he didn't die, she came out and called
me in, and that man died with my hands over his mouth and my
fingers on his throat. . . ."

The defense had had that kind of testimony to combat all
the way through. Pruiett was disconsolate when the jury went
out, and fearful of conviction. When they had been out two days,
he began to feel better, although he was drinking heavily to
sustain his ceaseless corridor pacing. He envisioned a deadlocked
jury and relished the visitation. He could give a lot of news-

paper interviews, and create a great deal of feeling in the public in the time which would elapse before another trial could be had. He remembered the damaging testimony and consoled himself with the thought held in readiness, for use in every case. You can't win 'em all; a hung jury is better than a conviction.

And then trouble marched into the courthouse. Lee Cruce, governor of the state which had absorbed the Indian Nations, hadn't gone to the field house to see the game. The contest had been over for two days, the umpires just hadn't posted their decision, when the governor arrived. The Guthrie Free Fair was in full country swing and the red and white yokel alike showing their yams and pop corn and trying to outwit the pitch men who manipulated walnut husks over inoffensive green peas. The governor was down to give that part of the citizenry which was still grieving over the loss of Guthrie's status as the capital a word of encouragement, and to make a little political swamp-root for himself by delivering a speech from the rail of the race track. Harry Houston, district judge who had heard the case, was to introduce him, and the governor's party had merely driven by to pick up the court.

Cruce pretended that he didn't see Pruiett pacing in front of the courtroom, as he ducked into the door of the judge's chambers. Pruiett walked into the bailiff's vestibule, outside the chambers, and dropped into one of the numerous empty chairs. No one else was in the room. With his eyes on the print of a country paper, but with his ears, and attention, focused upon the wide cracks around the door into Houston's office, he emulated interest in the smeared print. Cruce had already injured his case, so he was instantly suspicious of him when he saw him about the court.

"This is awful," he heard Cruce's voice after the trial judge had given him a profane explanation of the status of the case. "It's simply awful. That woman's guilty an' ever'one knows it. She should have been convicted long before this. It's awful."

"I can't help it," Houston answered, weakly. "I'm worn out, tryin' to hold that fellow Pruiett down. I've tried cases with him in 'em for fifteen years, way back in the territory courts at Ardmore an' the Valley, but he gets worse instead of better. I stopped court an' called him in here, an' told him I was goin' to lock him up if he didn't stay within the bounds of reason in cross-examinin' witnesses, but it didn't do any good. I jumped him for the same thing before the jury, an' he made a record of me that'll reverse the case as sure as hell if she's convicted, an' he takes an appeal. I don't know what to do."

"This case has been spread all over the country," Cruce growled. "It's news even in Canada, and we're being criticized for spendin' so much money on it. A lot of 'em up there think that we're wrong, and that she's innocent. A hung jury, where a quick conviction should be had, is goin' to make a joke out of the state, and this court, and," Cruce added, "the governor, too."

Pruiett heard Houston speak to the bailiff. "Go up and get Hancock, an' bring him here. Bring him in here; this office."

There was a short pause, with complete silence.

"Mr. Hancock, meet Governor Cruce; Governor, Bob Hancock, the foreman of the jury."

There was an exchange of greetings before Pruiett heard Houston continue. "Are you any nearer an agreement?" he asked.

"No, sir," came the reply. "There ain't been a vote change all day. We're hopelessly hung."

There was a weariness in the answer to give Pruiett hope. He wanted them to hang if they couldn't acquit; he didn't want any outside influence, even a governor's, to interfere with that order of results.

"Surely twelve sensible men can agree on as clear-cut a case as this one," he said. "These trials cost money; the state has spent a great amount on this one. Petty impressions should be set aside and the public good considered."

Pruiett gnashed his teeth as he fixed his stare into the little paper.

"The Judge is right," Cruce put in. "A verdict ought'a be reached in this case. We can't afford to try it again, or let the public know it has to be tried again. Can't you do anything to help this along?"

Hancock's answer was not immediately forthcoming.

"Well," he said slowly, "I might, but it is goin' to be hard. We might possibly agree,—but,—I—but—."

"This case should not result in disagreement. It should not be tried again. You intelligent men should agree, even if it is hard, as I have said—."

The judge interrupted him.

"Bob," he said, "I'm goin' to rely on you to line those men up. Bring us in a verdict—it can be done. Go back up there an' tell 'em the governor's waiting so I can go to the fair grounds to introduce him, and that I'd like for him to be present in the courtroom when they return a righteous verdict in this case. I want you to put an end to this quibblin'.''

When Pruiett took his ear from the keyhole he was purple with old fashioned Washita anger. While the judge, or the governor, had said nothing as to how they wanted the case decided, he knew that his client was having an instruction put in against her. The commendatory slap which he heard Houston bounce off Bob Hancock's back was as much as to say "Bob, old boy, the governor wants this woman stuck. Let's you and I and the boys give him what he wants."

When the jury filed into the box, rundown and bleary, Cruce and Houston were beaming. Pruiett looked like a prairie tornado just ready to swoop to earth for a havoc-wreaking instant. When that foreman announced that she was guilty, he was goin' to hear a denunciation such as no courtroom ever before had been privileged to hear. A certain judge and a certain governor were to be included. Pruiett was ready to scream.

The clerk read the verdict. "We find her not guilty." Houston looked like he had opened the election reports and found that his constituency had forgotten to remember that he was running for election. Cruce looked equally surprised, but there was a tinge of sheepishness about his expression. He realized how his attempt to influence a conviction had resulted in an acquittal, which otherwise would not have occurred.

The Daily Oklahoman carried the official report on the outcome. "The jury in the case of the woman, charged with helping James Chapman, a Negro farm-hand, murder her husband, on their farm near Stillwater . . . . brought in a verdict at 4 o'clock Saturday afternoon acquitting her of the charge. The case was brought to Guthrie from Payne County, . . ."

There was nothing in print about the star chamber session where the jury foreman, the trial judge and the governor discussed procedure without reckoning in the precepts of justice and civil liberties. No word was written on old Bob Hancock, who gave up his abiding opinion on the guilt of the accused in order that a verdict could be brought in while the governor was there to see it. The chronicle could have truthfully said: "The foreman and one other were for conviction, and would have so remained until the others had joined them, or they were excused from deliberations on the case. They gave up their position so that the state could be spared the expense of another trial."

CHAPTER FOURTEEN

Wherein the venerable Badger Game is turned into Blind Man's Buff, and Pruiett hastens to the aid of a sightless United States Senator. And how official Washington is startled by an expose of a back street chapter in its own story, as big-time politicians and lobbyists, revenge bent, cry for the complete discredit of a brother. And how the hush-money and bribery market hits the skids, the petticoats of the little woman in the case show soiled through their starch and lace, and the editorial comment of the National Press echoes the expression of the President of the United States—praise for counsel for the defense.

The Bond-Gore case, being tried in Oklahoma, was the unorthodox consequence of a fast first-round of the ancient indoor exercise known as the "badger game." The playground had been Washington, crowded with the curious throng which attended the Wilson inauguration in March, 1913, and stayed over to gawk and play, and look for jobs. The participants were: for a fall guy, United States Senator Thomas Pryor Gore of Oklahoma. For the closet peepers; two big time political organizations, one disgruntled over patronage, and the other over government business resisted by the Senator on the floor of the Senate.

Tom Gore was blind. His marble-white optics had received no sensation of light since he had been an eleven-year-old child, and in 1913 he was forty-two years old. The strength of his lost sense had fortified some of those which he retained, as is not unusual, and although sightless, he was gifted with a ponderous mind, and a matchless oral eloquence. His opposition in debate was not invited on the floor of the Senate, not even by the most able and keen eyed of the nation's statesmen.

And his sightless orbs, aided by the mind of a genius, could gaze beyond the grooved walls of the halls of state and see the rocks and shoals of the political sea.

"The court house shook with the stamping approval of hundreds of feet upon the floor today when Moman Pruiett, attorney for Senator Gore, in his speech to the jury exclaimed: "You, Senator Gore, are on trial here today because on the floor of Congress you stood between the helpless Indians of this state and the thieves and crooks who wanted to rob them. . . ."

Pruiett was talking about J. F. McMurray, of the Washington law firm of Mansfield, McMurray and Cornish, which or-

ganization had collected a single $750,000.00 fee for services in National Indian litigation. McMurray was a Texas product who had stopped long enough in the Indian Territory and the new state, as the latter was absorbing the former, to be able to identify himself as a citizen of both. Since he had gotten in the big money he confined his trips out of Washington to New York and adjacent points east, but he managed to keep his stick in with the delegations from the west. He was in on the ground with everyone but Gore, who didn't like him to start with, but who literally cut him to pieces on the Senate floor when the details of the three-quarter million dollars attorney fees, filched out of the Indians' buck-skin pouch, were made public, and plans of another, and larger one, were advanced.

The New York World had quoted from a speech made by Senator Ashurst of Arizona, debating on the Tariff Bill, to give a thumb-nail sketch of this J. F. McMurray. He was described as "the smoothest lobbyist I ever met" by the western senator.

"McMurray could carry a bundle of eels upstairs and never drop a one," Senator Ashurst said.

Continuing with the sketch the World had observed: "McMurray is a member of the law firm of Mansfield, McMurray and Cornish, which collected a fee of $750,000.00 for ridding the tribal rolls of the Choctaw and Chickasaw Indians of the names of 3,600 interlopers who sought a share in rich farming, mineral and timber lands. . . . In 1897 McMurray moved into the Indian Territory. The Dawes Commission was breaking up the rich tribal estates of the Five Nations. The government concluded the Atoka agreement with the Chickasaws and Choctaws a year later, undertaking to sell off their lands before 1907. Mansfield, McMurray and Cornish became the counsel for the Indians at an annual retainer of $10,000. . . . There were some 4,000 persons on the rolls who, in the view of the Redskins, were not entitled to share in the pro rata distribution of the proceeds of the sales of the lands. McMurray's firm undertook, for a consideration, to purge the rolls. The agreement was that, as every person put off the rolls meant $4,500 to the firm's clients, 9 per cent of the value of the lands thus added to the Indians' treasury should be paid to the lawyers. McMurray went to Congress and procured the creation by Congress of the Citizenship Court, and before this tribunal his firm drove out 3,600 persons from their Indian citizenship, adding to the value of the Indian owned lands."

As Pruiett said, with reference to the deal, "McMurray wasn't satisfied with makin' a fair fee ($750,000), he had to be a hog. He wanted to get rich, an' that's what he and the Senator fell out about."

". . . . McMurray and Senator Gore came to a clinch when Gore opposed a bill approving Indian land contracts, under which McMurray's firm was to collect a $3,500,000 fee." That was to be in coin of the United States Government, and not Indian wampum. Three and a half million dollars. ". . . Senator Gore, on June 24, 1910, arose to a question of privilege and told the Senate he had been offered a bribe of $25,000 to withdraw his opposition to the proposed legislation. The persons named by Senator Gore were exonerated by the Senate, but the McMurray laws were defeated."

There was that angle, and still another, to the attempted badger swindle. Wilson had to have a cabinet, and the west had long contended that it should have recognition, and representation, on that select board. Colonel Robert A. Rogers, of Oklahoma's Capital, who had left the south for the east when he was being educated, and who had sought the boundless traces of the Indian country when he had fulfilled the purpose of his quest, had all the qualifications for that office; at least, he acknowledged that he had them. He had the family background. He had land; money and lots of it, and he had been a graduating classmate of Woodrow Wilson when that prominent chinned student had marched with the others at Princeton commencement exercises.

It was real Alma Mater stuff, and Rogers knew that with a senatorial recommendation he would go over. Robert L Owen, Oklahoma's Cherokee Senator, had already gone on record for him. If Gore would go, the far west would have the cabinet post, a Secretaryship of the Interior, it was seeking.

Pruiett contended from the first that Rogers was the creator and principal backer of the plot to destroy the blind Senator. Rogers was no novice in playing badger; he had had a lot of experience and Pruiett knew it. The Colonel's experience had seen him in the place of the victim, instead of that of the victimized, but Pruiett surmised that a greater impression and knowledge of the intricacies had been gained from the position he had occupied, than from any other position or contact he might have with the old shake-down. Rogers had been successfully hooked for a large sum of money, and he would have lost more had it not been for the maneuvers of an apt attorney who stalled in court until he could compromise the compromising little widow who was after him. Coincidentally, Rogers's attorney in that case had been named Moman Pruiett.

The trial of the Colonel's case had been well under way on December 20, 1911 (about two years ahead of Senator Gore's difficulty) and was drawing its share of headlines and bold type on the News, published and circulated in Oklahoma City.

"Sensation was added to sensation in the case of Catherine Rogers against Robert A. Rogers, called for trial before Judge Oldfield in the Superior Court Tuesday. Catherine Rogers is suing for $100,000 alimony, and for $10,000 additional to pay for the education of her nine-year-old child, whom she claims is the son of Robert A. Rogers. . . . No case has been tried in the southwest which caused wider interest than the suit of the woman who calls herself Catherine Rogers, against Robert A. Rogers, a corporation lawyer of Oklahoma City, who is widely known in nearly all of the southern states. . . . When asked whether any marriage ceremony had ever been performed between them, Mrs. Rogers said: 'One time he asked me to go down on the beach at Galveston with him. One other woman went along. When we got down there he made me hold up my hand and swear to forsake all others and live with him. He told me if I ever broke that promise, I'd never see my mother in heaven. . . . Rogers was a classmate of Woodrow Wilson, and is the president of the Woodrow Wilson Democratic Club of Oklahoma.'"

Colonel Rogers maintained a mighty lobby in the city of the Potomac. He had the kind of money that it took to hire fast fixers, even after he had settled with Catherine, and he had them working. When they had failed, and they knew that they had failed, they took advantage of being already organized, and set out to scuttle the blind Senator's prairie schooner. Gore hadn't been able to see Rogers, either literally or figuratively, and the Colonel, and the crowd that saw good jobs winging with his failure to receive the appointment, knew that their loss was directly attributable to him. They moved over to the Ebbets House, mixed a few with Frank McMurray, and talked the situation over.

But the bait? What about the bait? Who ever heard of a badger sequence, even one with a blind villain, and with prominent politicians for heroes to appear in the nick of time, without a fair damsel to be rescued? With facial and physical pulchritude abundant in Washington, the producers of the drama picked a dumpy little matron of near middle age, whose sorrel hair and rats spiraled above her head like a bee hive, and who squinted at the world through a pair of thick lensed, pince-nez glasses. Setting the stage for a blind one must have been an exacting task for the revenge seeking job-seekers, who had the free advice and direction of such high priced producers as Mansfield, McMurray and Cornish.

Her name was Minnie. Minnie Bond was born Minnie Ballinger, and she had a husband. By strange coincidence her man had failed to catch any of the pie that the Gore wagon had been delivering, and there they were, a thousand miles away from home, broke, and with no jobs. Jim Jacobs, and Kirby Fitzpatrick, and Thaddeus E. Robertson, from their adjoining rooms in the Winston Hotel, had watched the coveted pastry with drooping lip, and looked apprehensively, as if in fear of cannibalism from their lank consorts, when the loaded cart had passed on and out of sight in the distance.

They were an able crew. Jacobs was an accomplished lobbyist. ". . . He had been there (Washington) a long time, and seemed to know the ins and outs; seemed to know where to hang his hat."

Fitzpatrick, until late enjoying plenty in the government land service, was a Tennessee adventurer who had seen the world, and had most recently soldiered in the Philippines. As he stoutly advised the Attorney General of the United States, after the Bond-Gore incident had begun to smell: "I am no vagabond; my people have not been strangers to the halls of Congress, nor laggards on the battlefield of the Republic; I followed the flag ten thousand miles from home and offered my life on the altar of my country's honor. I am a graduate of two universities and the governor of my state does not blush to call me friend . . . ."

Robertson, the fourth of the principal participants, was the youngest, and the most gifted. At 27 he was playing for big stakes and with the big boys. His stature, smaller than average, was surmounted by a large, swarthy-skinned head. He had a black, beady eye, and a quick answer. When Pruiett asked him what he was doing in Washington, he instantly replied, "I went there to see the inauguration, for one thing, and then I thought Bob Rogers would be appointed Secretary of the Interior, and I wanted to be in on the ground floor if he was."

"This is a plot to destroy me." Thus the sightless Senator labeled the lawsuit from the witness stand. But if he was going down, he wasn't going alone; he was dragging under, in his fierce and frantic clutch, all of the conspirators that were connected with it. When Gore had bowed his neck and refused to reconsider on the patronage proposition, Minnie Bond and the trio of eye-ball witnesses gave the story to the press. When Gore countered with charges of blackmail and attempted extortion, the conspirators had to make good, or suffer the consequences. They went to the District Attorney for the District of Columbia and gave information, and asked that the Senator from Oklahoma be arraigned on a charge of attempted rape. Their statements, as given to the officers of the district, and as they later developed in court, were as disconcerting to the political idealist, or moral idealist, as they were refreshing to the scandal-mongers and sensation-seeking court house loungers.

The District Attorney refused to file charges. The Senate declined to act, although each individual member was invited, in well-couched terms, to make an official inquisition in the matter. They gave their blind colleague a vote of confidence. Washington's lawyers wouldn't touch the civil angle of the case, although the Bond-McMurray-Rogers combine shopped the district. Back in Oklahoma, and just before election time, the Senator, on a visit to his constituency, received the greeting which apprised him that he had been sued by Minnie for damages, fifty thousand dollars worth of them, for assault, and for defamation of character. The trial, and its evidence developing ramifications, produced not only a sordid revelation of the official Washington manners and mannerisms, but revealed a back-street section of the life of the plaintiff Minnie Bond which had heretofore been studiously and successfully concealed.

But back to Washington, or rather to the events of Washington as they developed in the testimony of lobbyist Jacobs, on the witness stand. Jim, responding nicely to the careful handling of Minnie's lawyer, was beginning to tell how the trouble all began.

"On the 24th day of March, 1913, in the afternoon, I will get you to state if you had a conversation with Mrs. Minnie E. Bond?" The question was propounded by Mr. Lillard of Minnie's counsel.

"I did," Jim replied, truthfully.

"About what time was it, if you remember?" was the next question.

Jim had a good memory.

"My recollection is that it was between five and six o'clock," he promptly answered.

"What was the conversation, Mr. Jacobs?"

"I met Mrs. Bond in the little aisle that you come in, it would not be called a lobby, I don't think, about four feet wide on the first floor of the hotel, right where you start to walk up to the elevator, and she made a remark to me that she had an engagement with Senator Gore, and that she didn't know where she was going to talk to him. Well, I could understand why without her telling me; she went on to say, you see that both the men's and ladies' parlors are congested with people, stopping there, a lot of tourists stopping there, and very much congested at that time. I says, 'Mrs. Bond, take him to your room.' She says, 'Why no, I would not do that—I would not go to a private room anywhere with him.' I says, 'Why?' She says, 'You don't know Senator Gore.' I says, 'I will go along with you if there is nothing private you want to discuss.' She says, 'I would like to have you go, but I don't want to take you up to my room. I have unpacked everything to repack and it is not in proper shape for you to go in,' and she says, 'I am expecting him most any time.' I says, 'Take my keys and go to my room.' She says, 'Will you go up with us?' I says, 'No, I will either go up with you or come in afterwards and hang around and make it a point to be in if I don't go with you,'—so I left her the key and walked out on the streets."

Jacobs testified that he "just hung around the front of the hotel, talking with Bill Tilghman (the United States Marshal who was slain in his attempt to clean up the Cromwell oil field dance and gambling dives) until he saw the Senator come along. As he stated it:

". . . about that time I saw the Senator and his brother-in-law, the one the government has employed to lead him around, coming across the campus toward the hotel." The Winston was near First and Pennsylvania, across from the park of the Washington Botanical Gardens. When counsel asked Jacobs what he did then, he replied:

"Well, Fitzpartick was going by and I caught up with him and caught him by the arm and says, 'Fitz, let's go up to your room.' He says, 'All right.' I took him by the arm and walked part of the way towards the hotel from the corner of First and Pennsylvania Avenue, and held on to his arm I think until we got to the little alley—my recollection is—and when we got to that

I turned his arm loose and I says, 'Fitz, there is a matter I am going to watch.' I passed right on through and went on upstairs.''

The lawyer didn't like for him to stop there.

"What did you and Fitz do then?" he inquired, as if he didn't know what the answer was going to be.

"I went on ahead, and I met Robertson (Thaddeus E. Robertson) on the way. I says, 'Rob, let's go to your room.' He went ahead of me, unlocked the door, throwed it open, and he and I walked in."

Fitzpatrick and Robertson shared the room next to Jacobs', the one he had loaned Mrs. Bond for her interview with the Senator, and there was a door connecting the two rooms. The conference had already started when Jacobs and Robertson stealthily entered the latter's room.

Mrs. Bond testified and explained her business in the National Capital—how she had first contacted the blind Senator—and how they had reached Jacobs' room after making her general appointment at the hotel. Mr. Lillard was examining her.

"I will get you to state when was the first time you saw Senator Gore in Washington?" he asked her.

"I visited him in his office, in the Senate Annex," Mrs. Bond replied.

"And on what date, if you remember?"

"I don't remember the date, sometime between the 4th and 24th."

"For what purpose did you visit Senator Gore at his office?"

"To discuss Mr. Bond's appointment with him."

Lillard was being ponderous and methodical, as if he was much in the dark about the affair. The ground was being carefully covered.

"Did you discuss that appointment with Senator Gore at that time?" he inquired.

"I did," she answered.

"I will get you to state who, if anybody, was in his private office, at the time you had this first interview with him?"

"There was nobody in his private office," responded Mrs. Bond, with a significant, suggestive, toss of her head.

"Please state, Mrs. Bond, what occurred upon your entering Senator Gore's private office, and during this interview which you had with the Senator."

Mrs. Bond shifted about in her chair before answering. Her preparation was a suggestion of a spicy disclosure.

"On entering his office Senator Gore shook hands with me. I sat at the corner of his desk in a chair, and while we were discussing Mr. Bond's appointment, Senator Gore first reached over and took hold of one of my hands. I moved back a little bit, and then he put his hand on my knee. I shoved it off gently with my fingers, and moved back farther."

"What else occurred there?" Lillard took advantage of a slight hesitation to put another question.

"Senator Gore said he didn't have time to see Mr. Bond's references, although I urged him to see them. I was there but a few minutes when he reached down and took hold of my ankle, and after he held my hand and ankle, I decided it was time for me to go. I got up and said I didn't want to monopolize his time, and tried to get away without appearing to observe anything. When he went to shake hands to say good-bye he pulled me up to him. He said he didn't see how he could place Mr. Bond in that particular position, but that he would be very glad to have me call on him socially."

She was interrupted by another question.

"When did you see Senator Gore after that, or when did you have another conversation with him, either in person or over the 'phone?"

The witness studied for an instant.

"Well," she finally said, "I remember I called him over the 'phone to make an appointment with reference to the matter we had been discussing. He suggested that it was a matter he didn't care to discuss over the telephone. I said I expected to go away at a certain time, and asked him if he would come by the hotel."

"Did he invite you to his office?"

"Yes, he invited me to his office."

"Now, Mrs. Bond," Lillard persisted, "on the 24th day of March, I will get you to state if you had a telephone conversation with Senator Gore?"

"I did," she replied.

"What did he say in that conversation?"

"He asked me to come up, and I said I couldn't—I was busy; he said he thought he would be able to come down."

"Did you talk to him over the 'phone any more?"

"Yes, I talked to him at another time."

"What did you say in that conversation, and about what time was it?"

"I judge about three or four o'clock. I am not positive about the time. He said he had some people in his office he thought he would soon be able to get rid of, and that he would come to the hotel; he would call me before he did come."

Mrs. Bond continued to explain how her packing, and the return of her laundry, had caused her own room to be in temporary disarray, and how she aired her dilemma in the presence of compassionate old Jim Jacobs, on the mezzanine. She told of how Jim had given her his key, along with uncurtailed rights and privileges to use his room.

"Immediately afterward," she said, "and while I was downstairs, I just walked over to one side, and somebody remarked, 'there's Senator Gore,' or 'here is Senator Gore,' some such remark as that; . . . ."

"What did you do then?" catechized the ever curious Lillard.

"Senator Gore came on the inside," she answered, "I walked up to him and shook hands with him. He turned around, excused himself from his attendant, and walked with me to the elevator."

"Where did you go to?"

"When we got upstairs I told Senator Gore that we would go to that room, the parlors were all crowded. He said he had noticed the confusion. When we got upstairs we went down the corridor and into this room."

And so the little blind fly felt his way into the mesh of the spiders' adjoining webs. His hat and gold headed cane were placed upon the pillows at the head of the bed while he adjusted the lapels of his coat. The creases in his afternoon trousers were as true and immaculate as the black and grey stripes themselves, and there was an expression of benign patience on his child-like face as he turned his head from side to side, to better hear the swish of the petticoats as his little hostess bustled about the room. The shades were down, the lights were on, and a dresser had been pulled in front of the connecting door, to provide peeping space for the conspirators. It was as if they needed camouflage or cover to conceal them from their victim; Gore couldn't have seen them if they had lounged in the easy chairs under the reading lamps.

Jim Jacobs' version of the episode established that no lights were turned on in the Robertson-Fitzpatrick room when he and

Robertson stealthily entered it. He said that Robertson asked him who it was in his (Jacobs') room.

"I says," he testified, "It is Senator Gore and Mrs. Bond. I says, 'I am going to watch them.' About that time Fitz came in and I proceeded to ease the door open. The door is a connecting door—between Jacobs, and Robertson and Fitzpatrick's room, and the dresser set in my room in front of this door. They used to go back and forth to use my bathroom and sometimes we would leave the dresser moved enough for them to pass. I eased the door open a little tiny crack and proceeded to look in there. . . . When I got the door eased open Robertson was leaning against me. I looked around and there was Fitz, looking in through a crack. You see, the glass in that mirror hung on one of those apparatuses, a little hole, or groove, and all we could see of it we could see through this hole, for the dresser was three and a half or four feet high."

The blind Senator and bespectacled Minnie talked about the things that Senators and female applicants for jobs usually talk about in sequestered hotel rooms. "Mrs. Bond was sitting on the foot of the bed and Senator Gore was sitting in a rocking chair. . . . I noticed that he seemed to want to catch hold of her—he asked her some questions about her weight and looks. . . . . There was a scuffle and she sat back down on the bed. Senator Gore attempted to pull Mrs. Bond down on his knees, and she shoved herself loose from him, or rather shoved up and he pulled up with her, and in a very short while they were both over on the bed. . . . He had his hand on Mrs. Bond's face, his left arm—he took his right hand and placed her left here under his hand, no, under his right knee, and then crawled astride her; he then attempted to pull her skirts up and succeeded in getting them up about her knees . . . ." Such was a portion of Robertson's sworn version of the incident.

Jim Jacobs' account of the Senator's approach was slightly different in substance but essentially the same in conclusion. "Well, they talked along awhile there, he first tried to kiss her hand but she pulled it away and told him he must not do that. Then he caught hold of her arm and she would push it off and asked him to behave himself. He would say something back, I could hear his voice but could not distinguish what he would say. I think he finally put his hand up on her face—or up towards that way—and when he did that, and when she raised her back on the bed and she was not entirely laying on the bed, she caught hold of the foot of the bed with one of her hands. When she reached over she just was close enough to catch the foot of the bed and she made a remark, immediately when he got her down, that if he didn't let her up she would call the police. He jumped up and begged her pardon."

The ever helpful and oft-interrupting Lillard didn't recognize Jacobs' pause as a proper place to stop. He prompted him with another question.

"What did he do after jumping up?"

"Well," he said, "he sat back in his chair, and Mrs. Bond sat up a little more toward the head of the bed and then she began to reprimand him, said he ought to be ashamed of himself, and that she was not the kind of a woman he might think she was. Of course, he replied all the time but I did not understand anything he said. Then they went on talking again, about her uncle, friendship between them and so on, and they finally got this straightened up, this little episode, and commenced to talk about the position again. They talked on awhile about that and he made some kind of advance, I could not see on account of the dresser; my judgment from the demonstration that he made was that he commenced to catch hold of her feet. She said, 'Behave yourself, I want you to stop that.' He put his hand on her arm and put his other hand over her mouth and shoved her back on the bed and got right up over her. Fitz took hold of my arm and says, 'Boys, he's going to rape her in spite of hell.' "

The coy plaintiff had her own recollection of the events of which she made complaint.

"What did he say; did he or not ask you as to your looks, and as to whether or not you were good looking?" her counsel asked.

"He did," she answered tersely.

"After asking you that—and after your reply to him—what did he do; did he or not reach up to your face?"

"Yes, he reached up to my face."

"For what purpose?"

"I don't know what his purpose was, he didn't tell me . . . . I importuned him to keep his place, and he begged my pardon."

"What further conversation did he have with you as to the position in Washington?" That was the next question.

"He told me that if I were a little widow he would be able to take care of me in Washington." She said it with an emphasis intended to imply that such a declaration was not fully warranted by senatorial privilege.

"At that time had his actions become more marked?"

"They had."

"What did he do then?"

Mrs. Bond summed the situation up in her next answer.

"He caught hold of me and tried to push me on the bed," she said. "I told him I would call the police and that he would have a brass button to take away as a souvenir, if he didn't desist. He grabbed hold of me, shoved me down on the bed with his hand over my mouth, and piled down on top of me."

"What occurred then?" her counsel inquired, breathlessly.

"Mr. Robertson burst into the room. I held my clothes down with one hand and pushed him off with the other. When his hand slipped off my face, so I could, I gave a smothered scream. Then Mr. Robertson burst into the room."

". . . . He jumped up and asked who it was, and Robertson was saying, 'Robertson, from Oklahoma City.' 'How do you do, old man, how do you do,' the Senator replied. 'I am glad to see you, so very glad to see you.' "

When Minnie's attorney asked Jim Jacobs a rather delicate question, Jim proved his lobbyist's tact by the way he answered it.

In response to a question Robertson said that "the front of his trousers were unbuttoned. They were not open." After Robertson had hurried to the rescue, knocking down the dresser which set in front of the door, for the realistic effect it would give the charge, Minnie began to scream and blubber. The senator tried to get her to state, before Robertson, and Fitz and Jim Jacobs, who had followed Robertson into the room, "that everything was all right and that he had been a perfect gentleman." This Minnie declined to do. Robertson hustled Gore out while Minnie went into the bathroom, and it was while he and the blind man were waiting for the elevator that Robertson claimed he noticed the condition of the striped trousers, and it was there that the Senator straightened the situation up. "We were waiting for the elevator to come down and he asked me if his clothing was not all right, and I pulled his coat back to see. I noticed that his trousers were unbuttoned, and I told him so."

The storm of notoriety which started immediately after the incident and continued, for over a year, contained the various conflicting contentions of the various parties. The Minnie Bond backers, and there were plenty of them, contended that Gore sent a representative to the Winston the next day, and "asked her what she wanted, saying that she could get any job the Senator could give, if she'd keep her mouth shut." Fitzpatrick and Jacobs always maintained that they were offered lucrative positions in the government if they would respect the Senator's wishes for a complete silence in the matter. Gore and his backers claimed that the exposure never would have been made if certain demands for patronage had been met by him.

The more generally accepted, and more plausible, version of that angle of the case, was that the participants, who might have had some interest in getting a political job from the Senator, had no voice in the direction of the production after they had played their parts. Minnie's husband met Colonel Rogers, the man who could thank Gore for the loss of a cabinet position, in Memphis, and the two of them rode the train together to the National Capital. There was a midnight conference in the Jim Jacobs room at the Winston, where Fitz and Robertson, Rogers and Bond were present, and the names of Frank McMurray and Jake Hammon, the millionaire Republican politician from Ardmore, were mentioned. Rogers left the next afternoon for New York and Robertson followed him. These two met at the Martinique Hotel there, then journeyed to Baltimore, where they met Jacobs and Fitzpatrick. The large amount of cash which Rogers gave Jacobs for distribution amongst the group was called a loan by Jacobs— a payoff, by Pruiett. Minnie Bond and her husband went to the District Attorney's office and demanded that Gore be prosecuted. The press ate it up.

When the Bond story broke he had but one choice of program to adopt. He had to whip it so decisively that it could be used as campaign capital in his coming fight to be reelected, or he had to sit by and watch it as it overwhelmed and defeated him.

He employed Pruiett, when the retinue of talent already volunteered would gain his equivalent to an acquittal, along with relief from paying the fifty thousand Minnie prayed for, if legal ingenuity and skill could accomplish it. There was Charles B. Stuart, who had moved to the new state from Gainesville, Texas, when his law partner, Joseph Weldon Bailey, was elected to Congress and moved off and left him. A. C. Cruce, Pruiett's old alternating ally and adversary, was on the list, as was W. I. (Bill) Gilbert, who in later years acquired prominence as the leading legal light of the Pacific Coast, and who, in his suite in Los Angeles, advised the movie stars as to their rights and obligations, contractual, marital and otherwise. In a hotel room conference the lawyers agreed that Gore should know how, and by whom, he wanted his defense handled. The sightless Senator pecked the floor a few times with his fancy cane before he answered.

"The rest of you boys get the law ready, and take care of the detail. I want Moman to cross-examine their witnesses, and I want him to take charge of getting our evidence together. And another thing; I hired him to give this case to the jury."

Pruiett started after Minnie Bond in full cry. The plaintiff had had an unfortunate prior marriage or two, and a child born that didn't survive. A country town burial, with forced economy apparent in the utility of a shoe-box for a casket—and with the services of the embalmer and preacher dispensed with—gave him license to charge that she had murdered her progeny. On January 22, 1914, he took the sworn depositions of witnesses at Caddo, a hamlet in the old Choctaw bogs in the southeastern part of the new state, to expose a few of Minnie's apparent many indiscretions. His detectives had learned that she had lived in that community as the wife of Dr. Farrar, a dentist.

It was little wonder that the Oklahoma capital, where the case was being tried, was attracting the attention of the national paper-watching public.

" 'I knew they had framed up on me. I told Dr. J. H. Earp when he called at my office on the day following the occurrence that I would see them in hell before I would make terms with them. I did not tell Earp to hush Mrs. Bond and get her out of Washington. At no time, neither in my office nor in the Winston Hotel, did I ever offer Mrs. Bond any improprieties or take advantage of her.' So declared Senator T. P. Gore in testimony in his own behalf today in the $50,000 damage suit against him by Mrs. Minnie E. Bond." The St. Louis Globe Democrat had opened its daily two-column front in that manner. "Speaking in a loud, clear voice, Senator Gore denied every essential part of the testimony of Mrs. Bond, Dr. Earp and the other members of the alleged conspiracy against him."

". . . . The feature of today's events, other than the testimony of Senator Gore, was the appearance on the stand of Al Jennings, ex-outlaw and present candidate for governor on the Democratic ticket, as a witness for Mrs. Bond. Jennings contradicted the testimony of Mitch Bonner, Oklahoma City banker, and said that in Jacobs' conversation with Bonner, Jacobs did not say he would 'call off' the Gore charge for $25,000. . . ."

The St. Louis paper told the Senator's side of the story as he told it himself. ". . . . I talked with her only a few minutes. I told her I would have to go. I rose to start and extended my hand, and when she took hold of it she kind of seemed to go down on the bed. I said 'What does this mean?' She gave me some kind of an answer which I didn't understand and then I heard some one come in who said it was T. E. Robertson of Oklahoma City. We exchanged salutations. . . . Mrs. Bond began to make an outcry and carry on, and Robertson told her to 'stop that squalling.' He and she passed some remarks and she went into the bathroom. I told Robertson to get my hat. He did so and then I told him that I wanted to talk to Mrs. Bond. . . . I said to her, 'Mrs. Bond, what have you got to say about this?' . . . .I must explain here that my relations in the past with Mr. Robertson had been unpleasant. . . . She said, 'I don't want Bond to know you have been in my room.' I put the same question to Robertson and he had nothing to say. Neither made any suggestions of any impropriety. My intention was to summon the hotelkeeper if there had been any such suggestion."

The Kansas City Star likened it, editorially, to the New York scandal involving Funk and Sulzer. "The Gore case, like the case of Funk and Sulzer, has exposed once more the methods used by unscrupulous politicians to discredit men who are in their way. Sulzer they punished, not for his misdeed, but for his refusal to obey the mandates of the boss and turn over the state of New York to politicians to plunder."

The Associated Press to the Post Dispatch at St. Louis was able to glean a little of homely interest from the smelly bulk of the subject being considered. "On her arrival in the court room today Mrs. Gore brought with her hundreds of messages addressed to Senator Gore, from friends over the country and constituents, in Oklahoma, expressing their sympathy in 'his persecution' and their belief in his vindication by the jury."

SENATOR GORE, MRS. GORE AND THE TRIAL JUDGE
"***a blind man, high in the councils of government forced to meet the unmerited indignity of political persecution."

Argument of Moman Pruiett, Chief Counsel for United States Senator T. P. Gore, of Oklahoma, before the jury in the Minnie Bond damage suit case, on the 17th day of February, 1914, in Oklahoma City, Okla.

MAY IT PLEASE THE COURT—GENTLEMEN OF THE JURY:

"Now, therefore, go thou unto Pharaoh and speak, and I will be with thy mouth, and will teach thee what thou shalt say."

It is my duty and it shall be my pleasure to discuss with you in my meager way, the issues of a case which has assumed the proportions of a national disgrace, and has placed upon the fair name of Oklahoma a stain which you alone by your verdict can wipe away.

A United States Senator is on trial here today because on the floors of Congress he has stood between the helpless Indians of this state and the political crooks and thieves who wanted to rob them.

He is on trial because he has incurred the enmity of political vandals by refusing to appoint them to office; he is on trial because he brought down upon his head the wrath of such profligates as Jim Jacobs and the plaintiff in this case.

I am greatly embarrassed at the outset of this discussion by an almost overwhelming sense of responsibility and of personal inability to properly and fully discharge my duty to my client in saying to you all that I ought to say, all that ought to be said, at this time.

In the box where you sit, Gentlemen of the Jury, you have an unusual advantage over my friend and client, the defendant. You can see him but he cannot see you. He is in the dark. He cannot look into your faces and judge from your countenances what manner of men you are, whether you are his friends or his enemies,—whether you are all good men and true, or whether any or all of you may not be prejudiced against him by the false tale told you by the lying lips of a vile woman and her still viler co-conspirators and confederates.

He has had to depend upon me and upon my judgment concerning all and every one of you.

This worries me exceedingly. He tells me that he relies upon me implicitly to put his case truthfully and fairly before you in my argument. This also troubles me,—for how can he rely confidently upon another man whose face he has never seen?

There is another thing that stands in my way. My client is versatile and scholarly and has a profound knowledge gained from the many books which his wife has read to him and shown to the eyes of his mind.

On the other hand, I, his adviser and advocate, am unlettered and without the knowledge of books, for the only book I have studied is the book of human nature. From that book, and that alone, I do believe that I have learned how to judge correctly of a man's actions by his motives, and, conversely, to discover his underlying motives by considering carefully what he has done. From that book of human nature and a habit of long observation, I have grown to believe that I can very often read correctly the thoughts and emotions of men with whom I become acquainted and whose faces I can see, as I have seen yours for many days. But no man can always interpret correctly the thoughts of others by their faces, nor can man always speak the proper words to his brother.

My client requires me to speak the exact truth to you concerning the evidence in this case, and to misstate nothing. The imperfections of human recollection may lead one astray but I will do my best.

When the Lord appeared unto Moses at the burning bush and told him to go unto Pharoah, and to demand that Pharoah should let the children of Israel go out of Egypt and from the house of bondage, Moses answered and said: "Oh, my Lord, behold, I am not eloquent, neither heretofore, nor since thou has spoken unto thy servant, but I am slow of speech and of a slow tongue." And the Lord said unto him, "Who hath made man's mouth, or who maketh the dumb or the seeing or the blind?" "Now, therefore, go thou unto Pharoah and speak, and I will be with thy mouth and will teach thee what thou shalt say."

And I do believe that when a man is called upon to defend and protect the innocent by the words of his mouth, and he tries earnestly to do so, that help may and does frequently come to him from unknown sources, which enables him to speak effectively—to speak plainly, to call things by their right names, to denounce falsehood and conspiracy and to protect the innocent and the upright from the assaults of all the liars and the pimps and the prostitutes who are still outside of hell.

My friend Giddings said that he would stake his political future upon the activities he has displayed in this trial. Let me say to you men that Gid is placing very small stakes. Gid, you need not worry about your political future—you haven't any. You are merely chasing a Will-o'-the-wisp when you seek political preferment at the hands of an enlightened people. If you are not already politically damned, you will be at the end of the trial of this case.

In our opening statement we told you that we would show to you that Senator Gore has been made the victim of a "Hell-inspired Conspiracy", and in order that you may comprehend fully the force of that assertion, let me tell you about the conspirators themselves, the actors in this drama of crime.

First comes Jacobs, the arch-conspirator, who, with criminal ingenuity, created within his own perverted mind and debased soul the sickening details of this horrible crime perpetrated on Senator Gore. Jacobs, according to the testimony, was an eye-witness to the result of his own hellish scheme. He addressed a long written document to the Senate confessing his guilt and gloating over the fact that he had been successful in persuading others to take part in his high carnival of perfidy. With the sneaking malignity of the hyena, he has pressed on and on the wolf-dogs of persecution until today there is presented to the world the sad and sorrowful spectacle of a blind man high in the councils of the Government, who has hitherto led a life of honor, of merit and of truth, forced to meet the unmerited indignity of a political prosecution;—this man Jacobs the ringleader of a criminal gang; the brains and brawn of all that's dirty, that's low and debased; this monument of depravity whom they were afraid to put on the stand. We were loaded for bear on that if they had put him on the stand. He held off so he could turn state's evidence and save himself when these conspirators are arrested and prosecuted for this crime. Jacobs and McMurray are wily old coyotes, too cunning to be witnesses in this case, they planned it all, and cowardly like, they shirk in the shadowy background, and dare not deny Smith Chamber's testimony. In connection with this man Jacobs let me refer briefly to the testimony of Smith Chambers.

Chambers, a man who stands high in his community, who has been honored time and time again by the suffrages of his people; whose record as a good citizen and an honorable gentleman has not been assailed and whose testimony remains absolutely unimpeached—this man leaves the even tenor of his quiet vocation

MINNIE BOND AND HER HUSBAND
"She squinted at the world through a pair of thick-lensed, pince-nez glasses."

her throughout the long days of this trial. Her own sex has avoided her. She is a thing apart because of this shameful thing she has done. Even a scarlet woman would not touch the hem of her skirt,—this woman whose proposed victim was a blind man.

Can you doubt for a moment from the testimony the willing part she played in this infamous business? Can you doubt that she is clay in the potter's hands and that Jim Jacobs is the potter? Can you doubt the utter depravity of this woman whose life since childhood has been one continuous night of lewdness and shame; who has trod the path of unfaithfulness and violated the laws divine and human by depriving her innocent babe of its right to live, and who never inquired whether her first-born was a boy or a girl? Can you say that this woman, whose soul is steeped in the very fumes of hell, is the coy and bashful matron, the modest violet, the unsoiled flower, the eloquent gentlemen have pictured her to be? Can you, with any degree of sincerity, give serious consideration to the testimony of this creature who upon the witness stand showed not the least look of pity, the least sign of regret, the least feeling of sorrow as she sought to mulct from this defendant damages as a reward for her own criminal practices. I say that her testimony deserves no serious consideration at your hands. I say to give her one penny in damages would be turning this court into an instrument for the purpose of levying blackmail, and remove the legal shackles from the foul hand of extortion. It would paint the blackest page in the judicial history of this state and become an everlasting disgrace to this temple of justice.

Now let us divide our time with the great soldier in this case. Let us pay our respects to that distinguished military genius. Let us recall and let us not forget that he is a disappointed office-seeker.

Followed the flag ten thousand miles, did he? Let me tell you, men, he'd follow the bedraggled petticoats of a degraded woman ten thousand miles where he would follow the flag one. This brave soldier who stood there in that darkened room in a Washington hotel and peeped through a crack at a blind man who had been lured into a lighted room by a woman, a brave soldier indeed, peeping through a crack at a blind enemy! Fitz made a good watch dog for Jacobs, he played his part well, and has since used it to extol the virtues of himself and family.

Listen, men of Oklahoma County, I am appealing to the sense of duty of American manhood in the jury box.

You remember the testimony of Mrs. Bond in which she stated she told Jacobs in the hotel that she had an appointment with Senator Gore at three o'clock and asked Jacobs for the key to his room and Jacobs promising to be near her when she talked with the Senator. Jacobs gave her the key to his room and then waited in front of the hotel for Senator Gore to arrive. When the Senator appeared, Jacobs approached Fitzpatrick who was also near the front of the hotel, and in full view of the Senator he asked Fitzpatrick to come up to his room and said: "I have something I want you to watch." It will be remembered that Fitzpatrick never asked a question as to what he was to see or what was to take place. Jacobs on his way to the room then meets Robertson and tells him to come up to the room, that he has something for him to watch. The testimony was that a dresser was situated in front of the door leading to where Jacobs, Fitzpatrick and Robertson had placed themselves, but before the arrival of the parties it had been moved something like two feet, the door unlocked and left standing open about eight or ten inches. That Mrs. Bond, when talking to the Senator, could at the same time see three faces, of Jacobs, Fitzpatrick and Robinson not over six or eight feet away. Fitzpatrick made no inquiry as to what he was to watch for the reason that the scheme had been prearranged between the conspirators and each knew the part he was to play. There is no evidence here to sustain it, but I believe that I am justified in drawing the conclusion that Jacobs had a flag when he started to the field of his criminal operations, and Fitz just couldn't resist the temptation to follow it into that darkened room.

Then comes Robertson, the hero of this drama. This man who lunged into the room in response to the wild screams for help and admonished the woman to "stop that squalling." He who had sought to provide a Cabinet for the President; who had expressed the ambition to become the prosecutor of criminals—he was the man that grappled with the villain and saved the heroine from the dire calamity that was about to befall her. Bob would make a good prosecutor all right. He has had the experience. At prosecuting conspirators he ought to be made pastmaster and at placing upon the shoulders of blackmailers the cross of justice, he certainly could have no equal.

She tells you that when she first met Senator Gore in his

office that he wanted to play hands with her and tried to catch hold of her ankle. If that is a fact, she knew what kind of man he was. If she is the lady she would have you to believe her to be she would have felt unsafe in his presence. She would have shunned him like a bird shuns a snake. But the evidence shows that she called him constantly after this visit; that she insisted upon him coming to the hotel to see her. If she did not intend to entrap him, why did she renew her relations with the man, who had been guilty of gross improprieties toward her. If her purpose was not to carry out the wishes of Jacobs, why didn't she, like a lady, refrain from any further communication with the man who had shocked her modesty. Consider her actions throughout this infamous affair and you cannot sidetrack the conclusion that she sought to place this blind man in a position where the perjuring lips of Jacobs could assassinate his character.

Thus the actors appear to your view. Thus their own testimony presents them for your consideration. Jacobs: In the foul chambers of whose heart lurked the hissing serpent of motive and in whose depraved mind, the plot framed by him, became the deformed offspring of shattered political ambitions.

The Woman: "The Clay in the Potter's hands," and Fitzpatrick and Robertson, also "Potters" of unusual skill and ability. Thus they played their respective parts and the white light of God's purity spreads the panorama of their hideous offense before us.

I cannot, my friends, leave this subject without extending my respects to Bond—that apology for a husband. The man who would allow the woman he calls by the sacred name of wife to become merchandise in a court of justice; the man who would profit by the degradation of a woman, wanton though she be, ought to and will receive your public condemnation, your never ending execration, your unutterable loathing.

So far we have devoted our time to getting an insight into the characters of the actors. Let us now turn our attention to the perverted offspring of their concerted action. Let us look at the actual crime from the standpoint of the evidence introduced upon the part of the prosecutors. Let's view it from the time Senator Gore innocently walked into the arms of this dastardly conspiracy until this baseless fabric of a damage suit was filed some eight months afterward.

Senator, you were there, groping in the darkness of your blindness, surrounded by men whose souls were black as the dregs of hell and this woman, with her tainted record; you were there under the control of hands stained and blackened by the filth of infamy; you were there artfully led and cunningly entangled in the meshes of the spider web of political vampires— a net-work of hideousness; you were there the easy prey of their wicked desires, floundering helpless and defenseless, in a cesspool seething with the broth of perdition. Thus the drama begins.

She took him to the second floor, telling him she was going to the parlor. When she got there she excused herself a minute, as she told him, she was going in to see if the parlor was occupied. She was deceiving him there. She had roomed on that second floor for weeks and she knew there was no parlor on it. It was a bit of her deceit to prepare him for going into another room. She told him that the parlor was full of school children and she would have to take him to another room. That is the evidence here. That is her own story. Can you doubt now the purpose she had in mind? She did not take him to her room because there was no door there opening into another room where Jacobs, Fitzpatrick and Robertson might hide and pounce in at the right moment.

She tells you that she never was in that room of Jacobs' before. But the maid on that floor has testified that she saw Mrs. Bond often in that room. The bell-boy knew where to find her. He had a message for her. He looked for her in her own room and then went straight to Jacobs' room and found her. He knew where to look for her. He had found her there before.

She says she sat Senator Gore in a rocking chair and she sat on the bed because there was no other chair in the room, and yet the testimony of others is that there were three chairs there. Who ever heard of a great big hotel in Washington with only one chair in the room?

There he sat for about ten minutes in a well lighted room, the door unlocked, the corridor outside filled with romping students, there on a holiday, a bellboy coming to the door of the room and opening it, Mrs. Bond receiving a call over the telephone, and yet, in that public place in that brief time, they charge that he attempted to assault this woman. It is preposterous and impossible. The physical facts brand indelibly their accusation as a lie. He couldn't have done in that short space of time all the things they say he is guilty of. Yet they come here, their lips blistering with falsehoods—rank, foul and God-defying falsehoods— and ask you gentlemen to award this woman damages, when the surrounding circumstances and conditions disprove their every assertion.

By her story he had not asked her consent; he had not said a word to warn her of his purpose; she had not been given a chance to consent or deny. How did he know but that she would lock the door if he asked her to? Another thing. This attack is alleged to have been committed in March and this suit was not filed until eight months afterwards. Why? Because all through those eight months they were trying to levy blackmail upon Senator Gore. Thus you find the plaintiff's own words, the rank malice of her false accusations. Take her own testimony and turn upon it the light of truth and it is immediately discovered to be a hideous tissue of falsehood that has no truth or veracity. It is merely the vile exhibit of the lies cunningly contrived by the master hand of Jacobs.

And now my friends, here's where I get killed. Measure me for my coffin. Begin to dig my grave. This bad man Jennings, this outlaw who is making political capital of his every criminal act, who tenders his career as a horse thief and train robber as his chief asset for citizenship, has theatened to kill any man who dared to call him a liar. I call him a liar. I call him a perjurer. I say he is unworthy the respect of any honest man. I say this, and I say that Al Jennings will not dare to crook his little finger at me. To place any confidence whatever in what this self-confessed criminal has testified to would be placing a premium on perjury.

I have not attempted to make an elaborate analysis of the testimony of the plaintiff and her co-conspirators in this case, because it needs none. It explains itself, as the result of a vile conspiracy, colored with evil desires and tainted with perjury from beginning to end.

The plaintiff and her witnesses are all of the same litter, all spawn of the same kennel, and, now, at the close of this trial, they will all go hence branded, so that all men may hereafter know them for just what they are,—cowardly brigands who have tried to rob a blind man on the highway, of his good name and of his great and honorable reputation.

Concerning their counsel and legal advisers I shall have nothing beyond a mere suggestion.

"Oh, wad some power the giftie gie us,
    To see ourselves as others see us."

This brings me to a close. I have done my duty as my conscience has led me to see it. Just let me say in conclusion that a sadder spectacle was never presented than the spectacle of Senator Gore being dragged by malignant conspirators into this court to answer their vile and odious charge.

Talk about your Homers, your Miltons and all the blind men of the ages who have toiled and climbed through eternal night to high achievement. But this man, blind since he was a child, has outdone them all. He has groped his way with unseeing eyes to the floor of the Senate of the United States to a position second only to that of the President, and on that floor he has been able to meet in the battle for the right, the giants of debate.

For six days he has walked to and from this court house, the scene of his persecution, with his true and honored wife at his side, to meet fairly his false accusers. He has sat through the long days of this trial with her at his right hand; the light of her love beaming upon him and lending to his character that inexpressible charm that only the love of a wife can lend. In the early dawn of Grecian story, Homer told in immortal phrase the glories of Troy; her lovers and her warriors; in the twilight of a lovely wife, blind Milton pictured the pure joys of Eden and sung the world to sleep; and in the noonday of love, this blind defendant's fame encircles the globe, and he stands today the leading exponent of the people's rights. His name has become a synonym of liberty, of justice and of truth.

Homer and Milton were great in their age and realm. They were beloved by their people, because they discharged their duty— both public and private—in a way that merited approbation from mankind. But this blind man has outdistanced them. Living in an age and a country where the enlightenment of all former ages reinforces its new and modern civilzation, he has mastered all through the sense of hearing, his great diversity of learning stands as a wonderful achievement and his success as a statesman of the people is warranted by his absolute fidelity to public trust, his untiring efforts in behalf of his constituency, his love and patriotism for his country.

You are to be addressed in elaborate and powerful appeals by my adversaries learned in the law, cunning in debate. The praises of womanhood and virtue will be sung until the spacious halls shall re-echo their eloquent words. Let me ask you after all is said, to consider this case in the light of the facts, and by a

righteous verdict, to give back to the world unsullied by the assaults of a foul conspiracy, the name of Thomas Pryor Gore.
Delivered by Moman Pruiett.

After all arguments had been presented by counsel on both sides the climax of the case came later when the jury retired to consider the evidence and argument by counsel in the case, and returned within seven minutes with a verdict of "NOT GUILTY".

Moman Pruiett's argument to the jury, at the conclusion of the evidence and the reading of the law by the court, was typically his own. The satiristic scribe had said that he "touseled his hair and walked the jury-box on his hands." The National Press, commenting in a more serious vein, gave it such favorable notice that the author was swamped with calls, telegrams and letters, asking for reproduction of the speech. The none too modest Pruiett had it transcribed by the official reporter, and bound into an engraved booklet, with a bushy haired portrait of his own for a frontispiece. He spent two thousand dollars on the speech before the wave of orders subsided; that sum did not include the five hundred he paid for postage in sending it out.

One paper said: "Such a speech as that arouses the sympathy of even those who see the ridiculous character of the procedure. What he said is so essentially sound, the object of his strange eloquence is so fundamentally righteous that all his 'crouching like a tiger,' all his dramatics of removing his collar and tie, all his evident genius for going to the heart of an issue and appealing to the hearts of jurymen and onlookers seems to fit in well with the achievement of justice, if not with its administration."

The Joplin Globe, editorially, said:

"Probably the man who has profited most from the Gore case is the man who cared least about profiting. Moman Pruiett, one of the Senator's attorneys, won a lasting place in the hearts of every Gore sympathizer throughout the country by his burning castigation of the men behind the plaintiff. . . . There is no gentility to Pruiett's eloquence. Even his sarcasm is blunt and ragged; it has no razor edge. He simply strips a proposition naked and redresses it with homely, striking word pictures, or peppers it with trip-hammer blows of wilting invective. Naturally, he is deeply loved, desperately hated, and profoundly respected. And above all else, he is immensely interesting."

He kicked restraint under the counsel table and jumped upon "the hell-inspired conspiracy," as he calls it, and the conspirators.

The Baltimore Sun was prompt with its commendatory editorial. "We congratulate Senator Gore on the verdict which has so emphatically given the lie to the trumped-up charges against him. He performed a fine public service in refusing to make terms with the blackmailers, and fighting them in the open."

The Washington Post said: "All the men in public life will feel reassured by the outcome of the sensational trial in Oklahoma, in which Senator Thomas P. Gore was the defendant. He was properly exonerated. . . ."

The Press (Philadelphia) noted the outcome. "It looked like an attempt at blackmail from the beginning, and the contradicted testimony of the plaintiff and her witnesses did not remove that impression before the defense had said a word. Senator Gore bore himself with great dignity and good sense through his unpleasant ordeal. . . ."

In a letter bearing date of March 4, 1914, addressed "My Dear Pruiett," the blind Senator had a word of gratitude to offer. ". . . . It would be gratifying for you to know how many congratulations I have received and am still receiving from every quarter of the country and from every class of people, from the lowliest working woman to the President of the Republic. The President was especially enthusiastic in his congratulations, as was Colonel Bryan and other members of the Cabinet. . . . I am under deep and enduring obligations to you for your splendid faith and efficient service. Let me hear from you from time to time, and keep me advised as to the course of events. These people will of course exhaust every recourse in an effort to trump up some other cause of embarrassment, but all the world has now foreclosed the matter in our favor. . . . Truly yours, T. P. Gore."

Gore went back to the Senate. Standing before the roster of that great body he opposed the war policy of the President; he told his colleagues of what his sightless eyes could see across that horizon which blocked their view, but they abandoned him in an unpopular minority, to be defeated in the primaries of 1921. When his stand was justified by the development of historical events, he went back, and served another, his third term, as a member of the Senate. When he stepped down the second, and last time, he uttered an open letter to his constituency, which conveyed, more than anything else available on the life of the blind statesman, the quality which bound Pruiett, as a lawyer and a certain type of idealist, to him.

"At midnight, January 2nd, (1937) the curtain comes down forever on my political career. The people of Oklahoma have been generous to me, and I am grateful to them.

"As you know, I was defeated for the Senate in 1920 on account of my attitude toward the war. I had promised the mothers of Oklahoma that I would never vote to ship their sons across the sea to die in the bloody shambles of Europe. I kept my word, although it cost me my seat in the Senate. Some may doubt my wisdom, but they can hardly doubt my sincerity. When I left the Senate in 1921, I was confident that I would one day return. In 1930 my dream came true, but I now indulge no such dream as to the future. No one knows better than I do that politically my day is done; the people giveth and the people taketh away. . . .

"I repeat in parting that I love Oklahoma; I love every blade of her grass, I love every grain of her sands. I am proud of her past and I am confident of her future. I honor the Oklahoma Pioneer as I honor the American Pioneer. Their example is our richest heritage. The virtues that made us great in the past can keep us great in the future. We must march, and not merely mark time. We must indeed solve new problems, must meet new conditions with new measures, but they should be met with the same resolute and courageous spirit as of old. Anyhow, let us bet on America to win. Unless we quail we cannot fail. Whether I fought a good fight or not, I have kept the faith. . . . Goodbye and good luck."

CHAPTER FIFTEEN

Wherein Pruiett adds justification for patricide to his list of accomplishments, as he goes in style to the old Comanche-Kiowa Country, and tried a case which offers but little of early promise of success. And how his client, as usual, is saved by an absolute alibi, and the State's star witness charges the circumstances to a visitation of the supernatural. And where the outraged citizenry of the locality attempt to reverse the usual order of things by lynching the accused after the trial of the case, instead of before, and include in their plans an attack upon the lawyer, who had caused the liberation of the accused.

"L'affaire Hopkins" was one for the Pruiett legend; its locale was Lawton, in the Comanche-Kiowa country. The settlement had literally come into municipal existence through the spinning of the wheel of chance. Nestling amongst the rough slopes of the Wichita Mountains, so close that the shadow of each passing cloud, trailing its path across Mount Scott could be seen from the green courthouse square, the town was a mixture of the sturdy whites who had settled to a substantial, but not too opulent, existence and the long-haired Comanches who had given up their fight to retain control of the rocky upland.

By 1901 the land runs had become impractical. There were so many claimants for the limited Indian land remaining that a race would have precipitated a war—not a riot. "83,000 families were registered at Fort Reno for 13,000 homesites." The government took advantage of the sporting inclinations of the pioneers; they gave them numbers and rolled the wheel. The land-lottery gave homes to a few, disappointment to the multitude. Lawton was a hardy city and had produced some hardy citizens; Tom Gore had gone to the Senate from Lawton.

George Hopkins was tried in the brick courthouse there for the murder of his own father, and he was acquitted. To keep a mob from lynching him, Pruiett, the mouthpiece who had promoted the outrage, was spirited away with the defendant and out of town, an equal object of the mob's wrath. It was fitting that such an episode should occur in a chance-begotten city.

Old A. T. Hopkins, of fairly pure strain Scotch, had cracked the rocks of the rough hillsides, hoarded the trickling rains in the many gullies of his farm, and made money. His one extravagance had manifested itself in a love for horses, and with typical Scotch

[336]

ingenuity he had commercialized it. He owned a string of the finest race horses in the southwest, and in addition to the revenue he received from sale, trade and breeding, he entered them in race events over the country. His combined business and hobby was housed under the corrugated iron roof of the section's most complete and prosperous livery barn.

The roughest boulder on the hillside of Hopkins' thrifty existence had been an unsatisfactory family. Mary and George, his daughter and son, had been left motherless in early childhood by the death of his wife. They had passed through an adolescence of varying neglect and over-indulgence. No one could satisfactorily explain the passionate hatred which the girl developed for her father. George, the older of the two unusual offspring, concealed an utter disregard for the "old man" with an affected attitude of concern and consideration. This enabled him to avoid the restraints of the father's penuriousness, and to obtain funds at the same time, for the promotion of certain innate vices which ran the gamut of drink, females and gambling. Naturally, his pursuit of these devices required that he spend more than he had, or could get. He was alternately broke, flush, or in trouble for petty confidence ventures.

Mary had scarcely passed her majority before she married a young lawyer. She abandoned the sire she so cordially hated to the crudities of his humble tastes. George moved around. When confronted with an ordinary dilemma he would take a job and do a little work. If it was an emergency, such as the brig in the offing, he would petition the pater and invariably receive the discounted face of his request—for which he had made allowances—and the admonitory word of advice which would accompany it.

"What did you kill old man Hopkins for?" the assistant county attorney bawled at Tom Coley.

"I don't know nothin' about it, Mr. Froneberger," Tom answered.

Froneberger knocked him out of his straight-back chair with an open handed slap across the ear, then resumed his methodical, bigfooted pacing of the floor.

"What did you kill old man Hopkins for?" he howled again.

"I didn't do it, Mr. ———." Tom couldn't repeat his denial. Froneberger had hit him across the opposite ear, sending him whirling into the opposite wall of the room.

The methodical floor pacing was resumed and each time the prisoner was passed he dodged and cowered. Pausing before the swollen face, Froneberger placed his hands on his hips and glared balefully, as if waiting for the proper time to put the question.

"What did you—."

"Mr. George put me up to it," Tom interrupted him. "He paid me money, an' showed me how he wanted it done. He's the one that got me into this."

"Who do you mean, nigger?" inquired Froneberger suspiciously, "Who do you mean, Mr. George?"

"Mr. George Hopkins," chattered the Negro. "He's the one what done it. He give me the race mare an' a hundred dollars. He give me an axe an' brought me down here, too. It's a fact, Mr. Froneberger, Mr. George made me do it."

Froneberger stared incredulously. Nigger-whipping was but routine, and he had been about ready to let Tom go. He couldn't believe what he was hearing. "Then you was the one what did it?" he asked, doubtfully. "You killed the old man with the axe, an' took his pocket-book?"

"Yes, suh, I sure did, Mr. Froneberger, but I give the pocket-book to Mr. George. He was waitin' in the car, he was, an' we drove right on out of town. Mr. George he's the one what thought this up; he's the one what made me do it."

Froneberger suspected that Coley was lying about George and his participation in the crime. His deductive mind could already glean a motive sufficient to involve the confessing Negro.

"You used to work for old man Hopkins," he recited, "an' the old man fired you."

"Tell me about what?" asked Froneberger. "You mean that George and Mary and you layed up together the same way up there?"

"Well, you see, this what happened," the Negro said. "Mr. Hopkins sends me and Mr. George up to the Fair Grounds with the horses; an' we takes Mary along, like we usually do. Then Mr. Hopkins tells Mr. George to keep the horses in the Fair barns 'til some man gets his horses down from Chicago, an' they's goin' to run some races, horse for horse, you see? Mr. Hopkins told me to come back here an' go to work, but when I get ready to leave why Mary says she was stayin' with Mr. George. I jest decides I'd rather stay with them than have the job, so I didn't come back."

As the Negro's weird story unfolded, and as the testimony taken at the trial of the case confirmed him, George Hopkins lived with the Negroes in open disregard of convention. He slept in their various beds or on their floors and pallets, as conditions required. He ate the meals which black Mary prepared, from the oil-cloth covered table in her kitchen. Changing conditions, it developed, were governed by the excesses of the African guests of the evening and night before and by how many of the guests were unable—or indisposed—when time came to depart, and had laid down and gone to sleep where it was most convenient.

"He sure did, Mr. Froneberger," said Coley. "He took Mary right down to the grocery on the corner, an' told the man to sell her anythin' she wanted, an' jest put it on his bill."

"What about this killin'?" asked the officer. "How did you happen to decide on it? Did Mary have anything to do with it?"

"No," said Tom. "Mary thinks we better not do it. Mr. George, he said the old man was too tight with his money. He said it was all comin' to him anyhow, an' Mr. Hopkins, he done lived too long an' got too old. He said he'd help me, an' nobody'd ever think about me doin' it. He tol' me he's pay me a hundred dollars an' give me my pick of any horse in the barn. He said somethin' else, too. He says if I don't help him I get an axe in my own head."

"How long did you plan it?" asked Froneberger.

"'Bout a week," answered Tom. "We had to wait 'til Mr. George could borry a car from a friend of his'n. He gets us some corn, an' this car, it was a Hudson tourin' car, an' we left the city about dark. We got some eats about midnight an' drink a lot of whiskey. Mr. George, he done all the drivin'. We come down through the old reservation an' the fort, an' we got in Lawton about four in the mornin'."

"Who got the axe for you, Tom?" Froneberger asked. His manner indicated that he was beginning to believe the Negro. "Where did that new axe come from?"

"Mr. George bought it in the city," Tom said. "He got it an' had it aroun' the house the day before we left. He threw it in the back seat when we was leavin', an' he says, "Tom, this is what you make yourself a rich man with. You can fix Mary up an' show her off to your cheap nigger friends!'

"Mr. George tol' me what I was to do on the way down. I worked in the barn for a long time, an' I knowed when Mr.

Hopkins opens up. I'm to wait by the post in front 'til Mr. Hopkins swung the big gate an' got inside; then I was to go right in behind him. An' that's jest what I done, Mr. Froneberger. It was awful. I knows I killed him the first lick, but I kep' right on, jes' like Mr. George tol' me. He wanted me to be sure. I hacked him about ten times, I guess."

"What did you do then, Tom?" whispered the officer.

"Well," pondered Tom, "he was layin' on his face an' all I have to do is to take the pocket-book, 'cause that'd make folks think it was jes' a plain robber. An' I done jes' ever'thin' that Mr. George tol' me to do."

"Where was George Hopkins when you were doin' this job, Tom?" asked Froneberger. "Did he come up there, or drive up, to get you when you were through?"

"No, suh," answered Tom. "He waited for me in the auto. We was parked by a string of box-cars 'bout a block and a half from the barn. He was right there where he was when I left, when I gets back."

"What did he say when you got back?" inquired Froneberger.

"He asks me if I did a good job, an' says, 'Where's that pocket-book?' He says, 'Git in here an' let's get the hell out. Mary'll be worried 'bout us if we don't get back to town.'"

Judge Stevens had scarcely filed the Hopkins will for probate when he had a call from the police. George Hopkins was under arrest, being charged with murder. The police had a complete confession from Tom Coley, and part of the cash that George had paid him for the part he had played in moving him up in the livery stable business. Stevens, after a brief conference with his client, left the jail with a hopeless look. He started a long-distance contact for Pruiett as soon as he returned to his office.

George Hopkins, typical of the petty criminal apprehended in an attempt to cover too much territory, tried to talk, to explain, his way out of his difficulty. He made and signed a detailed statement wherein he attempted to show that Tom Coley had lied in every particular, and that the funds in Coley's possession had been actually stolen from him.

"Hell, no," he told Froneberger, "I never had nothin' to do with his wench. I never liked to have them niggers around me.

Tom stole that money from me, and cooked up this story to try to keep me from prosecutin' him."

"Where were you when you found out your Dad had been killed?" inquired Froneberger.

"I was out at the Fair Barn, workin,' answered George.

"Where were you the night before?"

"Let's see," mused George, seriously. "I was home all night. I was in my room, up in the city."

"And where did you say that was, George?" asked Froneberger.

"It was at the Allen Rooms," said George. "At Fatty Allen's Hotel on Broadway. That's where I stayed while I was in the city this last trip."

"Now look here, George," said Froneberger, "we got it pretty straight that you were stayin' with the niggers down on Noble Street. Tom Coley says so, and we got some witnesses' names; some white folks. You'd better tell the truth about this, because I've got to check up on you."

"A damned nigger never did tell the truth, John, an' you know it. You don't need to check me, but it's O.K. if you want to. But you ought to take my word in place of that nigger. He never told the truth, an' he never will."

George believed that his story would stand to discredit the Negro, without verification, for his alibi was being manufactured as he went along. He could expect no support from any of the pre-arrangements which the casually smart criminal would have provided for himself. The utter falsity of his statement, once checked and established, tended to indicate complete consciousness of guilt, and to entangle him more hopelessly in the web of circumstances.

Tom Coley had entered his own guilty plea and accepted a sentence of life imprisonment when, some four days later, Pruiett dazzled the square and court house with his presence. He was using an automobile, a long one, with his initials on the back door and a chauffeur to drive.

For an overnight stay out of town Pruiett would take a week's change of wardrobe. With the rear seat piled high with leather luggage.

There was a touch of gray in the black hair as he removed a soft felt hat and laid it on a dusty stand. He patted his moist brow gently with a silk handkerchief. It was exceedingly dry and warm in the daytime, although near winter, and the walk up the one flight to the second floor of the jail, and the lack of ventilation in the small room where he was about to interview George Hopkins, caused the beads of moisture to dot the scant forehead visible between the dark of bushy black brows and the black hair that dropped down before it began to reach back atop the head and about the ears.

Pruiett was past forty, but no sign of sparseness had appeared in the raven brush. It was more luxurious and abundant than it had been back on White River, when he had first become conscious of its comparative excellence, and began to groom it. It shone with an oily splendor which the constant care and studious grooming his prosperity permitted. He was tailored and attired to match the perfection of his natural ornament, in the neatest and finest raiment, and in the exactly correct style, of the period.

George Hopkins sat in a straight-back chair with both hands obscuring his face. He was weeping like a child. Pruiett eyed him with mild concern, unable to conceal all of the surprise and contempt he had for such a reception. The officer shook the prisoner roughly, and with a half-apology to the waiting lawyer, said that he would be waiting outside when the conference was over.

'Oh, God!" Mr. Pruiett," the miserable George bawled. "Can you save me from the chair. Can you save me? Can you save me?"

"Is that all you want?" Pruiett inquired, contemptuously.

"God, yes," Hopkins cried. "Just don't let 'em give me the chair. Judge Stevens said he couldn't save me, but you might do it. Can you save me?"

Pruiett's answer was indirect, going into the more material realm of what George had, and what he would be willing to put up. After a short conference he stepped to the door of the small, hot chamber. With a word to the waiting guard he hurried down the steps, and was soon talking to Stevens' office on the 'phone.

"Send your girl down here with a bunch of blank deeds and bills of sale," he said. "I'm about to take this case off your hands, an' I need some blank forms. Send a bunch of 'em, and be sure you give me a girl that's a notary."

When Pruiett walked into Stevens' upstairs office later that afternoon he carried title to every foot of ground and every item of personal property that Hopkins, senior, had owned when he died. Stevens, the family lawyer, had a startling report from the girl who spent the afternoon at the jail with George and the criminal lawyer. He intended to make an objection, but he was uncertain as to how to begin with it. Pruiett saved him the trouble.

"Well, I took the case," Pruiett said, carelessly. "It's a hell of a thin one, an' I've got a lot of things I'd rather do than try one like this. But we made a deal that's satisfactory."

"What did you take?" inquired Stevens.

"I took it all." The tone of the reply showed provocation, for he knew the girl had time to detail the events of the afternoon.

"You mean you took it all? All that property?" Stevens' tone and expression showed disapprobation.

"Hell, yes," said Pruiett, "Ever' damn bit, An' it'll be worth it before I get through."

"Look here, now, Mr. Pruiett," said Stevens with patronizing formality. "I represent the boy, and I have his interests to look after, even in his contract with you. I called you, you know, and I can't permit him to be fleeced in such a manner. That property will bring forty thousand at a quick sale, and you know it. I won't permit you to impose on his desperate state of mind, that way."

Pruiett stared at him in amazement.

"I'll be damned," he said. "You and John Young call me and beg me to come down here and take this mess off your hands—. You didn't say you were going to fix my fee, or guarantee I'd get one, even. I—."

"But you're taking all he's got—everything," Stevens interrupted. "You're leaving him penniless."

"What good will he get out of it if he burns?" Pruiett asked quickly. "You know he can't inherit the property if he's convicted and if he's acquitted I stand a chance of collecting a fee for my services."

"Well, he—."

"What right has he got to it? How did he get it?" The questions, with the second interrupting a stammering answer to the first, left Stevens speechless. Pruiett continued.

"If you mean to uphold this bird who killed his daddy; think he's got a right to keep any of this stuff, an' be conscientious in it, you'll be able to represent him yourself. In that case, you don't need me, an' you an' George can keep the property an' the plugs. But if I stay—the stuff stays with me. What do you think about that?"

He tossed the bundle of legal conveyances he had taken to the desk in front of Stevens in a gesture to emphasize his attitude of complete independence. Stevens pushed them back and shook his head. He knew that if he ran Pruiett out of the case after George had hired him, and something happened, he would be in a position as inextricable as was George himself. Pruiett was starting out in the case with his customary advantage.

Froneberger was detailed to check the purported Hopkins alibi. Arriving in Oklahoma City, he gained the assigned assistance of John Hubatka, plainsclothes expert of that department. They found the substance of the alibi false before they had fairly begun their investigation. Then they began to collect verification, which was plentiful, of the Tom Coley story as it pertained to conditions at and around the Coley house while the details of the plot to kill were being hatched.

The proprietor of the Allen Rooms was a portly person of perhaps two hundred and fifty pounds, whose short stature in connection with such prodigious weight made him a natural recipient for the nickname of "Fatty." Fatty kept a nine-stool "grease joint" on the ground floor with furnished rooms on the upper level. He had a tall, gaunt wife. They relieved each other at letting out the upstairs accommodations and serving up the unsavory food which an occasional customer called for across the counter.

"We're officers," said Froneberger crisply, showing a rusty badge stuck to the shoulder strap of his loose vest.

"Yes, sir," answered Fatty. Fatty had the same respect for authority that a petty thief had for a police uniform.

"Do you know George Hopkins?" inquired Froneberger.

"Hell, yes," answered Fatty.

"Seen him around lately?" was the next question.

"Hell, no," answered Fatty.

"How long's it been since you seen him?" asked Froneberger, casually.

"Been a hell of a time," said Fatty.

"Did he ever stay in your hotel here?" Allen was asked.

"Sure, a lot of times, but not lately," Fatty insisted.

"You keep any record here of roomers, and when they come in and go out?"

"I sure do," Fatty said, giving Hubatka the benefit of a big wink. "The law says I keep a register, an' I do just like the law says."

"We're checking up a little," explained the officer, "and we want to know if George was here in October. Where's the register book for October?"

"It's upstairs," said Fatty. "I'll go up and get it for you. Wait right here a minute."

"We'll go along with you, Mr. Allen," interrupted Hubatka. "We'll look at it upstairs."

A black bound ledger was laying on a home-made shelf, built desk-fashion along the wall at the head of the stairway. Hubatka and Froneberger reached it ahead of the proprietor, and studied for several minutes before turning to him with more questions.

"I see George was here on October 14th," said Froneberger. "I thought you said he hadn't been here for a hell of a time."

"That's a hell of a time in my book," grinned Fatty. "He ain't been here for over a month. You asked me was he in here lately."

Froneberger handed Allen the book. "Was George Hopkins in this joint on the night of November 7? Just last week?"

Allen studied the register, turning the pages slowly. "Nope," he answered, "he was with me just one night, an' that was last month, in October. It was October. It was October 14th, just like it shows up in the book."

"Is that Hopkins' signature?" asked Hubatka.

"Yep," answered Allen. "I seen him sign it. I know his writin' anyway, but I seen him sign that. I know it's his."

"Do you let people stay here without signin' up?" asked Hubatka. "Could Hopkins have stayed here without registerin'?"

"Hell, no, Mr. Hubatka. You know I wouldn't do that," wheedled Allen. "Anytime these guys stay in the Allen Rooms they put their John Henry right in that little book. I don't get myself in no trouble with the city laws."

"Do you remember about this George Hopkins?" persisted Froneberger, "do you remember when he was here, and how many nights he stayed, regardless of what the book shows?"

"Hell, yes," said Fatty. "He was here one night, just after the Fair closed and business fell off. I remember it was just after the Fair an' he was tellin' about his horses. I know damn well that it was close to Fair time, an' just one night was all he was here."

"Hopkins says he was here ever' night for three or four weeks, an' that he was here on November 8th, the day his old man was murdered down at Lawton. What do you say about that?" Froneberger was watching Allen narrowly as he talked.

"I say it's a damn lie," Fatty answered without hesitation. "I ain't seen him for a month, an' he ain't been in my rooms here but about twice in the last year. He's just a God damn liar if he says different."

"You won't alibi for these crooks, will you," Mr. Allen?" suggested Hubatka. "They don't use you that way, do they?"

"Hell, no," Fatty beamed, swelling with the compliment. "This is a respectable place, an' the crooks don't use Fatty's hotel for no alibi."

"Then I guess we'll have to make a witness out of you; you and your little black book," said Froneberger. "That is, if we have to try George. With the case we'll make he'll probably try to cop out, even if he has to take a chance on the chair. We got a signed confession by his buddy, an' this blows his alibi to hell. Can you take good care of this book, or shall we take it?"

"I'll take care of it, an' damn good care, too, I'll get me a new book an' put this one up in the trunk. When ya need it just call on old Fatty. He'll be ready to tell 'em what's what."

It was March of '16, the twentieth day of Oklahoma's windy spring month, when the George Hopkins trial was begun. The old man's daughter was unable to condone brother George's alleged liberty in murdering him, especially when she learned that the entire and rather bulky estate, went to George alone. She saw that her lawyer husband offered his service to County Attorney Orr as a special prosecutor. Calculating the customary outcome of a case defended by Pruiett, and in an attempt to avoid it, she arranged for the assistance of A. C. Cruce, Pruiett's old friend from Ardmore who had marched to prominence and success in his own line, along with Pruiett. He was the brother of Governor Lee Cruce.

Pruiett admired and respected this particular member of his opposition—even feared him—so far as his technique and courtroom ability was concerned. But he would give him no quarter, no matter how badly he needed it. Pruiett's objective in the trial of a lawsuit was victory, victory complete and at any price. He liked to win and he hated to lose. Those were his personal feelings in relation to triumph over his efforts to subvert it. His fierce fight for a client's liberty or life was a re-enactment of his struggling exit from the old Texas courtroom, when and where, as a boy, he had been dragged away to the miseries of a prison cell. His defense of a dangerous case was a figurative writhing, kicking and screaming, with claw and nail flailing in a fierce effort to find a vulnerable spot on his adversary.

"Witness after witness was introduced by the state in the trial of George Hopkins, Wednesday, in an effort to tighten the cordon of evidence around the defendant, attorneys for the defendant contesting stubbornly every inch of the ground covered." Thus the Lawton News viewed events. "Cross-examination of the witness in chief, Tom Coley, failed to materially weaken the force of the Negro's testimony. With a memory almost uncanny for an uneducated man, Coley repeated again and again on cross-examination, and almost word for word, his previous statements."

Pruiett's apparently casual defense of Hopkins was actually long calculated and carefully timed. It was pitched first on the proposition of discrediting Coley, impeaching the more or less immaterial portions of his confession and accusation, and then proving the defendant a positive alibi. There was Hopkins' signed statement to be reckoned with, the one the state had taken before counsel had been employed. He had to keep his witness-stand version fairly consistent with that, unless he intended to further discredit his client.

"I'll prove," said Pruiett, making his opening statement to the jury, "that Tom Coley is a motivated liar, and that his effort to incriminate my client is based on fear and spite. I'll prove that George Hopkins never was in the Coley house on Noble Street, like Tom says he was, while the plot to kill Hopkins was being hatched. My evidence will show that during the three weeks preceding the murder George Hopkins spent his days at the Fair Grounds race barn, and his evenings and nights at Fatty Allen's rooming house down on Broadway.

"By proving the one I'll automatically prove the other. If Hopkins was staying at Allen's, then Tom Coley's a liar when he says he was laying up with him and his friends on Noble Street." He gave the prosecution a half-defiant, half-contemptuous look as he said it. Cruce, who had just completed a narrative of what the state would conclusively prove, had said that he would offer the testimony of Allen, himself, to show not only that Hopkins was not there before and on the night of the murder, but that he had deliberately, and with guilty design, lied when he told the investigation officers that he had been there.

Tom Coley was the state's star, but Fatty Allen was given a distinguished supporting role.

"You say your name is Allen, and that you operate a rooming house in Oklahoma City?" County Attorney Orr inquired.

"Yes, sir," said Fatty.

"Mr. Allen," said Orr, "directing your attention to the month of October, last year, were you then engaged in the same business?"

"Yes, sir," repeated Fatty.

"Do you know George Hopkins, the defendant in this case?"

"I certainly do," said Fatty.

"How many times did the defendant stay in your rooms, if he did, during the month of October, 1915?" inquired Orr.

"He was there one night, and that's all."

"Do you remember the night he was there?"

"I remember 'cause it was just after the Fair shut down. That's how I remembered so well. It was the night of October 14th that he was there." Fatty was bolstering himself a little as he went along.

"Was Hopkins there on the night of the 15th, or the 16th, or the 17th, or any other night later that month?"

"No, sir, he wasn't. He certainly was not."

"Was George Hopkins there in your hotel during the early part of November, say during the first week of November?"

"Nope," answered Fatty. "He was there on October 14th and that's all. He hasn't been in the hotel a minute since then."

"Was George Hopkins in your hotel on the night of November 7th, or the early morning of November 8th, 1915? Was he there then?"

"He certainly was not." Fatty was emphatic.

Orr lifted a rough package from the counsel table. It was the register for the Allen Hotel, preserved by Fatty in a thick wrapper of newspaper. It was exactly as it had been when Fatty had put it in storage, that night after the Froneberger-Hubatka visit. Orr handed the bundle to the court reporter and had it marked as an exhibit. Then he handed it to the witness.

"Mr. Allen," he continued, very formally. "Do you keep a register, or guest entry book, in your hotel?"

"I sure do," answered Allen. "It's a city ordinance that says

I got to. I mean, it says, anybody what operates a roomin' house or hotel has got to keep a register. That's so the police, maybe, can check up on who's been stayin' there, an' whether they really have or not." He grinned knowingly at Pruiett and his client as he completed his explanation.

"This package," said Orr, has been marked as a state's exhibit. I will ask you to examine it, and then tell the court and jury whether or not you recognize it, or know what it is."

"Sure I do," the witness answered. "I know what it is. I brought it down with me from the city, like the subpoena I got told me to. Do you want me to say what it is?"

"No, not just now," answered the prosecutor. And turning aside to the court, he said, "We will reserve the offer of this item at this time. This is merely for preliminary identification. We may offer it later."

When Pruiett took Fatty Allen for cross-examination the Hopkins cause emitted a dire prognostication of the impossible; of Moman Pruiett losing a major case. Self-professed authorities observed that the defendant's chief counsel had tried to take in a little too much territory in his statement of what he intended to prove, and that his inability to make good on it was "goin' to do a sight of harm." The khaki clad youths from the post, who crowded about the jammed entrance-way, ribaldly remarked that the difference the outcome made was slight; that you might as well have that portion of the anatomy singed off at home as shot off at Metz or Verdun. While others had varying comment to offer, at least varying in form, it was not diverse in substance. The prevailing opinion was that George Hopkins was a goner.

"Mr. Allen," Pruiett inquired, respectfully. "Did you state on direct examination that the ordinances required you to keep a daily register of all the guests of your rooms?"

Pruiett had ample time to complete his regular analysis of the witness. He knew that he was a man of slight culture and of coarse taste and habit, who was enjoying the prominence which he believed was his by reason of his being a material witness in the trial of the case. His corpulence was attended by the usual physical distress accompanying such a physical condition, high and rapidly fluctuating blood pressure, shortness of breath, and a pronounced tendency to perspire. Spring had come early to the Wichitas, and in the early afternoon sunshine, with the crowd and the confinement of the old courthouse, Fatty was sweating copiously. Pruiett asked him a number of questions that were easy to answer. His purpose was to lead his ego out and exercise it. He might be out of condition by the time the hard pull began.

"I sure did," responded Allen, without apparent cranial exertion.

"Then why didn't you keep one?" There was a suggestion of an attempt to trap the witness, both in the suddenness of the query and a slight increase in the volume of his tone.

"I did; ever' day," said Fatty, looking about with a smirk, as if to placate the jurors, and assure them that he was master of the situation.

Pruiett assumed an air of slight chagrin, and hesitated, as if in a quandary.

"Then why didn't you bring it down here with you?" Pruiett finally came back.

"I did," Fatty cried, triumphantly. He was taking the bait like a gull. Cruce shifted uneasily in his seat. No one could make him believe that Pruiett didn't fully understand what was wrapped and tied in that newspaper package on the counsel table, even though Allen was gloating over the surprise and shock he was going to inflict if the stupid lawyer kept going in the same direction. Cruce began to feel that something was wrong. Pruiett feigned amazement.

"You did? You have the register, here? Well, where is it?"

"Right behind you, on the table." Fatty unfolded a pair of ponderous hands which he had kept folded across his bulging expanse of belly, and pointed a pudgy finger, with childlike glee, at the roughly bound package. It was some dumb lawyer that couldn't have guessed that he had just identified the book.

"Is this it? Is this the register book? Pruiett inquired doubtfully.

"Yes, sir, it sure is," replied Mr. Allen.

"How did it get down here?" Pruiett was examining the package, and questioning, as in idle curiosity.

"I brung it. I brung it down myself. That's what I just got through tellin' Mr. Orr."

"Well, what is it doing in this shape? You can't register guests with your book baled up like this."

Allen grinned indulgently, as if he was going to let Pruiett in on a big secret.

"Well," he said, "when Mr. Hubatka and the other gentleman came down and looked at it, and saw Hopkins' name wasn't in it, like he said it was, they said I was liable to have to be a witness, an' I said, 'will I have to have the book?' an' they says 'yes', so just to be sure, I gets me a new book, an' I tied the old one up, an' I locked it in my trunk. When the time comes for me to go to court, I gets the book out an' carries it along. I just want to be sure all the time that nobody fools with my register, you see?"

"If that's the case," said Pruiett, "this register ought to be just exactly the same now as it was the night Mr. Hubatka and Mr. Froneberger called on you, to check up on Mr. Hopkins' story?"

"Just exactly," said Fatty. "Nobody has it but me, an' nobody fools with it."

"When you checked it up, and showed it to Mr Hubatka and Mr. Froneberger, didn't you see Hopkins' name there for the night of November 7th, and for three weeks before, every night?" Pruiett was still being casual.

"I certainly didn't," said Fatty.

"Do you say now that your book doesn't show Hopkins was there, or do you want to change your testimony, and say it does?"

Allen was so astonished by the audacity of the suggestion that he didn't answer immediately.

"No, I don't, Mister," he said finally. "Allen don't change his story, now, or no other time."

Pruiett began to pace the floor in deep reflection. His right hand ran repeatedly, nervously, through his thick hair, and made it stand out farther about the square contour of his well shaped head. Finally, as if in desperation, he took the register and handed it to the witness.

"Mr. Allen," he said slowly, "will you untie this bundle so I may see what it is?"

"Do it yourself," said Allen shortly. "You look able-bodied to me."

Pruiett looked appealingly to the trial judge. He wanted Allen to feel that he was hurt, in addition to being completely at his mercy.

"You will accommodate counsel," advised the court. "Please do as counsel requests."

The witness produced a pocket knife. Slashing savagely at the heavy cords, and pawing the triple thickness of newsprint aside, Allen proudly produced the black ledger which he had previously used as a rooming house register. He handed it to Pruiett. Pruiett handed it right back to him.

"Is this the register you say you used at your hotel?" Observers, less involved with their own importance than with the witness, could have seen that Pruiett's demeanor had changed. The Pruiett scowl was stamped on a contracted brow and undershot jaw. The shaggy ends of his heavy hair seemed to snap and crackle like the sharp crisp words that flew from his throat.

"It ain't nothing else," replied Fatty flippantly.

"Turn to your sheet for October 14, the one day you say the defendant was there, and show me where he registered." The change in Pruiett's tone caused Allen to look up, but not to comprehend.

"Do it yourself, you—."

There was no appeal to the court this time.

"Do as I tell you," Pruiett cried, standing close and holding a taut finger in the witness' fat face. "Do as I tell you. Turn to your entry for October 14th, and show me where Hopkins registered on the night you say he was there."

Fatty glanced up and about; toward the jury, toward the court, toward Cruce at the counsel table, as if to see if something had occurred to upset his advantage, while he had received no notice of it, himself. Their somber faces seemed to bring him back to reality. He grinned weakly, mopped his brow, and opened the book.

"There it is," he said, when he had turned a number of pages. "Right there it is; George Hopkins, on the night of October 14th."

"Now turn to the fifteenth, the next day, and tell me if Hopkins' name is on that page." It was no request; it was a command.

"It ain't here, no more," said Allen, without attempting to obey. "It ain't here. I showed it—."

"Do as you're told," Pruiett roared at him. "Do as I tell you. Look and see if Hopkins' name is there on the next page, for the fifteenth."

Fatty acquiesced. Turning the page gayly, he glanced at Froneberger, sitting behind County Attorney Orr at the counsel table, and winked. Then he let his gaze wander idly over the lined page of the register. Pruiett was standing belligerently before him, his arms folded across his chest and a malignant black scowl on his countenance.

The witness gazed at the book for a full minute. Then he looked up slowly, toward the state's counsel and the officers, and after grinning weakly, jerked his head back for a quick second look at the book. Inserting a fat finger between his utterly wilted collar, he pulled lustily, in an eloquent gesture of stifling discomfort. He looked up at Pruiett, but found no understanding in the beetle-browed scowl which met his gaze. The silence of the courtroom was complete. Allen looked at the judge, who was squinting quizzically at him by that time.

"Judge, there's spooks in this God-damn case!" he said.

Pruiett wouldn't let random dumb wit detract from his climax. "Mr. Witness," he roared, "will you answer my question? Does the name of this defendant appear in your register for the date of October fifteenth?"

Fatty couldn't hear him. He was looking toward the only compassionate expression in the courtroom, that of the court, and clutching frantically at the wet collar which theatened to shut off his air.

"There's spooks in this God-damn case, I tell you, Judge, spooks. I never saw such a God-damn thing in my whole life—."

"I will remind you that you are in court, Mr. Allen, and that your alley language will not be tolerated." Such was the compassion of the court. "You will answer counsel's question, in seemly language, or I shall be required to penalize you for contempt."

"Answer my question, Mr. Allen," Pruiett shouted as he shook the saber-like finger in his face. "Does—."

"Yes," the witness interrupted the question which he had heard before, with a quick, weak, affirmative. "Yes."

"What about the next day, the sixteenth, do you see his name there?"

"There's spooks, Judge, I know there is. Spooks is in—."

"Read him the question, Mr. Reporter," Pruiett interrupted.

"Yes," was Fatty's same weak reply.

"Now, Mr. Witness," Pruiett continued, without looking toward the amazed Cruce and his colleagues, "I want you to direct your attention to this entry for the fourteenth of October. Is that George Hopkins' signature. I mean by that, did you see him sign it, himself?"

"Yes, sir."

"Does the name George Hopkins, you see written on the next page, appear to be written in the same hand?"

"It appears to be wrote by spooks," was Allen's dogged answer.

"Let's not be ridiculous, Mr. Witness," Pruiett cautioned him, as he would have reprimanded a child. "Does it appear to be the same hand?"

"Yes, it does," said Allen frankly, "but—."

"I know, spooks," Pruiet interrupted him as he waved him carelessly aside. He introduced the register into the trial record. In the defendant's undeniable scroll, the register was stamped for every day of the controverted period, including the day and night of the murder.

The attempt of the prosecution to recover was necessarily ludicrous. The register had been in the trunk in Fatty's attic; the defendant had been shivering through the gusty winter in the upstairs cell of the county jail. Fatty had severed the strand which bound the original wrapper about the volume, and then—. Allen swore on his redirect examination that the names, save one, had not been between the pages on that November eve when he tucked the precious book in and patted it good-night. Detective Hubatka, whom Fatty was so anxious to please, swore vehemently that he had examined the pages of the book, and that the pages had not had so much as a suggestion of a Hopkins signature. Froneberger chimed in with his denial of the existence of the registration, but it was all meat for Pruiett.

Suave and smiling, ultra-polite, he would require their recognition of the likeness between the first name, admitted to be the defendant's, and the others following. He called their attention to the varying positions of the entries on the pages, the color of the ink and its resemblance in shade to the established genuine. He tested their knowledge of the defendant's winter-long jail wait. Then he would casually inquire: "Do you believe in spooks?"

"The Hopkins case was closed by the arguments to the jury of two of the southwest's greatest lawyers, Moman Pruiett for the defense, and A. C. Cruce, for the state. Mr. Pruiett is recognized, and so characterized by Mr. Cruce, as one of the greatest criminal lawyers in the country, while, on the other hand, Mr. Pruiett in his address told the jury that he feared A. C. Cruce, his wonderful analytical mind and his power over a jury. Both gentlemen were but stating facts that were well known to the public. The Hopkins case is the 188th murder case in which Moman Pruiett has participated while A. C. Cruce was for years a prosecutor for the government, and has a reputation more than state wide."

The News was being prosaic and conservative, but just as well, for it would have been impossible to catch, in a word picture, an adequate reproduction of Pruiett in action. His timing was so superb, as he produced his thought and gesture, that he presented the intended drama of the moment in an exaggerated proportion, and what the one lacked, if it happened to be lacking, the other supplied. His every movement and expression was a continuing climax.

"Mr. Pruiett reviewed the testimony of practically every witness who had been placed on the stand, forcibly bringing to the front the substance of the witnesses for the defense and reducing to a minimum the substance of the state's testimony as he so capably knows how to do. He attacked the state's witnesses in roughshod language, and enlarged upon what he called a villainous conspiracy on the part of the state and the detectives employed by it to destroy a man for the greed of gold."

". . . . County Attorney T. B. Orr and Officer Froneberger of the city police force came in for a bitter arraignment at the hands of Mr. Pruiett. He grew eloquent as he referred to the love of George Hopkins for his father, and said that the state had not produced one scintilla of evidence to corroborate the testimony of Tom Coley with the main facts of the crime as required by law. . . .'"

Cruce, with all the admiration he had for his more daring and gifted adversary, detested defeat. He could see it settling its dark cloud around his shoulders, but he went down fighting.

"For almost three hours, Mr. Cruce argued to the jury, confining much of his attention to the defendant, for whom he said, he was surprised the attorneys had not contended insanity. With biting sarcasm he held before the jury a picture of the defendant as he strove to secure evidence which would smirch the character of his own sister, all for money. He said there were attorneys in the case whom two years ago would not have presented such a case as this one, not even for the twenty-five thousand dollars for which he was striving, and said that he believed that not only nations, but individuals were going mad."

The current press had carried the edifying intelligence of "the peaceful Meuse running red with the blood of the Germans and French." If his reference to cases and attorneys included Pruiett he was overlooking Red Fox and Rudolph Tegeler, and twenty-five grand was small change compared to what he had already taken from George Hopkins.

The jury took the case at 10:30 on Saturday night. Pruiett slept soundly and got up early, to drive with Dutch through budding vistas of Medicine Park and the contrasting martial bustle of Fort Sill. The post was teeming with the crop that was soon to sail for France. When he drove by his hotel at two in the afternoon he was told that he had been called from the courthouse, that the jury was ready to report. The word had circulated rapidly in the small town, and the curious were gathering, hurrying in across the shaded square from every direction.

The jurors returned a verdict of not guilty. The court excused them briskly, and Hopkins, who had been brought from the jail by the sheriff, pumped their hands with maudlin gratitude as they marched out. The trial judge congratulated Pruiett, avoided Hopkins and took his leave. The liberated defendant, his lawyer, and the sheriff were left alone. Pruiett and Hopkins were talking about leaving town, when a granite stone crashed through the window. Pruiett stood motionless; the sheriff hurried toward the break to peer out.

"You're in for trouble," he announced, as he came back. "It's a big crowd, a mob, out in front. They ganged a time or two before, when Hopkins was first arrested, but we were able to scatter 'em out. They're pretty sore."

Pruiett strode to the window. Another rock crashed through. As he peered cautiously over the sill he saw that a large crowd had gathered and was milling about beneath the trees below. He had some knowledge of mob conduct, and he realized that he stood in the same light, with them, as did the hapless Hopkins. He knew that if they went outside, or if the mob came in, he and his client would be roughly treated, beaten and stomped, or worse. He shuddered as he ruminated. If they had a rope, and they got started—. He was thinking of old Jesse West.

"I'll have to lock you up 'til we can clear this up," the sheriff said. "I can't take any chances of your gettin' hurt. We'd better get downstairs an'—."

Pruiett interrupted him. He was familiar with the courthouse and jail arrangement; the jail occupied a two-story brick wing on the west side of the building, making the general plan of the entire edifice irregular. The jail wing extended almost to the street on the west side of the square.

"Dutch'll see that crowd an' he'll know what to do," he said. "He'll drive to the only exit that's near the street, an' we can make it to the car."

They had been moving down the unlighted stairway all the time he was speaking. When they reached the main floor level, where they could see the light that streaked in from the three outside entrances of the building, they saw that the leaders of the muttering crowd were pushing through the east and north doors. The three men slid quickly through the adjacent openings into the jail wing. The barred gate, first, and then the pine door, slammed shut behind them.

Through the dirt stained and bar shaded windows of the sheriff's office, Pruiett could see that the south lawn, too, was cluttered with a milling, pushing throng of the excited farm and townspeople. He likewise noted, with an appreciative and understanding eye, that his car was moving slowly along the curb in the shaded street west of the square, toward the point, where in his mind's eye, the reliable Dutch knew he would need it.

"Sheriff," he said, "if we can get out of town you won't have any trouble. They may wreck your building, or some one may get hurt, if we stay here an' you have to protect us. If we can get out a window, or anyway, out this west side, my car's out there, an'—."

"The coal hole for the heatin' plant is right up against that street," the sheriff replied. "We can go to the basement, an' boost you out that way. If your car is there you can make it easy, an' there's no one on that side, yet."

Dutch had cased the job well. When the sheriff boosted the elegantly attired Pruiett, a little soot stained and mad, but otherwise his resourceful self, through the scuttle, the driver assisted him directly into the back seat of his own limousine. When Hopkins had followed him, and the door and scuttle were closed, Dutch drove quietly past the mob and away.

"Shall I drive by the hotel, Mr. Pruiett?" he inquired. "We have your bags there, and—."

"Hell, no," said Pruiett, savagely. "We might be killed tryin' to get 'em. Let's go out of this damned place as quick as we can, an' stay, as far as I'm concerned. They sure give you a hell of a reception when their own jury finds out they've had the wrong man in jail all winter. That's the way with our courts; they've raped justice an' persecuted the innocent so long that the people have got used to it an' like it. Yes, they demand that some one be convicted in ever' case. It's a great system, I'll say."

A Bohemian woman in a side road shack was getting rich peddling home brew to the boys in training at the post. They gulped her slop and joked about the champagne they would soon be having in Paris. She was hostess to Hopkins and his lawyer that night; the drinks were on Pruiett, for Hopkins was unqualifiedly broke.

Hopkins was happy. He had heard the hum of the dynamos and felt the first shock of the heavy death current. Breathing free air again was an experience he had not permitted himself to dream of during those endless nights of his pre-trial confinement.

Cruce and Diffendaffer, and County Attorney Orr, were pondering the events in the County Attorney's office. Ideas and theories were being advanced in an attempt to explain one problem, the reason for Hopkins' acquittal. That was, how did Hopkins' registration get in Fatty Allen's book?

"Allen may have been right," Diffendaffer said, sarcastically. "It might have been spooks."

"I see it all now," Cruce said. "We left that book layin' around here, and Pruiett slipped it into that big black brief case he had, and when the court let them use his office for a private session, they just had Hopkins sign it up. You know, he had Hopkins in there for a time or two, with the deputy guardin' at the door. That's how he did it."

"It's simple," said Diffendaffer. "They untied all that cord, unwrapped all that paper, made nineteen entries at the same time, wrapped it up again and brought it back and put it on the table, and none of us ever noticed it."

"They never were in there more than ten minutes at a time," Orr insisted, "and they couldn't have untied that much string in that time, alone. Besides, they would have changed the appearance of that wrapping so that Allen could have noticed it. I know, and I'll swear, that the book, wrapped, was on that table all the time they were in their private conferences. I saw it, and by God, I had it with me in my own hands, all the rest of the time."

"Yeah," said Diffendaffer, turning the pages of the offending register slowly. "And what about this ink. It's not fresh, an' it's not all the same. Not by the same pen, either. Maybe they slipped a little age to the ink, and to the paper while they had it in the chambers."

"Well, you can say what you want to, but that brief case of Pruiett's was too big; he got it for this particular purpose. I know he's had the book in it, and they just slipped it over on us, right before our eyes." Cruce was persistent, but the manner and tone of his delivery showed that he had not even convinced himself.

Pruiett maintained that Hopkins was innocent, and that the signatures in the register were genuine, both as to the signer and the dates of entries. The state introduced a girl wearing a polka-dot dress. She testified "that on several mornings she would go out on the back porch, pump her a drink of water, and look over into Tom Coley's house through the window, and see George Hopkins eating breakfast with Tom Coley, and his Negro wife, Mary. On cross-examination the polka-dot girl was positive as to the pump and the well under the rear porch of the house that she was living in. This house being the house west of Coley's something like 20 feet. She also acknowledged she occupied a connecting room with Charles McCloud, chief detective for the state, at the Midland Hotel, in Lawton, Okla., where the trial was being held. She was equally positive that the detective was guarding her. This witness came upon the stand immediately after Fatty Allen, and on cross-examination Pruiett asked her the question, "Do you believe in spooks?" Her answer was, "What do you mean?" Pruiett's next question was, "When did you see that house and the pump that you testified about?" "About ten days or two weeks ago," she answered. Pruiett again asked her, "Do you believe in spooks?" handing her a picture showing the house next to Tom Coley, the one that she lived in—showing the rear porch. In fact, he handed her three photos. One photo was a picture of Coley's house, showing the window through which she claimed to have seen Hopkins, Coley and his wife eating breakfast on several occasions. Pruiett asked her, "Are the pictures the pictures of her house where she lived at the time she observed Hopkins, Tom Coley, and his wife eating together?" "Yes," was her answer. Pruiett again asked her, "Do you believe in spooks?" A. C. Cruce objected to the question. The court sustained the objection. To the ruling Pruiett replied, "Your honor, with all due respect to the court, I'm compelled to, in the face of your ruling, to introduce another spook, and the question that I am now about to ask will convince your honor and the counsel for the prosecution." Cruce objected, stating that Pruiett was making an argument to the jury. The court instructed Pruiett to proceed with the question, whereupon Pruiett said: "Now, my polka-dot girl, show the jury where the pump was on the porch in this picture of the rear porch?"

"I don't see it in this picture," she answered.

Pruiett placed on the stand the photographer who made the picture, and two other witnesses who had been acquainted with the premises over a year, about which the polka-dot girl testified and they testified "that there was no pump on the rear porch," and thus another spook was introduced into the trial of George Hopkins, charged with the murder of his father. The polka-dot girl was an exceedingly beautiful woman, and admitted that she was fond of the frivolities of life.

CHAPTER SIXTEEN

Wherein, under the head of miscellaneous murders, Pruiett defends a Professor who killed a pupil; a woman who killed her brother; two women who killed their husbands; a storekeeper who slew an inoffensive patron; an aged man who killed his aged brother; and a rich man who killed a harpy; and how all were acquitted, but the aged man, who was innocent, is convicted. And how he vows that his client will never go to prison, and after an appeal turns unsuccessful, the old man makes good for him by committing suicide. And how disgruntled survivors of a murder victim assassinate a Mississippi lawyer, after Pruiett has maneuvered him out of confinement, and out of the shadow of the electric chair.

Professor Corley P. McDarment was a disciplinarian of the old school. "Spare the rod and spoil the child" had always been his slogan. When he drew a class of high school boys, larger than he in stature and handier than he with what it took to flourish the birch, he called upon his native Kentucky resourcefulness to help coin an appropriate amendment to his guiding precept. He ordered three of his rebellious pupils to a room in the school basement, and after following them there and bolting the door, produced a rod and began to apply it to them. The rod was of thirty-eight calibre, and would shoot six times in rapid succession. One dead and one seriously wounded was the score when the janitor broke down the door and disarmed him.

Pruiett was reading a week's accumulation of mail and soiling the polished brass of his own office cuspidors. His secretary slipped through the door and stood nervously before his desk. The Black Stud was not an easy task-master. "What you want?" he growled, without looking up.

"There's a man waiting to see you," she said. "He said—."

"I told you I didn't want to see any one," he snapped. "I got to get right on out of town. Let one of the boys take care of him."

"He won't see any of them," she replied. "He's been in several times in the last few days, and he says it's most urgent. He said it was a big murder case."

"Send him in," Pruiett said, but understand—I won't be in town the balance of this week, an' I don't want to see any one else."

"My name's Wright, Mr. Pruiett," the well-dressed man began. "I'm authorized to say that I represent the Teachers Association—."

"The school teachers?" Pruiett interrupted.

"Yes, the school teachers," the man smiled. "I know you're busy, so I'll be brief. One of our members is in jail, up in eastern Oklahoma, on a murder charge. We want to employ you to defend him."

"How bad do you want to employ me?" Pruiett asked. With murder waiting to be heard on a dozen dockets he couldn't afford to be tactful.

"We'll pay a thousand dollars," Wright said.

"I wouldn't touch it for two," Pruiett snarled. "Why hell's fire—you're talkin' about McDarment, aren't you?"

"That's the case," came the answer.

"The daddy of the boy he killed is a lawyer, an' one of my friends. His uncle is the district judge in that county, an' he'll probably try the case. I couldn't afford to get into it at all."

"It's a very unwholesome situation, for McDarment," Wright agreed. "That's the reason why our committee selected you. We figured that position and influence didn't make any difference to you."

"I'm awful busy," Pruiett argued, but Wright's smart flattery had not missed its mark. "They'd have the court an' jury both against you with that set-up. I don't want to get mixed up in it."

"I'll guarantee the payment of a three thousand dollar fee," Wright suggested. "I don't want to haggle."

"Will you put that in writin'?" Pruiett demanded.

"I'll be glad to," Wright replied.

"How long will it take you to pay off?"

"I'll agree to pay in full in ninety days."

"Pruiett pushed the buzzer beneath the desk ledge. "Call Tulsa an' get the county attorney; tell him I'm sick—I've had a stroke, or a fit, or somethin'," he said to the girl, "an' get that case over there passed." Then he turned to Wright. "Say, where are they holdin' McDarment?"

"At Muskogee," Wright smiled.

"See when's the first train to Muskogee, an' get me a ticket on it," he continued. "An' remember, I don't want to see anybody before I leave."

"Do you want me to outline the facts of this case for you?" Wright inquired.

"No," Pruiett answered, shortly. "Say, what the hell are you goin' to say for a professor that shoots hell out of the kids in his class. That's pretty stern teachin', isn't it?"

"I'll tell you," Wright began. "I'll tell you, if you'll hold on a minute," Wright said. "This McDarment is a small man; he doesn't weigh more than a hundred and thirty-five or forty. This happened in the high school up at Wagoner, up north of Muskogee, an' the boys involved were bigger than the teacher. Edgar Watts, the dead boy, weighed twenty pounds more than McDarment. Clay Moss, the one that got his eye shot out, weighed more than Watts. There was another one, named Dick Jones, and he was a big-armed bully, too. They——."

"I may be able to make the self-defense stick," Pruiett interrupted. He was so nervous that he couldn't be still. "These boys were bullyin' some of the little children, an' McDarment was tryin' to protect——."

"If you please, Mr. Pruiett," Wright persisted. "Let me give you the bare outlines; then you can add all the theory you wish. We'll pay you to add enough to keep McDarment from going to the chair. These over-grown yokels bragged that they wouldn't be bossed by a teacher that wasn't as big as they were. They barked like dogs and howled like cats, so that he couldn't hold classes. He was dodging beans and paper wads all the time, and they had a game that was called 'high and low,' where one would get on his hands and knees behind the professor, and another would push him backwards, over him. They told him when he got tired of it he could quit his job and leave town; that it'd be all right with them any time."

"That's bein' pretty hard on the professor," Pruiett agreed.

"They used to rough 'em up a bit down in Arkansas, but they never had the guts to get that rebellious. Did McDarment just get tired of it an' take his little pistol to school with him?"

"We don't know about that," Wright answered. "It seems like McDarment and these three boys were alone in a chemistry room they had in the basement of the school. We have two members who tried to teach in this school, who were driven out by these same boys, and they have reported the situation to us. We're sure McDarment was justified in taking the course he did, whatever it was. He's in jail, and so far none of us have had a chance to talk to him."

"Tell your membership that Pruiett don't give a damn about district judges an' state politics. All he's interested in is justice." He arose and held out his hand, the signal that the conference had been concluded. "Tell 'em McDarment's every legal right will be exhausted, an' not to let the fee matter drag along. Let's clear that thing up an' get it out of the way."

"Have you signed up a nice little statement for the county attorney?" Pruiett was squinting between steel bars as he asked the question. "No," McDarment answered. "I've had plenty of chances, but I told 'em I didn't care to make a statement until I had consulted my attorney."

"All school teachers aren't damn fools," Pruiett grunted. "Our Constitution says a man don't have to incriminate himself, but prosecutin' attorneys don't know anything about that. They usually take a signed statement, an' then add a little about 'this here can be used against me as evidence if the prosecution finds anything in it of value.' You know?"

"I know," McDarment agreed, listlessly.

"I like to have the co-operation of my clients," Pruiett said. "It helps to beat hell. Are you willin' to help me win this case?"

"Perfectly," McDarment answered.

"All right. Now: Who owned that pistol?"

"I did."

"Now look here," Pruiett objected. "I thought we was goin' to co-operate. It would be a hell of a lot better if one of the boys had brought that gun to school that day."

"I can't help it," McDarment replied. "It was mine and everyone around here knows it. We can't get anywhere going that way."

"You're right, if that's the case," Pruiett agreed. "What was you doin' down in that basement room with the three boys?"

"I sent 'em out of a classroom upstairs; told 'em to go down there, and then I followed them. That's—."

"Just a minute, now," Pruiett interrupted again. "That don't sound so good. We've got to be careful—. You are not feelin' well today," Pruiett said, stopping him. "There's no use discussin' it here. We'll wait 'til they have the preliminary next week, an' just fish out the facts they got against you. We're not puttin' you on the stand, see? Then—," Pruiett peered intently into the dim light of the cell. "Say, what's that stain on your sleeve? That one just above the elbow?"

"What does it look like?" McDarment countered.

"It looks like a burn, a scorched place, to me," Pruiett replied. "Did you have your coat on when this trouble came off up there?" Pruiett inquired. Before McDarment could reply, he reconstructed the question. "You didn't have your coat on, did you?"

"No," said McDarment. "I didn't have my coat on."

"Wait just a minute," Pruiett said. The Pruiett defense-delivering head was at work. Stepping down the corridor he called to the jailer and an assistant. He asked them to come down to the door of McDarment's cell. When they were there he asked the professor to stick his right arm through the bars. "Take this pen and put your initials on the sleeve of that shirt, up near the shoulder," he said, handing his fountain pen to the jailer. "That's all right, let it smear; just make 'em big enough so's they won't run together. That's it. Fine." He approved the way the bewildered officer made his mark, and then handed the pen to the other one, who was waiting. "Now you, please, sir," he continued. "Down here below, on the cuff. Put your initials. That's fine. That's it." Holding McDarment's arm out in the light as he placed his pen in his pocket, he pointed to the scorched place at the elbow. "You see that yellow burn? That scorched place right there?" he said to the officers. "That's what I want you to witness and remember. I've had you put your mark on the sleeve, so you'll know the shirt if you ever see it again. Now, Mr. McDarment, take it off so I can stuff it in this 'folio of mine. I'll see that you get another one right away."

That had been the substance of Pruiett's first interview with his client. The burned shirt had suggested something, possibly a remote likelihood of utility in the future, so he preserved it. If a place was made for it, and it fit, it would be heard from later. If not—. The most dutiful housewife scorches a garment occasionally. No harm was done.

"Professor C. P. McDarment . . . . instructor of Wagoner High School, was late yesterday afternoon, after preliminary hearing before Justice R. E. Doggett, held for the district court on the charge of murdering Edgar Watts, an 18-year-old student . . . . Two men and two boyhood companions of young Watts told their stories of what transpired behind the locked door of the High School laboratory on February 10 (1916) and when they had finished the tragedy remained as much a mystery as

ever." So did an early account of the case appear in the Muskogee (Oklahoma) Daily Phoenix. . . . McDarment himself
did not take the stand (at the preliminary). Neatly attired, he
sat beside his attorney throughout the day, seldom suggesting a
question to be asked. . . . Moman Pruiett, chief of his counsel,
thrilled the courtroom with dramatic declarations which gave inti-
mations of what the young teacher's defense might be."

"We got to be awful careful," Pruiett whispered behind his
hand to McDarment. "That's Thomas H. Owen, former member
of the Criminal Court of Appeals, that's in charge of the prosecution, an' the fellow with the big ears is Fred Branson. They're
both good lawyers, an' bitter prosecutors."

"What's the matter with the public prosecutor they had up
here?" McDarment whispered. "Isn't he supposed to have charge
of these kinds of cases?"

"Special prosecutors," Pruiett answered. "The interested parties are entitled to hire 'em if they want 'em, to back the state's
attorney up. They didn't need to hire 'em in this case. The
Wattses are so prominent up here they got a lot of volunteers."

"I think you can handle the situation," McDarment encouraged.

"I'll show 'em some tricks," Pruiett boasted, swelling with
the compliment. "Somethin' they can't pick up on an appeals
bench. Who's that kid they're bringin' in for a witness?"

"That's Clay Moss," McDarment said. "He's gettin' out
early."

"He sure as hell is," Pruiett agreed. "He must be perty
tough. Is he hurt as bad as that big bandage on his head would
make you think?"

"He lost his eye," McDarment whispered. "I'm glad it wasn't
worse."

"Moss gave a damaging account, damaging for McDarment,
of what had transpired in the High School basement room. The
state had the professor charged with deliberate, premeditated
murder, and Moss had received an injury at his hands. He made
a willing witness in support of the theory the state had to prove
if it was going to win its suit against the spare-built little school
teacher. 'Where were you the night before the tragedy?' Pruiett
demanded of Moss on cross-examination. 'At the basketball
game,' the witness answered. 'Did you see McDarment there?'
'Yes, sir.' 'Did you have a conversation with him that night?'
'All he said was that he wanted me to take charge of the game

and to referee. Then he gave me his whistle.' The witness mumbled his last sentence. Pruiett shot out of his chair. 'His pistol?' he cried. 'His whistle,' the witness corrected. 'I didn't know he had a pistol.' "

When Pruiett resumed the seat "he had shot out of," as the correspondent for the Phoenix had observed, the panorama of the McDarment defense was finally clear before him. The imperfect diction of the witness in answering, or his own inability to understand, had opened the door of credible explanation to him. He saw the dead cat. He heard the flap of the wings of his attending spooks. He conferred with McDarment, in whispers. before he resumed his cross-examination of Moss. "You did referee the basket ball game that night, didn't you?" he demanded.

"Yes, I did—."

"And isn't it a fact that Professor McDarment, or some other member of the faculty, usually acts as the official at the school games?"

"Yes, but—."

"You took the whistle out of McDarment's pocket?"

"He told me to. He said for me to get it out of his coat, hangin' on a post, an'—."

"McDarment was supposed to referee this particular game? He went there to act as referee, didn't he?"

"Yes, but—."

"And you and your friends Watts and Jones pushed the professor backwards a time or two, and told him if he didn't set up in the stands with the girls, where he belonged, that you were going to whip him, right there before the basketball crowd, didn't you?"

"No," Moss shouted. "Nothing of the sort. I—we—."

"That'll be all," Pruiett drawled, waving the witness aside. He arose to address the court. "I'd like to have this matter continued over until tomorrow, for further cross-examination of state's witnesses and possibly for some evidence for the defendant."

"We object," Tom Owen cried, jumping up. "We want to close our case now. After this hearing is over we are willing that he have fifteen weeks to manufacture his defense."

"I have never been handed such a beautiful bouquet of courtesy in my life," Pruiett said sweetly, making Owen a profound bow, "as my distinguished friend, the Judge of the Criminal Court of Appeals, has just presented me."

"The request for a continuance will be denied," the court barked.

"Thank you, your honor," **Pruiett** said, bowing again and smiling.

"I'm givin' you back nine of the fifteen weeks you offered me," Pruiett grinned at Owen and the prosecution as he swaggered into the district court courtroom before trial. "I'm announcin' ready." Owen and Branson, with others interested in the prosecution, pretended not to hear him. Pruiett looked closer to see that none of the family of the deceased were within hearing; he was always compassionate and considerate of those who survived his client's misdeeds. "I see you're runnin' for the Supreme Court," he continued, talking directly to Owen. "I'm glad to see it, an' I'm for you, a hundred per cent. Who shall I make my check to. I'm sendin' a little contribution to your campaign."

"Thanks," said Owen, indifferently. "Just send it to the office, if you're really going to the bother."

"I sure as hell am," Pruiett grinned. "I think we ought to have more public-spirited lawyers that're willin' to sacrifice the gain of private practice for the good of the people."

"Thanks," Owen repeated.

"I hope you win," Pruiett went on. "I hope you got a better chance of winnin' that judge's race than you got o'winnin' this case. You boys are off—." Owen got up and walked away. "I got his fire hot already," he beamed to McDarment. "Did you get that stuff I sent you to study?"

"I got it," McDarment answered.

"Have you got it straight? Want to ask any questions?"

"I understand it, I believe."

"I intend to reserve my openin' statement until the state has finished its case," he whispered. "We're goin' to coast on the cross-examination, just cut 'em a time or two, to let the jury know we ain't pleadin' guilty. We'll blast 'em when we put you an' our other witnesses on the stand."

"I'm sure your plan is a good one," McDarment agreed.

"When I start to make the openin' statement, act like you're too tired an' indifferent to listen, but have your ear over ever'-thing I say. I'm goin' over that statement I sent up to your cell, an' I don't want you to fall down. Follow it, close, in the statement."

When the state had concluded its case it had been established by Jones and Moss, who survived the basement fracas, that McDarment was the heartless aggressor. He had ordered the three boys from class, had directed them to go to the room in the basement, and after following them there, had bolted the door before he had made known the purpose of his private interview. Then he had drawn the pistol, and began to shoot.

Pruiett began his narrative of what the defense evidence would show. He was the embodiment of defiance, and assurance. His newly tailored suit, a trifle ash-cluttered, hung easily about his rugged frame. His black mop of hair was in faultless array, and shone brilliantly in the dim light of the courtroom. There was a trace of brown tobacco stains about the corners of his mouth, but he was close-shaven and freshly manicured. His voice was deep and booming. His gestures, his smiles of assurance and his grimaces of pathos, were always in harmony with the tempo of his restless footwork as he moved up and down in front of his listeners. The eyes of jurors followed him. They reflected his moods and feelings as he expressed them. "Gentlemen," he said, "you understand, from my cross-examination of state's witnesses that our defense is based generally upon the doctrine of self-defense. Our proof, which will follow this statement, will show that Edgar Watts was killed accidentally, in a struggle over a gun which might have caused the death of McDarment, or of the other boys, as well as it did of Watts. These boys had driven two teachers out of school, out of town, by their rough tactics, and they were enraged because McDarment had defied them and refused to give up his job. Professor McDarment didn't carry that gun to the basement room," he said, with tones and gestures which caressed his listeners' ears. "Our proof will show that—beyond all reasonable doubt." He made an oratorical play on the "reasonable doubt," and glanced slyly at Tom Owen as he let it roll out. Owen knew he was going to hear a lot about "reasonable doubt" before the trial was over, and he frowned. "McDarment sent the boys out of the class room so that he might have a talk with them in the privacy of the basement laboratory; to reason with them and to try to make peace with them. He wanted to try once more to show them that they were being unreasonable, and were wrong. He wasn't carrying a pistol. He had no design to commit an assault of any kind on the boys. The pistol was going to be the subject of the interview in the basement. The pistol was missing. There's going to be no contention that the gun that was used in this unfortunate affair was not the property of the defendant. He admits it. He will continue to admit it, but he didn't carry it to the basement on this fatal morning, and it was not in his hand when the tragic shots were fired." There was soul-stirring pathos in Pruiett's deep voice as he moved artfully toward his climax. "The professor had taken that pistol to the basketball game on the night before, to use it as a timing gun. In other words, when the half period was reached, and when the game was over, he would discharge the gun. The whistle was for stopping plays when the ball was out of bounds, and when fouls had been committed. I'm not familiar with the game, but it has been explained to me in that way. This pistol was in his coat pocket, just before the game started, hanging by the basketball court. The whistle was attached to a string, or little strap, and the professor carried it about his wrist or in his hand. The trouble came up about who was going to referee, and as it is partially in evidence, the Moss boy won the argument. He says that McDarment asked him to referee, and told him to get the whistle from the side pocket of his coat which was hanging there. That is not true, as our proof will show. Watts, Jones and Moss called McDarment aside, and told him that he was going to sit up with the girls, where he belonged, while Moss refereed the game. They told him that they were going to whip him, before the crowd that was coming in to see the game, if he went out on the court to referee. One of the boys grabbed the whistle and twisted it from McDarment's wrist. In confusion and embarrassment, and in an effort to avoid an embarrassing scene, McDarment withdrew, and permitted Moss to act as referee. He didn't think about the gun until he was on his way home, after the game, and it was then that he missed it. He didn't know whether it had been stolen, or whether he had lost it from his pocket. He intended to inquire about it, at school the next morning, merely to ask the students if they had found or heard of the gun being found about the school, but when he got there a girl student told him that she had seen Watts stick his hand into his coat pocket there at the basketball game, and take something out of it. Was it unreasonable for him to deduce that the incident explained the whereabouts of his missing gun? Yes, McDarment sent the boys to the basement. Does that show you premeditation of murder, sending three big boys, when he knew that one of them might be armed, down to a secluded room in the basement? Or you may think to ask me: 'Why did he send them out, and follow them away, as he did?' Our proof will show, gentlemen, that his acts were motivated by concern and kindliness for the boys. He will tell you that he didn't want to accuse them publicly of having robbed him; of having picked his pocket. He was going to ask them, privately, to return his property. Then he was going to demand its return, and then, if they refused, he was going to file a complaint against them, charging that they had stolen his pistol, and seek to recover it in a legal and proper manner. The boys went downstairs first. McDarment followed them. They were in the room first. McDarment will tell you that as he stepped into the dim light of that room the Moss boy moved in behind him, and slamming the door shut, bolted it. Before the professor had time to ask about the pistol Edgar Watts pulled it out and pointed it at him, held it right against his belly, and called him a bunch of vile names. He called him names that reflected upon the character of his mother and questioned the good purposes of his father, and told him that he had hung around their town too long. 'We don't like you and we've told you so,' they said to him, 'and we've told you to get out. Now we're going to beat the hell out of you, and you'll have to hire somebody to carry you out.' Watts held the gun on him while Moss aimed a blow at his head. The professor ducked and grappled with Watts, grabbing at the hand holding the pistol. As they struggled the gun went off; it was right between them. The first shot didn't hit any one. That's the one that lodged in the window frame near the ceiling. The next one grazed Moss' face; he had jumped into the fight, and he hollered, but kept right on swinging and slugging. It went off again, and the bullet went through Moss' eye; he fell unconscious, but Watts and the professor went on fighting, struggling over the pistol. There was another report, and the bullet went squarely through the boy's face. He fell to the floor—dead. McDarment stooped over, picked up the gun which had fallen from Watts' grasp, and the janitor pushed the barred door in. The gun which wounded Clay Moss, and which killed Edgar Watts, was in Edgar's hands all the time, during all the time that it was being discharged. We will offer for your consideration the testimony of the girl who saw the boys taking something from McDarment's pockets at the basketball game, the one who reported what she had seen to the teacher the following morning. We will have the testimony of firearms experts, who have made examinations of the shirt McDarment was wearing on the morning of this unfortunate occurrence. They will say that the shirt was scorched about the elbow of the right sleeve, and that with their microscopic examination they found tiny granules of burned gunpowder. That scorched place on Professor McDarment's arm was a powder burn, and if he had held the gun in his right hand, deliberately firing it into the bodies of his victims, as these victims have testified, it would have been impossible for the sleeves of his shirt to be scorched and burned by the blast."

Tom Owen mopped a fine film of perspiration from his forehead as Pruiett concluded his outline. Owen was a good lawyer; he knew a good defense when he saw one. The prophecy of acquittal was written across the dingy walls of the old courtroom, and the prosecution didn't need a prophet to interpret the message for them. The pilfering of the inoffensive whistle, suggested by the resemblance in the pronunciation of whistle and pistol, made a perfect base for the construction of Pruiett's defense. Owen saw why he was going to be beaten, at the same time the inevitable became apparent. He gnashed his teeth. Fred Branson cursed under his breath. The Black Stud leered and swaggered. Defense witnesses swore that Moss had slipped something from the professor's pocket. Moss said it was a whistle. The professor said he discovered that his signal pistol was missing after he left the ball game. What was the court going to say about reasonable doubt, when he instructed the jury? If there's a reasonable doubt in your minds at the conclusion of all the evidence, you must resolve it in favor of whom? The defendant? The accused? Why certainly. This here's the United States of America. This ain't revolutionary Russia. Will Pruiett think of that for his argument? Just you let Pruiett alone, and watch an' listen. You'll have some fun when he goes to burnin' the state in this case. The old jailer and his assistant came, under compulsion, to identify the scorched shirt which McDarment had yielded into Pruiett's brief case. The county attorney'll get us fired for this, but there's our initials on that shirt, an' that wild-eyed devil defendin' McDarment will hang a perjury rap on us if we try to back up on him. That's the shirt we signed, all right. Signin' a shirt! Who'd a thought of such a thing, except that brown-eyed Pruiett? That's the stain all right, right there by the elbow. It was there the day Pruiett came to the jail, an' it was the same shirt that the professor had on when he was brought into jail. Let 'em fire us. It's a hell of a lot better to be out of a job than to try to hedge with a wild man shakin' his fist under your nose, there in a crowded courtroom. We're tellin' the truth about that shirt.

And Pruiett was right about the ballistic experts. They came, and they testified. "Do you mean to tell this court and jury," Tom Owen screamed, "that a flaming pistol would make a different appearing scorch on a piece of fabric than a hot iron would?"

"No, sir, I don't," the expert replied.

"Then why are you so positive that this burned shirt shows powder burns, instead of some other kind of burns?"

"Because I made microscopic tests of the fabric, and I find particles of burned gunpowder in it, burned right into the scorched fabric."

Owen produced his big handkershief and began his deliberate, desperate, face mopping. "Could you take a piece of fabric that has been scorched in ordinary use, say as in being ironed, or coming too close to a hot stove, and after it had been discolored, fire a revolver in such proximity to it that particles of powder might become imbedded in the scorched surface of the fabric?" Owen was no fool.

"The witness pondered. "Well, yes," he answered. "I believe that it would be possible to imbed the powder in the fabric, with such a process."

Owen glared triumphantly with the admission, and stalked toward his chair. Pruiett gave him an insolent smile and wink. Was he going to let the jury convict a man on such an unreasonable hypothesis? Let him argue that the powder was a Pruiett trick. What was reasonable doubt in that old Constitution for, if they could get by with that kind of stuff?" Did the boy filch a pistol or a whistle? If he had stolen the pistol, would he admit it, in the face of the proportions of the tragic result which followed? Was a jury going to convict, when they couldn't ever decide, with definite certainty, what that kid had found in the professor's pocket? Pruiett was serene. He had acquired, in his rounds, something of a knowledge of homely human nature.

When the forensic fireworks, which came after the evidence, were over the jury went out—and came back. Pruiett's client was not guilty. McDarment pumped each juror's hand in gratification; Pruiett complimented each of them for a just verdict. Tom Owen and Fred Branson made strange muttering sounds under their breath as they tried to console the weeping, half-hysterical, parents of the dead Watts boy.

"Have you had any experience in shooting a gun?" A polite young clerk in a small town hardware store was leaning across the counter and asking the question of a plump, middle-aged woman. She wore a black dress and a black hat.

"No, sir," she answered, "but—."

"Then I would suggest that you get a shotgun," he said. "A mad dog, any kind of a dog, would be very hard to hit, and this small gun wouldn't be very satisfactory."

"I think I'll learn to use it all right," the customer answered. "Do bullets go with it, or do you have to buy them extra?"

"The cartridges will be extra," the man corrected. "How many do you want, a box?" "Just enough to fill it up," the lady in mourning replied.

When the clerk had loaded the gun, a short-barreled revolver, and cautiously complied with her request for information as to how to shoot it, she paid and walked out. Fifteen minutes later the crowd of farmers, who packed the town's principal store for the Saturday afternoon shopping, was in a panic. A woman, holding a pistol in both hands, was pumping it empty and into the body of a man who tried to stagger away from her. The killer was Callie Pence, the recently widowed survivor of Sid Pence, a farmer of the community. The victim, begging from the floor of the store was her own brother, Lee Sharp. Sharp was under indictment for killing Callie's husband in an argument which arose over the occupancy of a farm which Pence owned, but which Sharp farmed for him, on half-shares. He was out of jail on bond. Before all the "bullets" acquired in the neighborhood hardware store were exhausted, Sharp was fatally wounded, and two scurrying female bystanders had been less seriously injured. Pruiett took the case and a deed to the Pence property. Temporary insanity was the plea, and even the staunchest Pruiett supporter expressed a doubt as to whether or not he could explain around the cool premeditation which the hardware clerk's testimony was going to supply. It appeared that Widow Pence had fairly well decided to kill her brother before she began to put the decision into successful execution.

Callie's case came up for trial at Norman, county seat of Cleveland County. She was out on bond. A conference, pre-trial, was being held in local counsel's office near the old courthouse. "That hardware clerk is listed as a state's witness, an' he's goin' to testify about that mad-dog business," Pruiett said. "I am not sure whether I like it or not."

"I can deny I said it, if you want me to," Callie agreed.

"What other reason you goin' to advance for buyin' a six-shooter?" Pruiett asked.

"Whatever you say," Callie answered.

"I got a hell of a headache today," Pruiett said, pressing his temples between his finger tips. "My head's bustin'. I can't hardly think." Callie waited. She didn't need to inquire about his health. She was a woman of experience. "We won't bother to change it," he said finally. "You said a mad-dog, so we'll stay with it. I hate to have my witnesses change their testimony, anyway." Callie sat patiently. Pruiett arose, and pressing his temples again, began to pace the floor. "You had a dog out at the place that was acting mad, and you wanted to kill him. You came to town on Saturday afternoon, and bought you a little gun for shooting that dog, and you put it in your pocket-book. You was over at Rucker's store, doing some marketing, and in walks Lee Sharp. You didn't know that he was in town, and you wasn't entertaining no idea of giving him any lead treatment."

The testimony showed that Callie Pence accompanied the body of her dead husband, Sid Pence, and buried him in the old country church yard near their former home in Alabama. It was on the day she arrived in Norman, Oklahoma, after burying her husband that she purchased a pistol and cartridges. Testimony also showed she held her dead husband's head in her lap, and smeared her husband's own blood on the face of her brother, and told him in the presence of her dead husband that a righteous retribution would overtake him. It was designed killing all right, if designed killing constituted murder, but there was a lifetime of justification for it. Pruiett was back before a jury. "Callie and Sid grew old together," he whispered, leaning close to see if tears had started down the weather-beaten cheeks of his farmer jury's faces. "She was fourteen, he eighteen, when they married, penniless kids on a poor old Alabama farm, and in love." He paused to push a loose wisp of hair back into its black bulk, and to let his message sift down. The head would catch it, but the heart had to have it before it took effect. "Babies wouldn't come to them; they wanted them but they wouldn't come, so they directed the love that they would have had for their children back into each other. They lived alone, and worked hard, and loved one another. They had no one, nothing else to love." He was building slowly—carefully. "They moved out to this territory, and elbow to elbow, they toiled and saved. We know, you and I, of the hardships they endured. We were here with them, struggling as Callie and Sid were struggling, for the things that would make life in our declining years a bit softer—a bit sweeter. They relied on the comfort that the one would be to the other, in the eventide of life, as they struggled and saved and loved. Old Sid's hands were rough and work-worn. His face was wrinkled and seamed with the wear of age, and weather, and hard labor—but Callie loved him. He wore patches on his old overalls so that she might have a new churn, or a new gingham apron." Pruiett paused. They were coming, now. Number three in the back row was brushing them away with the back of his hand and trying to look unconcerned; he was feigning interest out the window. An old one in the front row, with gray hair, was indifferent about it. He let them drop off the end of his nose. "And they sent back to Alabama for Lee. Callie was kind-hearted, she cherished the recollections she had of childhood frolics on the old pine-studded Alabama hillsides. Lee wasn't gettin' along so well, and they had an adjoining farm they would let him have, and let him work it. Sid agreed, just because he thought it would make Callie happy, so they sent him money, and had him come on out to Oklahoma. Lee was Callie's brother, but let me tell you, my friends, that there's one thing stronger than the tie of family blood, and that's the bond of love that a man has for a woman, or a woman has for a man, that's been molded in the pit of joint-suffering and baked in the oven of self-sacrifice Selfish, little-minded Lee Sharp killed Callie's life-mate over a line dispute between the farms, an' the Pences owned both of them. He just took his shot-gun an' shot Sid to pieces. The law stepped in, and was going to prosecute Lee for it, I am sure, and I am sure that my client had no intention of interfering. By the force of her dull mechanical will she went on the train with the body; she carried Sid back to his Alabama hills, and saw him unloaded and dropped into the sandy ground. Did she come back here for vengeance, as the state contends? Did she come back here to slaughter and kill? It was her home here, the one she and Sid had suffered and bled for, and she had no other. She was an old woman—and she was alone. Her dreams of what was to come, the comfort that was to be hers, had been shattered." He spread his hands in an appealing gesture. "She had been awakened from her dream, but she moved about as if she were still asleep. Every ripple of the wind-blown grain field, the field that she and Sid had sown, was like a ponderous blow upon her heart. The sight of the trees he had planted, the fences he had built, were torture for Callie. She had to work to forget, or go mad, so she tried to run the farm. She didn't know Lee was in town. She had no desire to see him, or to harm him. She was going about the hard business of running her farms, and had been required to buy the pistol, when Lee Sharp had to march back into her tortured mind. The sight of him tore apart her last lines of understanding. The last fragment of reason and control snapped—and she couldn't remember."

The jury disagreed. A hung jury was half a victory, Pruiett always said, and it was an indicator. When he had hung a jury he had enough of the state's case in his mind to strengthen his next attack upon it, and he could make up for some of the flaws that had appeared in his defense. When he had produced the drama the second time the jury accepted it at par. Callie bought the gun to kill a mad-dog. The jury said that she was not guilty of murder, as charged.

Pruiett liked to play with that dangerous property called "temporary insanity." He invoked it in the defense of cases where other, and more feasible defenses, were available. On one occasion, when the wisdom of his program was being questioned by co-counsel, he made his typically frank outburst. "Hell's fire! I've got to have somethin' besides self-defense. I'm developin' rheumatism in my right shoulder from grabbin' at my hip pocket an' arguin' the old gun-pullin' act." He undertook the defense of Sam St. Mary. "As the result of a misunderstanding regarding the use of a telephone in the Gray-Graham Tailoring Company's store in the Skirvin Hotel Building, W. F. Henry, baggage driver, is dead, and Sam St. Mary, manager of the store, is in the county jail charged with murder. * * * The shooting occurred shortly before noon today. Spectators saw Henry run from the tailoring shop and turn the corner into the alley which flanks the Rock Island depot. As the fleeing man turned the corner, St. Mary is reported to have dashed from his shop with a 38-calibre revolver, and fired three shots which took effect at the base of Henry's spine. . . . Charles B. Selby was the prosecuting attorney. "I'll let Sam plead guilty an' recommend a life sentence for him if you'll save the state the expense of a trial," he said.

"An' relieve it of the chance of gettin' beat?" Pruiett inquired.

"There's not a chance of his gettin' away," Selby scoffed. "There was a noon-day crowd on the street, an' a big gang on the station platform waitin' for a train to come in, an' they all saw Sam shoot him in the back. I got fifty eye-witnesses in this case."

"I wonder what that crowd on the depot platform thought, when they saw that scared baggageman a-flaggin' down the bricks, an' old Sam burnin' his coat-tails with pistol bullets?" Pruiett laughed heartily.

"I don't know what they thought, but I do know what a jury's goin' to think. They'll give Sam the chair as sure as hell."

"I can't agree with you," Pruiett smiled.

"You'd better take this life sentence I'm offerin' you," Selby said, "before I change my mind. I can't leave a proposition like that open after I get the subpoenas out for my witnesses."

"Old Sam said he didn't want to go to the pen," Pruiett said. "He isn't very intelligent, but he's got that much sense. He gave me specific instruction to clear him. You ain't got a chance," Pruiett repeated, "but we are not pleadin' guilty, not even to a simple assault, if you wanted to reduce it to that. Me an' Sam'll be ready for trial when they call his case."

"Sam St. Mary found not guilty," the local press reported. How in the hell could a jury acquit a man under those circumstances? Shoot a man in the back, at high noon, before an army of witnesses, an' he's not guilty of murder? What's this guy Pruiett got? Can't the state get a conviction against him a'tall? The masses were grumbling. Charley Selby was tearing his hair. A week of rough and tumble Pruiett trial had left Charley distracted, but still confident of victory. Insanity wasn't going to work in this case; Pruiett was wasting a lot of his gas. When the verdict came in, and Pruiett was starting to grin across the table, Selby rushed out of the courtroom. Before Pruiett and his client could get out of the courthouse the sheriff had served another warrant on Sam, and was leading him off to the iron cells.

"I never heard of such a thing," Pruiett gasped. "How they goin' to keep holdin' this man after the jury's acquitted him?"

Selby smiled, weakly. "I went before the county judge an'

signed a' insanity complaint against him," he answered. "You
proved he was insane; brought the doctors an' others here to
swear to it, 'til you convinced the jury, an' me, too. I'm askin'
the county judge to send him to the hospital for the violent insane, for the rest of his no-good life."

"I'll be damned," Pruiett managed to say. "I never saw
such a pore loser. You aren't a sport at all."

"Not if lettin' that murderer run loose is a requisite for
sportsmanship," Selby agreed. "Bein' a public officer don't keep
me from complainin' against nutty folks, an' hadn't you just
proved he was nutty? I guess bein' his lawyer won't save you
from testifyin' in the sanity hearing."

"If I am not mistaken," Pruiett said, "a person that's accused of bein' insane is entitled to a trial by jury, the same as
when he's accused of anything else. Isn't that what the Constitution says?"

"Maybe it does," Selby laughed, "but you can't blow hot
an' cold at the same time. The judge, or the jury, is goin' to hear
the same evidence that this one heard that found him not guilty,
by reason of being insane. They can't find both ways."

Within a three weeks' period Pruiett twice produced his
jury-thunder; each time for Sam St. Mary. In the first case,
where Sam was charged with murder, Pruiett screamed that he
couldn't form the criminal intent necessary to make murder, because he was insane. In the second, where he was charged with
being insane, he maintained that he was mentally quite sound.
The doctors who had testified for him in the first hearing were
necessarily against him in the second. Testimony from the record
in the first case was read into the record of the second. The verdict, finding him not guilty because he was insane, was introduced
in evidence, and exhibited to the jury hearing the sanity complaint. "This is a farce," Pruiett roared, while the brass chandeliers in the room vibrated with the echo. "This is a fair example
of a petty-fogging attempt of a poor loser to misuse public office,
and public funds, to satisfy a personal desire for revenge. Charley
Selby's a poor loser, and he wants to get even. I took him to a
good trimmin' in a murder case less than a month ago, an' he
wasn't big enough to swallow it. He got it lodged in his craw;
let the cockleburr hang under his tail, so he thinks he'll spend a
little more of you tax-payers' money in parading his incompetence
—tryin' to get even with me an' Sam." It was plain language,
but it was Pruiett speaking. He didn't indulge in ambiguities.

He had bilked the state, and he might as well proclaim it. Wasn't he admitting it when he said he had trimmed him? He had gotten something he wasn't entitled to, but he could afford to acknowledge it because the law wouldn't allow a man to be twice placed in jeopardy. The murder case was a closed episode. The jury found Sam not guilty on the insanity charge. They found that he was sane, and they liberated him. Society ground its gold-filled molars and Selby started using the side streets and alleys. He was afraid that some one would make an insanity kick against him and have him picked up. He wasn't certain in his own mind, as to whether he could beat it or not. Pruiett brushed a curving section of the black plume back over his ears as he toyed with a tall drink. There was a sparkle in his brown eye and the trace of a half-smile about the corners of his big mouth. Was he thinking of the double fee the state had helped him earn by repeating its effort to take Sam St. Mary out of circulation? Or was he glancing into the dim chambers of years gone by, when the serpent's trail was visible on the western sands, and a theatrical threat of retribution was being uttered by a penniless, friendless boy?

Lee Bird was old enough to be held accountable for his own acts, however indiscreet, so the county officers drew murder charges against him, and filed them. He was 62 years old when he shot his 57-year-old brother to death. When running workmen from the industrial houses along the M. K. & T. tracks had arrived at the place where a number of rapid pistol shots had been heard, they found sour-faced old Lee with a pistol, and with blood running from a gaping wound on his left hand. Anderson Bird, his brother and partner, was lying dead on the rough floor. An unsatisfactory warehouse partnership had just been dissolved. The outcome of the Bird case was a stimulus for Pruiett's already cynical attitude toward the court and jury system. The old man was not entitled to be convicted. He had been attacked by a morbid and disgruntled brother, armed with a hatchet, and the shots which he had fired to stop him had begun only after he had suffered a vicious wound from the flailing weapon. Pruiett, in Bird's defense, presented the facts just as they were, witness for witness and circumstance for circumstance. The jury found him guilty of manslaughter, on one of the minor offenses embraced in the charge, and sentenced him to four years in the penitentiary. If Bird's counsel had slumbered or coasted as he negligently relied upon the prevalence of justice to protect his client at the trial, he made up for it as he presented his motion for a new trial, after the old man had been convicted. When he had concluded a lengthy and laborious tirade, which included a denunciation of the good faith of the individual jurors and the fairness of the trial court in instructing the jury as to the law, he arose to his toes and shook a menacing fist in the face of the trial judge. "An' I give you my word of honor as a lawyer and a gentleman, that old Lee Bird will never serve one second of this infamous sentence. The court may as well set it aside right now, and give him a new trial, for the dark walls of prison will never surround this suffering old man." The court understood Pruiett's meaning. He was saying that he would keep the defendant out on bond until he had completed an appeal, that he would reverse the conviction on appeal and that he would obtain his acquittal in another trial. He was skeptical and unimpressed, however, and the motion was denied. The Criminal Court of Appeals, passing on the Bird appeal almost a year later, affirmed the conviction. Pruiett had had the news long enough to take the bottle from the desk and have the battleship jaw outthrust. It galled him to lose any kind of a case, but in this one, with his courtroom threat and promise fresh enough to be revived with the publication of the outcome of the appeal, he was doubly annoyed. He didn't leave his office until after dark, and although he had imbibed freely during the afternoon, he could still see, by the light of the corner street lamp, that considerable notice was being given to the Bird decision. He had bought a late edition of the paper. Pruiett was pondering and scowling over the outcome of the case and its relation to his violent prediction, and trying to figure some technical way to continue the fight until he could make his word good, as he stepped into the living room of his home. "The coroner just called, Moman," his wife said, without the preliminary of a greeting. "Lee Bird's dead. He shot himself in the head with a pistol, and the coroner said it was despondency over his conviction that caused him to do it. He had a copy of the paper with the story of it by his bed, when they found him. The poor old man won't have to serve the sentence, after all, will he?"

"That fellow Guy MacKenzie was the sorriest little piker I ever saw, or ever heard of," Pruiett observed, as he spat and spewed. "If he'd a-been on the veldt in the days of Kimberly he'd a got him a job on the little sand dredge, an' scraped the surface for day wages, rather than take a chance of diggin' for a fortune in the diamond cuts." The boys who had dropped in to hear some Pruiett lore, from the Stud himself, listened in quiet anticipation. "There he was, a well-driller by trade, an' the big oil strikes around Tulsa had crude runnin' over the derrick tops an' floodin' the country, but old Guy just set still. Bill Skelly, an' Frank Phillips, an' Tom Slick borrowed a little money an' put a few extra lengths of stem on their drills, an' made millions of dollars. Guy goes right on drillin' water wells for a hundred an' a half a month, an' keepin' his friends' wives company when they was out of town or away from home."

"He got life for that killin', didn't he?" one of the fans inquired.

"Yeah," Pruiett answered, "an' the lawyer that defended him did a good job. I wasn't sure 'til it was over that they wasn't goin' to fry him. I couldn't get into the case on account of the one I got to try next week, but I was watchin' it awful close. That was a' awful murder."

"Did you know old Reuter, the one that got it?" some one asked.

"He was a personal friend of mine," Pruiett said. "He was a lawyer over there at Tulsa, an' a perty good one. He'd a been a rich man if that baggage hadn't a messed him up. He was a member of the school board, an' he'd organized his own oil company. They say that he had some good holdin's, but he was too swanky to drink city water. He made his big mistake when he started to have that well drilled in his back yard. I haven't never seen a well-digger you could trust."

"What's the real facts about it, Moman? Give us the dope."

"It's just exactly like it came out in the paper while they was tryin' MacKenzie," Pruiett answered. "Reuter had a wife that was gettin' middle-aged, but she had them perpetual youth ideas in her head. They had two kids, eight an' ten years old, an' old Charley didn't want any more, so he quit work. Laura, that's the wife, had saved her figger an' didn't want to be a sedate little housewife. She wanted to play, so when old Charley'd come home an' read his paper, an' go off to bed by hisself, she opens up for the well digger. Guy wasn't no piker when it came to housewives. He'd spud into a preacher's bedroom if he got a half a chance. Laura always had a sign so Guy could tell whether Charley was at home or not. When the shade in a back window upstairs at Reuter's house was down it meant that

DENVER, COLO., MONDAY, SEPTE...

Pretty Widow on Trial for Murder
Of Husband, Victim of Conspiracy

Mrs. Laura M. Reuter.

Reuter Home, Where Charles J. Reuter Was Slain.

Mrs. Laura Reuter Faces
Charge in Oklahoma
City Court.

Sweetheart Hires Thug to
Kill Man Who Stood
in His Way.

Charles J. Reuter and Their Children, Marcella and Johnny

DENVER POST DISPLAY OF REUTER PRINCIPALS
"***that well-digger would spud into a preacher's bedroom if he got half a chance."

Charley was at home, an' when it was up it meant that he was away an' the coast was clear. Charley found out about it, an' started to kill 'em both. He got to thinkin' about the kids, an' he was really that kind of a father, an' he decides to just keep his mouth shut an' get along the best he could. They lived in a great big house out on Cheyenne Avenue, an' Charley moved all his things into a single room up near the kids' room, an' stays away from Laura altogether. They lived there like that over a year before Charley got his head shot off. It was right in that room that Joe Baker shot him. Laura let Joe in the basement window, an' as soon as he'd killed Charley she jumped out on the roof by her window an' went to yellin' an' screamin.' They wanted to make it look like robbery, an' Joe grabbed all of Charley's diamonds. That was to be part of the pay, what he got off of Charley an' out of his room, except he had to split the diamonds with Laura."

"Where did the wife come in?" one of his listeners inquired.

"She was in it all the time. Ever'body knew Laura was mamma for Guy MacKenzie. They just rounded up Guy an' his gang an' started puttin' the pressure to 'em, 'til one squawked. They had a mixed-breed named Grover Bellew, he even had some Mexican in him, besides Greek, an' Choctaw an' freedman. He puked up a tubful, an' the show was over. Guy an' Joe Baker are down at McAlester doin' life, an' Laura's out on bond. That's one case that's got me worried."

"What's your defense?"

"We just don't know anything about it. Guy hasn't squealed, nor neither has Joe Baker. It's just Bellew an' some unfavorable circumstances about the house that's against us. I got the venue changed away from Tulsa; too much prejudice after tryin' Mac-Kenzie an' Baker, so we're tryin' it up at Bartlesville. It'll be bad enough up there."

"DETECTIVES FOIL PLOT OF HIRED GUNMEN TO ASSASSINATE BELLEW," proclaimed the Tulsa World in glaring red column heads. Acting on an underworld tip which advised that the half-breed wouldn't live to repeat the testimony he had given in the MacKenzie-Baker trial at Tulsa, but that Mrs. Reuter's defense plotted to have him killed, a group of special officers out of Tulsa County made an investigation. "Detectives Ed Egan and Charles McCloud, representing the prosecuting attorney's office of Tulsa County, searched the City (Bar-

tlesville) for desperate characters. They found the trio of gunmen (Blacky Anderson, Kid Glove Harry, and Tom Jones) in
consultation in the back room of a cheap rooming house. When
confronted by the detectives the men denied that they were here
to kill Bellew, but they agreed to leave town if spared arrest."
Pruiett denounced this damn detective propaganda to be most
unfavorable where his client's interests were concerned."

"A few weeks before the murder," said Ballew, "Guy Mac-
Kenzie mentioned to me about getting Joe Baker to murder Charlie
Reuter. I told him I didn't think Joe would do it, but he said
that Joe was hard up and he could get him to do it by showing
him that he would have the protection of Mrs. Reuter. . . . That
evening Guy told me that Joe Baker was going to do the killing
for $200 and whatever he found on Charlie. He said that Joe
had been over to the Reuter home that afternoon so Mrs. Reuter
could show him the house. . . . On Saturday morning just before
the killing I saw Joe Baker and he said he had been shown through
the Reuter house from basement to the top bedroom by Mrs.
Reuter. He said he was going to do the killing that night. He
was to get $200 and what money he found on Reuter, and Mrs.
Reuter was to get the diamonds back that he took from Reuter.
Guy said that Mrs. Reuter was to give an altogether different
description of the man than Joe was. She was to say that he
was a big man. (Joe was a runt.) He said Mrs. Reuter was
to place the key on the outside of her bedroom door, go to bed,
keep quiet and then, after the shots had been fired, to scream.
Guy said that Mrs. Reuter had said she would furnish plenty of
money for lawyers to defend him if he got arrested. Guy said
that after he got Reuter out of the way, he didn't know whether
he would marry Mrs. Reuter or not. He said her little boy
looked so much like Charlie that when he grew up he would
have trouble with him. He said Mrs. Reuter was to stake him
in business after the murder, and he was going to take me to
Mexico and start a horse ranch. Guy told me what I was to do.
I was to wait in the auto for Joe, drive him north of town about
a mile, where he was to burn the clothes he had on and to change
into the ones I had in the automobile. Then we were to go back
to town and I was to ditch Joe—then go on to MacKenzie's myself and go to bed. Guy was to be in Skiatook that night so he
could prove an alibi. The night of the murder we drove around
town for awhile. Joe and I went by the Reuter home and saw
a light burning and Joe seemed a bit uneasy. We went back to

MacKenzie's and got a suitcase Joe had brought up from his room, which had some clothes in it. He put on a pair of overalls, an overcoat, a mask, cloth gloves and some old shoes. It was about 1:00 o'clock Sunday morning then. Just as Joe left the car he says to me, 'If you cold turkey on me an' I ever see you again you're a dead one.' I went over to the orchard and pretty soon I heard a whistle and there was Joe, all out of breath. He had the money and diamonds in a handkerchief. I asked him how Mrs. Reuter acted and he said, 'Fine. She was screaming with all her might when I left.' We decided to take a different route than the one agreed on, so we went to the Pease ranch. We went up a canyon and burned all the clothes Joe had on, and the mask. He put on his other clothes. Joe told me he had done the job. He said he went into the house through the basement window, locked Mrs. Reuter's door on the outside and then poked his gun in Charlie's ribs and woke him up and told him to give him his money. Charlie handed him the money and then the diamonds, one at a time. Joe told him to turn around. Then he shot him in the back of the head. He shot the second time but the bullet went wild. The third time he shot him in the head as Reuter was lying on the floor. Then he left the house and ran to meet me at the orchard."

Glenn Condon, in a special to the Tulsa World, summed up the motive and execution in a crisp paragraph. "Guy MacKenzie wanted Reuter killed so that he could satisfy his passionate love for Laura Reuter; she was no unwilling participant in the purpose. It was she who set the stage and turned down the lights for the midnight tragedy which cast an air of mystery about the home on Cheyenne Avenue. . . ." The widow who had cast herself into mourning made good on her promise to "furnish plenty of protection and stand behind" her fellow conspirators. After MacKenzie and Baker had been convicted and had been moved to the state prison at McAlester, she disguised herself and slipped in on visitor's day to talk to them, and to pat Guy's hand through the bars. "Pat Oates, deputy warden of the Oklahoma State Penitentiary, testified this afternoon that Mrs. Reuter visited Guy MacKenzie and Joe Baker in the penitentiary two months ago. She represented herself to be a Miss Gordon, a famed detective in the employ of Moman Pruiett. . . ." Pruiett assured the jury that Laura was completely innocent, in spite of a "few circumstances that might look a little funny." Things looked too funny. The jury found her guilty, and she drew next to the maximum, the henceforward in confinement, at the state Penitentiary. But it was only the beginning for Pruiett. He filed his motion for a new trial, and Judge R. H. Hudson, who had tried the case, was so confused by the time the Black Charger had argued with him for two hours, that he didn't know whether Laura had received a fair trial or not. Laura's counsel, in no uncertain terms, charged that justice had been aborted. Resolving the doubt in the accused's favor, as old Thomas Jefferson had suggested that it be done in his document on the fundamentals of liberty and justice, the trial court set the conviction aside and assigned the case for trial again. The citizenry of the south and west, and especially that of the oil metropolis on the Arkansas River's brink, pulled frantic hairs. Pruiett slipped across the state line to the resort where the springs were hot and the guests from the east were strolling the hotel veranda. He had to have a little rest before the next murder trial. Laura stood trial again, but the details of a long story can be dispensed with and a much shorter treatment of the subject substituted. She was acquitted and restored to actual liberty. Her confinement, aside from the year's figurative restraint while under bond, had amounted to a total of 48 hours in jail, in Tulsa County.

Lottie Baker shot Lusco, her husband, on a downtown street in Oklahoma City. He died before he could be conveyed to a hospital. D. V. Monroe shot Margaret Ellis in a sporting house where Margaret was eking out what is reputedly a tough livelihood by merchandising her charm and virtue. Her death ultimately resulted from the wound. Both were charged with murder, both were represented by Moman Pruiett, and both were acquitted and restored to liberty by the juries which heard the cases. Lottie was a penniless waitress; Monroe was a wealthy business man and broomcorn planter. Monroe, although he knew it not, was helping to pay Lottie Baker's fee when he gave Pruiett seven thousand and five hundred dollars. But he was not getting full credit for it, for when Lottie's case was going to the jury Pruiett told them, in his pathetic, self-sacrificing manner, that he was serving her out of the kindness of his heart, that he was receiving no compensation for his services. Pruiett reached a new high for acrimony in his argument in Lottie Baker's case. He coined invectives which shocked the members of his own whiskey-consuming entourage. "He's unfit to preside while a female canine whelps her pups." he roared, speaking of the justice of the peace who presided at Lottie's preliminary hearing, and then came as a state's witness in the district court trial, to impeach her. "She had a perfect right to kill him," he howled, referring to dead Lusco. "If American manhood won't respect and protect its womanhood, then I say, let them take up arms and protect themselves. If any man had treated my daughter as Lusco did Lottie, I'd have taken my pistol—." He crouched, with his right index finger trembling taut in front of him, like a pistol barrel. He was re-enacting the incident, or the Doctor Threldkeld shooting. "I'd have taken my pistol and I'd have shot him through the heart, and as he fell to the earth I would have placed my ear over his bloody bosom, and listened with relish and satisfaction while I heard his soul yelpin' its way into hell'!"

When he concluded he was on his hands and knees before the jury, with his head cocked sideways like a listening pup. He was holding his ear over an imaginary bosom.

"A throbbing human drama was enacted late Tuesday afternoon in a room at 700 East Fifth Street. . . . Margaret Ellis, 22, girl of the underworld, paralyzed from the waist down and given four years, at most, to live, was a white thing, hardly distinguishable from the snowy linen of the bed. She faced D. V. Monroe . . . . wealthy merchant of Lindsay, who is under charge of assault with intent to kill. Since the night of Dec. 28, when Monroe shot Margaret Ellis in a resort at 9½ West California Avenue, the two had not met. . . . The meeting was the result of the justice court's desire to get the girl's story of the shooting, on which, more than anything else, Monroe's fate hinges. On the table near the girl's bed was a small leather-bound Bible. Near it was half an orange. Above her head was a picture of Cupid, armed with his bow and arrows. Other pictures were on the wall. . . . Attorney Moman Pruiett, head counsel for the defense, and reputed to be a bulldog when a point was to be gained, asked his questions of the girl as gently as if he were a nurse. . . .

"That girl's goin' to die," Pruiett said, as he and his client left the room.

"What'll happen then?" Monroe asked.

"You get plumb relieved of this assault an' intent charge you got against you," he answered, sarcastically, "an' you got a nice little murder charge against you instead. That's all that'll happen."

"I'm countin' on you to protect my interests in this," Monroe said.

"I've already told you we ought to pay off in the damage suit the girl's filed against you. She's got a perfect cause of action against you. You shot her, an' she's hopelessly and totally disabled as the result of it. A settlement before she dies will help to make dyin' a little easier for her, an' it'll make defendin' you for murder a sight easier."

"It's a shake-down," Monroe growled. "She's sued me for ten thousand, an' look at all the expense I've been to in this thing already."

"The fiddler always charges extra when he sees a' old man like you out tryin' to hop with the young folks," Pruiett said dryly. "If you get out of it with payin' all you got, but don't have to go to the pen, you can count yourself lucky."

"What makes you so sure I'm goin' to face a murder charge? How do you know she won't live a long time, or get well?"

"I been talkin' to her doctor," Pruiett answered. "That bullet hit half of her spinal cord. She's paralyzed from the waist down, now, but there's a gradual sloughin' of the balance of the cord, an' she won't live thirty days. They thought at first it might be a matter of years, but not now. She's a goner."

"What can we settle with her for, in the damage case?"

"I know her lawyer awful well, E. J. Giddings. I've tried lots of lawsuits with him. I think I can get a release for fifty cents on the dollar.

"That's too much," Monroe grumbled.

"Would you change places with her for five thousand?" Pruiett inquired.

"No," Monroe answered. "I ain't no whore—not a he one, No!"

"You just think you are not," Pruiett snapped. "What was you doin' in that whorehouse, then?"

"I ain't payin' you all this money to be insulted," Monroe sulked. "If you don't—."

"I'll get out an' let you get some one else to represent you if you want me to," Pruiett answered. "You're the head man, but if you was able to handle all the things that are goin' to come up in this case, or able to tell your lawyer how to handle 'em, you'd be a damn fool to pay out money for a lawyer's service. Either give me some authority to do what I think ought to be done, or fire me an' let me get out of the case."

Monroe studied. "I couldn't have anybody representin' me in this kind of a mess but you," he said. "Go ahead an' settle with her; get the best deal you can for me, an' I'll back you up in it. I'm sure you know best what ought to be done."

Pruiett stood beside the stricken girl's bedside again. "I haven't got any business bein' here," he said, abruptly. "I told the landlady that it might look bad for Mr. Monroe, me comin' here to talk to you, without your lawyer here, or any of the prosecutin' attorney's men."

"She told me," the girl said, "but I wanted to talk to you, an' I told her to go back an' tell you to come."

"What do you want?" he asked.

"Just to thank you, first," she said. "Mr. Giddings told me that you made Monroe settle with me for the injuries. The money I got is goin' to make me comfortable an' help me to do some things I wanted to do, before I go."

"Don't bother about that," he answered. "You don't need to thank me. Monroe's got plenty of money."

"I want to see my mother before I die," Margarite said.

"That's natural," Pruiett said, shortly. His eye was perfectly dry. "Where is she?"

"She lives in Indiana, at Gary," the girl whispered. "She's poor; lives up there with my step-father. I'd like to go back."

"What's holdin' you?" he asked. "I got the money for you. Why don't you go ahead?"

The girl smiled. She had lived the hard way; she was worldly wise, like Pruiett. "You ain't so tough," she smiled up at him. "You don't scare me with that loud mouth of yours. You're my friend. I trust you."

"What you got in your mind for me to do?" he demanded.

"I want you to go with me—to take me," she said. "I was in Mercy Hospital at Chicago, when I was a kid. I have dreams of goin' there; that maybe they might be able to save me, but if they can't, I'll be close to home. I've got the money, but I ain't got the strength. If I had some one like you, to cheer me an' bully me, and give me courage, then I'd be able to stand the trip. That's the main reason why I sent for you."

"That wouldn't be right, child," he said. She looked like a child, pale with pain and with fear of the ordeal approaching. The hard lines of life were gone from her face. In their place was the soft gleam of death. "I couldn't do that. I'm against you in all these things. I've got to try to justify what Monroe's done to you. He's paid me. We'd both be criticized for it; they'd say that you was sellin' out on the state, an' that I was influencin' you to keep you from makin' a statement against my client."

"I don't care what they say," she sighed. "I don't have a friend in the world—."

"You got your own lawyers," he argued.

"I wouldn't have had any help at all, if it hadn't a-been for you. You're the only one that's had a kind thought for me."

"I'm busy," he argued. "I got cases set for trial all over this country. I couldn't get away from business."

"I'm just askin' you to do me this favor, this last one," she whispered. "I'd forgive Mr. Monroe if you did. I really don't have to go, I guess, but—."

Pruiett went with the dying girl. He held her hand on the Pullmans to Chicago, and he stood by her bedside while the heads of the Mercy Hospital made their deliberate examination of her. He wiped the tears that trickled down her made-up cheek when they told her that she couldn't be saved; that she must die. In the cheaply furnished room at Gary, which was her mother's home, he was holding her hand when she died.

Monroe had to stand trial for murder. Pruiett put his painful recollection of Margarite's trust and devotion behind him as he plunged into the difficult defense. He could go soft, and let a distressed dame lead him out on a mercy errand if he wanted to, but when it came to murder, the state was always wrong. Pruiett's clients were never guilty. The sordid details of the shooting, and the events which preceded them, were preserved in a statement which Margarite Ellis signed at the hospital shortly after she was admitted there. "I am conscious and aware of impending death as I make this true statement," the paper began.

"It's incompetent. It's hearsay," Pruiett shouted. "Even if she was makin' a death-bed statement, which she wasn't, she was mistaken. She wasn't dyin'; she lived almost two months after she signed this outrage that the county attorney cooked up for her. It's not a death-bed declaration." The bloody document was read to the jury. "That girl didn't have any idea of what was in that paper when she signed it," Pruiett whispered to Monroe. "They talk about me doctorin' evidence in murder cases, but if

I ever pull a trick as raw as this one, I hope lightnin' strikes me dead. I'll fudge a little for mercy, but these devils that're supposed to be public officers are tryin' to fudge you into the electric chair." They fought it out before twelve men, elated with each sordid scrap which fell from the swinging scale in the hand of the blind goddess. That statement made it bad, but there's lots of ways of gettin' around incriminatin' evidence when you're tryin' your case to a jury. "Mister Monroe was met at the depot by runners from Gracie's hell-house," he told the jurors, commenting on the evidence after the court's instruction had been read. "Gracie Goode kept a few handsome girls like Margarite Ellis. I held her hand as she died an' she was as fair as a Grecian slave, God bless her soul; and Gracie kept a lot of illicit liquor. This evidence shows that through the wiles of this beautiful girl, Monroe was persuaded to get drunk. When they thought he was drunk enough to be rolled—for them to get his pocket book and all his money— Gracie came into the room, helped Margarite with that little job, an' was sneakin' out the door with it, when Monroe caught onto what was goin' on. He grabbed his pistol an' called for Gracie to halt. She kept runnin', an' he aimed at her legs to stop her, an' fired. Margarite screamed and stumbled into the line of fire, so that she received the bullet in her back which killed her." He paused and scratched his head in honest contemplation of the situation. "The court, in his instructions, told you what murder was. This is not murder; this is an accident, a wholly unavoidable accident, which, except for the related circumstances which cause clean minds to become prejudiced, would never be considered with the crime of murder. If he'd a hit Gracie, as he intended to hit her, it might have been murder. But he was stuck on Margarite— in his drunken state he held her in the tenderest esteem—and he would never have harmed her. So he had no intent, no premeditation, which the court tells you was necessary before the crime of murder can be complete. Can you agree, beyond all reasonable doubt—?" He launched into his highly developed analysis of reasonable doubt. He lashed them with logic. He captivated them with his eloquence, his gestures, and his pathos. Monroe was acquitted, and he went back to the country, sadder and wiser, and poorer by twenty-five thousand dollars. The victory celebration was in full swing. The drinks were on the Black Stud, and he was having plenty of drinks himself. "Now that it's all over," one of the boys suggested, "tell us why the hell Monroe wanted to kill a little doll like Margarite. I've heard all kinds of theories.

but none of 'em, not even the one you argued to the jury, sounds
right to me. What did he want to do it for?"

"You'll laugh your head off," Pruiett grinned. "A few of
his kind would make hustlin' a damn precarious occupation, now,
wouldn't it?" Pruiett inquired, innocently. A lusty whoop went
up around the table.

Mrs. Doctor Mehl, representing a committee of club women
of Oklahoma City, in a taxi cab, drove out to Pruiett's farm, and
appealed to him to defend Lottie Baker for the killing of her
husband, Lusco Baker, representing that they would raise for
him $500 to defend her. Pruiett reluctantly agreed to take the
case. He had one hour and 15 minutes to get into town from
his farm, which was nine miles at least. He changed clothes,
and when he arrived at the justice court, the justice announced
he had been waiting on him a half of an hour, and immediately
proceeded with the preliminary trial.

The defense of Lottie Baker had a catchy twist to it. Pruiett
threw the unwritten law into reverse, and using it as a background for a thin plea of self-defense, screamed Scriptures like a
traveling Holiness preacher, and won his case. Lottie was a
hard-working hasher. Lusco, the deceased, was a shiftless pimp
who offered to sell magazines for a blind. Agnes Smith, a police
court prostitute, who carried the alias of Dirty Breeches, held
down the pivot position in the triangle. Lottie killed Lusco because she caught him with Agnes. Agnes was the principal witness for the state. She was on the stand, and Pruiett was cross-
examining. "You say your name is Agnes Smith?" he inquired.

"Yes, sir," Agnes answered, meekly. She knew what was
coming. "You are generally known, about the police station, and
on California Street, as Dirty Breeches, are you not?"

"We object," the prosecuting attorney howled.

"What's the purpose of that line of examination?" the court
demanded.

"It would go to her credibility as a witness," Pruiett said.

"Overruled," said the court. "Go ahead an' answer."

"They call me that, but I don't like it, Agnes retorted, "an'
it ain't so."

"All right. You say it ain't so," Pruiett repeated, agreeable, as he turned to note the good-humored grins on the jurors'
faces. "Now you admit that you were in Lottie's room with
Lusco on the day of this fatal occurrence, don't you?"

Mrs. Lottie Baker, (above) shot and killed her husband, Lusco W. Baker, (below) at 7 P. m., Sunday, March 16, while church bells were ringing for evening worship.

One shot was fired, and the man fell dead at the alley entrance on N. Harvey st., between Main and Grand av.

Brandishing her pistol, Mrs. Baker is alleged to have forced Agnes Smith, the girl with Baker, to go to the police station where the gun was surrendered and the story told.

LOTTIE BAKER AND POOR DEAD LUSCO
"Pruiett threw the unwritten law in reverse, and screamed Scriptures like a Holiness preacher."

"Just like I said," Agnes answered. "I went up there to sign a contract to sell magazines for Lusco. We was there just a few minutes, an' we left to go up town an' have a notary stamp it."

"Going to have it stamped Sunday afternoon?"

"Yes."

"You mean you was there just a few minutes an' Lottie came in unexpectedly, an' you had to leave?"

"We was leavin' anyway," Agnes said. "Lusco took his magazines an' we started up town."

"Lottie asked him to stay there with her, didn't she?"

"She told him to, but he said he had to get his work done. He went out anyway."

"You went with him?"

"Yes, I went with him."

"An' Lottie followed you, didn't she?"

"Yes, she tagged right along behind us, cussin' me an' Lusco, an' threatenin' to kill us both. All I was tryin' to do was to get away from her."

"You've been layin' up with Lusco for a long time, haven't you?"

"I have not," Agnes answered, with feeling.

"You knew Lusco was a knife man, didn't you?"

"I knew he carried a knife, but I didn't know he was a knife man."

"Didn't you know he cut a playmate to death, when he was a kid, up at Paris, Illinois?"

"We object," the county attorney cried, bouncing out of his chair.

"Sustained," droned the court.

"I'll make my proof on it," Pruiett promised. "Did you know he cut a policeman to ribbons with a knife, up at Terre Haute, Indiana?"

"We object," the prosecution howled again.

"Sustained," said the court.

"I know what I'm doin'," Pruiett said, serenely. "Did you know that he was tried an' convicted of rape up at Terre Haute?"

"You'll have to offer that proof in the proper manner, if you've got it, Mr. Pruiett," the court interrupted, ahead of another objection.

"All right, your honor," Pruiett grinned. "I just thought

one time was as good as another for that kind of information.
Now look here, Dirty—I mean Agnes. When you got up there
about a block from the police station, Lusco turned on Lottie
an' told her to go back, didn't he?"

"Maybe he did," Agnes agreed, "he'd been tellin' her to
go back ever since we left the roomin' house."

"An' he started to pull out this long bladed knife he always
carried, didn't he?"

"He certainly did not," Agnes answered, indignantly. "Lottie
had been still for a minute, an' I thought maybe she had decided
to let us alone. Then I happened to glance back an' I saw her
close behind Lusco, with the pistol out. She shot him right in
the back of the head, an' he didn't know she was near to him."

"How many prostitution charges against you have the police
promised to dismiss for tellin' such a story?"

"Not any of 'em," Agnes came right back.

"Then they have got a few over you, haven't they?" Pruiett
grinned.

"Not very many," Dirty Breeches sulked.

The state offered the blood-spattered magazines, cheap pulps,
which Lusco had been carrying when Lottie assassinated him.
Household Magazine, with a red hen and a bunch of yellow
chicks on its front cover, was amongst the lot. Pruiett picked it
up and studied it. "Was this magazine in the bunch?" he demanded of Agnes?

"It was," she answered.

"It's a' old hen, lookin' after her brood, her little family,
isn't it?"

"That's what it looks like to me," Agnes agreed.

"Lottie was just tryin' to protect her husband from you,
wasn't she? Tryin' to get him away from you?"

"We object," the prosecutor cried.

"I'll withdraw the question," Pruiett said. "That's all of this
witness."

Pruiett produced an elaborate free defense for Lottie. He
brought the testimony of Captain Van Cleave, and Matron Catherine O'Donnel, to establish that departed Lusco had an unsavory
reputation at Terre Haute. It still stunk, on warm nights, up the
brick alleys of the old town. He proved that he'd raped a girl
and been convicted for it, that he'd carved an Indiana policeman
to shreds, and had killed a childhood playmate with a knife.

Was Lottie entitled to carry a gun, to protect her life, when she had business with Lusco? "Lusco got just what was comin' to him," Pruiett screamed at his jury. "He was a knife man. He dug his own grave with his own knife. There was poor, long-suffering Lottie, trying to hold her meager happiness, trying to keep her little home together," he whispered. He grabbed the Household Magazine and shook it, hen and chicks and all, in the jury's face. "O Jerusalem, Jerusalem, which killest the prophets and stoneth them that are sent unto thee;" he cried, plucking a passage from St. Luke from his unyielding memory, "how often would I have gathered thy children together, as a hen doth gather her brood under her wings, and ye would not!" He paused to mop his perspiring forehead. "And ye would not; and ye would not," he ruminated. "'Go away, Dirty Breeches, and let my husband alone,' Lottie begged, but she would not. She would not. 'Come home, with me Lusco! Abandon this whore and come back home with me!' But he would not. He would not. 'I'll take you back, Lusco, rotten and debased as you are, for you're all I've got an' you're mine; I'll gather you under my wing like a hen doth gather her brood and I'll work and slave for you,'— but ye would not; ye would not." He wheeled on Agnes, who was sitting with the spectators in the crowded courtroom. "The harlot looked from the casement of her window and discerned the weary youth, and she sought him; come, come to me, my bed is perfumed with aloes." He shook his fist at Dirty Breeches. "And the weary youth went straight like an ox to the slaughter." Pruiett's argument for Lottie Baker's acquittal lasted three hours and a half. Lottie was paying him nothing, so he received no more for his effort than he would have received for a five minute observation, except the victory.

Oral Argument of Moman Pruiett, Defense Attorney, to the Jury.
(Court Reporter's Notes)
Friday, June 13th, 1919, at 5:10 o'clock P. M.
———oOo———
By Court: Closing argument on behalf of the defendant.
———oOo———
By Mr. Pruiett: Your Honor please: Much has been said by the worthy county attorney, who is my personal and intimate friend, as to what Your Honor has done in the discharge of your duty. Much has been said as to what the sheriff has done in the discharge of his duty; and, much has been said as to what the

county attorney and his assistants have done in the discharge of their duty, in the preparation and prosecution of this woman.

Your Honor please: Before I go to the jury, I feel that I should say to the court and direct my remarks personally to you. I have known you a long time but this is the first, I think, I have ever had the pleasure of trying a case before you and I want to say, in good conscience, that, in my judgment—so far as Your Honor has the administration of justice—the rights of the defendant will always be protected and the laws of this state vindicated. I may differ with Your Honor as to what the law is and if Your Honor makes any mistakes, I know that it's not intentional; I know that you have tried, and made an honest endeavor to give this woman a fair trial.

You—Gentlemen of the Jury—you will not get from me any words of abuse. It is true that in my zeal, I may indulge in some criticism, and how well I know that if I do indulge and make criticism of an officer, or a witness, unless I am justified in that criticism, I know what the reaction will be with you twelve men. I am not going to try to be anything else in this case except human. And, in the selection of you twelve triers, I tried to select men who would be human. I tried, in behalf of this woman, to select men who carried their consciences and their hearts into the jury box. I tried to select men, as you said you would do and as you promised the county attorney you would do, that when it comes to the administration of justice, you would measure the testimony in this case by the same standards of justice you would if it was a man upon trial. That was proper. That was manly, manly answer for you to make, but, when you made that answer, it did not mean that you should disrobe yourself of all your human experience as to the characteristics of womanhood and place womanhood's characteristics upon the same plane that you would place man's characteristics. It did not mean, when you made the answers to the county attorney that you would try her as a calloused man; that you would disregard your human experiences and forget that one act that might move woman to action might never move man to action. The county attorney has referred, in this case, to the celebrated Thaw case; but, of all the millions of the hoarded gold that was behind him and where the plea of insanity was the defense; thank God, in this case, there is no hoarded gold; thank God in this case, there sits before you a common waitress, a common domestic, a common servant, and I am thankful of the fact that the testimony in this case shows that there is a paltry sum of three hundred and eighty-five dollars of money paid to a lawyer; to the lawyer, these criminal lawyers, that my friend Burns speaks of, who resort to tactics and whom he insults—me—his friend, by saying that it was upon my advice that she made certain statements. Men of manhood and men of Oklahoma County, you must stand behind the girls—the girlhood—here for the state and stand by it throughout the state.

I am here to defend this woman. Why? Because my mother was a woman and because she appealed to me in the darkest hour of her trial and if some man who is unfortunate enough to commit crime and is wealthy enough to pay the fee, I state to you upon my word of honor and my manhood, he shall pay the fee of this waitress, if he gets my services. That has been my pleasure for the last twenty years. This woman has a righteous cause. In the impaneling of you, Gentleman, I asked you certain questions: That if a defense was honestly presented to you and in good faith presented to you, would you consider it? You said: Yes. I—unlike my distinguished friend, if Your Honor please, Mr. Burns—I have faith in the manhood and integrity of this jury. I waived five of my challenges in the selection of this jury. Why? Your Honor, I thought it was unnecessary for me, like my distinguished friend, Mr. Burns, to stand before you for an hour and deliver a dissertation upon the duty of jurors. Why plead and beg with you? Why inject his personality into the jury box? If Your Honor please, he stood here and he said to this jury: "I am your county attorney and when I investigate a case and when I file the informations and when I and my assistants have done what we have done, then I have a right to demand, at your hands, as your county attorney." If Your Honor please, I say here and now, that I am just as much an officer of your court as Mr. Burns is and so long as my conduct is manly, so long as my conduct in this case is that of a reputable lawyer, Mr. Burns has no greater right to your consideration than I. We are all officers of the court. Just a few little rubbish and stuff before I go to the main facts in this case.

I want to say this to Your Honor: I don't know why Mr. Burns made the statement. Here, day before yesterday, I believe it was—I don't remember now whether the jury was present or not, or out—but, sometimes, lawyers give vent to statements that are misconstrued by jurors and by spectators. I cited the Litchfield case and Mr. Guyer made the remark that he

was in the Litchfield case and I says: "Yes, you got out of it."
Some of my friends on the outside wanted to know if that was
true and misconstrued my statement. I had reference to the
legal phase of that decision. I meant no reflections upon Mr.
Guyer when I made that statement. In view of the fact that two
or three misconstrued the statement, I tell it distinctly. I think
it's my duty to make this statement in open court instead of going
to him in private. So far as the conduct of the county attorney's
office or any of his assistants is concerned and so far as any
abuse is concerned, there will be no criticism come from my lips
except that criticism that is justly due them by virtue of their
conduct in front of you, Gentlemen.

Now let's see. What have we in this case? We have a woman
as a defendant. A woman who lived between the human mountain tops of what? Of love and fear and joy. Why, there came
a time when love almost melted away, particularly, after her
marriage with this man. Then what? Then came the destruction
or the attempted destruction of the virtue of her niece. Patience
then ceased to be a virtue. Love was struggling; love was beating
to the earth. Then it was that she exercised her rights as a
human being and what did she do, Gentlemen? Follow me a little
while and let us discuss this woman's history: Without a father
since she was two years old; just simply a human, painted upon
life's desert, tossed here and there. Her environments were such
that labor had to be the sequel of her success in life. Labor
meant to her a living. Marriage, and the cheery voice of a child,
the cradling, the desertion; the green-eyed monster of intoxication
made its appearance and with its forked tongue drove away
from her the first one. But, what kind of a woman is she? She
nestled in her bosom her first and new-born babe and from that
hour he is with her up until this crucial period. What has been
her history? Has it been like the history of Agnes Smith, the
police court character who's known as "Dirty Breeches"? No. Her
life history is that of a hard working girl. In all this record,
you may search, and, wherever you find Lottie Baker, you find her
laboring for him; you find her laboring for her child; you find
her laboring for her niece. And, Men of Oklahoma County, let me
say to you, when you go to your jury room, you find her laboring for whom? As she said, if Your Honor please, from the
witness stand: "Poor old mother; poor old mother." Who? The
mother of Lusco Baker, we find her sending back to Indiana—
it was only the common waitress's mite—it was only four dollars

Why, Mr. Burns, you talk to me about—because the time has arrived in this country, because politicians and statesmen have elected to give womanhood equal rights with men, you tell me, never shall the time come when womanhood will ever be placed upon the level and calloused plane of men. Why, Men of Manhood in the Jury Box, ever since the gray of creation's dawn drove back the flood of darkness, man has been fighting for the honor and virtue of womanhood. While I talk to you, now, for fourteen long years—up until two years ago—there sat in this court room an old, gray haired father and an old mother of Moman Pruiett to listen to every, every word he would say to the juries of his country and I would rather had them here than to have received the applause of all the men of Oklahoma or all of the women and I had my thought in this case, I stand here while I talk to you, I have not forgotten that this is a woman on trial. And I have not forgotten that the spirit of my mother, who is gone, is with me now and will ever be when I stand before twelve men presenting a cause for a woman like this. And then, they say, that you should forget that she is a woman. What are the facts?

Mr. Burns went back to Indiana; he went back there and took those depositions and Mr. Burns, let me hurriedly say back to him, when he said to the jury: You didn't know what an Indiana jury would have done. Bob, you fibbed, because, when we—you and I—were there, you learned what an Indiana jury would have done. I say that with all due respect and hand it back to Mr. Burns, as some times lawyers for the prosecution resort to tactics in order to win a case. Lusco Baker, in the city of Terre Haute, the police show there what they would do with a jury. Mr. Burns, since you have dropped it into this case; since you have directed the attention of these twelve triers of this woman to the public—I regret that he did that—he said to you that you could turn her loose if you wanted to and that you could say to the public, and that you could say to the women of Oklahoma and say to the citizenship of this county, that you had turned her loose. I say to you, Mr. Brns, if left to ninety-nine out of every hundred within the sound of my voice or who have read of this woman's awful, awful trials and tribulations, the verdict is already written, Mr. Burns; so far as the public is concerned, Mr. County Attorney. Mr. Burns had no right to do that, but since he did it, I am replying to him in kind.

Well, he spent about an hour and a half or a quarter, as he

said, on the defense of insanity, trying to convince you that this woman was not insane, and this court, is an illustration. Now, let's see: What is capable of driving a man or woman insane? What is necessary? Let me illustrate to you. Then I am going to show you, if I can, Gentlemen, in my feeble way, in analyzing this testimony that she didn't kill Lusco Baker because she was jealous of Agnes Smith; I am going to analyze this testimony; you may get tired but it's my duty to do it and I must do it.

Now, let's go back. First, let's see. Let's take Captain Van Cleave of the Terre Haute police force. Let's take Mrs. Catherine O'Donnell. Now, listen just a minute: Now, what was his reputation there in Terre Haute for being a bad and dangerous, violent and turbulent character? Bad. But, what else? Did he have a reputation, Captain Van Cleave, or did he have a reputation, Mrs. Catherine O'Donnell—that jail matron and an officer there for seventeen years—for any special line? Yes, what was it? A knife man. A knife man. Now, let's drop over from here just a minute and then go to Jack Gleason where he had his knife with a long blade, and then let me direct your attention to Frank Harrah, whose testimony is that he saw the knife with the long blade. A knife man in Terre Haute; had his knife here in Oklahoma City, but let's not stop there and it is undisputed; the testimony is— and it's undisputed—he killed a boy, when he was a boy, with a knife. A knife man, a criminal, a killer almost from youth. What else? Cut a policeman, and here is a certified copy of the record here and I will read it to you here before I get through; and a certified copy of his rape and I will read that to you before I get through; cut a policeman all to pieces; cut two other men; cut another man; cut a girl, Mrs. Terrell. Who knew of that? Who knew of that? Mrs. Baker. Mrs. Baker. But, after the rape, notwithstanding, but after the attempted assault upon this girl or the assaults; no married relationship from then on; but, what? A constant chain of assaults, a constant stream of abuses; not only her but her mother assaulted. What manner of man does Mr. Burns think you Gentlemen of the Jury are, by standing here and apologizing to you for prosecuting this woman? Why, he is not to be criticised; that's his duty. He is just seeking to explain to you he was just doing the best he could and he knew, in his own heart, and felt like he should not do it, but he give the impression to you he has got to do his duty while he is county attorney. Now, that's the honest truth; that's what his argument was. Now, that's all of that. All right. Finally, the

assaults in Paris, Illinois, became unbearable and what did she
do? She left Illinois and cast her lot in different fields. But, no,
there was no peace for Lottie Baker; there was no pillow upon
which she could lay her head in peace while the man Lusco
Baker, the knife man, lived. He died as many men die; some
dig their graves by pistols and some dig their graves with their
knives. But, the love of a woman's heart is peculiar, a part of
that peculiar piece of human mechanism. A woman's heart is
something that no man or no power has ever yet been able to
solve. And she wended her way to Oklahoma, into strange lands,
in order that she might enjoy some peace; away from that fear
and doubt, and torn away from that mountain of love that she
had on one occasion, but it seems as though there was something
left upon that little fabric; something left in that heart that
moved her on the first occasion, the belief that he would make
her a kind and loving husband, there was a little something left
there, and then, after she loved that little Harry. In the Van Swan
Room, who comes upon the scene? "Don't run; I'm here. You
can't get away from me now. I love you and I will follow you
to the end of the earth." Gentlemen: Do you understand womanhood? Do you know that a woman loves to have caresses? You
know that a woman loves to have her husband or her sweetheart
to say something kind to her? It don't make any difference
whether it's about love or whether it's about her household
duties or whether it's about her cooking; it may be about the pie
that she is baking; it may be about the cake she has baked; it
may be about the steak she is broiling; she loves to have some one
to say or appreciate and say something nice to her. I wish to
God that I really understood a woman's heart. And so it was
when Lusco Baker appeared upon the scene and said to Lottie
Baker: "Don't run, now; I love you and I will follow you to the
end of the world; you are going to live with me or die." Seems
as though there was something left, a little spark. Is she to be
condemned for it? Is she to be condemned if that spark was
still left there and Lusco Baker, by his mechanism, by his appeals,
fanned that spark into a blaze and caused it to blaze anew? Is
she to be condemned, if Your Honor please, because Lusco Baker
followed her here and fanned that spark? No. What does she
say?" In tears, she tells you: "I was out here in a strange place;
no one knew anything about our troubles and I loved him and
I feared him." Living between love and fear. She listened to
the appeal, and, to use her own language, she says: "I wanted

to give him another chance." Is she to be condemned for giving him another chance? Is she to have a jury to render a compromise verdict that would give her even one day in the county jail? No, men of manhood, don't do that; she doesn't deserve it. She gave him a chance. Yes, but they say that Lusco Baker was in a legitimate line of business; they say that he was working and actuated and moved by honest purposes and that his conduct should receive consideration at the hands of you twelve triers. The testimony in this case even, not only from her testimony here but from the letter that the poor woman wrote to Lusco Baker's sister: "I have tried to get him to do right." The statement was made to the newspaper reporters there: "I tried to get him to do right; I begged, I persuaded with him. I plead with him to do right; I tried to get him to leave this woman alone; I tried to keep him from spending the money that I gave him, on other women, going to the shows and the restaurants and he wouldn't do it." Finally, Jack Gleason says when he spoke about having a date and that the rain interfered with him, that he had a date with a "Jane" to go to the park and Gleason replies and says: "You have got a room; why don't you take a chance?" "I believe I will take the chance." The wife begging and pleading with him. Your honor, I wished I had John Howard Payne's "Peace" here, to read to this jury. This magazine—Your Honor, and you, Gentlemen of the Jury—introduced in evidence, reads like this: "The best stories you ever read. The Household. The Household." And on the front of this magazine is a picture of a little boy, not quite so large as little Harry, and an old hen and her brood. The testimony in this case shows, if Your Honor please, that Lottie Baker time and time again had begged and pled and so it is, as it is in the Book of all books; I may not quote it correctly but it's something like this: "Oh, Jerusalem, Jerusalem, Jerusalem! How oft would I gather up to Thy wings as a hen doth gather her brood and Ye would not; and Ye would not." So it is in this case. How oft, how oft has this woman begged this man; how oft has she pled with him, and he would not. Then, finally, when the cord of reason is snapped and on that occasion when he carried the harlot "Dirty Breeches" to the room, to the bed, that she toiled and toiled for the money in order to pay for a bed to sleep in; when he carried this harlot, this strumpet, to that room, what did he do? He set the brain on fire; he put Hell into her brain and mind and you may as well try to stop the waves of the sea as to have stopped Lottie Baker from following Lusco Baker. Here is a man—let's put him as a man—take any man in the audience and let him go home and find his wife with another man. By the eternal Gods, the woman in this case was as much entitled to and she be guaranteed, if Your Honor please, the right of the protection of the home as well as the man. Suppose a man goes to his home and finds another man in company with his wife or in there and just before they get in the door, she says—as his wife nudged the man—"There he is now." What did he do? He sets the brain on fire; in view of all the other transactions. Is it madness? Is it anger? No. No. With the pulse, and heart throbbing and beating as fast; as fast as electricity could turn the wheels of any machinery, the heart begins to throb, the bosom heaves, the brain is on fire, 'ust the moment the nudge. So it would be with a man. And the man says: "Who is this gentleman?" And she says: "It's none of your damn business." Sunday. They start out; and the husband says: "Can't I go along? Can't I go along?" She says: "No." Suppose the man didn't do anything but just even acquiesce in going, in going with the man's wife. You tell me that's not enough to dethrone a man's reason and he shoots the man to death without any overt act or anything else? The jury wouldn't be out ten minutes because, Gentlemen, the destruction of the family ties, the interference of the home, there is nothing on earth that dethrones reason like that; nothing in the world that dethrones the reason like the interference of your home. The same applies to woman, only a thousand fold stronger because a woman is so constituted and of that tender sex, they haven't the control—they haven't the will power—to control their impulses and their reasoning power, like men.

Your Honor: I have been talking, now, how long; an hour?

By Court: Fifty minutes.

By Mr. Pruiett: I would like to adjourn and finish after supper in a short time.

By Court: All right. We will take an adjournment, Gentlemen, until eight o'clock; during your absence from the courtroom, you will remember the admonition given you heretofore and go with the bailiff.

Note by Reporter: At 6:00 o'clock P. M., Court in recess until 8:00 o'clock P. M.

Friday, June 13th, 1919, at 8:00 o'clock P. M.

By Court (to Reporter): Let the record show the jurors are all present and the defendant is present. Proceed, Mr. Pruiett, with your argument.

——oOo——

By Mr. Pruiett: Gentlemen of the Jury: The last thing I believe I was discussing with you before supper was that women did not have the same will power, they are not so constituted to resist wrong done to them, like men. A woman, when once wronged, grieves over her wrong a thousand fold more than man. Now, why do I say this to you, Gentlemen? It's because Mr. Burns has said to you that he wants you to try her as you would a man. I want you, after you reach a conscientious conclusion so far as the administration of justice, in the administration of justice, to deal with her upon the same plane you would a man if you find her guilty, but you cannot disrobe yourselves and try her with all the woman's characteristics like you would a man. Why, I might say something to you or to you, Mr. Koontz (indicating juror), in the ordinary daily affairs of life and you might pass it over, yet, you might go home and say to your wife— the bosom companion of man that you had led to the altar and there took a marriage vow—she might pass it by like you; it would wound her feelings, it would hurt her, though, but you could pet her a little bit and say: "I am sorry," and she would forget it, for that one offense; but, suppose the next week, there comes another assault and there is the bruised cheek; that's the second time, and what is the testimony in this case? The entire history of this defendant is that this woman has borne her sorrows, has borne her abuse and humiliation and kept all of her troubles locked within her bosom. And when my hoary haired friend here (indicating Mr. Guyer) with his years of ingenuity and bull dog tenacity, for seven long hours kept this woman (indicating defendant) upon that witness stand, goading her minute after minute and hour after hour, there fell from the lips of this Tennessee daughter, what? Did you tell Mrs. Merkle? No. Did you tell the old man when he saw your eyes blackened back there in Paris, Illinois? Yes. Why didn't you tell Mrs. Merkle? I was ashamed. The only time the world ever knew of this woman's sorrow and the burden of her abuse was when this dead brute, this dead libertine, in open violation of law was apprehended by the officers of the law in Terre Haute, Indiana, as he pulled his murderous dagger that had sent one man to his grave; that had cut a policeman to pieces; that had cut two men to pieces.

and had this murderous dagger that had left the scars upon
the breast of another woman, was, when the officers of the law at
Terre Haute came to her rescue; then, it was, that it was made
public. Why am I discussing this with you? Not as my distinguished friend, the county attorney, says, that the court permitted it to go to you for the purpose of showing the mental
attitude of the defendant. First, if Your Honor please, I am addressing my remarks to you and the jury at the same time; you
admitted it for this purpose, to show whether or not the deceased was the probable aggressor at the time the fatal shot was
fired or what this defendant had the right to expect when the
fatal shot was fired and when this demonstration was made. And
before I am through, I will read the words of the court. And,
I say to you, this court's charge goes to this woman in her
darkest hour as the sweetest message she ever received in all
her life, and to the message, the dying words of Lusco Baker
comes now like a message from death and says to you: Apply
the court's charge to the evidence in this case and then say,
in good conscience, whether or not Lottie Baker shall suffer one
moment further punishment on account of the brutal acts and the
conduct of this libertine who now sleeps the sleep, and I for one,
pray that it be a sleep of peace. Is there anything to my argument? Am I appealing to your intelligence as I approach the
scene in this final tragedy which means life or death to Lottie
Baker? Do I approach it with fear or do I approach it with
confidence? Men of Oklahoma County, I say to you as an officer
of this court, I approach it with confidence; I approach the scene
of the tragedy when the fatal shot was fired with all the confidence that is within my being when I say to you that I stand
upon the testimony of that youthful boy, that horny-handed son
of toil, Kenneth Braugh, and he looked to me like a boy that
was intended for the life he espouses, because he came in contact
with the shadow of this harlot, Agnes Smith, when he said he
knew Agnes Smith, if Your Honor please, it carried me back
to that good Book once more where, over there in Proverbs, it
says: "The harlot looked from the casement of her window and
discerned the weary youth, she sought him; come, come to me;
my bed is perfumed with aloes, come, and the weary youth went
straight like an ox to the slaughter"; and so it was that Agnes
Smith had formed and made the acquaintance of this poor boy,
Kenneth Braugh; she knew Braugh and the other little fellow;
such women as she make the pitfalls for the youth of this

country; she makes killing possible because when such women as she invade the home, though the home be an humble one and though it be a common room in a common rooming house and though it be but a hard working waitress—Lottie, it was your home—and when this man Baker as he said to Gleason: "Took a chance." Let's see, Mr. Guyer, don't you tell this jury when you close this case that Lottie Baker killed Lusco Baker on account of jealousy. She didn't do that. Jealousy toils in the room, fired the brain and moved Lottie Baker to action. Jealousy toils in the room and all the powers of hell or heaven—a storm could not have been prevented, neither thunder, lightning, rain or storm—she would have wended her way and followed her husband on that afternoon so long as she saw that he was with her; no power on earth could have stopped or deterred her from following him. She had a right to follow him, Your Honor please. She had as much right as the wife of this libertine to follow him as the most fashionable society belle in Oklahoma City had a right to follow her husband with a harlot. She had a right to follow.

He nudged; he nudged her. Oh, My God! You place yourselves there. What am I asking of you men? Have you daughters? I have forgotten whether you have or not. I have one. I have one and my good friend who is to follow me has one; a lovely, beautiful family. John Guyer: If a man lived who was a husband of your daughter or mine and they had suffered abuses or assaults or beatings or floggings or of the taking of their money from their labor, especially spending it with harlots and going to shows and indulging in the things that he did, you and I would be driven crazy, we would have shot them to death and we, as he fell to earth, would have listened to his soul as it yelped its way into hell. Why, our reason would have been dethroned. Yes, sir, and there would be no rest nor peace until the object of destruction had been destroyed; and so it was, like Charlie White said: She was nervous, she would forget her orders, she would drop her dishes; it seemed like a great burden, a load, was upon her and after she got out of jail, the most beautiful, the most beautiful illustration of an abnormal mind I ever heard detailed in a courtroom. Why? Why? The object of her destruction, the object that had placed the burden, the object that had affected her mind, that incapacitated her, destroyed thought, destroyed happiness, destroyed everything, it was gone, it was dead; the burden was lifted. What else?

Yes. "I thought," with that same love, a spark of it left, "I thought I would give him another chance and I did; I did give him another chance."

What else? Then, just a short time before the killing. Poor little Florence Frailey: Virtue. The most priceless jewel that God could bestow upon a human body; Virtue. Virtue. Marked for life to wend her way through this world. Virtue. How did that affect her, when once aroused. Yes, and little Florence, her niece, that she had clothed as best she could, kept clothed, gave her pin money—spending money—spending money and bought her shoes, bought her her winter coat and came out here and then, he accosts her, little Florence; this libertine, this destroyer of virtue: "You damn little bitch"—with apologies to the ladies present—"You damn little bitch, if you ever tell what happened back in Indiana, I'll kill you and your Aunt Lottie both." Why? Oh, yes, he was plowing his trail; he was riding. Your Honor please, the black horse; he didn't know it; he was in a strange land; he was associating with virtuous girls; he was associationg with debauched girls. Yes, just as I told you before noon here. Why, it is: "The Household." That's one of his magazines. Yes. How oft! How oft! Would I have gathered; "Oh, Jerusalem! Jerusalem! How oft would I have gathered ye as a hen doth gather her brood and ye would not; and ye would not. How oft, How oft had this woman begged and plead with him and yet, he would not. It seems like that God has placed this magazine in this case. This magazine; the magazine like that: "The Household", in the hands of a libertine. Am I right about that? Am I too harsh? Am I stepping beyond my bounds? Am I taking the advantage of the position that I occupy as an honest lawyer when I say that? No. Why? Because there comes from the lips of that state's witness, Mr. Blackwell—and they introduced these magazines in this case—for the purpose of what? To mislead you (indicating the jury). Now, is that; is that going too far? Am I too cruel in the statement? Mr. Bartell, they put those magazines here to make you believe that this man was in a legitimate line of business (addressing an individual juror). Now, let's see if he was. Let's analyze this testimony; let's see if he was in a legitimate line of business, if that was his purpose on Sunday afternoon. Mr. Everest. Now listen to what Mr. Blackwell tells you. Where is your letter, Witt Badgett? If the prosecution in this case is sincere, if you have a just cause, when you get off this jury—whatever your verdict may be—Mr. Koontz, you go to Witt Badgett's and say: "Witt, did you know Agnes Smith?" Don't make any difference, now, whether you convict this woman or not or turn her loose, whatever your judgment be; if Witt tells you that he never heard tell of the harlot, come to me and I will write a letter and let the press publish it that I am the biggest liar that ever lived. Witt Badgett. It says, four business men. He came up those stairs and he nudged his concubine and he says: "There she is."

Another thing: I believe Mr. Sniggs discussed it with you, but I want to call your attention to it: Who was the closest human being to Lusco Baker and Lottie Baker when this fatal shot was fired? Agnes Smith. Agnes Smith. Gentlemen: I am by witnesses like I am by jurors. In all my experience, no bootlegger, no gambler, no thug or no thief ever sat upon a jury where Moman Pruiett appeared, either for the defense or prosecution, when I knew it. I want the best manhood the country produces and then I know that I will get a fair trial. And I am not a good man by any sense; I wish I was a better man than I am; but my experience has taught me that it doesn't help me to come even into contact with the very society of bad men. Now, he (indicating Mr. Guyer) will answer me. This is what you (indicating Mr. Guyer) will say, now: "Well, Pruiett had her on the stand." I wanted you (indicating the jury) to look at her for one purpose; I wanted you to see her face. I told you that we would prove that she had the reputation of being known as "Dirty Breeches." That was proven by an officer that Mr. Guyer put on the stand, himself; that was her nick name; and then, you, I believe Mr. Juror (indicating juror, Mr. Schroeffler), asked the question: "What hour of the night was it or what hour?" and Mr. Fields, the plain clothes officer, said, at the time he took her in charge down here but I may be wrong about that, taking her in charge, but questioned her, I think, was the language.

By Mr. Guyer: Go ahead.

By Mr. Pruiett: At about one o'clock in the front of the Terminal Station. "One o'clock," says one of the jurors, "day or night?" One o'clock in the morning. That's all right. Now, I did not propose to stand sponsor for anything she might say except this: I wanted an acknowledgment out of her—I am just as frank as I can be with you—that she was the woman that was there in the room that evening. Then, I wanted an expression of whether or not that was her baby's picture or if she had had any picture made of the baby. She answered: "No", and said her baby was in Tulsa. Of course, in this application the way Baker wrote it down—the poor fellow, it was his last writing; it was the last time, probably, he ever used a pencil in order to pave the way in order to satisfy his hellish lust—and then you, my friend Guyer, with your magazines and your application, and I had to threaten you with a duces tecum or whatever that Latin business is, to get you to bring it in and you never did pay any attention to me; you would pay some attention to me after you got that. And then, finally, you—after squirming and twisting like you had some oil of mustard in your seat—you brought it in and stuck it in, yourself, after I made you do it. I made you do it. Now, is that criticism? Is that irony?

Note by Reporter: Laughter and hand clapping in the courtroom.

By Court: Mr. Sheriff, keep order in here or clear the visitors from the room.

By Mr. Pruiett: Now then, Mr. Guyer: Mr. Burns says after they have worked as faithfully and has personally appealed to you gentlemen for co-operation and after he was informed against this woman, after he has done that, and then, enumerates all the things he has done, he says then, tells you what your duty is and you, Your Honor, you told this jury that that information should not be considered by them for any purpose. Now, that's in his charge here and I will get down to that after awhile. Now, as His honor told you: You must not consider that information for any purpose; it's only the means by which this woman is placed upon trial for her life. You don't know whether she is to be, whether or not she is guilty or not; whether she is guilty or not but Mr. Guyer when little Nellie Kinsley—now, she may not be, may not dress as fine, my good Irish friend (indicating Mr. Guyer) as your daughter or mine or some of these jurors' daughters; she may not go in the same select society that your daughter or my daughter or other good men's daughters like yourselves (indicating the jury) go; now, she works for a living but did you know that before I would propound the question to a good man and a good woman's daughter like Nellie Kinsley, questions you (indicating Mr. Guyer) propounded to her, before I would do it, well, I will tell you what I would do: I would ride across hell on a rotten rail, before I would do it. I don't know of any other way, if Your Honor please—with apologies for the rough and uncouth way I put it—but it expresses my conclusions for such questions propounded a daughter of a woman. Who was Nellie? Why, Nellie works for a living; she paints and sells her paintings. There is many a good man's daughter in Oklahoma City who works for a living and help their father and mother. But, that she works down there in selling drinks there in that theatre; where they have that root beer, as they call it, or, where they sell this root beer to the patrons of the theatre to quench their thirst. Another thing there; And why—if that child works there day after day and works for a living—why should you, my friend (indicating Mr. Guyer), stoop to the level to ask that child: "Did you ever go out there for immoral purposes into a rooming house? Did you ever go in a rooming house with him?" You was mad, John, or you wouldn't have done it; I will tell you what you was mad about. That child told this jury when you was offering the old hen and her little chickens and her little old coop and like little Harry here, when you was offering that in order to show that your man. You're what? Hero. Your knife man from Indiana; your killer; your dashing Lusco; your masher, to justify his cause and in the face of Blackwell's testimony, she testified that he offered her fifty dollars a week and expenses. Just think of it: Fifty dollars a week and expenses. Now, who was little Nellie Kinsley that he had offered fifty dollars a week and expenses to? Why, Nellie was the child that Mrs. Baker saw her husband with when he jumped behind the post. Another lie he went to his grave with because he told little Nellie—(a pause); no, let me get that right. Maybe he told her the truth because I think that if my memory serves me right, Nellie told you that he said he saw some one that he knew; I just told you that she said he saw some one, whom she saw, Your Honor, but, I believe her testimony was, he saw some one that he knew; and then it was that Nellie's suspicions were aroused and Nellie began to investigate. Now, Mrs. Baker saw him with Nellie and tries him again. Well, now, let's see. Suppose it was you, Mr. Rieves, or you, Mr. Shipman, or you, Mr. Schroeffler, and it had been—I don't mean anything personal about this but let's take it home; let's be human, as I say; all I ask is that you carry your hearts and your consciences into the jury box with you and be human; that's all and the lawyer, whether he be your prosecutor or not, has a right to assume of you that you will not strip yourselves of your heart and your conscience and be so inhuman in order to co-operate with the county attorney and his forces. Suppose that it had been one of you gentlemen and your wife. Now, a calloused man; a man with strong will power, not the tender sex; not with a woman's heart that begins to kick and plunge at the sight or thought of some one robbing her of her happiness, but a strong man. What would he have done? Why, it would have been just like touching a match to a powder magazine. Why, all hell couldn't have stopped either one of you. What am I asking you to do? I am asking you men of Oklahoma County to do by this poor girl just what you would have twelve (12) honest men to do by a daughter of yours under the same circumstances. Is that an unreasonable request? Did you have the right to follow? Now, let's get that. Let's go back a little bit further than that. Let's take on Tuesday when he beat her up; let's put it upon the broadest plane that the state can place it on. After he had blackened her, beat her, bruised her flesh on Tuesday, did she go get her pistol? Yes. All right. Now, let's go a little further. Did she tell the newspaper reporters: "I said that was the last time he would ever beat me up?" Now, listen, take it home to yourselves. Why? Because the court tells you—and I will get to the charge directly and read it to you—that you must view this from the standpoint of the defendant and the defendant alone. Now, I say in view of all these facts that she had gathered and that had come to her, as I believe I said before supper, you would as well try to stop the waves of the sea as to have stopped or kept that woman (indicating defendant) from following, that Sunday afternoon. Why? Listen: The first assault in Indiana, at Terre Haute; at Paris and Terre Haute. The assault when he attempted to stab her with a knife. The assault in the kitchen at Merkle's home. That second assault at the Merkle home. The other assaults. What else? The message that come from little Florence Frailey came to her. What else? The money she had given him when she saw him with that Smith woman. What else? Of having other women around, her money being spent upon women and bringing a woman there. All the things and all the wrongs done. With all that weight, that burden upon her mind, it all crowded into the brain and what? All hell couldn't have stopped or kept that woman from following. She had no reason. She acted; what upon? Everything that crowded into her brain. She followed. Unbalanced, abnormal as she was, she had a right to follow. She had a right to demand of this libertine who had sought to besmirch and debauch her with a harlot; she had a right to follow him and did and killed. But, oh, they say that she decided to kill him on Tuesday when he beat her up down there. No, that's not the testimony in this case; but, she did tell the reporters; "When he beat me up, I decided he would never beat me up again." And it's the law in this land; it's the law in every land; it's the law in all of the sea where nothing but beasts and sea life roam. The law of what? Self-protection. Self-protection. You step upon a worm and it will strike back. The law of self-protection; the law of self-defense; is not only known in humanity but it's an established fact upon animals. And she had a right with her bruised flesh, flesh that had so often been bruised; and, Gentlemen of the Jury, Mr. Schroeffler (indicating one of the jurors), she had a right, with sobs and tears and a trembling frame, as she went to her sister's and got the pistol and as she tells you, her sister begged her not to take the pistol; she had a right to arm herself with that pistol. Your Honor, please, is there any question about that? When the gentleman closes this case, I will ask an instruction from the bench if he takes issue with me on it. That in view of all of these assaults, that she had a right to arm herself with a pistol for the sole purpose of protecting herself. I say that when that woman left the room there, following Agnes Smith, this harlot and her husband, she was like a wild woman; she was unbalanced; she was abnormal. Why, they say she details in the most minute way everything that took place. Why, Gentlemen of the Jury, did you know that some of the most beautiful letters that were ever penned by man or woman are written by insane persons? I hope that there is some man on this jury that knows something about that. I happen to know because it comes very close to me. What was in that woman's mind? Stop. She had a right to follow. Here was a man that she had given the money to and boarding and feeding him; with all of these things in her own personal observation. I suppose my friend Burns wants you to view this case in the light of the ordinary criminal. I don't know whether you ever heard it or not but it's a story that fits Burns' position in this case:

A Kentucky Colonel was about seventy-five years old and he had a handsome valet. He had a young wife about twenty-two. The old Colonel—a grand old patriotic, practical, southern gentleman—walked in very suddenly on one occasion and found his wife in a very compromising position with the valet. She fell down on her knees and threw up her hands and she says: "Oh, my God! My good Colonel: Do you believe your eyes or do you

believe your baby?" He reached down, picked her up and said:
"I believe my baby."

Note by Reporter: Juror Schroeffler laughs out loud.

By Mr. Pruiett: So, I suppose my friend Burns is like the
old Kentucky Colonel and wants you to be that way.

Now, Mrs. Baker had personal observation of this man's
conduct on two (2) occasions. Gentlemen: You can't trifle with
a woman's love, with a woman's devotion; you should not stick
a dagger into the heart of a woman; it would hurt her worse
than to show ingratitude to her and to her loved ones.

Now, let's see. I say that there is the room. That woman
started out of the room in an abnormal condition because of
all these things. Why, this flashed through her mind just like
lightning flashed. What was it? As long as she saw that
woman Agnes Smith in this room, why, she saw every wrong;
she saw every wrong and every bruise and every lick. Why, I
imagine; I know that she could feel every lick and every assault
in Indiana and Illinois and in Oklahoma City and every lick, she
could feel it on her cheeks and on her eyes; and she followed and
she had a right to follow. Now, let's see. Did she kill him because
she made up her mind on Tuesday to kill him, as Burns says, or,
did she kill him because she said she never would take another
beating off of him? Now listen: If she killed him because she
tried to prevent him from ever giving her another beating or
hurting her or doing her bodily injury, then, you must acquit
her. Now, catch the distinction. I am trying to analyze this and
put it to you so when you go out to your jury room, it will be
just as clear as the A B C's.

If she killed him because he whipped her on Tuesday
and bruised her flesh and walked up behind him and shot, as
Burns had it, and killed him on account of him whipping her
on Tuesday, then she is guilty of murder. Now, listen: But, if
she killed him because she made up her mind that she would
never let him assault her and beat her up again; and what? And,
it was in order to prevent a repetition of such an assault, then
you should acquit her. Now, let's see. Let's see if I am analyzing
this testimony now.

Now, when she left the room, the testimony is and even
admit wandering Agnes—God bless her—I mean what I say. My
heart goes out in pity for that girl; she is a subject that the
Welfare League ought to look after; she has been the object of
deceit and there may yet be some rays of sunshine to beguile the

heavy clouds that now hang so lowly about her; I hope there is
and I am not using Agnes Smith in this case nor am I trying
to berate her or degrade her in order to help Mrs. Baker. I am
taking the woman as I find her in this case and presenting all of
the facts together for your consideration, Gentlemen. Now, she
followed and she overtook them twice. What did he say? "Go
back to your room." In the first place, what did he say in the
room? "None of your God damn business; don't start anything
here in front of this woman." Now, just before I get to that,
let me get to this point about Blackwell before I forget it. They
introduced these magazines. Mr. Blackwell—and that's the reason
why they are short on applications—now, let's see if I am justified
in this. Why did I keep this application back up here and then
go on the way I did? Because he (indicating Mr. Guyer) quarreled
with me and I made his old Irish blood boil up there and made
him half mad with me about it when he put his magazine in. Why
didn't he put his application in along with the other? Now, listen:
Mr. Blackwell said that the contract between he and Lusco Baker
was that he might take these applications and send the applicant
to his place of business and then, if he passed the applicant, if
they were of good moral character and he passed them and such
persons as he thought were proper, then he would issue a certificate properly signed before a notary and give to the applicant,
but what does Mrs. Baker tell you? She tells you that Lusco
Baker said: "I am going to take this woman before a notary
public." On Sunday. You tell me that you can fool a woman's
heart; you tell me that you can spurn a woman? There never
was yet the man born of a woman's womb who can live a double
life and deceive his wife.

Now, I don't endorse murder by any means. There is a large
bunch of old rakes in this town—yes, a lot of them—if they were
killed off, this community would be better off; that's what I have
got to say, on account of the treatment of their wives.

Now, you and I, we meet on trains and we may meet in lob-
bies of hotels; I may meet you at the farm, you in your place of
business and engage in certain conversations; we may be away
from home and indulge in things, Gentlemen, but listen: You are
occupying a position now; you are living in an entirely different
atmosphere from any you ever occupied before in your life except
it may be you, Mr. Shipman. We must take these things home in
all the solemnity that is within your power and then say: What

you would have done or what you would have your daughter to have done under the same circumstances.

Now, Mr. Blackwell tells you that Lusco Baker when he claimed he wanted to take this girl before a notary public, he lied about that. He died with another lie upon his lips. Because he had no authority to issue a certificate at all; there was no place on this application, either for any notary public's seal or acknowledgment. What did I do with that (speaking to his partner, Mr. Sniggs)? Going before a notary public. Gentlemen, I want you to look at that application (handing jury application marked Exhibit 13); no place. And Mr. Blackwell told you there was none; he had no authority for anything like that; he just was simply to send the applicant to him with that application and then, if he decided the applicant was all right, then he would issue the certificate. Now, so much for that.

Now, let's see: Did she kill him because, as Mr. Burns says, that she made up her mind on Tuesday she was going to kill him? No. Because they went down here; they stopped and had a conversation; he told her to go back to the room. Didn't she ask him up to the room: "Can't I go with you?" "No." Stepped down here: "Can't I go along?" "No; go back to the room." Ah! He was riding a black horse on Sunday evening; he was riding a charger. "No, go back to your room." "Come on," says he, to his paramour. Go on a little further. Now, listen, the only time—and when you (indicating Mr. Guyer) go to close this case—the only time he extended any invitation to his wife to go along, you will notice in the cross-examination, but when they got to the Mecca Cafe—turn to that transcript from Mrs. Baker's testimony and also White's and have it ready for me (talking to Mr. Sniggs)—when they got to the Mecca Cafe, he invited his wife to go in there with them to supper. No, she refused. And they went on and they got up to the corner. She says: "Why don't you go with me?" And he spurned her again. Do you have any idea how that affected that poor woman in the front of, in the presence of, another woman, that she had seen him with before at the Terminal Station? Do you gentlemen have any idea how that affected that poor soul who had been giving her money to this man? Have you any, Gentleman, have you any idea how she felt or the effect it had produced upon her mind, at that time? (Suppose it was you and your wife (indicating a juror)? Suppose that it was Pruiett and his wife and his wife would say: "Come on," like the man says? What about the woman? All right. They turned. She turned. Now, listen. She didn't kill him at the first stop but when he told her, "go back to the room," she could have killed him there. Then they parleyed. Then, haven't I the right to reason with you and show her purpose wasn't to kill him on account of him beating her up on the Tuesday before because she would have killed him at the first stop. But what kept her from killing him there when talking to him, face to face? Nothing in the world. All right. She didn't kill him at the second stop. Then they can't argue that she killed him because he had beat her up the Tuesday before at all because she didn't kill him at the second stop. Let's go a little further. Now, we are approaching right to the scene, at the time the fatal shot was fired. Now, remember. Just you remember Doctor Lawson's testimony. Mr. Koontz, the Doctor stood up this way (indicating) and Mr. Guyer asked him to place his finger where the shot went in and he put his finger just this way (indicating behind the left ear). He didn't put his finger this way (indicating); he placed his finger just this way (indicating). Now, I am arguing physical facts to you, now and I will drop back then to the other and apply them and then see, Gentlemen, whether I am analyzing the testimony in this case the right way or not, but he said, it went in about here (indicating behind left ear). Mr. Cooke, the undertaker, tells you he tried to probe the wound and he couldn't tell what way it ranged, whether forward, straight across or otherwise. Then, has the state the right to assume that she shot him, and that his head was to her, and that the shot went in this way (indicating straight back)? No. Well, hold on. Has the defense the right to assume that she shot him on the whirl, and as she stepped aside, as she says? Yes. Why? I will take your own witness, Kenneth Braugh, the boy from Stonewall or Ada, and thank God, the boy has gone home to Pontotoc County where there are no "Red Light Districts"; where there are no Agnes Smiths to greet him at the Terminal. Kenneth Braugh says, standing there within about ten feet (10′) of them and I said to him, I says: "Have you been a good boy?" And I looked at the boy's hands and I thought to myself: I will catch you now; you say, you are working on the farm and if you remember, Gentlemen, I got up while that boy was there (indicating witness stand) and walked up and I saw the boy's hands and saw the corns on his hands, on the inside of the palms. I took my seat and sat back down in my chair and I says "Have you been a good boy; never been in any trouble?" "Yes, sir." Because I knew that that boy was uttering the truth. What does Kenneth Braugh say? He says—at the scene of the shooting, at the time the fatal shot was fired—what? That Baker, the deceased, turned and said, some one was talking to his wife, of the woman who done the shooting; he turned his head and as he turned his head, the shot was fired. Listen to me. Let us go along this pathway of truth and look at a few circumstances here and there that will convince you whether or not this poor soul (indicating the defendant) is telling you the truth. Kenneth Braugh says they stopped and he turned and said something to the woman who shot him and just at that time he turned his head and the shot was fired. He—Braugh—turned his head, but this other boy, the Acres boy: All right. Now wait a minute. Now, let's take the state's strongest witness, Mr. Adair, the young man Adair. Adair says that he was in a very few feet of them and if you have any doubt about it, call for the record when you go to your jury room. That Baker said: "You are not going to follow me tonight." And what? "And something else I did not understand." And that he just turned his head that way (indicating). He said he hadn't kinda stopped but kinda checked, kinda delayed in their movements. I am quoting the exact language of the witness from memory. If I am wrong, call for the record. The other boy said that he was talking to Kenneth Braugh and that he looked but he had to look over Kenneth Braugh's shoulder to see the parties and that he saw him just turn his head that way (indicating) and the shot was fired. And here is the point: Mrs Baker tells you that he says: "You are not going to follow me tonight; I will cut your damn heart out," and made a demonstration and as he turned and said that, she stepped aside and fired. What was the language? I ask the state to tell this jury what were the words that the dead man uttered that this boy W. C. Adair did not understand? I will tell you what it was. It was "I will cut your damn heart out." Is that analyzing this testimony? Adair swears positively that he said something else but he didn't understand. Mrs. Baker tells you what it was. You (indicating Mr. Guyer) had Agnes Smith here and Agnes was standing by the side of this poor, degraded wretch. She might have enlightened this jury as to those remarks that W. C. Adair did not understand. Why didn't you let them hear what she had to say about it? How can you justify your conduct? Now, that's not abusive. Anybody, like my friend Burns said, lawyers might abuse.

There is one fellow, though, in this case that I am going to talk about and I hope he is here. He was standing back there, Your Honor, this afternoon; he was standing back here in the back of the crowd and I hope he is here tonight. I don't abuse people or take advantage of my position as lawyer in the court room unless I, in good conscience, feel wholly justified in doing it. I never saw a man in my life—listen here, just watch me— that ever talked between his teeth (counsel talking through his teeth with his upper and lower teeth closed against each other) but what was a damn scoundrel. You ever get one of them who talks between his teeth, you look out for him. He is expecting business from you (counsel indicating Mr. Guyer). He is expecting business from Burns. I, for one, declare here and now, so far as I am concerned, no knave or no crook can live and seek the relief in accord to his mouth in this community while I am here without my solemn protest. I am speaking of Earley. He is unfit to preside while a female canine whelps her pups. Listen to me because its abuse:

"BEFORE A. T. EARLEY, JUSTICE OF THE PEACE WITHIN AND FOR THE DISTRICT OF OKLAHOMA CITY, OKLAHOMA COUNTY, STATE OF OKLAHOMA.

"The State of Oklahoma, Plaintiff,
                    vs.
"Lottie Baker, Defendant.
            "Application for Change of Venue.

"Lottie Baker, of lawful age, being first duly sworn upon her oath, deposes and says:

"That she is the defendant in the cause above entitled, and that on account of the bias and prejudice of the above named Justice A. T. Earley, affiant verily believes that she can no have a fair and impartial trial on account of bias and prejudice of said A. T. Earley against her.

"That affiant also verily believes that on account of the bias and prejudice of W. P. Hawkins, another Justice of the Peace within and for Oklahoma City, Oklahoma, that it will be impossible for her to secure a fair and impartial trial before said Justice W. P. Hawkins.

"WHEREFORE: Defendant asks that this cause be sent

before some other Justice of the Peace in Oklahoma City, Oklahoma, other than A. T. Early and W. P. Hawkins.

"Mrs. Lottie Baker.

"Subscribed and sworn to before me this 19th day of March, 1919.

"H. D. Grout,
"Notary Public.
"My Commission expires January the 8th, 1921."

Note by Reporter: The above quoted paper is Exhibit No. 1 in the trial of said cause.

By Mr. Pruiett: Did you hear that man? Am I prejudicing this woman's cause on account of my criticism of Earley? Gentlemen: If I do, visit it upon me and not upon this poor soul (indicating the defendant). But what do you think of a man? What manner of man is that close-toothed scoundrel who would take the witness stand here and enumerate and study for two minutes in making up his answers to questions that would ultimately send that poor soul to the electric chair? In the face of all her other statements that she made to the newspapers and there to the reporters. She was frank; she was honest in telling them everything. Yet, that brute and miserable scoundrel placed into this poor soul's mouth (indicating defendant) words that he knew was as infamous as hell itself. I wish he would say something to me on the streets about what I am saying here in the court room because I don't believe in a lawyer taking advantage of the position he occupies in the court room and not back it up on the streets. I say that he is unfit to be a justice of the peace. That's all I have got to say about A. T. Earley. If any of you (indicating the jury) are his friends, I can't help it. A man, when, after that: after having locked in his power all those facts, and then, when that poor soul files that affidavit for a change of venue, to transfer the cause from his court, and then, he overrules it and goes ahead and tries this poor woman. Now, gentlemen, if that's your standard of justice that Earley metes out! Is it fair? Is it human? Is it right? Is it just? Now, he (indicating Mr. Guyer) is not to blame for it; Mr. Guyer is not to blame for it. Mr. Burns is not to blame for it. But what do you think of a justice of the peace that will go down there and "pump" and examine a woman for two hours? No, let it be said to the credit of Bob Burns, the county attorney, he went there like a manly man, like a gentleman, like a real officer of the law and he says: "No; no;

no, I don't; this woman has no lawyer here; I don't want to ask her any questions; I don't want to take any advantage of her." Judge Earley, you would sell your soul for a mess of pottage. That's what you would do. That's what you would. Yes, sir. And then, after all of that, he goes ahead and tries this poor soul and overrules her motion for a change of venue and tries her. With all that information locked in his bosom. A fine justice, isn't he? Your Honor, a fine justice. Fine scales that he holds, Your Honor. Why, do you know what a thing like that, the Criminal Court of Appeals of our state, if a district judge would talk to a defendant like that and then go ahead and try him, there is no difference, no difference in the world in the cause of the change of venue before Earley than it would be before Judge Phelps here; not a bit of difference; not a bit in the world; and, a district judge who would do a thing like that, the higher courts of this state, why they would brand him so he would be marked all the days of his life and every professional man throughout the country would know him by his mark; by the brand that the higher court would have placed upon him.

Well, now, let's see. Another thought: Did she kill him on account of jealousy? No. Not on account of jealousy. Her uncontrollable impulses, her brain on fire, couldn't check her from killing that husband. As far as her reason was concerned, she had no more power to control her reasoning faculties than a wild animal. Not a bit. Now, if she had gone there and killed on account of jealousy, what would the average woman have done? She would have killed the object that caused it. She would have killed the woman; she wouldn't have killed the man; she would have killed the woman. If that had been the purpose, she would have shot and killed the woman, Mr. Shupe (addressing an individual juror). If she killed on account of jealousy, she wouldn't have killed her husband. No, that which brought about his death was his conduct down there on that occasion. A person with her reasoning faculties gone, can act in self-defense as well as a sane person. Now, I am going to hurry on here.

I want to read this to you: For Assault and Battery for Lusco Baker and enters a Plea. That's in the case. He served ninety (90) days. That's a certified copy of a judgment back there in Indiana (handing Exhibit 15 to the jury). Here is the certified copy of the judgment for the Rape (handing jury the Exhibit 14). And here is a certified copy of the judgment; now, we haven't got the judgment here at the time he was sent to the penitentiary. As I told you, gentlemen, I thought Mr. Burns had it and we agreed to use these, but he just got the two judgments in these two cases, but the testimony, if you all remember, shows that he was sent to the penitentiary—and it's not disputed—for killing a boy when he was about fifteen (15) years old; shows he was a knife man from his youth up.

Note by Reporter: The jury examines the two certified copies of judgments, introduced in evidence as Exhibit 14 and Exhibit 15.

By a Juror: (to Mr. Pruiett): May we take these exhibits with us to our jury room?

By Mr. Pruiett (to the Jury): You gentlemen want any water?

By a Juror: Yes.

By Mr. Schroeffler (a Juror.) Your honor, may the bailiff bring me a glass of water?

By Court (to the bailiff): Get a pitcher of water and pass it to the jurors.

Note by Reporter: Mr. Pruiett ceases his argument while drinking water is passed to the Jury.

By Mr. Pruiett: Now, gentlemen, one of the jurors asked me; I want you to understand that as far as the defendant is concerned, we haven't the slightest objection.

By Mr. Guyer: What was it? I didn't hear it.

By Mr. Pruiett: Any of these exhibits; the defendant is willing that you take to your jury room and examine all of them.

By Mr. Guyer: The state is anxious for them to.

By Court: If the jury want them for their information.

By Mr. Guyer: If the jury want them for their information.

By the Court: The jury has a right to take to the jury room all of the exhibits.

By Mr. Pruiett: Certainly. Now, Gentlemen, see what we gather from this letter. Here is this letter about; now, the letter of March 13th; it's Exhibit 16.

Note by Reporter: Counsel states the letter is marked Exhibit 16, but the letter he refers to above is, in fact, marked Exhibit 18.

By Mr. Pruiett: Here is the letter that speaks of Lusco Baker's drunkenness. It doesn't say anything about his conduct with women. And why does Mrs. Baker—can a woman like that be a murderess when she sits here and tells you that she didn't want to worry poor old mother; that she had trouble enough and she didn't want to worry and burden her. Now, that's what she tells you and that's the reason. Now, this other letter. It's a frank, open statement; it's consistent and everything she has ever said, every word, and you can have all of these exhibits if you care to have them and the defendant is perfectly willing for you to take them and anxious for you to read them and take them.

Now, you heard this morning, Mr. White, when he was on the stand; he testified at the preliminary trial and he didn't notice the bruised cheek, the blackened cheek. You heard his testimony this morning that he noticed on one occasion at some time a discolored eye. Now, Mr. Guyer will probably read that to you. The point I want to make to you is this. Where is her—(statement not finished). You heard Mr. Guyer last night say to Mrs. Baker: "Well, when he threatened to cut your head off." Well, I let him go once. And the poor woman sitting there after being on the stand for seven (7) hours and pleading with her energy worn out, and: "Haven't you done so and so before that?" "Well, when he threatened to cut your head off." Now, this is my question. He (indicating Mr. Guyer) will try to make much out of it. Gentlemen, he did the same thing in the trial of Mrs. Baker when she was seeking bail before Judge Clark. Nowhere in the record and when he reads Mrs. Baker's testimony to you in his closing argument, here is what he is going to read:

"Q.   About how far do you think you was away from him, Mrs. Baker, when you fired?"

"A.   Well, I don't know."

"Q.   Have you any idea?"

"A.   Oh, I judge about the distance from here to that table."

"Q.   How many feet do you think that would be, ten feet?"

"A.   I judge that."

"Q.   About ten or twelve feet. As he turned his face towards you and raised—"

By Mr. Pruiett: Now, this is Guyer talking.

"Q.   '—and raised this knife, you shot him?'

"A.   Yes, sir."

Note by Reporter: Counsel reading from cross-examination of Mrs. Lottie Baker given in her application for bail before Judge Clark on April 10th, 1919.

By Mr. Pruiett: Now, take over here in her testimony or anywhere, about this big knife that Gleason testified about and that Frank Harrah testified about. And I says: "Did he ever try to use that knife on you?" and in her answer, she said: "Yes." And then, I said, "When?" She says: "That Sunday evening, at the time of the shooting." Now, what the poor soul meant to convey was that when he turned and run his hand, as she describes to you, that he was attempting to get the knife to use the knife on her. She never, at any time, said she saw the knife except where Guyer puts the question in her mouth like he did when he put the question in her mouth last night. I was saying: "Cut my head off", instead of: Cutting her heart out. "Q. About ten or twelve feet. As he turned his face towards you and raised his knife, you shot him? A. Yes, sir." Now, then, by Mr. Pruiett: "Q. What did you do when he made this demonstration with his hand?" (Reading from Transcript). She never at any time said anything about a knife or seeing a knife in his hand. Now, then the question, Gentlemen of the Jury, is this: It was unnecessary for any knife to be there. The court tells you in this instruction that the danger need not be real or actual, if apparent, viewed from her standpoint and her standpoint alone.

Now, you Gentlemen are getting tired. Mr. Guyer has got to talk to you.

By Mr. Guyer: No, he hasn't.

By Mr. Pruiett: You are not going to talk? Well, all right. I will just take my time.

By Mr. Guyer: Go right ahead.

By Mr. Pruiett: Because I can talk to you gentlemen all night. I was in hopes I would quit about now and let Mr. Guyer close the case and I am willing to do it and quit right now if he would close the case tonight. If you (indicating Mr. Guyer) want to do it, I will quit now, if you will close the case.

By Mr. Guyer. Take your time.

By. Mr. Pruiett: No, I don't mean; I don't want to crowd you; I don't want you to talk to a tired jury and if you will take the case and close it, I will quit. I am sincere in what I say. I know the jury will read the instructions.

By Mr. Guyer: Go ahead, Mr. Pruiett.

By Mr. Pruiett: Gentlemen of the Jury: I don't believe that I could say more for this defendant if I was to talk for six (6) months. I hope that I haven't said anything in my argument that will prejudice one of you gentlemen against my client's cause. I don't feel like that I can say anything more except a preference when you go out, to read the court's instructions which says that you are to view these circumstances from the standpoint of the defendant and her standpoint alone, viewed in the light of all the circumstances, assaults and everything that took place then and before; all of the conduct of the deceased, as to how that affected that mental condition on that night.

Gentlemen of the Jury: I am going to leave this case with you, with the request that you read the court's instructions. Take this case and may the Great God of the Universe, the Creator of the Conscience and Souls of Men, guide and direct you and each one of you in the rendition of a verdict in this case and if you permit that, Lottie Baker will have no fear of your verdict. Do not compromise away her liberty by giving her even one (1) hour in jail. The woman has suffered enough, as she said to the newspaperman: You might send her to the penitentiary for life, you might send her to jail, you might send her to the penitentiary for life but the punishment could not be as great as the punishment that she has undergone the last two (2) years.

Take this case, Gentlemen, and do with it as I know you will do with it and act honestly and in good conscience and this poor soul (indicating the defendant) will be satisfied. I thank you very much for your attention.

——oOo——

Note by Reporter: Mr. Pruiett closes his argument to the jury at 9:40 o'clock P. M., Friday, June 13th, 1919.

——oOo——

When the jury returned he heaved a tired, satisfied sigh. They agreed that Lottie was "free of guilt."

(J. M. Leggett case.) "To My Clients: This is to notify you that while I am burdened with the charge of murder against me and while this charge is of deep concern to me and my loved ones, yet I feel that the interests of my clients should be safeguarded and every right should be exhausted in their defense. I have employed Mr. Moman Pruiett, who will act in conjunction with my partner, Mr. George F. Short (who later became Attorney General of Oklahoma), in looking after their interests. This employment pertains to all criminal cases in which I have been employed, and I assure that your interests will be protected. (Adv.) J. M. Leggett." The Democrat-Record of Idabel, a town in the timbered Kiamichi Mountain section of Oklahoma—on the line the Frisco had cut and trestled from Rogers to Paris—was carrying a classified preamble to a Pruiett prowl on jury justice. "One of the most horrible tragedies that has occurred in Idabel since it was made an incorporated town, occurred here Saturday evening about 7:30 o'clock, when James M. Leggett, an attorney, shot

Hiram C. Strawn to death in the office of Esq. D. B. Price, in the second story of the DeBarry Building. . . . Just seventy-one days before the killing Virgil Strawn, a brother, was shot from ambush and killed in the northeastern part of the county, and A. W. Lail was charged with the murder. Leggett was the leading counsel for Lail, and had succeeded in getting him released on bail." Leggett, a Mississippian, had picked the booming Kiamichi lumber district for developing his legal talent, and he had been more than casually successful. Cash circulated freely through the hills. The big companies were shaving whole mountainsides at a swoop, and the old Frisco couldn't get enough cars to keep even with orders for hauling ties and lumber out of the camps. The accused lawyer had plenty of money, and a sensational state of facts involved in his case. Pruiett was interested. "Can't it wait a day or two?" Pruiett demanded into the transmitter. He was at the Baltimore Hotel in Kansas City, talking over long-distance to George Short. "This's the Fourth of July. We came up here where we could relax an' dissipate a little. You can—"

"I can't either," Short interrupted. "Jim's in a hell of a fix. It ain't like he was just charged with plain murder. It's not like a plain feud. This is a faction fight, an' Jim's killed one of the majority leaders. The sheriff's guardin' him out at his house at night, an' keepin' him in the jail in the day time. He's goin' to be lynched if we don't make bond and get him out of the country."

"How do I get down there from here?" Pruiett inquired.

"Take the Southern to Ashdowne, Arkansas," Short advised. I'll have a' automobile meet you an' drive you up here. Get yourself in shape for some work, 'cause there's sure a plenty of it waitin' for you."

Pruiett called the depot before he rejoined the party. "I haven't even got time to get a shave," he complained, as he slammed his dirty shirts, and a pair of large bottles, into his bag. "An' I need a Turkish bath. I wish to God the damn killers'd recognize a national holiday, like the rest of us, an' lay off. I'm gettin' tired of murder all the time."

"* * * Strawn, who is said to have been unarmed, was shot to death with a number of eyewitnesses to prove who did the killing. When Leggett went into the building . . . . he went back into the office of the justice, where he saw Hiram Strawn sitting in a window, and with some remarks began shooting. The first shots struck Strawn in the arm, and he attempted to get away from Leggett, who was still shooting, and got across the hall, when Leggett, who had followed him to the door, fired the last shot, the bullet striking Strawn in the back."

Judge Maben was with him in Kansas City, and Pruiett suggested that he might take him in the case with him. Bill Maben followed Pruiett down from Kansas City. He and Short, and Maben, were contemplating the case as they bumped over the hill roads toward Idabel. "I can't see much to hang self-defense on," Pruiett observed.

"Jim's got more than his own defense to worry him," Short said. "He's got a lot of law business pending around these parts, and he's not so sure that I can handle it just exactly to suit his clients. He wants to know, first thing, if you'll stay down here an' help me to straighten up his clients' affairs for them?"

"I can't do that," Pruiett objected. "I got so much stuff in my own office that I went stale; I just had to walk off and leave it. I got to get through here an' hurry home."

"You know how you're able to do that, an' get away with it?" Short countered. "You've got a reputation that's so well known that ever'body knows you got business conflicts all over the country. Counsel an' courts both know it, so they don't raise hell when you ask for a continuance like they do in other cases. It wouldn't take more than a month an' we could prepare Jim's case for trial in that time, an' wash the whole business up."

"I can't afford to," Pruiett answered.

"We don't want you to do it as a favor. We're cuttin' fees in all cases you handle, an' payin' you for defendin' Jim. You can make a year's pay out of it." Short was painfully persistent.

"Let's get us a campin' outfit an' open up headquarters on one of the foamy creeks," Maben suggested. "We'd be right close to town, an' it ought to be cool in these pine hills. We could fish, an' drink moonshine—."

"Have you got that writ ready to file, like I told you?" Pruiett asked.

"She's all ready to go," Short answered.

"Bill's got a good idea, finally," Pruiett said. "We'll open up defense headquarters up on Mountain Fork, an' you can take care of the office stuff in town an' handle the details for us. I was around these parts when I was a kid, an' I think I'd enjoy a little rest on the creek banks."

"I got a good camp man I'll send out to manage camp for you," Short agreed. "His name's Goggle-eye Smith."

"That's a good name," Pruiett said. "Does he know where the stills are?"

"He knows where his own is, an' it's big enough to take care of your demands. Ain't that enough?"

"That's plenty," Maben sighed from the back seat.

"That district court isn't goin' to allow bond in this case," Pruiett grunted from his seat on a log. His gaze wandered to a point above the tent top. "Who done that?" he demanded.

"I did," Maben grinned, as he calculated the subject of Pruiett interruption inquiry. "Me an' Goggle-eye did it. It looks real professional, don't it?"

"It looks like hell," Pruiett differed. Nailed across the stalk of a big pine was a yellow plank, bearing the inscription, "Moman Pruiett, Lawyer."

"It looks like the Valley," he said. "Where'd you get the lamp black?"

"It's burnt cork," Maben said. "Me and Goggle-eye thought you'd like it."

"I'd like it if I could make a little headway with this Leggett case," Pruiett muttered. "That Nelson, the county attorney, is the meanest guy I ever saw. An' these lawyers from Arkansas, Steel an' Lake that're helpin' him, they are real grudge fighters. This makes three writs, an' the court denies bond ever' time."

"George Short told you it was a faction fight, an' that Strawn was a big shot in the majority," Maben said. "What you think you'll do?"

"Jim Leggett says he's sick," Pruiett said. "If it looks like confinement is goin' to wreck his health the Criminal Court of Appeals will make 'em give bond. I don't think they'd turn me down in the state court if I could make a good showin'."

"He'll have to be some sick," Maben said.

"He put the jailer on the stand before a different judge, who set bond at $20,000. When Leggett's bond was approved and he was released, Pruiett was still dreaming on Mountain Fork. He was unwilling to break camp for home and old business. "I got things in good shape at the office," he said. "Ever'thing's bein' passed until I get my rest over an' my health back. Let's get it circulated around that Leggett ought to be tried right now instead of at the regular fall term of court. The natives would pick it up an' think it was their idea before night. They'd get a special judge appointed down here, which would beat the regular one, an' we could try the case an' have it over with. We could get ready right here in camp."

"Suits me," Leggett said.

"You're the doctor," Maben agreed.

"I'll go to town in the morning, then, an' send a telegram to the office, sayin' that if they don't set a special docket down here in a day or two, that I'll be in. I'll say that I hope to hell they don't, cause a delay of the case would help Leggett. That damn operator is kin to the prosecution, an' he's been givin' 'em copies of ever' wire I've sent since I've been here. They'll pick it up an' have a docket with a special judge workin' in three days."

"This looks more like a hardware store than it does like a court room," Pruiett whispered to his client. "There isn't a person here that isn't carryin' a gun."

"I know it," Leggett replied. "Harrison Branch, Strawn's brother-in-law, is carryin' a forty-five, an' he's said if the jury don't give me the chair he's goin' to drill me, right here in the court room."

"That guy next to him is workin' for me," Pruiett assured him. If he pulls a gun it'll be knocked down. But these prosecutin' attorneys are armed. I have never seen anything like this, not even in the Sandy Land Court."

"Nelson's carryin' his gun in a shoulder holster," Leggett observed. "That's why he keeps his coat buttoned up in this hot weather." "An' look at old Barrett up there makin' the state's opening statement. Smotherin' to death, an' keepin' his coat buttoned up clear to his chin. He's got one slung in his arm-pit." Pruiett was pondering as he talked.

"This imported judge don't know about the feud down here," Leggett said. "You think we ought to get a recess, an' tell him these lawyers are armed? I'd like to have a little protection, or the right to carry a gun myself."

"We'd have to amend the Constitution to get you the right to carry a pistol while you are bein' tried for murder," Pruiett grinned. "I got a' idea. I'll get 'em unarmed or get us both killed, an' ruin their damn prosecution at the same time. Wait 'till I make my statement." When Barrett had concluded Pruiett began to address the jury. He was making a narrative outline of what the defense proof was going to show. He was immaculate of manner and appearance. He smiled, and he nodded and he bowed as he interrupted himself and paused before the court's bench. "It's extremely warm in the court room, this morning," he observed, "and this promises to be a long trial. I wonder if your honor would grant me permission to remove my coat, and proceed in my shirt sleeves?"

"We have no formal rules here, Mr. Pruiett," the court said. "You may remove your coat if you care to." Pruiett slid out of his coat and draped it over the back of a chair. "You other gentlemen may do the same, if you wish," the court continued. "We might as well be comfortable—all of us. I think I'll take mine off." Pruiett watched the prosecutors, quizzically as the court stood up and peeled off his coat. They shifted uncomfortably, but made no move to unbutton their coats. "You can see, Gentlemen of the Jury," Pruiett continued, in a barely audible hiss, "that I am unarmed. With the might of right behind me, I'll deliver my innocent client from the shadow of guilt, unless I am struck down by a bullet in my back. That's the only way the state will stop me in this case. If the county attorney, and his special assistant, Barrett, were to remove their coats, they would display the arms which they deem essential to their program of intimidation and oppression. They may shoot me down, but—."

"Here, here," the court interrupted. "What kind of an opening statement is this? We're not up to arguments, and I won't stand to hear such charges being made against the state—."

"I demand that Nelson and Barrett be searched by the bailiff," Pruiett roared. Nelson grabbed a bundle of papers from the table and hurried toward the door into the court clerk's office. Barrett was close behind him.

A juror in the front row of the box leaped up. "I saw Nelson's gun beneath his coat, your honor," he cried. "I know about this feud and I've tried hard to keep out of it. If they're goin' to carry it into the courtroom, I'd like to be excused from service in the case. I got a family to support."

"An' so have I," cried another, rising. "They both had guns on. I seen 'em."

"We'll take a recess," the court ruled. "All attorneys in this case come into my chambers. I want to talk to you."

"The show's over," Pruiett whispered to Leggett. "That jury's on our side now, an' I'll see that they don't get away. I don't give a damn what they prove. That jury is goin' to turn you loose."

Leggett was acquitted. How, and why, will continue to be one of the mysteries of the system. When the evidence was all in, including the portion establishing that Strawn was shot in the back, a long-haired fashion plate with a demoniacal glare in his eyes began to parade before the enraptured jury. He defied God Almighty to strike him with lightning if his client wasn't innocent. He challenged the prosecuting attorney to shoot him in the back if they wanted to keep Leggett from being acquitted. Pruiett, Maben and Leggett slipped out of town before Branch and his surprised associates had time to pull their pistols. Leggett was a free man.

Pruiett and Leggett met a year later. They were in the Kingkade Hotel, in Oklahoma City, Oklahoma. "Where you headed, now?" Leggett grinned.

"I got to go to Lafayette, Tennessee," Pruiett answered. "I got to meet a boy named Jess Knight down there. He's charged with murder here, an' I'm to bring him in an' surrender him. I made the county attorney agree on bond when I agreed to surrender him."

"That sounds like a good deal," Leggett agreed. "Goin' to make a lot of money out of him?"

"Naw," Pruiett said, dubiously. "His father's a Baptist preacher an' I want to do somethin' for the church. They got his brother in jail now, they're both charged in the same killin', an' the old preacher got me to agree to represent 'em. I am not sure I'll be able to get my expenses back. Where the hell you been, an' where you goin?"

"I've been on a visit in my old home town, Hattiesburg, Mississippi," Leggett said. "There ain't a livin' for a lawyer down in that country. I'm goin' back to the Kiamichi, where there's some fun."

"You're not goin' to Idabel, are you?" Pruiett asked.

"I sure as hell am," Leggett grinned

"You won't last no time. Why, hell's fire, that Harrison Branch is a killer, an' he'll never get over wantin' to kill you. You're crazy."

Leggett continued to smile. "It's been a year," he said. "They've all forgot about the trial by this time. I want to get back down in those lumber hills an' make some money. I'm flat."

"You'll be a hell of a lot flatter, if you go back in that country," Pruiett said, with finality. "I am not your lawyer any more, but take my advice an' stay away from there."

"Much obliged," Leggett answered, "but I never was much of a hand to be a'scared. I can take care of myself."

"So long," Pruiett said, extending his hand gravely, for a farewell handshake. "Don't be hollerin' back across the river, an' tellin' me I didn't warn you. When you feel that hot lead a'cuttin' through your guts, just think of old Moman an' what he told you. So long, son."

Pruiett read about it in the paper when he arrived in Nashville, Tennessee. "I knew it," he said folding the paper and tossing it aside. "They shot him down before he had time to get his trunk out of the baggage office. Poor old Jim. I heard those bells ringin' in my ears ever since I saw him at the Kingkade Hotel."

CHAPTER SEVENTEEN

Wherein the Black Stud crosses the Arizona Desert to defend a train-robber with theatrical inclinations, and how the bells in his ears cause him to lose his case, but save his neck and the necks of his defense associates from the blade of a federal court indictment. And how he defends his office associate on a murder charge, and gains his acquittal. And wherein Pruiett's father and mother make a quiet withdrawal from the scene, and Pruiett with murder and draft exemption business on the docket.

"The Golden State train robbery case, for which Joe Davis and Jeff Spurlock are being tried in Federal Court, probably will go to the jury this afternoon, since United States Attorney Flynn had practically closed his address for the government before adjournment at noon. Judge Sawtelle's instructions will follow . . . . Attorney Moman Pruiett, of Oklahoma, sustained his reputation as an eloquent and able advocate in closing for the defense. He explained that the defense had introduced no evidence because they believed that the government had shown nothing against Davis and Spurlock except a mass of suspicion, which he believed unworthy of refutation. He then proceeded to argue that there was no direct testimony to connect the defendants with participation in the holdup, except that of Berthoff, the confessed bandit, and Hynes, the hobo soldier, and that they were unworthy of credence." It was the "Tucson Citizen," giving its current impressions of events developing at the Federal Building at Tucson, Arizona.

The Golden State's Limited, crack Pacific Coast unit of the Rock Island lines, had been stopped and looted in the fringe of the southern Arizona desert, near Aoache, in a throwback to the theatrical stage coach and train holdups of a quarter century before. The apprehension of part of the cash on one of the bandits, and a confession by him, had resulted in the arrest of Joe Davis and Jeff Spurlock. Davis called for Pruiett, who was the saltiest thing in the west, including Earl Rogers and the waning reputation he enjoyed with his local Los Angeles clientele. Spurlock had employed Charles Owen of El Paso, Texas. Owen was a lawyer of no mean ability, whose time was occupied, principally, in representing a certain nonresident named Pancho Villa. Pancho was encountering numerous legal complications in his operations on the upper side of the Rio Grande.

"I was late gettin' away," Pruiett said as he slid his suit case under the bed. "I just got checked in. Here—. One of you can sit on the bed."

"We were gettin' worried about you," Jack Davis said. He was the father of Joe Davis, whose trial was set. "We got a lot of work to do, an' just a couple of days to do it in. What was the matter?"

"My Maw's sick," Pruiett answered briefly. She's dyin'. I started once to wire you I wasn't comin', but I decided I might just as well. I figured she'd insist on my comin' if she was in any kind of shape. She always insisted I take care of lawsuits ahead of ever'thing else."

"No hope for her at all?" Owen inquired, sympathetically.

Pruiett shook his head. "Betty—I call her by her first name most of the time, like the old man—was about the best half of me. I can look back over my whole life an' the only bright spots in it are the ones where she was givin' me a wrinkled hand an' helpin' me over rough places. She told me one time—."

"What did she say?" Davis inquired, as he trailed off.

"It don't make no difference, now," Pruiett answered. "I am not going to bother others with my own private troubles. Let's get down to business. Is there any chance of gettin' severances, an' tryin' these cases one at a time?"

"Not a chance in the world," Owen replied, "And—."

"What's the chance of a continuance?"

"Not any better."

"We don't want no continuance," Davis cut in. "We got a bunch of witnesses here, an' it costs a lot of money. They're high-priced witnesses, an' we want to put 'em on an get it—."

"Shut up," Pruiett hissed, in a whisper. "I've had this room reserved ahead of time on a telegram. It may be tapped."

He turned up the mattress and examined the bed springs. He looked behind the pictures on the wall and in the drawers of the writing desk.

"Check that bathroom, an' be sure you do it good," he whispered to Owen, while he turned from the light-fixtures to the corners of the rug on the floor. Don't overlook anything. They got a bug in here."

"What the hell you so suspicious about?" Owen demanded.

"You an' me aren't charged with anything. You think they'd put a dictograph on us?"

"There isn't anything the government won't do to win this case," Pruiett declared. "I had a tip from a *con* that was on the train. He said that this town was as hot as that gold out of the Golden State's express car that they haven't found yet. He was a man I can rely on."

"Everything looks all right to me," Davis, senior, said from under the bed.

"I can't find a thing, but I can feel it, plain as hell," Pruiett grated. "Now, listen. Let's put this gabbin' off 'til tomorrow mornin', an' we'll meet in the cafe for breakfast. I'm all run down an' I got to get some sleep. We can—."

"We ain't got much time to—." Davis started to make an objection.

"We got plenty of time, 'til we locate that bug or get a place to talk where we won't be talkin' into some dick's ear," Pruiett rejoined. "An' do a little thinkin' about my suggestion that we continue this case, will you?"

"I been up a' hour," Pruiett announced, as Owen and Davis came up to his table in the restaurant.

"I didn't think the saloons opened up that early," said old Jack Davis.

"I didn't think you ever thought," Pruiett snapped. "Joe inherited all the brain you got, an' he's eatin' his breakfast out of a tin tray up in the federal jail."

"That stuff won't get us anywhere," Owen observed, stuffing his napkin in his vest. "Let's talk some sense. What're we goin' to announce when the government calls these cases?"

"Not ready, an' have a motion an' a bunch of affidavits for a continuance ready," Pruiett.

"I'll be damned if we do," Davis cut in. "I got a perfect alibi right here in town, an' it cost a'plenty. We're goin' to trial."

"I learned enough, while you was stuffin' your shirt-tail in this mornin', to satisfy me that we ain't got no chance tryin' to make a defense play work," Pruiett said. "That boy on the train said this place was hot as hell, an' he was just touchin' it. The guy that fixed my drink this mornin' isn't a regular bartender. He's a federal agent in there with his ears drooped over the counter, to pick up all the information he can. There was a punk at one of the front tables actin' drunk—but he wasn't. He's there to listen, an' he goes back to the can ever' few minutes to make a bunch of notes. Ever' joint's goin' to be the same way, an' ever' stranger in town is bein' watched and shadowed. My friend said there was four hundred dicks in here—Feds, express company and insurance company detectives—to try to find where the rest of that loot is, an' send ever'body connected with the defense to a Federal penitentiary."

"I don't believe it," Davis said.

"You won't believe nothin' I tell you, but Joe wouldn't believe anything anybody told him, either," Pruiett retorted. "That's the trouble with the whole bunch of you. Why, I saw a bunch of Mexicans goin' down the street—part of this celebration that's goin' on. What you call it?"

"Fiesta de los Vaqueros," Owen supplied.

"Yeah, the fiesta," Pruiett continued. "An' they was pullin' them red an' green shawls up around their tight little seats an' lookin' back like they was expectin' a knife in their backs. Ever'-body's scared; ever'body's suspicious. I can feel the tension in the atmosphere; the bells are ringin' in my head, an' I know it isn't no time to go to trial."

"We'll either try it with you or without you," Davis snapped.

"Can you do anything with him?" Pruiett inquired of Owen.

"I couldn't if I wanted to," Owen answered.

"You mean you want to go to trial in this mess?"

"Might as well, an' get it over with."

"It's two against one," Pruiett announced. "I'm willin' to announce ready, an' let the boys get a good long stretch, if you two insist, but I'll be damned if I'll let the two of you insist that I'm goin' along with 'em. That phony alibi is out. We'll let the boys tell the stories they told in the beginnin'; follow the statements they gave the government, an' stand on it. We are not offerin' no corroboration."

"Oh, yes, we are," Davis said, looking toward Owen for support.

"Davis," Pruiett said patronizingly, "anyone listenin', an' I am not so sure that they are not, would think I had hired you to give me advice, instead of vice versa. Now get this . . . . It's my final expression in this case. I won't offer a word of that stuff that's been cooked up, an' I'll bet you five hundred that any one that does is goin' to the Federal penitentiary, right from the court room or the witness stand. I can see it, an' I can smell it, an' I can hear the bells ringin' in my ears. There's the damndest system coverin' the preparation of this trial that was ever got together. My room's wired, whether I can find the bug or not. Yours is too, both of you, an' all your witnesses have been makin' up a volume of information for the prosecution durin' these last two or three days, but they don't know it. We'll try it straight, on what we got, or old Moman don't even go to the courthouse."

"Quittin', are you?" Davis sneered.

"You're damned right I am," Pruiett snapped.

"I guess we can get along without him, can't we judge?" Davis inquired of Owen.

"I won't stay in the case without Pruiett; he's been the head man all the way through," Owen said. "If he withdraws, I'm makin' application to the court to get out myself."

Pruiett picked up the check. "I'm walkin' around on the street for a few minutes, an' then I'm goin' to my room," he said. "Let me know before time to get ready for the noon train, what you want to do about it."

Davis and Spurlock were convicted and given 15 years apiece. As Pruiett was hurrying out of the building toward his train he was stopped by Flynn, the District Attorney in charge of the prosecution.

"Pruiett," Flynn said, as he extended his hand, "I've heard a lot about you, and I've wondered about you a lot since I found that you were going to be active in the trial of these cases. I've enjoyed meeting you and trying the case with you."

"Thanks," Pruiett said, dryly. To himself he said: "What you heard wouldn't be to my credit, but I don't give a damn."

"The government was prepared to resist a studied attempt to acquit these men," Flynn said, as if his dictograph was hooked to Pruiett's head, and he was hearing him think. "We had authentic information showing that a perjured conspiracy was being considered. And we have information that you are the one who prevented it and kept the defense on a clean, and safe, plane. I want to commend you, and thank you."

Pruiett watched him closely. He didn't know whether Flynn was sincere, or sarcastic.

"Davis's people ought to thank you, too, and a few others— some lawyers," Flynn went on, significantly. "If that thing had gone on, if they hadn't listened to you—there would have been twenty-five indictments out in connection with it by this time. We would have played their perjury back to them on phonograph records, and—."

"Thanks for the information, old man," Pruiett interrupted, as he grabbed his hand and gave it another hurried shake. "I've got to go. Got to make a train. Stay on the level, is my motto . . . Always stay on the level. I'm glad to have met you, Flynn, and glad to have had this little chat."

Pruiett's mother was not dead when he got back, but when he called on her she took his hand and uttered "God Bless You, Son, you are here," and then she died.

He took her to the Valley, to the plot beneath the marble shaft he had raised over the grave of his first wife, "Lilly Belle Pruiett;" his brother "White Pruiett" and his son "Stilwell Russell Pruiett," and as he heard the last rites being said over her casket, he supported the stooped, trembling husk of the old Captain, his father. The lingering look which the Captain gave the spot as they guided him away was as much as an assurance to the fresh remains that it would not be long until he was back with her. Fourteen months later, when the May zephyrs were whipping the blooming branches of the redbuds along the Washita, the Captain returned, and he was lowered to the place which had long been waiting for him.

Pruiett was 45. The gusts which disarranged his bared black plumage as he stood there beside his father's grave, were unable to expose a single fading strand. His stance was straight and square, and his emotion, as always, was concealed by the straight line of his set lips and the advanced, defiant jaw. He stole a glance about while the benediction was being read. There was Colonel Garvin's Choctaw widow, hiding her grief with typical aborigine stoicism. Her presence made him conscious of the absence of old Colonel Sam, and Grant, the banker. And there was Jeff Aiken, and Cal Stewart with all the lineaments of old men, looking on with expressions of dutiful sadness. He had saved them both from the gallows. And could it be, was it possible, that the coarse-dressed slattern, worn and shapeless, was the lithe cross-breed who had once been his client? A look of added sadness crept across his countenance. The years had been unkind to Izora. It was his client, Izora Alexander.

Grief had to be combined with business on the docket. Congressional ratification of President Wilson's war proclamation made the United States an ally of the European majority. The machinery of the selective draft revolved about the drive of one Hugh Johnson, an Oklahoman, and an intimate friend of Pruiett's;

a country-school classmate of Pruiett's wife. It was whispered that Pruiett could get things done in Washington. He never made an appearance before the exemption board, but the majority of the clients who contributed to the expense of his constant travel between Oklahoma and the national capital received favorable consideration. He had taken a lesson from his trip in the Bias case, and learned where to hang his hat.

While Pruiett had been traveling in the Pacific northwest in 1906, and making his plans for scraping the Valley mud from his boots, a Valley jury had convicted Dr. Price Patterson of manslaughter, and had sentenced him to confinement in the penitentiary for ten years. The doctor had stalled the conviction through a four year appeal, and upon an unsuccessful conclusion, had managed to get a parole from the governor.

His boy, Orban, had finished law school, and on account of Dr. Patterson's personal appeal, Pruiett found a place for him in his law office, because his father, W. L. Sullivan, Dr. Young and other good men highly recommended the boy Orban to Pruiett. "I'd like to see you make yourself into a lawyer," Pruiett said. "Get the feud ideas out of your head an' work hard. I'll help you get started."

"I'll try to make myself handy," Patterson said. "How long's it been since the old man killed Doc Harrod?"

"It's been almost ten years."

"Maybe it's over, but them Valley feuds don't usually die so quick; they raise somethin' besides good cotton an' broom corn up them Washita flats, an' they're tough hombres. It isn't but a jump from Mayesville over to Lindsay."

"That's right," Patterson agreed.

"Ever hear of my client Monroe from up that way?" Pruiett grinned.

"I'll say I have," Patterson answered.

"They call him the chippey's nemesis around here," Pruiett laughed. "But no jokin', I figured, from the day your daddy shot old Doc Harrod in two with that shotgun, that there'd be a string of killin's follow it. That's the way things usually went down in the Valley."

Patterson smoked in silence. He was a tall youth who looked dreamily away when office clerks and loungers poked fun at his old fashioned habit of wearing a pistol, his height, in excess of six feet. The exceeding roundness of the outline of his small head was not interrupted by the sparse, fine hair which he brushed so close to it. His eye was keen; black, and straight and cold. His sallow complexion harmonized with the inevitable cigarette which he nervously fingered or sucked, and while he seldom spoke, when he did it was with a queer finality which discouraged disagreement.

"Old Bill Murray made a' awful dirty speech about me over at Mayesville," Pruiett ruminated, re-lighting his frayed cigar. "Your paw heard it, an' told me about it, an' durin' the conversation I asked him if he wasn't scared of old Harrod's kinfolks, or friends, down there."

"The old man ain't scared of nothin'," Patterson said without hesitation. He was not boasting.

The buzzer in the office began to rattle. Pruiett grabbed up the telephone. "Pruiett!" he bawled into the transmitter. "Pat? Yeah, he's in here. Sure. Here, son, it's for you."

Patterson put the receiver to his ear and answered the call, softly. "Is that so?" he inquired. "How long ago? Well . . . . well, I guess I'd better come down. Yes . . . . I'll see you before long."

Pruiett, with his feet in the window ledge, blew smoke rings and looked inquiringly up at Patterson as he took his coat from the back of his chair and started to put it on.

"Got to go?" he inquired.

"Yeah," Patterson answered, evenly. "Wade Williams shot the old man up. He's dead."

"The hell," Pruiett cried, jumping to his feet. "When? How did you find out?"

"That was Sis called," Patterson replied. "She just told me. It just now happened, down home."

"Are you goin' down there—now?" Pruiett asked, watching him intently. There was an unnatural air of unconcern about the young man.

"Sure, I'm going down there," Patterson replied. "I'm going down there—now."

Pruiett took his arm and turned him around, so that the two pair of beady dark eyes crossed their beams within a short, blunt radius.

"I'm a lot older than you are, son, an' I've seen a hell of a lot of this stuff. I've been close to it all my life an' I know what I'm talkin' about. Don't do it. Don't do what you are thinkin' about doin.' Take my advice and let the law take care of it, an' don't make matters any worse by another killin'."

Patterson made no change of face. "You want me to let him get away with it?" His eyes were unwavering. "You think I should do nothin' about it?"

"That's what I said," Pruiett snapped. "I'm givin' you some good advice. Don't do any killin'."

"Mr. Pruiett," said Patterson, with mock formality, "I understood you was from Kentucky. That don't sound like Kentucky counsel you're givin' me."

"I'm your friend, son, an' I'm talkin' to you like I would to my own boy. Let the law handle this case. Keep your hands out of it."

"All right, Mr. Pruiett," he said. Patterson had looked him searchingly in the face before he replied. He prefaced his dry answer with a wan smile. "I'll take your advice. I'll follow it— at least for awhile."

When word come to the office that Wade Williams had been acquitted at his trial for killing the doctor, the young lawyer sat quietly by the window, smoking his cigarettes and looking away, not even glancing up when Pruiett stopped by to reiterate his word of warning and advice. No visible change in his demeanor appeared, when, two months later, his sister, Verna Patterson, was found dead in the old Terminal Hotel at Oklahoma City. A dose of self-administered poison had produced her death. The two sealed notes which she had written and left on a dresser in the room were pocketed by Patterson; any questions regarding their contents were met with a patient shake of his head.

"I'd like to see you forget that hog leg, some morning; leave it at home on your baby grand," Pruiett joked with Patterson. "It's liable to go off an' hurt somebody."

"Maybe," Patterson answered, without looking up from his desk.

"Let's get these blood and thunder ideas out of our heads," Pruiett persisted.

"I don't want to be disrespectful, Mr. Pruiett," Patterson said, rising, "but I'll have to ask you to let me handle things that don't pertain to office business in my own way."

"I've been burned up with hate all my life," Pruiett confessed, "an' I think I'd a been better off if I'd a taken a few people into my confidence. I'm your friend. If you got to nurse these grudges, let me help you. Tell me about 'em."

"I'm not much of a hand to talk," Patterson said, "but you can't see your people killed off like I've seen mine, and expect a pistol bullet in your own back, an' not burn inside over it. I can't work, for thinkin' about it."

"Has the Williams jumped the old grudge up this late, you suppose?"

"Hell, yes," Patterson said. "They been hatchin' it since they was sure the old man was goin' to stay out on his parole. Wade stood across the street from the bank an' watched Dad come out, an' then shot him down like a dog. An' it's the old man Sam Williams that's responsible. He's been trainin' the boy, Wade, ever' since Harrod was killed, to do these jobs they been doin'."

"They didn't have anything to do with your sister's death, did they?"

"You're damned right, they did," Patterson answered, bitterly.

"What was the truth about that?" Pruiett demanded. "What was the matter, that she killed herself like she did?"

"That's something I can't discuss, not even with you," Patterson answered. "Don't ask me."

"So that's it," Pruiett mused, scratching his chin. "The old man wasn't in on that, though."

"He's the devil's granddaddy," Patterson gritted. "He's fixed up the parties an' furnished the liquor, an' got the young people together. An' he was—."

Pruiett waited. Patterson didn't want to disclose any more.

"That old man's been raising hell and killing up an' down the South Canadian River for twenty-five years," Patterson said. "He was with old Matt Wolfe in a lot of 'em, an' that Williams bank at Purcell never did get the reputation of bein' the farmer's friend."

"He ain't done no killin', himself, but he's engineered a dozen of 'em, just like he did the old man's," Patterson said. "When you want to stop the wolf pack, why, head off the leader. Ain't that right?"

"Get those ideas out of your head," Pruiett said, slapping him on the back. "By the way, when I used to make Purcell, the old banker was carryin' a little pearl handled thirty-two in his side pocket, all the time. Come in an' see me any time you get stuck on any of these cases."

"Sam L. Williams, banker and ranch owner of Purcell, Oklahoma, was shot and almost instantly killed by O. C. Patterson, an Oklahoma City attorney, at 10:45 this morning." The afternoon Times was advising the populace of the western city, still stunned by the nation's entrance into the war and the first drawing of the selective draft, of what had occurred on the crowded downtown intersection. "The tragedy took place on North Robinson Avenue, near the intersection of Main Street. Patterson shot Williams when the two met at a point twenty feet north of the Main Street line. . . . The shooting is said to be the result of a feud of long standing between the Williams and Patterson families."

". . . . Wade Williams, son of Sam L. Williams, killed Patterson's father, Dr. Price Patterson, at Maysville, last October. The killing is also reported to have resulted from alleged relationships of Williams, and his son, with one of Patterson's sisters. When tried, Wade Williams was acquitted by the jury."

"Miss Verna Patterson, a sister of Patterson, is said to have committed suicide at a hotel here several months ago. . . . After shooting the contents of his pistol into Williams, Patterson stood beside the body and lighted a cigarette. . . . Patterson will plead self-defense, according to Moman Pruiett, Patterson's law partner. Pruiett has been engaged to defend Patterson."

In subsequent reports on the case it appeared that "When asked in regard to a letter one of his sisters is said to have received from Sam Williams some time ago, Patterson said the matter would all be threshed out at the trial." As one account stated, "Justice of the Peace A. T. Earley, who performed the inquest on the body of Verna Patterson, who committed suicide at the Terminal Hotel last March, declared that the girl had tried several times to call a man named Williams over the telephone before she committed suicide." And in another, "A letter addressed to Wade Williams, which was found by her (Verna's) side when her body was discovered, was turned over to young Patterson, and is still in his possession, according to Moman Pruiett, Patterson's attorney."

The panorama of the trial-defense was in his mind when he started to the jail to see Patterson.

"Well, son, how you feelin'?" Pruiett greeted through the bars.

Patterson looked dreamily through the tobacco smoke of his cell. "Did you ever pick cotton, Mr. Pruiett, an' drag a heavy sack 'till you thought your neck was goin' to break, an' keep watchin' the sun and hopin' it would go down, so you could quit and get that awful load off your back?"

"Hell, yes," Pruiett laughed, "I've picked lots of cotton. Why, I've—."

"And then," Patterson interrupted, "the sun got clear out of sight, and it began to get dark—real slow like—and you could see the old man and the wagon at the end of the row, hitchin' up to go home. An' then you got to the end of the row, an' you took that strap from across your shoulder and around your neck, and you stood up straight, an' took a deep, free breath. Did you ever do that?"

"Hell, yes," Pruiett repeated. "Lots of times, why—?"

"Well, you asked me," Patterson replied. "That's how I'm feelin'. I'm feelin' awful damned good."

The foundation for Patterson's self-defense plea had been set when the coroner produced a small automatic pistol from the dead banker's pocket. The defendant's own testimony, well corroborated, would justify the first shot. What bothered Pruiett was a satisfactory explanation for emptying the smoking cylinder into the writhing body while it was prostrate on the concrete. He anticipated that the abundant proof on that phase of the case, which the prosecution meant to stress, would cause trouble after the trial judge had instructed on how far a person, once attacked, could reasonably go in repulsing the attacker and defending himself.

Colonel Jake Hodges had observed that self-defense was best; that the unwritten law was often adequate and effective, and that temporary insanity was better than a plea of guilty. The Pruiett corollary, formulated in a dark cell at Rusk and developed in the cow country courts while apprehensively looking about so as to be able to dodge a pistol ball headed for his back, had tended to combine all of them.

Patterson wasn't guilty because the old man, shifting his cane from his good hand so as to clamp it under his paralyzed arm, had meant to pull the little gun and inflict severe bodily harm, possibly death, upon him. He had wronged his sister, had broken her heart and caused her to take her own life, and that was of itself an act a true southwestern gentleman could not honorably overlook. The combination of the overt agencies produced by the dead man, the murder of Dr. Patterson, the wrong to his sister, fear for his own safety, mortal fear, dread and hate,

all aroused with the single view of Williams, had caused a break-
down of his reason and intellect. He temporarily lost control, and
in the blackness he continued, as witnesses glibly established, to
snap the pistol in the direction of the dead man long after the
last cartridge had exploded.

Pruiett scornfully ignored a valuable talking point in the
Patterson trial. The accused was big, young, single and able-
bodied. "Tell them the country needs men, he's already been
drawn in the draft, to send him to the front. He'll probably be
executed in France; make the Huns waste some powder and
lead on him." Those were some of the many suggestions which
Pruiett received as he was preparing to go to the jury with his
final appeal.

"I don't beg 'em for a damned thing," he growled. Patterson
feels that he'd already done the world a greater service in killin'
the head dog of the Williams kennel than he would have if he'd
captured the Kaiser. He's got some good stuff in him, it appears
to me."

The years since Rusk and Little Rock had proven Pruiett's
theory. John Evans and Doc Wilson stood at the head of his
proof column, beckoning to the host that floundered in a mire
of blood. What did it take to convince a jury? . . . . Credible
proof! What did it take to overpower a jury? . . . . The psychological thrust at the psychological moment! Where would
Maggie Miller have been if he hadn't produced credible proof?
Would Clarence Douglas have walked out into free air if the
jury hadn't been startled into belief, with his twin knife trick?
Didn't pulling his coat off at the right time ruin the carefully
prepared murder case the state had built up against Jim Leggett?

Pruiett played a jury like the piper played his piccolo. The
astonishing recollection; his amazing ability to act and imitate; the
power which permitted him to pull appropriate poetry out of his
head; to remember testimony, word for word and never to forget
a face, had stored up a profound panorama of murder-trial experience behind him. By inclination and instinct, and knowledge
based upon a process of elimination, he knew what to offer to
this jury, and what to offer to that one. Pruiett genius had
reached his zenith. He knew how to stage the perfect murder
trial.

Patterson's trial was simply a more highly developed reproduction of a hundred others which had preceded it. It was Pruiett,
jerking his laughs, tears and jeers as he willed them. He toyed

with the state's attorneys and encouraged them, until he was ready to shatter them with his favorite blow; the unearthly eloquence of his final speech to the jury. The local reporter used old copies of the paper for notes; they changed the old names and dates, and left the Pruiett in. One composed a page of doggerel, as he casually watched the state's witnesses march up to the sacrificial stand for Pruiett's cross-examination:

"The courtroom was crowded and quietness reigned
As lawyers from witnesses, slowly obtained
The tale of how Patterson, armed with a gun,
Discharged all its bullets, which struck, to a one—
How Williams wheeled back, how he fell, how he died,
While Patterson calmly stood off to the side."

"The scene in the court as the story they sought,
Displayed little love, and of happiness naught.
The sorrowful women, the stolid-faced men,
Presented a scene for the pessimist's pen.
The talking continued, the wrangling kept up,
When through the small gateway there toddled a pup;
A pup! Yes, we mean it—a wee little hound
That clumsily tumbled and sniffled around."

"A spectator grinned and a baby cried Goo!
His Honor looked solemn—what else could he do?
The hearing went on, and the lawyers all pored
O'er the books on the table—the dog was ignored.
'Til wandering around he pulled up at the feet
Of Pruiett—Yes, Moman—the lawyer complete."

"The latter leaned across his chair
And stroked the puppy's shaggy hair.
The doggy knew he had found a friend—
His tail vibrated to the end.
He stood upon his hindmost paws
And smiled between his doggish jaws,
While Moman Pruiett, lawyer, sat
And gave the pup a kindly pat."

"Have you wondered at the power which this Pruiett
    does command
When he takes a case to try before the court?
Have you wondered why he's able when he takes it in
    his hands,
To deliver it across in finest sort?"

"Now perhaps here is a reason—it's the fiber of the MAN,
Who though leader of a case of much import,
Found the time to stroke a doggy for a little moment's span,
As the creature wandered friendless through the court!"

Patterson came clear. "We the jury drawn, empaneled and
sworn in the above entitled cause do upon our oaths find Orban
C. Patterson, NOT GUILTY. (signed) M. R. Thornton, Foreman." Charles B. Stuart was attending court. He had been a
former law partner of Joe Bailey, in Texas, and was respected
in the southwest as a man of character, and a lawyer of great
ability. He met Pruiett in the corridor of the court building as
he came out. The two shook hands. Stuart ventured, "I've
watched you and the cases you've tried with a lot of interest.
I never tried a murder case by myself in my life; it's out of
my line, but I've been before plenty of juries. The way you handle
a jury and win your cases is most remarkable. I still hear people
talking about your argument in the United States Senator Gore
case."
    "I guess I have been fortunate is all, Judge," Pruiett an-
swered, with a modesty not entirely characteristic of him. "No,"
Stuart disagreed, "there's something that helps you along, that
holds you up, and you must know what it is. If you wouldn't
mind, I'd like to have you tell me what it is that you attribute
your success to in the trial of jury cases?"
    Pruiett studied, then smiled. "It may sound a little strange
to you right here, Judge, but I believe in giving a fair answer
to a fair question. I never enter a courtroom to try a case without
offerin' up a prayer; not a prayer to win the case, understand,
but a prayer to be directed to try it right, so that my client will
have the best chance of gettin' what he needed, when he showed
confidence in me, by hiring me." Stuart was nodding slowly as
he passed on. There was neither surprise, disbelief nor scorn in
his expression as he went into the courtroom.

CHAPTER EIGHTEEN

Wherein Pruiett made the greatest speech of his career to a Federal Judge for a client who was charged with a violation of the Mann Act, and breaks from a gallop to a trot, as he declines to go to the defense of the handsome woman who killed his friend, the Republican National Committeeman, Jake Hamon, and how a pistol ball finds a vital spot in the body of a bootlegging Negro client, and Pruiett, the dean of the felon emancipators, makes his own bond under a technical charge of murder. And how he comes clear in the court, and he suffers defeat in his defense of the worst murder case in the annals of Rocky Mountain criminal history. And how he gains the acquittal of a coy little widow of a wealthy gambler, who was charged with making herself a widow, and coins, in the trial, invective and abuse more scurrilous than any he had originated theretofore in his career—Annabelle Edwards.

Pruiett's deliverances of Sam St. Mary and Orban Patterson were classic. Nothing could have been added to perfect their records and further their desired results. No word or move was omitted which might have detracted from the theme of the defense. From the time the jurors were called to the box to the time the verdicts were read, the scowling, black haired lawyer dominated the scene. Sauve and sarcastic, or explosive and belligerent, each syllable, sentence and gesture was timed and produced to fit into the picture he had learned to create—the perfect murder trial. Ten days of his enchanting excellence, and the juries, the mere men who came to try the ones accused but who only watched, and marveled at the technique of their counsel, were under his spell.

Pruiett, as he was in those cases, would have saved Sacco and Vanzetti from the New England hot seat. He would have produced some justification, some circumstance of mitigation, for William Edward Hickman's bestial Pacific coast conduct; he would have robbed the maw of San Quentin's hungry gallows of its insignificant morsel. Leopold and Loeb, with cringing pleas of guilty, resting secure on the practical decision of a judicial mind, were not tried a la Pruiett. Was their crime less justifiable than Maggie Miller's? Was the probability of their technical guilt less certain than that of Red Fox, or George Hopkins? Pruiett would have mixed them up a batch of temporary insanity in the Sam St. Mary manner, and with a jury, a group of human beings with souls, feelings and emotions, he would have commenced the dangerous game of lives and liberties. His game was winner take all.

The towering pine exposes more of vulnerable surface to the elements than the scrub. When it reached its full growth and height, the weight of its own structure causes it to sag and split, and with each opening a vulnerable spot is made for the entrance of a parasitic body. Decadence proceeds from excellence more inexorably than it does mediocrity. The symphony is complete and a master is acclaimed. The campaign of application, and concentration, and sacrifice, and self-denial is over. Real genius does not stumble over his objective; he has fought for it and pursued it, and he holds it, for at last it is his. With the joys of success come the correlative pain of practical understanding. There is but one pinnacle. The classic cannot be improved.

In the defense of Joseph Goldstein, charged with a violation of the Mann Act (transporting a female, with immoral intent, across a state boundary), the accused had experienced apprehension over the way his case was being handled. He was a wealthy merchant, unable to see his mischieviousness, indiscretion at best, in the criminal light turned upon it by the district attorney. The girl had been young and inviting. He had spent his money for clothes and food for her, and that, in the old Jew's opinion, was justification for using her how, and where, he was able. But could his high-priced counsel present the case so that the court would see it his way, and understand? Pruiett stood steadily, adjusting the knot of his silk necktie. His argument was in his eyes, not in his voice box.

"An old man, an old fool," he mused dreamily in his smoothest tone, "but still human."

He resumed his seat at the counsel table. Nine soft words, from the throat and mouth capable of producing a thunderous volume. Spectators wondered. Goldstein glared. There was mayhem in his face, and it remained there, until he was startled in realization with a deliverance. The speech, in a single sentence, had moved him out of the shadow of Leavenworth's grim walls.

And there were other appearances of decadence, if temporary lapses from complete abandoned ferocity could be called decadence, in the demeanor of bloody murder's best friend. Jake

L. Hamon, millionaire oil man, Republican National Committeeman from Oklahoma, and an intimate of the President of the country, was shot to death in his hotel room by a concubine whom he took on tour and passed off as a member of his family. The defense was offered to Pruiett. What could have been sweeter a decade or two before? A beautiful client. A shy, softly sweet, witness. Cash! Stacks of cash, and national eye-catching notoriety. Pruiett in his former days offered his services to a lowly washerwoman just for the opportunity to fight and win. How he would have relished, in that day, the offer Clara Smith extended for services in the case where she was charged with killing wealthy Jake.

Pruiett turned her down. "Assailing Clara Smith as a modern vampire, Moman Pruiett, noted criminal lawyer, today set at rest rumors that he might aid the alleged slayer's defense when he sent a telegram to Mrs. Jake L. Hamon, as follows: 'I think it is an outrage that no voice has been raised in behalf of the dead. I know more about this unfortunate tragedy and what led up to it than any man living, and I cannot longer remain silent when this modern vampire is preparing for the movies and seeking a one-fourth interest in Jake's estate.' " It was strange talk for the man who had dedicated his life to empty prison cells and rotting gallows ropes.

Jake Hamon had been one of Pruiett's closest friends. Pruiett had made a convert of him in his defense of U. S. Senator Gore, where Hamon was discovering the efficiency of the political outlet for surplus cash. Hamon was putting up a lot of the money that the Bond-McMurray-Fitzpatrick combine was spending to discredit the blind Senator. When it was over and there was no question about who had won, Hamon went directly to Pruiett.

"We made our mistake in not havin' you on our side," he said after he had complimented Pruiett on his victory.

Pruiett didn't answer.

"I'd like to feel that I could call you when I need a lawyer in this part of the country," Hamon said. "I can let you make some money, an' I'll feel a lot safer with you lookin' after me and my business."

"You can call me," Pruiett replied with slight cordiality. "I'm in the business."

Their next meeting had been in a room in the Kingkade Hotel in Oklahoma City. "They've had me before the grand jury all day," Hamon opened the subject with little preliminary. "I think I'm goin' to be indicted."

"What do you want done?" Pruiett asked. "What d'you think I can do?"

"I think you can block it," Hamon replied coolly. "I'm new in this politics business, and I like it, for a plaything. I don't want to be indicted."

"I never saw any one who did," Pruiett laughed.

Hamon opened one of the top drawers of the dresser in the room. "Well, I don't want to be indicted," he repeated. He was tossing little oblong packages from the drawer to the corded counterpane. "Here's somethin' for you to work on."

Hamon laid out ten thousand dollars in hundred dollar bills, two bundles of them, with fifty crisp notes to the bundle.

"Yes," Pruiett grinned, "I see you don't want to be indicted."

An indictment had been returned against Hamon when the two had their next conference, in a room in the same hotel. It was Pruiett's turn to toss out the green packages. Hamon thumbed them glumly as they landed on the bed beside him, taking a quick, professional inventory.

"You brought it all back," he said when he had concluded his count. "Didn't you do anything to block this business?"

'I sure as hell did, plenty, but it couldn't be stopped," Pruiett replied. "I may get yanked up myself for what I've done. An outfit like that would indict Jesus Christ on hearsay. I just couldn't stop it."

"How much did you spend?" the astute Jake inquired, watching close for the expression that would come with the answer.

"Three dollars, an' I had a hell of a time doin' that."

"Well," Hamon persisted, "you didn't hold out anything for legal services. Don't you value your services at anything?"

"Not when I don't produce." Pruiett responded. "I'm always willin' to let my client put the fee up in the bank, or give me a note payable when they get their results." His mind was in the Valley, plugging for a win-or-you-don't-collect fee in the Sam Ashton case. "When I lose I don't care about the pay."

Hamon handed him one of the packages. It was five thousand dollars. Pruiett was about to make an objection to taking it when he was interrupted by a knock on the door.

"Come in," Jake called. A beautiful young girl walked in.

"Mr. Pruiett, meet my niece," Hamon said, very softly.

"Really?" the worldly Pruiett drawled. His remark was dripping with skepticism. "I'm delighted."

"Clara Hamon," Hamon continued.

Pruiett made another bow, more formal and sincere than the first. His apologetic manner was a confession of the doubt he had of actual relationship.

The girl was twenty-three or twenty-four years old; radiant, stalwart, voluptuous. The V at her throat was a trifle low and the hem of her skirt a trifle high, Pruiett thought, for a young woman to wear for a call on her middle-aged uncle. Pale, tan freckles across the bridge of her nose and high on the smooth cheek detracted nothing from her natural charm. They added a natural accompaniment to the picture of health which her superbly developed figure suggested. Her reddish brown hair was loose and wavy. The white toothed smile which she bestowed so opulently upon Uncle Jake seemed slightly out of proportion to the esteem, or restraint, usually accompanying meetings between those so closely related.

"I'll fix us a drink," Jake said, as he tugged with the top of a ginger ale bottle.

"Your niece is a handsome girl," Pruiett observed, eyeing her frankly as she crossed her legs and reclined in a big chair.

"Ain't she," Jake beamed. Clara took a package of cigarettes from her hand bag.

"How many drinks you fixin'?" Pruiett demanded.

"One apiece," Jake laughed. "You ain't so old fashioned you won't let a little girl take one, are you?"

"Not me," Pruiett grinned, trying to conceal some of the surprise he felt at Jake's attitude. What the hell kind of a fellow was he—with his kinfolks?

"This is keen," Clara cooed, sipping the cold highball and blowing a blast of white smoke through her delicate nostrils.

"It's a good drink," Pruiett agreed.

"Jake knows how to fix 'em better'n anybody," Clara declared, as she got up and walked toward the men on the bed. She rested her weight upon Hamon's thick knee, and carelessly let the hand holding the cigarette steal across his shoulder and behind his fat neck.

"I got to be goin," Pruiett announced, after he had bolted his drink. "I got an appointment I got to keep. I'll mail you a receipt for the money, an' I'll call you sometime."

Bill Maben dropped in from Tulsa. Pruiett was out of the city. "What the hell does he mean poppin' off about Clara Smith Hamon?" he inquired. "Why don't he grab off that case an' go to town?"

"He's been actin' queer about a lot of things, here lately," Patterson answered. Pat's mind was clinging to business since he had dispatched the leader of the Williams wolf pack and Pruiett had cleared up the likelihood of his having a penalty to pay for it.

"I thought maybe he had a' offer from the Hamon estate," Maben said. "They'll be hirin' a special prosecutor or two in it, won't they?"

"They offered it to Pruiett, but he turned it down," Pat answered. "What they offered him was equal to the runs of a Healdton gusher, an' you know what he says? He says 'Hell, no. I see old Jake across the river, an' he's shakin' his head an' tellin' me not to touch it.' Can you believe it?"

"He's been leary of them prosecution cases ever since he tried Pete Thompson," Maben mused. "He poured it on old Cecil Mingle, an' they gave him life. Then he sent that amateur Romeo that was a justice of the peace up state for a life sentence, an' he didn't seem to mind that. But when that jury gave Pete a death sentence, Pruiett looked sicker'n Pete. He ain't no prosecutor."

"Hell, no he ain't," Patterson agreed. "He got so burnt up prosecutin' Pete that he forgot how strong he was goin'. He lost twenty pounds worryin' about the state burnin' a man on his help."

"Just the same, I don't understand him landin' on Clara Smith, an' then turnin' down a whale of a fee from the Hamons. He could grab the gravy, an' pull short on the punches, couldn't he?"

"He could," Pat agreed, "but he wouldn't. There's somethin' about the damn case I don't understand. Some of the boys from down Ardmore way was up to see him, an' they had a hell of a session. I think maybe he was afraid to cut any cake. He thought he might choke on it."

"I'd believe he had a heavy conscience before I'd believe anybody bluffed him out of a part," Maben scoffed. "You know how him an' Jake was—an' Clara, too, for that matter. The three of 'em was stayin' in the same suite at the Raleigh at Washington, an' they went to New York an' California together two or three times. I heard Pruiett say that old Jake was the best hand to hustle a bootlegger in a strange town he ever saw."

"An' I've heard him tell how Clara used to pull their shoes

off an' spread the foot blanket over 'em, after he an' Jake had passed out," Patterson recollected. "He made two or three settlements between Jake an' Clara after they started gettin' tired of their arrangement, an'—."

"It takes a woman to make a final settlement," Maben laughed. "Give one of 'em a thirty-eight an' a close shot an' she'll draw up a' agreement that'll hold."

"Pruiett's strong for his friends, like he is poison for his enemies," Patterson reminded. "He was tryin' a case one time an' I was helpin' him empanel the jury. I came in a little late an' saw a guy in the box that was no good, an' I felt like I ought to tell Pruiett about it. 'That guy in the third seat in the back row's a dirty cur,' I whispered in his ear. 'I know he is,' Pruiett comes back, 'but he's MY cur. I'm goin' to keep him.' That's the way he is."

"Maybe he thinks too much of Jake, that's why he's blastin' Clara, but it don't sound right. Well . . . . he's got plenty of murder cases waitin'. Maybe he ought to keep out of at least one around here."

"Ropey" O'Brien of Chicago, a prosecutor who was trying to hang as many murderers on the Great Lakes as Pruiett has managed to liberate to the south and southwest, took the Hamon hook. When he stepped onto the station platform at Ardmore, a tall man with a big hat and double hip-bulge sauntered out to meet him. It was Buck Garrett, the pride of the cattle land grown rich with oil drenched pastures; the same Garrett whom Pruiett had liberated those fifteen years before, after his indiscreet gunplay in the sporting house over the hardware store. Buck was chewing, and whittling, and looking carelessly about as he approached lawyer O'Brien.

"You Mr. O'Brien?" he inquired casually.

"Why, yes, I'm O'Brien," the lawyer replied, with surprise.

"Are you the lawyer from Chicago that's going to work in the Smith case?" The lank sheriff chipped splinters from a wooden block in his hand with a narrow, long bladed knife.

"Yes, sir, I am," O'Brien responded. "Did you have a message for me?"

"Why, yes, I did," Garrett drawled. Looking him intently in the eye he let the block drop and clatter to the bricks of the platform, while his left hand extended to grasp the lawyer's flowery necktie. With a firm grip on it he lashed out with the knife hand, severing the tie just below the knot at his throat.

"I'm tellin' you that you ain't wanted here, an' that it ain't healthy for you to stay. That's about all I got to say."

No imported talent was chargeable with the loss of the Clara Smith case. The mild efforts of the local prosecutors were ineffective. She was restored to liberty.

The leg of lamb rose up and smote the butcher with a shiny cleaver. The pony stood on its hind legs in the center of the ring, puffing a cigar and popping a long whip while a male biped on all-fours, with big-tent mustaches and patent-leather boots, galloped 'round the ring and jumped clumsily through the big hoop. Everything was in reverse. The war and the armistice, prohibition and bath-tub-gin, had upset the universe. Moman Pruiett, the dean of the felon emancipators, was led into court behind counsel, held on a technical charge of murder.

Pruiett had been defending murderers for almost a quarter of a century. His business confined him to contacts with murder. His reputation limited his conversations to murder. It was as natural for a casual acquaintance, as for an old friend, when meeting him on the train or on the street, to talk of that which they presumed would be of the most interest to him—murder. He lived, ate and slept murder. He knew the signs and sequels of murder like the old settlers on the Washita knew nature's signs of the seasons.

When Cal Stewart slew Ben, his brother, after Pruiett had obtained a joint acquittal for both of them, for murdering old Doctor McCarrol at Enville, Pruiett nodded understandingly. He knew that he would have to defend one of them for the murder of the other, and that in all probability Cal would beat Ben to the punch. He defended Cal, and he came clear. When news came to the Main Street of Marietta that Cal had killed Ben, Pruiett showed no surprise or concern. Liddell was the son of the marshal who had been slain by Hancock on the Thackerville depot platform in 1899. Pruiett knew when he cleared Hancock that when the Liddell kids grew big enough, one of them would avenge the marshal's death.

The bells were ringing in his ears again.

Joe Patterson, a burly Negro ex-convict, was stopped in his unsavory prime by Pruiett lead. The soft-nosed slug smashing against his leather-tough chest and rough ribs flattened and spread as big around as a silver dollar before it exploded his heart. Writhing, kicking and cursing, the dying outlaw crawled and flopped from the kitchen of his bootlegging joint to its front porch, where, in final resignation, he rolled down the steps and sprawled motionless in death.

Joe ran a spot in "nigger town," the east side colored settlement along the Rock Island railroad tracks in Oklahoma City. Cold home brew was thirty-five cents, three bottles for a dollar. Corn liquor that would strip the enamel from the molars as it rushed by was a dollar a pint. If a storage squab-chicken was seduced from the back porch ice box and fried up in the quick grease, it was two dollars more. And like all guys in luck, Joe didn't know when he was well off. He had to do a little hi-jacking, and buy and sell hot diamonds, in between times and on the side. His fondness for carrying a pistol caused his downfall.

Pruiett and pistol-totin Orban Patterson packed their artillery into Joe's, shortly after supper time on Sunday night. Patterson was still watching from his eye-corners for Wade Williams. Rush McGaffey, a Negro protege of Pruiett's, who drove his car, oiled his pistol cylinder, and operated a Kelly pool game and policy racket in a Pruiett owned building, was along. The Negro Patterson, who was a client of Patterson, Pruiett's junior partner, didn't like Rush McGaffey; neither did white Patterson, the junior partner.

Joe decorated the worn oil-cloth of the kitchen table with four sweating bottles before he sat down in the one vacant chair remaining. Pruiett, expensively tailored, and with his black mop competing with his finger and tie diamonds for shine and splendor, showed the strain of a deep suspicion of the two Pattersons, his dark eyes twitched spasmodically. There was a noticeable gap between his white collar and his neck.

"Get me another bottle of beer, Joe," Pruiett commanded in an unpleasant tone.

"Let Rush get it, he ain't too damn good," interrupted Orban Patterson.

Joe sat and looked defiantly for an instant; he uttered a slight sniff of contempt as he rose to obey. There was insolence in the way he slammed the fresh bottle down on the table before the lawyer after he brought it. Rush McGaffey squirmed uneasily.

"I guess I'd better go on home, Mr. Pruiett," Rush said. "It ain't very far an' I'll just walk."

"Hell, no," said Pruiett. "You're drivin' my car, an' stayin' with me. When I go you go, an' not before."

There was a difficult silence which lasted for several minutes. "Joe," Pruiett said, deliberately, as he eyed him through optics that were almost closed, "I've worked out all I owe you for drinks. You don't get any more free service; I don't get any more free service; I don't get any more free drinks."

"That's good for me," Joe answered. "What suits you suits me. I guess there's plenty of lawyers, just like there's plenty of bootleggers." He grinned understandingly at Pat, sitting sour-faced and silent beside Pruiett.

"Pat don't represent you, not if he stays in my office, if that's what you mean," Pruiett corrected him. "I told you about those diamonds, and I meant what I said. You went right ahead an' fenced 'em."

Joe shot a quick look at Rush McGaffy. "Damn you, Rush, did you—?"

"I ain't said nothin,' Joe, not a word," Rush said, half-rising, "Mr. Pruiett's been fussin' all evenin' an' sayin' I was in on it too, but I ain't, an' I ain't told him nothin'."

"Hell, yes, he did, the black rat," said Orban Patterson. "He's the one that squealed, an' it ain't the first time he's done it. He's a regular snitch."

Joe's massive lip curled with contempt. "You always was a damned rat," he growled at McCaffy, "an' I ought to kill you."

"Get me another bottle of beer, Joe," Pruiett interrupted.

Joe Patterson glared at McGaffy for a full instant before he gave a sign of hearing Pruiett. He looked defiantly at Pruiett, again, as he arose. The evil look which was apparent on his face as he headed for the back-porch cooler was suspiciously absent, and supplanted by a fictitious grin, when he returned.

"No use to get mad at me, Mr. Pruiett," he said. "Ol' Joe is goin' to listen to his lawyer. He ain't got the best one in the country for nothin.' Ol' Joe ain't that dumb."

Pruiett nodded and studied the rising foam on the slightly wild brew. He might be drunk, and he might suffer from chronic ego, but he wasn't goin' to be fooled by a murderous nigger. He understood the situation instantly and it told him to watch out for evil action.

Black Joe changed the subject; switched to a tale of World War ribaldry. McGaffy, frightened and uneasy, forced a smile, then an African guffaw, at the smutty climax.

Joe Patterson didn't resume his seat. Instead he stood beside it, on one foot, with the other foot pointed squarely in the seat of the chair. "What kind of a gun's that you're carryin' tonight, Rush?" he asked. "Is it the same one as you always had?"

Rush laid his hand on the table. "Yeah," he said, as he touched the table. McGaffy was unarmed. Orban Patterson's hand crept toward his belt. He was wearing his pistol in the waistband.

"Rush," Pruiett barked, "don't do it! Don't move your hand. They're gonna kill you."

McGaffy turned a pale brown. His hand froze on the table.

"Put it on the table," Joe Patterson said, with a menacing movement toward his side. "Put it on the table. You reached for it, an' you don't get no drop on me. Lay it out here."

McGaffy was as white as Pruiett or Orban Patterson. Unable to move a muscle, he could only look appealingly at Pruiett by rolling his big eyes.

"Don't move, Rush," Pruiett said. "If you start to move your hand they'll shoot you. That's all they want to do. Don't move."

"It's a showdown," Joe Patterson gritted. "An' I don't take no chances. Do you bring it out, or do I let you have it now?"

Joe was standing directly across the table from Pruiett. His gun was on his right hip, which was slightly distorted by the position of his right foot, resting as it was on the seat of the chair. He didn't suspect that Pruiett was armed; that he had a pistol in the band of his trousers.

Joe Patterson started to drag his foot across the bottom of the kitchen chair. He was going to drop it to the floor, and draw his gun at the same time.

"Don't move, Rush," Pruiett whispered. "They'll kill you, sure." As Joe Patterson's foot went down Pruiett leaped up. Joe Patterson said, "You and the judge both die together." Two pistols spoke. It was Pruiett's and Orban Patterson's. The force of the big slug from Pruiett's gun knocked Negro Patterson almost out of the kitchen door. Mortally wounded, bleeding terribly, he crawled back past the transfixed trio in the room, through the house and out the front door, whimpering and mumbling like an ailing pup. Orban Patterson's shot just missed Rush McGaffy's head. McGaffy grabbed Orban Patterson's pistol, and Pruiett rushed in and assisted him in disarming Patterson. The unexpected turn of events stunned Orban Patterson. He was standing pale and rigid, watching the wounded Negro, his friend when Pruiett's attention was attracted by a movement at his side.

and discovered that McGaffy had Patterson's pistol pointed at Patterson. Pruiett cocked his big pistol again. "Don't shoot, Rush," he cried. "Don't you kill Mr. Patterson. If you do I'll blow your head off."

Patterson looked around into the menacing muzzle of his own gun, trained full on his head by McGaffy, Pruiett was at the Negro's side, holding a cocked pistol in both hands, within a foot of McGaffy's head. "I'll kill you as sure as hell if you shoot," Pruiett repeated. "Put that gun down; take it off of Mr. Patterson. You're as dead as hell if you don't."

McGaffy seemed to reflect for an instant, not looking toward the man who was threatening his life so soon after saving it; he was sighting all the time down the groove of the pistol barrel. In the tense atmosphere he seemed to casually seek the preponderance. He wanted to kill Orban Patterson. Was it worth what it would cost if Pruiett meant what he said? Rush dropped the gun to the table-top. Patterson slumped into a seat.

"You better go on home, Rush, or somewhere out of here," Pruiett said. "Me and Pat'll take care of things. Maybe you better call me at the office in about a' hour. I've got to call the sheriff, an' I may need you."

"PRUIETT HELD ON CHARGE OF KILLING NEGRO."

It was 34 point type in the Oklahoma's headlines, announcing another sensational move on the part of the irrepressible Pruiett. "Joe W. Patterson, Negro," said the story which followed, "was killed Sunday night at 9 o'clock in a shooting affray at his home, 615 East First Street, in which Moman Pruiett, Orban Patterson and Rush McGaffy are alleged to have been participants . . . ."

"According to W. P. Lindsay, under-sheriff, Pruiett called the county jail immediately after the shooting and announced that he had 'shot a man,' and was ready to give up. . . . When they arrived they found Joe Patterson dead near the front steps. . . . Pruiett, in a statement to Carl Glitsch, chief of police, said at the jail that he had shot Joe Patterson in self-defense, following a disagreement between Orban Patterson and Rush McGaffy, in which Joe Patterson is alleged to have interfered. . . .

"Information gained by county officials, that a murderous plot was nipped in the bud when Attorney Moman Pruiett wheeled and killed 'Negro Joe' Patterson at his home Sunday, kept charges from being filed Monday against the attorney, it was declared. . . .

"The mystery of the shooting rests solely in the hands of Rush McGaffy, Negro bootlegger and gambling king, who operates a pool hall in a building owned by Pruiett. . . . Bertilion Expert Lee Mullenix rushed to the place from the police station, and declared Monday that 'all parties had been drinking heavily.' . . . .

"Both Attorney Patterson and Moman Pruiett were released on personal checks of $1,500 each as bond pending investigation by the county attorney. . . . 'Negro Joe' Patterson was considered a 'bad actor.' Together with Rush McGaffy, the control of the gambling and bootlegging element among the Negroes fell to the pair."

"Moman Pruiett was justified in killing Joe Patterson, alleged Negro bootlegger and gambler, Sunday night . . . In instructing the jury McWilliams (Justice of the Peace A. W. McWilliams) said that he believed that it was their duty to exonerate Pruiett."

"The said jurors," read the entry on the magistrate's docket, "upon their oaths do say that the said Joe Patterson came to his death by gunshot wounds, said gun in the hands of one Moman Pruiett, and that said Moman Pruiett was justified in said act, and was acting wholly in self-defense. . . . (Signed) R. Weesner, Foreman."

It was a hum-drum existence. Annabelle Edwards was insisting that at least a fraction of his time be devoted to the preparation of her case, coming on for trial in a fortnight. The Hill murder case, for trial at Brighton, Colorado, was set, and in no uncertain terms had the court and the prosecution told him that his application for a continuance would be denied. Napoleon Buffalohead, Osage Indian at Newkirk, who had paid him $4,500 to defend him in a murder case, couldn't understand why his counsel had to kill a nigger on the night before his case was to be tried, nor why he didn't come on up, and help his office assistants, after the coroner's jury had promptly absolved him of blame.

"The 10-year-old girl found murdered by drowning near Eno, Adams County, late Saturday, was Helen Maxine Short, daughter of Mrs. Thelma Hill, this city. This is the bare statement of last night's development in probably the most brutal murder case Adams County police annals show. Evidence found by Sheriff E. A. Gormley and Coroner E. J. Jones of Adams County, weights tied to the child's neck by wires, the clutching position of her hands, the marks made by the wires on her throat, showed, the authorities believe, that the little girl was thrown into the water alive and left to die," said the Rocky Mountain News of Denver.

"Circumstantial evidence and information given by Mrs. Hill here started a search for William Riley Hill, her second husband, who, she said, is a half-breed Indian, as the alleged slayer of the child."

William Riley was the son of old John T. Hill of the Valley; his mother was a Chickasaw Indian. They were Pruiett's friends and clients of a more wholesome era, who held land on the Washita, and raised cattle to augment their already substantial wealth. Pruiett was employed.

"KNOW ALL MEN BY THESE PRESENTS: That I, William Riley Hill, son of John T. Hill, deceased, of Pauls Valley, Garvin County, Oklahoma, ... do hereby grant, bargain, sell and convey unto Moman Pruiett of Oklahoma City, Oklahoma, all of the following described real estate situated in Garvin County, Oklahoma, to-wit:

"Approximately four hundred and fifty (450) acres of land situated from two and one-half to three and one-quarter miles east and south of Pauls Valley;

"Approximately nineteen hundred (1900) acres of land situated about eight miles east of Pauls Valley; all of the above land being situated in Garvin County, State of Oklahoma, and being included in the Estate of John T. Hill, deceased, of Pauls Valley, Oklahoma, described as follows: . . . ."

The utterly original explanation offered by Hill didn't help Pruiett as he strove to make out a credible defense for him. "Hill still maintains that he gave the little girl to a foreigner near Derby, who promised to take her back to Denver in his automobile. He admitted that the child was with him in the vicinity the day before the murder is supposed to have occurred." Pruiett had never liked to see a witness change his testimony; tell your story and stick to it, regardless of how improbable it may seem, had been his advice to his clients. Callie Pence profited by his program. He built his defense around Hill's hastily concocted statement, given to the police immediately after his arrest.

The flattering notices given him by the mountain press failed to rouse or elate him. "Pruiett gained prominence when he defended Senator Gore of Oklahoma in the sensational damage case brought against him a few years ago," said the Denver Post. "His (Hill's) leading counsel is Moman Pruiett of Oklahoma

City, a criminal lawyer of wide reputation in Oklahoma and Texas," said the Brighton Blade. "Mr. Pruiett has been the chief counsel for the defense in two hundred and sixty-nine murder cases." He was weary, and tired, and bored. He'd rather have a continuance than have the case go to trial. Maybe he'd feel better, more like trying it next term. He was beginning to suggest a delay in every case being called to trial.

But the account of the conclusion of the trial, printed in Denver's Rocky Mountain News, disclosed that there was the customary rally just before the whistle blew. "The Oklahoma Lawyer was perspiring profusely, and stopped long enough to remove his collar. . . . The attorney then delved into the testimony, dissecting it and assembling it to his client's credit. . . .

" 'I am appealing to you men,' he said, whirling again to the jury. 'I am appealing to you not to be swayed to a rabid sentiment built upon a false fabric.' . . . . Then turning and shaking his finger at Sheriff Gormley, he cried at the top of his voice, 'Gormley, you sleuth hound, with your ambition for re-election, why didn't you bring the station agent of Barr into the courtroom. This defendant asserts he talked with him. Why didn't you bring the agent in to testify?' Then whirling again to the jury, 'Gormley thinks he has a cinch on this case,' he said, 'but gentlemen, I've known dead things to crawl. There is nothing to fear but maudlin, damnable sentiment that ought to be in purgatory rather than in a court of justice.' "

But the Colorado jurors wouldn't be whiled away from a true verdict in such an obvious case. They found Hill guilty of murder and sentenced him to life imprisonment in the penitentiary. When Pruiett entered the district courtroom at Oklahoma City two days after the verdict, ready to try the Edwards case, every one was congratulating him.

"That was a good job, Moman," the lawyers and courthouse employees observed. "It was a great victory. We knew that was all you expected to do; save him from hanging. It was a terrible case."

"Sure," Pruiett agreed aloud. "It was a' awful tough one."

Annabelle Edwards paid Pruiett five thousand dollars for his services. She was charged and tried for the murder of Billy Edwards, her gambler husband. In rage and disgust, she charged him with stupid conceit, but her psychological analysis was not as true as her aim with a thirty-eight (poor dead husband Billy). Her counsel merely despaired because her case was so routine. There were no new fields for him to invade.

The Black Charger bustled into the office of E. D. Oldfield, District Judge. His pocket was bulging with an assortment of legal papers.

"Got your writs all ready?" the judge inquired, smiling.

"I am not interested in a writ, yet," Pruiett grinned.

"Annabelle isn't goin' to wait trial in jail, now. Don't tell me that."

"Not unless I lose my taw," Pruiett returned. "We got somethin' more important than tryin' to bust the state's investigation hold while they wait on Billy to die. We're suin' him for a divorce, an' I got orders here for tyin' up a couple bank accounts, an' a safety deposit box."

"That's kind of rough, ain't it?" Oldfield inquired. "Shoot a man up an' put him in the hospital, an' then file a lawsuit against him? She just wanted to be sure she'd have him where she could get service on him, is that it?"

Pruiett grinned again. "This is the first shootin' case I ever got into where I started out with a divorce petition instead of a writ of habeas corpus," he admitted. "But this is a' unusual case from a lot of angles. She alleges in her petition that this cash is community, Billy's folks are liable to grab it out of the bank, an' beat her out of it. We want some restrainin' orders, to keep ever'body away from that stuff 'til we can get a hearin'."

"You ain't tryin' to restrain a little security for a' attorney's fee, are you Moman? Oldfield inquired, as he attached his signature to the orders.

"It's goin' to be high if Billy dies, an' I'll bet you two to one he isn't alive tomorrow night," Pruiett said. "If I'm right about that, you'll see me in here with the writ. We'll have to persuade the county attorney to agree to bond, or make him do it in court."

Billy Edwards writhed and twisted under a restraining sheet while a deputy sheriff served the summons in the divorce case on him. He was dead by nightfall, and Pruiett filed his writ to compel Annabelle's release on bond. The bond was steep, but he made it, and preparation for trial was commenced.

"More shooting took place at 910½ North Dewey Avenue, Billy Edwards apartment, Tuesday night. . . . Following a report of shots heard there, police rushed to the place and found Moman Pruiett, attorney, and Mrs. Edwards. . . . Pruiett said some one was eavesdropping at the apartment, and that the shots were fired by Mrs. Edwards' guard. No arrests were made. Pruiett said he did not fire the shots."

"What's the trouble?" a plain-clothes officer demanded, as he came to the top of the stairway.

"Nothin' a'tall, chief, nothin' a'tall," Pruiett assured him. "Mrs. Edwards and I came out here to pick up some private papers of hers, an' to reconstruct the tragedy for her defense, an' some one tried to sneak up on us. Dutch was waitin' in the car, an' he tried to stop 'em. When they ran, he took a couple of shots in the air, just to scare 'em."

"Where's Dutch now?" the officer asked.

"I sent him away," Pruiett answered. "I don't like that kind of stuff. I told him to go away an' let us alone."

"What's the matter with Mrs. Edwards?" he asked, next.

"She's under a strain; you know how it is, an' I guess the shootin' upset her more," Pruiett said. He was steadying the girl with a tight grip, while she trembled and shook with sobs.

"I'm leavin' it with you," the policeman said, after a deliberate study. "Let's have things quiet around here from now on. The neighbors are raisin' hell about this place all the time."

"O. K., Chief," Pruiett agreed. "I won't bust a cap if they mob me."

"I'm glad he didn't look inside, an' see all the bullet holes we got in here," Pruiett said, as he pushed Annabelle into the apartment and locked the door. "What the hell's the matter with you?"

"I wanta' die," Annabelle sobbed. "Give me that gun back, an' let me alone for a minute, an' I'll see that I do."

"Brace up," Pruiett soothed.

Annabelle sank to the bed crying hysterically. "I'll get the chair; I know I will," she bawled. "I paid you a fortune to defend me, an' I get death. Oh, God! Let me have that gun so I can end this misery."

"You'll send me to the chair," she groaned. "You just mark my word, I'll be convicted. I know I will."

"You won't if you'll give me half a chance to defend you," Pruiett answered, "You'll come clear. You know it?"

He took a big handkerchief and wiped her tear-smeared rouge. She smiled and sniffled. Pruiett had a way with his clients.

J. B. A. Robertson, who managed to last his four-year term without being impeached, was Governor. Jack Walton, his successor who didn't fare so well with the Senate, sitting as a court of impeachment, was the mayor of Oklahoma City. Pruiett didn't like them or agree with them politically, and as the Edwards case contained a rich graft and corruption element, he decided to unload it on them.

"The defense will prove," Pruiett said in his opening statement, "that the dead Billy Edwards paid the Governor $5,000 for a pardon for George Parrish, who was his first lieutenant in the vice and liquor business, and who is the state's principal witness in this case; that Jack Walton's police force winked at open violations of law as Billy and his gang of gamblers and bootleggers paid tribute to him."

"Pruiett, following his attack on Robertson, Walton and a number of gamblers and bootleggers, all of whom he asserted were in conspiracy against this woman on trial, declared he not only feared for her life, but for his own as well. 'They may get me, some dark night,' he said in a broken voice, 'but if they do, I hope that some other will take up the torch and carry on the fight. . . . 'I'm only 49 years old,' he added, 'but I'll be ready to go. I've already lived a hundred and forty-nine years in my lifetime.' "

"A brawl and near-fight between defense Attorney Moman Pruiett and George Parrish, erstwhile gambler, was the entertainment presented to hundreds of murder fans at the re-opening of the Annabelle Edwards trial Monday. . . . Parrish accused Pruiett of frequenting city gambling halls; Pruiett denounced the witness as a liar, and both men were out of their seats. Judge E. D. Oldfield quelled the disorder before either had a chance to follow up the hot words."

"George Parrish was put on as the first prosecution witness. The brawl with Pruiett came near the end of his testimony. 'Didn't you operate gambling houses with this unfortunate man, Edwards?' Pruiett demanded. 'No,' Parrish retorted. 'I was at some places where gambling was going on, just like I've seen you at such places.' . . . 'That's a lie,' Pruiett shouted, banging the table at his side. 'I haven't played cards for 16 years.' . . . 'You wouldn't call me that outside this courtroom,' Parrish answered, as Oldfield rapped for order and other attorneys moved in to quiet them. Pruiett was determined to fire a parting shot. 'Mr. Parrish,' he inquired, suavely, 'Isn't it a fact that you regularly and recently, purchased eight and ten 100 pound sacks of sugar?' Parrish turned even redder than before. 'What about that grocery store at 23rd Street and Robinson?' the attorney demanded. 'I bought five sacks there,' the witness admitted. 'But I bought them for a friend.' "

Those were the days of home brew and sugar whiskey. Mash-fed hogs brought good prices on the market; there was a ready sale for the liquor. Pruiett drank it in case of emergency, when he couldn't get the high-priced stuff which he usually imported from Kansas City.

Behind the back of the straw man of graft and corruption which he had set up, to beguile the jurors away from the real issue, he had his inevitable little plea of self-defense.

" 'He came upstairs and said, "You God dam bitch, get your duds on and get out of this house," ' Mrs. Edwards said in telling of the shooting. 'He walked to the dresser and opened the drawers. I walked over to him. He snatched a diamond lavalier from my neck and struck me. My hand struck the side of the table. I had been sick and wasn't well enough to fuss or fight. I backed away. My hand touched a gun lying on the table. He made a movement as if to reach for a gun. He was left-handed and always wore his gun on the right side under his vest—.' " At this point she choked and sat silent for a moment. " 'Well, what did you do?' asked her attorney. . . . 'I fired,' was the answer. 'When I picked up the gun I didn't know whether it was loaded or how many shells were in it. I intended to scare him, but he kept coming. I knew by the look on his face that he would kill me. I shot to protect my life. I fired twice; his gun fell to the floor.' "

That was all there was to the Annabelle Edwards case, except Moman Pruiett, counsel for the defense and the forensic fireworks which went with him. He managed to drag the trial of the case out over fifteen full days. He took five hours to sum it up in the final argument to the jury. Even the trial judge was looking sheepish and apologetic when Pruiett had concluded his denunciation of the enforcement offfcers and state prosecutors who had been so ignoble as to try to perform their sworn duty. A holy light, like the nimbus over a madonna, glowed about the head of the little woman in the prisoner's dock.

Pruiett warmed up by telling the jury that the Governor of their state was "as crooked as a pan of hog guts."

"God deliver me from coming in contact with the shadow of this Governor us yellow Democrats are so proud of," he bawled.

"I wouldn't trust Jack Walton (the mayor) or the Governor, handcuffed, to carry their own grips to the depot."

And poor old George Parrish, the state's star witness, had hesitated before attending the trial, apprehensive of being picked up on an old criminal complaint. The prosecuting attorneys had written him, and, in diplomatic terms, had given him to understand that bygones could be bygones, even with the majesty of the Law, and especially when Pruiett was hot on their heels. Pruiett's extensive underworld intelligence service had brought news of the deal back to him, and he had exposed it in the trial of the cause.

Having paid his respects to the Governor, and the Mayor, he turned to the prosecuting attorney's office. Jerking his coat off and slamming it into an empty chair he dashed a splash of perspiration from his face and wheeled upon the hapless prosecutor with the same movement.

"There never was a more dirty or contemptible deal made, with a perjuring skunk, than your letter indicates you made with this dirty pig," he roared. "Give ME the authority of county attorney, and give me this Edwards case, and I'll put more crooked thieves and officers in the penitentiary than there are this side of hell."

The able E. J. Giddings, his adversary in a hundred bad cases, who had fought so valiantly to discredit blind Senator Gore seven years before, was special prosecutor. He had been hired by dead Billy's parents to insure the conviction of the woman who had killed their son. Giddings was desperate. By preference he had joined the whispering school that said, "Pruiett is slipping; he's drinking himself to death." He felt and hoped, may have even believed, that at last his opportunity for victory, and revenge, had arrived. He made a vigorous and effective argument to the jury, but not one that Pruiett couldn't answer in his own inimitable manner.

"That is the gentleman, Annabelle, honey," Pruiett soothed, as he pointed the trembling finger at Giddings, "who called you a harlot and a prostitute, without one scintilla of testimony to support it. The dirty, damnable scoundrel who brands a woman as a harlot is unworthy of the consideration of any jury, especially when he does it without one scintilla of evidence to justify it. When any lawyer says that a woman laid flat on her back, in the absence of proof, in old Kentucky—that lawyer is either mentally deranged or he is as mean and dirty as hell. Where is there testimony in this case that this poor little soul has ever laid flat on her back?"

Pruiett stood defiantly beside his pitiable client, caressing her shoulder tenderly. He glared at the jury, then in the direction of Giddings, and then back at the jury.

"He talks to you of the North," he continued. "I care not from what clime you come. I care not if you live upon an island in the sea; I care not if you be a Yankee, with a blue stripe around your belly six inches wide; I care not whether you hail from Georgia (he pronounced it Jaw-Jaw) or old Alabamy, or whether you are from the state that produces the blue granite, as cold and relentless as it looks. You're a man if you're a man, whether you came from Wharton County, Kentucky, or not, and in the breast of every real man there is a resentment against murderous and slanderous assaults against the defenseless woman, and a natural inclination to come to the defense of a helpless, ninety-five pound woman."

"You talk to me about the Fatherhood of God and the Brotherhood of Man, and how it is abroad in this land. You talk to me about peace on the earth, and good will toward men. But let me ask you, where can that peace ever exist when men like Giddings can take the floor and stultify pure American womanhood, and pardons are bartered and sold by our public officials at $5,000 per each?"

The sweat which sifted through his pores and saturated every garment over his body gave off a pungent odor. His eyes were fixed and glassy, and with every wild vehement gesture the billowing black mass of hair atop his head rocked and rolled. His eloquence was fierce—painful. No one, not even the presiding court, dared to interrupt him. Every eye in the room was trained upon him, and not even as much as a labored breath could be heard during his dramatic pauses. And, as if his scurrility was not strong enough, he half apologized to the tense jurors for the mildness of his language.

"I wish I could coin a word to describe that man Parrish," he cried. "Do you know, I studied all night? I told my wife, 'for God's sake, honey, give me something; get the dictionary, so we can find some word to describe him.' 'Well,' she said, 'you once said "A lizard of lies," what does that mean?' I says, 'that don't describe him at all.'"

"He said 'I am a farmer—I have got 20 acres of land; I get $90.00 a month from the Government. No wonder you lie,

God bless your heart. (Laughter, reported in official notes.) There wasn't any use for him to do it—but listen, the dirty liar, he wouldn't weaken. The dirty skunk—but skunk isn't a good name for George. Did you ever go to the mouth of a sewer, with fecal matter? Well, it is one of those live things, that is what George Parrish is."

"Your Honor, I have heard that on the equity side of the docket, before they can get anything from you or the rest of the judiciary, that they must come in with clean hands, but it looks like, in these piping times of bootlegging and gambling, that in the PROSECUTION, you can come in with just any old kind of hands.

"Look at Parrish. 'What did you feed those hogs out there —sugar?' and he says, 'I didn't carry any sugar out to those hogs.' 'What are you doing buying 10 sacks of sugar a week out there on North Robinson Street?' and he says, 'Judge, do I have to answer it? . . . . I bought that for a friend.'"

When he was ready to conclude he stood quietly in eloquent stillness, close to the front row of jurors, near to the center of the box. In a mild tone, without gesture, he started to speak again.

"In God's name, I beg you; I beg you in the name of Him who came to save, in the name of Him who met the woman at the well, be just. If the spirit of Christ and the goodness of the hand of God can penetrate this jury box, we can have no fear. Let the Godly spirit combat and destroy the wickedness, and the evil in this case—Annabelle, God bless your little heart—you need have no fear."

The conclusion of the trial was orthodox. It was chronicled for posterity by a representative of the fourth estate, who witnessed it with his eyeballs.

" 'Gentlemen,' inquired the court, 'have you reached a verdict?' 'We have, your Honor,' replied the foreman. . . . 'Hand it up please, Mr. Foreman,' said the judge. . . . There was a stir, than an intense hush. 'We find the defendant, Annabelle, not guilty,' read the judge. 'Gentlemen, is this your verdict?' . . . . 'It is,' came the unanimous statement from the jury box. . . . Annabelle Edwards smiled a little smile of relief—and the flowers fell to the floor. 'Three cheers for Moman!' shouted some spectator near the doorway. The bailiff thundered for order. 'Who was that man that got noisy' growled the judge—but the man had left hurriedly."

CHAPTER NINETEEN

Wherein Pruiett proficiency in matters civil is demonstrated, cnd account is given of his conduct in the trial where the sad eyes of Lincoln save a murderous vagrant from the penalty usually imposed for taking human life. And how the recollection of the ill-considered action which cost the life of a fellow man presses upon him. And how he justifies the activity of a millionaire oil man who slew a nationally prominent army aviator, and prevents a stain from attaching itself to the name of the accused's wife, by acquiring a verdict of exoneration for him. And how the death sentence is passed at last—not upon a Pruiett client—but upon the Washita Stallion himself, and he puts his house in order before going to old Havana, to sit by the bay and watch the sun go down.

When Uncle Joe Adams died on the fender of a Santa Fe locomotive, after a very commonplace crossing collision, Aunt Nancy would hear of having no one but Moman Pruiett for "suin' the company."

"It's out of my line," Pruiett told her. "I'm a—."

"I know—you're a criminal lawyer," Aunt Nancy supplied. "That's what some of my neighbors said, an' that you wouldn't try this kind of a case, but I know better. You have to try it to a jury, don't you?"

"Yeah, it's a jury question," Pruiett agreed. "But—."

"Uncle Joe wouldn't a' had anybody but you for a lawsuit," Nancy maintained. "You got to take this case an' try it for me. The company's goin' to pay me plenty."

"Look, Auntie," Pruiett argued, "there's plenty of ambulance chasers that know how to win a railroad-crossin' case with their head in a bucket. They try 'em all the time, just like you see me tryin' murder cases all the time. It isn't that I don't want the business; I just don't want you to take a chance by havin' a lawyer tryin' your case that don't know his stuff. Get the idea?"

"What's the difference?" Nancy demanded. "A lawsuit's a lawsuit, ain't it?"

"This case of yours has got a lot of involved negligence law mixed up in it," Pruiett argued. "Just because Uncle Joe is dead don't mean that you can recover. You got to prove that the company was guilty of negligence, an' that Uncle Joe didn't con-

[471]

tribute to his own death. I'd have to look up a lot of law before I'd be wise on that."

"Uncle Joe said you was the smartest lawyer in the country," Nancy answered. "You've got the case. I'm leavin' it to you to get me my money."

Pruiett prepared for trial at Eva Rush's roadhouse in the Mulligan Garden district, west of Oklahoma City. An office assistant gave him a short memorandum of a brief and two books on negligence law the night before the trial of the case. He announced ready when the case was called the next morning.

Uncle Joe's survivors and their floundering counsel made enough of a case for the trial court to let the issues go to the jury. Pruiett, under the impression that the customs of civil procedure limited him in the lengths he could go in arguing the facts, made a quiet and conservative, although analytical and effective, speech. He wanted, in a way, to show that he could restrain himself in court and be as much a gentleman in the trial of a case as the corporation's counsel opposing him. The Santa Fe's staff had quietly enjoyed the discomfiture which Pruiett exhibited in the trial. He was obviously not familiar with the civil procedure. They had the bad taste and judgment to drop a word about it at the close of their argument.

"Pruiett is a little off his course in this case," the defense attorney told the jury. "He doesn't know just what to do with himself. He doesn't recognize the elements of negligence, and what it takes to make liability in this kind of an action. If it was a MURDER trial, he'd know what to do, but here the poor old boy has just stumbled around, and made a miserable failure of making a case. He ought to stick to murder. Yes, sir! Old Moman Pruiett just doesn't fit in where there's anything involved besides a brutal, bloody, sensational murder."

The last word went to the plaintiff. When the defense had concluded its arguments, Pruiett still had time for a short reply. He came out crouching, with mane bristling and eyes snapping. Dignity and decorum were forgotten.

"Murder?" he bellowed. "Did I hear some one say somethin' about murder? Murder? MURDER? MURDER?" Each inquiry was made with increased volume, until he had reached a rafter-shaking roar.

"Good God Almighty," he screamed. "What is this if it isn't murder? What in the name of God is murder? Why—. The books have always told me that murder was the takin' of human

life without the authority cr justification of the law. Old Uncle
Joe's dead, isn't he? He was killed, wasn't he? They took his
life, I guess, if they killed him. Does the law say you can slip
up on people at death-trap crossin's and crush their bones, and
tear their flesh apart, just because you've got millions of dollars—
because you're a big corporation—an' stole a lot of land from the
government along with your millions from the pee-pul? MUR-
DER? Does the law tell them to ring their bells and blow their
whistles, so to give poor folks like Uncle Joe a little warnin' at
the crossin's, as they tear through the country, after more money,
an' after more gold?

"An' he says I do all right in a murder case," he reflected.
"Well, let me tell you, that this is the damndest, meanest, most
cold-blooded case of murder I ever got mixed up in in my life,
an' as a murder specialist, I feel perfectly at home here tryin' it."

The jury charged the railroad $7,000 for his speech. Prui-
ett reflected at Eva's as they read him the verdict over the 'phone.
"Maybe I been wastin' my time," he mused. "Maybe I been tryin'
the wrong kind of murder cases."

"Moman Pruiett, Attorney, sprung a surprise Tuesday in
the Haines murder trial following the convening of court after
the noon-day recess, when he admitted that his client, A. H.
Haines, charged with the murder of Claude O'Conner at Garber
on the night of January 5, last, was guilty."

That was news. The fire hydrant had dribbled on the dog.
It was the first Pruiett client in twenty-five years who wasn't
outraged in his complete innocence.

"Give your sheriff the credit and the honor for arresting the
man who did the shooting," Pruiett said. "As for the deceased,
O'Conner, I have nothing to say in censure of him, but may
God have mercy on his soul."

The listening, and doubtlessly surprised, jury was beginning
to see more—and further. Pruiett's client was guilty, but with
reservations. The deceased had done something, his conduct had
been objectionable, and base, that big-hearted Pruiett was concerned about his chances in the hereafter. An experienced observer would have sensed in an instant that it was the Pruiett
prelude to a ripping old unwritten law defense.

"O'Conner proclaimed his plan of leaving for California
and wrote a note to Lucy Haines, this defendant's wife, asking
her to go with him. She wrote him a note in reply, asking him

not to bother her. When Haines learned of the note he asked his wife why she had deemed it necessary to reply in writing."

Pruiett was warming up to his task with relish. Haines was surely entitled to be just a little suspicious of such conduct. "He didn't get a very satisfactory reply. He followed O'Conner to the pool hall and there asked him to show the note his wife had written him. Either he or O'Conner proposed that they step out the back door. After they had reached the outside Haines again asked to see the note his wife had written, and O'Conner said, 'All right, I'll give it to you, and I'll give you something else, too.' With this O'Conner moved as if to strike Haines, and Haines fired the shot that killed him."

The case was being tried at Enid, the old Cherokee Strip post which had developed into a handsome prairie town with tree-lined avenues leading away from a well planned public square. It seemed to Pruiett to be the constant host to Temple Houston's ghost. He remembered the town by the Houston Episode, and it was with displeasure, for he had suffered two decisive and unwarranted courtroom defeats there at the Texas master's hand.

The Haines-O'Conner killing had occurred at Garber, a mushroom camp in the Garber-Covington petroleum production area, where millions were spouting for the settlers who had participated in the last of the great free land rushes. The defendant was a pimp who had brought himself from the poor, piney districts of West Virginia. Lucy, whom he claimed was his wife, may have been; she was unquestionably his stock in trade. Pruiett didn't care. Someone had paid him a fee, and the way he would make it look, their family life and relations were spotlessly clean.

Written instructions of the law had been read to the jury, and final argument had been continued until the following morning.

The fading interior of the old courtroom was of average country-courthouse simplicity. The dung-brown walls were two-tone, light dung above a dust catching molding rail half way down the wall and dark dung from the rail down to the floor. The judge's rostrum, straight, unornamented and ugly, relieved a little the monotony of design at the south end of the room. Directly above the bench, and balancing precariously upon the molding rail, was a warped and faded chromo in harmonizing brown, as dour and drab and dingy as the balance of the interior of the room. It was a whiskered portrait of Abraham Lincoln.

"When I saw the Lincoln picture I remembered I was in a

belt of Republicans; that it was a Republican congressional district, an' that they gave the Democrats hell around there all the time," he said, describing his motives which directed his strange conduct at the conclusion of the case.

Jurors were dozing or gazing out the window. The accused was shifting uneasily in his chair. Such lame forensics were not what he had bargained for when he paid his money for representation, or what he had expected from the highly touted Pruiett. The March gale, rattling a loose splinter in the window frame so that it sounded like a neighbor's boy practicing on his cornet in the distance, was attracting more attention than the purportedly eloquent lawyer. "These Republican devils can stand a lot of Abe Lincoln," Pruiett resolved to himself.

"Look, men!" He struck an heroic crouch in the center of the floor as he startled them back to attention with a stentorian shout.

"The sad eyes of Lincoln!" he roared. "The sad eyes of Lincoln are upon us. The spirit of Lincoln is hovering about us today!" He held his left hand outstretched, with fingers spread wide, like a master muting the bass section, while he led their attention with an eloquent pointing finger to the melody—the faded chromo perched on the wall. "Look! Behold! the sad eyes of Lincoln!"

The jurors in the box were startled. Their quick, scared glances furnished the poor old picture (the remains of what had been an insurance company's calendar) with an atmosphere of the artistic, and of reality. Judge Cullison, sitting beneath the likeness, and immediately in front of it, had to turn and twist, dangerously, in his highbacked swivel chair to look, like everyone else in the crowded room, at what was causing Pruiett so much evident concern. As the judge craned and twisted, and the drapes of obesity which fell from his ample jowls, partly obscuring the collar of his shirt, were drawn tight and tense, his sinus ailment attacked him, and a series of prodigious tears began to course down his face. "That jury thought he was touched; that his memory of Old Abe was breakin' his heart," Pruiett said. "They thought he was weepin' for me and my client."

Pruiett, with his clenched right fist held high above his head, began to advance upon the jury, holding them with the strange fanatical glare which seemed to create an ominous spell over those whom it encompassed. He began to recite the lines he had stored in his memory almost ten years before when he had read them in a little Kansas paper while he waited for a shave in a Topeka barber shop.

"Sad eyes that were patient and tender, sad eyes that were steadfast and true, and warm with the unchanging splendor of courage no ills could subdue."

He interrupted his recitation with an extemporaneous insertion. "The spirit of him with the great heart and the sad expression, who so loved the liberty of a million slaves that he sacrificed his own life, is present now with you. I can feel his presence like the warmth of the sun, the soothing caress of a spring breeze. What would he do, my friend, if he was in your place today?"

It was indeed a ponderous problem, what Lincoln would have done with the West Virginia boy murderer. When Pruiett described the magnitude of the responsibility in such terms, the upland farmer began to look at the case in a different light. What the hell would Lincoln have done?

"Eyes hard with the dread of the morrow, and woe for the day that was gone, the sleepless companion of sorrow, the watchers that witnessed the dawn. . . ."

"Those sad eyes will be watching for you and your return with a just verdict, like they were for the presence, the symbol of liberty on Sumter's ramparts," he shouted. "The sad eyes stand guardian here today over the rights of this American citizen who had the courage to stand against the assaults of a defiler of his home, an assailer of his person, and fight for those rights which Lincoln promised, and guaranteed to the true American citizen. What would Lincoln have done? You do that which he would have done, by your verdict."

The Republican brothers found their departed leader's mind in a typically opulent state that afternoon. They declined to convict Haines for the crime charged but did convict him of manslaughter, and gave him four years in prison, and looked cautiously up at the faded chromo, as if for approbation, as the court read the verdict. Pruiett, chuckling as he gathered his note pad and papers, nodded cordially, in gratitude, toward the likeness of the Emancipator, and stalked out of the courtroom.

He struggled on, shouldering the heavy burden of work and worry. The city of Tulsa reflected its refinery fires in the turgid Arkansas, as men took wealth from beneath its sandy banks and put it back into towering buildings on the hill above its sweep.

Its citizenry emulated Pruiett and his own homicidal conduct on an enlarged scale. The race riots, which raged there, took a heavy toll of life, especially from black bodies and consumed a proportionate toll in property destruction. When the National Guard had restored a semblance of order, the civil authorities began their customary inquiry for fixing responsibility.

Will Robinson, an educated Negro man, was indicted for riot on the theory that he was the principal instigator of the mass destruction. While he was accused of but one specific killing, by inference, he would be tried at once for a hundred or more of them. An organization of Negroes, designing to serve their race generally, and Will Robinson particularly, raised a fund for the employment of counsel. They met to decide to whom the employment, and the fee, should be offered. A great fundamental principle was involved. If Robinson was cleared, the blame against their race would be materially lessened; the pressure of prejudice would be relieved. Correspondingly, if he was convicted, condemnation against the race would be more definitely fixed. Serious complications might develop. Their man must be represented by the most able; by the one most likely to secure an acquittal.

Lawyer Pruiett of Oklahoma City was able, but he had killed a member of their race in a beer-joint shooting. Perhaps the Negro had been wrong; maybe Pruiett had been right, as the white man's jury had decided, but still, Mr. Pruiett didn't have any right to be over there. The Negro had been shot down in his own home, and the Constitution said that color or previous condition of servitude didn't make any difference where a man's rights were concerned, especially around his house what the white folks called his domicile.

And Lawyer Pruiett was being mentioned in the papers in a way to make them believe he wasn't taking care of his business. He was goin' out too often, and drinkin' too much. What about that? Even if we are black, even if we are plain niggers, we got to have a man we can rely on. We got to have a man that can bring Will Robinson out clean. They've got good lawyers in Kansas City, an' Chicago. There's thousands of us, an' we've all to worry us. Who shall we get to defend Will?
chipped in a little, so we've got plenty of money. That's no item

Record for record, accomplishment for accomplishment, the sick, fading Pruiett stood out in bold relief. He got the offer and he took the job. In one brilliant plea before the district court at a hearing on Robinson's petition for a writ of habeas corpus, he showed that he knew his law like he knew his human nature in the jury box. With empassioned brilliance he interrupted his intemperance long enough to decisively defeat the prosecutors, and walked from the courtroom with a black man, free, where before he had been held without bond on the most difficult and dangerous of criminal accusations.

"The charges of grand larceny, which were preferred against G. L. Roberts and W. I. Ritchey, of Fredonia, alleged bank robbers, were dismissed this morning by County Attorney Arch F. Williams." So said the El Dorado, Kansas, Times. "Immediately after the dismissal of the charges here, Roberts and Ritchey, and their attorney, Moman Pruiett of Oklahoma City, Oklahoma, went to Eureka, where preliminary hearings are being held this afternoon for Roberts and Ritchey on charges of robbing the Piedmont State Bank last winter. The defendants have been out on bond of $15,000 each since their arraignment at Eureka several weeks ago. . . ."

"The visit of Mr. Pruiett to El Dorado recalls that he recently was employed for the 268th time, in his career as a criminal attorney, to defend a man under a shadow cast by a deadly shot he fired. . . . This time the defendant is Jean P. Day, wealthy lawyer, politician and oil man, who killed Lieut. Col. Paul Ward Beck on April 4, (1922) when he surprised Beck attempting to attack his wife. . . ."

"Pruiett, with his flowing shock of hair that gave him the nickname of 'the Black Maned Maverick of the Washita,' has fought opposite prosecutors in practically every county in Oklahoma, and has defended slayers as far west as Aberdeen, Washington. . . . His is the frontier type, grown up with the west, and though Oklahoma population has changed greatly in 30 years, Pruiett has never lost the keen perception and knowledge of people in every community that makes him clever at jury-picking and shrewd at presenting testimony."

His reputation trailed him wherever he went. Up to the time he killed Joe Patterson, he gloried in it. Afterward, he tried to slip in and out of strange places, and to avoid contact with the press. God, wasn't he glad that old Doc Threldkeld hadn't died that time he shot him. This thing of havin' killed a man, even a Negro, was something he'd rather the public would forget. If they would, and wouldn't be forever writing it up, usually wrong, in their papers, maybe he could forget it himself.

Murderers. Bank robbers. Dope smugglers. What was it old Walter Ferguson had said about him in his column years ago? The chicken thieves and petty criminals were turned away from his door? That he specialized in murder and defended only the big horse thieves? Maybe Ferguson was right. He said that he was the toughest hombre in the toughest Indian town in the territory. That was right, then. He'd been tough.

He should take a rest. He ought to see a doctor, and if the doctor said go away and rest up, he should do it. Every one had some suggestion to make; they all agreed that he looked bad; that he didn't act like the old Pruiett. He cut down on the work. Just the choice cases nowadays. The ones with the heavy dough in 'em, a bank loot, or a rich murderer, or something like that. Not so much to do, and a little more time for rest. But the rest let him think; it made him think, an' he couldn't stand some of the things that made him think of them. So the liquor bottle came out, and the cycle began all over again. Where was he goin'? Where was he goin' to get off? What in the hell was goin' to happen to him?

The little old Kansas sheet that had to garble up the shooting story told about Jean P. Day, as "the last case for him to take employment in." While Pruiett didn't know it at the time, it was his last murder case, the last one for him to participate in, for a long time.

"On Tuesday morning, last (April 4, 1922) the entire state was shocked by the news of a tragedy that involved two of the most prominent citizens within the confines of the state." Forrest L. Hughes, County Attorney for Oklahoma County, was having a formal statement published in the local press.

"The deceased, Paul Ward Beck, was one of the most prominent aviation officers in America. The man who fired the fatal shot was not only one of the ablest lawyers in the state but one of its most highly respected citizens. . . . Since this tragedy occurred I have been quoted in a number of papers as saying things I little dreamed of. Owing to this fact I now take the opportunity of making my first official statement relative to this fatal occurrence.

"I am frank to admit that I have had the highest regard for Judge Day, both as a citizen and as a lawyer. However, immediately following his statement to me he requested me to forget that friendship and not hesitate to file a murder charge against him if I thought it my duty to do so. His attorney later reiterated this request and statement." (Pruiett was Day's counsel.)

The case made national news. "Jean P. Day, former State Supreme Court Justice, President of the Foursome Producing and Refining Company and Vice-President of the Continental Asphalt and Petroleum Company, is being held at his home, 411 West Nineteenth Street, in the custody of a deputy sheriff, following the shooting to death of Lieut. Col. Paul W. Beck, commandant of Post Field, Fort Sill, at 3 o'clock Tuesday morning. . . . . Lieutenant Colonel Beck was one of the first four army aviators in the United States. . . . Day returned home and found his wife struggling in the arms of the army officer, according to a statement authorized by Judge Day, made by a friend of the family." So said the Washington, D. C., Post. "On the witness stand Day and his wife told, with emotion, of the slaying of Lieut. Col. Beck. In a broken voice, but with a gleam of determination in his eye, Day said he killed the army aviator accidentally when he sought to drive Beck from his home, after finding him attempting to attack Mrs. Day."

"I saw Colonel Beck holding Mrs. Day on the divan," said Day. "She was fighting him. He had his right arm around her. His other hand was about her knee."

The unusual events had followed a late party in the Day home, where a group of the oil elite were amusing themselves on apricot cordial—"non-intoxicating." "Judge Day denied a statement of W. R. Withington, evidence man, that empty bottles and a glass found on the mantle in the room after the bridge party had contained intoxicants. . . . The bottles had contained nothing stronger than nonintoxicating apricot cordial, he said. Beck was sober at the time of his alleged attempt on Mrs. Day, the judge declared, denying emphatically there had been any drinking."

"Moman Pruiett, defense counsel, gave forth a statement Wednesday, ... He said it was he who advised the Days to make a sworn statement of the tragedy wherein Day invoked the 'code of Oklahoma,' that a man's home is inviolate, and shot Beck when he alleged Beck had attempted Mrs. Day's honor. 'I wanted to save them the humiliation of appearing before the coroner's jury and satisfying morbid curiosity,' Pruiett said in the statement."

Mrs. Day's theatrical account of the affair was good copy. "Mrs. Jean P. Day, Washington and Oklahoma City society woman, half-hysterical and distracted, Tuesday night told at her home what she remembered of the tragedy early Tuesday morning. . . . Mr. Day had gone to take the other guests home. . . . I sat on the couch, Colonel Beck facing me from a chair. Suddenly he sprang from his seat and came to my side. 'I must tell you,' he said—! . . . Then he poured out an impassioned plea that I submit to him. He grasped me, clutching me to him. I screamed aloud for him to release me. He did not heed. Instead he held me closer, crying out that he would have me. I fought with all my strength, but he was too powerful for me. The events which followed are but a blank. I was still struggling, his arms about me, his face pressed to mine, when I saw the form of my husband before me. I ceased to struggle then, and only then, for I knew I was safe. I knew no more until I saw Beck's body there dead at my feet."

The way it looked from out west, and the way the Los Angeles Examiner put it, "I did not see the shot fired. I did not hear the report," Mrs. Day testified. "I looked down and saw his lips move," she continued, "I lifted his head, then I put his head back down and the blood surged out. Then my hands were covered with blood. . . ."

" 'When he was struggling with you and he asked you to come to his room, you didn't think he was trying to do anything wrong then?' asked County Attorney Hughes, explaining that he wanted to bring out the intent in Beck's mind. '. . . . I didn't know,' Mrs. Day replied. 'What would you think?' "

Pruiett conducted his prominent client's defense in his customary manner. The army board had its findings to make, and Pruiett insisted on going before them with Judge Day. They had their own way of doing things, what they called the rules of the military court, and Pruiett had what he had long shouted was the "constitutional right of an American citizen."

"The morning session was consumed in the examination of Judge Day. The new angle of the case that was developed, it was said, was the introduction of several letters by Moman Pruiett, Day's attorney, concerning the alleged relations of Beck with women at other posts where he had been stationed. This came as a surprise to the army men, it was said, who expected the defense only to answer questions put them."

The findings of the military board, conducted under Maj. Thomas George Lanphier, were slightly ambiguous. "The board does not believe the version of the Days as to the conduct of

Lieutenant Colonel Beck on the fatal morning was true. However, it does not believe the testimony introduced at the inquest would justify filing a charge of murder against Jean P. Day."

Lieutenant Paul Ward Beck, Jr., son of the slain officer, viewed the conduct of the military court disconsolately, and with disapprobation. " 'My father was always an honorable man, an officer and a gentleman, and I still believe he remained so to the last,' young Beck said. . . . Coupled with the son's statement came the intimation that a searching investigation will be instituted by the War Department, to clear up certain confused details in connection with the death of the officer."

For a swan song, Pruiett gained a figurative double-acquittal at the trial of one case. Said Judge Day: "The jury did exactly what they ought, and it is absolutely a just verdict." Said Mrs. Day: " I feel grateful over the verdict. It is an honest one, and the only thing the jurors could have done. The evidence has thoroughly vindicated me, and left my name stainless. . . ." But Pruiett says that: "The Blue-Barrow will continue to squeal in the Day case."

The stoop and forward pitch of Pruiett's posture, first noticeable as he ambled in to testify at his own murder preliminary, didn't disappear when the coroner's jury decided, and said, that they wouldn't bind him over for a trial in the district court. Pruiett slowed down, perceptibly, almost overnight.

In less than two weeks after the final hearing in the Jean P. Day case, Pruiett went to a new doctor. It was not for a recurrence of the dungeon stiffness; his knees and ankles had ceased their painful assaults upon his motion almost ten years before. His years between forty and fifty had been, fortunately, the most vigorous and healthful of his life. But his throat had developed a great huskiness, a great pain, and the once stentorian roar, responding with his impulse, was modulated overnight to a raspy whisper. Passing food from his mouth to the stomach was torture.

"Doc," he said, "I got a lot of confidence in you. When a fellow can't believe a lot of specialists, he goes to his friends, the ones he knows he can trust. I want you to check me over, an' give me a fair verdict."

"All right, Moman, I'll decide your case," the smiling doctor replied.

Pruiett was talking to Dr. Oscar M. Marchman, in his office

in Dallas. Marchman, member of the Southwest Clinic of Dallas, staff doctor at the Baylor Baptist hospital, was an established throat specialist in the southwest. Pruiett smiled back at the doctor, but shook his head.

"It's not as simple as that, Doc," he replied. "I'll agree that your recommended course of treatment is good, but your diagnosis is incomplete. I'm sick as hell. They say I'm goin' to die."

Marchman laughed again. "You're too tough to think about it," he said. "Let me put you to bed and clean you out. Give me a week, 'till I can get the water I run through you to come out pure, and I'll have you ready to go back to work."

"I got a hole in the roof of my mouth, Doc." Pruiett complained, with a trace of a quiver in his voice. "It's as big around as a nickel an' it keeps gettin' bigger. It's plugged up with wet cotton now, or I couldn't even talk. I'm in a hell of a shape."

The doctor's face and manner changed. He became grave. "I'm sorry, Moman," he said. "I didn't understand. Let me see now, how long has it been bothering you?"

"Six weeks, maybe a little longer," Pruiett replied. "I can't work. I can't sleep."

"I'm sorry," Marchman repeated. "What do the doctors at home say about it? What do they think?"

"Cancer," said Pruiett laconically. "But I don't believe a damned word of it. There never was a cancer in my family. I know damn well it isn't a cancer."

Marchman had to laugh again. "I'll dress you in and run you through the clinic. You ought to stay three or four days. A certain laboratory test I know of will tell me right off what's the matter with you."

"If it's a Wassermann you're talkin' about," Pruiett said, "they are not worth a damn. I've had nine of 'em in the last four weeks an' ever' damned one comes back negative. That's why they say it's cancer."

Marchman's amazement was obvious. "Nine tests, and all negative? All by the same technician, or at different place?"

"Three doctors; three tests apiece," Pruiett answered. "Ever' damned one negative."

"It's no use then, running you through," Marchman said, shaking his head. "What could I do?"

"It isn't what I haven't got, it's what I have got, that I want to know. That's what I want you to tell me."

The Dallas doctor was more puzzled at the close of the three

day clinical examination than he had been after he had taken
Pruiett's history of the case. Two Wassermann tests showed
negative. There was no disease in the blood. Diagnosis by elimination, supported by some clinical evidence, suggested cancer, but
Marchman, like Pruiett, didn't think it was cancer.

"Disregard the laboratory and take regular course of treatment for your blood. I'll graft the palate back in, when you
begin to respond, and make you well again. I'll make you so
well you can go back to screaming at juries again. If I do, you
pay the regular fee. If I don't, you don't pay me a cent."

"That's the way I handle cases," Pruiett said. "Win 'em
or you don't collect. I believe you, Doc, but I'm just not satisfied. I think I'll shop around a little more, and see if maybe
some one else can't figure this out."

Baltimore was the next stop. Pruiett was dressed in at
Johns Hopkins, to endure the trial of a thirty day clinic. The
black mane, that had showed its first tinge of gray as he limped
up the stone steps to Marchman's office at Dallas, had turned
iron gray. His stoop was decided; his step halt. He carried the
little paunch which he had permitted to develop under the inside
angle of his stoop and the brown eye, once so sparkling and
sharp. He would have been meat in the revengeful hands of
the old prosecuting clique in the southwest, who had so long
predicted that Pruiett was through. He was so completely out
that he didn't think in terms of murder trials and criminal defenses. "Give me something, anything, to relieve this damn pain."

"Judge," the diagnostician at Johns Hopkins was saying,
"your frank question requires a frank answer. The infection in
your mouth is malignant. It's cancer. If you take care of yourself, you may last a year. But at best, it's just a year; you can't
live any longer than that."

"Tell 'em to bring my clothes in. If a man's only goin' to last
a year an' he's got to be in such pain as this, what difference
does it make, I'm getting out of here."

The doctor's answer was an unconcerned shrug as he turned
to walk away. Bellevue at New York concurred with Johns
Hopkins.

"We can keep you, and treat you, Mr. Pruiett, and take your
money," the staff-man at Bellevue told him, "but we can't do
any more than your wife could do for you at home. That's a
cancer. You can't impeach the Wassermann like you can a poor

witness; you simply don't have syphilis. At the rate it's going, it will kill you within a year, and as we feel we should in these kinds of cases, we're warning you so that you can put your things in order."

"Will this pain get worse?" Pruiett inquired.

"I'm sorry, but it will, much worse," the doctor said. "But wherever you are, you can get prescriptions to relieve that from reputable physicians, of course."

"It was merely a suggestion, Mr. Pruiett," the doctor answered. "I can understand how you feel."

"I'm not criticisin' you, son, for the suggestion. If I got to die, it's all right. Two or three lifetimes wouldn't help me a hell of a lot now, for I've been ever'where an' seen ever'thing. I may get on junk, but if I do it won't be because I think it'll make my life any longer. I don't care about that. It's this damn pain all the time that I don't like. It's so useless, like killin' a man by inches when you can do it all at once by shootin' him."

"I only wish we could do more than give you temporary relief," the doctor said. "But at the same time, think what a blessing the diseased have received since morphine an—."

Pruiett returned to the west after leaving five thousand dollars on the Atlantic seaboard. He received nothing for it but definite information that he had a cancer in his mouth and that he would be dead within a single year. The black flag was down. A halting step and a weary stoop had supplanted the belligerent strut which had been so characteristic of him in his prime. One landmark, the grizzled and out thrust jaw, remained unchanged. The power was gone, but the spirit was intact. One look at Pruiett's countenance and one knew that his attitude was unchanged. "I haven't got cancer, they're either wrong about it, or they're a bunch of damned liars."

Thomas H. Owen, who had survived the Pruiett assault in the McDarment case, had become justice of the Oklahoma Supreme Court. Pruiett made him trustee of his property and accounts, with his wife and daughter as beneficiaries, and taking out twenty-five thousand in cash for himself, moved on to Havana. He was thinking, although rebelliously, about the Bellevue doctor's reference to the prescription. Pruiett knew where and how the dope came into the country from southern Europe. He knew that the West Indian Islands, with Havana and Nassau as import centers, relayed the stuff into the Florida Keys, and that from there the runners moved it northward.

Pruiett put the bulk of his cash in a Dallas bank. He thought of the miserable watery-eyed addicts he had heard whine at him through the iron bars as he interviewed clients in jail corridors. He remembered their furtive, shifting movements as they jerked and scratched, and flaunted the miserable poverty which they endured for the sustenance of their terrible habit. All hell could turn its misery loose upon him; slow fire and the medieval wheel might scar and grind him, but it would be easier than going on the junk. He decided that there was one easy death he would pass up.

Palm tree shadows across sun swept boulevards and lattice stripes of swinging doors across saloon entrances endeared Havana to the failing lawyer. He had a year, possibly a little more, possibly a little less, to live. He had to suffer every waking minute of the residue, and as the high priced specialists had frankly told him, the pain he now had would gradually increase, until the time came, when relief was near, he would have to have prescriptions— take the needle—to lift him over it. But the needle was out. He had set the square jaw and eliminated the needle. They could start with the roof of his mouth and tear him apart an inch at a time, but he wouldn't die a damned, sniveling dope head. Hell, no, he wouldn't. That was out.

Pruiett had plenty of money. There were no worries, or regrets about his family, except those of natural compunction at leaving them. His fatalistic attitude toward life was real, not an assumed one that would crumble with his own exposure to the reality of death, and leave him cringing in abandoned loneliness. Where he had started with nothing, he left a trust that would amply provide for his wife and child. He would deny them the right to make the sacrifice he knew they longed to make, that of being with him and comforting him as the spectre of death stalked slowly, but relentlessly in for him.

It was selfishness, in a sense, for he knew that they would be no comfort to him, only stimuli for the lapse into morbidity which he could tolerate only in his solitude. What they would suffer in knowing that he was suffering, and dying, out of their arms, or the correlative satisfaction their service to him would give them, he refused to seriously consider. He made definite arrangements to stay, so long as the thread of life would permit, in old Havana, Cuba.

CHAPTER TWENTY

Wherein Pruiett returns from Havana, Cuba, where he had been for his health, and with the aid of the miracle of modern medicine, stumbles through the dim halls of half-life into vigorous health again. And how the invisible empire takes a new lease on life with him, and together, they unseat a Governor who had not previously enjoyed favor in Pruiett's fancy. How he fills his sack, prior to departure for the south, with what he considers the last of western tribute. How he trades diamonds for a villa on Biscayne's blue bay, Miami, Florida.

Routine delays and charges in the exchange, drawing on his deposit in the Dallas bank, had chafed his already irritable nature. With the specific intent of withdrawing his money, placing it in his pocket and carrying it to Cuba with him, where he could reach it and spend it as he chose, he took the boat for the mainland and the train for Dallas. The fates that had permitted him to survive as a premature infant, who had deposited such a prodigious brain in his skull and such matchless courage in his belly, who winked at his adolescent folly and turned the key in the dungeon locks to restore him to his liberty, who fouled the cap on murderous old Doctor Threldkeld's cartridge and who furnished him with an inspiration of deliverance in every emergency, were still attending him. From his room in the Adolphus Hotel, Dallas, Texas, he called his friend and medical aid, Doctor Oscar M. Marchman.

"My God, Moman," the doctor cried. "What in God's name has happened to you?"

Pruiett had the cotton plug removed. The opening between his mouth and the nasal chambers was unobstructed, so that he could only talk with a great deal of effort and pain.

"It's that damn cancer," he whispered. "I been to Baltimore, an' New York, too. I told you I was a sick man, an' they backed me up in it. I'm gonna die—," he glanced around as if to see if any one was watching, or listening. "The fact is, Doc, I'm done dead. This isn't old Moman you're talkin' to, now."

Dr. Marchman's eyes were ablaze when he saw his friend before him in Pruiett's room.

"Where's your wife, Moman? Where's your family? What are they thinking about, letting you get yourself in this condition?"

"They are not with me," Pruiett mumbled. "I'm dead, an' I'm buried down in Cuba. I'm a rummy, Doc, but I'd rather be an old rummy than a dope head. What do you say, Doc?"

"How long have you been in Dallas?" the doctor asked.

"Two or three days. Just came up to get my money out of your damn bank. Seems like they don't want old Moman to write checks on his own money." He thrust his hand into his trousers pocket, as if to produce a roll in substantiation of what he had said.

"Don't do that, Moman," Marchman restrained him by a gentle pressure on the arm. "Let's get in a cab, and go out to the clinic. I want to talk to you."

"Nope," said Pruiett. "I got to buy me some new clothes, an' get outa here. I don't like it. I'm goin' back where they let a man do as he pleases, an' he can get all the rum he can pay for. I'm a damn rummy, Doc." He put his arm around the doctor again, confidentially. "It's a damn good place down there, Doc, an' I like it. It's a damn good place—to die."

One of the most devout Christians Moman ever knew, Dr. Marchman, contemplated the sick man hopelessly. "You owe me the courtesy of one more visit, Moman," he insisted. "We may never meet each other again, and we've been good friends. We *have* been friends, haven't we?" Marchman knew how to wheedle a sick friend.

"You're right, Doc, we been friends—but a man hasn't got no right to his friends when he get a cancer in his face," Pruiett argued. "He hasn't got no right to his wife, or his kid, or nobody else. He's just got a right to a lot of pain, that's what, an' a lot of lonesomeness. But Doc, I'm not on the needle; I'm no junker, an' I want you to remember that."

His tired whisper was trailing. A cab swerved to the curb in answer to the doctor's wave.

"Go out with me for just a short visit, Moman," he urged. "We can talk, and maybe I can help you." When Pruiett continued to hold back he leaned close to his ear. "I've got some good stuff out there; it's prescription, not bootleg. I can fix some hot toddies while we talk." The sick man's resistance faded.

Marchman put Pruiett to bed. Two days later he was able to carry on an intelligent conversation with him.

"I quit fightin'," he said. "I know I'm dyin' but I still don't believe it's cancer. It's something just as bad, maybe worse, so it doesn't make much difference. An' don't feel bad about the way you found me, Doctor. I'm not down and out. I've got plenty of funds. Rum and whiskey kill the pain, and it doesn't matter how you look when you're full of that stuff. I'll be all right 'til it's over."

"But Moman," Dr. Marchman said, "there's no sense in quitting. It's not like you. I told you before you went east that I thought you had an infected blood stream, regardless of what the Wassermann showed. I told you I'd give you the treatment to correct it, and if I was wrong, there would be no charge."

"That's damn nice of you, Doc," Pruiett answered wanly, "but I don't see any use. Seven or eight months, an' I'm a dead duck, here, or Havana, or somewhere else. I don't want to burden my friends, or my family—."

"Moman, you've given up before the verdict's read," said Marchman. "Did you ever try a tough case, a real tough one; one so tough that you thought you were going to lose it, so while the jury was out, you slipped up to the trial judge and offered to plead guilty? Offered to plead guilty and throw your client on the mercy of the court, just because you thought there was a probability of gettin' stuck. Did you ever do that?"

"Hell, no, I never, and you know it, Doc. Pruiett lost a few cases, but he never lost a client. An' he never lost his nerve, either. Check me up on that."

Dr. Marchman had made his point. "That's what you've done to yourself, Moman," he whispered. "You never weakened on the other fellow, but you did on yourself. You quit fighting before the verdict was in."

The sick man's eyes shone. He said, "I see what you mean. I believe you're right. I'm not so old yet; I'm 52. I'm not worn out, am I Doc?"

"No, you're not, Moman; you've got a lot of murder cases left in you, unless I'm mistaken. What do you say about letting me experiment on you?"

"What are the requirements?" What are the rules?"

"Complete obedience to my directions, is the first one. Complete rest, that means, stay in the hospital, in bed, is the next one. Make up your mind that I'm going to cure you, that you're going to get well, and—no liquor! Absolutely no liquor!"

"You won't make me suffer too much, will you, Doctor? You won't drag it out too far, will you? Promise me that when you know you can't make it, you'll tell me, so I can make my own plans from there on." Pruiett was pleading and directing at the same time.

"That's a bargain," Marchman answered.

"And listen, Doc," Pruiett charged. "I don't want no damn morphine. I made up my mind I won't be no hophead. Do you understand?"

"I understand," said Marchman.

Pruiett kept the faith with his doctor; Marchman's treatment restored him to health, and after a delicate operation, grafting the palate and roof back into his mouth and throat, his vigorous roar began to echo across Baylor Hospital's wide halls.

There were a few words, and a few tears, as Pruiett and Dr. Marchman clasped hands in the hospital lobby on July 14, 1923. Pruiett was being discharged. He was well; cured.

While Pruiett had been alternately engaged in trying to die and trying to get well, John Calloway Walton, more familiarly known as "Jack", had been engaged in getting himself elected governor of Oklahoma. He was the same Walton, who, as Mayor of Oklahoma City, "couldn't be trusted, handcuffed, to carry his own suitcase to the depot." He took the gubernatorial reins from the hands of J. B. A. Robertson, whom, Pruiett so bluntly averred, "was as crooked as a pan full of guts."

And while Pruiett was away, strange events, in addition to the Hall-Mills trial farce in New Brunswick, and James A. Stillman's paternity squabble, at Carmel, New York, were occurring, something stronger than the West Indian rum had been shot into the long dormant organs and glands of the Knights of the Invisible Empire. The hillsides and creek banks from Penobscot to Bakersfield were flickering in the light of a multitude of fiery crosses; the cotton sheet market was enjoying a decided upturn as white-hooded regalias waved themselves back into flower.

And not all being published about the rejuvenated order was to its credit. "The Klan springs from the memory of post-Civil War lawlessness, when the Negro was disfranchised by terror. It proclaims its purpose to maintain white supremacy and to protect womanhood, the two customary cloaks for lynching. Its leaders assert its purpose to protect the security of the people 'in the absence or inadequacy of the forces of law and order.' Its membership form discloses an unmistakable anti-Jewish and anti-Catholic bias. . . . Over the whole has been thrown an amazing haze of mumbo-jumbo, with its Imperial Wizards, its King Kleagles. its Grand Dragons, Ghouls, Goblins, and Cyclopses, its fiery crosses and the rest. It was inevitable that all this would have attracted those most easily stirred to mob action . . . . and should have led to repeated outbreaks."

The New York World's expose of the Klan gave it a million members—paying five million dollars for hooded night shirts. (Five dollars per suit, f.o.b. the Klan-owned manufacturing company.) Its realms and domains, extending their influences into every state in the Union, had contaminated fair Oklahoma, and was alarmingly "threatening white supremacy and the purity of womanhood," or at least so Governor Walton averred. Although conditions were not so bad in Texas, where "a young white woman was seized on a hotel porch by masked men wearing white uniforms, taken several miles into the country, undressed, tarred and feathered and returned to town," nor in Birmingham, Alabama, where "a Klansman killed a Catholic Priest in cold blood on his own doorstep, and was acquitted at the trial amidst the plaudits of the mob," they were serious enough to cause the new governor to look around and about for counsel on the extent of his authority with martial law behind him if the hooded props for law enforcement began to interfere with things, the way he thought they should be managed.

A half-page display ad in the Oklahoman, at Oklahoma City, announced that "The Ku Klux Klan will hold a great Open Air Initiation at the Fair Grounds, Wednesday, October 4 (1922) at 8 P. M." On the following day and in the news side appeared: "With fiery crosses outlined against the sky and white robes appearing ghostly in the darkness, the Invisible Knights of the Ku Klux Klan gave Oklahoma City a glimpse of its strength and the nature of its rites at a public ceremonial at the fair grounds. A crowd estimated between 20,000 and 25,000 watched the initiation of 400 candidates into the mysteries of the order. . . ."

Florida, like Texas, Alabama, Oklahoma and every other state in the Union, was suffering from Klanitis, and as the press put it, "Just before election day 500 members of the Ku Klux Klan marched in costume through the streets of Jacksonville, Fla., following the fiery cross, 'supposedly,' according to the New York Times, 'as a warning to Negroes to attempt no lawlessness at the polls on Tuesday.' It is of record that few colored people voted in Jacksonville on Tuesday. 'White Supremacy' was maintained."

While Governor Walton's courage was commendable, his judgment was unquestionably subject to criticism. The brand which he picked up and attempted to brandish was hot clear down to the handle. The wily Klansmen had him on the ropes and out before the first bell rang, but the fight, while it lasted, was one to excite the interest and admiration of a true fight fan— even of Florida-bound Lawyer Pruiett. Pruiett, after his recovery, proved, as a witness before the Senate impeachment court, that he had been right again when he so frankly appraised Walton's virtue while arguing for "poor little Annabelle" Edward's freedom.

Retiring Governor Robertson had left no Ku Klux good will in the gubernatorial closet for pro-papal Walton to utilize. As the annals of his waning months in power disclose, "Governor J. B. A. Robertson testified before the State Supreme Court Tuesday that he would have been mobbed by the Klan in Okmulgee had not the National Guard officers accompanied him when he was there, seeking to testify before the grand jury which indicted him on a charge of accepting a bribe to permit the continued operation of the Guaranty State Bank, after it had become insolvent."

In addition to inheriting Robertson's Klan fight, the conduct of neighboring Governor Allen, in Kansas, abetted Walton in his injudicious warfare against the hooded order, and his plunge into political self-destruction. "The Kansas battle against the Ku Klux Klan, started by Governor Henry J. Allen, drew George C. McCarron of Oklahoma City, head of the K. K. K. activities in Oklahoma, Kansas, Missouri, and Nebraska, into its center Tuesday. . . . While Governor Allen, keeping up his campaign since last Saturday against the Klan was making a statement against the 'Invisible Empire,' McCarron from the Kansas City office of the Klan was answering Allen and indicating more strength than is generally known for the K.K.K. in Kansas. . . ."

Divisional director McCarron, making answer to the Sunflower State's governor's threat to drive the Klan out of Kansas, and in no ambiguous terms, said that "it will be about as hard as driving out the Knights of Columbus."

While Pruiett was in Baylor Hospital and he failed to observe it, the fight waxed warmer. Beneficiaries of Walton's executive clemency, and there was a host of them, were being flogged, along with other miscreants, by bands of prowlers dressed as goblins. By the time Pruiett had recovered from his illness and been discharged from the hospital, Walton had half emptied the state penal institutions, had the state under martial law, and was directing his adolescent guards as they patrolled the corridors of

THE DAILY OKLAHOMAN, THURSDAY, OCTOBER 11, 19

JAMMED COURT ROOM WAITS VERDICT IN JEWETT CASE

The Trial of the Grand Dragon

"'All's well on the Potomac,' cried the Klan."

the Capitol to prevent an impeachment session of the state legislature from convening. Machine guns protruded from windows abutting the courthouse and city hall in Oklahoma City. When Jack Walton said that civil authority had ended, and that his martial law edicts should stand in lieu thereof, he meant just exactly that.

The local papers spared enough of the front page, being pressed as they were by news of Walton's impeachment and juicy revelations of his remarkable official conduct during the brief time since his inauguration, to announce the Pruiett departure. "Oklahoma and the southwest will lose its best-known criminal lawyer within a few months. . . . Moman Pruiett, known in many states for his ability to bring tears of sympathy for unfortunate persons charged with murder, will leave the first of the year for Miami, Florida, where he plans to practice law. . . . For the past year, Pruiett has been missing from courtrooms, due to a prolonged illness. Murder cases were postponed from last winter's court term because he could not appear for the defense. . . . About two weeks ago Pruiett resumed active practice, and in that time has tried five murder cases. He is now representing W. A. Joslyn, on trial for the murder of Anna Stewart, in District Judge T. G. Chambers' court. . . . Born on a river boat in the broad Ohio, Pruiett has often remarked that he is a native of no state. As for law colleges, he says that they are mighty nice, but not necessary. . . . For years he has specialized in murder cases, and his record for acquittals is not approached, perhaps, by any other lawyer in the United States."

If the writers of the article knew what Pruiett had in place of law college, and why he thought it was not an absolute necessity, they tactfully kept it to themselves. References to Little Rock, and Rusk, were taboo. They were still his fightin' words.

Joslyn came close to disaster. He was charged with being an abortionist who had been caught red-handed, so the state claimed. Current accounts stated that his victim, dying in agony, signed her name to a prepared accusation by guiding a pencil held in her teeth. Pruiett was selling out, leaving Oklahoma for good, when Joslyn engaged him to go right into the trial of the case. Any style or plan of defense, other than Pruiett's would have been unsuccessful, and Joslyn knew better than anyone how narrowly he missed having them. His efforts procured a prompt acquittal,— the hard way, tried to a jury of twelve fathers and husbands.

"N. C. Jewett, Grand Dragon of the Oklahoma Klan, and L. L. Rhode and C. Whitlock of El Reno, were cleared of charges in connection with the whipping of E. R. Merriman, March 7, 1922. . . ."

The actual substance of that news item had contained the punch which knocked out a hard hitting governor for the count,—and out of a job so select that only forty-eight of them were available in the entire nation. The military court, directed by the state's executive as commander-in-chief of the national guard, has fostered the procedure which resulted in the "riot and insurrection" charges being filed against the three men. A conviction of those charges would amount to some justification for the martial law, and the high-handed invasions of civil liberties which Governor Walton claimed were required to suppress the Klan and its depredations. An acquittal was to be a reliable indicator to the contrary, a civil rebuke to Walton's martial regulation of the populace.

"Senational charges of 'darkroom,' third degree methods, used by Walton henchmen to obtain confessions, tensed the large audience to absolute quiet in the final moments of the trial," said the papers.

The charges and counter-charges flew. Walton's military court had contended that a band of hooded Klansmen went into Merriman's Carbarn cafe on the night of March 7th, held a gun on the operator while he was being handcuffed, and then drove him to a secluded place in the country where they administered an old-fashioned mule whipping. "Merriman, Charles Wallace, cook in the cafe, and Gus Marlatt, employee of the Oklahoma Railway Company, testified on the stand that Whitlock and Rhode were the ones who held the gun on Merriman." A rather disreputable Mr. A. A. Maupin completed the evidence against the rioters by swearing that Mr. Jewett, the Klan's head man, took him into his confidence and told him that he "had told him of leading the whipping party on March 7, in the Klan's offices in the Liberty National Bank Building."

Pruiett, as counsel for the defense, had an alibi for every one. The hand and mind that had delivered George Hopkins from the very jaws of retribution wouldn't be confounded with so simple a situation. "Jewett, and Cliff Saffell, his assistant secretary, said that the offices had been moved from the Liberty National to 139½ West Third Street, before March 1st, 1922."

"Rhode and Whitlock proved that they were in El Reno on the evening of March 7, 1922, by several witnesses. Chief among these were R. D. Thompkins, secretary of the Knights of Pythias Lodge, which had held a meeting that night, attended by Rhode, and A. J. Kivette, mayor of El Reno, who declared that Whitlock, a special policeman, had been at the police station at the time Merriman was taken out and flogged."

"While Maupin was on the stand he was made a target for scathing questions by Pruiett. 'Did you use dope before coming up here to testify?'

" 'I'll scratch my face, or any other part of my body when I damn please,' came the hot retort." It was a boner for Pruiett. He was familiar enough with addict characteristics to know that the witness' wit was at its peak. He backed away from that line of examination.

"The courtroom was packed during the entire trial and toward the last spectators crowded close to hear every word of evidence. . . . Not even an indistinct murmur was heard when Whitlock told his story of how he had been arrested without a warrant, brought under armed guards to Governor Walton's residence, and then placed in a dark room at the Huckins Hotel, where he was asked to tell his story and go free, by an alleged friend and member of the Klan."

Late in the afternoon on the day of the acquittal of the alleged insurrectionists, Pruiett answered the 'phone at his home. An old friend and acquaintance was calling.

"It's a little party for you, tonight," he was told. "All in your honor; call it a farewell party, if you got to have a name for it. We'll have a car pick you up in front at ten o'clock."

Pruiett got into the rear seat of a large touring car beside a prominent local business man. Two others, well known to Pruiett, were riding in the front seat. The car headed westerly from the downtown sector.

"Where's Charley?" Pruiett inquired, making reference to the man who called to invite him out.

"He couldn't come, but he's out there. He'll be there when we get there."

"Where's the blow-out goin' to be?" Pruiett asked.

"Well," came the hesitant answer from the man beside him,

"that's kind of a secret. You see, this is kind of a surprise party, and we can't tell you. But we'll be there soon. It's not far out."

The car was passing through a residential section. All the occupants had relaxed into handy corners, and were saying nothing. The man in the back seat interrupted the silence.

"You see," he began, "this is kind of a surprise. We got to surprise you, not let you know where you are, see? Before we get too close, we're supposed to blindfold you." He produced a black cloth from the corner of the seat behind him. "We better put it on; we're getting pretty close to there."

Pruiett laughed. "It's all right with me, boys, if it's a party, but remember, I'm leary of this mystic hokus-pokus stuff. I'm not used to it. You'll have to go easy, and not scare me too much."

After being led through a door, a series of halls and up a short flight of steps, Pruiett was ushered into a room. He knew by its heavy silence that it contained a multitude of people. Without a word the guides who held each arm released him, and he felt the bandage, which had been tied about his eyes, being jerked away. There was no perceptible difference. He was in complete darkness, as impenetrable as had been the blackness of the blindfold.

He waited, standing motionless. Then he saw a light flicker opposite him in a large room, which wavered and grew. He saw that it was a match, first scratched, then applied to a taper. As others were lighted around the room their wavering beams began to reflect upon the white bulks in the background, rounded trunks with pointed hoods above them. Some had crimson crosses and insignia across the white fronts while others were of plain white. He was amongst the Knights of the Invisible Empire and at what appeared to be a solemn and secret ceremonial.

He stood and grinned, unable to identify any of them for a more appropriate or direct greeting.

"Mr. Pruiett." A voice well known to him came from the depths of an ornate nightgown. It was that of his client of the day; Jewett, the Grand Dragon. "We are indeed honored by your attendance."

Pruiett's reply was a profound bow, made more profound by mockery.

"Our principles require that we recognize, and acknowledge signal service," the spokesman for the group continued. "We have asked you here for one purpose, to thank you, and to attempt to show our genuine gratitude to you."

"It is my honor, gentlemen," Pruiett replied, with another, and more profound bow.

"We have abrogated every rule and regulation of our order in bringing you here in this way and in this manner. May I say that you are the first non-member, not a subject of discipline, of course, to attend an executive session of this group." When he referred to discipline there was a titter from the ranks. "We hope to impose upon your generosity once more today by asking that you lend your efforts to us in correcting the breach of our regulations which we have made in admitting you here tonight."

"I am at your service, gentlemen," said Pruiett, a trifle mystified. "I hope your requirements are not so difficult that I cannot comply with them."

The leader of the hooded band continued. "This group lives and breathes for the public good. The maintenance of law and order, the protection of the underprivileged, is what we strive to preserve. Membership is open to Americans, of good character, who are sympathetic with the high ideals which our cause fosters. We do not solicit membership. Membership is awarded to deserving applicants after their qualifications are investigated, and determined."

The leader paused, as if trying to catch the line of a committed speech which had temporarily eluded him. Not understanding, Pruiett remained silent.

"We are your friends. We have watched your fight for health with interest, and had sympathy for you in your absence and distress. When you returned, we watched for your application for membership in our order, with hope. We read of your decision to move to Florida with regret.

"By official action I am prepared to offer to you an unsolicited membership in the Ku Klux Klan. We know you have the qualifications for membership. Your acceptance of it will correct all irregularities with reference to your attendance here tonight. You will serve us and make us happy by being a brother!"

Pruiett walked up to the speaker with hand outstretched. "ALL'S WELL ON THE POTOMAC," Jewett cried.

"All's well on the Potomac," Pruiett echoed.

There were two hundred solemn handshakes with solemn gravity, before the new member could work his way through the then dehooded throng to the tables where refreshments were being served.

Pruiett was making hay while the ground was in shape. He wanted more than carfare to Florida; he wanted to have his sack full, for he knew something about that tropical rainy season. It took more for that than it did for an ordinary rainy day. The South Atlantic boom looked good, but he didn't know whether he would find such lush pickings there, or anywhere else, as there were in his old haunts after a year's absence. He even made a contract to procure a pardon for Xenophon Jones, a long-term murderer, when he knew he had to work through his arch enemy, Jack Walton. Jack was then flailing and floundering before his senatorial accusers. The case was infested with money, and for that stuff, in sufficient amounts, Pruiett was prepared to put his pride behind him, and apologize to Jack. Maybe he (Walton) *could* be trusted to carry his luggage as far as the depot, even with the handcuffs left off.

Xenophon, whose mention always brought forth a scandalized whisper—that he was half white and that his father was a wealthy member of the Oklahoma Supreme Court, was actually supposed to be half Negro and half Creek Indian. Rumor and pedigree were of little assistance when appearance was considered. He looked like a full-blood nigger. The makers of the Creek tribal rolls didn't try to minutely determine the ratio of black to red when they were being made up. Xenophon's allotment was belching oil over its own, and adjoining, scrub timber acres, and his bank balance was prodigious. But there he was in McAlester pining away for little luxuries which he could afford, but which the inconsiderate warden refused to let him have. "Hell, who wouldn't want out, under those circumstances?" Pruiett observed, while the facts of the case were being submitted to him.

"Jones was sentenced to 25 years imprisonment when a jury found him guilty of shooting and killing Guy F. McIntyre, a white man, in 1917." (Pruiett would have been glad to have acquitted him, win-or-you-don't-pay style, for half of the fee the lawyers collected who bungled the case, and let old-fashioned justice prevail.) "After the shooting he was placed under a $75,000 bond for appearance at preliminary hearing. . . . He appealed from the district court verdict, and was placed under $10,000 appeal bond, which he forfeited, and went to Tia Juana, Mexico. . . . The wealthy Negro had one of the most colorful

careers in Oklahoma criminal annals. Many attempts have been
made to secure his freedom, and reports were that as much as
$100,000 had been offered for a pardon. . . ."

The Pruiett contract was contingent on his procuring "Zen"
a pardon, not on the prisoner being restored to liberty. The details of how a duly executed pardon was presented to the warden,
and to every other state official who might be connected with the
State Penitentiary, only to be turned down, were aired before
the committee investigating impeachment charges against Governor
Walton.

"Testimony of Martha Jones, wealthy mother of the Negro
slayer, before the house committee, was revealed. . . . The Negro
woman told of a contract she entered into, about October 20, with
Moman Pruiett, Oklahoma City attorney. By it, she testified, she
was to pay $10,000 in cash, to be deposited in a bank, and was
to turn over 120 acres of land in Tulsa County (with potential
oil production) valued at $25,000."

Speaking editorially, the Times for Oklahoma City inquired
and said: "Does any one think Xenophon Jones would have been
pardoned if he had not had much money at his command? There
is no apparent reason for clemency in his case. His brutal crime
deserves punishment. But there was a fortune behind him equal
to paying $25,000 for 'Counsel.' That much has been revealed
by the investigation,—and that the pardon was issued. It happened to be one of the pardons that came too late, and Xenophon
still is in prison—which is exactly where he belongs."

So there, Mr. Xenophon! With a handsomely embossed certificate in your lawyer's pocket and your coffers considerably de-
pleted, you are still behind those nasty old prison bars. Acting
Governor Trapp, standing at attention before the Ku Klux review,
tells the warden that his name must be on the paper now, because Mr. Walton has been suspended from office by the act of
his once loyal and cheering senate. If the impeachment court
acquits, the pardon will be worth par value. If they convict? The
pressure will be too strong, I fear. We'd better keep you where
you are, Mr. Xenophon, right where you are, for just a little
longer.

The uproar succeeded in involving Mr. Pruiett officially. He
was called as a witness to testify before the State Senate, sitting
as a court of impeachment for its suspended governor. Wesley E.
Disney, young Tulsa county attorney and member of the lower

house, was hard and fast on his way to congress, prosecuting the
hapless executive. He conducted the examination of Pruiett.

"Xenophon Jones is your client in the matter of a pardon?"
Mr. Disney inquired.

"Yes, sir," said Mr. Pruiett.

"You visited McAlester (home of the State Penitentiary) at
the call of Martha Jones?"

"Twice."

"A week or two ago?"

"Well, once at her call, and once at my calling her."

"The first time you went there, Mr. Patterson didn't go did
he?"

"No."

"Who went with you?"

"I went by myself. Now, I will explain that to you. I had
an appointment with the Hayes boys who I defended there for
murder, and I went to the jail, saw the Hayes boys, and after
.going to the jail, I went to the penitentiary."

"You talked with Martha Jones and Xenophon Jones there
at McAlester?"

"Yes, sir."

"Relative to representing him in a pardon matter?"

"Yes, sir."

"As I understand it, you didn't definitely fix the matter of the
fee that day?"

"We did not. It was agreed on, the matter of the fee."

"To refresh your recollection, didn't you meet Martha at the
station?"

"Yes, sir."

"Now, who was the man who had the pardon—whom you
told her had the pardon there in their grip, or portfolio?"

"I didn't tell her that. I had it right here where I have it
now." (Indicating coat pocket.)

"That was a week or two before the fee was definitely arranged for?"

"Yes, we had agreed on it that day. If you gentlemen will
allow me, I will just tell it in my own way."

"Well, just tell it in your own way."

"I want a sweeping investigation, so far as I am concerned
about it, because I have lived here a long time, and they haven't
caught me touching the hem of a jury's garment, or with the
shadow of the subornation of perjury, and I am going to leave.

(His "viller" was beckoning.) Now Martha Jones was over here. I don't remember the exact date, and while here some nigger woman by the name of Jennie, an old nigger that I defended for murder, and two or three of them came up to my office, and said that Martha, the mother of Xenophon Jones, was here, and she wanted a pardon. And they told me about Xenophon Jones. I had read that in the press, of course, with all the great publicity given it. In fact, I had read about it during Robertson's administration, and read of it, about Garrett carrying him over there when you gentlemen investigated it. At that time, though, I told this bank, or those people who came to me, I would be glad to help her if I could, but my attitude with the administration was such that I didn't think I could help much, but I named some gentlemen I thought might help them, and among the parties I named was Orban Patterson. (Patterson was his law partner.) I thought that I knew Jack Walton's chief virtue and his greatest fault, and I knew the connection between Patterson and Walton, and I told these parties that Walton could get the pardon."

"You mean that Patterson could get the pardon?"

"Patterson could get the pardon. I don't know whether it was the day before or two days before, I told Patterson that he had better get that pardon if he expected to make any money out of it; if he expected to get the fee. I cautioned him in every way I could to be very conservative about his remarks; that the investigation was on and I didn't want to see him have any shadow cast on him in any way about the transaction. I told him there would be great publicity through the press. I think it was on the day that the governor was suspended, I'm not sure whether it was the evening before, that I told Mr. Patterson if he expected to get it he had better get it. On the day the governor was suspended, sometime that evening, I don't remember the— sometime around five-thirty or six o'clock. Whatever the time may have been, at one-forty, before he was suspended I saw the pardon, and I only know by hearsay as to when he got it."

"Where did you see it, Mr. Pruiett?"

"I saw it in Mr. Patterson's office."

"You didn't know who delivered it to him of your own personal knowledge?"

"No, I don't. I would be glad to tell you anything in the world, I know about it."

"Do you know anything on earth that Ruth (Charles H. Ruth was a suspended state supreme court commissioner) had to do with it? The question of the validity of the pardon is not before us, you understand."

"Yes, I know what I heard. I don't mind telling you. When these niggers came to me, some nigger by the name of Jennie, I don't know—I can't tell her name now—but Jennie somebody— there was three of them telling me that Martha was here, you understand. They told me that Ruth said he had it in his pocket, and that he could deliver it. Well, I told them if that was true, if Ruth or anyone else had the pardon in his pocket, that the culprit had the right to that pardon; they didn't have the right to peddle it around over the country, for the purpose of commercialism, or otherwise. That is what I told those niggers."

"To refresh your recollection, wasn't it an Indian woman by the name of Jennie Fields, instead of a Negro? Jennie Fields, George Field's wife?"

"Yes. Well, I had forgotten, because when I came back here from the hospital, I just finished trying eight murder cases, and I have been awful tired;—these things just come to me, in fact, I knew Patterson and Walton were good friends, and I thought if he could make the fee by getting it, why let him get it. That is my attitude in the matter, exactly."

"Do you know anything further, by hearsay, about Ruth's connection with it?"

"I think that Martha Jones, when she came over here, went to Judge Thomas H. Owen. (The same Tom Owen who had tried to prevent Pruiett's delivery of Corley McDarment, and who was supposed to be, at the time, trustee for Pruiett's property and estate.) 'I think she talked to him, in other words, sought advice about it, because when these parties—the reason I have an independent recollection of this matter is, when these niggers, or Indian women or whoever it was, came to me and talked to me about the matter, I wanted to find out, if I could, the financial ability of Xenophon Jones and his mother, and I told Mr. Patterson that I would go and try to find out. I went to Judge Owen. I asked him about the financial condition. He said he had attended to the business of Martha Jones, for, oh, I think something like twenty-four or twenty-five years. He told me of the condition of Xenophon Jones—of an allotment he had. He said the value of it was very much exaggerated. It was located somewhere in Tulsa County. It was after that that Martha Jones called me and at her bidding I went to McAlester. Now, in that conversation there in the jail with Martha Jones, I got this information. The poor old Negro woman, she looked at me and said, 'Now, Judge, of course I know you have been working on this case, but how many of you gentlemen got the pardon?' Well, it was such a scream of humor that I couldn't help but laugh. I said, 'Martha, I don't know how many gentlemen have got the pardon, but I know I have been working in harmony, as you know I have, trying to get it.' She said, 'Is there more than one out?' I said, 'I don't know; I am not so sure; but I think there is more than one out.' Well, it struck me so forcibly that before leaving the penitentiary—there was a mailman there, who handles the mails, and I happened to know him. He said, 'Moman, I saw you talking to Xenophon Jones and his mother.' I said, 'Yes.' He said, 'Well, I understand you have a pardon for them.' I said, 'Yes, I have got it here in my pocket.' He said, 'How many is out?' I said, 'Well, it don't make any difference, I have got the pardon.' He said, 'Well, I understand there is another one out.' I am giving you gentlemen all the information I have.'

"Did you ever talk to Ruth about it?"

"No, I don't talk to him, I don't deal with men of his ilk. You can put that in the record. My attitude is this way—they came to me and I know that Orban Patterson had went around here and worked his head off. He and I married sisters and I was fixing to leave here; I just thought I would help him out if he could get the fee—I would put him onto it. So that is the history of it. I would be glad to come back in the morning and give you further information, as long as you will learn of it this afternoon. I would like to do it. It is no secret; it will be made public, because people who are connected with this pardon must give their testimony here or affidavits before the Secretary of State. I have nothing in the world to conceal. At the time of my first conversation with Martha Jones and Xenophon Jones, the first conversation in the penitentiary, I stated to Martha and Xenophon that I had the pardon and it mattered not whether they kept their contract with me or not—that he was entitled to the pardon, and it was to be delivered to Judge Thomas H. Owen, whether they kept the contract with me or not."

The most amazing part of the Pruiett testimony, its background and its effect, was the sincerity of it. Pruiett's peculiar viewpoint was properly reflected in his disclosures. He saw no evil in his own purveying of pardons. The governor was the only one who was guilty of the wrong. He saw nothing objectionable in taking money from Martha Jones and Xenophon. They were

Negroes, in the first place, and they had too much money, in the second. Patterson's fee was half his, they were partners, but his own open enmity for Walton justified his denial of having any direct connection with the case. Pruiett was jealously proud of what he considered a spotless character and reputation; he considered the testimony which he gave before the Senate as nothing but support for them.

"You get a splendid view of the bay here, and it's delightfully cool all the time," the young man with the white panama hat was saying. "That's the Nunnelly property there, and the Candler estate over here. And you see the big place across the point there, with the pink tinge to it? On the island? That's—," he stepped closer, lowering his voice into a confidential undertone. "That place is sold, but the buyer insists that his name be kept secret. But just between us, it's Mr. Capone, of Chicago. Al Capone. It's one of the finest properties on the bay."

"I don't think me and that son of a gun would make very good neighbors, but I don't know," the elder man replied. "How much do you want for this dump?"

A pained expression passed across the young salesman's face. "Twenty-five thousand dollars, and it's our best bargain. These values are increasing, and the adjoining properties are being constantly improved. Mr. Capone is spending—."

"Who gives a damn about Capone?" the prospect interrupted. "Will you take some good diamonds in on the deal?"

The salesman started. The closer scrutiny he gave the man he was trying to sell, after such an inquiry, disclosed a medium sized man a little past fifty, with broad shoulders and dark, sun-tanned face and neck. His jaw was square and hard. A wide, thin-lipped mouth, drawn wider as it encompassed a huge cigar and rolled it in its extreme corner, suggested an unsympathetic, probably cruel, nature. Shaggy black brows shaded dark eyes, almost black, which were deep set and inscrutable. The broad-brimmed panama, setting carelessly aslant on his large head failed to conceal all of a billowing mass of iron gray hair which bulged from beneath it and fell shaggily about his ears and the back of his high collar. As he gazed into the cool breeze, out into Biscayne's blue, his eyes shone with the light of youth, and the extreme vigor in the expression caused the younger man to look again at the long gray locks, as if in contemplation, and suspicion, of a disguise. The reference to diamonds startled him.

"The Viller"

"Pruiett tossed cigar butts and spat into its rippling fountains with impunity."

"Well, we might consider diamonds on the deal," he said cautiously, "but, you know—."

"They're clean. Nothin' hot about 'em," the older man interrupted, correctly reading his thoughts. "I got fifteen thousand dollars worth of 'em."

"We can talk about it with the manager," the salesman said. "What did you say your name was, please, sir?"

The gray haired man darted him a look of contempt. "It isn't Capone, an' it isn't Jesse James, either," he growled. "It's Pruiett. Moman Pruiett, an' I'm from Oklahoma."

"Oh, yes, Mr. Pruiett. I read about you in the paper, last week. I didn't understand it when we met at the office. You are an attorney, I believe the article said."

"Hell, no," Pruiett said, "I'm no attorney. I'm a lawyer—just a plain one-gallus lawyer. An' this place is not what I wanted, but I'm gettin' tired of lookin', so I'll take it. Get your manager and come by the Ta-Miami. I got my diamonds in the hotel safe. If they'll take the rocks at a fair price, I'll buy your little viller."

The Miami News had published glad tidings. "An important addition to legal circles in Miami shortly will be the location of Pruiett and Patterson, of Oklahoma City, who have been engaged in practice for 26 years and have been interested in some of the most important criminal trials ever held in the southwest. Moman Pruiett, head of the firm, and Orban C. Patterson, one of his associates, are at the Ta-Miami hotel, where they have spent the last week arranging for office space in a downtown building and looking for desirable residences for their personal use.

"Mr. Pruiett handles murder cases, principally, but his firm does a general legal business. He represented Jean P. Day, ex-member of the Supreme Court [Commission] of Oklahoma, who killed Col. Paul Ward Beck. When United States Senator Thomas P. Gore was sued for damages by Minnie E. Bond, Mr. Pruiett was chief counsel for the Senator. He also defended Clarence P. Douglas, former editor of the Muskogee (Okla.) Phoenix, when Douglas was placed on trial charged with the murder of James Williams, editor of the Ardmore (Okla.) Chronicle. . . . . Discussing Florida Mr. Pruiett said: 'Florida is the only state left unscratched. It is the only section for youth and talent to meet its reward; it is almost what the Indian Territory was thirty-five years ago. There is no question about the wonderful future of this city and state, and no question but that the government will recognize its claims to become an important seaport with ample ship channels. As to climate, I have not suffered from heat since coming here, although the temperature reached 107 in Oklahoma City recently. . . ."

The old Pruiett capacity for making the headlines was unimpaired. Two days later the News bowed to him again. "Thursday afternoon proved to be a gala occasion at the range of the Miami-Hialeah Gun Club at Hialeah, where distinguished visitors were amongst those present. . . . Outside of the Club's own George D. Williams, back in Miami from a northern trip for a few days, interest centered particularly in Moman Pruiett and Orban C. Patterson of Oklahoma City, who have come to Miami to make their home. Mr. Pruiett is probably one of the most famous criminal lawyers in America, specializing in murder cases, and who has handled some of the country's most sensational ones. . . . Interest of club members centered in the two visitors as the result of a rumor preceding them to the range, to the effect that gentlemen from Oklahoma never ventured forth without high-top boots, a sombrero and a pair of 45's strapped to their belt. (Black Joe Patterson's fresh ghost, or old banker William's more mature one, may have had something to do with starting the rumor.) It turned out, however, that neither Mr. Pruiett nor Patterson sported any of the three articles mentioned, but did know how to shoot, and tallied a good score of clays with deft handling of the guns."

Pruiett was back in the criminal law business. From a very sick man walking the streets of Havana, Cuba, he had risen in a year to fight and overcome disease, and regain his place at the top of his profession, as if his absence had been but a holiday out of the office. His conduct in his recovery, as always, had been fantastic and unorthodox, and unexplainable.

CHAPTER TWENTY-ONE

Wherein the rejuvenated Pruiett enters upon the Florida Boards, and lives up to the flashy press notices by clearing a Catholic with a Klucker jury, notwithstanding the victim had been a Klucker, and had been ruthlessly dispatched, before witnesses, on the stoop of the Miami Post Office. And how he demonstrates his point, after charging that Darrow had mistried Leopold and Loeb, by pleading self-defense for a hi-jacker with a record, who shot a uniformed policeman from his motorcycle on a downtown thoroughfare, and successfully defies a jury of twelve men to electrocute him. And, wherein, his technique is labeled "Hokum," and Florida is advised to auction its electric chair pending his continued stay on the peninsula.

When handsome Hattie Freckleton shot her husband to death on a crowded street in the Miami business district, she was merely impelled by those ordinary passions of hate, viciousness and self-pity which invariably concur to produce such extraneous conduct. But she was rendering the lawyer Pruiett an inestimable service. She was setting the stage for his comeback; was giving him his chance to perform in the light of the flashy notices lavished by the Florida press since his permanent location in Miami.

The Pruietts were at home in the "viller" at 59th Street and the Bay Shore. The fountains, three of them, gurgled on the front lawn, in the sun room and on the patio. Pruiett tossed cigar butts and spat his brown expectoration into their rippling basins with impunity. Pruiett, attorney, had offices in the Calumet building. "Were they fixed up? Why, I paid three thousand dollars for the rugs we had in the place; three thousand for the stuff we wiped our feet on," Pruiett boasted.

Legend had labeled him the wheel horse of the Washita, as he ploughed through a quarter century of murder trials. He was on the ascent of his second Matterhorn. He had risen and fallen. The heights which he had attained were the loftiest; the depths to which he had dropped had been like the ocean's floor. His accomplishments and his defeats were illustrative of his nature. They contained the utmost of the good and noble; an equal content of honor and courage was there. Only such a nature, in such a physical structure as the indomitable Pruiett possessed, could have survived the rigors of exertion of body and mind and the excesses to which they had been subjected. It was for such a man to rise again, to scale the second, always the more difficult and forbidding, pinnacle; it was him to write the second masterpiece; to compose the second symphony.

Slightly bent and slightly gray, he jerked about with youthful vigor. The bustle of the extravagantly promoted land boom, with its hustlers and suckers, inflated values and deflated characters, reminded him of the old Valley on Saturday afternoon, when the ranchers and Indians were packed so tightly on the muddy main street that buckboard wheels interlocked, and drunken cursing vibrated like thunder, warning of a storm, before the bullets began to fly. The sandy stretches of the wastes along the coast looked all the world like the dry, sandy bed of the South Canadian during the long summer drouths. Green citrus groves, with tangled tropical foliage along the ditches and bordering the fences, were like his Washita, in full green to match the dark vistas of alfalfa fields, ready for their first spring cutting along its muddy banks.

He had the same desire—the inspiration and fight—which had propelled him to Washington for Charley Bias. The courage and ingenuity which the liberation of Sam Ashton and Doc Tyree had required, was hot within him. It was the old Pruiett. He was ready, and aching, for a fight.

The Freckletons, Hattie and Joseph, lived in Miami's Cocoanut Grove section. Joseph was an artist, a designer and decorator, who had moved south from Jersey when the Florida boom and the building of the big places along the bay offered a tremendous field for his kind of service. He was a Protestant. Hattie was a Roman Catholic. Special dispensation had been made by her church before the marriage had been performed. Their existence, agreeable or otherwise, was little noticed in the booming peninsula, until Hattie put the ball through his skull which left a mural, in some unidentified capitalist's palace, unfinished. Then the entire populace seemed to know all about them, and just how they had gotten along together in their bungalow in the pines on Douglas Road.

Ku Klux Klan popularity was at its height. The order's impressive victory over Governor Jack Walton, marked by his impeachment and complete condemnation, had quieted executive opposition in other parts of the country. The Kansas governor's fight had been placidly postponed. Candidates for office, the

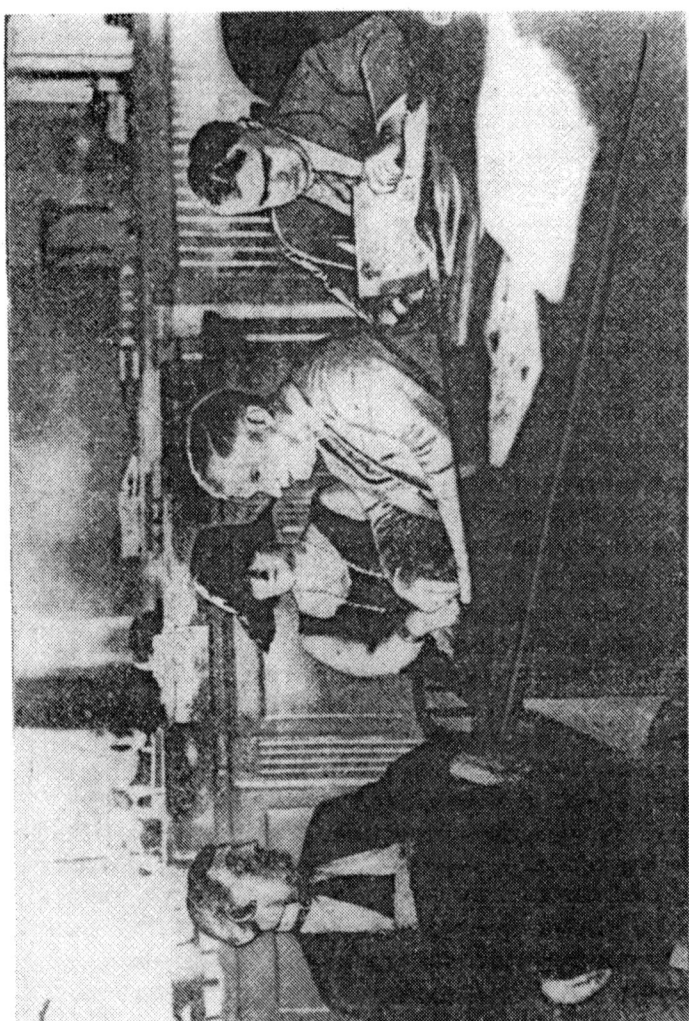

COURT SCENE—THE HATTIE FRECKLETON TRIAL

"Pruiett was on the ascent of his second Matterhorn; all he had to do was prove that husband-killing didn't amount to murder."

nation over, adopted new campaign plans and procedures. What they would normally have invested in advertising they put up in an attempt to purchase Klan endorsement, which was the equivalent to election.

Conscientious members would limp across town for a package of cigarettes or a box of cough drops, to buy them from a brother in the lodge, when a Jew or a Catholic was running a drug store next door to them. And outside of its closest calculations, the

Klan was stimulating the Negro population. The whites were foraging no more after night. They stayed at home and went to bed early, and layed up with their own wives as an incident to the necessity. Black babies were being born with greater frequency.

The Miami Klan had lost one of its most active members with the demise of Brother Freckleton. He had kept Hattie's past completely quiet, and starting with the early rejuvenation of the order, he had worked himself up, for personal and business reasons, to an enviable kleagleship. When news of Hattie's religious affiliation came out, following the killing there was an executive session of the white robed fraternity. With solemn deliberation the case was tried and the ballot taken. Hattie Freckleton was condemned to die, by the Klan, in the state's electric chair. The old Goblins and Kleagles were pretty crafty.

Pruiett's honorary Klan card reposed in his bulky bill fold. He had not elected to establish his membership or affiliate himself with the Florida organization.

"We ought to join up with these Kluckers," Patterson said to him, in their office. "You got your card, and you can get me in. We won't get any business around here unless we do."

"I'm beginnin' to feel the same way about it," Pruiett said. "They're worse here than they were at home, an' if you don't think that's bad, write your old pal Jack Walton a letter," he chuckled.

"Well, make a move; we can do a lot better if we start gettin' some of the Klan business," Patterson. "We got to make some money."

"Did you ever stop to think," Pruiett inquired casually, "that every damned lawyer in Miami, except a few Jews, is a member of the Klan. They stick together, all right, but when one of those guys gets a little law business, he's goin' to take it to the lawyer member he knows best; that he's known the longest. We've just got to wait, an' get acquainted. It'll take a big case to put us over."

"We don't get started any younger," Patterson replied. "I say, join up and find out who the big boys are. Get acquainted as members, not outsiders."

"Use your head a little," insisted Pruiett. "Non-membership is goin' to get business, too. While we're decidin' on just what's best, we may get some good business, that a Klan member couldn't take, or get. Did that ever occur to you?"

"Freckleton was shot to death near the Real Estate Building on First Street, near North East First Avenue," said the Miami Tribune. "Immediately following the shooting the wife was arrested by police and later released to county authorities." When Pruiett saw her, on the same date, she was in the old jail behind the Dade County courthouse.

"Do you belong to this Klan, Mr. Pruiett?" That was the first question she asked him.

Pruiett evaded her. "I've only been here six months," he said. "I don't even know who the Klan is."

"I'm a Catholic, Mr. Pruiett, and my husband was a member of the Klan. He was a powerful member, too. The sheriff, the judges, the court employees, they all belong to the Klan." She was talking fast—half hysterically. "They'll have a Klan jury, too, Mr. Pruiett, and I won't get a fair trial. Oh, God, what can I do?"

"You can trust me, for one thing," Pruiett told her promptly. "I don't belong to the Klan, this Klan down here," he corrected himself, "but if I did, I've still got my oath to uphold the Constitution of the United States. I'm under obligation to no one in Florida, nor any lodge or fraternal order. I'm a free lance lawyer."

"Will you swear it? Will you swear to me that no matter what else you belong to, that you have no connection with this gang, this Klan that Freckleton belonged to?"

"On my honor as a lawyer and a gentleman," Pruiett said. He wanted her case and wanted it badly. He could see the reflection of his picture on the front page of the News and the Herald, as he looked through the bars into Hattie's tear-stained visage.

Pruiett got the case. In brief, simple terms, his client had killed her husband by shooting him through the head with a thirty-two pistol and bullet. All he had to do, besides avoid the difficulty which she, a Catholic, might expect from a Klan jury, if the jury was a Klan jury, was to prove that technically, such killing did not amount to murder.

"At the beginning of the afternoon session Attorney Moman Pruiett, who is acting as counsel for Mrs. Freckleton, stated the case as it would be offered by the defense. He told the jury that

it would be the contention of counsel to show that Mrs. Freckleton is 32, that Mr. Freckleton was 40; that they had been married
about five years at the time of the homicide and were happy until
after the time Mrs. Freckleton made a trip to the North for an
operation; that following her return trouble existed between them;
that he mistreated her; that she was allowed to come to Miami
only a few times during the four years they lived at Cocoanut
Grove; that she received a blow at his hands from which she
has suffered continually since; that he filed divorce proceedings
against her and that the matter was adjusted, and they became
reconciled.

"Following this reconciliation, they became estranged and he
again started to sue for a divorce. She was attempting to effect
another reconciliation just before the killing, but he cursed her
and finally offered to strike her, causing her to fire the shot, in
self-defense, which ended his life.

" 'We expect to show that she was distracted—an abnormal,
woman,' Mr. Pruiett concluded. 'And if we show you these facts,
and I have tried not to exaggerate them, we confidently expect
you men of the jury to acquit this defendant.' "

Pruiett was making that opening outline to a jury composed principally of members of the Klan. He had engaged local
counsel, not a Klucker, who knew, by reputation and street corner
talk, about who was who in the Klan. All his associates, and his
client, had presumed that he was getting such information so
that he could challenge Klan members as they attempted to qualify.
Instead, he challenged the non-members, and accepted those whom
his client, and co-counsel, said were Klansmen.

"My God, Mr. Pruiett," Hattie whispered frantically, "we've
got ten Klan members in the box; what in the world are you
doing?"

"From now on," Pruiett answered, "I'm waivin' my peremptory challenges. I got you a damn good jury. No more challenges."

"But the Klan, they've sworn to avenge Joe," she rasped.
"You've got to get 'em off; do something, not let 'em murder me."

"I'll try your case for you, Mrs. Freckleton," Pruiett told
her. "That's what you hired me for. Now, please, don't bother
me. We'll have our final conference on your testimony just before
the state finishes its case."

The accused leaned back in her chair with a fixed, frenzied
stare in her eyes. She was convinced that the counsel, to whom

she had deeded her bungalow and given an assignment of poor Joseph's life insurance policies, was in with the all-powerful Klan. She could see the double cross, instead of the fiery cross, sending her to death in the wired seat.

Pruiett seemed oblivious of her hostility—of her lack of faith in him. He cross-examined the state's witnesses with old time territorial ferocity. He stalked and strutted and ranted, building his defense foundation step by step, and using for it the same stones the state had produced for building a death dungeon for unhappy Hattie.

The state, with numerous incriminating offerings, proved by its officer Scarborough that following the shooting he rushed to the body and demanded to know who had committed the act. He said that Mrs. Freckleton stepped forward, and said: "Oh, I did it. He's my husband." The state contended that her declaration was with perfect candor, as if the marital ties entitled her to take such liberties she had just taken with her spouse's skull. And it is probable that Hattie meant it just as it sounded.

Pruiett saved the best until the last. All of his evidence was in before he put Hattie on the witness stand. Her attitude had noticeably brightened since a long conference in the consultation room of the jail, at mid-trial, but she was still nervous and ill at ease. Pruiett began to question her, casually.

"Are you a native of the South, Mrs. Freckleton?" he inquired.

"Oh, no," she assured him, "I was born in the North; up in Jersey."

"And your husband, Mrs. Freckleton? He was born up there, too, I presume?"

"Oh, no, Mr. Pruiett," she said. "He wasn't born in this country; he was born in Sicily, you know."

"What?" demanded Pruiett, affecting such surprise that he flounced from the reclining position in his chair. "What did you say, Mrs. Freckleton?"

"I said that Mr. Freckleton was born in Sicily," she repeated. "He came to this country when he was a young man."

"Well," Pruiett seemed to muse, "he was naturalized, I suppose. He was an American citizen?" He had the corner of his eye on the alien-hating Klan majority in the jury box.

"No, he was not, Mr. Pruiett. I talked to him about it lots of times. I begged him to take out his naturalization papers, but he wouldn't do it. I just couldn't persuade him to take them out."

The coy witness daubed a perfectly dry eye with her handkerchief.

"Yes," Pruiett said, breathlessly, as if to say—"keep it up, for Christ's sake don't stop now."

"He refused," she continued. "He said that if they got his name on the books, he'd have to do military service, and—."

"We object," howled Swink, the prosecuting attorney. "It's immaterial."

"Sustained," droned the court.

"Was your husband a veteran of the late war, Mrs. Freckleton?" he asked.

"We object," howled Swink again. It's—."

"Sustained," said the court.

Hattie's pathetic look was equivalent to a negative reply. It carried even more weight with the jury, and the jury was beginning to take interest in what the defendant was offering.

Then Pruiett and Hattie got down to business. Freckleton was a sadistic beast in a ceiling decorator's smock. He beat her and he kicked her and he cuffed her. He denied her enough clothes to wear or enough food to eat. Her evening caress was rewarded with a fist in the face. Her prostrate supplications for consideration, and affection, were met with brutal kicks. He whipped her when she laughed and he whipped her when she cried, but his uncontrollable frenzy, with bestial attacks, came when she objected to his sending his money away when she needed it so badly for groceries and a few clothes.

"Is that so," Pruiett asked innocently. "What did he do with his money? Who did he send it to?"

"I never was able to find out who it was, for sure," she whined. "It was a foreign name; he sent it back to Sicily."

"Did he have people in Sicily?"

"I don't know, Mr. Pruiett. He had no relatives in this country at all; it may have been that he had folks in Sicily, but I think it was a business associate, a painter. As fast as he received pay on a contract, he took just enough to keep us, that is himself, for he had no regard for me, and the balance he sent to Sicily."

"Didn't you ever receive letters from the old country?"

"He did; not I," she corrected. "He did, quite often."

"And who were they from?"

"I don't know, Mr. Pruiett; he destroyed them. He burned them just as soon as he opened them and read them."

A shapely shank and a coy manner were Hattie's natural attributes. The Sicily story and all the rest was narrative. If an innocent person could be convicted, a guilty one could be acquitted, and no rule, law or prohibition, could stop him if his client would give him a semblance of co-operation. Hattie Freckleton worked with him like a true disciple of the doctrine.

It was privation—and Sicily. It was cruelty—and Sicily. It was want—and Sicily. Americanism in the jury box was being invited again, as when it was inducted into the robed order, "to approach the portal of our beneficent domain and join in the sacred duty of protecting womanhood, to maintain forever white supremacy in all things, to bless mankind and to keep eternally ablaze the sacred fire of a fervent devotion to a pure Americanism." Americanism and Sicily? Americanism, with beating a hungry wife, preliminary to sending hoarded American wealth to a bunch of damned lower Italians? What the hell is Americanism? Hattie was seeing and understanding Pruiett's motive in keeping the Klansmen, her avowed persecutors, on the panel.

Florida saw its first fanatical forensics in the courtroom when Pruiett argued the Freckleton cause to the jury. "Mr. Pruiett, who came to Miami recently from Oklahoma, where he was attorney in a large number of important murder cases, held the rapt attention of a courtroom which was, this time, crowded to its capacity. The defendant sat motionless, almost as pale and immovable as a marble statue, while her counsel paced back and forth, hurling his bursts of oratory at the jury, or extending hands pleadingly—only to turn a moment later and shake his fist at the state's attorney."

"Mr. State's Attorney," he roared, "I throw the challenge back at you. Try her as if she were a man. Forget she is a woman. Suppose a man were on trial and had been repeatedly beaten, choked, abused, threatened, and assaulted. Would you not say that he would be justified in protecting his own life? Talk of compromise, if you please, Mr. Swink. Spread before the jury's eyes the smooth visa of a prison sentence. Never! In this case it must be either the extreme penalty, or an acquittal. There can be no middle ground.

"My friends, since in the beginning of time, when the gray of creation's dawn began to drive back the flood of darkness, the true male of the specie has endeavored to love and protect womanhood, not oppress, mistreat and degrade it. The real issue in this case," he cried, "is American manhood in the jury box, protecting American womanhood from the depredations of an alien beast!

There is to be no compromise. If Mrs. Freckleton is a human tigress, she is guilty and she must pay the penalty. If she is not, she is innocent and you must find her not guilty by your verdict."

"Give her liberty or give her death," he challenged.

"They say she lived in Cocoanut Grove? Nay! She lived in Lonesome Valley, between the mountains of dread and hate. They tell you she lived on Douglas Road, but she lived on the road of fear. All she had for companions were cats and dogs, and lonesome pines. This man was a brute, and when I say 'brute' I will assume the full responsibility for the use of the word."

When he had screamed of chivalry, the sanctity of the home and the purity of a good woman's breasts, of blind wifely devotion and compelling mother love, and everything else that could possibly tend to excite patriotic feeling in a male structure, he mopped the perspiration away with a huge silk handkerchief and made as if to sit down. Then, with an afterthought, he rushed to the rail in front of the first row of jurors.

"When our American mothers tuck our American children in their little beds tonight, let them be able to kiss the little frowns of care from their innocent faces, and assure them, and the Maker she looks to for guidance and counsel, THAT ALL'S WELL ON THE POTOMAC!" He gave the rail a resounding slap, as if punctuating his sentence with an exclamation point. Then he stalked defiantly to his seat.

"Mrs. Hattie Freckleton was acquitted of a charge of first degree murder for the slaying of her husband, Joseph Freckleton, on N. E. First Street near the Real Estate Building, on September 29, 1924. The jury in Judge H. F. Atkinson's circuit court, which was given the case at 2 o'clock, returned its verdict of not guilty at 5:10 o'clock. . . . Following her acquittal, Mrs. Freckleton was released from the county jail, where she had been since the time of the shooting, and was taken to the home of Attorney Moman Pruiett, on the bay shore at Fifty-Ninth Street, where she will remain for some time to rest."

Pruiett, with Charley Ketcham, past Grand Master of the Masonic Lodge, who had driven from Key West to hear him try his case, went to the Ta-Miami Hotel for dinner. After dining they lounged in the lobby, smoking cigars.

"Judge Pruiett?" A uniformed hotel employee had approached him.

"Yes," he said.

"A gentleman says he's holdin' a 'phone call for you in the game room. Shall I tell him you'll take it there?"

"Yes, I'll take it. Show me how to go," Pruiett replied.

The boy led him through the back lobby to a stag room used for cards; the current craze called for hearts, but poker and rummy equipment was available. The boy stopped at the doorway. As Pruiett walked in the door was closed behind him.

"Hello, Judge." A grinning man dressed in a light tan suit offered his hand. It was the foreman of the jury that had acquitted Hattie. Pruiett looked about as he accepted the shake. He thought he saw the entire jury present, although there were actually only ten of them—the ten that he knew were Klansmen. Possibly as many as a dozen other men were in the small room.

A portly man with gray hair, almost as thick as Pruiett's, took charge of the meeting. "Grab him, boys," he directed.

Two or three of them, closest to him, attached themselves with restrained grips to each of his arms. "Shake him down, now, an' see if you can find it. See if he's got it on him," the leader directed.

A man stepped forward to begin a methodical search. When it had proceeded as far as the left hip, to a bulging billfold, the search ended. The searcher held up the Klan identification card triumphantly. "I told you he was a Klucker," he cried.

"Why didn't you identify yourself a long time ago?" the leader demanded.

"I wanted to establish myself," Pruiett laughed. "I wanted you to learn somethin' about me before I pulled the card on you."

The jury foreman stepped up. "Was Joe Freckleton really born in Sicily?" he demanded.

"Hattie said he was," Pruiett laughed. His merriment was a shaking roar before he concluded. "Hattie swore it; you heard her."

"Boys," the chief said. "You've been hooked. You've been double-crossed. He talked you out of doin' what you started out to do, and made you think you were doin' your duty. It's a hell of a note."

"It's a treason, that's what it is," said another. "A member defendin' a Catholic woman who killed a brother member, to a Klan jury, and gettin' her off. Oh, God!"

"What's to be done with him?" asked the leader. "Do we revoke the card and give him the strap, or act on his application for transfer of membership?"

"Who said he applied for transfer?" chimed a voice.

"I did," said the leader. "When he said 'All's well on the Potomac' before that jury, he was puttin' in his bid. If he wasn't, he's in a hell of a bad fix now."

"I'm ready to join up, or get the boot, either one," Pruiett grinned. "It's the Constitution of the United States first with old Moman, and fraternal affiliations next. If it suits you, I'd like to come in."

"Was Joe Freckleton really born in Sicily?" insisted one of the members of the jury.

"You heard what I said about it," evaded Pruiett.

They voted him in. "It reminds me," Pruiett began, as they handed him his third drink, "of the old Sam Ashton case. Now that was a case where I had a tough jury, an' a hell of a bad client. We started out—." He told them about Pruiett here and there—in murder cases. When subsequent inquiry established that Joe Freckleton had been born in Davenport, Iowa, and had some respectable relatives living in the north, they declined to vote as was suggested, on removal, and Klan discipline, for Pruiett.

The assistant warden at Raiford brushed out the death cell and ordered an overhauling for the electric chair. The signs from down Miami way were as conclusive of death business coming, as the palmtree stalks, snapped half-way up, were of the recent visit of a gulf storm. Company was surely on its way.

The extreme quiet around Toledo, Ohio, had driven young Walter Valiton out. From petty to great thievery, he went with little more than a parental rebuke. Drifting across and below the Ohio he swiped himself an automobile at Somerset, Kentucky, but received only a suspended sentence and a mild rebuke from a kindhearted judge. With the Kentucky experience for guidance, he went back to Toledo and pulled the same kind of a job. He received the same kind of lenient treatment after being apprehended.

With this experience in his mind, his appreciation for the court's good will and leniency in his heart, and a stolen automobile in his hands, Valiton sought the more agreeable clime of Biscayne's sunny bay. Napolenically, he went post-auto, taking fresh mounts as whim and convenience permitted, at intervals along the route. Car owners and insurance companies were distracted by the time he reached Daytona, where he stole his last,

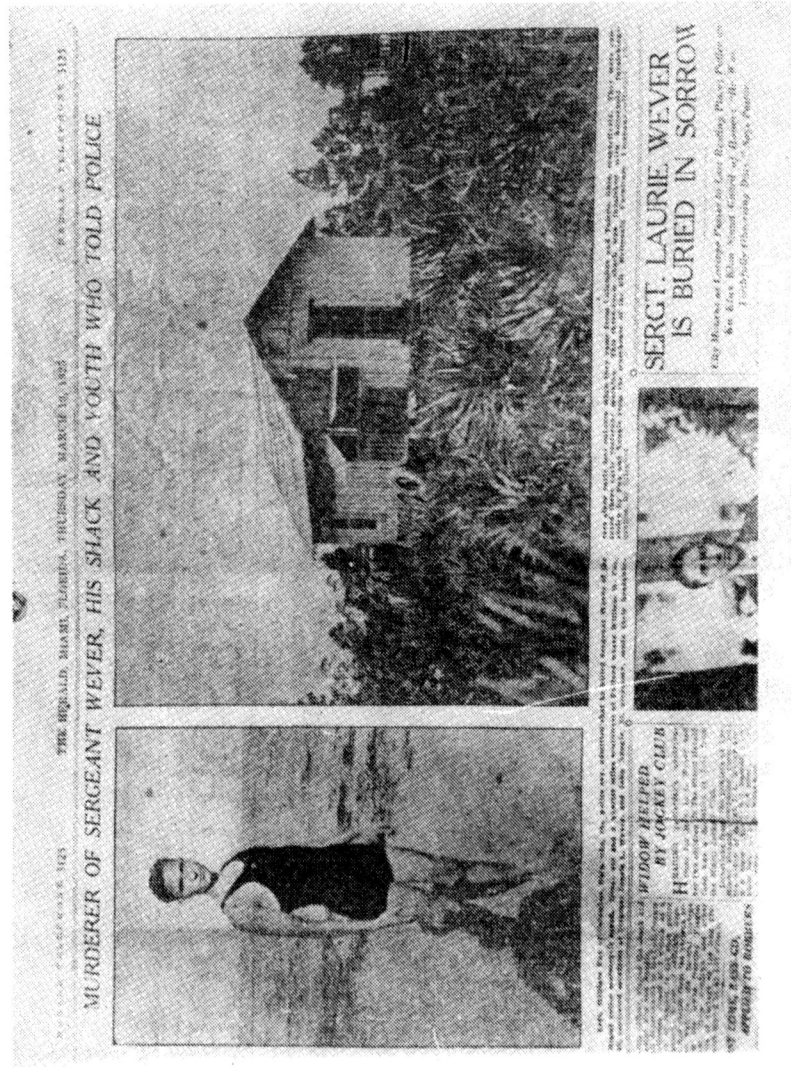

THE SHACK IN THE PALMETTO SWAMP, AND ITS MURDEROUS OCCUPANT
"Valiton stood for bigger and better crime in Florida."

a box-backed Essex, to carry him into Miami. There he began to put into effect his plans for bigger and better crime in Florida.

"The little devil was tougher than a boot," opined Pruiett, who was to become his mouthpiece. Building into the weak and already criminally inclined crackers of the poor piney land, Valiton got himself a pal and a few girls. From an abandoned shack in a palmetto swamp, surrounded by enough substantial earth to support thick pine woods, he began his program of hi-jacking, pilfering and burglarizing. John Naugle, a misguided kid who had run away from a poor home in Jacksonville, received a first lieutenant's commission from the Toledo outlaw.

The warehouse of the Eli McDonald furniture company suffered an unusual violation. Enough furniture to furnish a small house, in selected items, was stolen with the currency and checks from the office safe. The leaky floors of the shack in the swamp, thereafterward, were covered with oriental rugs, and handsomely carved mahogany pieces rested awkwardly in its well-ventilated corners. Valiton and Naugle, in silk shirts and bell-bottomed trousers, smoked imported Cuban cheroots and drank expensive Jamaica liquor.

The carbide light of Police Lieutenant Wever's motorcycle reflected from the rear of a slow moving sedan with an Ohio license. It was 2 o'clock in the morning, and police business was bad. The chief had been raisin' hell about the wave of burglaries and hi-jackin's that had the county half-terrified, and the strong language of a recent departmental bulletin on the subject was running through his mind. Here's a good one to ivestigate, Wever decided.

"Pull over there, you; pull over and stop." Wever had ridden to a position beside the driver. When the car stopped two stylishly dressed boys stepped out. "What's the trouble?" the one who had been driving inquired.

The street light from the corner, by the Savoy Hotel, gave Wever a good view of them, but he augmented the illumination with the beam of his flashlight. "Kind of late for joy riding, ain't it?" he asked. "What you doin' out this time of the morning?"

The driver flashed him a personality smile. "We took our girls home, and then had a flat tire," he said. "It took quite a while to fix it, so we're late. We're just on our way home."

Wever's light continued to play on them. "You didn't get your hands very dirty, changin' that tire, or your clothes, either. How about that?"

"Oh, we washed up at the filling station—washed our hands up," the spokesman said glibly, with just a little more smile. "I'm pretty good at changin' 'em, anyway."

The patrolman wasn't satisfied. "Mind if I look in your car?" he inquired, watching them closely in the light.

"Help yourself. Drive it around the block, if you want," chirped the flip speaker.

The little light arched its white ray into the back seat of the sedan. Wever switched it around, pulled the rear cushion out onto the floor with one hand, and studied the display within the beam for several minutes.

"What you use these kind of tools for?" he asked.

"Tires," said one of the boys.

"First time I ever saw any tire irons that shape, or size," the policeman replied. "And what's the use of so many. Have a lot of flats, do you?"

His hand was on the butt of the service revolver which hung on his Sam Brown belt as he walked back to where the boys were standing. "Do you always carry so much soap, an' perfume, an' cigarettes, when you're going home from seein' some dames?" he asked.

The boys didn't answer. "Got guns?" asked Wever. There was still no reply. "Hold your hands up a little, while I look around." Wever walked behind them, his hand still on the handle of his own revolver, and began a methodical search by running his hand down the exterior of their light clothing. After he had inspected the front seat and compartment of the car, by illuminating it with his little light, he turned to the boys, still standing under the street light.

"Get in an' drive down to the station," he directed. "You look hot to me, an' I'm goin' to have you checked up. I'll follow on this motor, an' remember; no monkey business. You turn right two blocks down for the station."

Two blocks down the Essex failed to turn. With a slight increase of speed it continued straight ahead. Wever pulled up on the driver's side. "What the hell's the matter with you," he bawled, "I told you to turn right back there——."

The driver, with one hand on the wheel, was holding a blue thirty-eight in his lap with the other. He had slipped it from under the front seat cushion, where Wever's flashlight had failed to penetrate, as he had driven from the scene of the policeman's search. Laying it professionally on the crooked elbow of his driving arm he pointed it square at the motorcycle rider's chest, and began to fire.

"I was shot by a highwayman," Wever managed to gasp to fellow officers before he died. Three days later a posse, composed of officers and incensed citizens, stormed the shack in the swamp, which was in truth a little fortress. They met no resistance from the two occupants. Valiton adopted the alias of William Fox, and credited Columbus, instead of Toledo, with his origin. He modestly confessed to having killed Wever, giving the deputies, who took an occasional random swing at him, or jabbed him with the point of a pocket knife, all of the intimate details.

".... When Valiton was brought to the jail he was spattered with blood, his lips and face were bruised and he appeared badly battered up . . . ." said the Miami News. " 'I took Valiton,' said the warden, 'placed him in a padded cell and told the officers that I would kill anybody who started anything.' "

"While a constantly growing crowd milled around the court yard and county jail yesterday morning," observed the Miami Herald, "eager to secure a glimpse of Fox and Naugle, the prisoners were spirited away before their eyes by deputy sheriffs posing as garbage collectors. . . . 'Make way for this truck there, men,' called the driver of one of Dade County's big trucks, used in road-repairing. 'Move that automobile out of there.' . . . . The crowd paid little attention to the truck or the attendants who brought forth from the jail the large garbage cans with the lids clamped down. . . . The men were deputies from Sheriff Henry R. Chase's staff. Inside one garbage can huddled Fox, confessed slayer of Sergeant Laurie Wever. Inside the other crouched Naugle, Fox's accomplice."

".... The prisoners were removed from the county jail at 9:30 this morning," the sheriff's office notified the steadily increasing crowd at 3 o'clock in the afternoon. "Whether they went by water, automobile or rail, we are not at liberty to state. . . . The sheriff decided that under all the circumstances it was best to remove them from Miami. They will likely be kept at the place to which they have been removed until their own case is called to trial."

Startling revelations tumbled over each other as they began to come out in the case of State of Florida v. Walter P. Valiton, alias William Fox, and John Naugle. "Money came easy for Fox and Naugle, and it went just as easily as it came, according to their admissions to the police. Cards, liquor, women and the races claimed their money, which they obtained through the strong arm method."

"Eleven hundred dollars, taken by Fox and Naugle from the

safe in the office of the Eli McDonald Furniture Company, was squandered on the races, pool games and other forms of betting, and two hundred dollars taken from the safe of Ye Wayside Inn, obtained by them when they tied up the night watchman, went the same way. . . . They confessed yesterday that they had in their automobile loot from a drug store which they had just robbed when overtaken by Sergeant Wever. Fox declared he did not want to be taken to jail, and shot in a frenzy of fear. He said that he had been drinking."

The automobile abandoned in the swamp was the beginning of a well marked trail to the hideout. The clumps of palmetto along the way, and the thick, adhesive morass, yielded up separate articles of loot, then the suitcases used for carrying it. Word of suspicious acting occupants in the abandoned hut, and careful description of the occupants, harmonized with the indications made by the flight and the trail of loot. "At exactly 2:10 o'clock yesterday morning 14 policemen in charge of Chief Quigg and detective Nelson set out from the police station in three automobiles. All were heavily armed. The party continued as far as Fulford, then turned west on the trail leading to the shack housing the two slayers. Then parked their automobiles."

"Six of the men, revolvers in hand and ready for instant action, crept up the trail about a quarter of a mile and surrounded the house. . . . In the meantime the remainder of the party, on signal, approached the house. Without lights of any kind Chief Quigg drove his automobile through the underbrush to the front of the shack, then flashed the headlights and spotlight directly on the house. . . . At the same moment, Detective L. H. Haddock, with William Beechey and Detective Pearce immediately behind him, threw his full weight on the door, which soon gave way. Four men dashed into the room, revolvers and flashlights in hand."

"The two men were asleep in the front room of the house. Fox on the west side of the room and Naugle on the east side. While the three companions of Beechey covered the two men with their guns, Beechey jumped on Naugle and handcuffed him, as he said: 'Did you kill Wever?' . . . . Naugle, somewhat dazed and nervous, replied, 'No, I didn't, but he did,' pointing to Fox."

"A careful examination of the house revealed a large box of dynamite caps and several boxes of electric fuses. Throughout the house was a complete network of wires, which terminated at a point near the dynamite box. Over each door two wires termi-

nated, and it is believed that they could be so arranged that if
the door was opened the dynamite would be ignited by a spark
from several dry batteries. The circuit was disconnected when
the men were in the house, and in their absence the men would
close the circuit, leaving a death trap for intruders."

"Two truck loads of stolen property were hauled away from
the small shack, including articles of every description. A large
quantity of perfume, soap and other articles sold in drug stores
was found. . . . A complete set of yegg's tools, including a
ratchet drill, hack saws, copper headed sledge hammer and a
large collection of keys were found in a box in the back room of
the house. Acids used extensively by yeggs on safes and as a
neutralizer for nitro-glycerin composed part of the kit. . . .Dis-
patches yesterday from Columbus, Ohio, stated that police in
that city have no Bertilion record of Fox. . . ."

Miami turned out en masse for popular officer Wever's
funeral. His bullet scarred motorcycle was draped with black
and mounted on a truck, and paraded about the city behind the
hearse carrying his body. A quick trial and a speedy execution for
his assassins was the oft expressed hope and opinion. The Klan,
in executive session, considered a private everglade hanging for
them, they reflected on the rather irregular liberation of Hattie
Freckleton, who had slain one of the brothers. Wever had been a
member. But the electric chair at Raiford, Florida, needed a work-
out, and Pruiett was a member, now. There would be no slip this
time; so just let the law take its course. No official action was
taken.

Valiton's mother and father, on their arrival from Toledo,
hired Pruiett to defend their precocious killer. The Kluckers
winked and grinned when the gray-haired mouthpiece who had
tricked them once told them in tones that could be heard in Key
West, "the Constitution of the United States comes ahead of any
oath I took to any secret society, and I'm goin' to the front for
that kid." Let him go, as far as he wanted. Valiton would fry
as sure as the tides would be in in the evening.

It was a tough case, but not Pruiett's first one. Loeb and
Leopold were becoming familiar with the regulations at Joliet,
after their uneventful trial. Its outcome had been easily predict-
able. A news hack, half inquiring and half suggesting, approached
Pruiett.

"Are you going to follow Clarence Darrow's plan of defense

in this case, Mr. Pruiett—as he defended Leopold and Loeb?"
he asked.

"Hell, no," said Pruiett briefly. "There will be no Clarence
Darrow stuff in this case. . . . And you can make the most of
that statement. These defendants will go to trial on the real
issues."

He had been fighting the system too long to lay down and
beg for mercy now. He'd plead them not guilty, and chance the
chair trying to clear them. Any one could plead guilty and cop
life.

On the trial date he filed a volume of pleadings. There was
a twenty page motion for a change of venue, with attached copies
of every article, editorial and illustration the Miami papers and
magazines had carried on the crime, the capture, and the Wever
funeral. He complained of the threatened mob violence which required the removal of the prisoners from Miami. He filed a fifty
page motion for a continuance of the trial, and a volume of
accusations against the regularity of the jury panel, which he
charged, "was drawn by the Ku Klux Klan with the purpose
and intent of convicting, and electrocuting my client."

"It's treason," whispered the scandalized Klansmen again.

"Attorney Pruiett, in his demand for a change of venue,
stressed the fact that public sentiment had been so aroused by
the press and by wealthy relatives of Sergeant Wever that the
sheriff was forced to spirit Valiton out of the jail to the north
to prevent possible violence, immediately following their arrest.
. . . . 'The public has been given only one side of this story,'
cried Pruiett, trembling as if shaken by violent emotion. 'Walter
Valiton is not guilty of the crime charged; he has been forced to
confess to this deed by being brutally beaten by deputy sheriffs,
and threatened with even more serious harm. The public does not
understand; it has been given an untrue version of the story.'"

". . . . Pruiett pointed out that the young men were strangers
in a strange city; that at the time of their arrest they neither
had money nor opportunity to hire lawyers to advise them, and
that after a third degree their only course could have been to
confess to anything—to prevent mistreatment. 'Why,' he exclaimed,
'many attorneys who were asked to defend these young men
pleaded other business. On the other hand, many of the most
prominent attorneys volunteered to prosecute them. And more
than $2,000 has been raised to assist their prosecution.'" But
Dade County didn't want to lose the right to burn the jelly-bean

killer, and it didn't want to lose the Pruiett production of the defense. They knew it would be futile, but if the Hattie Freckleton forensics were any criterion, they knew it would be good.

"MARTIN PLEDGES TROOPS TO GUARD MIAMI SLAYERS," announced the Daily News on Monday, March 30th. The type of the bulletin covered the upper half of the front page. "National guardsmen will be called out in Miami to preserve order in event of a mob outbreak against Walter Valiton and John Naugle, confessed slayers of Sergt. J. L. Wever, Gov. John Martin notified Moman Pruiett, attorney for the pair, by telegraph Monday night. Shortly before noon, Pruiett wired the governor, who is at Tallahassee, that in case a change of venue to another county is granted, he feared the two confessed slayers would be in danger of violence at the hands of a mob, presumably infuriated because of the removal of the pair to the courts of another county, and asked that proper precautions for their safety be made. . . . Shortly afterwards, Judge H. F. Atkinson refused the defense plea for a change of venue, and ordered that the trial resume Thursday in the Dade County court. Apparently still concerned over the safety of the two youths, who are being held in the county jail, Pruiett did not revoke his plea for state protection for the prisoners. . . . About 9 p. m., the answer of the governor to the attorney's plea came by telegraph. The telegram said: 'Advise sheriff take every precaution, keep down mob violence. If necessary, will call militia. (Signed) John W. Martin, Governor of Florida.' "

"Pruiett wired the Governor," advised the Herald. "During the argument for a change of venue in the beginning of the trial yesterday of Walter Valiton, Attorney Pruiett, for the defense, without consultation, so far as it has been ascertained, with any constitutional official of the county, sent the following telegram to Governor Martin: 'My firm defending Walter Valiton, charged with murder of Sergeant Wever. Motion pending for change of venue. Believe same will be granted. In that event, I fear mob violence. Will you communicate with officers here and take such steps as may be necessary? (Signed) PRUIETT.' "

During the Washita charger's brief term as a citizen of Florida, he had already placed himself in a position where he could take liberties with the governor, and identify himself by merely signing "Pruiett" to the communication. His dinner with the governor, at the Flamingo in Miami Beach, had been but a resumption of a friendship which had begun in Washington.

A PRUIETT NOTICE IN THE MIAMI NEWS
"Keep 'em awake. Carry the baby or shoot off blank
cartridges. Give that jury a show."

"Where I can do anything for you, Moman," the governor had
said as he left Miami, "don't hesitate to call on me." Pruiett
had suggested that he put Florida's principal city under martial

law, with but slight hesitation. "And if he thought it was necessary, or that I needed it, he sure as hell would have called them soldiers out," Pruiett laughed, reviewing the incident after the conclusion of the trial.

"At no time, during the day's hearing," continued the Herald, "was there any indication that aid might be needed in the preservation of order. It was obvious, of course, that should any disturbance occur, now or at any future time, the sheriff would not hesitate to ask for help from the governor. It is UNUSUAL FOR AN ATTORNEY TO MAKE SUCH A MOVE. The telegram sent by Pruiett was dispatched at an hour when absolute quiet prevailed. . . ."

If boom-bounding Miami and vicinity wasn't going to approve of the unusual, it was going to have to rid itself of the irrepressible Pruiett. The right way, or the orthodox, was the one way he wouldn't go if he could avoid it. No one was concerned with the commonplace. He had long since learned that what roused the slumbering populace, and made them act the way he wanted, and needed, them to act, was the unusual, the unexpected and sensational. The front page ad which his two dollar telegram acquired would have cost an orange grove development, or a yacht sales agency, fifty thousand. And maybe it would put the prosecutors on their toes. He wanted some competition in the trial of this little old case.

Pruiett was putting on proof in support of his motion for a change of venue. "John Talbot, deputy sheriff, the last witness to testify on the change of venue petition to the Valiton trial, climaxed the morning session when he declared that Moman Pruiett, principal attorney for Valiton, was the only man he had heard utter a threat against the prisoner. . . . Talbot emphasized that the threat was uttered before Pruiett was retained as counsel by Valiton's parents. Pruiett himself arose and placed in the record the phraseology of the threat originally spoken near the kitchen of the county jail while Valiton and John Naugle were at Jacksonville for safety. . . . 'If they bring those men back to Miami, old Moman, for one, will be athirsting for their blood,' Pruiett said were his words."

Talbot had steadfastly denied that he had heard any threats made against Valiton. Pruiett persisted, trying to break him down. "The incident sent the spectators, judge, attorneys and court attaches into gales of laughter, punctuated by a spatter of applause. Even young Valiton, shadowed by the law, smiled, as did his parents, through their astonishment. . . . Only the taciturn, poker-faced Talbot, and Pruiett himself, refrained from displaying any mirth. . . . The defense lawyer unsuspectingly pulled the forensic trigger that fired Talbot's surprise shot. 'Did you ever hear any man utter threats of violence against the life of the prisoner?' . . . . 'Yes,' Talbot replied dryly. . . . 'Tell the court and jury about it,' urged the lawyer. . . . 'It was you, Mr. Pruiett,' continued Talbot. 'You were the one man I heard speak words of violence against the life of the prisoner.' "

"For one moment Pruiett was dumbfounded by the sudden turn. Then he sprang to his feet to make the best of it. . . . 'Then you did hear a citizen of Dade County,' he thundered at the witness, 'in the act of threatening violence upon the defendant?' "

His motion for a change of venue was denied, but his appeal for a reasonable continuance—in order to prepare for trial—was granted. On the last day of the proverbially ill-fated month of March the Christians filed into the arena to view the gory drama. "Harland Miller, Miami Daily News staff writer, is reporting the Valiton-Naugle trial for the News. Mr. Miller covered the Loeb-Leopold murder trial in Chicago. He has written the story from the packed courtroom in the Dade County courthouse." So speaks the Daily, editorially.

"Lack of Jurymen May Delay Trial of Murder Pair," announced the Miami Tribune. "All Jurors Challenged," reported the Herald. "Lawyer Defending Valiton Declares Whole Panel Illegal." The news item, written under the foregoing column heads, tended to demonstrate that correspondent Harlan Miller knew whereof he spoke when he observed that "Pruiett had begun to swing the shield of a complex defense, without an apparent loophole," between his client and the Raiford prison's electric chair.

"Pruiett announced to the court his challenge of the entire list of veniremen summoned, and moved that the indictment against the defendant be quashed. In his motion to quash the attorney said: 'Dade County had a population in January, 1925, as shown by the last census, of 85,000. Under the laws of the state of Florida, the board of county commissioners is required to provide a list of not less than 2,500 to 3,500 persons to serve as jurors. We allege and maintain that the board of county commissioners has failed to comply with the provision of the law by its failure to provide such a list of qualified jurors, and the panel therefore is illegal. . . . This entire panel of 750 jurors, instead of the 2,-500 required under the law, is disqualified. . . ."

Perhaps the point was a trifle technical for a self-educated territorial lawyer to raise. The court overruled him. But it didn't discourage the movant, or endear the trial judge to him. Thence forward the court came in for his share of the arraignment which Pruiett usually reserved for the prosecuting force and the arresting officers.

"Your Honor," said Pruiett, "since reports and modern law are not sufficient to convince you, let me read this Florida case. It supports my contention precisely."

"You may as well sit down, Mr. Pruiett; I have decided the point against you," replied the court.

"I know it, but I just wanted to show you how ignorant the members of Florida Supreme Court are," Pruiett replied.

"Yesterday, the third day since the court called Walter C Valiton to the bar for trial, was occupied entirely with the selection of the jury and the questions and arguments of attorneys. . ."

"Very few of the men examined said they had formed no opinion as to the guilt or innocence of the accused, and of those who said they had formed such opinions several declared their opinions were of such a nature that they could not render a fair and impartial verdict according to the evidence. Some said their opinions were so strongly formed that it would require convincing evidence to overcome them."

". . . . Scruples against the death penalty caused many jurors to be excused by the court . . . . When questioned by the state's attorney, E. C. Miller, a resident of Dade County during the past 30 years admitted he had formed and expressed an opinion, but said this opinion could be swayed by evidence favorable to the accused. Questioned by Pruiettt he said he would go into the jury box with his opinion fixed, and that convincing evidence would be required to change that evidence."

"In reply to questioning by Judge Rose, Miller said his opinion was not so strongly fixed as to prevent his rendering a fair and impartial verdict exclusively on the evidence he heard from the witness chair. Miller admitted expressing his opinion on one occasion."

"Pruiett objected to Miller's acceptance, but the court overruled his objection. The jury was sent out of the courtroom and

arguments of counsel began. Pruiett objected to the court questioning the jurors."

"This court must be extremely careful," Pruiett cried, shaking
his finger in the judge's face, as if he was cross-examining an
alley witness. ". . . . If this court is going to lean at all, he
should lean toward the defendant. The Constitution says a man
is presumed to be innocent, until proven guilty, and our appellate
courts have construed that to mean that a reasonable doubt must
be decided in favor of the accused."

The prosecutors blanched. The great crowd in the room was
hushed. It was worse than treason; it was contempt. The little
murderer's counsel had the same as accused the trial judge of
leaning, of being biased and partisan. He was going too strong;
he wouldn't get by with this.

"Do you realize what you infer, Mr. Pruiett?" the judge demanded sternly.

"I am as conscious of every syllable of my remarks as I
am of the terrible responsibility which rests upon my shoulders,"
Pruiett roared at him, never retreating a step. "I'm defending
the life of an American citizen and I want every word I am
saying to go into the record of this case. No man will ever say
that Moman Pruiett was derelict in his oath to our Constitution,
or his duty to his client."

"Watch your language," barked the court.

"The record will watch my language," howled Pruiett. "And
let me say, that this court has no right to interfere, and question
jurors, as it did this man Miller." The prosecutors gasped again.
"The state is well and ably represented here by its attorneys, and
they are questioning these veniremen properly. You are the judge.
When you go to examining jurors, you are having an influence
over them, and depriving this defendant of his right to a fair
trial." The exasperated court had to recognize the logic of his
argument and the correctness of his position. Miller was excused."

"After exhausting a panel of 250 talesmen from the box
and a special venire of 70 others, a jury was at last selected and
the state began the presentation of its case. . . ." Keep the line
open to Raiford. Don't let the dynamos get cold.

"Nostrils aquiver and lips tightened with mature fear of a
whipping, 18-year-old Walter Valiton, the stigma of neurosis
shadowed on each feature of his face, watched his lawyer attempt
to swing the shield of a complex defense between him and the

death penalty, as the trial opened. . . . 'There will be no Clarence Darrow stuff,' Moman Pruiett, the prisoner's attorney had said, and Monday morning he laid a foundation for a defense that left not a loophole unguarded. . . .''

So much for Harlan Miller's comparative impressions on Pruiett's technical efficiency. Speaking more intimately, and personally, he said: "Pruiett is of the type so tremendously effective with a jury. Juries, as a rule, are filled with men who prefer their dramatics mellow; and Pruiett gives them what they want. He paces back and forth, whispers and roars at them alternately in intimate nearness. Very nearly he caresses them with persuasive phrases and gestures, and pours pathos on their susceptibilities. He is master of the histrionics of the homicide trial; deft in his appeal to home and fireside, to patriotism and community pride. Watching him face twelve of his peers, one sees him, in the mind's eye, addressing a Fourth of July crowd, or memorializing the soldier dead on Decoration Day."

Pruiett philosophy had long held that a guy who would steal, or murder, would squeal. He was all set for the leniency-dispensing prosecution to prime an accomplice against him—to turn state's evidence—as the stock phrase put it. "Stunning news that Naugle had turned state's evidence went through the packed courtroom as deputies brought him into the room at 12:05 P. M., and it flashed through the courthouse and out on the streets, bringing crowds which could not jam their way into the already filled courtroom. . . . As Naugle went on the stand he threw one long look toward Valiton, a look which caused one spectator to murmur, 'He seemed to say, "I'm sorry, but I've got to do it." ' Valiton exhibited signs of nervousness as his erstwhile companion walked into the courtroom and as Naugle sat down in the witness chair, Valiton's hands were shaking and his hair, usually polished close to his head, was rumpled from his fingers which had been pushed through it."

It took Pruiett to plead self-defense for a hi-jacker who had admitted shooting a uniformed policeman off his motorcycle. "Yes, I shot him," he told a jury in the circuit court, where he is being tried for murder in the first degree. "I shot him because I believed he was going to shoot me. . . . He threw his light into my face and into John's and then he went from the left side of the automobile to the right side and examined it. He looked under the seat and saw the tool box and asked what it was. I told him we had been changing a tire."

" 'Drive on down to the police station,' he said. He never told us he was a policeman, or said who he was. He never said we were accused of any crime, or told us what he wanted. He just said, 'drive to the station.' . . . . He was standing on the right side of the automobile when I started up the motor. Then he said: 'Pull up to that curb or I will kill both of you.' He reached to his right and pulled out a gun. I thought he was going to shoot. I did not mean to kill him, but just wanted to scare him, because I thought he was going to kill me."

The crackers whispered in the courtroom and on the streets. "Where does that Oklahoma lawyer think he's goin' with that kind of stuff? It's sickenin'. He's fryin' the kid as sure as hell; such a defense is ridiculous." But Pruiett wasn't lost; he just didn't have anything better to offer. The flimsiness of the story was indicative of the load he was going to carry when he went to the jury for the last time. Anything was better than a guilty plea, for with that, the court would discharge the jury and direct the application of the current himself. He just wanted an issue, something to keep away from a directed verdict, and self-defense was all he could think of.

But was he giving up? Valiton was trying to keep away from an unsavory record; he lied about his previous convictions. But Swink and Pine had the goods on him, official records of his car thefts and suspended sentences, and the squawk of another old buddy.

"Did you plead guilty to stealing an automobile in federal court at Toledo, Ohio, on July 1, 1924?" Prosecutor Pine inquired politely.

"No," Valiton answered shortly.

"Did you plead guilty in federal court, to stealing an automobile at Somerset, Kentucky, on April 19, 1924?"

"No," Valiton insisted. "I have never been arrested on any charge whatever."

"Then Moman Pruiett, chief of defense lawyers, jumped to his feet with a motion to strike from the record the testimony given Friday by Police Chief Quigg, in which the chief recounted a statement made to him by Sergt. Laurie L. Wever, for whose slaying Valiton is being tried. Chief Quigg had said that as Wever lay dying in the hospital the wounded man told him: 'I was shot by a highwayman.' . . . Pruiett now contended that the state had no right to introduce this testimony, as Sergeant Wever did not know whether or not his assailants were highwaymen. . . .

Then Fred Pine prepared for his smashing thrust at the very heart of the defense's plea that Valiton was not a highwayman, had never been arrested, and is now on trial for the only offense of his life."

The first thrust was the witness's own criminal record. The second was the testimony of young Cleo Butler, Valiton's cousin, "who testified that he came to Miami from Toledo with Valiton, and stayed here one month." "What was Valiton's occupation?" . . . . The defense objected. Then Butler answered. "His occcupation was—stealing."

Pruiett's efforts to shake him, on cross-examination were unsuccessful. "He had no occupation except as a thief," Butler insisted.

"Did you help him?" Pruiett asked.

"Yes, I did on two occasions," Butler answered.

"Then you are a thief yourself?" Pruiett surmised.

"No," the witness replied. "I am not a thief." He was entitled to his opinion, and he was going to stick to it.

And Pruiett's professed fidelity to his Constitution—superior to that he had for any fraternal oath—had to come out.

"Parker Henderson was the third witness called by the state in its rebuttal testimony. He testified that he was driving north on N. W. Second Avenue on the night when Wever was shot. He said he saw a large crowd in front of the Savoy Hotel and stopped there. He saw Wever, and added that he saw the policeman's pistol and holster, with the pistol in the holster."

"This testimony was brought out by the state, it is believed, in answer to Valiton's assertion that he saw Wever draw his pistol, and fired in self-defense. The fact the pistol was in the holster after the wounded sergeant fell to the ground is considered by the state as proof that he had not drawn it before Valiton fired."

"Then Pruiett started cross-examining. 'Did you belong to the same secret society as Wever? 'I am not sure,' Henderson replied. 'Don't you know for a fact that you do belong to the same society?' Pruiett insisted. 'I refuse to answer,' said Henderson. 'You may answer,' Judge Rose interposed. 'I do not belong to the society,' he said. 'Don't you remember,' asked Pruiett, 'that you and I and Wever were present at the lodge rooms together on one occasion?' 'No, I was not there,' repeated Henderson. As Henderson left the stand he threw a dirty glance at Pruiett, which was seen by almost every person in the courtroom. There was some laughter, and applause. Judge Rose cautioned the spectators to keep silent."

Pruiett swung the heavy load across his back and started up the hill. He looked the hostile jury in the face and without a blush declared that the state had failed to make out a case of murder; that his client was guiltless, and that they ought to turn him loose. "Arraigning the attorneys for John Naugle (Valiton's squalling partner) as subjects for a whipping boss, and State's attorney Swink and Assistant's State Attorney Pine as crying for blood, not justice, Moman Pruiett closed the argument for the defense with one of the most bitter, personal attacks made in the history of Dade County courts."

The staid southerners would have to insulate with asbestos if the pride of the Chickasaw Nation was to continue to try cases in their midst. "The prosecution thought they were ready for what was comin', but they weren't. They thought they would send that boy to the electric chair, but I knew damned well they wouldn't. Another thing, I wanted to show Harlan Miller that Clarence Darrow didn't try Leopold and Loeb right. Hell, what's the bar comin' to, when it pleads a fellow guilty, and then crawls and begs for leniency?"

"Is there no God in Florida?" he screamed at them. "Is there no Christ in Miami? Are the monsters of hell really lurking in the everglades, ready to crawl out and breathe fire from their nostrils on your dance of death, while you gloat over this friendless boy's death agonies, like a swarm of cannibals?"

He revived his old Jephtha story for them. They could acquit Valiton and send him home to mama and papa, if they had the guts and stamina of a Biblical bastard. The way the Valiton case was put to them, they were bastards if they did and bastards if they didn't.

"The money changers need to be chased from the Temple," he added, then turned on State's Attorney Swink and Assistant State's Attorney Pine with the challenge that they had made electrocution and vengeance a personal matter, going back to the old Mosaic law of 'an eye for an eye, a tooth for a tooth.' Since that law was written, I have heard of a New Testament, and of a Christ who was crucified on the cross."

He paused, deliberately taking the cue for his next thrust from his own reference to the Scriptures. "On the cross? . . . . On the cross? . . . . On the cross!" He had graduated from a gaunt whisper to a buxom roar. "Your actions in deciding this case will be guided by the sign of the cross. Perhaps you can, perhaps you may, weigh the issues of human flesh and blood, of a human being's soul, in the shadow of the cross—the FIERY CROSS. But by the memory of my mother's prayers, offered up for the guidance of my feeble childhood steps, I'll cling to the Cross of Calvary, where Jesus died for weak, misguided mankind."

He was so utterly sincere and devout, or so utterly vicious and abandoned, that he never failed to startle his listeners. Before the jury took up the issue of the case they tried to decode Pruiett. "What the hell kind of a man is he? One that can make me feel that way—I've never felt like gettin' religion before—must have somethin' on the ball. How can he be so good, an' so tough at the same time? Can a body that can generate such viciousness have any good, at all, in it, or is that Bible stuff all a part of his act?" Each deliberation over Pruiett was an advantage—for Valiton. The old partridge was crippling down the hedge row, leading the hunter away from the nest.

"Is Walter C. Valiton in the courtroom?" Judge Rose asked.

"He is. Your Honor," answered Bailiff Garnett.

"Let him stand up," said the judge. To Valiton he said:

"You, Walter C. Valiton, have been found guilty of murder in the first degree, and the jury has recommended you to the mercy of the court. Have you anything to say why the sentence of the law should not be imposed upon you?"

"I am sorry all this happened," said Valiton. "I know I am not a murderer in my heart."

"You have had a fair trial by an impartial jury," Judge Rose continued. "You were protected by the court in your legal right. Your counsel was zealous in his defense of your rights. Their verdict was fully warranted by the evidence in the case. The evidence, in the opinion of the court, showed a cruel and unprovoked murder of an officer in the discharge of his duty. . . . Under the law, whoever is convicted of a capital offense and recommended to the mercy of the court by a majority of that jury in their verdict, shall be sentenced to imprisonment for life.

"It is therefore considered, and it is the judgment of the court that you, Walter C. Valiton, be imprisoned by confinement in the State Penitentiary for the remainder of your natural life." Valiton did not quail as he heard the sentence pronounced.

SERGEANT WEVER'S OFFICIAL FUNERAL
"Pruiett used self-defense for the car-thief who shot
an uniformed policeman off his motorcycle."

Miami Life made the last official lament. In its current editorial it arraigned Pruiett, and the brothers in the lodge who were
so derelict in their instructed duty. "What the jury gave Valiton

is, as a matter of precedence and fact, a sentence of eight or ten years, and we venture the prediction right now that Valiton will never serve longer. . . . Just the same as there are otherwise sane jurymen who will allow a wildly gesticulating criminal lawyer to pervert their judgment with hokum, there are mildly imbecilic men and women who conceive it their highest duty, the moment anyone is imprisoned for murder, to start pleading with the governor and pardoning board for his release.

"Hokum—and we say this with all due respect for the court and the lawyers, for no one knows it better than they—saved Valiton from the chair. And hokum will free him in a few years. . . . . Miami Life is going to petition Governor Martin to sell the electric chair that was recently installed. Junk it, blow it up— do anything to get rid of it. Erase the law authorizing capital punishment. After the Valiton trial, we are convinced that we have no use for either."

CHAPTER TWENTY-TWO

How Pruiett, on the other side of the table as special prose-cutor for the State's Attorney, convicted Forrest Cecil Mingle for killing an inoffensive woman, and how he defeats the Governor of Oklahoma on the Governor's Message to the Legislature on the question of crime, lawlessness and the reformation of the Code of Criminal Procedure of the State, by distributing thou-sands of copies of a speech he made to the "Oklahoma Electric Club," around over the State. How he consoles an old friend, the managing editor of the "Daily Oklahoman," on how NOT to become famous after the editor had been kicked out of the "Hall of Fame" by his political enemies, and how this same editor re-members Pruiett in an editoral forty-one years after Pruiett had become the leading citizen of Pauls Valley (at that time the Indian Territory), Oklahoma.

"ARGUMENT to the jury in the case of the State of Okla-homa vs. Forrest Cecil Mingle. By Moman Pruiett,—Special Prosecutor."

"Forrest Cecil Mingle, or Harry Parker, writhes with emotion as prosecution tells him in words which burn like tips of flame that Pearl Pearson's blood stains his hands."

"Mingle branded as slayer of defenseless woman."

"Eye for Eye," and "Tooth for Tooth," says State's Attor-ney, bitterly denouncing the defendant for murder. Accused pales under scathing attack of prosecutor.

"Shall the cooing and prattling of a babe drown the message of truth as it came from the lips of the dead woman, with the rattle of death in her throat?"

"Shall the manifestations of parental love here to a babe,— who is an off-spring of a self-confessed libertine, destroy the force and effect of a message, which to all law-abiding ears and honest men sounds now like a message of truth blown from death's pale realm?—'Harry Parker did it;—don't forget the name!'"

——oOo——

The above excerpts from the argument of Moman Pruiett, Special Prosecutor, appeared in the Daily Oklahoman immediately after they had been delivered to the jury.

——oOo——

This argument was not reported in full; but the following

[541]

notes were made at the time of its delivery. Mr. Ross Lillard had just preceded Pruiett in his address to the jury. Lillard called on the jury for mercy.

———o0o———

"GENTLEMEN of the Jury: Mercy! Mercy! Why shouldn't this defendant ask for mercy, knowing, as he does, that he is guilty?"

"I feel, in this solemn hour, that I would not do justice to this court if I did not say something about the justice which it has dealt out during the past two weeks. I feel certain that so long as Your Honor sits upon the bench the rights of defendants will be protected, and the laws of the land fully and completely vindicated.

"The last remark of my young friend Ross Lillard was 'Mercy! Mercy!' He spoke of the actions of the defendant in the courtroom, and called your attention to the love and devotion here exemplified by this defendant toward his young wife and babe.

"Gentlemen of the Jury, shall the cooing and prattling of a babe drown the message of truth as it came from the lips of the dead woman with the rattle of death in her throat? Shall the manifestations of parental love, shown in this courtroom, to a babe that is the off-spring of a self-confessed libertine, destroy the force and effect of a message which, to all law-abiding ears and honest men,—sounds now like a message of truth blown from death's pale realm? 'Harry Parker did it; don't forget the name!'

"You are to turn this man loose, according to Lillard, because he called on God to sanctify his remarks. The man who will murder a woman and then rob her, and ten minutes later begin to manufacture the story of his defense, is cunning enough to call on God to witness the truth of his assertions!

"Unbroken by any link in this chain of circumstantial evidence, it is the innocent man who would tremble when giving evidence regarding himself;—but when you have the hardened criminal, as this defendant,—he can go upon the witness stand, with the blood of a woman upon his hands, and say: 'God being my judge, Mr. Giddings, I never killed that woman!' But as I begin to throw the steel into him, you gentlemen could not help seeing the hell in his eyes. You saw all there was to arouse the hell and venom in him. Why, this defendant has more brains in a minute than Mr. Giddings and Mr. Lillard will have in a thousand years. This is nothing new to him.

"Cecil Mingle, you didn't have to lead and decoy this poor helpless and defenseless woman to a lonely ravine to kill her, where nobody but God's all-seeing eyes could look down upon you. There were other places closer in where escape would have been more certain. But, whether, according to the dying woman's statement, there was more than one purpose, there was at least one purpose on your part, and that was to slay that woman and get these letters and cards which she possessed.

"Gentlemen of the Jury, I am going to present to you, link by link, a chain of circumstances which will place the black cap of death upon the head of this defendant, Forrest Cecil Mingle, so that the citizenship of Oklahoma County can say that there has been one jury in this land that possessed the manhood and courage to render a verdict encouraged by the facts.

"Gentlemen, here is the pocketbook that is supposed to have contained the mystic messages over which the deceased was killed. She wore it, something like this (fastened to her belt), and, after the fatal shot was fired, this defendant tore it from her in a manner something like this;—and this defendant knows something about the way it was done.

"I do not care whether you be Protestant or Catholic; Methodist, Baptist or Campbellite; I do not care what your religion is,—there is no place for sentiment in this case. Here is where the iron hand of the law should lay hold and set an example for all who shall live in the future. I say it here and now, and you can herald it far and near,—that while I stand before the courts of my country,—I shall try to do my duty. Not one criminal in one thousand, convicted of murder, is innocent. The theory of the state in this case is 'an eye for an eye—a tooth for a tooth.' We do not want to do this defendant an injustice. There may be some mistake as to the man, but I do not believe there could be a mistake. His eye minutely describes such a man as the murderer of poor Mrs. Pearl Pearson.

"I would be merciful, rather than do him an injury or an injustice;—but, Gentlemen of the Jury, I invoke the doctrine of the ancient law;—'An eye for an eye, a tooth for a tooth, an ear for an ear, and a life for a life,—he who sheddeth man's blood by man shall his blood be shed.'

"I hope that, in trying to forge the links in this case of circumstantial evidence, I shall not become tiresome to you men. I have my duty to perform in this case, as well as the court and you men; but the facts I am going to place before you are very important. They are important to the defendant as well as to the state,—and it is important that I make no mistake against that man. As I stand here, I wish to say, that I hope, in all future years, no man or set of men will call upon me to prosecute a fellowman. I do not belong on this side of the table;—my feelings are always with the unfortunate one in a criminal case. But I do say that wherever duty calls me I want to do my duty, and if I feel justified in asking the life of this man upon the facts in this case, I will do it irrespective of what the results may be.

"Forrest Mingle, why did you lay your coat so gently on the wire fence at the home of Mrs. Waring? You man of iron,— you man of steel? You man of nerve! While you were fleeing from the scene of your crime? Call upon God as your witness, if you please, for an honest analyzation of the facts produced by an honest prosecution. All these facts will be considered by an honest jury, and an example will be set in this community that all men may profit thereby.

"Behold, Gentlemen, the weapon of death! The pistol that wrought the deed of shame! And this defendant knows something about how deadly it is.

"Mr. Giddings, you may be the leading man representing the profession in which I am engaged, but when you accuse Sam Campbell, sheriff at Enid, or his brother, of perjury in respect to their testimony relating to what was found in this defendant's gun when arrested at Enid,—you are treading upon dangerous ground. If you persist in that the men of this jury will have no respect for you. No honest men or women under the sun and within the hearing of my voice will have any respect for you. Murderers may go unwhipped of justice, but so long as I have the God-given power to analyze testimony when it is my duty,— let no man say that I have failed to do it properly.

"Is there a missing link anywhere in this chain we have woven about this defendant? Here are the shoes which were worn by this defendant on the day of the murder. The sole of a shoe cannot lie. There is a sole that speaks the truth, as well as the soul that made its flight into eternity on the fateful afternoon of September 16, 1908. This is the sole that follows the murderer from the spot where the fatal shot was fired until the present moment.

"Gentlemen, they seek to destroy that which illuminates this entire tragedy from the beginning to end,—the diamonds,—the brilliancy of which has made plain as day the pathway of this defendant from the scene of this awful tragedy to a verdict that will speak the truth.

"Gentlemen, you may compromise your verdict and give this defendant a sentence of life imprisonment; but if you do I beg you to arrange someday whereby there may be written upon his brow, in deathless letters of blood, these words: "MURDERER—LIBERTINE," so that in future years, if he should escape, all decent mothers and virtuous daughters may know him as he approaches them,—and will shun him as they would a leper.

"Better that this beautiful metropolis be stricken with the bubonic plague; better that a 'yellow jack' be placed on every home indicating yellow fever; better that every train bring a special coach full of physicians to attend the ills of the afflicted than for this man to be turned loose. Medical science can check the plague and cure the afflicted, but there is only one remedy that can check this man in his career of crime—and that is death."

"Take this case, gentlemen, and let the Great God of the universe, the Creator of the consciences and the souls of men be your guide. And when you do so, the State of Oklahoma will have no fear that this or any other community will ever again be burdened with the presence of this defendant. Manhood and womanly virtue will be safe, and communities will not be aroused by the piercing screams of a murdered woman. Grandmothers will not be forced to take little daughters upon their knees and rear them through life as motherless children. There are other babes in this case besides the one which is fondled in your presence for the purpose of distracting your minds from the awful chain of circumstances which bind this defendant hand and foot. My God! Mingle, if the voice of your victim; if the voice of the motherless child had played upon your heart you could have saved all this,—and wiped out every heartache. You could have saved the wail of an orphan; you could have saved the appeal of a wife and sister-in-law; you could have saved the bringing here of a tottering father-in-law, who is on the brink of eternity.

"Gentlemen of the Jury; however awful these statements may sound to you, do your duty and do it right. Do what you think should be done. There is but one thing that you can neither face nor flee from, and that is the consciousness of a duty disregarded. So, viewing this case from every standpoint from the hour of the fatal shooting until this present moment, I ask the Great God of the universe to give you light to see your duty well, and the courage to sustain your conviction.

"Gentlemen, I thank you for your kindly indulgence and patient attention."

———oOo———

The following letter from a former warden of the Oklahoma State Penitentiary will show that Pruiett's judgment of Mingle was correct. Mingle was paroled and later convicted in California of killing a man for his diamonds. The story of his trial and conviction in California is told in the August, 1944, issue of Headline Detective magazine.

June 27th 1944

Hon. R. R. Connor,
Warden,
State Penitentiary,
McAlester, Oklahoma.
Dear Warden:

I am writing you this letter at the request of Moman Pruiett. I do not know what Moman wants; but I do know Moman, and have known him for fifty-five years, he has practiced criminal law for fifty-seven years. I think he is the greatest judge of human nature of any man in this country or any other country.

While I was Warden, your records should show he recommended many prisoners for trusty-ship, and no man he ever recommended violated his trust. I remember one instance I was favorably impressed with the application of one convict, Forrest Cecil Mingle. Pruiett refused to recommend him and said if I made him a trusty that he would murder my wife and daughters for the two or three diamond rings they had, in other words he claimed he was a kleptomaniac on diamonds. I never made him a trusty, he was finally pardoned or paroled, killed a Jew in California for his diamonds and I understand died in San Quentin prison having been sent there for life.

I do not believe that Pruiett would recommend a man to you for trusty-ship unless he sincerely believed the man would keep your trust.

I hope you and your subordinates are functioning in a way

that society will be protected and a reformation may be brought about among many of your subjects.

Yours Very Respectfully,
R. W. DICK
Former Warden.

——oOo——

SPEECH
by
MOMAN PRUIETT
to the
Oklahoma Electric Club,
Oklahoma City
Feb. 21, 1927
"The Relationship of Old Black Gold
to Law Enforcement"

——oOo——

"They are slaves who fear to speak
For the fallen and the weak;
They are slaves who will not choose
Hatred, scoffing and abuse
Rather than in silence shrink
From the truth they needs must think;
They are slaves who dare not be
In the right with two or three."
—James Russell Lowell.

——oOo——

A few days ago the Honorable Governor of this State, for whom I voted, both at the primary and general election, for whom I made speeches, and for whose integrity I have the most profound respect, delivered a message to the joint session of the Legislature wherein he dealt at length with the momentous question of Crime, Lawlessness and the Reformation of the Code of Criminal Procedure of this State.

He mentions the questionnaire sent out by the National Economic League from which he has learned that the most important problem of the American people today is the administration of justice.

Gentlemen, I have always been of the opinion that the greatest problem confronting this or any people, of this or any age, is the administration of justice. I consider that to be the great interest and purpose of men on earth, and the only interest and purpose of men on earth. I never knew before that it was left for some "Meddlesome Mattie League" to send out a questionnaire to ascertain that great fact. I consider that as being a fundamental proposition so deeply grounded in the hearts of intelligent men as not to call for a questionnaire. Yet this questionnaire makes plain one proposition and that is that the "Meddlesome Matties" are at work; it also shows who their play tools are.

But, gentlemen, this message covers many phases, and deals at length with the question of reforming the Criminal Code.

I read it with interest, astonishment, and amazement; and when I finished perusing it, I read the Code of Hammurabi, written two thousand years before the birth of the Nazarene.

Gentlemen, I consider the message of Governor Johnston as being a message of blood and terror, and if enacted into legislation would be the greatest step backward toward the Hammurabi code of righteousness that man has ever made. I consider it as being the most vicious abortion of justice that has ever been penned by the Chief Executive of any free untrammeled people.

It indirectly thrusts the very saber of tyranny into the most fundamental rights of our American people. By subterfuge it would destroy the most vital spark of our trial by jury.

The Governor believes that the same right to disqualify a trial judge should be accorded unto the state as well as to the defendant. This has ever been the right and privilege under our form of government which has been accorded only to the defendant. The state is the prosecutor, and her judges are her ministers elected by her people, and if they are prejudiced toward their masters they should not only be disqualified but forever barred from judicial service and there is no other cause for the disqualification of a judge, save prejudice, whether brought by political, financial, or personal interest.

This law is hinged on the principle that if, for any reason a judge is prejudiced against the defendant, that defendant has the right to disqualify the judge to sit in judgment at his trial. This condition can arise often, and often does arise.

The governor further asks that defendants charged with conspiracy should be denied the right of severance at trial, notwithstanding that the nature of their defenses may materially differ.

This principle of law has ever hinged on the theory only that defenses may materially differ and it has ever been considered good law to grant a severance of trial where the defense has a material variation. These laws were made and enacted to protect the rights of the individual and that the less guilty should not suffer as severe a punishment as those who are more guilty.

The Governor further asks that the Legislature enact a law making the defendant a competent witness in his own behalf, and if he fails to testify, permit his failure to be commented on by the court, jury and attorneys in the case. Under the ancient laws of all savage nations defendants were forced to bear testimony against themselves. Brutal and pitiless instruments of torture were used by the officers of the law to force from the lips of the defendant words of self-condemnation. The rack and thumbscrew, the gibbet and the stock were instruments by which the brave and valorous were forced to recant and admit their guilt as adjudged.

But in America we have ever considered this as being the work of savage beasts and we have shrunk from these brutal instruments as we have shrunk from the monarch's heel; and as a righteous reaction from the ancient code of infamy and savagery, we have placed in our Constitution provisions that have for their purpose the preventing of prosecutors from forcing defendants to bear testimony against themselves. The wise Fathers of this great republic—men of foresight, vision, and governmental genius who peered into the future as far as human eyes could see, saw the furies of the morrows, all the hatreds yet to be—knew that such men would walk the earth in the future as they had in the past, who would be willing that the defendants should bear testimony against themselves; wherefore they enacted as the Fifth Amendment to the Federal Constitution the provision that no person shall be compelled in criminal cases to be a witness against himself.

Gentlemen, I consider that demand of our Governor as being one of the most brutal stabs at the right and prerogatives of the defendant that the world has ever heard. Our Governor further asks that the Legislature provide for the privilege of taking depositions for the prosecution as well as for the defense. This is in direct contradiction to the great landmark laid down in the Sixth Amendment of the Constitution of these United States, which provides, among other things, for a public trial by an impartial jury and that the defendants may be confronted in that self-same public trial by the witnesses who are their accusers.

In the dark ages that have slumbered in the vicious vistas of the days of long ago, when the individual had no right for which to fight and for which to contend—when the prerogatives belonged to the Monarch, Governor Johnston's theories were in vogue. But man has advanced in many ways and we may well assume that if there is anything now settled or ever to be settled in our courts of justice as an act of procedure, it is, let us hope, that the defendant shall ever have that glorious right and sovereign prerogative of a public trial, and then and there in open court to be confronted by his accusers. This law has ever hinged on the principle that these trials are to be public—that these witnesses are to appear in this self-same public court and then and there be subject to cross-examination. Under the ancient savage laws, most trials were conducted when the defendant slumbered in some dark and desolate dungeon while his accuser in royal regalia wrote out the verdict of his destiny.

The Governor further asks the increase in power for the trial judge that he may become an agency of justice rather than a mere referee of a contest, and he asks that the judge be authorized to analyze and comment upon the testimony, in a method that shall be free from vindictiveness, malice and ill will. Shame be upon the age! Shame be upon the principle! When such an unrighteous thrust shall be made at the very fundamental, underlying principles of the trial by jury system. If the trial judges are to be permitted to use their exalted position to instruct a jury and comment upon the testimony, we may as well assume that his comment will be in close accord with his malice and vindictiveness. If they are to be accorded this extraordinary privilege, then what will be the ultimate annihilation of the prerogative and right of the defendant to be tried by a jury of his peers?

In this country it has ever been considered the most sacred principle of our administration of justice that the defendant should be tried by twelve good men and true, who are to be the sole judges of the testimony as it comes from the witness stand; and he who would seek by legislation to pollute that sacred stream of the jury trial and the principles of procedure involved therein is both unworthy of our considerations and the fit subject of our fears.

If Governor Johnston should secure by legislation the enactment of his demands, the Bill of Rights becomes a hollow joke, and our Constitution but ropes of sand. We have on our statute books today enough laws to safeguard our substantial rights, yet each new administration sees fit to make new requests and demands of the law-making body, calling for reform, until the reformers have become more or less deformers.

Our honorable Governor further recommends that the statute of limitations be so amended that the same shall not commence to run against any public officer for official misconduct until the expiration of the term of years of office of said person. Gentlemen, I take the position and maintain that the statute of limitations should never run against any officer for any crime he may perpetrate.

The people repose extraordinary confidence and trust in their public officers and who pollutes and breaks that faith should suffer the consequences thereof whenever the commission of his offense shall have been ascertained. The statute of limitations should no more run against officers who have violated their public trust than against the man who commits malicious murder; for politics and politicians do so mingle that protection is oftimes given to those who prostitute their offices for personal or political gain; and, further, time does tame the thief in high places.

During the last few years, the forces of fanaticism have made great progress in this country, and the "deformer" and his associates, the various snooping syndicates throughout the land, have been trying to deprive the working man of his only day of enjoyment by trying to close on Sundays theatres, ball parks, and other places of enjoyment and amusement.

Nothing breeds vice like an attempt to promote virtue by force, and eternal vigilance is still the price of liberty! Yet, we have such organizations to thank for this age of graft, lawlessness, crime and the reign of the bootlegger. Their triumph has made sneakery, hypocrisy and disrespect for the law popular; it opens the flood gates of vice, drunkenness and crime; it nullifies constitutional provisions for the protection of individual liberty, and is ready, in the administration of government, to replace democracy with absolute despotism.

Man is a fighting animal, that fights for life, for love, for fame and glory, for his rights and liberty, for property and power; the fight starts at his conception and ends at the tomb.

Were the Legislatures of the various states of America to enact a few messages such as Governor Johnston requests, in a few short years man would have nothing for which to fight.

Gentleman, I say, beware of regulators and deforming reformers; beware, in this age, of snoops, sneaks and meddlesome spies; beware of those in high places who seek to subvert the ancient landmarks of the nation, and cite as their authority, the statistics of an aggregation of crazy fanatics.

Oft times in the past, many, many crimes perpetrated in the construction of a few miles of highway were concealed, while the attention of the public was called to some special prosecution in some case, not especially interesting to the public coffers or making any special strain on the people's pocket book.

In the past, tainted bonds, Liberty, municipal, county and state, have not been brought to light and dragged from their hiding places; neither has the searchlight of truth been turned properly upon corrupt commissioners.

Gravel pits in this state have been likened to the sparkling diamond fields of Africa; cement plants have been likened unto the gold mints.

Justice has been thwarted on account of granting of pardons and directing prosecutions. Why? All for Old Black Gold.

Gentlemen, I do not understand and cannot conceive how anyone who believes in the principles laid down by the meek and lowly Nazarene can ask for the enactment of laws that would rob the individual of every right in an open court of justice. I do not understand how anyone who believes in the principles set forth by Him who died on Calvary can say to the world: We will imprison them for life; we will take away their names, we will disgrace them before the world, we will number them and mark them as eternal outcasts unworthy of citizenship and association. We will place them in coal mines in less than ten days, we will try them summarily and take from them their present rights that conviction may be sure and certain. We will make of their body a bloody sacrifice that the world may know that we of Oklahoma propose to enforce the law to the letter, for we propose to demand the last drop of blood, and the last pound of flesh; then if they will not submit, we will burn their bodies in an electric chair and stand by in happiness and glee and watch their poor lives ebb out in a whirling wreath of smoke.

Gentlemen, that is what they propose, that is what they demand!

I look into the past and I see Man, mad with hate, selfishness, envy and greed; I see him building dungeons wherein he incarcerates from light his fellowman; I see him building the scaffold upon which the unfortunates of the world must hang; I see the thumbscrews, rack and gibbet; I see the auction block and whipping post and a thousand other instruments of torture—dreadful souvenirs of ignorance and hate. All this has been.

But I look again and all this has gone; I see a race comely

and fair; I see men practice fraternity toward his fellowmen; I
see him invent instruments with which he may penetrate into the
curious bastions and the winding halls of the human brain and
decipher the languages of virtue and vice; I see men delve into
the human heart and hear her mysteries. I hear men say and
practice what the Master said, "Come, I will give you rest."
All this shall be; and in the future let us strive and work to do
away with all instruments of torture; let us assist in destroying
all instruments that tear and rend human flesh. Let us work for
and usher in the eternal day when "Truth will not be forever on
the scaffold, and wrong forever on the throne."

In the great open spaces of the great Southwest, we find
a fair city with a varied citizenship. This city has her Main
Street (as curious, peculiar, spectacular, antique and modern as
any that has ever traversed any city's heart); this city, too, has
her Broadway, where the garrulous and gay find full hilarity.

But, this city has other streets wherein the mean, morose,
maligning moods of men, and the wiles and ways of women find
full exemplification. Main Street, too, has her bagnio and Broadway her brothel.

This city has great buildings (fitting tributes to the genius
of architecture), and yet dedicated to the industry and commerce
of the world.

This city has great homes of magnificent structures and
of beauty in design, fit abodes for the Olympian Gods, and might
well be compared with the dwellings on the fabled isles of Greece.

A system of education exists here that may well vie with any
that we find throughout the broad dominion of the world.

Churches of wonderful structure lift their spacious spires
unto the skies, whereon may play the long days through, the angel
babes.

Yet, here where wealth and culture, genius, religion and education have their happy home and habitations, we find the Open
Gates—the play grounds of infamies, crime and sin. Here we
find the places where infamies are matured, and crimes are sustained in freedom. Here we find the officers are but poor execu-
tors of their sworn duty—sleepy administrators of the law—and
we wonder why.

Is the God of Mammon more potent than He who pled for a
righteous cause? Is the lust for old black gold to outweigh the
consciousness of duty? Is a bootlegger converted into a Blackstone the most lofty disciple of the law?

Yet, all this we find. We find the gates open to a thousand crimes. We find men once paupers becoming wealthy through infractions of the law. We find ex-bootleggers now bedecked with sheepskin and pleading the cause of law, to the exclusion of lawyers who were made so by industry, study and toil.

We find that dreaded specter that has ever haunted the brain of man; the dope-trust, with its falcons red, that pierce the very soul of its weak-willed victims. We find it protected at so much "PER" shake, and we find that if this is not forthcoming, then they are turned to the "Federal."

"DOPE," that does eat upon the soul and heart and brain and sinewy nerves of his victims till they become veritable maniacs, walking, stalking ghoul-eyed goblins and finally end their suffering days in the asylum for the weak-minded—for insanity through pity does ofttimes end their pain.

Yes, dope, that frightful power, that they draw out the poppy's subtle blood, that paints upon the easel of the brain colors and forms that do entrance and lead the victim whithersoever it will with their glaring eyes and vicious brain.

Yet, we find this protected, and the same Mammon extended protection to its cruel, heartless, purveyor that protects the liquor crime and the gambling den and brothel house of shame.

But who opened the gates? Who turned the silent key? Have the ghastly hands of Mammon turned the gates upon their austere hinges and permitted bootlegging, gambling, dope-peddling, burglary, robbery, bribery, extortion and bawdy brothels to run rampant with OPEN GATES?

We think that this but the waning hiss of defeated candidates, blighted politicians, corrupt office holders and impure administrators of the law.

We think that there is a hand to close these gates, and we summons it to do its duty. We would summon it to drive from high places the untrue office-holder, the bribe-taker, the receiver of blood money, the extortioner—all those who demand and accept BLACK GOLD that crime may run with OPEN GATES.

Whenever America can say: "My poor are happy; neither ignorance nor corruption is to be found among my public officials; my jails contain only prisoners placed there by the due process of law—a law enacted by a Christian people who have discarded all remnants of the savage ages, and who have learned of a Christ who said: 'It hath been said of old, "An eye for an eye, and a tooth for a tooth," but I say Nay;' the aged are not in want, the taxes are not oppressive, the rational world is my friend, because I am the friend of its happiness"—when these things can be said, then may this country boast of a government whose officials have never bowed before the Golden Calf of Mammon, and whose hands have not been stained by the filth of old BLACK GOLD.

——oOo——

Copied from: OKLAHOMA CITY TIMES, November 20, 1936.
"DOG HOUSE OF FAME."

Old Friend Moman Pruiett, a Man Who Can Take It, consoles us with some dandy reading mostly on How Not To Become Famous. He should buy up a batch of asbestos and write a book. There's a title for him—"The Dog House of Fame."

——oOo——

Editor of the Times:

Why are you raising so much hell about a man's conduct who has not been in Oklahoma long enough to get a sun bath?

Let me tell you a little incident that I have never forgotten. Riding along with my old Uncle Haden Moorman, in Hardin County, Kentucky, we passed a polecat.

I said, "My goodness, Uncle Haden, that's one of those stinking cats."

He said, "Listen, little man, whenever you smell that kind of a cat, don't dignify the cat by saying anything about it, just hold your nose tight."

So I suggest to you, you are too big a man, too good an editor to dignify the cat. Why, Walter, what do you care about not being in the Hall of Fame.

Look at me, I had a county named after me, Moman, and during the Constitutional Convention, your paper published an interview that I gave out in which I criticised the members of the convention and dubbed them as sycophants when I said they were building a Chinese wall around Oklahoma to keep out capital to develop the state. I predicted that article 9 and section 9 would be repealed in ten years from the time of its passage. It was.

Did you know after I gave the interview referred to about the constitutional convention, a resolution was offered to change the name of Moman County and it could be changed only by unanimous vote. You know when Bill Murray put the vote to the convention, there were 25 or 30 no's, but Bill did not hear the no's. With his gavel he knocked a hole through the desk declaring the resolution carried unanimous. You know, I didn't like that, but hell, I go down to Broken Bow and go political coon hunting with Bill ever now and then. And Walter, I never disturbed that cat for changing Moman County.

I'm not in the Hall of Fame, Walter, but oh, hell, what's the use!

———oOo———

Say, Walter, I defended one of your brother editors for killing a brother newspaper editor. The jury acquitted him at Purcell and packed me up on their shoulders and carried me halfway to the Love hotel from the courthouse in Purcell, and this editor belongs to this Hall of Fame that you are raising so much fuss about, and offers resolutions about moving the old decayed bones. In other words, another board would be created to buy the ground for a miniature Arlington, and to employ vandals to go to work. Anything, oh God, for new boards and new jobs for some, even to the extent of commercializing on the dead.

Say, Walter, do you really know anything about fame? Your Times in July, 1935, published to the world that I was at one time the greatest criminal lawyer in the Southwest. You quoted one of the judges of the Supreme Court's statement to that effect. Why, you don't know anything about fame. You said and published that I was a drunkard; that whisky had destroyed me; you published everything about me from a visit to the President to visit to a Negro bootlegging joint in Negro town; you published that I was 84 years old, and you know I was born in '72, but I didn't disturb the cat.

I am never going to be in the Hall of Fame, I'm not kicking, why are you, Walter? You say the Governor doesn't like you. You're mistaken. He just doesn't like your policy, doesn't like to be disturbed.

———oOo———

Now, Walter, I think you ought to suggest to your brother editor who belongs to that association that some of them ought to suggest the name of Pete Drake, for that gentleman sure has made some history in Oklahoma. Now all I have to say about Pete being placed in the Hall of Fame is that I raised ducks all my life and I have been very fond of ducks with but one exception. I never had any use for a wabbling quacking drake, for they always seem to be apparently more wise or pompous than the rest of the ducks. Now I don't dislike Pete, but I don't like his policy. He is one duck that has only been here long enough to get a sun bath, but if it is popular for this class to be in the Hall of Fame, let's make him chairman of the board who will have the purchasing of the ground and upkeep of the new Arlington for Oklahoma.

Say, Walter, Judge Robert L. Williams and I had a murder case down in Durant. It was the Whitledge murder case. It was to be tried in the United States court before Judge Humphrey. I had been to Washington working for statehood, drinking Scotch whisky, playing poker and eating chicken lobsters with rich butter sauce for about two months. When I arrived in Durant, my face was all broken out with eczema. Bob at that time, as we all knew him as Bob, called at my hotel, wanted to know what was the matter with me. I remember this was an awful murder case and Bob and I wanted to win it. Bob rushed from the hotel, explained to the judge that I had smallpox. The Whitledge case was not tried at that term of court. I was rushed out of town before I was quarantined. Bob can tell you the rest of the story. Didn't this incident make Judge Williams and me famous?

———oOo———

Now, Walter, if you really want to be famous, I tell you what you do, read up a little about people in Pennsylvania in the Matthew Quay and Penrose days, then drop back to your own home town and analyze the conduct of some of the politicians. Lay before the Legislature the conduct of some of these people, then you surer than hell will disturb the cat, for the tactics of Matthew Quay and Penrose are abroad in Oklahoma today.

Walter, I do not want to clothespin you, nor do I want you to clothespin me. My only purpose in writing you this letter is to show you how ridiculous we can make ourselves by disturbing the cat just in order for both of us to be famous and get our names in the Hall of Fame.

Your friend,
MOMAN PRUIETT.

———4———

"WHEN OLD SETTLERS MET: There is nothing new in these reunions of old settlers out here in Oklahoma." (The Daily Oklahoman in an editorial by Luther Harrison, September 4th, 1941.) "The old timers have been foregathering for many, many years. Forty-one years ago today pioneers of the Washita valley staged a reunion of old settlers at Hull's Crossing near Pauls Valley. That was only eleven years after the run of 1889.

It was seven years before Oklahoma entered the Union. Even then there were old timers to meet together to tell the stories of past hardships and triumphs and to speculate upon the uncertainties of the future.

"Those old timers who met at Hull's Crossing seemed to be more than ordinarily interested in the future. *At least they listened to an orator of the day who devoted his time to a forecast of what the future had in store. Moman Pruiett was younger then than he is today. Just forty-one years younger,* and he could only guess what the coming years would bring forth. *But he guessed with remarkable accuracy.*

"It would be child's play for an orator of 1941 to stand at Hull's Crossing and talk of what had been accomplished in the past forty-one years. For we now have statehood and we have had nearly a half century of additional development. The state stands far advanced among the great agricultural commonwealths. It has its population of nearly 2,500,000. It has its impressive University and its other institutions of learning. It has its ribbons of concrete and asphalt and gravel to bind the 77 counties into a well articulated unit of common interests. But it had mighty few of those great possession forty-one years ago.

"*Never the less Pruiett foretold nearly everything important that Oklahoma now possesses.* We who have seen those things created and developed from nearly nothing into their present impressiveness may feel that the orator had an easy task. But it is never easy to forecast the future accurately. It is not easy in 1941. Who of us can read the riddle that is spread all over the international skies and foretell what the state of our people will be forty-one years hence or even five years hence? Prophecy was as hazardous in 1872, when Mrs. Betty Pruiett prayed for a son that would some day become a great lawyer, and when that son, Moman Pruiett, in 1900, prayed that the community in which he lived would some day become a part of a great state, which was then Pauls Valley, Indian Territory, both prophecies came true. Now, what?"

CHAPTER TWENTY-THREE

How Pruiett obtains the acquittal of a man charged with slaying his sweetheart while she is confined in jail, and how the experience crystallizes his previously entertained ideas of abandoning the Gay Coast. And wherein, he expresses his disapprobation with the locality, and predicts its destruction, almost on the eve of the blast which blew a land boom away and materially reduced the status of the precocious peninsula. And how gentle nature takes a hand to obtain the result for which enforcement bodies and public prosecutors had long striven, and the intrepid Moman makes an humble and unostentatious exit.

The reflecting light of the Flamingo Hotel's thousand windows were multiplied into millions as calm Biscayne's mild ripples sparkled them across the bay. The Pruietts were watching in quiet darkness as they sat on the veranda of their shore home.

"It won't work, Leda," Pruiett said. "It isn't meant to be, so it won't be. This place won't last."

"It's heavenly," she murmered. "What I have dreamed of, and prayed for. There's no place on earth like it. No—."

"No, and it won't be here long, either," he interrupted. "There never was so much wickedness, and so much evil, got together on God's earth before—an' I don't suppose you dreamed and prayed for any of that."

"Moman," she said softly, ignoring the harshness of his tone, "what's come over you? What's happened to turn you against Florida—against Miami? The way business has been, and the way things have gone, I was sure you were contented here."

"Why, hell yes, I'm satisfied, but that isn't it," he persisted, "a coral reef isn't strong enough to make a foundation for such a structure of sin and degradation. There isn't no sound basis for this place. We've got a fortune involved here—I know it's small compared to what the others around here have got—but we can't afford to stand a loss like they can." He waved generally toward the Candler, and Capone, and Nunnally estates.

His wife laughed. "That's funny, from you, Moman. You sound like an evangelist. Leave off the courtroom act for me; let me understand you. What's bothering you?"

Pruiett chewed his unlighted cigar savagely before making

answer. "I want to sell out and get out of this damn place. I want to go back west, to Oklahoma, somewhere."

"Not for anything in the world," she replied. "This is the first place where we've found peace, and contentment. No references to your misfortune; no slurs at me in connection with it. No cold; no dreariness. It's the first place where I've had happiness, and I won't give it away, at least without a reason. Do you see hell fire and brimstone descending on the palm groves?" She was trying to cheer him.

"Do you remember the trip we made to the Lewis and Clark Fair, up in Oregon state? The one we made with old Sam Garvin and Mrs. Garvin, right after we was married? That was twenty years ago; can you remember it?" He asked the question softly, musingly.

"Why, yes," she replied, "I'll never forget—."

"An' remember the week in San Francisco, when we took all the excursions, and went to all the old joints and dives?"

"Yes, I remember," she said.

"An' we went to China Town, an' Barbary Coast, an' old man an' old lady Garvin was so shocked by what we saw, an' the whiskey I drank?"

"Yes, Moman, I remember all about San Francisco."

"Well," he said, raising his voice, "can't you remember what I said, when we were on the train comin' home, about San Francisco?"

There was a moment of silence. "No," she finally answered, "not particularly. What do you mean?"

"Hell," he said, with provocation. "I told you, right before the Garvins, that damned place was too wicked. I said it's like Sodom and Gomorrah; God Almighty won't let it stand. He'll wipe it off the earth, right level with the ground. Wasn't that what I said, an' wasn't it about six months later that I carried the paper in to you, and showed you the picture of what God done about it? Everything that wasn't shook down was goin' up in smoke. Didn't I tell you that very thing?"

"Yes, dear, you did," she replied, slowly, "but that was nature; that was the law of nature. What the people of San Francisco were doing had nothing to do with that earthquake, and the fire."

"Why, hell no, and neither did the people of Sodom have anything to do with what happened to them, and their damn town. But she was leveled off, shook apart and burned up."

"You were guessing; any one might have said the same thing. And you were drinking, too. You were more surprised than anyone else, that your prediction came true. If you had believed in it yourself, the realization of your power, your gift, would have driven you crazy."

"Just a minute, honey," he interrupted, "I didn't guess at it, and I didn't know it. I felt it, like the damned bells I hear ringin' in my ears. I felt old Doc Threldkeld tryin' to kill me, an hour before he pulled the pistol. I felt the destruction of that wicked city, an' I feel the destruction of this one. She just can't last."

"Will it be an earthquake," she inquired, with mock interest. "Will the Lord shake the walls of Miami apart, and burn the ruins 'til they slide back into the swamps. What does my soothsayer see?"

He chewed his cigar silently, as if intending to ignore the sarcastic question. "Typhoon," he said, laconically, "damn gulf twister, an' she'll blow the whole damned works away."

Mrs. Pruiett laughed. "Right away?" she inquired. "Will I have time to pack my bags, and run for it?"

He ignored her levity again. "Maybe this season; maybe next; maybe next after that. I don't know, but they've been gatherin' in the Carribean for centuries and centuries, and comin' this way ever' once in a while. An' when they come, they'll put the ground where the water belongs, and blow the water up where the ground used to be. They can't fix the foliage up after one of 'em; they will have to grow a new crop; palm trees and all. It's just a matter of time 'til another one comes by."

"Oh, we've had storms since we've been here, but nothing like that; nothing to do great damage," she rejoined. "I—."

"I'm talkin' about a hurricane, not a tropical shower; a wind that'll blow a wall of water a mile high across this peninsula, an' carry a mahogany saw-log across from Cuba an' blow it into the side of that Flamingo Hotel, an' knock the hell clear out of it. One that'll strip the tillable top off this ground, an' leave twisted pine stalks on white sand dunes. That's what I mean; where the ones that live to tell about it will be damned few, an' damned lucky, an' where there won't be a house or buildin' standin', like in San Francisco."

"I never heard of Miami being in the storm belt. Wouldn't some record of hurricanes be kept, if they came here?"

"Who'd keep 'em? The Seminoles? The pirates? the outlaws? This is a damned sand bar, I tell you, an' there's been nobody here, capable of keepin' a record, till this crazy boom came. Blow a Seminole off in the swamps an' he'll forget it, if it don't kill him, before he can tell another generation about it. The pirates an' outlaws, that are hidin' out down here, don't write in an' tell about the bad weather. Maybe it's been twenty-five years, maybe thirty, since the pine groves had to start all over again, but that isn't no sign the storms have quit. It means, to me, it's about time to start watchin' out. It's about time for somethin' to cut aloose."

"I can't believe it," she persisted. "We—someone would have heard of it—."

"Well, what about Galveston? Ever hear of it?"

"Yes, but it wasn't like that in Galveston, and there was an economic reason for it, too. That was a flood, and Galveston was reclaimed from a swamp, a sunken island. They might have expected that."

"I don't know whether God Almighty had anything to do with that one or not, but we got our entire fortune right here on a reclaimed stretch of sandy land, layin' on a dead fish foundation. An' look at those boats out there; them yachts. Hear that?"

He paused to listen to a snatch of music, floating up to where they sat.

"Their empty bottles, an' their rags, will drift in, in a few days, an' hungry kids'll pick 'em up, an' sell 'em for a few pennies, for bread. Millionaires, an' yachts, an' liquor an' women. This is no place to live; this is the devil's outdoor assignation house. That's all it is. It's a damn good place to play, but a damn poor one to live."

"Is my Moman reforming? Has he turned against dissipation, an' loose living? I'm startled."

"No, honey," he said earnestly, "don't misunderstand me. I'm no hypocrite. If I'd had a little different start, I might have been somewhere else right now, but that isn't the point. I've made lots of mistakes. I've lost more money gamblin', an' I've throwed away more money on parties, an' liquor, than a lot of these tinhorn millionaires ever will, but when I got sobered up, or went broke, I went home. I've kept my respectability. I never did live in a house of disrepute. I didn't keep my office in no gamblin' joint. I didn't sleep in jail with my crooked clients. I kept a respectable home, an' went to it. That's my point. We're livin', an' got our business, in a little part of God's earth that a bunch of tin-horns has made into an assignation house. That's the best way I can put it. When the raid comes, they'll make bond an' go home, like I've done for them lots of times. But us? We're stuck. We've got no place to go."

"I don't agree with you," she said shortly. "You said yourself that the government ship channels would make this a commercial center, and that the climate would make it a healthy place for people to settle, and for capital to come in with improvements. Why, you said it was as good as the Washita Valley, in the old territorial days."

"I was lyin'," he muttered. "I was lyin', an' tryin' to fool myself. I was in the Silent Night last week. Charley Moreau pays me $250.00 a month to represent him an' that joint. He's got a hundred thousand invested in rugs, an' drapes, an' roulette wheels; all on a damned old scuttled steamer, anchored on a pier. He's playin' the same bunch we are, an' he's makin' a hell of a lot of money, but are you goin' to tell me he'll last? He's got to fold, an' so have I. But what I'm tellin' you is, we've all got to. Values here aren't normal, an' if God don't wipe her away, a panic will. I want to sell out, an' get out."

"You've got yourself in a panic; that's the only panic I can see," she laughed. Get a few days' rest; collect a nice fee in a good case, and then try to tell me what you have tonight, all over again."

He shook his head. "Sodom and Gomorrah went down. God Almighty won't stand for such wickedness. I can feel it. Didn't old Julius Fleishmann laugh like hell when he paid Charley off what he lost on the wheel that night, an' thousands of these damned crackers down here went to bed hungry? An' didn't I see him fall off his horse at the polo field dead, with heart failure? What does that add up to?"

"It adds up to heart failure," she answered. "Mr. Fleishmann was too fat for such exertion; his doctors had told him that. If God Almighty, as you say, had anything to do with the case, Mr. Moreau was the one that was entitled to fall dead. That's the way I look at it."

"God Almighty's got some funny ways of workin' out His wisdom, I'm told," Pruiett chuckled. "I don't hope to understand it, so I don't question it."

"Where have we ever been so contented, and so fortunate, Moman?" she asked. "What would we do? Where should we go? And why should we leave?"

"I've got a hell of a lot of real estate down here; took most of it in for fees, an' it's ten times as high as it used to be, or'll ever be again. I got that orange grove up at Stuart, all those lots in Coral Gables, an' the houses an' lots in Cocoanut Grove. I got two hundred acres in Jasper County that's a swamp, got alligators all over it, but I can get a hundred dollars an acre for it now. I can get twice what I paid for this villa today; some bird in Pittsburgh wants to buy it so he can throw about three parties a year in it. He'll keep his gal in a flat up north the rest of the time. Honey, we can get two hundred and fifty thousand, a quarter of a million, out of this stuff we've picked up down here, an' get out. I'm gettin' old. I can't try lawsuits, like that Valiton case, all my life. I got to slow down."

"I think you're wrong about Florida," was her dogged response. "We have our health, and our peace of mind, to consider. Let's not be hasty about makin' a decision. Let's enjoy this bay breeze, and the sunshine while we think it over."

Then murder came by again. Pruiett undertook the defense of John Gobel, wealthy real estate dealer.

"Gobel was charged with murdering Mrs. H. B. Hunt last August following the woman's death in a hospital after she had swallowed a quantity of deadly poison. She had been confined in the county jail on a larceny charge. The charge had been preferred by the real estate dealer."

Norman Miller had selected the stage of an abandoned opera house for the production of his little murder. J. E. Crowe had elected to start shooting at Nick Kaufman while he was being booked at the police sergeant's window, and Jim Leggett had shot Hiram Strawn to death in the justice of the peace court, but it took old Gobel to surpass them all in the selection of a bizarre place, and manner, for the execution of the statute book's most serious offense. He has his victom arrested, and then was charged with killing her while on a visit in the jail.

"What did you have me put in this dreadful old place for, Daddy?" the demure little matron whined. She was talking to him in the run-around of the Dade County Jail, where prisoners could visit with callers. "I didn't think you could be so mean to me."

"I hated like hell to do it, but by God, I want that diamond back. I can't be givin' a dame a three thousand dollar ring. I got to have it back."

"But you gave it to me, it was my present. You can't be takin' it back now."

"I was drunk, an' you know it. You got me drunk, just to get that diamond. I suspected you, and watched you, all along, an' I know I didn't give it to you. You pulled it off of my finger. Now—."

"No, honey," she said, "you gave it to me. You said it was to be the symbol of our love—."

"Love, hell," Gobel grated, "I signed the complaint against you, and by God, I'll prosecute you for that ring. I won't be hooked by no bitch. You'll go to the pen for it as sure—."

"You'll just have to appear against me, then," she sighed, mournfully. "I had it, all right, for a day after you gave it to me, but I lost it. I can't give it back."

"You pawned it," he suggested, hopefully. "Tell me where. Give me the ticket. I'll pay it out and settle up the court costs. I won't be mad; I'll get you out of here."

Mrs. Hunt shook her head. "Honest, honey, it's lost. I drank a lot myself; see how I'm shakin'? You'll never know how I've suffered in this terrible jail since you had me locked up. Terrible. But I can't get it back for you; I lost it."

"Gave it to your pimp, huh?" He glared at her balefully. "I'm the big chump; the sucker. I ought to—."

Gobel checked himself, looking about apprehensively. "I didn't come here to quarrel with you, honey. I didn't mean to do that, but I got to have that diamond back. I got to, understand? Tell me where to get it now, and let's have it over with. No more fuss; no more trouble."

He was begging.

"It's gone, Daddy, gone," the little woman sighed sadly. "I wish I could give it back, but I can't. It's just gone."

The man was silent for a period, gazing at the rusty bars along the far side of the enclosure.

"Well," he mused, "if it's gone, it's gone. There's no good in pushin' you around, if I can't get my ring back. I guess I'd better tell the district attorney to call it off, an' turn you loose."

She grasped his arm affectionately.

"I knew you would, Daddy," she said. "Let me get out, and get straightened up, and we'll have some parties, won't we?"

"Yeah," he agreed, watching her narrowly, "how you feelin' today?"

"Just terrible," she replied, holding a hand and arm out

in front of her. "See it shake? I been havin' the most terrible hang-over I ever had. Where did you get that stuff we was drinkin'?"

"It was good stuff; came in on a boat," he said, with the same strange look in his eye. "It knocked hell out of me, though, too. I went to a doctor. He gave me some stuff that was awful good for it."

"I wish I had somethin'," she said. "I sure have suffered, somethin' terrible for two or three days."

"I got some of the stuff that Doc gave me, here in my pocket." He pulled a short glass bottle from his coat. "It tastes like hell, but it'll knock the shakes out of you quicker'n anything I ever saw. Want me to fix you one?"

"What is it?" she asked, mildly curious.

"Oh, some fancy name attached to it. I can't say it or spell it either. But it's hell on the bucks. It'll straighten you up right now, an' I mean, right now."

"Just a pill?" she inquired, looking at the bottle.

"One ain't enough for a bad case," Gobel said. "I'll fix you up a dose."

A water cooler was setting on a wooden stand in the steel enclosed square. Two tin cups were setting beside it. Gobel drew a quarter of a cup of water, and shaking a half dozen of the pills from the bottle into the cup, he began to stir it with the gold head of his vest pencil.

"This way they work quicker," he said. "Dissolve 'em, then toss 'em off quick, like a bad drink, an' then it's all over. It'll fix you up."

"I need it," Mrs. Hunt advised him.

"It tastes like swamp scum, so drink it quick. I got a chaser here for you in the other cup. All at once now, an' I got to go. You'll be all over the shakes by the time I have you out of here."

The prisoner followed her visitor's directions, and accepted his hurried kiss on a wry, puckered countenance. Gobel had scarcely gone from the jail before her screams began to rattle the barred windows and doors. She lived long enough to make an incriminating deathbed statement, and then she died. Gobel was given a cell fronting on the jail run-around. He was charged with murder.

"His arrest followed a visit with Mrs. Hunt in the jail. As Gobel left the institution Mrs. Hunt summoned deputy sheriffs and told them she had been poisoned. Her dying statement, in the hospital a short time later, implicated the man who had been instrumental in her arrest."

"Attorneys for Gobel based their defense on the presence of poison tablets in Mrs. Hunt's cell prior to the man's visit."

That was it. Remorseful, disconsolate Mrs. Hunt had decided to put an end to herself, but why make it just an ordinary suicide? Here was a revengeful boy-friend who had played her a dirty trick, had given information against her and had her confined as a common thief, and made her suffer the horrors of breaking a bender in a dirty, noisy jail. Wouldn't it be smart? Wouldn't it be subtle, to tell the deputies and the hospital orderlies, as the lights were going out, that he had slipped her the drops? Maybe they'd cause him some trouble. Maybe he'd get some time, on the same lousy mattress. Maybe they'd burn him. That was the answer. A trifle deep, but nevertheless, a sufficient motive, for attacking a deathbed statement.

Hadn't old Rudolph Tegeler beat the chair by claiming that Lila Meadows and husband Jim conspired against him by burying an unidentified stiff in a cornfield, and then Lila telling the cops that she helped him to murder her husband? And all the time Jim was stringin' 'phone wires on the Panama Canal Project, and enjoying the trouble Rudolph was having in trying to keep out of the hot seat.

"John Gobel, Miami real estate dealer, was acquitted yesterday afternoon in Dade County Circuit Court of the charge of poisoning Mrs. H. B. Hunt, last August, while she was a prisoner in the county jail. The jury returned a verdict of 'not guilty' twenty minutes after Judge Will H. Price completed his charge."

"The courtroom was crowded with spectators when the climax of one of the greatest legal battles in the annals of Dade County was reached. Many women were in the room and eagerly listened for the words which meant death or freedom for the accused. Tenseness gripped each spectator as the jury filed into the box and they watched closely as the slip of paper upon which the verdict was written was passed from the jury to Judge Price and then to Clerk Trammel. A perceptible feeling of relief swept through the room as the verdict was read."

"After Judge Price had declared court adjourned, friends and defense attorneys congratulated the man who, a few minutes before, had stood in the shadow of the electric chair. His brother,

Frank Gobel, hugged him affectionately, and Attorney Moman Pruiett, of defense counsel, placed his arm around him and buried his head on his shoulder."

There was no victory celebration at the Ta-Miami or the Flamingo after the Gobel verdict. There was whiskey, of course, great quantities of it, for Pruiett, but no speeches. The Pruietts were at home, sitting in the darkness and watching the rippling lights upon the bay.

"You were wonderful in your final argument to the jury, Moman," Leda told him. "Wonderful. It made me think of Rudolph Tegeler, and Agnes Gilbert, and the way you tried those cases. And it made me think of something else, of the way you used to have the bailiffs fix an easy rocking chair inside the rail for your mother, and father, so that they could come down and hear your closing arguments. I don't believe you've been so completely in charge of a case, since your mother died, until today. It was like old times."

Pruiett prolonged the silence which followed with a deep, deliberate drink.

"Funny," he mused, "how those things come up. I haven't had my mother on my mind much, since I was in Havana, 'til this trial started. I was tellin' myself that mother was sittin' there, listenin',—while I was goin' to that jury. That's just what I had on my mind."

"She would have been proud," Leda replied.

"Yeah?" he inquired skeptically. "Of what? Of me?

"I can't understand you, Moman," his wife said with a dubious shake of her head. "Quit drinking so much, and getting yourself into these morbid states. You're beginning to give it to me. You're back on top, selecting the cases you want and getting the fees you ask for. What more do you want?"

"We'll take that old Hunt girl," Pruiett answered, "she probably liked the smell of this rotten atmosphere as well as you and I. Continuing, he stated that: "Colonel Paul Beck was entitled to live, and so was old man Hopkins. What saved every damned one of their killers? Take a pencil and paper, and sit all night some night, write down their names as you think of them, and you will find that there is several hundred of them that I have saved from burning or hanging. There is no end to the number, and what is it that's done it, what?"

Leda replied that "It was your analysis of the evidence and the law in their defense, the Moman Pruiett philosophy."

"Moman," she whispered, "is it your conscience? Are you afraid?"

"Hell, no," he answered, "my conscience is my best friend; it's the only one I got, except you, my dear, and Gail. I just like to tell the truth once in a while, to keep from forgettin' how."

"I'm proud," she whispered again, "and your mother would be, too, for she'd understand. You got to remember; you can't forget, now, the things that have kept you up and made you go. And you must have been right, dear. I've heard you say so much of divine retribution, I believe in it. It wouldn't have been possible to accomplish what you have, if the right wasn't on your side."

"You'll find the right, honey, where the brains are, an' the guts," he stated complacently, "the scales of justice never were tipped by a lunk-headed prosecutor, but a fast one has hung many a' innocent man. God Almighty can't see around the rail of a jury box, but I've sustained myself so long on my philosophy of life, an' you've heard it so much, that we both believe it, most of the time. If some of these Florida editors would analyze it, they'd find it to be about ninety per cent right at that."

"That sounds more like you, and it sounds better to me," Leda observed. "I hate to see you strike these morbid periods."

"Sam Harris named me the black wheel horse; remember?" he mused. Well, he'd have to call me the old gray horse. Why, hell, Leda, I'm fifty-six. Fifty-six years, and how much of it's been in any kind of quietude, or contentment. I'd burnt up the energy I was born with when I was thirty. I fought through the thirties, an' I staggered through the forties. I gave up once, and quit, but somethin' made me come back. That was the very first time, after thirty-three years of practice, that I suspected that there was an underlying retribution guiding me."

"Just don't think so much, or think about things that will inflate you. Practice a little suggestion, for the sake of your health, and peace of mind."

"I want to talk to you about sellin' out and leavin'—."

"Please don't dear," she interrupted. "I can't think of it."

"When I was barking in that jury's face, an' when I listened to blubbering old John Gobel after the verdict, I knew I was gettin' out of here. Did you see me put my head on his shoulder, there? I had to hide my face from the court. When the jury reported, old John looked real sanctimonious, and said, 'Truth crushed to earth will rise again.' I thought, Hypocrisy. Deceit. Fraud. Sham. That's all there is here, an' the dread of what will wreck it is gettin' me. Somethin's goin' to happen, 'cause those damned bells keep ringin'. I got to go."

"We're not going," came the flat reply.

"I hate to leave you, the way I feel about Miami, but I got to do it. I'll take about a week to get ready, and out I go. I can open up an office back in Oklahoma somewhere. I guess I can still catch a murder case once in awhile around the capital. But I'd rather sell out here and kind of quit. I could feel real disaster while I was pleadin' for Gobel. It was somethin' tellin' me to quit this rotten business."

"You need a rest, a long one," she said. "Let's take a trip, back home, and visit our old friends. We can take a month, two months, to rest and plan, and then if you still feel the same way, if you haven't changed your mind, I'll quit holding out for Florida. I'll do whatever you say."

He patted her affectionately. "I knew you'd stay with me," he said. "It's a deal. If I can shake these bucks that are on me, we'll stay with the ease of the palmy shores. If not—. Then we'll stick to the west. I got a good farm on the Washita, you know, an' one right near Oklahoma City. The way I been feelin', I'd like to get me a few goats an' a hoe an' a rake, an' let somebody that's a little younger worry over murder for awhile."

"I want to spend a few days with Doc Marchman in Dallas, on the way back," he mused. "There's about a half dozen killers that owe their lives to Doc, only they don't know it. I'll surprise him, an' thank him for Hattie, an' young mister Valiton."

While Pruiett's automobile hummed a rhythmic farewell north and west, the poker chips and the balls on the roulette wheels continued to rattle in the silent night on the shores of the famous moon-filled Biscayne Bay, and the ripples therefrom carried up empty flasks with ornamented labels with pinched sides, while the music and harsh laughter floated from the Ta-Miami and Flamingo Hotels to the dimly lighted yachts anchored in the bay, where music and laughter re-echoed back from the drifting crafts to the resorts on the shore.

Domestic bootleg was high; the fancy-bottled imported stuff from the Indies was higher. It took money to acquire, and operate, the brass-trimmed yachts and speed boats. Jawbone alone wouldn't support parties at the Flamingo. The play-boys, mindful of their good things, had a weather eye on the status of the stock market and the welfare of the old bankroll.

Weather-eyed Pruiett was right; "Erratic fluctuations in cotton continued Friday, but prices moved in a narrower range, as was the case Thursday. Instead of the 40 point changes, an early improvement of less than 10 points was followed by a decline of 20 points and at the end of three hours the list was slightly under Thursday's close. . . . The cause underlying market gyrations was more definite information regarding the progress of the tropical disturbance near Nassau, which brought storm warnings to the Florida coast. . . ."

Were the bells ringing? Yes; the emergency bells, and the warning sirens were screaming their excited throats raw, but no one, save the distressed, could hear. The gale which snatched up their feeble wails and carried them inland to fuse their identity with the swish of the bending pines and palms had driven aside the telegraphic and 'phone connections with the mainland to the north. There was a hell of a disturbance going on in the Indies.

"FLORIDA COAST IS SWEPT BY FIERCE TROPICAL HURRICANE"

The Associated Press advised its multifarious subscribers.

"Miami Flooded, Cut Off From Rest of World, Wires Down and Trains Stopped," came the subheads. "A hundred mile wind spread ruin over a wide area. The devastating fury of the tropical storm which swept the south Florida Coast Saturday morning has transformed Miami into desolate Venice, with streets inundated, buildings wrecked, light and power gone, and untold property damage."

Pruiett paced the floor of a hotel room in Oklahoma City, pausing long enough occasionally to stir a fresh drink with a shaking hand, or to curse an operator for her inability to get a call through to Miami, or Jacksonville. He had to have news of the situation. He feared that he was about to see his prediction come to pass. His fortune was being buried under a gale-driven chain of dunes. Why couldn't the papers get information, or come oftener with what they had?

"55 Die in Hurricane! 38,000 Homeless in Florida! Property Damage $125,000,000!" Good God! The whole damn peninsula wasn't worth that kind of money. The works must have blowed right over west into the Gulf of Mexico. There won't be a pound of stucco left out of the viller. It's good-bye to that classy orange grove."

"A hurricane which came out of the West Indies swept over the lower east coast of Florida Friday and Saturday, causing a death list estimated at more than 500 persons, destroyed property valued at more than $125,000,000 left 38,000 people homeless and passed into the Gulf of Mexico."

"Military control was ordered in the stricken City of Miami by City Manager Frank H. Warden. More than 300 extra policemen were sworn in, after looting had taken place in certain parts of Miami! . . . ."

Pruiett growled as the paper shook in his trembling hand. "The evil buzzards. They brought it on themselves, an' now they'd steal from their own dead."

"Miami Bay front was subjected to a terrified battering as the violent windstorm struck from a more dangerous angle. The bay crept high over its accustomed level and raced like a mill pond, waist deep, from the Miami River northward toward the county causeway. Mountainous waves broke over Miami Beach . . . . . hurling abandoned automobiles into the bay and destroying many homes. . . ."

When the true proportions of the tragedy became known, as the disrupted rail connections were replaced, and wire communications were resumed, President Coolidge issued a proclamation declaring a state of emergency, and urging the nation "to organize relief for the overwhelming disaster."

"Cal had better get some relief to that white-headed Pruiett up on the sixth floor," a wag in the lobby observed as he read the latest bulletin. "He's been up there now for five days, burning the wire for news."

When Pruiett finally blinked in the sunlight he knew the worst. He had talked over long distance with an associate in storm-torn Miami. The villa was down. The coast along the Jupiter lighthouse was stripped bare, so hope for the orange grove was gone. Miami was desolate. Deserted. The only activity there was the desultory plugging of the salvage and wrecking crews, and the exodus of the disillusioned. The great bonanza had played out.

"Refugees from Miami and its environs continued to move upstate to Jacksonville, where they entrained for the homes they left during the long months of the big boom in Florida. Six hundred left Palm Beach during the day and hundreds of others were preparing to get away."

Less than two months before he had known it, as surely and as terribly as he knew it then. He could have unloaded, sold out, and left the doomed strip to the wicked and the unwise. Now he knew it, and the press was advertising the exodus to the world. Everyone knew it now. Value had dropped from the top to the bottom. The creeping scrub pine, and the alligators, and the tax collectors, could have it. He'd never go back for the salvage..

That was the end of the man who took the teeth out of the law which prohibited the wanton taking of life. He didn't die, not Pruiett. God's wrath, a breath blowing a hundred miles an hour, could scarcely bend the spirit hovering about the cold body which stalked from Rusk's dungeon. He had his fierce convictions, and he had that indomitable will which wouldn't recognize defeat.

CHARGES HAD BEEN FILED AGAINST MOMAN PRUIETT FOR FILING AN ALLEGED UNLAWFUL LAWSUIT AGAINST ONE Roberts, and one Wells, owners and managers of the Wells-Roberts Hotel, in Oklahoma City, Okla.

"Hell, no, I am not going to quit," he growled, when Bill Maben came to town and inquired about his plans. "I may be broke, but I am not any broker than I was when I was shinin' shoes in Fayetteville and Fort Smith, Arkansas. I lack a lot of bein' through."

"You're goin' to have to be careful," Maben suggested. "Things are not like they used to be. The old boys we used to work with are dyin' off, an' the boys we broke in are gettin' a lot of power. I notice we're gettin' an integrated bar, with a disciplinary committee an' an enforcement board for keepin' our ethics straight."

"Yes, they got a damn judge on the Supreme Court to guard their own crookedness," Pruiett stormed.

"All the short cuts the little fellers like us took in a lifetime wouldn't average up to the corruption of one of these big corporation lawsuits. The white collar buzzards are not gettin' rich fast enough, so they throw up some ethics smoke to hide the robbin' and riflin' they got planned to do. Why, there has been more subornation of perjury committed in the trial of seven lawsuits at Tulsa and Sapulpa, Okla., than has ever been committed by any ten lawyers in the trial of murder cases before statehood, and up to this good hour. Yes, all for filthy lucre, but not a voice raised for mercy in behalf of a human being."

"You got some new ideas on the subject, ain't you?" Maben inquired.

"Just got a new way of expressin' 'em," Pruiett answered. "Did you ever see a big utility swindle, or a municipal graft, that wasn't engineered by high-priced corporation counsel? Why, hell no! They got to have their big law firms back of 'em, an' they split the swag in what they call payin' counsel fees. You show me an apprehended swindler or a tax-dodger, an' I'll show you a guy with a corporation lawyer's philosophy that's paid out half of what he's been stealin' to fast lawyers."

"It ain't illegal to represent your client," Maben said.

"Not if you're in with the right bunch—the ones with the white collars an' plush bottoms," Pruiett agreed. But let'em catch a criminal lawyer with one foot off the base—tryin' to save some poverty-stricken devil from a livin' death in the penitentiary— an' after that poor unfortunate devil they call the criminal lawyer, and they start to give him some discipline. Isn't that right?"

"I guess subornation of perjury is the same in a murder case as it is in a land title case," Maben agreed.

"Hell, yes, it is," Pruiett gritted. "They holler about me clearin' Maggie Miller. I did that for mercy; I was conscientious about gettin' her out of a heart-breakin' situation. Civil lawyers robbed a hundred thousand ignorant Indians. Made over a million dollars in one fee, an' they didn't have any purpose in mind but fillin' their own big greasy gut. Selfishness! Lustful robbery! An' the public's forgot about that. All they can holler is Maggie Miller, an' George Hopkins, an' John Gobel."

"You've been very successful, Moman," Maben reminded.

"Sure I have," Pruiett agreed. "I started out with a sincere purpose, an' I accomplished it. I made a lot of money, but I never turned down a criminal defense 'cause the accused didn't have the money to pay me. Maybe I have been indiscreet in my time. Maybe I have been a hypocrite, in some of the acts I've put on before juries, but let me tell you this. All the crookedness I ever poured into all the lawsuits I ever tried wouldn't amount to a tenth of what any of these big railroads or oil companies has crammed into a single case, just to cheat honest landholders out of their just rights. I can look 'em in the eye an' tell 'em to go to hell. I done mine for mercy. They done theirs for greedy gold."

There were flashes of the Washita fight. There were recurrences of St. Mary and Volitan brilliance. But with each fat fee collected there was a recess. He came back to the bar with stamina and power. He was up and he was down. He was cited for contempt. The committee on the enforcement of ethics objected to his manner of handling an alienation of affection suit —it smacked of extortion—they claimed, and lawyer Pruiett, an old man, was suspended. And this man Busby has appeared before the Bar Association and delivered an address on professional and judicial ethics immediately after writing the opinion of suspension.

He fought it through the appellate court. Hell's fire! Was he goin' to let a bunch of white-collared young pups railroad him without a battle, even if he was old and broke? Not the old Moman. "I can't get a fair trial in that damn Supreme Court," he bawled. "There's old Doc Threldkeld's son-in-law, Orel Busby, settin' as one of the Associate Justices, an' that family's still sore at me for shooting holes through the old drunk. And Busby wrote the opinion."

The conviction was affirmed but the punishment was modified. Disbarment was changed to a year's suspension from practice.

"Isn't that hell?" Pruiett swore. "What if they was to catch me with kin-folks on my jury? Wouldn't they scream? An' here these ethics-watchers censure me—convict me—with the son-in-law of a man I shot settin' on the court. What did I tell you about 'em coverin' up their own corruption with a big stench over the little feller's ethics?" The black mane had turned to a soft white. The strut, the stride, the loud profanity, the color that was Pruiett, was gone. The rumble of the real Moman was but an echo—a memory.

While the alleged charge of filing an unlawful lawsuit was pending before the Supreme Court of Oklahoma, Pruiett defended Sam and Margaret Wilkerson, who had been arrested and charged with killing I. E. Hemmingway.

Spread across the front pages of the daily papers in Oklahoma City, the following headlines, and articles were printed relative to the Wilkerson murder case:

"Standing room was at a premium in the Oklahoma County District Courtroom Monday (January 17th, 1933) as the trial of a murder charge against Sam Wilkerson, farmer, in connection with the death of I. E. Hemmingway, a loan broker, was started. Mrs. Margaret Wilkerson, his wife, was also charged with murder in the case, but Mrs. Wilkerson's trial is not scheduled until after her husband's."

———oOo———

"It was in the early part of November, 1932, Isaac E. Hemmingway, disappeared. He was a cold-blooded money lender, and not a philanthropist as some newspapers and magazines gave him credit for being. Sam Wilkerson, a son of a highly respected minister of the Church of Christ, was a confirmed bootlegger and a whiskey maker. Sam owned a farm nine miles northeast of Oklahoma City, Oklahoma, which he had bought from Hemmingway. Hemmingway had Wilkerson to borrow a part of the purchase price from the School Land Department of the State of Oklahoma. Hemmingway then took a second-mortgage on the farm, from Wilkerson for the balance. In the deal Hemmingway was taking a second mortgage which was a net profit on the farm. He had received from Wilkerson the amount of money that he had borrowed on the land from the School Land Department, which was more than the gross value of the land to start with."

The theory of the state was that on a Sunday afternoon Wilkerson came into Oklahoma City, and kidnapped Hemmingway, took him to his farm, and under fear of death had him to write a check of nine hundred ($900.00) dollars; another check to the School Land Department for fourteen hundred ($1,400.00) dollars, and write and sign two letters addressed to A. J. Cofer, a business associate. He also prepared a release for the mortgage, and had Hemmingway to sign it releasing the mortgage. Wilkerson then came to town on Monday and got a notary public, returned to the farm, and the release was properly acknowledged. There at the farm after the notary had left, the Wilkersons held Hemmingway a prisoner. Wilkerson went to the town of Sulphur, Oklahoma, mailed the letters, and returned to his farm. The letters to Hemmingway's friends said he was not feeling well, and that he would remain in Sulphur for a few days.

"At the time of Hemmingway's disappearance there were two men working on a levee on the west side of the Wilkerson farm. The levee was being built to protect his own farm. While the men were at work on the levee near the noon hour, Hemmingway holding on to some tall sun flowers staggered up to where the men were at work, blood streaming down his shoulders. The men made inquiry, but Hemmingway was unable to answer them. They began to hitch up a mule to take him to a hospital, when Wilkerson appeared upon the scene and made inquiry: 'Have you seen an old man staggering around here?' 'There's an old man sitting on the spring-seat,' one of the men answered, 'we were just fixing to take him to a hospital.' There was a gate leading from Wilkerson's hog lot to the levee where the men were at work."

Wilkerson says, "I'll take him to the hospital myself, help me take him over to the gate where my car is." The two men assisted Wilkerson in taking Hemmingway to the car and put him in it, when they immediately returned to the levee. There was a long shed boxed up on the west side. This shed was between the levee, where the men were at work, and Wilkerson's residence on the east side of the hog lot. The shed would have obstructed the view of a Ford car going to the Wilkerson house. Wilkerson claimed that Hemmingway's nephew came and took him away.

"Pruiett's defense was that Hemmingway was alive and left with his nephew.

"On that evening about dusk a young lawyer by the name of Judd Black and an oil broker by the name of Kirkpatrick, who had been squirrel hunting down the river testified that they had parked their car earlier in the day at the southeast corner of Wilkerson's farm, and on returning to their car on the levee looking east as they traveled south to their car they had observed two men digging and shoveling in the hog lot, but they could not recognize either one of the men.

"Knowing Sam Wilkerson's reputation as being a bootlegger, they decided to go by his house and get a bottle of whiskey. When they arrived there Wilkerson was at home, but claimed that he had no whiskey.

"The theory of the state was that Sam Wilkerson had returned home from Sulphur, after mailing the letters, and that Hemmingway had attempted to make his escape in his absence, and that his wife had shot Hemmingway in the back of the head, and thought that she had killed him. Whereupon, Wilkerson grabbed his winchester rifle and started out to find Hemmingway. And after finding Hemmingway and putting him in his car beat his brains out on the east side of the hog lot with a hammer, and afterwards buried him in the hog lot.

"The body of Hemmingway was later located by the state

authorities. Wilkerson and his wife were both arrested and placed in jail without bond for the murder of Hemmingway. Sam Wilkerson was tried first, convicted and sentenced to prison for life."

Later Mrs. Wilkerson was tried, and it was the theory of the state that Hemmingway was kidnapped, carried to Wilkerson's home, and there held a prisoner by Wilkerson and his wife Margaret. And the facts sustained the theory. "On Monday Wilkerson went to town and secured a notary public, and returned to his home with him. The notary public testified that when "he and Wilkerson arrived at the Wilkerson home no one was there but Mrs. Wilkerson and Hemmingway, that when he and Wilkerson returned to town Hemmingway remained in the house with Mrs. Wilkerson."

The testimony of the two men on the levee was that "Hemmingway told them that he was kidnapped and forced to sign papers." The theory of the state was that when Wilkerson was away from the house Mrs. Wilkerson was doing the guarding of him, and that when Sam Wilkerson returned from Sulphur after mailing the letters, that he was informed by Mrs. Wilkerson what had taken place between her and Hemmingway; that she had fired the shot in the back of Hemmingway's head while he was trying to escape. That after she had so informed her husband he immediately went to the levee where the men were at work, and there found Hemmingway.

There was a much stronger case made against Mrs. Wilkerson than there was against her husband. The Wilkersons had two little twin daughters, nine years old.

This was Pruiett's last major murder case, which was tried in March, 1933, and his last words to the jury were; stepping back—placing his hands on Mrs. Wilkerson's head, he said: "DAUGHTER OF TEXAS, MOTHER OF TWINS, HAVE NO FEAR." The jury brought in its verdict, "NOT GUILTY."

An old man with bushy hair dozed in a court-room pew. It was Pruiett. Lint from cottonwoods on the lawn drifted through the open window, and in the spring haze the purple of the Washita woods could be seen dim on the horizon. A young man with stylish clothes and a Greek-letter pin on his vest was storming and raging in a languid jury's face.

"That boy's a bear, ain't he?" a man in overalls whispered, nudging the old man with his elbow.

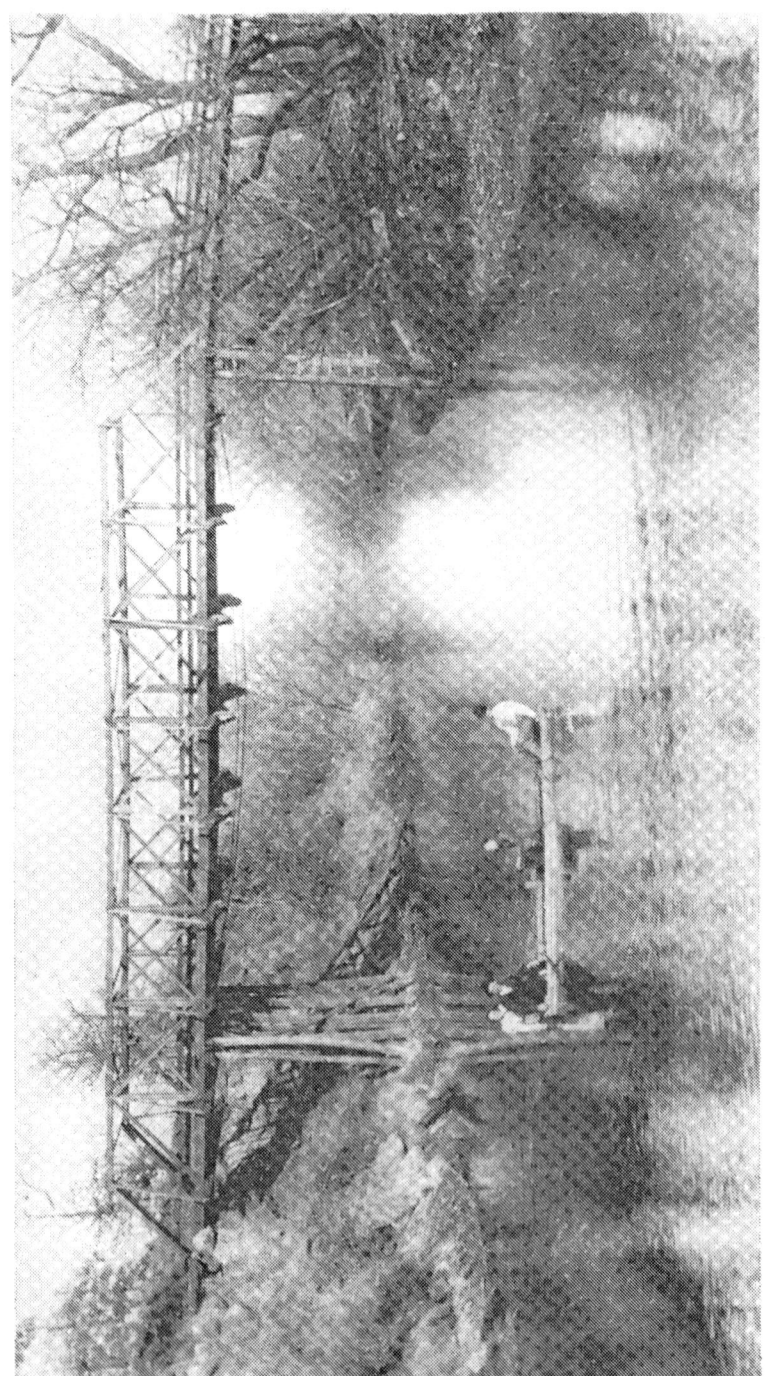

THE WASHITA
"That little old river is as crooked as a pan of hog guts."

"How's that?" Pruiett inquired, opening his eyes.

"That boy's a bear," the man repeated. "He's a regular Moman Pruiett."

"He's a what?" Pruiett repeated. "Who was Pruiett?" Pruiett inquired.

The farmer gave him a withering look. "Did you never hear of Moman Pruiett, the CRIMINAL lawyer?"

Pruiett shook his head, sadly.

"He was the greatest lawyer that ever banged a table," the man whispered. "I heard him try cases in this very courtroom an' win 'em, when he was defendin' blood-guilty murderers. He made a million dollars an' went down to Florida, an' died down there, I guess. We kind of lost track of him. He tried a murder case ever' week, an' he never lost a one of 'em."

The old man with the white hair and round shoulders thumped his cane toward the exit.

"No use tryin' to explain anything to an old man like that," the farmer muttered. "Never heard of Moman Pruiett, the criminal lawyer. Jesus Christ!"

MOMAN PRUIETT—AGE 73—JULY 12, 1945

CPSIA information can be obtained at www.ICGtesting.com
Printed in the USA
BVOW010334191011

273940BV00012B/3/P

9 781163 184240